Lecture Notes in Computer Science 6835

Commenced Publication in 1973
Founding and Former Series Editors:
Gerhard Goos, Juris Hartmanis, and Jan van Leeuwen

Rudolf Mester   Michael Felsberg (Eds.)

Pattern Recognition

33rd DAGM Symposium
Frankfurt/Main, Germany, August 31 – September 2, 2011
Proceedings

Volume Editors

Rudolf Mester
Johann-Wolfgang Goethe University
Visual Sensorics and Information Processing Lab
60054 Frankfurt/Main, Germany
E-mail: mester@vsi.cs.uni-frankfurt.de

Michael Felsberg
Linköping University
Department of Electrical Engineering
58183 Linköping, Sweden
E-mail: michael.felsberg@liu.se

ISSN 0302-9743   e-ISSN 1611-3349
ISBN 978-3-642-23122-3   e-ISBN 978-3-642-23123-0
DOI 10.1007/978-3-642-23123-0
Springer Heidelberg Dordrecht London New York

Library of Congress Control Number: 2011934378

CR Subject Classification (1998): I.5, I.4, I.3.5, I.2.10, I.4.1, I.2.6, F.2.2

LNCS Sublibrary: SL 6 – Image Processing, Computer Vision, Pattern Recognition,
and Graphics

Typesetting: Camera-ready by author, data conversion by Scientific Publishing Services, Chennai, India

Printed on acid-free paper

Springer is part of Springer Science+Business Media (www.springer.com)

Preface

Welcome to the proceedings of DAGM 2011, which was held in Frankfurt am Main, an international financial hub within Germany with a vibrant cultural and historical tradition. The Johann Wolfgang Goethe University was founded by the wealthy citizenship of Frankfurt in the early twentieth century. The university, which currently has about 39,000 students, is today best known for its law school, the department of economics, its medical school, but also for a rich spectrum of life sciences and nature sciences. Research activity in visual pattern recognition received a significant boost in Frankfurt through the formation of a Bernstein Focus Neurotechnology (BFNT) research cluster emphasizing "vision in man and machine" through BMBF funding within the Bernstein network for computational neuroscience. The research program brings together an interdisciplinary team of computer scientists, neuroscientists, psychologists, machine learning and systems engineering experts to build an integrative framework for computer vision systems.

This year, for the first time, the annual symposia of the German Pattern Recognition Association (DAGM) and the German Classification Society (GfKl) were held in conjunction. This offered a forum for scientific exchange and contact between researchers in the two fields. We hope this provided a stimulating experience for each participant in the joint conference.

The technical program of DAGM 2011 was a joint endeavor between the VSI group of Goethe University and the Computer Vision Laboratory at Linköpings Universitet and was supported through a grant from the Swedish ELLIIT excellence initiative. The technical program covered all aspects of pattern recognition such as early vision to machine learning and robot vision. The present proceedings are the result of a multi-step process of paper solicitation, double-blind review, and careful selection. The DAGM 2011 call for papers resulted in 98 submissions from authors in more than 24 countries. Each paper was subjected to a rigorous double-blind review process and assessed by at least three Program Committee members. Subsequently, a moderated per-paper discussion among the reviewers led to a rating profile and a recommendation that summarized the views of the reviewers. During a Program Committee meeting held in Frankfurt in May 2011, the rating profiles, reviews, the discussion results and, where necessary, additional review reports were evaluated. On this basis, the Program Committee selected a total of 42 papers, corresponding to an acceptance rate of below 43%. The Program Chairs assigned 20 papers for oral and 22 papers for poster presentation, and grouped the papers into sessions. All accepted papers are compiled in the present proceedings. We express our appreciation and thanks to all the members of the Program Committee as well as the external reviewers for their valuable service to the community. We would also like to express our thanks to all authors who submitted papers, for it is the vivid response of authors to a conference call that makes a strong program possible.

We were proud to be able to present two invited talks from internationally renowned scientists:

- Donald Geman: "Image Interpretation by Entropy Pursuit"
- Yann LeCun: "Learning Visual Feature Hierarchies"

These talks were complemented by a number of keynote talks invited by the GfKl. Furthermore, four tutorials held by recognized experts were arranged:

- Tensors in Computer Vision and Image Processing, by Klas Nordberg
- Random Field Models for Natural Image and Scene Statistics, by Stefan Roth
- Higher-Order Feature Learning: Building a Computer Vision "Swiss Army Knife," by Roland Memisevic
- Convex Optimization for Computer Vision, by Thomas Pock and Daniel Cremers

Meanwhile, it is almost a tradition to have a Young Researchers' Forum at DAGM, where a carefully jury-selected ensemble of young researchers presented their Master thesis work during the conference. This appreciation of theirs hopefully acts as an incentive for further noticeable scientific contributions.

For the first time, an "Adverse Vision Conditions Challenge" was initiated as a satellite event to a DAGM conference, addressing the important area of implementing computer vision on real-life video material which suffers from different strong degradations of image quality. The submitted contributions had to comply with the same selection procedure as for the rest of the DAGM papers, and four papers were selected for a particular AVCC poster session.

The technical program was complemented by a workshop on New Challenges in Neural Computation (NC^2), which was organized by Barbara Hammer and Thomas Villmann on behalf of the GI-Arbeitskreis Neuronale Netze and the German Neural Networks Society.

We would like to express our gratitude to all the kind people who contributed to making DAGM 2011 in Frankfurt a success. This refers in particular to the members of the Visual Sensorics and Information Processing Lab at Goethe University, and to the members of the Computer Vision Laboratory of Linköpings Universitet, Sweden. We are indebted to Holger Friedrich, Christian Conrad and David Dederscheck for their help with all local organizational matters, for Web support and technical assistance, to the indefatigable Liam Ellis at Linköpings Universitet for operating the Conference Management Tool (CMT) and author communication during the review phase and while assembling the proceedings, to Florian Meyer (Marburg University) for setting up the registration system, to Kerstin Werschnik, Nicole Stender (Frankfurt) and Birgit Strassheim (Marburg) for back-office work concerning communication, social events, and accommodation issues, and finally our students and PhD students for a virtually uncountable set of small and larger jobs along the way. Finally, we thank our sponsors, and appreciate the initiative of Microsoft to provide the CMT conference management system to the scientific community for free.

It was an honor for us to host the 33rd Annual Symposium of DAGM in Frankfurt am Main in 2011, and we look forward to DAGM 2012 in Graz.

August 2011   Rudolf Mester
                                                                    Michael Felsberg

Organization

General Chairs

Rudolf Mester   Universität Frankfurt, Germany, and
Linköpings Universitet, Sweden
Michael Felsberg   Linköpings Universitet, Sweden

Local Organization

Holger Friedrich   Universität Frankfurt, Germany
Christian Conrad   Universität Frankfurt, Germany

CMT Management

Liam Ellis   Linköpings Universitet, Sweden

Program Committee

Chairs

Michael Felsberg   Linköpings Universitet, Sweden
Rudolf Mester   Universität Frankfurt, Germany, and
Linköpings Universitet, Sweden

Members

Horst Bischof   TU Graz, Austria
Thomas Brox   Universität Freiburg, Germany
Joachim Buhmann   ETH Zürich, Switzerland
Daniel Cremers   Technische Universität München, Germany
Andreas Dengel   DFKI, Germany
Joachim Denzler   Universität Jena, Germany
Gernot Fink   TU Dortmund, Germany
Boris Flach   Czech Technical University, Czech Republic
Wolfgang Förstner   Universität Bonn, Germany
Uwe Franke   Daimler AG, Germany
Peter Gehler   Max-Planck-Institut für Informatik, Germany
Michael Goesele   Technische Universität Darmstadt, Germany
Fred Hamprecht   Universität Heidelberg, Germany
Joachim Hornegger   Universität Erlangen Nürnberg, Germany
Xiaoyi Jiang   Universität Münster, Germany
Bernd Jähne   Universität Heidelberg, Germany

Awards 2010

Olympus Award

The Olympus Award 2010 was given to:

Stefan Roth

for his outstanding work in statistical approaches to image modeling, motion estimation, human tracking, and object recognition.

DAGM Prizes

The main prize for DAGM 2010 was awarded to:

Sven Grewenig, Joachim Weickert, and Andrés Bruhn:
"From Box Filtering to Fast Explicit Diffusion"

Further DAGM prizes for 2010 were awarded to:

Alexander Barth, Jan Siegemund, Annemarie Meißner, Uwe Franke, and Wolfgang Förstner:
"Probabilistic Multi-class Scene Flow Segmentation for Traffic Scenes"

Fuxin Li, Catalin Ionescu, and Cristian Sminchisescu:
"Random Fourier Approximations for Skewed Multiplicative Histogram Kernels"

Julia E. Vogt and Volker Roth:
"The Group-Lasso: $l_{1,\infty}$ Regularization versus $l_{1,2}$ Regularization"

Table of Contents

Object Recognition

Poster Session 2

Adverse Vision Conditions Challenge

Shape and Matching

Segmentation and Early Vision

Robot Vision

A Bayesian Approach for Scene Interpretation with Integrated Hierarchical Structure

Martin Drauschke[1] and Wolfgang Förstner[2]

[1] Institute of Applied Computer Science, Bundeswehr University Munich, Germany
[2] Institute of Geodesy and Geoinformation, University of Bonn, Germany
martin.drauschke@unibw.de, wf@ipb.uni-bonn.de

Abstract. We propose a concept for scene interpretation with integrated hierarchical structure. This hierarchical structure is used to detect mereological relations between complex objects as buildings and their parts, e. g., windows. We start with segmenting regions at many scales, arranging them in a hierarchy, and classifying them by a common classifier. Then, we use the hierarchy graph of regions to construct a conditional Bayesian network, where the probabilities of class occurrences in the hierarchy are used to improve the classification results of the segmented regions in various scales. The interpreted regions can be used to derive a consistent scene representation, and they can be used as object detectors as well. We show that our framework is able to learn models for several objects, such that we can reliably detect instances of them in other images.

1 Introduction

Scene interpretation is a very active research field in computer vision. Hence, hierarchical approaches can be found for categorizing images and detecting (complex) objects in images, cf. [1–6], where often instances of general classes, such as, e.g., *airplane*, *building*, *cloth*, *dog*, *face* etc. are to segment and to recognize. A different also very challenging task is the detailed interpretation of terrestrial facade images, i. e., the derivation of a scene description with information about the parts of the recognized building. This task has been attracted by the computer vision community due to the fast developments of virtual 3D city models. So far, such city models with several hundred thousands of buildings are only used for visualization, but the integration of semantics would significantly enrich their purpose. Obviously, the interpretation of facade images should be performed automatically.

Buildings and their parts as windows, doors and balconies are very challenging objects due to their large variety in shape, size, color and texture. To detect such objects in images, many different approaches have been proposed in last years. E.g., main authors (see [7, 8]) try to classify pixels or larger patches using Markov Random Fields (MRF). While their focus lies on separating *building*, *ground*, *sky* and *vegetation* from each other. The contextual scene interpretation by considering different object sizes and therefore image scales for object classification has already been applied in [3, 7, 9], but these approaches either suffer under too simple regions, e.g., patches which cannot be used for describing complex shapes, or they have a very high complexity.

R. Mester and M. Felsberg (Eds.): DAGM 2011, LNCS 6835, pp. 1–10, 2011.

The spatial arrangement of facade elements is also considered in [10, 11] where the authors propose to use spatial grammars for their scene interpretation. In [12–14] the authors propose more ore less successful strategies for recognizing windows in facade images, but rely on the rectangular shape of windows with strong contours and distinctive corners, or they consider the repetitive structure of many windows in building facades. A very simple blob detector has been proposed by [15] who apply a saliency based image analysis. In experiments, they obtained promising detection rates for windows, but other facade parts, especially the smaller ones, have relatively low detection rates.

The success of the window detectors leads to the question, if we could also design reliable detector for other facade parts as roof, doors or balconies. These objects are more challenging due to their more variable appearance in images and their lower frequency. Thus, we are pessimistic that this is a promising strategy. Instead of spending much effort into modeling detectors for such objects, we propose to integrate segmentation results in the scene interpretation. Thereby, we focus on object hierarchies, believing that we obtain better classification results in case we integrate classification results of higher image scales when analyzing lower image scales, e.g., we do not want to look for windows or doors where we believe to see vegetation.

We propose a scene interpretation framework, which can be trained to detect instances of various types. Therefore, we segment image regions at several image scales and arrange them in a hierarchical order. [5] use their hierarchy to derive features from various scales, which are used to build a feature vector for regions of the lowest scale only. In contrast to [5], we also want to classify the regions at higher scales, thus we individually derive features for each segmented region. We improve our classification by an additional analysis using the region hierarchy, which we realize as a conditional Bayesian network. Since Bayesian networks only infer hierarchy information, we also integrate context knowledge by extracting features characterizing the neighborhood of a region. This synthesis of methods enables us to develop a very flexible data-driven scene interpretation approach.

The paper is organized as followed. In sec. 2, we present our concept of a conditional Bayesian network which is constructed by using a hierarchy of segmented regions. Further details to our approach are given in sec. 3. Then, we present our results in sec. 4. In sec. 5, we discuss an extension of our approach for more general scene interpretation tasks. Finally, we summarize our approach and discuss possible extensions of it in sec. 6.

2   Concept for Conditional Bayesian Network

We want to develop a methodology, which is able to detect instances of different classes. These classes may describe well-shaped things, such as *buildings* and their parts as *windows* or *doors*, and formless stuff, such as *sky* or *vegetation*. Due to the facts that we look of objects which can be arranged hierarchically and we are interested in interpreting man-made scenes where we often find precisely detectable object contours, we propose to segment distinctive image regions which are hierarchically ordered to obtain image evidence for further classification. This further step consists of three steps: extracting features for each region, classifying it by a conventional classifier, and finally we construct a conditional Bayesian network to infer information through the hierarchy of regions. At we end, we have consistent classification of image regions, and the classification results can be visualized in the image. Fig. 1 shows at the left side the input image of a building scene in suburban environment, and below of it, the ideal classification results of *building* and *window* are shown. At the right of fig. 1, we show a hierarchy of manually segmented image regions.

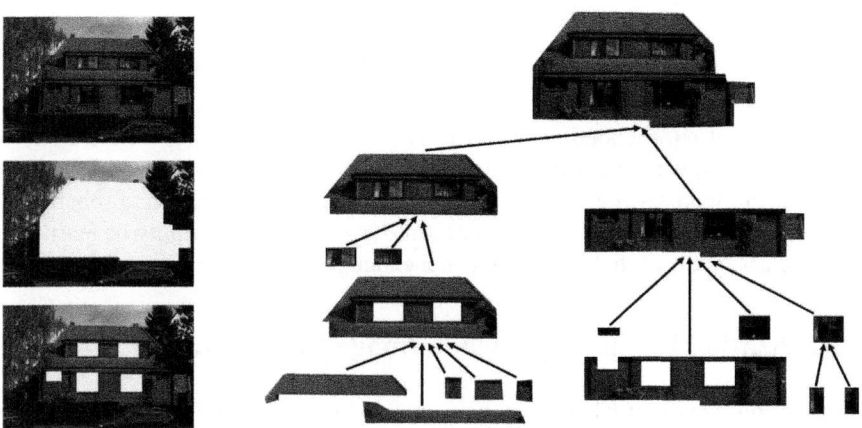

Fig. 1. Left: Facade image (top row) and manually marked objects of class *building* (middle row) and class *window* (bottom row) in yellow. Right: Hierarchical segmentation of *building* object with parts of *roof*, *wall*, and *window*.

We call a segmented image region S_m, and note their hierarchical order by the parent-relation π. I.e. for each region S_m we find exactly one parent $S_{\pi(m)}$, and the parent-relation does not exist for top regions in the hierarchy. Usually, hierarchies are defined by inclusion of smaller elements by larger ones. Hence, the parent of a region $S_{\pi(m)}$ holds information on region S_m and of a distinctive neighborhood. In our point of view, this is more realistic than learning about neighborhoods of all directions as typically done in MRFs.

We derive a block of features F which consists of feature vectors F_m extracted from region S_m. We use the region hierarchy and the block of features F to construct a Bayesian network, as visualized in fig. 2. If we have segmented M regions, the graph of the Bayesian network consists of $M + 1$ nodes. For each region, we introduce M random variables x_m which are modeled discrete with C states, which describe the probability for the m-th region to belong to one of the C classes. The additional node in the graph is F which is treated like an observed random variable, because the features do not change when inferring in the Bayesian network. Thus, F makes our network to a conditional one.

We obtain the best result for our scene interpretation, if we maximize the probability $P(\underline{x}_1,\ldots,\underline{x}_M,F)$, which we can approximate by

$$P(\underline{x}_1,\ldots,\underline{x}_M,F) \tag{1}$$

$$= P(\underline{x}_1,\ldots,\underline{x}_M \mid F)P(F) \tag{2}$$

$$= P(F)P(\underline{x}_1 \mid F) \prod_{m>1} P(\underline{x}_m \mid \underline{x}_{\pi(m)},F) \tag{3}$$

$$= P(F)P(\underline{x}_1 \mid F) \prod_{m>1} P(\underline{x}_m \mid \underline{x}_{\pi(m)})P(\underline{x}_m \mid F) \tag{4}$$

$$\doteq P(F) \prod P(\underline{x}_m \mid F) \prod_{m>1} P(\underline{x}_m \mid \underline{x}_{\pi(m)}) \tag{5}$$

$$\propto \prod P(\underline{x}_m \mid F) \prod_{m>1} P(\underline{x}_m \mid \underline{x}_{\pi(m)}). \tag{6}$$

The right side of eq. 6 contains only two terms, which we want to derive from training data. Thereby, we approximate $P(\underline{x}_m \mid F)$ by learning a classifier κ on the basis of region-specific features, i.e. by $P(\underline{x}_m \mid F_m)$. Then, classifier κ returns probabilities of region S_m to belong to class c. The other term $P(\underline{x}_m \mid \underline{x}_{\pi(m)})$ can simply be learned from counting class labels of the training data dependent on the region hierarchy.

3   Realization Regarding Facade Image Interpretation

In this section, we describe how we have realized our concept for interpreting facade images. We applied segmentation, feature extraction and classification methods which are either designed with respect to that domain, or they are simple and efficient.

3.1   Hierarchical Segmentation

Several general and domain-specific approaches have recently been proposed to segment facade images. While the authors of [16] proposed a domain-specific strategy with subdividing the scene into rectangles, we developed a more flexible segmentation earlier, cf. [17]. There, we determine watershed regions in a dense scale-space with 41 scales. To reduce the number of regions, we proposed only to select stable regions, i. e. we obtain $M \approx 1000$ stable regions S_m. In experiments on facade images [17], we showed that we are able to detect small objects, such as windows, and larger ones, such as buildings. Furthermore, we showed that the hierarchy of stable regions reflects the object structure.

3.2   Features of Regions

For each region S_m, we extract a D-dimensional feature vector with $D = 65$. We use region-specific features as its area, circumference, form factor, and aspect ratio. Others describe the region and the difference to its neighborhood, e.g. mean and standard deviation of the color channels as well as the color differences. Furthermore, texture features derived from Haar transform, characteristics of the gradients similar to HoG-descriptors by [18], and characteristics of the generalized region by a 4-corner-polygon

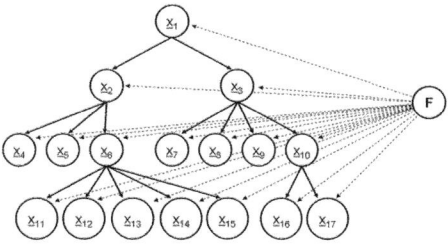

Fig. 2. Conditional Bayesian network derived from hierarchical segmentation of Fig. 1

as its angles or its area ratio to the original region. In preliminary tests, we evaluated that these features are sufficient good for separating different objects. The corresponding class label of each region, the best fitting label $\hat{x}_m$, is derived from manually labeled annotations, cf. sec. 4.

3.3 Classification of Regions

Here, we describe how we design the classifier κ. Usually, at smaller scales, small regions are segmented, which have homogeneous color or texture, but no characteristic shape. At higher scale, this turns around: shape is often more informative than color or texture. Therefore, we divide our set of segmented regions into subsets. Stability of a region is defined in [17] by only slight changes of a region over several scales. Thus we find each detected region in at least one of our five reference scales in scale space ($\sigma = 1, 2, 4, 8, 16$). The lowest one defines the subset membership for classification.

For each training data subset, we perform a Linear Discriminant Analysis (LDA) which determines the optimal feature subspace for separating the classes. There, we determine class-specific probability density functions (PDF) by mixtures of three Gaussian distributions (GM). Three GM are more reliable than just one, because we must expect very heterogeneous data, e. g., building may have a homogeneously colored wall, and they can be textured by their bricks. Then, we determine for each sample the PDF for each of the C classes, and we obtain the probabilities for the sample's class membership $\underline{x}_m$ after normalization. The class with the highest probability is taken as result of the classification noted by $\widetilde{x}_m$.

3.4 Learning Probabilities of Hierarchy

For applying our conditional Bayesian network, we further need to determine probabilities for class appearances in the region hierarchy. Again, we designed the probability by depending it on the scale of region S_m. We derive the probabilities from counting the relationships of targets of hierarchically ordered regions.

The class hierarchy itself might not be sufficient enough. E.g., if you recognize a dark region in a red roof-region, then it is more likely a window than roof tiles, which would be red again. Hence, we decided to specify the probabilities more detailed, and we integrated the features of both regions, S_m and its parent $S_{\pi(m)}$. For each feature, we model the PDF by class-dependent histogram with ten equally filled bins w.r.t. both regions, yielding in a 2D matrix of 100 entries. Evaluating the improvement of the classification by the conditional Bayesian network, we are able to decide which feature to choose for testing our algorithm.

3.5 Conditional Bayesian Network

The segmented regions are arranged in a hierarchy which forms a forest of trees. In the Bayesian network, we model a random variable for each segmented region, which has two parents: the random variable of the parent's region and the random variable describing the region's classification in the LDA-subspace.

Now, we want to determine the best probabilities of all random variables, i.e. the best classification results of all regions. Therefore, we apply the inference algorithm of polytree-structured Bayesian networks as proposed in [19]. Since our structure of hierarchically segmented regions only consists of trees, the inference algorithm is very simple. As result we obtain vectors with C elements, each one reflecting the inferred probabilities for a region's class membership. The class label with the highest probability is noted by $\widetilde{x}'_m$ and selected as new classification result.

4 Experiments

4.1 Setup Up of Our Evaluation and Used Data

In the previous sections we described our concept and explained how we have realized it. Now we want to show some results, and evaluate our approach. We tested our classification framework on the benchmark data set by [20], where also regions of objects and the relations of parts are available. The data set contains of 60 facade images and their manually labeled annotations, showing buildings of various sizes and styles, mainly acquired in Germany and Switzerland. We divided the data set into five equally sized subsets with 12 images, which were used for testing, while the other 48 were used for training the classifier and learning the probabilities on hierarchy. By performing a cross validation test, we managed each image being a test image exactly once.

For assigning target values for the regions, i.e., the best fitting class label $\widehat{x}_m$, we first check the manually labeled pixel-wise annotations of [20]. If there is one most dominant class label, we select this label as target for the region. Otherwise, we check, if the region overlaps with different objects, then we call the region *mixture*. Simultaneously, we check, if the regions overlaps with different objects where one is part of the other, then it gets the class label of the superior class. Finally, if the region shows too much image content, which is not labeled in the annotation, we assign this region to be *background*. After determining the target of each region, we merge all classes together, which appear less than 3%, and form a new class *others*. So, we hope to avoid many misclassification due to the low appearance of some classes. In total, we will perform a classification of regions considering the $C = 7$ classes *building, window, vegetation, car, mixture, background, others*. The class *others* contains the regions with the original class labels *door, pavement, ground* and *sky*.

Table 1. Success and misdetection rates s and d of original classifier κ (LDA with GM) and s' and d' of classification with Bayesian network). p marks the portion of true samples of whole data set.

class	p	s	s'	d	d'
building	0.319	0.488	0.648	0.457	0.4
vegetation	0.245	0.759	0.811	0.427	0.331
window	0.237	0.593	0.729	0.527	0.386
others	0.91	0.215	0.323	0.56	0.392
background	0.40	0.66	0.77	0.833	0.709
car	0.37	0.239	0.227	0.687	0.497
mixture	0.31	0.15	0.002	0.854	0.873

Fig. 3. Four scenes from Berlin (Germany) and classification results from the conditional Bayesian network. Top row: results w.r.t. classes *building*, *window*, and *car*, respectively. Bottom row: w.r.t. classes *building*, *vegetation*, and *window*, respectively.

4.2 Results

In total, our segmentation algorithm segments 131 060 stable regions in 60 images. We tested our approach and obtained the two classification results $\tilde{x}_m$ and $\tilde{x}'_m$ for each region and compared them to the the region's target $\hat{x}_m$. We determined the number of true and false positives, respective, and we define their portion of all true respectively all positively classified samples as success-rate (s or s') and mis-detection rate (d or d'). The prime indicates the classification after inferring the Bayesian network. With classification by classifier κ (LDA and GM) we obtained a success of $s = 0.514$ correctly classified regions, after inferring the information in the Bayesian network, we could improve our success-rate to $s' = 0.620$. The class-specific success-rates of our classification are shown in table 1.

Table 1 also shows the bad classification results for less occurring classes. In our data set, we have 80% of all regions with a label *building*, *vegetation* or *window*. Thus,

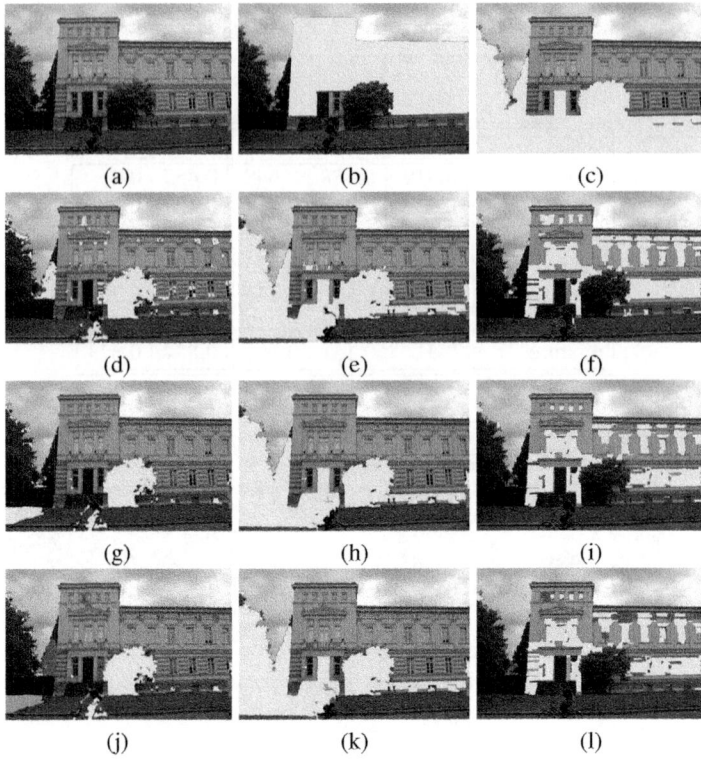

Fig. 4. Scene in Bonn (Germany). In the top row, (a) shows the original image, (b,c) the output of *building* and *vegetation* at the highest scale, respectively. In the next row, (d,e) show the κ-output for *vegetation* at two different lower scales and (f) the κ-output for *window* at a lower scale. In the bottom row, (g,h) show the output of the Bayesian network for *vegetation* at the same scales as a row above and (i) the output of the Bayesian network for *window* at the same scale as a row above. Last row shows differences between CBN-output and κ-output. Red regions are no longer classified, green regions are newly classified as vegetation or window, respectively.

classifiers typically perform better, if they perform well on these classes. Consequently, low occurring classes as *background*, *car* and *mixture* have very low success rates.

Fig. 3 shows three results from Berlin, Germany, where we obtain really good results with respect to one class. Here we see, that our classification scheme could be used for object detection in images as well. For further visual inspection, we prepared images showing the output of the classifications in fig.4. Within the image part visualized as *building* in (b) the classification results in the lower scales (d,e,f) compared to (g,h,i) improve significantly.

5   Adaptation of the Concept

Our concept for a Bayesian network used for scene interpretation as presented in sec. 2 only relies on (i) ground truth annotations, (ii) a hierarchical segmentation of the scene, (iii) the extraction of features for segmented regions including characteristics on their neighborhood and (iv) a classifier which returns probabilities regarding the region's class membership. Our proposed Conditional Bayesian network remains, although the other components may get changed. So far, we chose these components with respect to the domain of interpreting man-made scenes, where we want to recognize complex objects, such as facades, as well as their parts including their structure.

We are confident that we could transfer our concept to more general scene interpretation tasks as segmenting and classifying objects using the MSRC data set [21] or ImageNet [22]. These data sets do not use overlapping classes, i. e. objects and their parts (building resp. window), but show symbolic image descriptions with a single class for each pixel. The mapping between the segmented regions can be easily adapted, maybe our additional label *mixture* can be dropped. Furthermore, our segmentation could be exchanged by [9, 23], because the analysis of image partitions at a few scales might be more efficient for general recognition tasks than working with selected, but stable regions from various scales. Then, our feature vectors could get extended by additional features, e. g. [18] or [21], and a more powerful classifier as random forests or logistic regression could get integrated. Consequently, the classification results of a reference scale should be selected for its evaluation.

6   Conclusions

We propose a methodology for scene interpretation which combines the hierarchically ordered output of image segmentation and classification on the basis of region-specific features. The tree-structure of the segmented image regions is used to construct a conditional Bayesian network, and we may apply a very efficient inference algorithm. In the conditional Bayesian network, we combine the probabilities reflecting the region's class membership by a common classifier and the class-specific coherences within the hierarchy to improve the classification of segmented regions.

We presented reasonable results for detecting building parts and other objects in terrestrial facade images using the benchmark data set [20] and working with seven classes. We have increased the classification performance of our segmented regions from 51% (ordinary classification) to 62% (classification with conditional Bayesian network). Our approach is very efficient, because we may learn fast the needed probabilities on the hierarchy and the region-specific classification, and the inference of the network is simpler than in common MRFs.

Finally, we discussed how our approach can get generalized for application in other scene interpretation tasks. Further developments w.r.t. the domain of facade images could be done by integrating our results as input of a grammar-based approach. In our point of view, this extension should further improve the results, because they also consider the spatial arrangement of facade elements, e.g., the repetitive structures of windows.

References

1. Epshtein, B., Ullman, S.: Semantic Hierarchies for Recognizing Objects and Parts. In: CVPR (2007)
2. Fidler, S., Leonardis, A.: Towards Scalable Representations of Object Categories: Learning a Hierarchy of Parts. In: CVPR (2007)

3. Schnitzspan, P., Fritz, M., Schiele, B.: Hierarchical support vector random fields: Joint training to combine local and global features. In: Forsyth, D., Torr, P., Zisserman, A. (eds.) ECCV 2008, Part II. LNCS, vol. 5303, pp. 527–540. Springer, Heidelberg (2008)
4. Ladický, L., Russell, C., Kohli, P., Torr, P.H.S.: Associative Hierarchical CRFs for Object Class Image Segmentation. In: ICCV, pp. 739–746 (2009)
5. Lim, J.J., Arbeláez, P., Gu, C., Malik, J.: Context by Region Ancestry. In: ICCV (2009)
6. Ommer, B., Buhmann, J.: Learning the Compositional Nature of Visual Object Categories for Recognition. PAMI 32(3), 501–516 (2010)
7. Kumar, S., Hebert, M.: Man-made Structure Detection in Natural Images using a Causal Multiscale Random Field. In: CVPR, vol. I, pp. 119–226 (2003)
8. Verbeek, J., Triggs, B.: Region Classification with Markov Field Aspect Models. In: CVPR (2007)
9. Plath, N., Toussaint, M., Nakajima, S.: Multi-class Image Segmentation using Conditional Random Fields and Global Classification. In: ICML, pp. 817–824 (2009)
10. Dick, A.R., Torr, P.H.S., Cipolla, R.: Modelling and Interpretation of Architecture from Several Images. IJCV 60(2), 111–134 (2004)
11. Ripperda, N., Brenner, C.: Evaluation of Structure Recognition Using Labelled Facade Images. In: Denzler, J., Notni, G., Süße, H. (eds.) Pattern Recognition. LNCS, vol. 5748, pp. 532–541. Springer, Heidelberg (2009)
12. Lee, S.C., Nevatia, R.: Extraction and Integration of Window in a 3D Building Model from Ground View Images. In: CVPR, vol. II, pp. 113–120 (2004)
13. Reznik, S., Mayer, H.: Implicit Shape Models, Self-Diagnosis, and Model Selection for 3D Facade Interpretation. PFG 2008(3), 187–196 (2008)
14. Čech, J., Šára, R.: Languages for Constrained Binary Segmentation based on Maximum Aposteriori Probability Labeling. Intern. J. of Imaging and Technology 19(2), 66–99 (2009)
15. Jahangiri, M., Petrou, M.: Fully Bottom-up Blob Extraction in Building Facades. In: PRIA (2008)
16. Burochin, J.P., Tournaire, O., Paparoditis, N.: An Unsupervised Hierarchical Segmentation of a Facade Building Image in Elementary 2D-Models. In: ISPRS Workshop on Object Extraction for 3D City Models, Road Databases and Traffic Monitoring, pp. 223–228 (2009)
17. Drauschke, M.: An Irregular Pyramid for Multi-scale Analysis of Objects and Their Parts. In: Torsello, A., Escolano, F., Brun, L. (eds.) GbRPR 2009. LNCS, vol. 5534, pp. 293–303. Springer, Heidelberg (2009)
18. Dalal, N., Triggs, B.: Histograms of Oriented Gradients for Human Detection. In: CVPR, vol. I, pp. 886–893 (2005)
19. Pearl, J.: Causality: Models, Reasoning, and Inference. Cambridge University Press, Cambridge (2000)
20. Korč, F., Förstner, W.: eTRIMS Image Database for Interpreting Images of Man-Made Scenes. Technical Report TR-IGG-P-2009-01, IGG University of Bonn (2009)
21. Shotton, J., Winn, J.M., Rother, C., Criminisi, A.: textonBoost: Joint appearance, shape and context modeling for multi-class object recognition and segmentation. In: Leonardis, A., Bischof, H., Pinz, A. (eds.) ECCV 2006. LNCS, vol. 3951, pp. 1–15. Springer, Heidelberg (2006)
22. Deng, J., Dong, W., Socher, R., Li, L.J., Li, K., Fei-Fei, L.: ImageNet: A Large-Scale Hierarchical Image Database. In: CVPR, pp. 248–255 (2009)
23. Arbeláez, P., Maire, M., Fowlkes, C., Malik, J.: Contour Detection and Hierarchical Image Segmentation. PAMI 33(5), 898–916 (2011)

Multi-view Active Appearance Models for the X-Ray Based Analysis of Avian Bipedal Locomotion

Daniel Haase[1], John A. Nyakatura[2], and Joachim Denzler[1]

[1] Chair for Computer Vision
[2] Institute of Systematic Zoology and Evolutionary Biology
Friedrich Schiller University of Jena, 07743 Jena, Germany
{daniel.haase,john.nyakatura,joachim.denzler}@uni-jena.de

Abstract. Many fields of research in biology, motion science and robotics depend on the understanding of animal locomotion. Therefore, numerous experiments are performed using high-speed biplanar x-ray acquisition systems which record sequences of walking animals. Until now, the evaluation of these sequences is a very time-consuming task, as human experts have to manually annotate anatomical landmarks in the images. Therefore, an automation of this task at a minimum level of user interaction is worthwhile. However, many difficulties in the data—such as x-ray occlusions or anatomical ambiguities—drastically complicate this problem and require the use of global models. Active Appearance Models (AAMs) are known to be capable of dealing with occlusions, but have problems with ambiguities. We therefore analyze the application of multi-view AAMs in the scenario stated above and show that they can effectively handle uncertainties which can not be dealt with using single-view models. Furthermore, preliminary studies on the tracking performance of human experts indicate that the errors of multi-view AAMs are in the same order of magnitude as in the case of manual tracking.

1 Introduction and Related Work

Understanding animal locomotion is a crucial part of countless problems ranging from the field of biology over motion science to robotics. To name but a few, these problems include gaining a better understanding of evolution [1], the development of mathematical models of locomotion such as the *spring-mass model* [2], or building walking robots. To answer open questions in the field of locomotion research, avian bipedal locomotion provides an appropriate testbed. One reason for the suitability is that bird species exist in countless variations of important locomotion parameters like body mass and limb proportions and exhibit a large range of walking and running speeds.

To gain a profound and detailed insight into terrestrial bird locomotion, many different specimen of various species need to be studied. Nowadays, these studies are often entirely based on high-speed x-ray videography. As opposed to external marker based methods, the key advantage is that all important parts of the

R. Mester and M. Felsberg (Eds.): DAGM 2011, LNCS 6835, pp. 11–20, 2011.

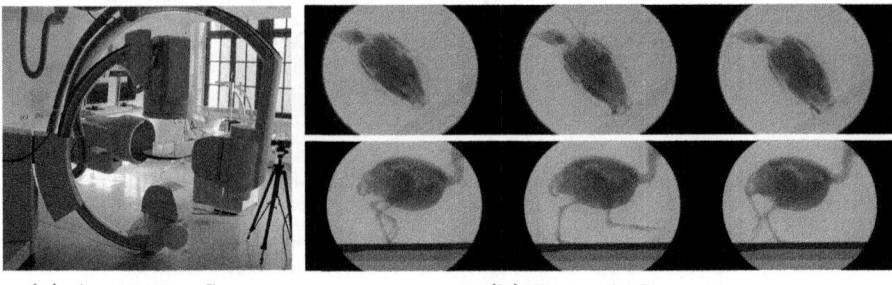

(a) Acquisition System   (b) Example Sequence

Fig. 1. (a) Biplanar high-speed x-ray acquisition system (Neurostar®, Siemens AG). (b) Example sequence of a quail (*Coturnix coturnix*) for the dorsoventral (*top row*) and lateral (*bottom row*) camera view acquired with this system.

locomotor system can be observed directly [3,1]. A state-of-the-art x-ray acquisition system is shown in Fig 1a. The system consists of two movable x-ray image intensifiers (C-arms) which are positioned around a table and allow for recordings at a high temporal and spatial resolution (1536 × 1024 pixels at 1 kHz). For the recording of animal locomotion sequences, a non-metallic treadmill is placed on the central table. In Fig. 1b, the locomotion of a quail (*Coturnix coturnix*) acquired using this system is exemplarily shown.

The evaluation of the locomotion sequences is mainly based on anatomical points of interest (*landmarks*), as for instance the *femur* (thighbone), the hip joints or the knee joints. Example landmarks used for a quail are shown in Fig. 3. Until now, the landmarks have to be located manually by human experts. Due to the high temporal resolution, however, this is a highly time-consuming task which has prevented the realization of large-scale studies up to now.

Therefore, there is urgent need to automate the task of anatomical landmark tracking for this application at a minimum of user interaction. At first sight, this might seem to be an easy task, as key point tracking is a well-researched topic in computer vision. Yet, there are several issues which tremendously complicate the procedure. The main problems are the severe and continuously changing occlusions in the x-ray images in consequence of the motion of the animal and the imaging process. This effect causes local image areas around anatomical landmarks to be extremely variable. Thus, local tracking techniques like optical-flow tracking [4], KLT-tracking [5], region-based tracking [6] or SIFT-tracking [7] are rendered impossible [8].

Model-based global approaches, on the other hand, explain each image as a whole and hence are less prone to local disturbances. A prominent example in this context is the registration of a given 3D computer tomography (CT) data set to a 2D image [9,10,11]. In our scenario, however, this is a very difficult task, as for each specimen a full-body CT scan plus a skeletal model would be necessary.

Active Appearance Models (AAMs) [12,13,14] offer another way of global modeling. They are entirely based on given training images having annotated landmarks, and a global model of shape and texture is learnt automatically. The

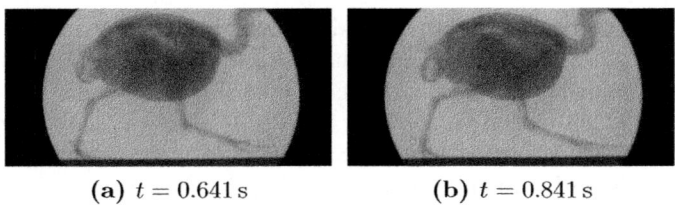

(a) $t = 0.641$ s   (b) $t = 0.841$ s

Fig. 2. Example for possible anatomical ambiguities. (a) and (b) depict the images 641 ($t = 0.641$ s) and 841 ($t = 0.841$ s) of a quail sequence, respectively. Both images seem to show the identical pose of the walking bird. However, in the first image, the quail's right leg is ahead of the left leg and in the second image it is vice versa.

general suitability of AAMs for the present tracking task is shown in [8], where a proof-of-concept is given and the impact of preprocessing methods and the choice of training images are analyzed. Further difficulties of the tracking task at hand which are not already covered in [8] are anatomical ambiguities, especially for parts of the locomotor system. An example for this case is shown in Fig. 2, where two approximately identical images are shown, which however represent opposing states of a walking period. To resolve these ambiguities, either temporal modeling or further context knowledge is necessary. Because one goal is to keep the amount of user-interaction and hence the number of training images small, a temporal model as described in [15] is not applicable. Instead, in the following we analyze the suitability of using both camera views at a time to resolve these uncertainties. For this task, we employ multi-view AAMs [16,17].

The remainder of this paper is organized as follows. In Sect. 2 we first give a brief overview of basic AAMs and then describe the application of these models for the current tracking task. Thereafter, we describe the adjustments presented in [16,17] to achieve a multi-view model. We present our experiments and results in Sect. 3. At the end we conclude our findings and discuss future work.

2   Active Appearance Models

Active Appearance Models (AAMs) [12,13,14] are well-known statistical models which are used to represent the appearance of objects in digital images. In the following, basic AAMs, their application on locomotion data and the extension on multiple camera views are described.

2.1   Training Step

In the training step of AAMs, the goal is to learn valid appearances of an object based on exemplary images. As the appearance is influenced by both shape and texture, it is necessary to model these two in a combined framework. Thus, the training step consists of building a *shape model*, a *texture model* and a *combined model*. The training data consist of N training images $I_1, \ldots, I_N$ and M two-dimensional landmarks $l_n = (x_{n,1}, y_{n,1}, \ldots, x_{n,M}, y_{n,M})^{\mathrm{T}}$ for each image I_n.

Modeling Shape. The goal in this step is to determine the joint movements of the given landmarks in a statistical manner by using Principle Component Analysis (PCA). As first step, all shapes are aligned with respect to scale, rotation and translation. Then, the landmarks are combined into the matrix $L = (l_1 - l_\mu, \dots, l_N - l_\mu)$, where $l_\mu = 1/N \sum_{n=1}^{N} l_n$ is the *mean shape*. The PCA is applied on L, which gives the matrix P_L of *shape eigenvectors*. By this means, an arbitrary shape l' can then be described by its *shape parameters* $b_{l'}$ via

$$l' = l_\mu + P_L b_{l'}, \quad \text{where} \quad b_{l'} = P_L^T \left(l' - l_\mu \right). \tag{1}$$

Modeling Texture. The combined variations of the gray values are analyzed in a similar manner as in the previous step. The object textures of the images I_n are shape-normalized to fit a common reference shape, forming the texture vectors g_n. Afterwards, a PCA is applied on the matrix $G = (g_1 - g_\mu, \dots, g_N - g_\mu)$, where $g_\mu = 1/N \sum_{n=1}^{N} g_n$ is called the *mean texture*. The result are the *texture eigenvectors* P_G, which can be used to represent an arbitrary texture g' by its *texture parameters* $b_{g'}$ by means of

$$g' = g_\mu + P_G b_{g'}, \quad \text{where} \quad b_{g'} = P_G^T \left(g' - g_\mu \right). \tag{2}$$

Modeling Appearance. In the third sub-step, the shape parameters b_{l_n} and the texture parameters b_{g_n} are concatenated into a new vector $c_n = (w b_{l_n}^T, b_{g_n}^T)^T$ for each training image I_n. Here, $w \in \mathbb{R}$ is a scaling factor to account for the different units of shape and intensity. Then, a final PCA is applied on $C = (c_1, \dots, c_N)$, which yields the matrix P_C of *appearance eigenvectors*. Each object instance with shape parameters $b_{l'}$ and texture parameters $b_{g'}$ can then be described by its *appearance parameters* $b_{c'}$ via

$$c' = (w b_{l'}^T, b_{g'}^T)^T = P_C b_{c'}, \quad \text{where} \quad b_{c'} = P_C^T c'. \tag{3}$$

By restricting P_C on the leading eigenvectors with a certain amount of the total variance, the number of model parameters can be reduced dramatically.

2.2 Model Fitting

To fit a trained model on new data, the necessary parameter updates δc are predicted based on the texture difference δg between model and image. For this purpose, a linear model $\delta c = R \delta g$ is used. The coefficients R are estimated using multivariate regression by systematically displacing the known model parameters of the training images. For a previously unseen image, the AAM can then be fitted by iteratively adapting the model parameters according to R and δg.

2.3 Application on Locomotion Data

For the application of AAMs to the task of landmark tracking in locomotion data, several issues have to be considered. A fundamental question is concerned

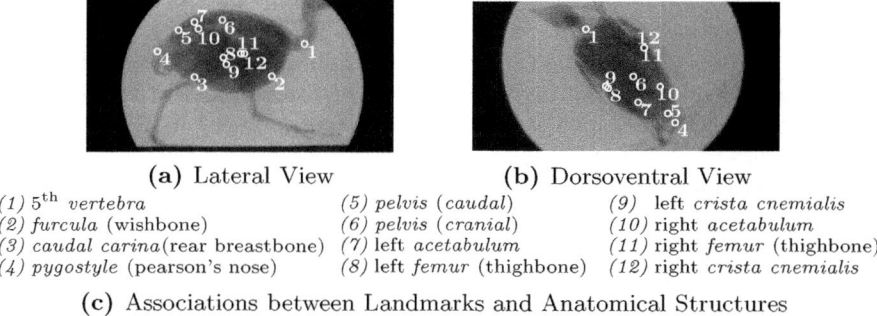

(a) Lateral View   (b) Dorsoventral View

(1) 5th vertebra   (5) pelvis (caudal)   (9) left crista cnemialis
(2) furcula (wishbone)   (6) pelvis (cranial)   (10) right acetabulum
(3) caudal carina(rear breastbone) (7) left acetabulum   (11) right femur (thighbone)
(4) pygostyle (pearson's nose)   (8) left femur (thighbone)   (12) right crista cnemialis

(c) Associations between Landmarks and Anatomical Structures

Fig. 3. Overview of the anatomical landmarks used in the two camera views of the employed quail data set

1st shape parameter   2nd shape parameter   1st shape parameter   2nd shape parameter
(lateral model)   (lateral model)   (dorsoventral model)   (dorsoventral model)

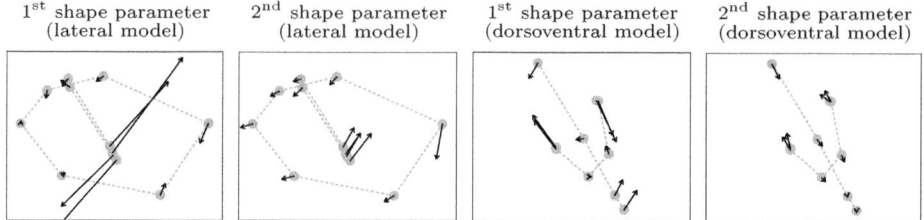

Fig. 4. Influence of the shape parameters of the lateral and dorsoventral shape models. The arrows indicate the movement of the landmarks for positive parameter values. For negative values, the orientation of the arrows is the other way around. The shown landmarks are described in Fig. 3.

with the selection of training images and the resulting scope of the model. Possible options range from generic inter-species bird models over specimen-specific models to models for each individual locomotion sequence. Due to differences in anatomy, annotated landmarks and the experimental setup between multiple recordings, we concentrate on sequence-based AAMs.

In this case, annotated images taken from the sequence to be analyzed are used for training. Note that this is an important difference compared to standard AAMs which are usually trained on a set of independent object instances (e.g. a face database in the context of face modeling). As a consequence, the resulting AAM becomes a basic locomotion model which expresses the dynamic variation of the landmarks over time. An example for this effect on the quail data set (see Fig. 3) is shown in Fig. 4. It depicts the influence of the first and second shape parameters for a lateral and a dorsoventral AAM. It can clearly be seen that for both models the first shape parameter governs the movement of the thigh bones. The second parameter mainly represents the typical cervical movement of the quail which occurs during locomotion.

Another area of concern for this application is the huge shape non-stationarity (cf. [18]) which is induced by the movement of the landmarks during locomotion.

As at least a certain degree of shape stationarity is assumed for AAMs, currently only the torso, the knee joint and the hip joint landmarks (see Fig. 3) are considered for automated tracking. In general, simply including the toe landmarks, for instance, will lead to a drastically decreased tracking performance.

More details on the topics described above can be found in [8].

2.4   Multi-view Model

The extension of AAMs on multiple camera views is presented by [16,17] in the context of medical image analysis. If we denote the number of camera views to be modeled by K, then the nth training example consists of the images $\boldsymbol{I}_n^{(1)}, \ldots, \boldsymbol{I}_n^{(K)}$ and the landmarks $\boldsymbol{l}_n^{(1)}, \ldots, \boldsymbol{l}_n^{(K)}$ in these images. As first step, the landmarks $\boldsymbol{l}_n^{(k)}$ of all training examples are aligned camera-wise just like in the single-view case. Then, all training images have to be shape-normalized, however still independently for each camera view, yielding $\boldsymbol{g}_n^{(k)}$. The main idea is then to simply concatenate the landmark vectors and the texture vectors of the camera views for each training example $1 \leq n \leq N$ in the sense of

$$\boldsymbol{l}_n = \left(\boldsymbol{l}_n^{(1)\,\text{T}}, \ldots, \boldsymbol{l}_n^{(K)\,\text{T}} \right)^{\text{T}} \quad \text{and} \quad \boldsymbol{g}_n = \left(\boldsymbol{g}_n^{(1)\,\text{T}}, \ldots, \boldsymbol{g}_n^{(K)\,\text{T}} \right)^{\text{T}}. \tag{4}$$

In this way, each training example actually consisting of multiple shapes and textures can effectively be reduced to just one landmark vector $\boldsymbol{l}_n$ and one texture vector $\boldsymbol{g}_n$. The subsequent steps exactly follow those from the case of the single-view model, and the multiple views are modeled implicitly.

3   Experiments and Results

In the following we experimentally analyze the benefits of multi-view AAMs in comparison to single-view AAMs for the present task of anatomical landmark tracking. As the main goal is to achieve sound tracking results at a minimum of user interaction, the essential questions to be answered are:

- Can multi-view AAMs substantially resolve anatomical ambiguities which can not be overcome using single-view models?
- Is a reduction of the amount of training data possible with multi-view AAMs?
- How do these models perform compared to manually tracked landmarks?

To answer these questions, all experiments were conducted on a real data set for which comprehensive ground-truth landmark positions are available. This data set shows the locomotion of a quail from two camera views (*lateral* and *dorsoventral*, see Figs. 1 and 3) and has a length of 2245 images (2.245 s recorded at 1 kHz). As a rescaling of the original images (1536×1024) to a size of 25% does not lead to a substantial loss of tracking quality [8], all experiments were conducted on the smaller versions for performance reasons. The evaluations, however, were performed with respect to the original image size in any case. Ground-truth landmark positions obtained from experts are available for 81 frames evenly spread over the entire sequence and allow a systematic evaluation.

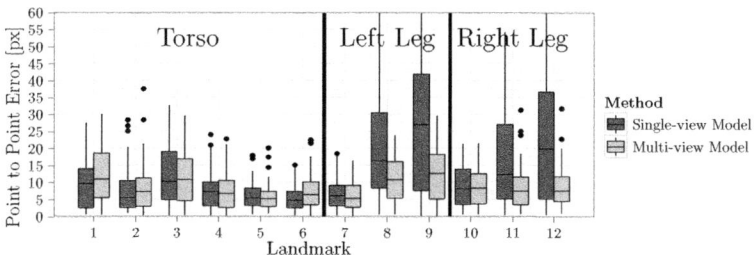

Fig. 5. Comparison of the tracking results between a single-view and a multi-view AAM for the landmarks of the lateral camera view. Using a multi-view model, anatomical ambiguities can be substantially resolved. As a result, the tracking quality of the knee landmarks 8, 9, 11 and 12 is drastically improved.

The quantitative evaluation of the results is based on the Euclidian distance between tracked and ground-truth landmark, which is known as *point to point error* [19].

3.1 Resolving Anatomical Ambiguities

In the course of this paper we presented an example for anatomical ambiguities which can arise in locomotion sequences (see Fig. 2). Furthermore, we stated that these uncertainties can not be resolved using single-view AAMs and that the application of multi-view AAMs is inevitable. To support this hypothesis, we trained two single-view AAMs on the lateral and dorsoventral view of the data set and compared the results with an—in other respects identical—multi-view AAM. For training, 15 images from one walking period at the end of the sequence were selected. Due to the ambiguities described above, the single-view model of the lateral view has severe problems of locating the knee landmarks correctly and even occasionally mixes the landmarks for the left and right knee up. The comparison of single-view and multi-view model is given in Fig. 5. It can clearly be seen that the multi-view model drastically improves the tracking results of the knee landmarks (8, 9, 11, 12, see Fig. 3). Small errors, as, for instance, indicated by the 25% quartiles, are reduced observably, however, the major enhancements are present in the larger error regions. The median error for the right knee landmark (12) is, for instance, reduced from 20 px in the single-view case to 8 px in the multi-view case.

For the torso landmarks, however, no substantial improvement is observed. This result can be explained by the fact that the torso landmarks usually have a low ambiguity due to low interference with parts of the locomotor system.

3.2 Reduction of the Amount of Training Data

One very important goal is to keep the human interaction spent for landmark labeling at a minimum to allow for a large amount of data to be processed. Therefore, the amount of training images is an important factor. However, less

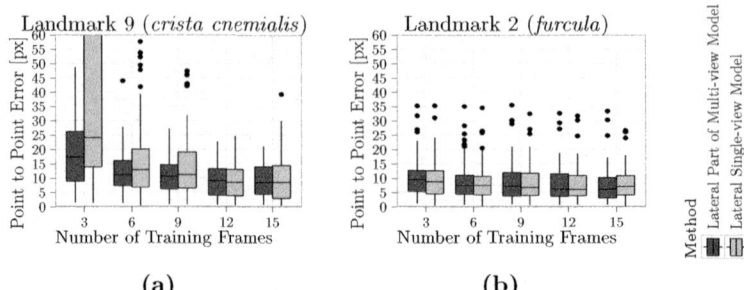

Fig. 6. Influence of the reduction of training data on single-view and multi-view AAMs. The results are shown for (a) an exemplary knee landmark (*crista cnemialis*) and (b) an exemplary torso landmark (*furcula*).

training images usually cause greater uncertainties and hence greater errors during tracking. As discussed in the last subsection, the multi-view model is capable of reducing uncertainties. For this reason, an interesting question is whether multi-view AAMs can be used to decrease the necessary amount of training data.

To answer this question, we compared the tracking results of single-view and multi-view AAMs with identical parameters for varying numbers of training frames. The frames were chosen from the third walking period of the quail in the middle of the sequence. As in the last subsection, the results vary considerably between torso landmarks and landmarks of the locomotor system. In Figs. 6a and 6b, example results for both cases are shown. The former depicts the case for a knee landmark (landmark 9, left *crista cnemialis*, see Fig. 3). Here, it can be seen that the errors of both the single- and the multi-view model increase as the amount of training frames is reduced. However, the errors for the single-view model rise much more rapidly. In the case of the torso landmark, the results remain approximately constant for both the single- and the multi-view models. Again, this can be explained by the low ambiguity of this kind of landmarks.

Above results indicate that multi-view models can be used to decrease the necessary amount of training frames. While the uncertainty of the torso landmarks can not be decreased substantially as they are not subject to anatomical ambiguities, the uncertainty of the locomotion landmarks can be reduced.

3.3 Comparison to Manual Landmark Tracking

Tracking Time. For the multi-view model presented in Subsec. 3.1, a total time of 38.20 min (15.21 min training, 22.99 min tracking) was required. As the sequence has a total number of 2245 images per camera view, this corresponds to a time of 0.51 s per image. Human experts, on the contrary, usually need at least about 45 s per image, which results in speed-up factors greater than 90.

Accuracy and Precision. To allow for a meaningful comparison between automated tracking results and manual tracking, currently a large-scale study on the accuracy and precision of human experts is in progress. Here, four experts are to label one and the same locomotion sequence, three times each, and independently of one another. Unfortunately, not all results are available to date.

Yet, first comparisons between multiple labelings of two experts for the given data set indicate that the typical human errors are in the range of about 0.5 px (min.), 5.5 px (1st quartile), 9 px (median), 14 px (3rd quartile) and 40 px (max.). Taking these preliminary results into account, we can state that the errors of the multi-view AAM shown in Fig. 5 are in the same order of magnitude as the manual errors.

4   Conclusions and Further Work

In this work we analyzed the benefits of multi-view Active Appearance Models for the application of anatomical landmark tracking in biplanar x-ray locomotion sequences. We showed that multi-view models perform substantially better than comparable single-view models in situations of high uncertainty, e.g. for frames with anatomical ambiguities. Furthermore, we compared single-view and multi-view models for varying amounts of training data and demonstrated that the latter can be used to reduce the necessary amount of user labeled training images. Finally we stated that, based on preliminary studies, the performance of multi-view AAMs is in the same order of magnitude as in the case of manual tracking.

An interesting point for future work is to expand the presented approach on landmark configurations with a substantially larger non-stationarity, as for example shapes including toe landmarks. Also, local refinement methods could be analyzed in order to obtain an even more accurate adaptation to the anatomical structures. The preliminary studies on the precision of manual tracking should be continued to enable a more profound comparison to automated methods.

Acknowledgements. The authors would like to thank Alexander Stößel from the Institute of Systematic Zoology at the Friedrich Schiller University of Jena for providing the labeled quail dataset.

This research was supported by grant DE 735/8-1 of the German Research Foundation (DFG).

References

1. Gatesy, S.M.: Guineafowl hind limb function. I: Cineradiographic analysis and speed effects. J. Morphol. 240, 1097–4687 (1999)
2. Blickhan, R.: The spring-mass model for running and hopping. J. Biomech. 22, 1217–1227 (1989)
3. Brainerd, E.L., Baier, D.B., Gatesy, S.M., Hedrick, T.L., Metzger, K.A., Gilbert, S.L., Crisco, J.J.: X-ray reconstruction of moving morphology (XROMM): Precision, accuracy and applications in comparative biomechanics research. J. Exp. Zool. A 313A, 262–279 (2010)
4. Horn, B.K.P., Schunck, B.G.: Determining optical flow. Artif. Intell. 17, 185–203 (1981)

5. Baker, S., Matthews, I.: Lucas-kanade 20 years on: A unifying framework. Int. J. Comput. Vision 56, 221–255 (2004)
6. Hager, G.D., Belhumeur, P.N.: Efficient region tracking with parametric models of geometry and illumination. IEEE T. Pattern Anal. 20, 1025–1039 (1998)
7. Lowe, D.G.: Distinctive image features from scale-invariant keypoints. Int. J. Comput. Vision 60, 91–110 (2004)
8. Haase, D., Denzler, J.: Anatomical landmark tracking for the analysis of animal locomotion in X-ray videos using active appearance models. In: Heyden, A., Kahl, F. (eds.) SCIA 2011. LNCS, vol. 6688, pp. 604–615. Springer, Heidelberg (2011)
9. Rohlfing, T., Denzler, J., Gräßl, C., Russakoff, D.B., Maurer Jr., C.R.: Markerless real-time 3-d target region tracking by motion backprojection from projection images. IEEE T. Med. Imaging 24, 1455–1468 (2005)
10. Bey, M.J., Zauel, R., Brock, S.K., Tashman, S.: Validation of a new model-based tracking technique for measuring three-dimensional, in vivo glenohumeral joint kinematics. J. Biomech. Eng. 128, 604–609 (2006)
11. Brainerd, E.L., Gatesy, S.M., Baier, D.B., Hedrick, T.L.: A method for accurate 3D reconstruction of skeletal morphology and movement with CTX imaging. Comp. Biochem. Physiol. 146, 119 (2007)
12. Cootes, T.F., Edwards, G.J., Taylor, C.J.: Active appearance models. In: Burkhardt, H., Neumann, B. (eds.) ECCV 1998. LNCS, vol. 1407, pp. 484–498. Springer, Heidelberg (1998)
13. Edwards, G.J., Cootes, T.F., Taylor, C.J.: Face recognition using active appearance models. In: Burkhardt, H., Neumann, B. (eds.) ECCV 1998. LNCS, vol. 1407, pp. 581–595. Springer, Heidelberg (1998)
14. Cootes, T.F., Edwards, G.J., Taylor, C.J.: Active appearance models. IEEE T. Pattern Anal. 23, 681–685 (2001)
15. Bosch, J.G., Mitchell, S.C., Lelieveldt, B.P.F., Nijland, F., Kamp, O., Sonka, M., Reiber, J.H.C.: Automatic segmentation of echocardiographic sequences by active appearance motion models. IEEE T. Med. Imaging 21, 1374–1383 (2002)
16. Lelieveldt, B., Üzümcü, M., van der Geest, R., Reiber, J., Sonka, M.: Multi-view active appearance models for consistent segmentation of multiple standard views. International Congress Series 1256, 1141–1146 (2003)
17. Oost, E., Koning, G., Sonka, M., Oemrawsingh, P.V., Reiber, J.H.C., Lelieveldt, B.P.F.: Automated contour detection in x-ray left ventricular angiograms using multiview active appearance models and dynamic programming. IEEE T. Med. Imaging 25, 1158–1171 (2006)
18. Das, S., Vaswani, N.: Nonstationary shape activities: Dynamic models for landmark shape change and applications. IEEE T. Pattern Anal. 32, 579–592 (2010)
19. Stegmann, M.B.: Active appearance models: Theory, extensions and cases. Master's thesis, Technical University of Denmark, DTU (2000)

A Fully Implicit Framework for Sobolev Active Contours and Surfaces

Maximilian Baust and Nassir Navab

Computer Aided Medical Procedures and Augmented Reality (CAMPAR)
Technische Universität München

Abstract. We present a convenient framework for Sobolev active contours and surfaces, which uses an implicit representation on purpose, in contrast to related approaches which use an implicit representation only for the computation of Sobolev gradients. Another difference to related approaches is that we use a Sobolev type inner product, which has a better geometric interpretation, such as the ones proposed for Sobolev active contours. Since the computation of Sobolev gradients for surface evolutions requires the solution of partial differential equations on surfaces, we derive a numerical scheme which allows the user to obtain approximative Sobolev gradients even in linear complexity, if desired. Finally, we perform several experiments to demonstrate that the resulting curve and surface evolutions enjoy the same regularity properties as the original Sobolev active contours and show the whole potential of our method by tracking the left ventricular cavity acquired with 4D MRI.

1 Introduction

Several problems in computer vision, such as image registration, segmentation, stereo, and denoising, can be formulated as energy minimization problems. If the modeled energy is convex, several global solution techniques can be used to find a solution, e.g. [10,16]. There are, however, some cases where local techniques, such as gradient descent, have to be used:

- The energy to be minimized is not convex, e.g. special energies for vessel segmentation [11].
- The energy is convex, but the global minimum does not correspond to the desired solution.

A typical example for the latter scenario is the usage of the Chan-Vese model for tracking applications, e.g. [18]: this energy can be convexified [3], but its global optima may not correspond to meaningful results and thus local methods, such as gradient descent, have to be used.

During the last two decades, the idea of Sobolev gradients [12] has turned out to be a powerful advancement in gradient descent based optimization and it has been applied quite successfully to several computer vision problems, such as deformable registration [21], image segmentation [20,6], and image denoising [4].

R. Mester and M. Felsberg (Eds.): DAGM 2011, LNCS 6835, pp. 21–30, 2011.

Put simply, the idea of Sobolev gradients is to project the standard L^2 gradient of an energy, which is obtained via the calculus of variations, into a subspace of L^2 which contains more regular functions, i.e. a Sobolev space. Projecting the gradient usually requires the solution of an elliptic partial differential equation (PDE) and has to be done in every iteration step. The computation of Sobolev gradients for active contours and surfaces is even more involved, because one needs to solve this PDE on evolving curves or surfaces, respectively. While the computation of Sobolev gradients for contours can be done in linear complexity [20], the computation for surfaces enforces the solution of an equation system due to the elliptic character of the problem. Although it has been demonstrated by [6] and [8] that Sobolev type surface evolutions are computationally feasible, there is still some space for improvements, which shall be demonstrated by this paper:

1. In contrast to related approaches for surface evolutions [6,8] we will employ a geometrically motivated Sobolev-type inner product, which allows the user to weight the translational and the deformational component of the computed gradient. This inner product is related to the ones that have been proposed for active contours by [20,19].
2. All previous approaches for Sobolev type curve and surface evolutions use either no implicit surface representation at all [8], or an implicit surface representation only for projecting the gradient [20,6]. In contrast to this, we use an implicit representation throughout the whole paper, which yields a convenient framework for Sobolev type curve *and* surface evolutions.
3. In order to solve the projection step in a computationally efficient manner, we propose to turn the resulting elliptic PDE into a parabolic one, which corresponds to a continuous gradient descent. We further split the elliptic operator in such a way that a standard semi-implicit time discretization can be used. If desired, one can even use operator splitting techniques, e.g. [22], in order to obtain an approximative Sobolev gradient in *linear complexity*.

Before we explain the theory of Sobolev spaces on implicit surfaces in Sec. 3, we briefly review the classical L^2 framework for variational level set based segmentation in Sec. 2. In Sec. 4 we derive the proposed numerical scheme and in Sec. 5 we verify the expected properties of the proposed method experimentally.

2   The Classical L^2 Framework

The considerations in the remainder of this paper are based on a signed distance representation of the evolving curve or surface $\mathcal{S} \subset \Omega \subset \mathbb{R}^d$ $(d = 2, 3)$:

$$\phi(x) = \begin{cases} -d(x, \mathcal{S}), & \text{if } x \text{ is inside } \mathcal{S}, \\ 0, & \text{if } x \text{ is on } \mathcal{S}, \\ +d(x, \mathcal{S}), & \text{if } x \text{ is outside } \mathcal{S}, \end{cases} \tag{1}$$

where $\phi : \Omega \subset \mathbb{R}^d \to \mathbb{R}$. In the following we will use the well-known property $|\nabla \phi| = 1$ in order to simplify the notation whenever possible.

We assume that our segmentation problem is modeled as a minimization problem of the form

$$\min_{\phi} E(\phi). \tag{2}$$

In order to make the following derivations more illustrative we further assume that E is a linear combination of a region and a surface integral, e.g.

$$E(\phi) = \frac{1}{|\mathcal{S}|} \int_{\Omega} H_\epsilon(-\phi) f \ dx + \frac{\alpha}{|\mathcal{S}|} \int_{\Omega} \delta_\epsilon(\phi) g \ dx, \tag{3}$$

where

$$H_\epsilon(\phi) = \begin{cases} 0, & \phi < \epsilon, \\ \frac{1}{2} + \frac{\phi}{2\epsilon} + \frac{1}{2\pi} \sin(\frac{\pi\phi}{\epsilon}), & |\phi| \le \epsilon, \\ 1, & \epsilon < \phi, \end{cases} \qquad \delta_\epsilon(\phi) = \begin{cases} \frac{1}{2\epsilon} + \frac{1}{2\epsilon} \cos(\frac{\pi\phi}{\epsilon}), & |\phi| \le \epsilon, \\ 0, & |\phi| > \epsilon, \end{cases} \tag{4}$$

are first-order accurate approximations of the Heaviside function H and its distributional derivative δ, cf. [13]. Note that this energy is made scale-invariant by normalizing it by the surface area $|\mathcal{S}|$. Computing the first variation $F(E, \psi)$ of E yields

$$F(E, \psi) = \frac{d}{dt} E(\phi + t\psi) \Big|_{t=0} = -\frac{1}{|\mathcal{S}|} \int_{\Omega} \delta_\epsilon(\phi) \left[f + \alpha \mathrm{div} \left(g \nabla \phi \right) \right] \psi \ dx = 0, \tag{5}$$

where ψ is an arbitrary variation of ϕ. Taking a closer look at (5) we identify the L^2-type inner product

$$F(E, \psi) = \langle -\left(f + \alpha \mathrm{div} \left(g \nabla \phi \right) \right), \psi \rangle_{L^2} = 0, \tag{6}$$

where

$$\langle u, v \rangle_{L^2} = \frac{1}{|\mathcal{S}|} \int_{\Omega} \delta_\epsilon(\phi) uv \ dx. \tag{7}$$

The key observation, first made by [20] and [6], is that the gradient of the energy, i.e. $- \left(f + \alpha \mathrm{div} \left(g \nabla \phi \right) \right)$, depends on the choice of the inner product and we thus write

$$\nabla_{L^2} E = -\left(f + \alpha \mathrm{div} \left(g \nabla \phi \right) \right). \tag{8}$$

This gradient is usually used in a continuous gradient descent

$$\partial_t \phi = -\delta_\epsilon(\phi) \nabla_{L^2} E \tag{9}$$

in order to evolve the contour or surface towards the desired configuration.

The problem of $\nabla_{L^2} E$ is that it inherits the local behavior of the image data to be segmented, cf. Fig. 1. This makes any curve or surface evolution based on $\nabla_{L^2} E$ very local and prone to get stuck in an undesired local minimum [20]. By using an inner product in (6) which enforces the computed gradient to be more regular, i.e. to be an element of a Sobolev space, we can solve this problem.

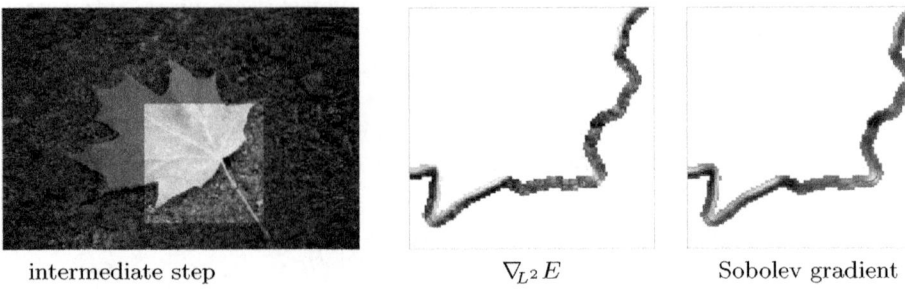

intermediate step	$\nabla_{L^2}E$	Sobolev gradient

Fig. 1. We compare the classical L^2 gradient and the Sobolev gradient visualized in the narrow band around the contour. Note that the Sobolev gradient is much more regular than the L^2 gradient. (The image data taken from [1].)

Before we proceed, we want to briefly discuss the computation of the first variation in (5). It has been demonstrated in [7] that computing the first variation with respect to the embedding function, as done in (5), is different to computing the first variation of E with respect to the surface itself. The technique presented in [7] for converting level set gradients to shape gradients is, however, only available in two dimensions. If a similar technique becomes available for three dimensions, it would also make the proposed framework more geometric, but until then we rely on computing the first variation with respect to ϕ.

As a consequence, our definition of $\nabla_{L^2}E$ is slightly different to the usual convention of defining $\langle u, v \rangle_{L^2} = \int_{\Omega} uv \, dx$ and $\nabla_{L^2}E = -\delta_\epsilon(\phi)\left[f + \alpha\text{div}(g\nabla_\phi)\right]$. This way, the inner product defined in (7) can be interpreted as an approximation to the L^2 inner product for functions defined on $\mathcal{S}$ rather than functions defined on Ω. Thus, $\nabla_{L^2}E$ as it is defined in (8) shall be interpreted as a function defined on $\mathcal{S}$. This interpretation would, of course, give rise to the question of how $\nabla_{L^2}E$ has to be extended to the support of δ_ϵ in order make the evolution in (9) well defined, but since the definition of $\nabla_{L^2}E$ makes sense for all points in Ω this extension is naturally given.

3   Sobolev Spaces on Implicit Surfaces

As discussed in the last subsection, carrying out the computation of the energy gradient in a Hilbert space which contains more regular functions would lead to more regular gradients, cf. Fig. 1. A natural choice are Sobolev spaces, because they enforce not only the L^2 norm of the function itself, but also its derivatives to be finite.

3.1   Sobolev Spaces

The Classical Sobolev Space H^1. In [6,8] a Sobolev space of the following type has been used for obtaining more regular gradients:

$$H^1(\mathcal{S}) = \left\{ u \in L^2(\mathcal{S}) : \|u\|_{H^1} < \infty \right\}, \tag{10}$$

where $\|u\|_{H^1}^2 = \langle u, u \rangle_{H^1}$,

$$\langle u, v \rangle_{H^1} = \lambda \langle u, v \rangle_{L^2} + \frac{1}{|\mathcal{S}|} \int_\Omega \delta_\epsilon(\phi) \nabla_{\mathcal{S}} u \cdot \nabla_{\mathcal{S}} v \, dx, \quad \lambda > 0. \tag{11}$$

Noting that the unit outward normal is given by $\eta = \nabla \phi$ we can write the intrinsic surface gradient as

$$\nabla_{\mathcal{S}} u = (I - \eta \otimes \eta) \nabla u, \tag{12}$$

which is a projection of ∇u onto $\mathcal{S}$, cf. [2]. In contrast to [6,8] we decided to weight the zero order component of $\langle \cdot, \cdot \rangle_{H^1}$, because this will allow us to better compare H^1 to the following Sobolev space.

The Geometrically Motivated Sobolev Space $\hat{H}^1$. The reason why we propose to use a different Sobolev space is that the zero order component $\langle u, v \rangle_{L^2}$ of H^1 has no geometric interpretation. Inspired by [20] we propose the following Sobolev space

$$\hat{H}^1(\mathcal{S}) = \left\{ u \in L^2(\mathcal{S}) : \|u\|_{\hat{H}^1} < \infty \right\}, \tag{13}$$

where $\|u\|_{\hat{H}^1}^2 = \langle u, u \rangle_{\hat{H}^1}$,

$$\langle u, v \rangle_{\hat{H}^1} = \lambda \bar{u} \cdot \bar{v} + \frac{1}{|\mathcal{S}|} \int_\Omega \delta_\epsilon(\phi) \nabla_{\mathcal{S}} u \cdot \nabla_{\mathcal{S}} v \, dx, \quad \lambda > 0, \tag{14}$$

and

$$\bar{u} = \frac{1}{|\mathcal{S}|} \int_\Omega \delta_\epsilon(\phi) u \eta \, dx. \tag{15}$$

The benefit of this Sobolev space is that the zero order component of the inner product has a geometric interpretation, $\bar{u}$ is the translational amount of u. This geometric meaning can also be observed experimentally, cf. Sec. 5.

3.2 Computing Sobolev Gradients

Fortunately, Sobolev gradients can be computed easily from the standard L^2 gradient by means of the Riesz representation theorem [9]. In order to simplify the notation we define $u = \nabla_{H^1} E$, $\hat{u} = \nabla_{\hat{H}^1} E$, and $w = \nabla_{L^2} E$. We further define

$$\fint_\Omega \cdot \, dx = \frac{1}{|\mathcal{S}|} \int_\Omega \delta_\epsilon(\phi) \cdot \, dx. \tag{16}$$

Computing $\nabla_{H^1} E$. Applying the representation theorem we obtain:

$$\langle w, v \rangle_{L^2} = \fint_\Omega wv \, dx = \fint_\Omega [\lambda uv + \nabla_{\mathcal{S}} u \cdot \nabla_{\mathcal{S}} v] \, dx = \langle u, v \rangle_{H^1}, \tag{17}$$

where v is chosen arbitrarily. Noting that $\mathcal{S}$ is a closed surface and applying integration by parts we obtain

$$\fint_\Omega wv \, dx = \fint_\Omega [\lambda u - \Delta_{\mathcal{S}} u] v \, dx, \tag{18}$$

where
$$\Delta_S u = \mathrm{div}\left((I - \eta \otimes \eta) \nabla u \right) \tag{19}$$
is the intrinsic surface Laplacian, i.e. the Laplace-Beltrami operator, cf. [2]. Applying the fundamental lemma of calculus of variations we obtain
$$w = (\lambda I - \Delta_S) u. \tag{20}$$
In order to solve this surface PDE we impose homogeneous Dirichlet boundary conditions $u|_{\Gamma_\epsilon} = 0$, where Γ_ϵ denotes the boundary of the support of δ_ϵ, which we denote by $\Omega_\epsilon = \{ x \in \Omega : \delta_\epsilon(x) > 0 \}$.

Computing $\nabla_{\hat{H}^1} E$. Again, we apply the representation theorem:
$$\langle w, v \rangle_{L^2} = \int_\Omega wv \, dx = \lambda \bar{u} \cdot \bar{v} + \int_\Omega \nabla_S u \cdot \nabla_S v \, dx = \langle u, v \rangle_{\hat{H}^1}. \tag{21}$$
Inserting the definition of $\bar{v}$ yields
$$\int_\Omega wv \, dx = \int_\Omega \left[\lambda \bar{u} \cdot (v\eta) + \nabla_S u \cdot \nabla_S v \right] \, dx. \tag{22}$$
Integrating by parts and using the fundamental lemma we end up with
$$w = \lambda \bar{u} \cdot \eta - \Delta_S u. \tag{23}$$
As $\bar{w} = \bar{u}$, we finally have
$$w - \lambda \bar{w} \cdot \eta = -\Delta_S u. \tag{24}$$
Similar to (20) we impose homogeneous Dirichlet boundary conditions on Γ_ϵ.

4   Numerical Treatment

Once we have computed $\nabla_{H^1} E$ or $\nabla_{\hat{H}^1} E$ numerically, we can use it to evolve the embedding function by
$$\partial_t \phi = -\delta_\epsilon(\phi) \nabla_{H^1} E, \quad \text{or} \quad \partial_t \phi = -\delta_\epsilon(\phi) \nabla_{\hat{H}^1} E, \tag{25}$$
respectively, where we use $\epsilon = 1.5$, as suggested in [14]. We approximate the time derivative with a standard forward Euler discretization and interleave this evolution with a few iteration steps for reinitializing the signed distance function, where we use the method of Peng et al. [15] in our experiments. A more geometric way of maintaining a signed distance representation would, of course, be given by the method of Chen et al. [7], which is unfortunately only available for two dimensional problems. However, it should be noted that ϕ deviates much less from a signed distance function during the evolution when we use Sobolev gradients instead of classical L^2 gradients.

The only question remaining is how to compute $\nabla_{H^1} E = u$ or $\nabla_{\hat{H}^1} = \hat{u}$ numerically, if $\nabla_{L^2} E = w$ is given. Our strategy will be to turn the stationary PDEs (20) and (24) into time dependent ones and split the elliptic operators in such a way that a standard semi-implicit time discretization for parabolic problems can be used.

Computing $\nabla_{H^1} E$ Numerically. At first we note that (20) may be interpreted as the gradient of the energy

$$\frac{1}{2} \int_{\Omega_\epsilon} \|\nabla_{\mathcal{S}} u\|_2^2 + \lambda u^2 - 2uw \; dx. \tag{26}$$

A continuous gradient descent for this energy yields the parabolic problem

$$\partial_t u = \Delta_{\mathcal{S}} u - \lambda u + w. \tag{27}$$

Next we split $\Delta_{\mathcal{S}}$ which yields:

$$\partial_t u = \Delta u - \operatorname{div}(\eta \otimes \eta \nabla u) - \lambda u + w. \tag{28}$$

Finally, we employ a semi-implicit time discretization leading to

$$(I - \tau \Delta) u^{t+\tau} = u^t - \tau \left[\operatorname{div}(\eta \otimes \eta \nabla u^t) + \lambda u^t - w \right]. \tag{29}$$

Computing $\nabla_{\hat{H}^1} E$ Numerically. Similar to the previous considerations, we note that (24) may be interpreted as the gradient of the energy

$$\frac{1}{2} \int_{\Omega_\epsilon} \|\nabla_{\mathcal{S}} u\|_2^2 - 2(w - \lambda \bar{w} \cdot \eta) u \; dx. \tag{30}$$

The corresponding continuous gradient descent then reads

$$\partial_t \hat{u} = \Delta_{\mathcal{S}} \hat{u} + (w - \lambda \bar{w} \cdot \eta), \tag{31}$$

and after splitting $\Delta_{\mathcal{S}}$ we obtain

$$\partial_t \hat{u} = \Delta \hat{u} - \operatorname{div}(\eta \otimes \eta \nabla \hat{u}) + (w - \lambda \bar{w} \cdot \eta). \tag{32}$$

Finally, we employ again a semi-implicit time discretization:

$$(I - \tau \Delta) \hat{u}^{t+\tau} = \hat{u}^t - \tau \left[\operatorname{div}(\eta \otimes \eta \nabla \hat{u}^t) - (w - \lambda \bar{w} \cdot \eta) \right]. \tag{33}$$

Remarks The presented numerical schemes allow us to perform a gradient descent with a comparatively large step size in order to compute the Sobolev gradients. In all our experiments in the next section five iteration steps with $\tau = 2$ were sufficient in order to obtain a good approximation. Finally, we want to mention that weighting the first order component $\int_\Omega \nabla_{\mathcal{S}} u \cdot \nabla_{\mathcal{S}} v \; dx$ by $\lambda > 0$ results in operators of the form $(I - \lambda \tau \Delta)$, which leads to an unnecessary coupling of the discretization parameter τ and the model parameter λ.

5   Discussion of the Experiments

The main advantage of Sobolev gradients is that curve and surface evolutions which employ Sobolev gradients are much smoother than the ones based on classical L^2 gradients. In order to demonstrate that the Sobolev gradient obtained

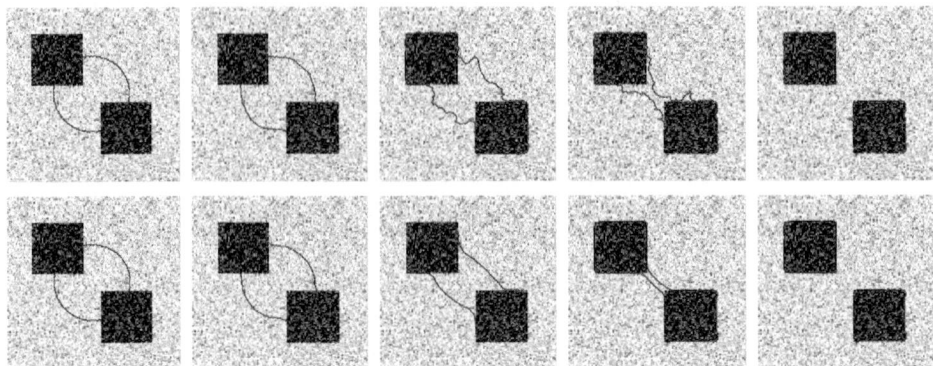

Fig. 2. In contrast to the curve evolution based on L^2 gradient (upper row), the evolution based on $\hat{H}^1$ gradients is much smoother, even in the case of topological changes

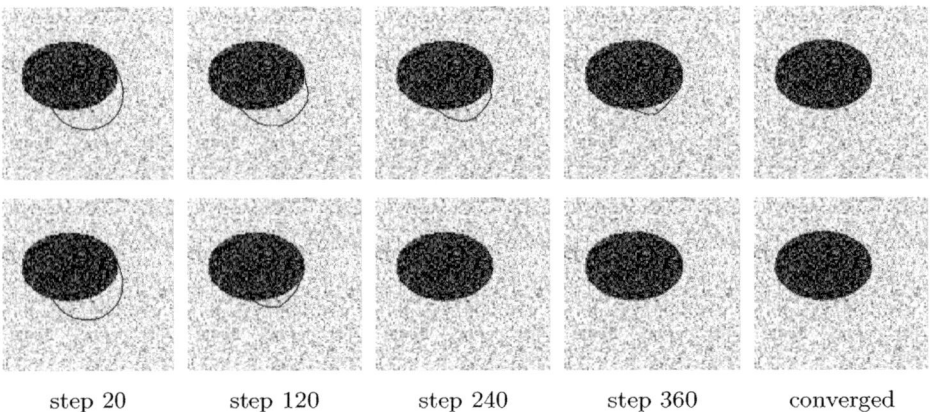

step 20	step 120	step 240	step 360	converged

Fig. 3. The H^1 driven curve (upper row) is only able to segment the object by deforming itself. In contrast to this, the $\hat{H}^1$ driven curve can also capture the object by translation and it thus reaches to object much earlier, compare step 240 and 360.

with the proposed numerical scheme have the same advantageous properties we compare $\hat{H}^1$ evolution to a classical L^2 evolution in Fig. 2 by minimizing the standard Chan-Vese model without penalizing the curve length [5]. As expected, the $\hat{H}^1$ evolution is much smoother than the one based L^2 gradients.

In Fig. 3 we illustrate the difference between the H^1 evolution and the $\hat{H}^1$ evolution by minimizing the same energy. In both cases we chose $\lambda = 0.5$ and used the same step size for the curve evolution. We can see that the curve evolved by the $\hat{H}^1$ gradient (lower row) moves much earlier to the object than the curve evolved by the H^1 gradient, which is only able to capture the object by deformation.

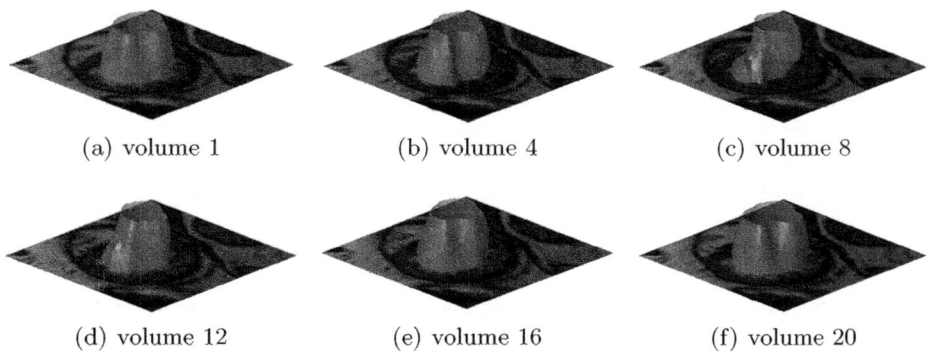

(a) volume 1   (b) volume 4   (c) volume 8

(d) volume 12   (e) volume 16   (f) volume 20

Fig. 4. Tracking of the left ventricular cavity acquired by 4D MRI [17]

Our last experiment in Fig. 4 shows the applicability of our framework to real world problems. We track the left ventricular cavity in 4D magnetic resonance imaging (MRI) data (taken from [17]) by taking the segmentation result from one volume as the initialization for the following one. Again we use the Chan-Vese model without length penalty and apart from that we employ no regularizer which ensures that the subsequent segmentation result is somehow close to the previous one. Note that the image quality in 4D MRI data is usually inferior to the quality of static 3D MRI. Please refer to the supplementary material for the full video showing the segmentation of 20 consecutive volumes.

6   Conclusion

We have presented a convenient and efficient framework for Sobolev active contours and surfaces, which is derived in a fully implicit manner. In contrast to previous approaches [6,8], we employ a geometrically motivated Sobolev type inner product. The performed experiments clearly show that the Sobolev gradients obtained with the proposed numerical scheme lead to smooth curve and surface evolutions. If desired, one can even use operator splitting techniques, e.g. [22], in order to compute the Sobolev gradient in linear complexity. Further work might include the usage of more sophisticated inner products, such as the ones described in [19] as well as the incorporation of the ideas presented in [7].

References

1. Alpert, S., Galun, M., Basri, R., Brandt, A.: Image segmentation by probabilistic bottom-up aggregation and cue integration pp. 1 –8 (17-22 2007)
2. Bertalmio, M., Cheng, L.T., Osher, S., Sapiro, G.: Variational problems and partial differential equations on implicit surfaces. Journal of Computational Physics 174(2), 759–780 (2001)
3. Bresson, X., Esedoglu, S., Vandergheynst, P., Thiran, J.P., Osher, S.: Fast global minimization of the active contour/snake model. Journal of Mathematical Imaging and Vision 28

4. Calder, J., Mansouri, A., Yezzi, A.: Image sharpening via sobolev gradient flows. SIAM Journal on Imaging Sciences 3(4), 981–1014 (2010)
5. Chan, T.F., Vese, L.A.: Active contours without edges. IEEE Transactions on Image Processing 10(2), 266–277 (2001)
6. Charpiat, G., Maurel, P., Pons, J.P., Keriven, R., Faugeras, O.: Generalized gradients: Priors on minimization flows. Int. J. Comput. Vision 73(3), 325–344 (2007)
7. Chen, S., Charpiat, G., Radke, R.J.: Converting level set gradients to shape gradients (September)
8. Eckstein, I., Pons, J., Tong, Y., Kuo, C., Desbrun, M.: Generalized Surface Flows for Mesh Processing. In: Symposium on Geometry Processing, pp. 183–192 (2007)
9. Evans, L.C.: Partial differential equations. Graduate Studies in Mathematics, vol. 19. American Mathematical Society, Providence (1998)
10. Goldstein, T., Osher, S.: The split bregman method for l1-regularized problems. SIAM Journal on Imaging Sciences 2(2), 323–343 (2009)
11. Gooya, A., Liao, H., Matsumiya, K., Masamune, K., Masutani, Y., Dohi, T.: A variational method for geometric regularization of vascular segmentation in medical images. IEEE Transactions on Image Processing 17(8), 1295–1312 (2008)
12. Neuberger, J.W.: Sobolev gradients and differential equations. Springer, Berlin (1997)
13. Osher, S., Fedkiw, R.: Level Set Methods and Dynamic Implicit Surfaces. Springer, Heidelberg (2003)
14. Osher, S., Paragios, N.: Geometric Level Set Methods in Imaging,Vision,and Graphics. Springer, Heidelberg (2003)
15. Peng, D., Merriman, B., Osher, S., Zhao, H., Kang, M.: A pde-based fast local level set method. J. Comput. Phys. 155, 410–438 (1999)
16. Pock, T., Cremers, D., Bischof, H., Chambolle, A.: Global solutions of variational models with convex regularization. SIAM Journal on Imaging Sciences (2010)
17. Radau, P.: Evaluation of cardiac mr segmentation (2010), http://sourceforge.net/projects/cardiac-mr/files/
18. Sundaramoorthi, G., Yezzi, A., Mennucci, A.: Coarse-to-fine segmentation and tracking using sobolev active contours. IEEE Transactions on Pattern Analysis and Machine Intelligence 30(5), 851–864 (2008)
19. Sundaramoorthi, G., Mennucci, A., Soatto, S., Yezzi, A.: A new geometric metric in the space of curves, and applications to tracking deforming objects by prediction and filtering. SIAM Journal on Imaging Sciences 4(1), 109–145 (2011)
20. Sundaramoorthi, G., Yezzi, A.J., Mennucci, A.: Sobolev active contours. International Journal of Computer Vision 73(3), 345–366 (2007)
21. Trouvé, A.: Diffeomorphisms groups and pattern matching in image analysis. International Journal of Computer Vision 28(3), 213–221
22. Weickert, J., Romeny, B., Viergever, M.: Efficient and reliable schemes for nonlinear diffusion filtering. IEEE Transactions on Image Processing 7(3), 398–410 (1998)

Implicit Scene Context for Object Segmentation and Classification

Jan D. Wegner[1], Bodo Rosenhahn[2], and Uwe Soergel[1]

[1] Institute of Photogrammetry and GeoInformation
[2] Institut für Informationsverarbeitung
Leibniz Universität Hannover

Abstract. In this paper, we propose a generic integration of context-knowledge within the unary potentials of Conditional Random Fields (CRF) for object segmentation and classification. Our aim is to learn object-context from the background class of partially labeled images which we call implicit scene context (ISC). A CRF is set up on image super-pixels that are clustered into multiple classes. We then derive context histograms capturing neighborhood relations and integrate them as features into the CRF. Classification experiments with simulated data, eTRIMS building facades, Graz-02 cars, and samples downloaded from Google™ show significant performance improvements.

1 Introduction

Our aim is to segment and classify objects in images. We want to assign a label to each pixel of an image. Context knowledge may add valuable information if local object descriptors deliver ambiguous results in complex scenes. We learn contextual relations between single objects of a scene and introduce them as a prior. Local object descriptors and contextual knowledge are combined in a CRF framework and each pixel is labeled with the most likely object class.

Much research has already focused on how to exploit contextual prior knowledge for object classification in images. In [9] and further related publications Kumar and Hebert extended Conditional Random Fields (CRF), originally proposed in [11], to two-dimensional data and applied them to object detection in images. They consider contextual knowledge through pair-wise potentials that are weighted with features. CRFs provide a highly flexible framework for contextual classification approaches. Torralba et al. [18] use Boosting to learn the graph structure within a CRF framework. Spatial arrangements of objects in an image are learned with a weak classifier and object detection and image segmentation are done in a combined way. Shotton et al. [17] propose an approach based on features derived from texton maps they call "TextonBoost" to achieve joint segmentation and object detection applying Boosting within a CRF framework. Murphy et al. [12] use CRFs for joint object detection and scene classification within a CRF. This classifier learns that particular object categories are more likely to occur in certain scenes than in others. False alarms due to ambiguous local features may be reduced because, for example, polar bears are not likely to

R. Mester and M. Felsberg (Eds.): DAGM 2011, LNCS 6835, pp. 31–40, 2011.
© Springer-Verlag Berlin Heidelberg 2011

appear in a jungle scene. However, this approach considers context on a global scene level but does not model relations of single objects. He et al. [5] introduced the use of a multi-scale CRF for scene segmentation and classification incorporating contextual features at regional and global scene level in addition to local features at pixel-level. Rabinovich et al. [14] formulate a CRF based on image regions that encodes co-occurrence preferences over pair-wise object categories. This allows them to distinguish between object categories that often appear together in the same image and, more important, categories that do usually not appear within the same scene. Calleguillos et al. [3] develop this method further by introducing contextual interactions at pixel-level and at region-level in addition to semantic object interactions via object class co-occurrences. Gould et al. [4] add a spatial component by modelling relative locations between object classes and introducing them into a CRF as additional potential.

Kohli et al. [7] generalize the classical pair-wise Potts model to higher order potentials that enforce label consistency inside image regions. They combine multiple segmentations generated with an unsupervised segmentation method within a CRF for object segmentation and recognition. Related works of Ladicky et al. [10] propose a hierarchical CRF that integrates features computed in different spatial units as pixels, image segments, and groups of segments. They formulate unary potentials over pixels and segments, pair-wise potentials between pixels, and between super-pixels and also a connective potential between pixels and the super-pixels they are contained in.

Heitz and Koller [6] exploit context contained in the background class through what they call the "thing and stuff" (TAS) approach. The main idea is to, first, cluster image super-pixels based both on local features and their ability to serve as context for objects of interest and, second, to integrate this context prior into a rigorous probabilistic framework for object detection. They combine a window detector for local object detection with context that adds predictive power for that particular object category. Savarese et al. [15] compute histograms of so-called correlatons capturing correlations between pairs of pixels based on visual word indices as function of distance. They learn exemplar histograms for each object class from training data and test images are then assigned to the nearest histogram in feature space.

1.1   Contribution

The key idea of our approach is to capture context of the background class of partially labeled images via histograms to support object segmentation and classification. With partially labeled we mean that only a small portion of the object categories existing in the data are semantically annotated in training data. All categories not explicitly labeled are contained within a joint background class. Inspired by the "thing and stuff" (TAS) concept of Heitz and Koller [6] and the "shape context" histograms of Belongie et al. [1] we introduce implicit scene context (ISC) to CRFs. We seek a more general formulation and capture background context and its relation to object classes via histograms (similar to [15]) and integrate it as a potential into a CRF. This is done without major changes to the general CRF framework in terms of training and inference. We do neither add an additional potential nor introduce any complex graph structure but exploit the flexibility provided by the definition of the association potential which depends on all data globally [9].

- Characteristic patterns within the background class of partially labeled images and their relation to labeled object classes are learned.
- Contextual patterns are formulated in terms of histograms. We achieve rotation invariance and the use of multiple context scales ensures good performance for both small and big objects.
- Although we model it as a unary potential within a CRF framework it can generally be utilized (with minor changes) with any kind of non-contextual classifier like Support Vector Machines, too.

This novel approach is generally applicable to any kind of image scene, for example, aerial images, terrestrial images, and medical images.

2   CRF Classification Framework

In the following, we denote scalars in normal face type and vectors in bold face type. CRFs are discriminative models and thus directly model the posterior distribution $P(\mathbf{y}|\mathbf{x})$ of the labels $\mathbf{y}$ given data $\mathbf{x}$. The label of the node i of interest is y_i and y_j the label of node j it is compared to. We have to formulate a cost function which is usually written as an energy term $E(\mathbf{x}, \mathbf{y})$ that encapsulates unary potentials and pair-wise potentials. In order to gain a posterior distribution $P(\mathbf{y}|\mathbf{x})$ we need to turn the energies into probabilities by normalizing them through the partition function $Z(\mathbf{x})$. Making use of sufficient statistics of the exponential family we may then write the posterior distribution $P(\mathbf{y}|\mathbf{x})$ as:

$$P(\mathbf{y}|\mathbf{x}) = \frac{1}{Z(\mathbf{x})} \exp\left(E(\mathbf{x}, \mathbf{y})\right) \tag{1}$$

Following the notations of Kumar and Hebert [9] we can express the energy term $E(\mathbf{x}, \mathbf{y})$ as the sum of association potentials $\mathbf{A}_i(\mathbf{x}, y_i)$ and interaction potentials $\mathbf{I}_{ij}(\mathbf{x}, y_i, y_j)$:

$$E(\mathbf{x}, \mathbf{y}) = \sum_{i \in S} A_i(\mathbf{x}, y_i) + \sum_{i \in S} \sum_{j \in N_i} I_{ij}(\mathbf{x}, y_i, y_j) \tag{2}$$

The association potential $\mathbf{A}_i(\mathbf{x}, y_i)$ measures how likely a label site i is labeled with y_i given the data $\mathbf{x}$. It contains all unary potentials defined over cliques of size one and this is where our implicit context will be incorporated. The interaction potential $\mathbf{I}_{ij}(\mathbf{x}, y_i, y_j)$ models the pair-wise potentials that are defined over cliques of size two. It describes how two label sites i and j interact and we will leave this term almost unchanged.

Both potentials, unary and pair-wise, have access to all data $\mathbf{x}$ of the set S of all image sites. Additionally, the pair-wise potentials also have access to all labels

y globally because the neighborhood N_i of site i of $\mathbf{I}_{ij}\left(\mathbf{x}, y_i, y_j\right)$ may potentially be the entire image. Those properties of CRFs provide a high degree of flexibility and we can thus introduce context from very local to global scales into both terms of the energy term in Eq. 2. However, the standard modelling of the association potential $\mathbf{A}_i\left(\mathbf{x}, y_i\right)$ and the interaction potential $\mathbf{I}_{ij}\left(\mathbf{x}, y_i, y_j\right)$ (e.g., [9]) does not fully exploit the possibility of considering labels **y** and given data **x** globally. Much research effort has gone into finding a more general and global formulation of context through label comparisons in the interaction potential (e.g., [14,7,3]). Our focus is on exploiting the full flexibility provided by the CRF definition of the unary potentials of $\mathbf{A}_i\left(\mathbf{x}, y_i\right)$. We seek a more general and global incorporation of all data **x** as done, for example, by Murphy et al. [12]. If we model the association potential $\mathbf{A}_i\left(\mathbf{x}, y_i\right)$ as a linear model the standard formulation is:

$$A_i\left(\mathbf{x}, y_i\right) = y_i \mathbf{w}^T \mathbf{h}_i\left(\mathbf{x}\right). \tag{3}$$

Node features $h_i\left(\mathbf{x}\right)$ generated from data **x** are contained in vector $\mathbf{h}_i\left(\mathbf{x}\right)$ and the corresponding weights, which are tuned during the training process, are contained in vector $\mathbf{w}^T$. We will integrate ISC through the feature vector and thus $\mathbf{h}_i\left(\mathbf{x}\right)$ will be replaced as we will explain in section 3.1. The interaction potential $\mathbf{I}_{ij}\left(\mathbf{x}, y_i, y_j\right)$ determines how two sites i and j should interact regarding all data **x** (see Eq. 4). Using again a linear model we can write:

$$I_{ij}\left(\mathbf{x}, y_i, y_j\right) = y_i y_j \mathbf{v}^T \boldsymbol{\mu}_{ij}\left(\mathbf{x}\right). \tag{4}$$

$\boldsymbol{\mu}_{ij}\left(\mathbf{x}\right)$ contains all edge features and $\mathbf{v}^T$ the weights, respectively. Edge features $\boldsymbol{\mu}_{ij}\left(\mathbf{x}\right)$ can generally be chosen based on any kind of feature derived from data **x**. They should however somehow reflect and model the relationship of the nodes i and j that are compared. The standard approaches consist of either concatenating the feature vectors $\mathbf{h}_i\left(\mathbf{x}\right)$ and $\mathbf{h}_j\left(\mathbf{x}\right)$ of both nodes or of subtracting them element-wise. We choose the latter one and $\boldsymbol{\mu}_{ij}\left(\mathbf{x}\right)$ is:

$$\boldsymbol{\mu}_{ij}\left(\mathbf{x}\right) = \left|\mathbf{h}_i\left(\mathbf{x}\right) - \mathbf{h}_j\left(\mathbf{x}\right)\right|. \tag{5}$$

3 Implicit Scene Context (ISC)

The idea is to exploit spatial patterns contained in the background class of a partially labeled image to support object segmentation and classification. We can then benefit from very large image databases where images are only partially labeled and learn context although we do not explicitly know all object classes. In addition to the object classes that have been explicitly labeled for training we can use patterns existing in the unlabeled part of the data (i.e., labeled as background class).

The following requirements have to be met: We should be able to cope with very local to global context scales. In addition, we want to keep ISC generically applicable to multiple kinds of scenes. For example, it should capture context in terrestrial images of building facades where usually sky is above the facade

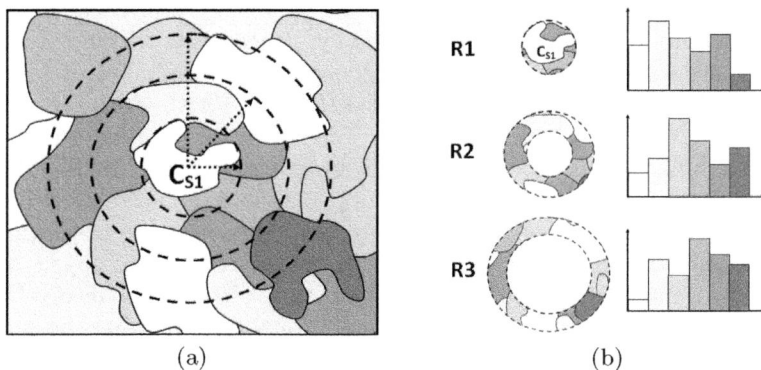

(a)   (b)

Fig. 1. Principle of implicit context: (a) ranges around the centroid C_{S1} of image super-pixel $S1$ (grey levels indicate different labels appointed to the super-pixels with k-means during training or NN during testing), (b) histograms of cluster labels of the three ranges $R1$, $R2$ and $R3$

and vegetation below but also in aerial images of buildings where no preferred ordering with attributes like "above" and "below" exists. Thus, we do not want to rely on any kind of preferred direction. Finally, we want to achieve computational efficiency and avoid the computation of co-occurrences. In order to meet these requirements we take the following steps that will be explained in detail in the following paragraphs:

- multi-scale image segmentation into super-pixels and feature computation,
- unsupervised k-means clustering and nearest-neighbor (NN) classification of the super-pixels based on the previously generated features,
- generation of context histograms in three different ranges per super-pixel,
- input as feature vector to the CRF unary potentials.

3.1   Context Potential within CRF

During training we first perform an unsupervised classification of all super-pixels. We could use any kind of unsupervised classifier but for means of speed and simplicity we chose a k-means clustering followed by a NN classification. As input to the k-means clustering we use all features $h_i(\mathbf{x}) \in \mathbf{h}(\mathbf{x})$ that were computed per super-pixel. The exact cluster centers $\mathbf{K}$ we compute with the k-means clustering $\mathbf{K} = K_{means}(\mathbf{h}(\mathbf{x}))$ are used for the following processing.

Each super-pixel is labeled with $y_{us,i} \in \mathbf{y}_{us}$ where $\mathbf{y}_{us}$ contains all unsupervised labels corresponding to the number of chosen cluster centers k. Label $y_{us,i}$ of the super-pixel i of interest is determined via NN and is thus a function of the minimum mean distance between feature vector $h_i(\mathbf{x})$ and the cluster centers $\mathbf{K}$. Each super-pixel i is assigned the cluster center $\mathbf{K}_c$ (where $c = 1...k$ is the cluster center with k the total number of all cluster centers) that is the closest in feature space. The resulting labeled super-pixels (e.g., with $k = 6$) are shown schematically in Fig. 1(a). Next, the centroid C_S of each super-pixel is determined and histograms of labels $hist_R(\mathbf{y}_{us})$ occurring within three different ranges R around each super-pixel are generated. The number of label occurrences $\mathbf{y}_{us}$ within each range R is counted (Fig. 1(b) with three ranges $R1$, $R2$, and $R3$). We can choose either short or long ranges depending on whether we would like to incorporate local or global context, respectively. It should be noted that longer ranges do not lead to any more complex graph structure because no graph is set up at this point. Furthermore, the number of the ranges and either coarse or fine scaling enables us to capture the distribution of object categories contained in the background class as a function of their distance to the node of interest. Then, various moments and additional information representing the contextual patterns in the environment of a particular super-pixel are derived from the histograms. We use qualitative, quantitative, and spatial context features $\mathbf{C}(\mathbf{h}(\mathbf{x}))$ (e.g., most often occurring label). For testing we apply exactly the same processing steps but drop the k-means clustering. The cluster centers $\mathbf{K}$ that were determined during training are passed to testing and the NN cluster centers to the nodes of the test data are computed. Thus, all super-pixels of the test data are labeled corresponding to the unsupervised classification performed during training. The implicit context features $\mathbf{C}_i(\mathbf{h}(\mathbf{x}))$ of the test data are computed and introduced into a linear model:

$$A_i(\mathbf{x}, y_i) = y_i \mathbf{w}^T \mathbf{C}_i(\mathbf{h}(\mathbf{x})) \tag{6}$$

We can then either determine the class of each super-pixel i merely based on implicit context features $\mathbf{C}_i(\mathbf{h}(\mathbf{x}))$ or also add the local node features $\mathbf{h}_i(\mathbf{x})$ to the feature vector. The pair-wise potentials only change in such a way (cf. Eq. 5) that the element-wise absolute differences between nodes i and j in the graph are now computed based on the corresponding implicit context features:

$$\boldsymbol{\mu}_{ij}(\mathbf{x}) = abs(\mathbf{C}_i(\mathbf{h}(\mathbf{x})) - \mathbf{C}_j(\mathbf{h}(\mathbf{x}))) \tag{7}$$

We do not perform any normalization of the label count in the histogram, for example, based on the size of the super-pixels because tests show that the importance of a super-pixel does not necessarily increase with its size. In other words, small super-pixels may be characteristic context features and thus are of high relevance for a particular object class.

4   Experiments

We perform several experiments with partially labeled data in order to assess the benefits of ISC-CRF. Only one object category is semantically annotated in training data and all other categories are labeled as background. First, we demonstrate the performance improvements achieved with ISC-CRF compared to a standard CRF for different object classes and background patterns (4.1). Second, we evaluate the impact of different cluster center numbers and, third, we assess the robustness to noise (4.2). Quickshift [19] is used for super-pixel

(a)   (b)   (c)   (d)   (e)   (f)

(g)   (h)   (i)   (j)   (k)   (l)

Fig. 2. Results with simulated data, eTRIMS [8] facade images, algae, and Graz-02 cars [13]: true positives (green), false positives (red) and false negatives (blue) without implicit scene context (b, e, h, k) and with implicit scene context (c, f, i, l)

generation. If a super-pixel extends across an object boundary it may not be repaired later on in the process. We thus over-segment all images to ensure consistency of object boundaries and super-pixels. In order to avoid unstable feature distributions of too small super-pixels we generate a segmentation in three different scales. Super-pixels sharing a common boundary at the highest scale are linked with edges in the graph. Features of coarser-scale super-pixels are written to the vectors of the highest-scale super-pixels they contain. As features $h_i(x)$ of a super-pixel we compute the first two moments of the color information and oriented gradient histogram features. We select those very simple features for reasons of transparency and ease of replicability. A subset of different benchmark data sets (nine images out of each) is used to verify the proposed ISC-CRF concept. A quadratic expansion of the feature vectors is done as described by Kumar and Hebert [9] in order to introduce a more precise quadratic decision surface. We apply the quasi-Newton method limited-memory Broyden-Fletcher-Goldfarb-Shanno (L-BFGS) for parameter estimation and loopy belief propagation for approximate inference using Mark Schmidt's toolbox [16]. Cross-validation is performed with two thirds of the data for training and one third for testing (as recommended by Crowther and Cox [2]) in order to compute true positive rate (TPR) and false positive rate (FPR) pixel-wise. The TPR is the percentage of all correctly labeled object pixels and the FPR is the percentage of all background pixels that are misclassified as object.

4.1 Classification of Objects in Different Scenes

In order to verify the general applicability of the implicit scene context we perform tests with four different object class scenes: with simulated aerial images of an urban scene, with facade images taken from the eTRIMS benchmark data [8], with Google^{TM} images of algae and with car images of the Graz-02 benchmark

Table 1. TPR and FPR in % of standard CRF and ISC-CRF

Data	CRF		ISC-CRF	
	TPR	FPR	TPR	FPR
Simulation	85.9	**6.8**	85.9	**0.8**
eTRIMS facades	86.9	**22.1**	88.1	**7.3**
Algae	75.7	**37.0**	84.5	**23.7**
Graz-02 cars	86.6	**16.4**	88.1	**4.3**

data [13]. Those four object class categories are chosen because they represent different spatial object and background distributions. Many small objects (buildings) embedded into background context are contained in the simulated urban scene (Fig. 2(a)). Small irregular objects entirely surrounded by background context are the cars (Fig. 2(d)), single very large objects (facades) with clear straight boundaries and with background context only above and below are the building facades (Fig. 2(g)) and large but frayed objects partially surrounded by background context are the algae (Fig. 2(j)). A good performance of the implicit scene context approach for all tasks would support the claim of general applicability to any kind of image scene.

The classification performance results of the test data are summarized in Table 1. Example images and the corresponding results are shown in Fig. 2. In all four cases the ISC-CRF decreases the FPR significantly in comparison to the standard CRF. On an Intel[TM] Core i7 2.4 Ghz CPU, 12 GB RAM the computation time using the implicit scene context potential does only marginally increase by several seconds per image.

4.2   Parameter Assessment with Simulated Data

The context ranges, the number of k-means cluster centers, and the segmentation scales are currently adapted manually to each data set. The previously introduced simulated urban scene (see example in Fig. 2(a)) is used to evaluate the impact of varying cluster centers because we know the exact number of object categories contained in the data: buildings (red and gray rectangles), trees (dark green circles), grassland (light green background) and streets (light gray lines). The buildings are our labeled object class and all other object categories are contained in the background class. Only color features are used for these tests leading to five distinct clusters due to the building class consisting of red and dark gray buildings. We use three different ranges (10, 20, and 30 pixel radii) and perform tests with five up to 50 cluster centers. The FPR of each test is displayed in blue Fig. 3(a) whereas the FPR of the standard CRF is displayed in red. The FPR varies about 1 % (from 0.8 % to 1.8 %) and no significant trend is observable. Changing the number of k-means cluster centers has a very small impact on the classification performance but of course on computation time. A rather small number of cluster centers is beneficial. The radii of the context ranges and the segmentation scale are adapted to each scene separately because both parameters depend on the scales of context and objects. This makes the

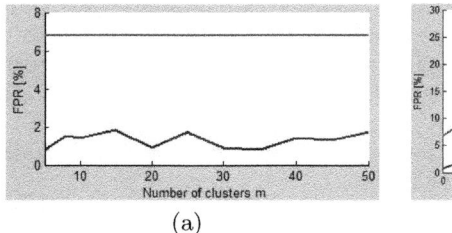
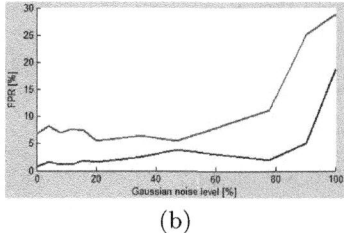

(a)   (b)

Fig. 3. FPR of ISC-CRF (blue) and standard CRF (red) classification of simulated data: (a) with varying numbers of k-means cluster centers and (b) with different noise levels

ISC-CRF highly flexible and easy to adapt to new scenes. Both parameters could also be introduced into the learning step without major changes to the general framework.

Second, we test if the ISC-CRF is robust to image noise and whether we gain robustness compared to a standard CRF. Several gaussian noise levels with mean zero and standard deviations up to 100 % (corresponding to 256 in our case of 8 bit RGB channels) are generated and added to the RGB channels of the simulated data, which is then cropped in order to keep all values between zero and 255. Cross-validation tests with CRF and ISC-CRF is done and FPR is recorded. In figure 3(b) FPR of the standard CRF (red) and FPR of ISC-CRF (blue) of all tested noise levels are displayed. For all noise levels the FPR of the ISC-CRF stays below that of the standard CRF. Furthermore, the ISC-CRF is slightly more robust to noise because its FPR starts increasing later (approx. 90 % vs. approx. 80 %).

5   Conclusions and Future Work

In this paper we have introduced the concept of implicit scene context to learn context in an unsupervised way from the background class. Tests with four different scene types have shown that the ISC-CRF decreases the FPR while increasing the TPR compared to a standard CRF. We have demonstrated that different spatial object and background distributions can be captured via the context histograms. In future work we want to integrate more complex features and feature combinations, test our method on complete benchmark datasets, and learn those parameters that are currently chosen empirically.

References

1. Belongie, S., Malik, J., Puzicha, J.: Shape Matching and Object Recognition Using Shape Contexts. IEEE Transactions on Pattern Analysis and Machine Intelligence 24(24), 509–522 (2002)
2. Crowther, P.S., Cox, R.J.: A Method for Optimal Division of Data Sets for Use in Neural Networks. In: R.K., et al. (ed.). LNCS, pp. 1–7. Springer, Heidelberg (2005)

3. Galleguillos, C., McFee, B., Belongie, S., Lanckriet, G.: Multi-Class Object Localization by Combining Local Contextual Interactions. In: CVPR (2010)
4. Gould, S., Rodgers, J., Cohen, D., Elidan, G., Koller, D.: Multi-Class Segmentation with Relative Location Prior. International Journal of Computer Vision 80(3), 300–316 (2008)
5. He, X., Zemel, R.S., Carreira-Perpiñán, M.: Multiscale Conditional Random Fields for Image Labeling. In: CVPR (2004)
6. Heitz, G., Koller, D.: Learning spatial context: Using stuff to find things. In: Forsyth, D., Torr, P., Zisserman, A. (eds.) ECCV 2008, Part I. LNCS, vol. 5302, pp. 30–43. Springer, Heidelberg (2008)
7. Kohli, P., Ladicky, L., Torr, P.H.: Robust Higher Order Potentials for Enforcing Label Consistency. International Journal of Computer Vision 82(3), 302–324 (2009)
8. Korč, F., Förstner, W.: eTRIMS Image Database for interpreting images of man-made scenes. Tech. Rep. TR-IGG-P-2009-01 (April 2009)
9. Kumar, S., Hebert, M.: Discriminative Random Fields. International Journal of Computer Vision 68(2), 179–201 (2006)
10. Ladicky, L., Russell, C., Kohli, P., Torr, P.H.: Associative Hierarchical CRFs for Object Class Image Segmentation. In: ICCV (2009)
11. Lafferty, J., McCallum, A., Pereira, F.: Conditional Random Fields: Probabilistic Models for segmenting and labeling sequence data. In: ICML (2001)
12. Murphy, K.P., Torralba, A., Freeman, W.T.: Using the Forest to See the Trees: A Graphical Model Relating Features, Objects, and Scenes. In: Thrun, S., Saul, L., Schölkopf, B. (eds.) Advances in Neural Information Processing Systems. MIT Press, Cambridge (2004)
13. Opelt, A., Pinz, A., Fussenegger, M., Auer, P.: Generic Object Recognition with Boosting. IEEE Transactions on Pattern Analysis and Machine Intelligence 28(3), 416–431 (2006)
14. Rabinovich, A., Vedaldi, A., Galleguillos, C., Wiewiora, E., Belongie, S.: Objects in Context. In: ICCV (2007)
15. Savarese, S., Winn, J., Criminisi, A.: Discriminative Object Class Models of Appearance and Shape by Correlatons. In: CVPR (2006)
16. Schmidt, M.: UGM: A Matlab toolbox for probabilistic undirected graphical models, http://www.cs.ubc.ca/~schmidtm/Software/UGM.html (accessed July 15, 2010)
17. Shotton, J., Winn, J.M., Rother, C., Criminisi, A.: TextonBoost: Joint appearance, shape and context modeling for multi-class object recognition and segmentation. In: Leonardis, A., Bischof, H., Pinz, A. (eds.) ECCV 2006. LNCS, vol. 3951, pp. 1–15. Springer, Heidelberg (2006)
18. Torralba, A., Murphy, K.P., Freeman, W.T.: Contextual Models for Object Detection Using Boosted Random Fields. In: Saul, L.K., Weiss, Y., Bottou, L. (eds.) Advances in Neural Information Processing Systems, pp. 1401–1408. MIT Press, Cambridge (2005)
19. Vedaldi, A., Soatto, S.: Quick shift and kernel methods for mode seeking. In: Forsyth, D., Torr, P., Zisserman, A. (eds.) ECCV 2008, Part IV. LNCS, vol. 5305, pp. 705–718. Springer, Heidelberg (2008)

An Estimation Theoretical Approach to Ambrosio-Tortorelli Image Segmentation

Kai Krajsek, Ines Dedovic, and Hanno Scharr

IBG-2: Plant Sciences
Forschungszentrum Jülich
52425 Jülich, Germany
{k.krajsek,i.dedovic,h.scharr}@fz-juelich.de

Abstract. This paper presents a novel approach for Ambrosio-Tortorelli (AT) image segmentation, or, more exactly, joint image regularization and edge-map reconstruction. We interpret the AT functional, an approximation of the Mumford-Shah (MS) functional, as the energy of a posterior probability density function (PDF) of the image and smooth edge indicator. Previous approaches consider AT or MS segmentation as a deterministic optimization problem by minimizing the energy functional, resulting in a single point estimate, *i.e.* the maximum-a-posteriori (MAP) estimate. We adopt a wider estimation theoretical view-point, meaning we consider images to be random variables and investigate their distribution. We derive an effective block-Gibbs-sampler for this posterior PDF based on the theory of Gaussian Markov random fields (GMRF). The merit of our approach is multi-fold: First, sampling from the posterior PDF allows to apply different types of estimators and not only the MAP estimator. Secondly, sampling allows to estimate higher order statistical moments like the variance as a confidence measure. Third, our approach is not prone to get trapped into local minima as other AT image reconstruction approaches, but our approach is asymptotically statistical optimal. Several experiments demonstrate the advantages of our block-Gibbs-sampling approach.

1 Introduction

In this paper, we examine the Ambrosio-Tortorelli (AT) functional [1] for image segmentation from an estimation theoretical point of view. Instead of minimizing an energy functional in the original formulation, we interpret the AT functional as the energy of a posterior probability density function and derive an effective block-Gibbs-sampler for approximating the minimum mean square and the minimum medium estimator.

The Mumford-Shah (MS) [7] functional is maybe the most well-known constraint used for image segmentation. A major difficulty in using it is the handling of inner image borders as lines, being circumvented by Ambrosio and Tortorellis [1] approximation. They introduce a smooth edge indicator function

R. Mester and M. Felsberg (Eds.): DAGM 2011, LNCS 6835, pp. 41–50, 2011.

$v(x, y) : \mathbb{R}^2 \rightarrow [0, 1]$ instead of the original line-like edge indicator, with $v(x, y) \approx$ 1 on the edges, and $v(x, y) \approx 0$ on smooth regions.

$$E_{AT} = \iint\limits_R (\beta(u - g)^2 + (\alpha(1 - v)^2\|\nabla u\|^2) + (\frac{\rho}{2}\|\nabla v\|^2 + \frac{v^2}{2\rho}))\mathrm{d}x\mathrm{d}y \qquad (1)$$

where g is the observed noisy or incomplete image, u its smooth reconstruction, and $\alpha, \beta, \rho \in \mathbb{R}^+$. For $\rho \rightarrow 0$ energy E_{AT} converges to the original Mumford-Shah functional. Unlike many other approaches, *e.g.* using level-sets [8], open boundaries can be handled easily. Using such a functional, image segmentation is understood to be joint image regularization and edge-map reconstruction. Previous approaches to MS able to handle open boundaries (see *e.g.* [10]) or approaches to AT segmentation [9] minimize the functionals, or, equivalently, maximize the posterior PDF resulting in the MAP estimate. In contrast to this, we interpret image and edge-map as random variables and sample from their posterior PDF derived from the AT energy. Sampling is done using block-Gibbs-sampling. Pixel-wise Gibbs sampling has its origin in image processing [2], where it was already used for image restoration / segmentation together with a model including a line process. However, sampling each pixel value individually has the disadvantage of a much slower convergence to the target distribution than block-Gibbs-sampling [11].

1.1   Related Work

Pätz and Preusser [9] recently showed, how to use the AT functional for segmentation of stochastic images. Stochastic images are a representation, where each pixel value is handled as a random variable and its distribution is modeled explicitly. Even though they model probability distributions, finding a solution of the AT functional is still done deterministically using its Euler-Lagrange equations together with a conjugate gradient solver. This is in contrast to our stochastic approach.

  Pock and Cremers [10] propose a fast primal-dual algorithm to compute the solution of a convex relaxation of the MS functional. They report that their results are independent of start conditions and better than results received by the AT approach. We therefore perform some experiments on the same images they used, in order to show that quality restrictions do not apply as local minima are not an issue of our estimation theoretical approach. In addition to a point estimate, we are able to give information on its distribution, *e.g.* error variances. Efficient block-Gibbs-sampling of Gaussian Markov random fields (GMRF) has been introduced by Rue and Held in a general statistical setting [11]. In a computer vision context, *i.e.* the estimation of diffusion tensor images, GMRF block-Gibbs-sampling has been applied by Krajsek *et al.*[5]. To the best of the authors knowledge, GMRF block-Gibbs-sampling has never been used in any segmentation approach so far.

2   Bayesian Estimation Theory in a Nutshell

In this section we give a brief overview of the main principles of Bayesian estimation theory as used here, for a broader overview we refer to [4]. We formulate our AT estimation problem on a regular discrete image domain $\mathcal{G}_h$ with grid size h. Discrete images then can be represented as column vectors $\boldsymbol{u}, \boldsymbol{v}, \boldsymbol{g} \in \mathbb{R}^N$, respectively. Gradients ∇u, ∇v are approximated by finite difference operators that can be described by matrices acting on the column vectors.

For an estimation theoretical view of the AT energy functional, one interprets images as random vectors, *i.e.* each element of the vector is a realization of a random variable. The task is to estimate the image $\boldsymbol{u}$ as well as the edge indicator $\boldsymbol{v}$ from (possible noisy and incomplete) observations $\boldsymbol{g}$. For notational convenience we combine image and edge indicator to a target variable $\boldsymbol{z} = (\boldsymbol{u}^T, \boldsymbol{v}^T)^T$. Let us further denote with $\boldsymbol{\varepsilon} = \hat{\boldsymbol{z}} - \boldsymbol{z}$ the error between the estimated images $\hat{\boldsymbol{z}}$ and the particular true realization $\boldsymbol{z}$ of the target vector.

Bayesian estimators are characterized by means of their *risk* $\mathbf{R}(\hat{\boldsymbol{z}}) = \mathbb{E}[L]$ defined by the expectation of a loss function $L : \mathbb{R}^{2N} \to \mathbb{R}^+$, $\boldsymbol{\varepsilon} \mapsto L(\boldsymbol{\varepsilon})$ with respect to the posterior PDF $p(\boldsymbol{z}|\boldsymbol{g})$. The Bayesian estimator (with respect to a specific loss function L) of the target variable is then given by the value $\hat{\boldsymbol{z}}$ minimizing the risk

$$\hat{\boldsymbol{z}} = \arg_{\tilde{\boldsymbol{z}}} \min \mathbf{R}(\tilde{\boldsymbol{z}}) \tag{2}$$

Obviously, different loss functions lead to different Bayesian estimators. Prominent estimators are given by the quadratic loss function $L(\boldsymbol{\varepsilon}) = \|\boldsymbol{\varepsilon}\|^2$ leading to the minimum mean squared error estimator (MMSEE)

$$\hat{\boldsymbol{z}} = \int \boldsymbol{z} p(\boldsymbol{z}|\boldsymbol{g}) d\boldsymbol{z}\,, \tag{3}$$

the (vector) hit and miss loss function $L(\boldsymbol{\varepsilon}) = 0$ for $\boldsymbol{\varepsilon} = \boldsymbol{0}$ and $L(\boldsymbol{\varepsilon}) = 1$ for $\boldsymbol{\varepsilon} \neq \boldsymbol{0}$ leading to the maximum a posteriori (MAP) estimator,

$$\hat{\boldsymbol{z}} = \arg_{\boldsymbol{z}} \max p(\boldsymbol{z}|\boldsymbol{g})\,, \tag{4}$$

and the absolute error loss $L(\boldsymbol{\varepsilon}) = \sum_i |\varepsilon_i|$ leasing to the minimum medium error estimator (MMEE)

$$\hat{z}_i = \operatorname{median} p(z_i|\boldsymbol{g}) \tag{5}$$

$$= \operatorname{median} \int p(\boldsymbol{z}|\boldsymbol{g}) d\boldsymbol{z}_{\dashv i} \tag{6}$$

where $\boldsymbol{z}_{\dashv i}$ denotes the random vector without element z_i. Most prominent among these estimators is surely the MAP estimator. Its popularity might come from the fact that it can be computed by a pure optimization task. Other estimators require computation of (usually high dimensional) integrals which in most cases cannot be analytically computed but require some approximation. However, we will demonstrate in the following that such approximations can effectively be obtained for the AT segmentation problem by means of Markov chain Monte

Carlo (MCMC) techniques. We approximate the MMSEE as well as the MMEE by generating n samples z^j from the posterior PDF $p(z|g)$. The MMSEE is then simply obtained by its sample mean, MMEE by its sample median. This means that we transform the original AT image segmentation problem into an estimation problem *without the need for any optimization step of a highly non-convex energy functional.*

3   AT Segmentation as an Estimation Problem

In the following two subsections we describe the core of our segmentation algorithm. First, we rewrite the AT energy in a probabilistic setting followed by the numerical details.

3.1   A Probabilistic Interpretation of the AT Energy

The first step of our approach is to approximate the AT energy functional on a discrete grid. To this end, we consider image values $z = (u, v)$ at the knots of the grid

$$E_{AT}(u, v) = \sum_{i=1}^{N} \beta(u_i - g_i)^2 + \left(\alpha(1 - v_i)^2 \|(\nabla u)_i\|^2 \right) + \left(\frac{\rho}{2} \|(\nabla v)_i\|^2 + \frac{v_i^2}{2\rho} \right) \quad (7)$$

Gradients are approximated by finite differences.

In a next step, we consider (7) as the energy of the posterior PDF $p(u, v|g)$ of image u and edge indicator function v. Unfortunately, integrals required for the MMSEE as well as for the MMEE are not analytically tractable with this posterior PDF and direct sampling from $p(u, v|g)$ is also not possible. However, fortunately, due to the seminal work of Metropolis *et al.*[6] and Hastings[3] we know that we can approximatively sample from $p(u, v|g)$ by sampling from a suitable proposal distribution. In particular, if we could find a partition of the target vector $z = (a, b)$ such that we can sample from the conditional pdfs $p(a|b, g)$ and $p(b|a, g)$ in turn

$$a^{j+1} \sim p(a|b^j, g) \quad (8)$$
$$b^{j+1} \sim p(b|a^{j+1}, g), \quad j = b_n, ..., K \quad (9)$$

Metropolis [3] tells us that each sample of (8) and (9) is – after a considerable *burn in phase*[1] – an approximative sample from the posterior pdf $p(u, v|g)$. This approach is denoted as a *block-Gibbs-sampler* [11].

The conditional PDFs $p(a|b, g)$ and $p(b|a, g)$ can be derived from the full posterior PDF $p(a, b|g)$ by means of the basic multiplicative rule of probability theory as $p(a|b, g) = p(a, b|g)/p(b|g)$ and $p(b|a, g) = p(a, b|g)/p(a|g)$, respectively. Thus, the conditional PDFs $p(a|b, g)$ and $p(b|a, g)$ can be obtained from

---

[1] Meaning that we disregard the first $b_n - 1$ starting samples.

the posterior PDF $p(\boldsymbol{a}, \boldsymbol{b}|\boldsymbol{g})$ by setting one variable fixed combined with suitable normalization.

What is a suitable partition of the target variable $\boldsymbol{z}$ for our AT segmentation problem? By investigating the posterior PDF $p(\boldsymbol{u}, \boldsymbol{v}|\boldsymbol{g})$ of the AT energy, we recognize that by fixing $\boldsymbol{u}$ or $\boldsymbol{v}$ the resulting AT energy becomes a quadratic function of the other variable and consequently the corresponding conditional PDFs become Gaussian distributions from which samples can be obtained directly.

To make it more concrete let us first fix the edge indicator $\boldsymbol{v}$. To consider the symmetric nature of the AT functional (1), we approximate the gradient expressions by forward and backward differences and taking its average as[2]

$$\|\nabla u\|^2 \approx \frac{1}{2} \sum_i \left(\|\boldsymbol{B}_{x_i^+} \boldsymbol{u}\|^2 + \|\boldsymbol{B}_{x_i^-} \boldsymbol{u}\|^2 \right) \tag{10}$$

$$= \boldsymbol{u}^T \boldsymbol{D} \boldsymbol{u}, \quad \boldsymbol{D} = \frac{1}{2} \sum_i \boldsymbol{B}_{x_i^+}^T \boldsymbol{B}_{x_i^+} + \boldsymbol{B}_{x_i^-}^T \boldsymbol{B}_{x_i^-} \tag{11}$$

$$\|\nabla v\|^2 \approx \boldsymbol{v}^T \boldsymbol{D} \boldsymbol{v}, \tag{12}$$

yielding the energy of the conditional PDF

$$E_{AT}(\boldsymbol{u}) = \beta \|\boldsymbol{g} - \boldsymbol{u}\|^2 + \alpha \sum_i \boldsymbol{u}^T \boldsymbol{D}(\boldsymbol{V}) \boldsymbol{u} + c_1 \tag{13}$$

with

$$c_1 = \sum_{i=1}^{N} \left(\frac{\rho}{2} \|(\nabla v)_i\|^2 + \frac{v_i^2}{2\rho} \right), \quad \boldsymbol{V} = \boldsymbol{I} - \mathrm{diag}(v_i) \tag{14}$$

$$\boldsymbol{D}(\boldsymbol{V}) = \sum_i \boldsymbol{B}_{x_i^+}^T \boldsymbol{V} \boldsymbol{B}_{x_i^+} + \boldsymbol{B}_{x_i^-}^T \boldsymbol{V} \boldsymbol{B}_{x_i^-} \tag{15}$$

Applying quadratic complementation allows to transform the energy

$$E_{AT}(\boldsymbol{u}) = (\boldsymbol{u} - \boldsymbol{m}_u)^T \boldsymbol{Q}_u (\boldsymbol{u} - \boldsymbol{m}_u) + c_1 + c_2 \tag{16}$$

with

$$\boldsymbol{Q}_u = \beta \boldsymbol{I} + \alpha \boldsymbol{D}(\boldsymbol{V}) \tag{17}$$

$$\boldsymbol{m}_u = \beta \, \boldsymbol{Q}_u^{-1} \boldsymbol{g} \tag{18}$$

$$c_2 = \boldsymbol{g}^T \beta \boldsymbol{I} \boldsymbol{g} - \beta^2 \boldsymbol{g}^T \boldsymbol{Q}_u^{-1} \boldsymbol{g} \tag{19}$$

and finally results in the Gaussian Markov random field (GMRF)

$$p(\boldsymbol{u}|\boldsymbol{v}, \boldsymbol{g}) \propto \exp\left(-\frac{1}{2} (\boldsymbol{u} - \boldsymbol{m}_u)^T \boldsymbol{Q}_u (\boldsymbol{u} - \boldsymbol{m}_u) \right) \tag{20}$$

---

[2] Central differences are avoided as such approximation are known to lead to checkerboard artefacts as shown in [12].

Applying the same procedure when holding $\boldsymbol{u}$ fixed yields the GMRF

$$p(\boldsymbol{v}|\boldsymbol{u},\boldsymbol{g}) \propto \exp\left(-\frac{1}{2}(\boldsymbol{v}-\boldsymbol{m}_v)^T \boldsymbol{Q}_v (\boldsymbol{v}-\boldsymbol{m}_v)\right) \tag{21}$$

with

$$\boldsymbol{L} = \alpha \mathrm{diag}\left((\nabla u)_i\right), \quad \boldsymbol{e} = (1,...,1)^T \tag{22}$$

$$\boldsymbol{Q}_v = \boldsymbol{L} + \frac{\rho}{2}\boldsymbol{D} + \frac{1}{\rho}\boldsymbol{I} \tag{23}$$

$$\boldsymbol{m}_v = \boldsymbol{Q}_v^{-1}\boldsymbol{L}\boldsymbol{e} \tag{24}$$

Having obtained an appropriate number of samples using the scheme (8) and (9) with the conditional PDFs (20) and (21) allows us to approximate different estimators as described in Section 2. The MMSEE is approximated by taking the mean of each variable and the MMEE by taking the median. The estimated variance of each variable serves as a reliability measure of the point estimates.

3.2   Numerical Issues

As explained in the last section, the challenge is to sample from a Gaussian distribution with known mean value and known precision matrix. Due to the neighborhood relation of the finite difference approximation the Gaussian distributions under considerations reduce to a Gaussian Markov random field (GMRF) which means that the precision matrix is sparse and has a band-limited structure [11]. We start with sampling from a zero mean Gaussian random vector $\boldsymbol{q}$ with identical covariance matrix, *i.e.* each element of $\boldsymbol{q}$ is the realization of an independent zero mean Gaussian random variable. Gaussian random variables can be generated from uniformly distributed variables by means of the Box-Muller algorithm; we used the Matlab function 'randn'. Secondly, the Cholesky decomposition $\boldsymbol{L}$ of the precision matrix is computed, *i.e.* $\boldsymbol{Q} = \boldsymbol{L}\boldsymbol{L}^T$. In the third step, we solve the linear equation system $\boldsymbol{L}\boldsymbol{y} = \boldsymbol{q}$ by back-substitution. Finally, we add the known mean to $\boldsymbol{y}$. Inserting $\boldsymbol{p} = \boldsymbol{m} + \boldsymbol{L}^{-T}\boldsymbol{q}$ in the definition of the covariance matrix directly proofs that $\boldsymbol{p}$ is a sample from $\mathcal{N}(\boldsymbol{m},\boldsymbol{Q})$.

We implemented the Gibbs sampler in MATLAB using standard build-in functions and performed all experiments on an AMD Phenom II X6 1055T processor running at 3.5 Ghz. For an 128×128 image our block-Gibbs-sampler requires about $0.3s$ for each sample, *i.e.* a sample of the image or the edge indicator function. A typical estimate of $K - b_n = 1000$ samples with $b_n = 500$ burn-in samples thus requires about $2 \cdot 0.3(1000 + 500)s = 900s$ which is in the same time range reported for the estimator proposed in [10]. However, in [10] a GPU implementation is considered running on a NVIDIA Tesla C1060. The implementation of our approach on parallel optimized harware/software is topic of future research. We compute the MMSEE and MMEE for the $K - b_n$ samples. As we found no significant differences between them we report only the results of the MMSEE in the following.

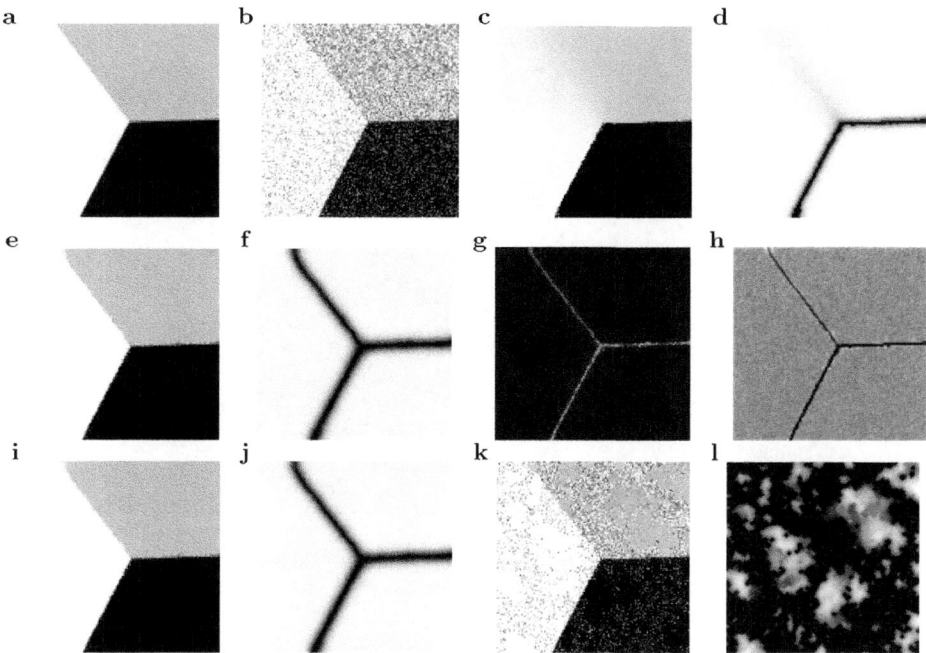

Fig. 1. a original image; **b** degraded with 20% Gaussian noise ,*i.e.* $\sigma_{noise} = 0.2$ when the noise free image values are scaled between 0 and 1; **c, d** results obtained using the classical, deterministic AT approach with random initialization, **e,f** results obtained with our MMSEE approach with random initialization, **g,h** standard deviations of estimated image and edge-map of **e** and **f**, respectively, **i,j** results obtained with our MMSEE approach initialized with observed image and observed edge indicator function, **k, l** results obtained using the deterministic AT approach with observed image and observed edge indicator function (parameters: $\alpha = 6000$, $\beta = 12.5$, $\rho = 0.8$).

4   Experimental Results

4.1   Stochastic vs. Deterministic AT Segmentation

In Figure 1 results for a noise reduction and edge detection at a triple junction are shown using the deterministic AT [1] and our stochastic approach. We observe that the deterministic approach gets stuck in a local minimum when initializing with the observed images (**k,l**) as well as when initialized with random images (**c,d**). Our stochastic approach (**i,j,e,f**) correctly finds the edges and in addition gives information on the underlying distribution irrespective of its initialization. Our approach also allows to estimate standard deviations of image (**g**) and edge-map (**h**). As expected, variances are high for edge positions in the image, as gray value information there obviously depends on the noise. Variances are low for edge positions in the edge map, as there the edge signal is highest and most certain.

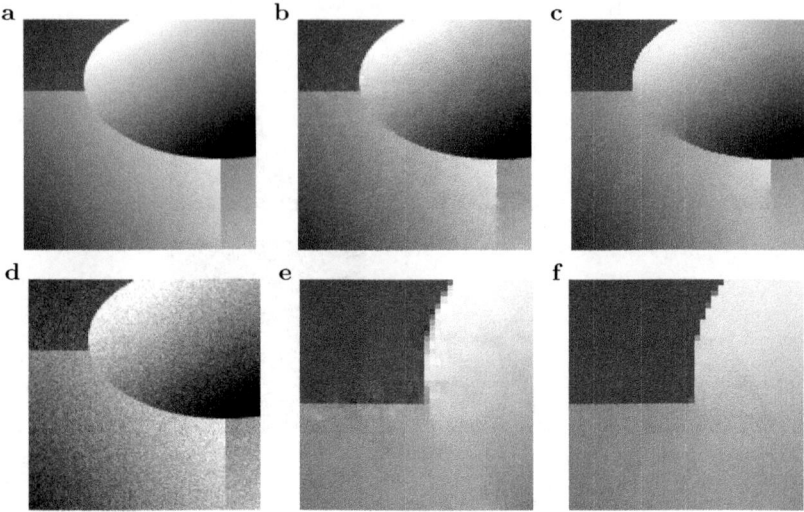

Fig. 2. **a**, **d** original and degraded image with 5% Gaussian noise; **b**, **e** smoothed image and close up with parameters: $\alpha = 1000$, $\beta = 200$, $\rho = 1.2$; **c**, **f** parameters: $\alpha = 4000$, $\beta = 70$, $\rho = 0.3$

4.2   Piecewise Smooth Images and the Crack-Tip Problem

Pock and Cremers [10] compare the original AT approach to their MS method, which we consider to be the current reference method concerning achievable image quality. They show two experiments which we redo in the following. The first experiment using a synthetic piece-wise smooth 128×128-image with 5% Gaussian noise added (see Figure 2 **a** and **d**, and [10], Fig. 4) focuses on visual noise artifacts. Pock and Cremers state worse results for the deterministic AT approach, visible as noise pattern close to image edges. In Figure 2 the same experiment is redone for two different choices of ρ, however now using our stochastic AT approach. In the close up views Figs. 2 **e** and **f**, we see that using $\rho = 1.2$ we get similar artifacts as reported in [10], which however nicely vanish if ρ is reduced to 0.3 and smoothness weight α is increased.

The last experiment is the so-called Crack-Tip experiment (cmp. Figure 3 and [10], Fig. 6), an inpainting experiment nicely demonstrating how the deterministic AT optimization approach gets stuck in local minima, depending on initial conditions. The synthetic image I (Fig. 3a) is given by $I(x,y) = \sqrt{r(x,y)}\sin(\theta(x,y)/2)$ where $r(x,y)$ is the Euclidean distance of a point (x,y) to the image center and $\theta(x,y)$ is the angle of the point (x,y) to the horizontal line. The red circle in Fig. 3d presents the covered/missing part of the image. Inside the circle parameter β is set to be 0 and outside ∞. The classical AT method works well in a case of good initial conditions, but in other cases it does not always come close to the global minimum of the AT energy (Figs. 3**b**, **e**). Our stochastic approach visibly comes close to the true underlying image independent of initial conditions, even locating the tip of the crack close to the

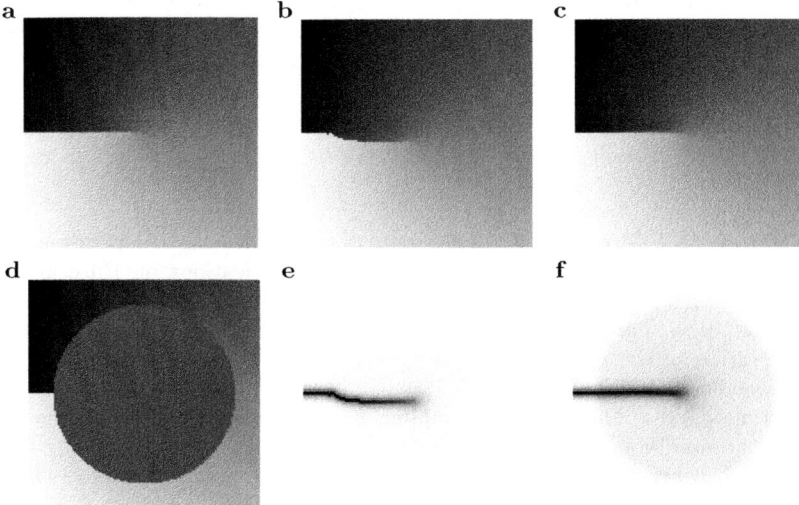

Fig. 3. a, d original image and observed image with a circular gap in the middle; **b, e** image and border using deterministic AT approach and a random image as an initialization, **c, f** our result

center (Figs. 3c, f). Thus, we conclude that when applying a suitable estimator, the AT functional delivers highest quality results, well comparable to the ones reported in [10].

5 Summary

We presented a block-Gibbs-sampling approach to AT image segmentation. In our approach the usual AT energy is interpreted as a posterior energy analogously to the pioneering work of Geman and Geman [2]. But instead of applying a pixel-wise Gibbs sampler within a discrete energy model as done in [2] we derived an efficient block-Gibbs-sampler for the continuous valued AT energy which allows us to sample the whole image or the whole edge-map at a single blow. MMSEEs and the MMEEs are subsequently obtained by the sample mean and sample median, respectively. No minimization of non-convex functionals is necessary within this estimation framework. In addition, obtaining samples allows us to calculate standard deviations of images and edge-map as a confidence measure easily. This is also achieved by the method of Pätz and Preusser [9], however using a gradient descent scheme sensitive to local minima. The results we get are visually of the same quality as the ones of Pock and Cremers [10], and also independent of the initial condition. In contrast to Pock and Cremers' approach, we do not need to quantize gray values, allowing for better results on continuous-valued images. We conclude, that we presented the first AT method combining high quality results, independence of initial conditions, and error estimation.

Acknowledgement. The research leading to these results has received funding from the European Communitys Seventh Framework Programme FP7/2007-2013 Challenge 2 Cognitive Systems, Interaction, Robotics under grant agreement No 247947 GARNICS.

References

1. Ambrosio, L., Tortorelli, V.: Approximation of functionals depending on jumps by elliptic functionals via γ-convergence. Communications on Pure and Applied Mathematics 43, 999–1036 (1990)
2. Geman, S., Geman, D.: Stochastic relaxation, Gibbs distributions and the Bayesian restoration of the images. IEEE Transactions on Pattern Analysis and Machine Intelligence 6, 877–885 (1984)
3. Hastings, W.K.: Monte Carlo sampling methods using Markov chains and their applications. Biometrika 57(1), 97–109 (1970)
4. Kay, S.M.: Fundamentals of Statistical Signal Processing, Volume I: Estimation Theory. Prentice Hall Signal Processing Series (1993)
5. Krajsek, K., Menzel, M.I., Scharr, H.: Riemannian Bayesian estimation of diffusion tensor images. In: Proceedings of the 12th IEEE International Conference on Computer Vision (ICCV), pp. 2327–2334 (2009)
6. Metropolis, N., Rosenbluth, A.W., Rosenbluth, M.N., Teller, A.H., Teller, E.: Equation of state calculations by fast computing machines. The Journal of Chemical Physics 11(21), 1087–1091 (1953)
7. Mumford, D., Shah, J.: Optimal approximations by piecewise smooth functions and associated variational problems. Communications on Pure and Applied Mathematics 42(5), 577–685 (1989)
8. Paragios, N.K., Deriche, R.: A PDE-based level-set approach for detection and tracking of moving objects. In: Proceedings of the Sixth IEEE International Conference on Computer Vision (ICCV), pp. 1139–1145 (1998)
9. Pätz, T., Preusser, T.: Ambrosio-tortorelli segmentation of stochastic images. In: Daniilidis, K., Maragos, P., Paragios, N. (eds.) ECCV 2010. LNCS, vol. 6315, pp. 254–267. Springer, Heidelberg (2010)
10. Pock, T., Cremers, D., Bischof, H., Chambolle, A.: An algorithm for minimizing the Mumford-Shah functional. In: Proceedings of the 12th IEEE International Conference on Computer Vision (ICCV), pp. 1133–1140 (2009)
11. Rue, H., Held, L.: Fast sampling of Gaussian Markov random fields with applications. Journal of the Royal Statistical Society, Series B 63, 325–338 (2000)
12. Scharr, H., Black, M.J., Haussecker, H.W.: Image statistics and anisotropic diffusion. In: Proceedings of the Ninth IEEE International Conference on Computer Vision (ICCV), pp. 840–847 (2003)

Combined Head Localization and Head Pose Estimation for Video–Based Advanced Driver Assistance Systems

Andreas Schulz[1], Naser Damer[2], Mika Fischer[3], and Rainer Stiefelhagen[3]

[1] Robert Bosch GmbH, Leonberg, Germany
andreas.schulz3@de.bosch.com
[2] TU Kaiserslautern, Institute of Signal Theory and Control Engineering
naser_i_damer@hotmail.com
[3] Karlsruhe Institute of Technology, Institute for Anthropomatics
{mika.fischer,rainer.stiefelhagen}@kit.edu

Abstract. This work presents a novel approach for pedestrian head localization and head pose estimation in single images. The presented method addresses an environment of low resolution gray–value images taken from a moving camera with large variations in illumination and object appearance. The proposed algorithms are based on normalized detection confidence values of separate, pose associated classifiers. Those classifiers are trained using a modified one vs. all framework that tolerates outliers appearing in continuous head pose classes. Experiments on a large set of real world data show very good head localization and head pose estimation results even on the smallest considered head size of 7x7 pixels. These results can be obtained in a probabilistic form, which make them of a great value for pedestrian path prediction and risk assessment systems within video-based driver assistance systems or many other applications.

1 Introduction

The field of video-based pedestrian detection has gained a lot of interest by researchers during the past years. One reason for that is the huge demand of car manufacturers to reduce harmful injuries of pedestrians caused by accidents with a nearcoming car or even to avoid those. Advanced driver assistance systems not only try to detect pedestrians but also try to perform the best action to react properly according to the underlying scene. As one can expect, a lot of difficult scenarios and reactions have to be considered and figured out. To support such approaches the head pose of pedestrians can provide a very important hint. A pedestrian looking in the direction of the car may be aware of it and thus is less likely to cause a critical situation than pedestrians just walking towards the street without regarding the environment. The head pose indicates the pedestrians' awareness of the vehicle existence but it also helps to predict the intended movement direction of the pedestrian for a further use within tracking methods or risk assessment systems. Head pose estimation using a vehicle

R. Mester and M. Felsberg (Eds.): DAGM 2011, LNCS 6835, pp. 51–60, 2011.
© Springer-Verlag Berlin Heidelberg 2011

mounted camera, has to deal with low resolution, lack of color images, as well as high variations in illumination and background. Such a system also needs to be robust to large variations in pedestrian and head appearances and guarantee a high degree of reliability.

1.1 Previous Work

As this work integrates the head localization and head pose estimation problem, related literature dealing with both problems is discussed here. Moreover, we present approaches on pedestrian orientation estimation due to its application similarity to pedestrian head pose estimation. Face localization is a specific type of face detection, where the number of faces in a given image is already known. In comparison, face detection usually deals with frontal poses of human heads, while head localization tries to localize the head in any given pose. Nevertheless, the approach of this work is largely related to the problem of face detection in general. One of the major contribution in this field is the work of Viola&Jones [20], where a cascade of boosting classifiers based on Haar-like features is used to detect faces in gray–value images. In [10] they present a generalized method to detect faces under various orientations and heads under various poses. Another major approach to face detection is the use of the Modified Census Transform (MCT) to describe binary structures around pixel positions, see [7]. Recently, [22] suggested an extended 12-bit MCT feature set for low resolution face detection in color images. Others [17] propose the Haar Local Binary Pattern feature, a hybrid between Haar-like features and Local Binary Patterns (LBP, similar to MCT), to achieve an illumination–invariant face detection.

Head pose estimation approaches are usually application driven. [13] present a survey of existing head pose estimation approaches for different scenarios and variable kinds of input data. Applications in human machine interaction [19] e.g. require more precise pose measures but provide a higher head resolution and sometimes depth information using a stereo camera system. These approaches mostly consider the frontal face poses. Applications in surveillance [3,9,15], rough gaze estimation [16] and video driver assistance systems provide lower resolution images under harsh conditions, but demand a discrete pose estimation with larger pose steps including the full pan angle. Regarding the camera setup and available information, many approaches use a network of two or more calibrated cameras [2,4,14,21]. Nevertheless, some approaches are based on conventional 2D image signals [1,3,9,15,16]. To estimate the head pose, different algorithms are presented. Some works estimate the head pose by measuring the similarity to discrete appearance templates [15] while others try to detect facial features and then estimate the head pose according to the geometrical positions of these features [19]. Others use detection techniques to predict one of several discrete head poses in an effort to detect heads under various poses [21]. Concerning our requirements, we deal with discrete, relatively wide pan angle steps (45°) that cover the full head pan angle (360°) in low resolution images. Similar conditions are also given in the works of [3,15,16]. [3] use Ferns to determine skin and non-skin segments of the head, based on color information. In a second step they estimate the head pose to be one of eight pose classes. [15] creates pose template models by calculating a mean image for each of eight head pose images. A similarity distance weighting map is constructed as a pose descriptor. Finally, a given head sample is classified by a support vector machine (*SVM*).

From an application point of view, in video driver assistance systems the head pose is used as a pedestrian intention cue. Some works discuss the pedestrian body pose as an alternative measure of a pedestrian's intention and gaze in order to improve tracking algorithms [6,8,18]. Most of them assume already detected pedestrians and try to estimate their orientations [8,18]. Others integrate the pedestrian detection and orientation estimation within a probabilistic framework to achieve better results [6]. [18] use Haar-like features to train *one vs. all SVMs*, while [8] train *one vs. one SVMs* using Histograms of Oriented Gradients (*HOG*) [5]. [6] also use HOG features combined with support vector machines, as well as adaptive local receptive fields (*LRF*) in combination with a multilayer neural network. Evaluations on their test data show the positive effect of the integrated detection and orientation estimation in comparison to the results of [8,18].

Because of the low resolution images and the wide pan angle used in this work, head pose estimation based on facial features detection will not be suitable. A template based approach does not perform well when dealing with very diverse appearances and background variations. The lack of color information also prevents the use of color histograms. In comparison to pedestrian orientation estimation, where the pedestrian's movement direction does not indicate the real pedestrian's awareness of nearcoming vehicles a priori, with the head pose estimation, we are really able to predict the person's intention.

1.2 Proposed System

This work proposes an integrated head localization and head pose estimation approach. The method builds its decisions based on confidence values provided by pose associated classifiers. These classifiers are based on state–of–the–art object detection approaches, each of which is trained separately under a modified one vs. all framework to achieve a high localization rate and ensure a stable training process. Assuming a pre–defined pedestrian hypothesis (bounding box), the provided algorithm searches in the upper region followed by a head localization and head pose estimation block. The head

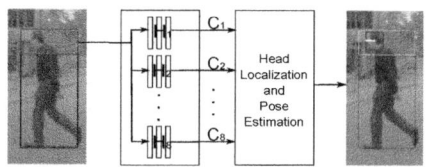

Fig. 1. Approach overview. Different head pose associated classifiers H_m, $m = 1...8$, evaluate all possible windows in the head search area (red) of a pedestrian detection (blue). The outcoming confidence values $\mathcal{C}_m$ are used to perform the head localization and pose estimation.

pose of interest is set to be one of eight discrete poses distributed over the full pan angle of 360°. Figure 1 shows an overview of our proposed system.

2   Methodology

The system developed here consists of eight separate classifiers associated with the different head pose classes. These classifiers are built under a modified one vs. all framework (see Sec. 2.1). Each classifier consists of a cascade of boosting classifiers and produces a classification confidence, when a test sample is evaluated. Given a pedestrian detection, the head pose classifiers are searching for head correspondences in a specific area (Sec. 2.2) on the top of the pedestrian image, using a sliding window technique on different scales. This results in eight confidence values per search location, which are normalized to be comparable among each other (see Sec. 2.3). The head localization and pose estimation is achieved by comparing the confidence values for all windows at all different scales, assuming the presence of exactly on head per pedestrian hypothesis (see Sec. 2.4).

2.1   Training Procedure

This work tries to map the continuous full head pan angle into a discrete set of eight pose classes. Therefore problems generating the training data may appear in separating border elements of neighboring classes. In other words, we are facing the problem of a training set with fuzzy borders between the different classes, see Figure 2. A conventional one vs. all training [18], where a certain class classifier is trained against all the other classes, may lead to an unstable

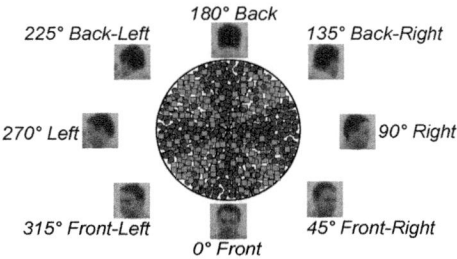

Fig. 2. Distribution of the manually labeled training samples with fuzzy borders between different pose classes

training process, especially when using outlier–sensitive boosting algorithms. To prevent this problem we use a modified one vs. all training procedure, where a special pose classifier is trained against all the other poses, except of its direct neighboring poses. Experiments showed, that this yields more stable classifiers and higher localization rates. Additionally we include areas around the head and background images recorded in inner city scenarios into the negative set. Figure 3 shows some examples of our training data. The number of samples in each pose associated training set differs due to the distribution over pedestrian appearances in our scenario. The setup of the classifiers we use will be explained later in the experiments (Sec. 3).

2.2   Head Search Domain

Detected pedestrian images are the input to the head localization and pose estimation system developed here. The system will search for the pedestrian head in the upper part of the pedestrian hypothesis. On average, the head represents

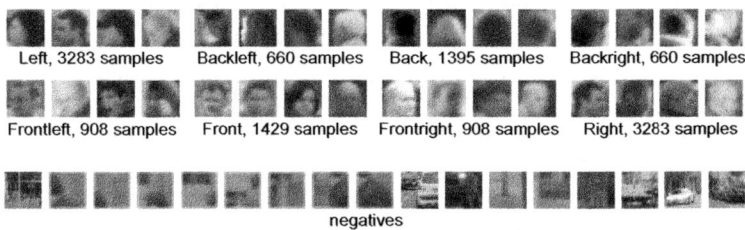

Left, 3283 samples   Backleft, 660 samples   Back, 1395 samples   Backright, 660 samples

Frontleft, 908 samples   Front, 1429 samples   Frontright, 908 samples   Right, 3283 samples

negatives

Fig. 3. Examples of the training data for eight pedestrian head pose classes and negative samples

approximately 1/7 of the total human height. If a perfectly aligned pedestrian detection is assumed, the mentioned value would be fine. In practice however, pedestrian detectors sometimes will detect a pedestrian resulting in a detection box that is not perfectly bounding the pedestrian. To handle this problem, we consider a head search domain having the same width as the pedestrian detection box. For the height we choose 2/11 of the pedestrians box height resulting from previous experiments. This area is scanned on different scales to detect heads on different sizes. An example is given in Figure 4.

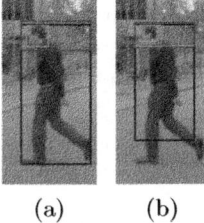

(a)   (b)

Fig. 4. Pedestrian detection (blue), head search domain (red) and search windows (green). The ideal height for the head search domain of $\frac{1}{7}$ of the pedestrians height (a), does not hold for imperfect aligned pedestrian detection hypothesises (b).

2.3 Calculation and Normalization of Confidence Values

Classifying a certain region of an input image, using a sliding window, results in eight confidence values per search position. These values are used later in a comparative manner to determine the localization and the pose of the pedestrians head. Since the eight pose classifiers are trained independently, the different confidence values are also independent, thus have different ranges. To bring the different outcomes to a comparable level, we perform confidence normalization. For this we first evaluate each pose classifier on its training data and compute the mean output confidence value $\bar{C}_m$. To normalize the different classifiers' confidence value ranges, the mean confidence values $\bar{C}_m$, $m = 1, ..., 8$ need to be equalized. This can be achieved by multiplying these values by normalization coefficients α_m such that $\alpha_m \bar{C}_m = \alpha_n \bar{C}_n$, $m \neq n$. Normalization with respect to the highest mean confidence value will yield

$$\alpha_m = \max_{n=1,...,8} \{\bar{C}_n\}/\bar{C}_m. \tag{1}$$

The outputs $C_m(l)$ of the different classifiers, on a special location l, are then normalized by the corresponding coefficient α_m, i.e.

$$C_{m,\ norm}(l) = \alpha_m C_m(l). \tag{2}$$

In the following we assume normalized confidence values and ignore the additional label.

2.4   Head Localization and Pose Estimation

The search for the head of a given pedestrian hypothesis is limited to the defined domain in Section 2.2. This area will be scanned by a sliding window at different scales, where each position l_h is evaluated by the different pose classifiers. As a result we get eight normalized confidence values per search position. We consider a Bayesian decision and assign the sample x the position $\hat{l}_h$ and pose class $\hat{\theta}$ with the highest a posteriori probability:

$$(\hat{l}_h, \hat{\theta}) = \operatorname*{arg\,max}_{l_h, j \in \{1,\dots,8\}} P(l_h, \theta_j | x), \text{with } P(l_h, \theta_j | x) \approx \frac{C_j(l_h)}{\sum_k C_k(l_h)},\ l_h \subset x. \tag{3}$$

Thus, the head localization and head pose estimation is performed by simply taking that particular position and pose, which scores the maximum confidence over all pose classifiers, positions, and scales. I.e. the classifier outputs are used twice, for head localization and estimation of the head pose.

3   Experiments

3.1   Experimental Setup

The proposed method is tested using classifiers based on different kinds of features, that proved to be very useful in the fields of pedestrian– and face–detection as well as for head pose estimation problems. All the classifiers are trained with the same training parameters on the data mentioned in Section 2.1. First, we use a boosting cascade of *Haar-like* features, as proposed in [20,12]. The second type of classifiers are based on the *Modified Census Transform* [7]. These features proved to outperform the Haar–like features concerning the problem of face–detection. As we have proposed a method to estimate the head pose of a pedestrian, we are dealing with head images at a very low resolution. Concerning this point, we evaluate our classifiers on test samples with different resolutions in order to get a dependency between the performance of our classifiers and the image resolution, which is directly related to the distance between a pedestrian and an approaching vehicle. Obviously, the effort on our system is to detect the pedestrian's intension as soon as possible. Thus, for evaluation we consider pedestrian detections with a maximum height of 140 pixels (head size $\approx$20x20 pixels) and a minimum height of 50 pixels (head size $\approx$7x7 pixels). The test samples are collected from 24 inner city video sequences à 200 Frames. In total our test set consists of 10290 pedestrian samples, covering the eight head pose classes.

3.2   Head Localization Performance

Being aware of the fact, that we already assume the presence of a head within a pedestrian hypothesis, it is possible to achieve very high head localization rates in general. We assume a head localization to be correct, if cover and overlap [11] of annotated ground truth data and detection hypotheses results in values higher than 0.5.

Figure 5 shows the head localization rates for the different classifiers at different image resolutions. All configurations achieve very good correct localization rates, scoring over 92% even when evaluating on the lowest considered resolution of 50 pixels of pedestrians' height. The MCT-based features seem to perform slightly better for higher resolutions than the Haar-like features, resulting in a correct localization rate of nearly 98% for head sizes of 20x20 pixels. For smaller resolutions the performance of the MCT features breaks down and is comparable to Haar-like features. We explain that with the loss of structures within a 7x7 pixels patch in comparison to a 20x20 pixels head image. Figure 8a shows some sam-

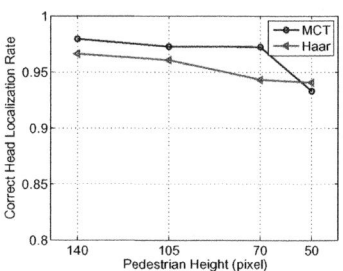

Fig. 5. Correct head localization rates for different pedestrian heights in image pixels. The corresponding head sizes cover a range from 20x20 pixels to 7x7 pixels.

ples of mislocalized heads at different resolutions. Most of these errors occur, when the structure of the background has a high similarity to the head appearance.

3.3   Head Pose Estimation Performance

The correct estimation of the head pose is a more difficult task than the localization itself. We are scanning the upper part of a pedestrian detection with eight different pose classifiers, so that it is likely, that at least one of those results in a very high confidence at the correct head position. For the head pose estimation we would take the pose related to that particular classifier. However this could probably fail concerning the difficulties of our fuzzy multi–class problem on low resolution images. We represent our results using confusion matrices as proposed in [6,15]. Higher values concentrated on the diagonals are related to a better performance of a multi–class detection algorithm. Figure 6 shows the confusion matrices for the considered feature types and resolutions. All configurations achieve satisfying correct decision rates, even when evaluation is performed on very low resolution images. The MCT–based approach reaches an overall correct decision rate over 60% for head sizes of 20x20 pixels, where the use of Haar–like features achieves 49%. The best accuracy up to 76% is reached by the left and right pose MCT–classifiers. For head sizes up to 7x7 pixels, the overall performance breaks down to a correct decision rate of 42% for the MCT–classifier and 44% for the classifier based on Haar–like features. It can be noticed that the MCT–classifiers

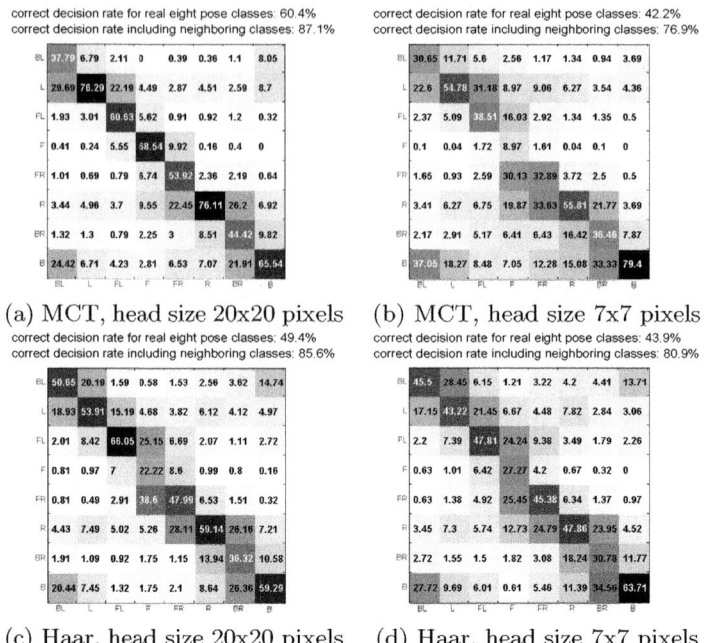

(a) MCT, head size 20x20 pixels   (b) MCT, head size 7x7 pixels

(c) Haar, head size 20x20 pixels   (d) Haar, head size 7x7 pixels

Fig. 6. Confusion Matrices for MCT– ((a), (b)) and Haar–classifiers ((c), (d)) for head sizes of 20x20 pixels and 7x7 pixels

score higher correct decision rates for higher resolutions when compared with the classifiers based on Haar–like features. The use of Haar–like features results in a slightly better performance only on the lowest considered image resolution. This may be explained, as for the localization results, by the nature of MCT–based features that rely on the pixel level structures, which may disappear in low resolution images. Haar–like features measure intensity differences between larger areas and are therefore unlikely to face this problem. Figure 6 also shows, that most of the confusions of one particular head pose occur with the direct neighboring head poses. Therefore we also considered a pose estimation to be correct if the predicted pose is identical to the true pose or one of its direct neighboring poses. In this way, it is possible to get correct decision rates at a minimum of nearly 76% for head images of 7x7 pixels and a maximum of 87% for head sizes of 20x20 pixels using MCT features. In the case of the real eight–class problem, the classifiers using Haar–like features tend to confuse the neighboring poses more than the classifiers based on the MCT. However, when dealing with modified eight–class problem, they seem to slightly outperform the MCT–classifiers, especially on the lowest resolution. Figure 7 displays samples of correct head pose estimation results for heads of 20x20 and 7x7 pixels size using our MCT-based method. The approach using Haar–like features results in similar images. To get an impression of the complexity of head pose estimation in very low resolution images we show samples of wrongly estimated orientations in Figure 8b.

(a)   (b)

Fig. 7. Correct results using MCT features for pedestrian heights of 140 pixels (a) and 50 pixels (b). White stripes indicate the pedestrians' head pose direction.

(a) Samples of mislocalized heads using MCT features in different image resolutions

(b) Samples of wrongly estimated head poses using MCT features in different image resolutions

Fig. 8. Samples in different image resolutions, where the proposed system using MCT features fails. (a) mislocalizations, (b) wrongly estimated head poses.

4 Conclusion

This work dealt with the integrated problem of pedestrian head localization and head pose estimation under the harsh conditions of low resolution gray–value images, full pan angle poses and high dynamic scenarios taken from a moving camera. A solution of this problem was achieved by using a detection–based approach, where two state–of–the–art face detection techniques built the basic block. Head pose classifiers were trained in a modified one vs. all framework, that guaranteed a good localization rate over the continuous head pose pan angle and prevented instabilities during the training process. A sliding window at different scales was used to collect classification confidence values all over the head search area. Based on the normalized confidence values, the head could be localized and the pose be estimated in a probabilistic manner. We evaluated the developed system on a large and diverse dataset. Results were presented considering confusion matrices and showed a very good performance for head localization and head pose estimation, even when dealing with very low resolution images including heads down to a size of 7x7 pixels. The probabilistic form of the head pose estimation results provides a suitable type of information for further integration within video–based driver assistance systems.

References

1. Ba, S.O., Odobez, J.-M.: A probabilistic framework for joint head tracking and pose estimation. ICPR 4, 264–267 (2004)
2. Bäuml, M., Bernardin, K., Fischer, M., Ekenel, H.K.: Multi-pose face recognition for person retrieval in camera networks. AVSS 7 (2010)
3. Benfold, B., Reid, I.: Guiding visual surveillance by tracking human attention. In: BMVC, vol. 20 (2009)
4. Canton-Ferrer, C., Casas, J.R., Pardàs, M.: Head orientation estimation using particle filtering in multiview scenarios. In: Stiefelhagen, R., Bowers, R., Fiscus, J.G. (eds.) RT 2007 and CLEAR 2007. LNCS, vol. 4625, pp. 317–327. Springer, Heidelberg (2008)
5. Dalal, N., Triggs, B.: Histograms of oriented gradients for human detection. In: CVPR, pp. 886–893 (2005)
6. Enzweiler, M., Gavrila, D.M.: Integrated pedestrian classification and orientation estimation. In: CVPR, pp. 982–989 (2010)
7. Fröba, B., Ernst, A.: Face detection with the modified census transform. In: IEEE FG, vol. 6 (2004)
8. Gandhi, T., Trivedi, M.M.: Image based estimation of pedestrian orientation for improving path prediction. In: Intelligent Vehicles Symposium, pp. 506–511 (2008)
9. Hirata, J., Morimoto, M., Fujii, K.: Estimating face direction from low resolution images. In: World Automation Congress, WAC 2008, pp. 1–6 (2008)
10. Jones, M.J., Viola, P.: Fast multi-view face detection. In: CVPR (2003)
11. Leibe, B., Seemann, E., Schiele, B.: Pedestrian detection in crowded scenes. In: CVPR, pp. 878–885 (2005)
12. Lienhart, R., Maydt, J.: An extended set of haar-like features for rapid object detection. In: International Conference on Image Processing, pp. 900–903 (2002)
13. Murphy-Chutorian, E., Trivedi, M.M.: Head pose estimation in computer vision: A survey. IEEE TPAMI 31, 607–626 (2009)
14. Niese, R., Al-Hamadi, A., Michaelis, B.: A stereo and color-based method for face pose estimation and facial feature extraction. ICPR 1, 299–302 (2006)
15. Orozco, J., Gong, S., Xiang, T.: Head pose classification in crowded scenes. In: BMVC (2009)
16. Robertson, N.M., Reid, I.D.: Estimating gaze direction from low-resolution faces in video. In: Proc. IEEE European Conference on Computer Vision, vol. 9 (2006)
17. Roy, A., Marcel, S.: Haar local binary pattern feature for fast illumination invariant face detection. In: BMVC (2009)
18. Shimizu, H., Poggio, T.: Direction estimation of pedestrian from multiple still images. In: Intelligent Vehicles Symposium, pp. 596–600 (2004)
19. Vatahska, T., Bennewitz, M., Behnke, S.: Feature-based head pose estimation from images. In: 7th IEEE-RAS International Conference on Humanoid Robots 2007, pp. 330–335 (December 2007)
20. Viola, P.A., Jones, M.J.: Rapid object detection using a boosted cascade of simple features. In: CVPR, pp. 511–518 (2001)
21. Zhang, Z., Hu, Y., Liu, M., Huang, T.: Head pose estimation in seminar room using multi view face detectors. In: Proceedings of the 1st International Evaluation Conference on Classification of Events, Activities and Relationships, pp. 299–304 (2007)
22. Zheng, J., Ramírez, G.A., Fuentes, O.: Face detection in low-resolution color images. In: Campilho, A., Kamel, M. (eds.) ICIAR 2010. LNCS, vol. 6111, pp. 454–463. Springer, Heidelberg (2010)

Towards Cross-Modal Comparison of Human Motion Data

Thomas Helten[1], Meinard Müller[1], Jochen Tautges[2],
Andreas Weber[2], and Hans-Peter Seidel[1]

[1] Max-Planck-Institut für Informatik
Campus E1.4, 66123 Saarbrücken, Germany
thelten@mpi-inf.mpg.de
[2] Bonn University, Institut für Informatik II
Friedrich-Ebert-Allee 144, 53113 Bonn, Germany

Abstract. Analyzing human motion data has become an important strand of research in many fields such as computer animation, sport sciences, and medicine. In this paper, we discuss various motion representations that originate from different sensor modalities and investigate their discriminative power in the context of motion identification and retrieval scenarios. As one main contribution, we introduce various mid-level motion representations that allow for comparing motion data in a cross-modal fashion. In particular, we show that certain low-dimensional feature representations derived from inertial sensors are suited for specifying high-dimensional motion data. Our evaluation shows that features based on directional information outperform purely acceleration based features in the context of motion retrieval scenarios.

1 Introduction

There are many ways for capturing and recording human motions including mechanical, magnetic, optical, and inertial devices. Each motion capturing (mocap) technology has its own strengths and weaknesses with regard to accuracy, expressiveness, and operating expenses, see [4,14] for an overview. For example, optical marker-based mocap systems typically provide high-quality motion data such as positional information given in joint coordinates or rotational information specified by joint angles. However, requiring an array of calibrated high-resolution cameras as well as special garment equipment, such systems are not only cost intensive but also impose limiting constraints on the actor and the recording environment. On the other side, in recent years low-cost inertial sensors, which can be easily attached to the body or even fit in a shoe, have become popular in computer game and sports applications [7,9]. Another use of inertial sensors is shown in [8], where the inertial sensor data is used to regularize marker-less tracking results. However, inertial information such as joint accelerations, angular velocities, or limb orientations, is often being of less expressive power and affected by noise.

R. Mester and M. Felsberg (Eds.): DAGM 2011, LNCS 6835, pp. 61–70, 2011.

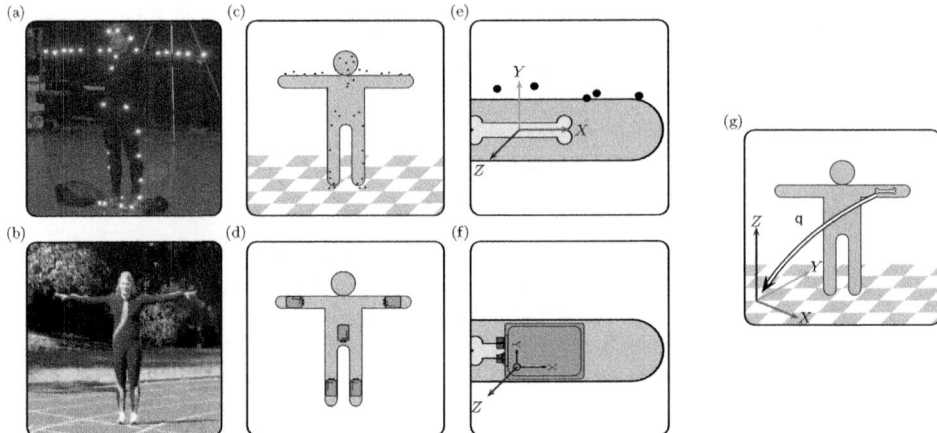

Fig. 1. (a) Actor wearing a suit with 41 retro-reflective markers as used by an optical mocap system. (b) Actress wearing a suit with 5 Xsens MTx Sensors. (c) Positions of 41 markers provided by the optical system. (d) Locations of the sensors. (e) Limbs' positions and orientations defined by the positions of markers. (f) Inertial sensors measuring the orientation of the limb they are attached to. (g) Limb orientation expressed with respect to a global coordinate system.

In this paper, we address the issue of cross-modal motion comparison investigating the expressiveness of various motion representations in the context of general motion identification and retrieval scenarios. As one main contribution, we introduce various mid-level feature representations that facilitate cross-modal comparison of various motion types. Here, the main challenge consists of finding a good trade-off between robustness and expressiveness: on the one hand, a mid-level representation has to be robustly deducible from the data outputted by different mocap systems; on the other hand, the representation has to contain enough information for discriminating motions within a certain application task. In particular, we show that certain low-dimensional orientation-based motion features are suited for accurately retrieving high-dimensional motion data as obtained from optical motion capturing.

The remainder of the paper is organized as follows. In Sect. 2, we describe different sensor modalities and discuss some of their properties. In particular, we go into more detail on acceleration and orientation data as obtained from recent inertial sensors. Then, in Sect. 3, we introduce various mid-level feature representations that can be derived from the different sensor modalities. In Sect. 4, we study the performance of these mid-level representations in the context of cross-modal motion retrieval. Finally, in Sect. 5 we conclude with an outlook on future work. Further related work is discussed in the respective sections.

2   Sensor Modalities

In this paper, we focus on two types of mocap systems, optical and inertial systems, which differ largely in acquisition cost, in the requirements on the recording conditions, and in the kind of data they provide. We now summarize some of the fundamental properties of such systems, while introducing several motion representations and fixing some notation.

2.1 Positional Motion Data

Optical marker-based mocap technology, as used in the passive marker-based Vicon MX system[1] or the active marker-based PhaseSpace system[2], allows for recording human motions with high precision. Here, the actor is equipped with a set of active or passive markers, which are tracked by an array of calibrated high-resolution cameras. From synchronously recorded 2D images of the marker positions, the system can then reconstruct 3D coordinates of marker positions or other skeletal kinematic chain representations. One particular strength of optical marker-based systems is that they provide positional motion data of high quality. However, requiring an array of calibrated high-resolution cameras as well as special garment equipment, such systems are cost intensive in acquisition and maintenance. Furthermore, many of the available optical mocap systems are vulnerable to bright lighting conditions thus posing additional constraints on the recording environment (e. g., illumination, volume, indoor). In our experiments, we use a set of 41 retro-reflective markers which are attached to an actor's suit at well defined locations following a fixed pattern, see Fig. 1 (a).

2.2 Inertial Motion Data

In contrast to marker-based reference systems, inertial sensors impose comparatively weak additional constraints on the overall recording setup with regard to location, recording volume, and illumination. Furthermore, inertial systems are relatively inexpensive as well as easy to operate and to maintain. Therefore, such sensors have become increasingly popular and are now widely used in many commercial products. On the downside, inertial sensors do not provide any high-qualitative positional data, but only accelerations and rate of turn data given in the sensor's local coordinate system. Note that these measured accelerations always contain, as one component, the acceleration caused by gravity. Therefore, the measured acceleration a can be thought of a superposition $a = \bar{q}[m + g]$ consisting of the gravity g and the actual acceleration m of the motion. Here, the quantity a is given in the sensors's local coordinate system, while m and g are given in the world coordinate system. The term $\bar{q}[\cdot]$ represents the transformation from the global coordinate system to the sensor's local coordinate system (see below). This fact is often exploited in many portable devices such as recent mobile phones to calculate the device's orientation with respect to the canonical direction of gravity [2].

In the context of cross-modal comparison of optical and inertial data, one could integrate over the inertial data to obtain 3D positions. This, however, is not practical since inertial data is prone to noise leading to very poor positional

---

[1] www.vicon.com

[2] www.phasespace.com

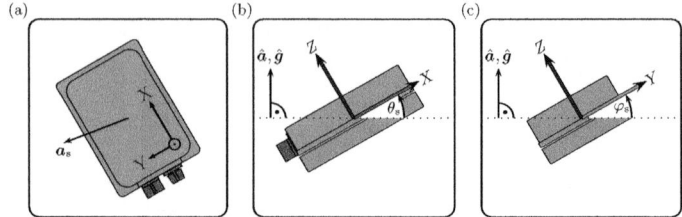

Fig. 2. Illustration of the different feature values. (a) Measured acceleration a_s with respect to the sensors local coordinate system. (b) Pitch θ_s of a sensor with respect to the plane defined by $\hat{a}$ respectively $\hat{g}$. (c) Roll φ_s of a sensor with respect to the plane defined by $\hat{a}$ respectively $\hat{g}$.

data when being integrated [13]. Therefore, inertial data is often used indirectly to influence and control certain parameters within a motion generation engine. For example, inertial information may be used to identify and retrieve high-quality motions that were previously recorded by optical mocap systems [11]. Here, to make the 3D positional data comparable with inertial information, one obvious way is to suitably differentiate the 3D positional data to obtain velocities and accelerations. Such data, however, is very local in nature with respect to the temporal dimension thus making comparisons on this level susceptible to short-time artifacts and outliers. In the following sections, we investigate this issue in more detail and introduce mid-level representations that facilitate a more robust cross-modal comparison.

In our experiments, we use inertial sensors supplied by Xsens[3]. Each MTx unit contains an accelerometer, a rate gyro, as well as a magnet field sensor. These units combine the information of the contained sensors to calculate their full 3 degree of freedom (DOF) orientation q with respect to a global coordinate system, see e. g. [1,3]. In the following, we refer to such a combination of inertial and additional sensors as inertial unit. In order to express the orientation q we use rotations expressed as unit quaternions (see [10]). Each such quaternion defines a 3D rotation $\mathbb{R}^3 \rightarrow \mathbb{R}^3$, which we also refer to as q. Let q$[x]$ denote the rotated vector for a vector $x \in \mathbb{R}^3$. The inverse rotation is referred to by $\overline{q}$.

3   Feature Representations

In order to compare human motion data across different sensor modalities, one needs common mid-level representations that can be generated from the data outputted by the different sensors. In the context of this paper, our goal is to retrieve full-body motions from a database containing motion data captured by an optical mocap system using 41 markers, where the query is given in form of a motion clip captured by five inertial sensors $s_1, \ldots, s_5$ placed at the hip next to the spine (s_1) both lower arms (left s_2, right s_3) and both lower legs (left

---

[3] www.xsens.com

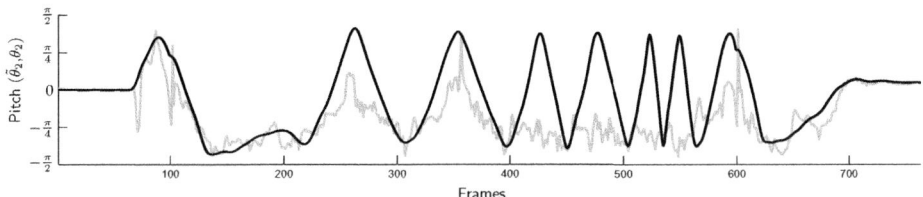

Fig. 3. Motion sequence consisting of six arm rotations, where the speed of the arm rotations increases with each repetition. The pitch of the left forearm is shown, calculated by using $\tilde{\theta}_2$ (gray) and θ_2 (black).

s_4, right s_5), see Fig. 1 (d). Since all information supplied by the five inertial sensors can be simulated using the 41 marker position (as shown in Sect. 3.1), we use features close to the inertial data as common mid-level representation.

3.1 Virtual Sensors

Local accelerations and directional information as provided by inertial sensors can also be defined from positional information coming from an optical mocap system. To this end, for a given inertial sensor fixed to a limb in a specific way, we use a suitable combination of markers to define the location and local coordinate system of a corresponding virtual sensor, see Fig. 1 (e). The orientation q of a virtual sensor is then the transformation from the local coordinate system to the global coordinate system (see Fig. 1 (g)), while the global acceleration m is obtained by double differentiation of the virtual sensor's global position. By adding the gravity g and transforming this quantity to the virtual sensor's local coordinate system using $\bar{q}$ one finally gets the local acceleration $a = \bar{q}[m + g]$.

3.2 Local Acclerations

As a first simple feature representation, we directly use the local accelerations as outputted by the accelerometers. Using five inertial sensor units $s_1, \ldots, s_5$, this results in five local accelerations $a_s \in \mathbb{R}^3$ for $s \in [1 : 5] := \{1, \ldots, 5\}$. We then simply stack these five acceleration vectors to form a single vector

$$v_a = (a_1^T, \ldots, a_5^T)^T \in \mathbb{R}^{15}. \tag{1}$$

3.3 Directions Relative to Acceleration

A more robust motion representation is obtained by measuring directions rather than magnitudes. To this end, we define a global up-direction using the direction of the gravity vector g. We are now able to define a two degrees of freedom orientation of the sensor's local coordinate system relative to this global up-direction. Inspired by aviation, we call these two parameters *pitch* θ_s and *roll*

φ_{s}, see Fig. 2. In many applications these quantities can be approximated using only the measured acceleration $\boldsymbol{a}_{\mathrm{s}}$. These approximations denoted by $\tilde{\theta}_{\mathrm{s}}$ and $\tilde{\varphi}_{\mathrm{s}}$, are defined as follows:

$$\hat{\boldsymbol{a}}_{\mathrm{s}} = \frac{\boldsymbol{a}_{\mathrm{s}}}{\|\boldsymbol{a}_{\mathrm{s}}\|}, \tag{2}$$

$$\tilde{\theta}_{\mathrm{s}} = \arccos\left\langle \hat{\boldsymbol{a}}_{\mathrm{s}}, (1,0,0)^{T} \right\rangle, \tag{3}$$

$$\tilde{\varphi}_{\mathrm{s}} = \arccos\left\langle \hat{\boldsymbol{a}}_{\mathrm{s}}, (0,1,0)^{T} \right\rangle. \tag{4}$$

Here, note that if the sensor's local Y-axis is perpendicular to the global up-direction, the pitch is determined by the rotation around the Y-axis. The resulting angle can be approximated by using an inner product between the X-axis and $\hat{\boldsymbol{a}}_{\mathrm{s}}$ approximating the up-direction, see Fig. 2 (b). Similarly, the roll can be derived from the inner product between the Y-axis and the upward direction, see Fig. 2 (c). We refer to the resulting pitch and roll features as *acceleration-based directional features*. Again, we stack these features for all five sensors $s_1, \ldots, s_5$ to form a single vector

$$\boldsymbol{v}_{\hat{\boldsymbol{a}}} = (\tilde{\theta}_1, \tilde{\varphi}_1, \ldots, \tilde{\theta}_5, \tilde{\varphi}_5)^{T} \in \mathbb{R}^{10}. \tag{5}$$

Here, pitch $\tilde{\theta}_{\mathrm{s}}$ and roll $\tilde{\varphi}_{\mathrm{s}}$ are calculated using $\boldsymbol{a}_{\mathrm{s}}$ as approximation for $\boldsymbol{g}$. Recall from Sect. 2.2 that each measured acceleration is a superposition $\boldsymbol{a}_{\mathrm{s}} = \overline{\mathsf{q}_{\mathrm{s}}}[\boldsymbol{m}_{\mathrm{s}}+\boldsymbol{g}]$. Thus $\tilde{\theta}_{\mathrm{s}}$ and $\tilde{\varphi}_{\mathrm{s}}$ are only good approximations if $\boldsymbol{m}_{\mathrm{s}}$ is negligible. However, for fast and dynamic motions, the component $\boldsymbol{m}_{\mathrm{s}}$ is large, which leads to corrupted pitch and roll values, see Fig. 3

3.4   Directions Relative to Gravity

To address the above mentioned problem, one needs to approximate the global upward direction in a more robust way—in particular during dynamic phases, where $\boldsymbol{m}_{\mathrm{s}}$ is not negligible. To achieve such an estimation, simple accelerometers do not suffice. We therefore use an inertial unit that outputs not only the local accelerations but also the sensor's orientation with respect to the global coordinate system, see Sect. 2.2. Then, the direction $\hat{\boldsymbol{g}}$ can be estimated by transforming the direction of the global Z-axis by means of the sensor's orientation q_{s}. More precisely, we define

$$\hat{\boldsymbol{g}}_{\mathrm{s}} = \overline{\mathsf{q}_{\mathrm{s}}}\left[(0,0,1)^{T}\right], \tag{6}$$

$$\theta_{\mathrm{s}} = \arccos\left\langle \hat{\boldsymbol{g}}_{\mathrm{s}}, (1,0,0)^{T} \right\rangle, \tag{7}$$

$$\varphi_{\mathrm{s}} = \arccos\left\langle \hat{\boldsymbol{g}}_{\mathrm{s}}, (0,1,0)^{T} \right\rangle. \tag{8}$$

As before, we stack the pitch and roll features for all five sensors $s_1, \ldots, s_5$ to form a single vector

$$\boldsymbol{v}_{\hat{\boldsymbol{g}}} = (\theta_1, \varphi_1, \ldots, \theta_5, \varphi_5)^{T} \in \mathbb{R}^{10}. \tag{9}$$

The components are referred to as *gravity-based directional features*. The values θ_s and φ_s exactly define (up to measurement errors) pitch and roll as introduced in Sect. 3.3. The improvements in the case of highly dynamic motions are illustrated by Fig. 3, which shows the values of $\tilde{\theta}_2$ and θ_2 over a motion sequence containing six arm rotations (between frames 210 and 575). Here, the arm rotations are performed at increasing speed, where the last rotation is performed almost three times faster than the first one. While θ_2 clearly shows the periodic fluctuation of the pitch during the rotation, $\tilde{\theta}_2$ fails to display any meaningful information when the motion becomes faster.

4   Cross-modal Comparison

In this section, we evaluate the feature representations in the context of a cross-modal retrieval scenario, where we search in a database which comprises high-dimensional 3D mocap while using low-dimensional inertial sensors as query input.To this end, we assembled two databases DB_{xse} and DB_{c3d}. Each of the databases contains ten instances of the ten motion classes shown in Fig. 4 (a), which results in a total of 100 motion sequences per database. While the database DB_{xse} was recorded using five inertial sensors set up as shown in Fig. 1 (d), the database DB_{c3d} was assembled from excerpts of the HDM05 database which consists of high-quality motions recorded by a 12 camera Vicon optical mocap system, see [6]. Finally, we computed virtual sensors for DB_{c3d} as described in Section 3.1 matching the sensor setup as used for DB_{xse}.

4.1   Class Confusion

Depending on the used feature representation, we now examine how well high-dimensional motion sequences in DB_{c3d} can be characterized by low-dimensional sensor input from DB_{xse}. To this end, we rank the motion documents from DB_{c3d} according to their similarity to a given query document from DB_{xse}. More precisely, we consider a document from DB_{c3d} a match when it is an instance of the same motion class as the given query document from DB_{xse}. As similarity measure we use the classical dynamic time warping (DTW) distance described in [5], where, in our case, the highest ranked motion document has the smallest DTW distance. By considering the distribution of motion classes among the ten best-ranked documents one gets a good impression how the motion classes are confused under a given feature representation. A common means to visualize this are *confusion matrices*, which are shown for the three feature representations v_a, $v_{\hat{a}}$ and $v_{\hat{g}}$ in Fig. 4 (b). The rows of a confusion matrix represent the motion classes of the query, whereas the columns represent the motion classes of the ten best-ranked documents. Dark entries indicate a large percentage of a motion class, whereas light colors indicate a low percentage. For example, the matrices show that most of the motion classes are confused with the motion class CW (first column) when using the feature representation v_a. Here, the reason is that the motion class CW shows a lot of variance among the different motion instances

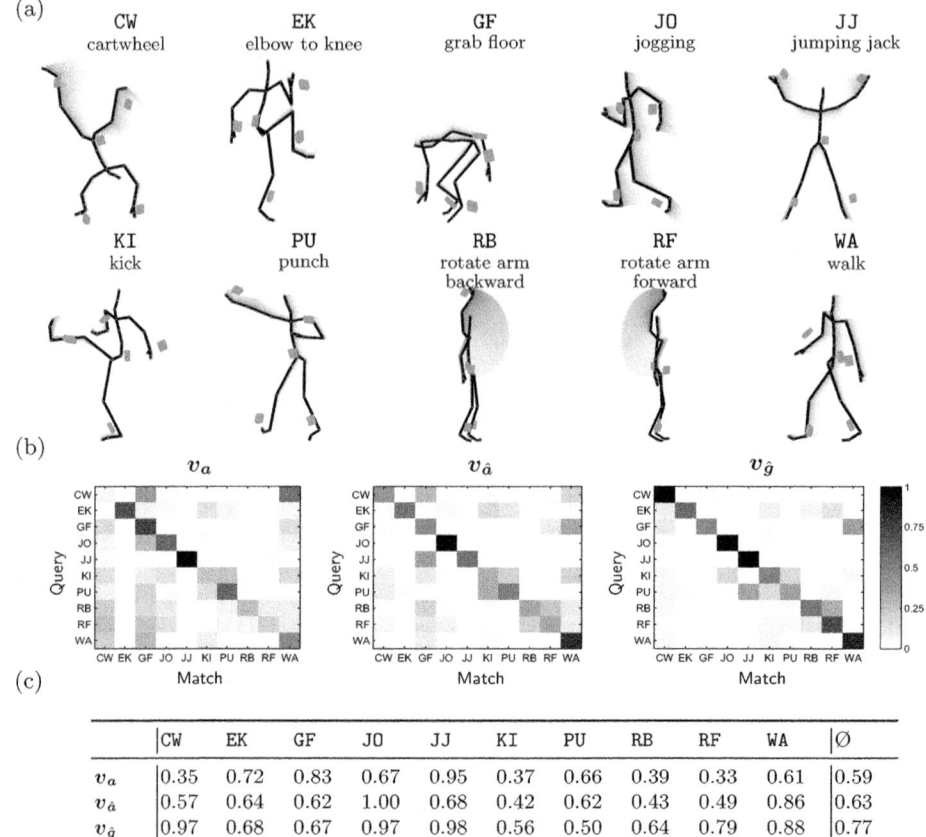

Fig. 4. (a) Motion classes used for the experiments in Sect. 4. (b) Confusion matrices (left) and true match distributions (right) of the three different feature representations. (c) Averaged maximal F-Measures for every feature representation and motion class. The last column shows for every feature representation the average over all motion classes.

even when performed by the same actor. In particular, the risk of confusion with the motion class CW is high for dynamic motions classes such as KI, PU, RB, and RF, because dynamic motions under the feature representation v_a have a very noisy character without much characteristic features. In contrast, using the directional feature representation $v_{\hat{g}}$ this confusion is reduced significantly.

4.2   F-measure

To further quantify the retrieval results, we use another measure from the retrieval domain referred to as *maximum F-measure*. Let k, $k \in [1:K]$ be the rank of a given document, where K is the maximum rank (in our case $K = 100$). Now, for every k, *precision* P_k and *recall* R_k are defined as $P_k := |T \cap M_k|/|M_k|$ and $R_k := |T \cap M_k|/|T|$. Here, M_k is the set of all documents up to rank k and T the set of all possible matches (in our case $|T| = 10$). Combining precision and recall values for a given rank k yields the (standard) F-measure $F_k := 2 \cdot P_k \cdot R_k / (P_k + R_k)$. Now, the maximum F-measure is defined as $F := \max F_k, k \in [1:K]$. The table in Fig. 4 (c) shows the averaged maximum F-measure for each motion class,where the was calculated by averaging the maximum F-measures over all queries of each motion class, and every feature representation. Finally, the last column shows the average over all motion classes. The better a given feature representation discriminates a motion class against all other motion classes the larger is the corresponding entry in the table. It can be seen that the feature representation $v_{\hat{a}}$ is well suited to identify instances of motion class JO (1.00), whereas the feature representation $v_{\hat{g}}$ performs particularly well for the motion classes CW (0.97), JO (0.97), and JJ (0.98). Furthermore, the identification rates for the class CW show a drastic improvement under the feature representation $v_{\hat{g}}$ (0.97) in comparison to v_a (0.35). Also, the arm rotations RB and RF are much better characterized under the feature representation $v_{\hat{g}}$ (0.64 and 0.79) compared to the acceleration based feature representations v_a (0.39 and 0.33) and $v_{\hat{a}}$ (0.43 and 0.492). Interestingly, there are some exceptions where $v_{\hat{g}}$ does not outperform the other two feature representations. For example, in case of motion class PU, $v_{\hat{g}}$ (0.50) is worse compared to $v_{\hat{a}}$ (0.62) and v_a (0.66). Here, on the one hand, the orientations of both arms—including roll and pitch—shows large variations among the actors. On the other hand, all punching motion exhibit characteristic peaks in the acceleration data, which can be captured particulary well by v_a. However, in general, one can notice that $v_{\hat{g}}$ is much better suited to identify most motion classes than the feature representations v_a and $v_{\hat{a}}$.

5   Conclusions

In this paper, we have presented a systematic analysis of various feature representations in the context of a cross-modal retrieval scenario, where inertial-based query motions are used to retrieve high-quality optical mocap data. Because of the increasing relevance of motion sensors for monitoring and entertainment purposes, the fusion of various sensor modalities as well as cross-domain motion analysis and synthesis will further gain in importance. For example, first approaches have been presented that allow for identifying high-quality 3D human motions from sparse inertial sensor input [11,12]. The reconstruction of high-quality 3D human motions using database knowledge has become a major principle used in computer animation and the gaming industry. Here, our analysis results and methods constitute a suitable foundation for estimating the performance of the various motion representations. For future work, following [11,12], we plan to investigate which kind of inertial sensor input and which amount of database knowledge is actually required to facilitate a robust and efficient reconstruction of complex 3D full-body motions.

References

1. Kemp, B., Janssen, A.J.M.W., van der Kamp, B.: Body position can be monitored in 3d using miniature accelerometers and earth-magnetic field sensors. Electroencephalography and Clinical Neurophysiology/Electromyography and Motor Control 109(6), 484–488 (1998)
2. Lee, J., Ha, I.: Real-time motion capture for a human body using accelerometers. Robotica 19(06), 601–610 (2001)
3. Luinge, H.J., Veltink, P.H.: Measuring orientation of human body segments using miniature gyroscopes and accelerometers. Medical and Biological Engineering and Computing 43(2), 273–282 (2005), http://doc.utwente.nl/61405/
4. Maiocchi, R.: 3-d character animation using motion capture, pp. 10–39 (1996)
5. Müller, M., Röder, T.: Motion templates for automatic classification and retrieval of motion capture data. In: Proc. ACM SCA, pp. 137–146. ACM Press, New York (2006)
6. Müller, M., Röder, T., Clausen, M., Eberhardt, B., Krüger, B., Weber, A.: Documentation: Mocap Database HDM05. Computer Graphics Technical Report CG-2007-2, Universität Bonn (June 2007), http://www.mpi-inf.mpg.de/resources/HDM05
7. Ohgi, Y., Ichikawa, H., Miyaji, C.: Microcomputer-based acceleration sensor device for swimming stroke monitoring. JSME International Journal Series C Mechanical Systems, Machine Elements and Manufacturing 45(4), 960–966 (2002)
8. Pons-Moll, G., Baak, A., Helten, T., Müller, M., Seidel, H.P., Rosenhahn, B.: Multisensor-fusion for 3d full-body human motion capture. In: Proc.IEEE CVPR, pp. 663–670 (June 2010)
9. Sabatini, A., Martelloni, C., Scapellato, S., Cavallo, F.: Assessment of walking features from foot inertial sensing. IEEE Transactions on Biomedical Engineering 52(3), 486–494 (2005)
10. Shoemake, K.: Animating rotation with quaternion curves. ACM SIGGRAPH Computer Graphics 19(3), 245–254 (1985)
11. Slyper, R., Hodgins, J.: Action capture with accelerometers. In: Proc. ACM SCA (July 2008)
12. Tautges, J., Zinke, A., Krüger, B., Baumann, J., Weber, A., Helten, T., Müller, M., Seidel, H.-P., Eberhardt, B.: Motion reconstruction using sparse accelerometer data. ACM TOG, New York (to appear, 2011)
13. Thong, Y.K., Woolfson, M.S., Crowe, J.A., Hayes-Gill, B.R., Jones, D.A.: Numerical double integration of acceleration measurements in noise. Measurement 36(1), 73–92 (2004)
14. Zheng, H., Black, N., Harris, N.: Position-sensing technologies for movement analysis in stroke rehabilitation. Medical and Biological Engineering and Computing 43, 413–420 (2005)

Indoor Calibration Using Segment Chains

Jamil Draréni, Renaud Keriven, and Renaud Marlet

IMAGINE, LIGM, Université Paris-Est, France

Abstract. In this paper, we present a new method for line segments matching for indoor reconstruction. Instead of matching individual segments via a descriptor like most methods do, we match segment chains that have a distinctive topology using a dynamic programing formulation. Our method relies solely on the geometric layout of the segment chain and not on photometric or color profiles. Our tests showed that the presented method is robust and manages to produce calibration information even under a drastic change of viewpoint.

1 Introduction

Many tasks in computer vision[1] , such as structure from motion, expect a set of features matched across images to register cameras in a common coordinate system. For decades, corner detectors such as Harris and KLT detectors represented the *de facto* features in computer vision literature. Recently, a new breed of features appeared in the literature. Pioneered by the seminal work of David Lowe [9], this new generation of feature detectors brought two major capabilities that lacked in the previous generation: geometric invariance and a descriptor. The first aspect is often achieved by using a scale-space framework [8] and data normalization, whereas the addiction of a feature descriptor yield a better matching repeatability.

However, in low texture scenes such as man-made environments (Fig.1), feature point perform poorly. In such scenes, 2D features run short in favor of line segments and yet, they have not been used extensively as features for image registration because of the difficulty of matching them. The later stems from the fact that, segments vicinity are textureless and usually not distinctive which precludes histogram-based (gradient, color, . . .) description. Even if a segment vicinity shows some variety, defining a neighbourhood zone is not tractable because a segment does not bear a natural scale, as it's the case with feature points. Last but not least, segment's endpoints are seldom accurate thus, using them as distinctive features is often error-prone.

In [3] authors used Kalman filters to track line segments. Their formulation is akin to features tracking in video sequences and assumes short baselines.

Schmid and Zisserman [10] used epipolar lines bundles to constrain putative matches followed by an intensity similarity check (using SSD along the segments)

---

[1] This work was partially supported by the Fondation d'entreprise EADS, contract no 3610.

R. Mester and M. Felsberg (Eds.): DAGM 2011, LNCS 6835, pp. 71–80, 2011.

Fig. 1. A pair of indoor images used in this paper

to identify correct matches. Though fast and accurate, their method assumes a known epipolar geometry which makes it unsuitable for camera calibration. In [1], a segments matching method with an application to wide baseline stereo is presented. Here, feature points (SIFT, HOG,...) are extracted and used as anchor points. The actual segments pairing is performed by first, grouping putative matches using their color profiles.Then, anchor-point/segment sideness consistency is exploited to sort out the matches. Obviously, if no or few feature points were detected and paired, the segment matching will rely solely on color profiles which are known to be unstable. The idea of using supporting 2D features was also proposed for segments matching in [5] and more generally for untextured regions matching in [4].

In [11], the authors proposed an approach where segments are assigned a descriptor computed from the layout of neighbouring lines (length ratios, relative angles). As pointed out in [5], line signatures are subject to instabilities because they rely on segments endpoints locations which are known to be inaccurate.

In this paper, we present a new method for segments matching. The proposed method is suitable for camera calibration in an indoor environment and is based on the fact that indoor scenes are often composed of segment chains. While individual segments might not exhibit saliency, we show how segment chains topology have a distinctive layout that can be exploited for matching. In this work, segment chains are extracted and matched using dynamic programming. The result is then used to compute the epipolar geometry induced by the camera motion.

The rest of the paper is organized as follows. Section 2 presents the algorithm used for segments detection. The core of our algorithm is detailed in Section 3 while experimental results are reported in Section 4. Finally, we draw our conclusion and discuss further improvement Section 5.

Fig. 2. The Line Segment Detector (LSD). Line support regions are gathered recursively if they fall within a certain orientation tolerance.

2   Segments Extraction

There are numerous ways to extract line segments in images. The classical approach consists of applying the Canny detector [2] to the image to extract edges. These edges are then clipped at high curvature points. Along the curve that connects two high curvature points, a line is fitted by either a least squares method like in [1,5] or using a robust method such as the M-estimator technique. In this paper, we used the Line Segment Detector (LSD) recently introduced in [6]. We would like to point out that our matching procedure is independent of the underlying line detector and conveniency was the main motivation behind this choice since an implementation of LSD is freely available on the author's web page. In the following we will summarize the LSD detector.

As depicted on Figure.2, line extraction starts by computing the edge map of the image. Then, starting from a random position, line-support regions are formed by grouping adjacent pixels that share the same gradient orientation within a certain tolerance. The formation of the line-supports is done recursively in a flood-fill fashion. Even though this procedure is based on a greedy algorithm, the simple operations behind it makes it very fast. As a result, LSD outputs the coordinates of the each segment endpoints along with the width of the associated line-support.

Once the segments are extracted, an orientation will be assigned to each of them according to the direction of their supporting gradient. Namely, a segment will be oriented such as the darkest region will always lie on its right side. The purpose of the orientation assignment is to form consistent segments chain as it will be explained later. It could also be used to leverage matching ambiguities when cameras orientations are available[2].

2.1   Segments Merging

Segments detected by LSD are often fragmented because of noise. In order to simplify the matching step, we post-process LSD output by merging the segments fragments that share the same orientation (up to a tolerance) and whose endpoints are close. This is illustrated in Fig.3.

---

[2] Most modern cameras provide this information in the image header.

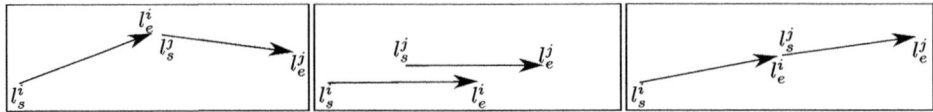

Fig. 3. Segments merging. Segments i and j are identified by their start and endpoint. Left) No merging is done here because angle difference is large. Middle) No merging neither because the distance between endpoints ($\|l_e^i - l_s^j\|$) is large. Right) Merging is done because the segments are well aligned and close to each other.

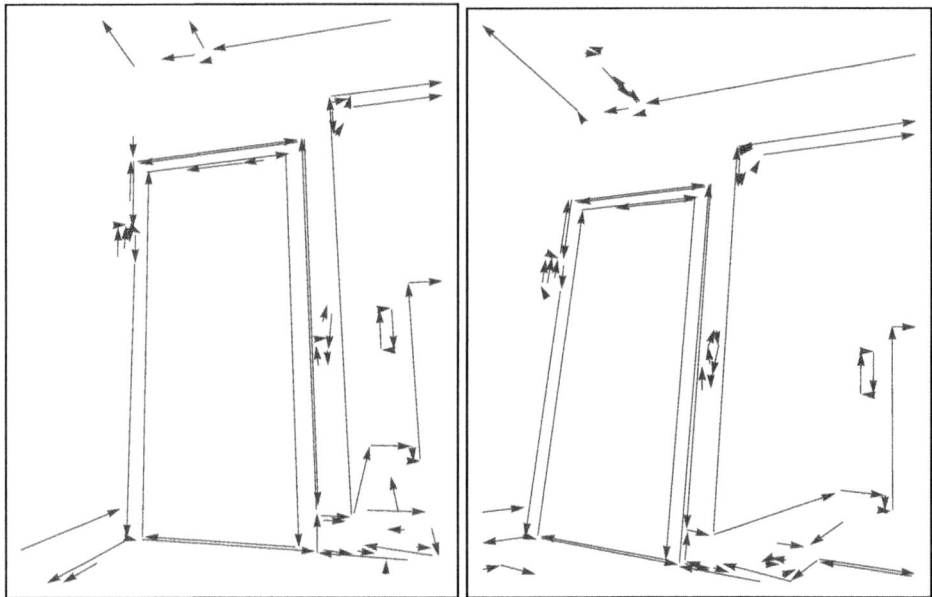

Fig. 4. LSD output after post-processing (see text)

The result of this process is a set of neat segments more suitable for our matching procedure. As an exemple of such sets, running the merging procedure on the sequence in Fig.1 is depicted in Fig.4.

3   Segment Chains Matching

In this section, we will give the details of our segment chain matching method. Starting from an image, we use LSD to extract segments and merge fragments as explained in the previous section. We then, form segments junctions by connecting salient segments in quasi-intersection situation. Such segments are most likely to be 3D-coplanar, thus their intersections are the projection of real 3D points that can be further used for camera calibration. At this stage, segments in T-junction configuration are avoided as they presage occlusions.

Fig. 5. Three extracted chains. The added segments must preserve the global orientation of the chain (clockwise or counterclockwise) and its continuity.

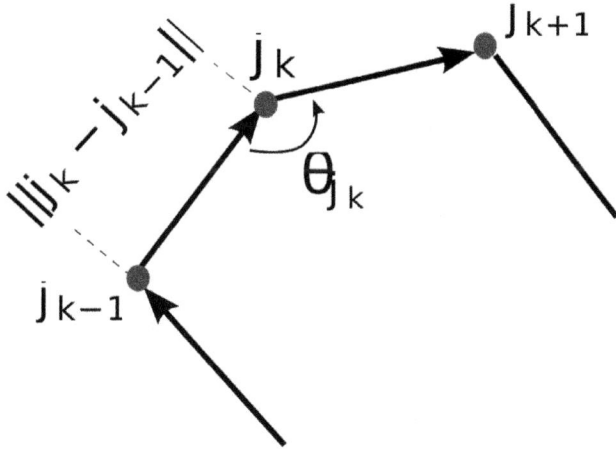

Fig. 6. The incident angle θ_{j_k} of a junction j_k and the length of its inward segment

Starting from a junction that connects two salient segments, we form an initial 2-segment chain. This chain is recursively grown by adding continuous segments that preserve the overall orientation. Three such chains are depicted in Fig.5. Even though the extraction procedure is greedy, the running time is small thanks to the low cardinality of the segments present in indoor scenes.

Once segments chains isolated in both images, matching can take place using a dynamic programing scheme presented in the following.

3.1   Dynamic Programing Formulation

Let C and C' be two segments chains to match, given as a list of their junction points. We define the cost of matching two junctions $j_k \in C$ and $j'_l \in C'$ in terms of their incident angles $(\theta_{j_k}, \theta_{j'_l})$ as:

$$match(j_k, j'_l) = |\theta_{j_k} - \theta_{j'_l}| \tag{1}$$

The cost of skipping a junction j_k is given by the length of its inward segment:

$$skip(j_k) = ||j_k - j_{k-1}|| \tag{2}$$

See Fig.6 for further explanations.

The optimal cost of matching the junction $j_k \in C$ with the junction $j' \in C'$ is formulated recursively as:

$$cost(j_k, j'_l) = match(j_k, j'_l) + \min \begin{cases} cost(j_{k-1}, j'_{l-1}) \\ cost(j_{k-1}, j'_l) + skip(j_k) \\ cost(j_k, j'_{l-1}) + skip(j'_l) \end{cases} \tag{3}$$

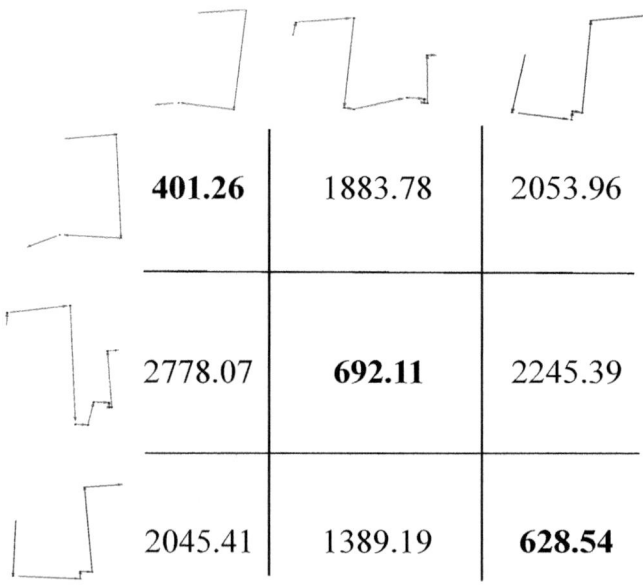

	401.26	1883.78	2053.96
	2778.07	**692.11**	2245.39
	2045.41	1389.19	**628.54**

Fig. 7. Matching cost. The cost of cross-matching 3 different chains. We can see that real matches have a very low cost compared to other combinations which precludes a winner-takes-all scheme.

Fig. 8. Estimated epipolar lines on the first sequence along with 2 segment chains (blue and red)

Because we do not know in advance the corresponding segment chains from an image to another, we simply cross-match all the chains using our dynamic programing formulation and assign matches using a winner-takes-all scheme. Because the number of chains is low, this procedure is fast. To show the effectiveness of this procedure, the cross-matching costs of the 3 chains depicted in Fig.5 is reported in Fig.7 .

3.2 Camera Calibration

Once segment chains matches have been determined, junctions matches are trivially extracted. However, theses matches are only putative because, unless they result from coplanar segments, they are not the projection of the same 3D points. To circumvent this, a RANSAC routine is used to randomly select 7-tuples from putative junction matches and robustly estimate the fundamental matrix as explained in [7]. Of course, in the calibrated case, one would prefer estimating the essential matrix in order to extract the rotations and translations of the cameras.

Our experiments showed that indoor scenes exhibits few outliers. Indeed, in such scenes, adjacent segments are likely to be coplanar, thus most junctions turn out to be real features.

4   Experiments

In this section we show the results of our experiments to demonstrate the effectiveness of the proposed method. All images were shot with a hand-held iPhone.

Fig. 9. Second sequence. Top: Original images. Bottom: Detected segments after fragments removal.

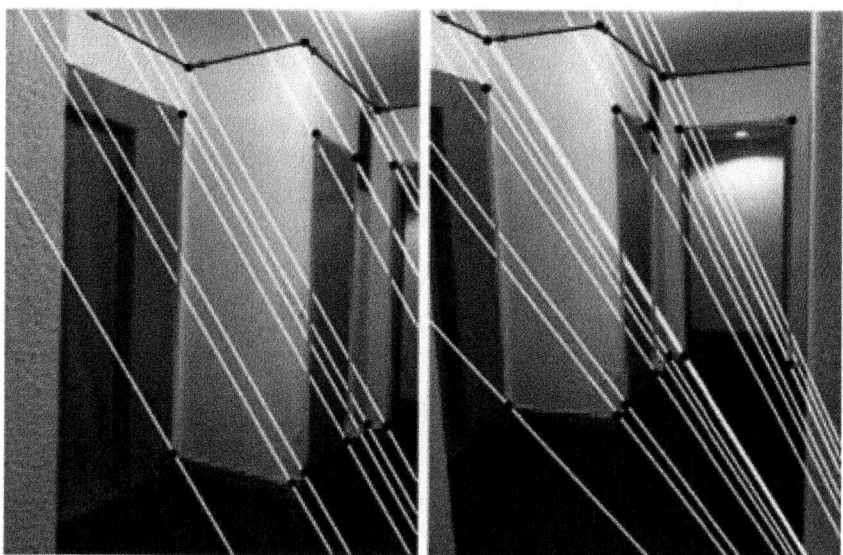

Fig. 10. Estimated epipolar lines and 2 segment chains from the indoor sequence

The images were downscaled to a resolution of 1200×800. The estimated epipolar geometry from the first sequence (see Fig.1) is depicted in Fig.8. Notice the precision of the epipolar lines despite the camera motion.

We also ran our algorithm on a second sequence (see Fig.9). As it can be seen, this sequence is challenging due to the amount of occlusion and the lack of texture. The resulting epipolar geometry is shown on Fig.10.

The method was implemented on Mathematica and still, the running time for each sequence was under 5 seconds on a 2.13 Ghz computer.

5 Conclusion

In this paper we presented a novel method to match line segments in an indoor environment. Instead of building descriptors per segment, we considered segment chains for their rich geometric topology that makes them very distinctive even in presence of occlusions and severe viewpoint change. We also presented a simple dynamic programing formulation to efficiently match such chains based solely on geometric properties. In fact, our method is completely intensity-blind as no photometric information was used to achieve the matching.

Moreover we think that our method could be successfully used to reconstruct interiors from images and furthermore to produce building outlines.

Finally, we are convinced that our system could benefit from advances in graph theory field to better explore the network of segments and efficiently extract meaningful chains. In fact, topics such as graph partitioning techniques are already in study.

References

1. Bay, H., Ferrari, V., Van Gool, L.: Wide-baseline stereo matching with line segments. In: CVPR 2005: Proceedings of the 2005 IEEE Computer Society Conference on Computer Vision and Pattern Recognition (CVPR 2005), vol. 1, pp. 329–336. IEEE Computer Society Press, Washington, DC (2005)
2. Canny, J.: A computational approach to edge detection. IEEE Trans. Pattern Anal. Mach. Intell. 8, 679–698 (1986)
3. Deriche, R., Faugeras, O.D.: Tracking line segments. In: Faugeras, O. (ed.) ECCV 1990. LNCS, vol. 427, pp. 259–268. Springer, Heidelberg (1990)
4. Dragon, R., Shoaib, M., Rosenhahn, B., Ostermann, J.: NF-features – no-feature-features for representing non-textured regions. In: Daniilidis, K., Maragos, P., Paragios, N. (eds.) ECCV 2010. LNCS, vol. 6312, pp. 128–141. Springer, Heidelberg (2010)
5. Fan, B., Wu, F., Hu, Z.: Line matching leveraged by point correspondences. In: CVPR, pp. 390–397. IEEE, Los Alamitos (2010)
6. Grompone von Gioi, R., Jakubowicz, J., Morel, J.-M., Randall, G.: LSD: A fast line segment detector with a false detection control. IEEE Trans. Pattern Anal. Mach. Intell. 32(4), 722–732 (2010)
7. Hartley, R.I., Zisserman, A.: Multiple View Geometry in Computer Vision, 2nd edn. Cambridge University Press, Cambridge (2004) ISBN: 0521540518
8. Lindeberg, T.: Scale-Space Theory in Computer Vision. Kluwer Academic Publishers, Norwell (1994)
9. Lowe, D.G.: Distinctive image features from scale-invariant keypoints. International Journal of Computer Vision 60(2), 91 (2004)
10. Schmid, C., Zisserman, A.: Automatic line matching across views. In: IEEE Conference on Computer Vision and Pattern Recognition, pp. 666–671 (1997)
11. Wang, L., Neumann, U., You, S.: Wide-baseline image matching using line signatures. In: Proc. International Conference on Computer Vision. IEEE, Los Alamitos (2009)

Multilinear Model Estimation with L^2-Regularization

Frank R. Schmidt[1], Hanno Ackermann[2], and Bodo Rosenhahn[2]

[1] University of Western Ontario, Canada
fschmidt@uwo.ca
[2] Leibniz University Hannover, Germany
{ackermann,rosenhahn}@tnt.uni-hannover.de

Abstract. Many challenging computer vision problems can be formulated as a multilinear model. Classical methods like principal component analysis use singular value decomposition to infer model parameters. Although it can solve a given problem easily if all measurements are known this prerequisite is usually violated for computer vision applications. In the current work, a standard tool to estimate singular vectors under incomplete data is reformulated as an energy minimization problem. This admits for a simple and fast gradient descent optimization with guaranteed convergence. Furthermore, the energy function is generalized by introducing an L^2-regularization on the parameter space. We show a quantitative and qualitative evaluation of the proposed approach on an application from structure-from-motion using synthetic and real image data, and compare it with other works.

1 Introduction

To detect a model based only on observed images constitutes one of the central tasks in computer vision applications. Problems like structure and motion estimation as well as 3D or even 4D reconstruction can be formulated as a model fitting problem. Assuming temporal coherence leads to a smoothness prior on some variables. In this work we will focus on problems that are given as a *multilinear model* and we will show how the introduction of an L^2-regularizer leads to better solutions which can even be computed more efficiently.

Fitting a model with only a few parameters to observed data is the base of the well understood method of *principal component analysis* (PCA). It is used, for instance, for computation of eigenfaces [13], image matching [20], pose and shape estimation [12], rigid structure and motion (SfM) estimation [19] or non-rigid SfM [2]. *Singular value decomposition* (SVD) is often used to compute a PCA. Since SVD can be computed quite easily, it is very popular for dimension reduction approaches. However, SVD requires all measurements to be known. In many applications in computer vision, for instance structure and motion estimation, points cannot be observed because of occlusions or tracking failures.

In [19,3], missing observations are dealt with by solving complete sub-sets and propagating these solutions while an EM approache is favored in [18]. Both

R. Mester and M. Felsberg (Eds.): DAGM 2011, LNCS 6835, pp. 81–90, 2011.

types of algorithms work well for low noise or low amounts of missing values, but they fail for realistic problems. A different approach to estimate the multilinear model is the *power factorization* or *NIPALS* approach [22,11] which minimizes an L^2 energy function. It estimates solutions starting from the complete data, *i.e.* it does not begin on any sub-set of the data.

In [16,17] Newton and Gauss-Newton approaches were considered which were later generalized to weighted data [9,4]. To be more robust to errors that are related to missing or corrupted data, different error norms are used in [6,15,8]. Another approach to cope with corrupted data is to enforce additional constraints that are specific to the problem. Constraints on individual projection matrices were used in [14], consistency with epipolar geometry was imposed in [1] and the smoothness of camera trajectories was enforced by means of a Kalman filter in [10].

In this work we will minimize the common L^2 energy function of [22,11,16,17,4] by a gradient descent technique. The difference to power factorization is that this gradient descent jointly optimizes both sets of variables thereby avoiding accidental maximization and other numerical pitfalls.

Furthermore, we include a smoothness prior into the L^2 energy. This leads to the minimization of an energy E that is a convex combination of the L^2 energy E_{data} and the smoothness prior E_{smooth}. At the presence of a strong data term, the smoothness term has only a small effect. Otherwise (due to missing data), the smoothness term takes over control by extra- and interpolating information that are driven by neighboring data. Therefore, our approach is different from a Kalman filter approach in the sense that we do not *indiscriminately* enforce smoothness but only if there is insufficient data. As a result, non-smooth models can be estimated if the data information is very strong. Smoothness on the other hand is stronger in areas of missing data and is weaker in areas that are well defined by the observed measurements. A second difference to the Kalman filter is that we do not process the data sequentially. While the L^2-regularizer depends on a specific temporal order of the observed images, the overall energy functional E depends on all observations at the same time and will not change during the optimization process.

The difference to the Gauss-Newton variants of [4] is that we only impose smoothness on one set of variables. In the context of 3D-reconstruction we can thus enforce smooth camera trajectories yet allow for non-smooth surfaces or vice versa. Our experimental evaluation will show that the proposed method performs superior.

Overall, we present the following contributions in this paper:

- A global energy is minimized by gradient descent thus avoiding problems caused by starting from some sub-set of the data.
- The data term is extended by a smoothness term that governs those areas with few measurements.
- We do not enforce smoothness on all variables indiscriminately, but only smooth selectively. Thus partially non-smooth solutions can be obtained.
- We will demonstrate the proposed algorithm for simulated and real data.

This paper is organized as follows. In Section 2, we derive the gradient descent algorithm and discuss the advantages compared to power factorization. Section 3 generalizes the functional to include a smoothness prior. A quantitative analysis with synthetic data is conducted in Section 4. Real image experiments with challenging sequences are conducted in Section 5. In the same section we briefly discuss future work. Section 6 provides a summary.

2   Energy Minimization Formulation

In this section, we will formulate the multilinear model estimation as an energy minimization method and derive the gradient of this energy functional. We will then discuss in which sense a gradient descent deviates from the popular *power factorization* [11]. After presenting these two approaches, we will in Section 3 introduce a generalization that incorporates an L^2-smoothness term into the here presented energy functional.

First let us start with the general problem of multilinear model estimation. To this end, we have a set of observations that are encoded in a $m \times n$ matrix W. This can be understood as n observations of dimension m. The idea of a multilinear model is it now to incorporate the knowledge that the observations do not form an n-dimensional but rather an r-dimensional subspace with $r \ll m$.

Hence, we have r model vectors $x_1, \ldots, x_r \in \mathbb{R}^m$ and $y_1^\top, \ldots, y_r^\top \in \mathbb{R}^n$ that form a left and right base of the r-dimensional model space. Let $x_{i,k}$ and $y_{k,j}$ denote the kth coordinate of vector x_i and $y_j^\top$. Every element W_{ij} of W can then be written as a linear combination of x_i and $y_j^\top$ and we obtain for $W_{ij} = \sum_{k=1}^r x_{i,k} \cdot y_{k,j}$. If we now put the vectors x_i and $y_j^\top$ into the $m \times r$ matrix X and the $r \times n$ matrix Y, we receive the following equation

$$W = X \cdot Y. \tag{1}$$

In the perfect noiseless case, W has rank r, but since measurements are usually perturbed by noise, matrix W can also exhibit ranks which are larger than r. In practice, Equation (1) can thus not be solved exactly and is often reformulated as the following least squares problem:

$$\min_{X \in \mathbb{R}^{m \times r}, Y \in \mathbb{R}^{r \times n}} \|W - X \cdot Y\|_{\mathrm{fro}}^2 \tag{2}$$

where the Frobenius norm $\|A\|_{\mathrm{fro}} := \sqrt{\sum_{i,j} a_{i,j}^2}$ is the canonical norm on matrices. In order to solve this problem, we can simply use the SVD of $W = Q_1 \Sigma Q_2^\top$. This results in the solution $X = Q_1 \Sigma^{\frac{1}{2}}$ for the left subspace and $Y = \Sigma^{\frac{1}{2}} Q_2^\top$ for the right subspace, respectively.

As SVD requires each entry of W to be known, for most real computer vision problems it is not applicable. If some entries of W are unknown, we also have a visibility mask $V \in \{0,1\}^{m \times n}$ which encodes the information whether the entry w_{ij} is a valid observation ($v_{ij} = 1$) or not ($v_{ij} = 0$). Equation (2) then becomes

$$E_{\mathrm{data}}(X, Y) := \frac{1}{2} \|(W - X \cdot Y) \odot V\|_{\mathrm{fro}}^2 \tag{3}$$

where the operator $\odot$ denotes the element-wise product. In Section 3, we will add a smoothness term to this data term in order to obtain better results, but for now we will stick to this data term.

To minimize Eq. (3), we can use a gradient descent approach. In order to do this, we have to compute the gradient of E_{data}. The next lemma states that this task is easy in the sense that in only involves elementary matrix operations.

Lemma 1. *The gradient of E_{data} can be computed as*

$$\nabla E_{data} = \begin{pmatrix} \frac{\partial E_{data}}{\partial X} \\ \frac{\partial E_{data}}{\partial Y} \end{pmatrix} = \begin{pmatrix} [(XY - W) \odot V] Y^\top \\ X^\top [(XY - W) \odot V] \end{pmatrix}.$$

Proof. We will only show how to compute $\frac{\partial E_{\text{data}}}{\partial X}$. The computation of $\frac{\partial E_{\text{data}}}{\partial Y}$ can be done analogously. Now denote the columns V by v_j. Then, we can write

$$\frac{\partial E_{\text{data}}}{\partial y_j} = \frac{1}{2} \frac{\partial}{\partial y_j} \left[\sum_{j=1}^n \| (w_j - X \cdot y_j) \odot v_j \|^2 \right]$$

$$= \frac{1}{2} \frac{\partial}{\partial y_j} \| V_j (w_j - X \cdot y_j) \|^2$$

with the diagonal matrix V_j consisting of the entries of v_j.

$$= \left(X^\top V_j X y_j - X^\top V_j w_j \right)$$

$$= X^\top \left((X y_j - w_j) \odot v_j \right)$$

$$\Rightarrow \frac{\partial E_{\text{data}}}{\partial Y} = X^\top \left((XY - W) \odot V \right) \qquad \qquad \square$$

Since E_{data} is neither convex nor quasi-convex there is no obvious way of finding the global minimum efficiently. In [22,11], Eq. (3) was minimized by iteratively solving for $\frac{\partial E_{\text{data}}}{\partial X} = 0$ and $\frac{\partial E_{\text{data}}}{\partial Y} = 0$ while keeping the other set of variables fixed. However, this method can get trapped in a local extremum: at every iteration, a potential local extremum at least for one of the two variable X or Y is chosen and thus the vulnerability that a local extremum for E_{data} is found increases dramatically. Of course, we like to believe that this local extremum is at least a local minimum. But this is not true in general. Since E_{data} is not a convex function, every iterative update step can even *increase* the energy that we want to minimize. If for example $\frac{\partial^2 E_{\text{data}}}{\partial^2 X}$ is negative definite or even indefinite, the update w.r.t to X will move Y into a local maximum or a saddle-point.

To overcome these problems, we perform a gradient descent approach which jointly optimizes X and Y. After each update of X and Y, X is projected to an orthonormal representation as classical power factorization does. This has several advantages:

1. The gradient descent approach will always decrease and thus we will omit any local maximum.
2. Gradient descent methods tend to not get stuck in saddle-points. This is because the area that will lead neighboring points via gradient descent into the saddle-point form themself a zero set in the definition domain.

3   Introducing L^2-Regularization

Many real problems provide further constraints on the model. In this section it will be shown how Eq. (3) can be generalized to include a smoothness prior on the coordinates X. In the context of 3D-reconstruction we want to allow for non-smooth surfaces hence we do not enforce smoothness on the variables Y.

X can be understood as a path in $\mathbb{R}^r$ which corresponds to the temporal coherent observation in $\mathbb{R}^m$ encoded by the rows of the observation matrix W. Therefore, X can be understood as a discrete sub-sampling of the following trajectory:

$$c : [0,1] \to \mathbb{R}^r$$
$$c\left(\frac{i-1}{m-1}\right) = (x_{i,1} \cdots x_{i,r})^\top \qquad \forall i = 1, \ldots, m.$$

With this formulation, we can now introduce the L^2-regularization on c via $E_{\text{smooth}}(c) = \frac{1}{2} \int_0^1 c'(t)^2 \, dt$ which becomes for its discrete representation X the following backward difference:

$$E_{\text{smooth}}(X) = \frac{1}{2} \frac{1}{m-1} \sum_{s=1}^{r} \sum_{i=2}^{m} (x_{i,s} - x_{i-1,s})^2. \qquad (4)$$

By weighting the importance of the smoothness term over the data term by a non-negative number λ, we can formulate the *multilinear model estimation with L^2-regularization* as minimizing the following energy function:

$$E(X,Y) = E_{\text{data}}(X,Y) + \lambda \cdot E_{\text{smooth}}(X) \qquad (5)$$

As in Section 2 we want to minimize this energy via a gradient descent approach. In order to do this, we have to compute the gradient of E_{smooth}. It turns out that also this gradient can be computed by easy matrix operations:

$$\frac{\partial E_{\text{smooth}}}{\partial x_{i,s}} = \frac{1}{m-1} \left(-x_{i-1,s} + 2x_{i,s} - x_{i+1,s}\right) \qquad (6)$$

Instead of matrix multiplication as in Lemma 1, we only need to compute a simple linear combination of neighboring rows in the matrix X. Combining Equation (6) with Lemma 1, we can find a minimum of E by projected gradient descent.

4   Evaluation for Synthetic Data

For experimental evaluation, we draw on an application from structure from motion: it was shown in [19] that feature trajectories of a rigid body over several images taken by *affine* cameras are constrained to span a low-dimensional linear subspace. Due to the incomplete trajectories, centroids cannot be computed, thus

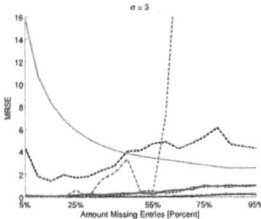

Fig. 1. Mean root square error (MRSE) of 10 trials between the estimated matrix and the ground truth. The solid blue line indicates the proposed method, the dashed blue line power factorization, the solid (dashed) red line Kalman-EM with (without) specified variance, the solid green line nuclear norm minimization (NNM), and the magenta dash-dotted line the regularized Gauss-Newton scheme.

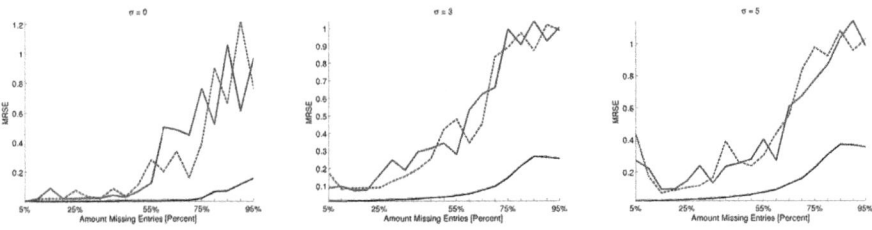

Fig. 2. Average mean root square error (MRSE) with ground truth data of 10 trials. The solid blue line indicates the proposed method, and the solid (dashed) red line Kalman-EM with (without) specified variance.

the standard rank-3 constraint used in [19] must include the unknown center, hence generalizes into a rank-4 constraint [1,18] in Eq. (2). We simulated 200 3D-points distributed on a cylindrical surface. The points were translated, rotated, and projected onto 20 images. For projection, an affine camera model was used, thus avoiding non-Gaussian noise induced by estimating an incorrect model. We experimentally determined that the functional obtains a global minimum for $\lambda = 3 \cdot 10^8$.

The proposed method was further compared with the power factorization (NIPALS) algorithm, the Kalman-filtering EM approach, a method which minimizes the nuclear norm [5][1], and a Tikhonov-regularized Gauss-Newton scheme from [4]. Power factorization, the Gauss-Newton scheme, and the proposed gradient descent were randomly initialized 50 and the best result taken. The Kalman-EM-algorithm was executed twice: once with specified variance (see below), once with a generic variance of 1. For the nuclear norm minimization (NNM) there are several parameters to specify. We set them to values which are very conservative according to the authors.

---

[1] The code is provided at `svt.caltech.edu`

Occlusion was simulated by randomly removing parts at the beginning and the end of trajectories. We thus had trajectories only visible on a more or less narrow band on the diagonal of W increasing the difficulty [2]. We increased the amount of invisible data from 5% until 95% in steps of 5%. Visible measurements were perturbed with normally distributed noise with standard deviations $\sigma = \{0, 3, 5\}$. For each combination of noise and missing observations, we simulated 10 different realizations of W, *i.e.* perturbed and sampled its entries, and computed average errors and computation times.

Figure 1 shows the average Frobenius error per pixel between the the estimated matrix and the ground truth, *i.e.* a mean root sum of squares error (MRSE). The noise level was $\sigma = 3$. The solid blue line indicates the proposed approach, the dashed blue line, the solid red line Kalman-EM with known variance and the dashed red line Kalman-EM without known variance. The green solid line indicates NNM. Lastly, the magenta dash-dotted line indicates the Tikhonov-regularized Gauss-Newton scheme of [4]. The NNM approach usually converged to solutions of rank larger than 4. Since the physical model requires rank 4, we then truncated the estimated left and right subspaces which caused large errors. We varied its parameters yet could not find a more successful combination. The Gauss-Newton method performed poorly for large amounts of missing data. Other variants from this box achieved similar results. Both Kalman-approaches (KF) and the proposed solution both achieve low errors. Our approach performs superior to all other methods including power factorization.

The plots in Figure 2 compare both KFs and our method. The left plot corresponds to $\sigma = 0$, the middle to $\sigma = 3$, and the right to $\sigma = 5$. The blue error curves look similar for $\sigma = 3$ and $\sigma = 5$, yet differ slightly. For noise-free data, all three methods achieve similar errors if less than 40% of the matrix is known. For larger sampling ratios, the proposed algorithm performs more than twice as good. For noisy data, the proposed method is between 2.5 and more than 14 times more accurate.

5   Real World Applications

In this section we show successful application of the proposed method to two real image sequences containing large noise and even a few outliers. While regularized energies have already been applied to 3D reconstruction [7,21], the problem that we address here is different from prior work. In [7,21], camera calibration including intrinsic and extrinsic parameters is known, while the current work considers unknown calibration information. Furthermore, regularization is not applied to the 3D-points. Instead, we regularize the camera path.

The scene shown in Fig. 3(a) shows a corner of a historic building. A total of 2000 trajectories were observed over 60 images with 68.6% missing features. While there are no obvious outliers, noise is very large. Four images of the 3D-reconstruction are shown in Fig. 3(b). The color of the pixel in the image it was

---

[2] Due to the random occlusion, trajectories have to be permuted properly to make the band-diagonal structure of W visible.

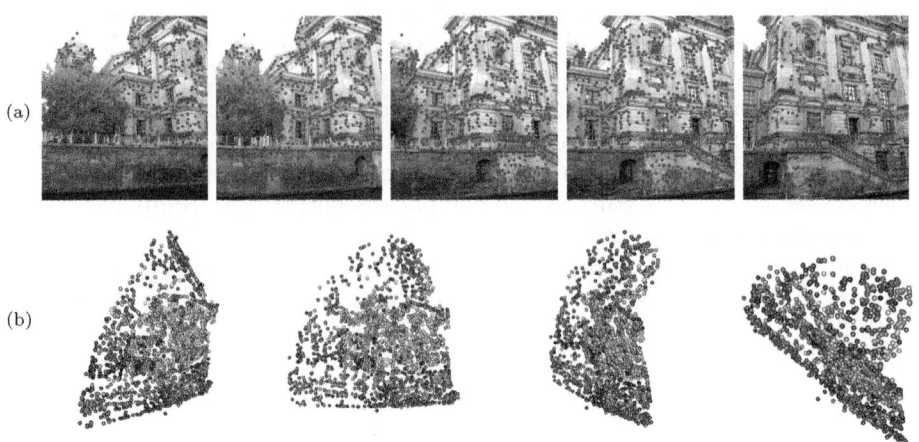

Fig. 3. (a) Five images of a 60 image sequence with 2000 trajectories. 68.6% of the data is missing and there is large noise. Red points indicate the feature found in each image. (b) Four views of the reasonable 3D-reconstruction.

first observed in was assigned to each 3D-point. The overall reconstruction looks reasonable, only the depth of the scene is underestimated. This error is due to the affine camera model which cannot handle significant scene depth compared with the the distance to the camera.

The second sequence consists of 672 trajectories over 10 images[3]. A single image is shown in Fig. 4, left. A total of 57.7% of the data matrix is unknown.

Since there are several outliers present in the data, we adopted a RANSAC approach on minimal subsets.

Four images of this 3D-reconstruction are shown in the left images of Fig. 4. The ground plane is not rectangular with the wall of the house, and the right side is heavily distorted. Considering the affine camera model, the reconstruction is reasonable.

The achieved results look reasonable considering the affine camera model and the fact that the shown squences have significant depth variation whereas the assumption is that all 3D-points have similar depths. Approaches for projective or Euclidean bundle adjustment can achieve better results yet require good initializations which can be provided by the proposed algorithm. Furthermore, such software packages are much more complex than the proposed algorithm.

It is known that the L^2 error metric defined by Eq. (3) is not entirely suitable for 3D-reconstruction. Nonetheless, the L^2 metric is quite general and can be directly applied to many other problems [13,20,12]. For SfM, we therefore like to interpret the used error as an approximation of the prefered metric. Future work will focus on studying more descriptive errors which better suit 3D-reconstruction. For the general problem of multilinear model, we would still advocate the Frobenius error because it is a very general error which is consistent with the proposed L^2-regularizer.

---

[3] This sequence is provided at http://www.robots.ox.ac.uk/~vgg

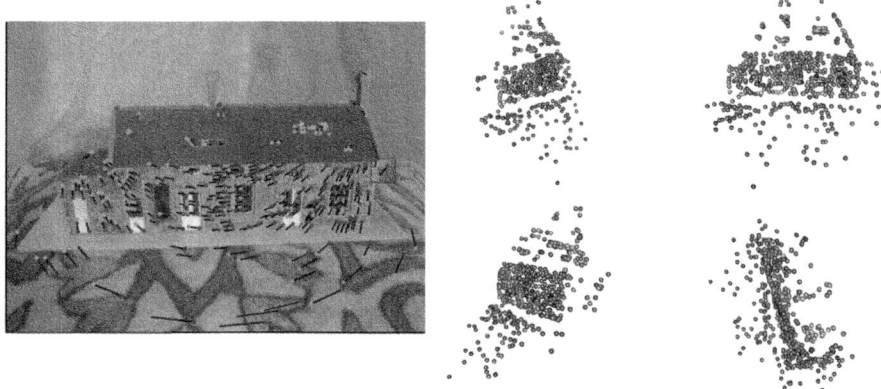

Fig. 4. Left: One image of a 10 image sequence with 672 trajectories and 57.7% unknown features. Red points indicate features in the current image, green points correspondences in the next image. Red boxes indicate apparent outliers. Right: Four views of the 3D-reconstruction. Overall, it looks reasonable. The angle between ground plane and house is not orthogonal due to the strong perspective distortion of the points close the to camera which the affine camera model cannot handle.

6 Conclusion

In this work, a factorization algorithm for partially known matrices was presented. It uses a globally invariant energy function which was generalized to include a smoothness prior. This prior penalizes non-smooth models only if the data term is locally insufficient. Using the generalized energy functional, a gradient descent method was derived. Using simulated data, we showed that this algorithm is more accurate than all other methods even if significant parts of the matrix are unknown. Using real image data, reasonable 3D-reconstructions were presented. The proposed solution can be used to initialize a bundle adjustment. Although structure and motion estimation was presented as application the proposed algorithm is general and can be applied to any PCA problem [13,20,12,19,2].

References

1. Ackermann, H., Rosenhahn, B.: Trajectory Reconstruction for Affine Structure-from-Motion by Global and Local Constraints. In: CVPR (June 2009)
2. Brand, M.: Morphable 3d models from video. In: IEEE Computer Vision and Pattern Recognition (CVPR), Kauai, Hawaii, USA, pp. 456–463 (2001)
3. Brand, M.: Incremental singular value decomposition of uncertain data with missing values. In: Heyden, A., Sparr, G., Nielsen, M., Johansen, P. (eds.) ECCV 2002. LNCS, vol. 2350, pp. 707–720. Springer, Heidelberg (2002)
4. Buchanan, A., Fitzgibbon, A.: Damped Newton Algorithms for Matrix Factorization with Missing Data. In: CVPR, Washington, DC, USA, pp. 316–322 (2005)

5. Cai, J.F., Candès, E.J., Shen, Z.: A singular value thresholding algorithm for matrix completion. SIAM Journal on Optimization 20(4), 1956–1982 (2010)
6. Candès, E.J., Recht, B.: Exact matrix completion via convex optimization. Foundations of Computational Mathematics 9(6), 717–772 (2009)
7. Cremers, D., Kolev, K.: Multiview stereo and silhouette consistency via convex functionals over convex domains. IEEE TPAMI (2010)
8. Eriksson, A., van den Hengel, A.: Efficient computation of robust low-rank matrix approximations in the presence of missing data using the l1 norm. In: CVPR, San Francisco, USA (2010)
9. Gabriel, K., Zamir, S.: Lower rank approximation of matrices by least squares with any choice of weights. Techonometrics 21(4), 489–498 (1979)
10. Gruber, A., Weiss, Y.: Factorization with uncertainty and missing data: Exploiting temporal coherence. In: NIPS, Vancouver, Canada (December 2003)
11. Hartley, R., Schaffalizky, F.: PowerFactorization: 3D Reconstruction with Missing or Uncertain Data. In: Australia-Japan Advanced Workshop on Computer Vision (June 2002)
12. Hasler, N., Ackermann, H., Rosenhahn, B., Thormählen, T., Seidel, H.P.: Multilinear pose and body shape estimation of dressed subjects from image sets. In: CVPR, San Francisco, USA (June 2010)
13. Turk, M.A., Pentland, A.P.: Face recognition using eigenfaces. In: CVPR (1991)
14. Marques, M., Costeira, J.: Estimating 3d shape from degenerate sequences with missing data. CVIU 113(2), 261–272 (2009)
15. Peng, Y., Ganesh, A., Wright, J., Ma, Y.: Rasl: Robust alignment by sparse and low-rank decomposition for linearly correlated images. In: CVPR, San Francisco, USA, pp. 763–770 (June 2010)
16. Ruhe, A.: Numerical computation of principal components when several observations are missing. Tech. rep., Dept. Information Processing, University of Umeda, Umeda, Sweden (April 1974)
17. Ruhe, A., Wedin, P.: Algorithms for separable nonlinear least squares problems. Society for Industrial and Applied Mathematics Review 22(3), 318–337 (1980)
18. Sugaya, Y., Kanatani, K.: Extending interrupted feature point tracking for 3-D affine reconstruction. In: Pajdla, T., Matas, J(G.) (eds.) ECCV 2004. LNCS, vol. 3021, pp. 310–321. Springer, Heidelberg (2004)
19. Tomasi, C., Kanade, T.: Shape and motion from image streams under orthography: A factorization method. IJCV 9(2), 137–154 (1992)
20. Ullman, S., Basri, R.: Recognition by linear combinations of models. IEEE TPAMI 13, 992–1006 (1991)
21. Vu, H.H., Keriven, R., Labatut, P., Pons, J.P.: Towards high-resolution large-scale multi-view stereo. In: CVPR. Miami (June 2009)
22. Wold, H.: Estimation of principal components and related models by iterative least squares. In: Krishnaiah (ed.) Multivariate Analysis, pp. 391–420 (1966)

Optimization of Quadrature Filters Based on the Numerical Integration of Improper Integrals

Andreas Krebs[1], Johan Wiklund[2], and Michael Felsberg[2]

[1] Dept. Aerodynamics/Fluid Mech., BTU Cottbus, Germany
krebsa@tu-cottbus.de
[2] Computer Vision Laboratory, Linköping University, Sweden
mfe@isy.liu.se

Abstract. Convolution kernels are a commonly used tool in computer vision. These kernels are often specified by an ideal frequency response and the actual filter coefficients are obtained by minimizing some weighted distance with respect to the ideal filter. State-of-the-art approaches usually replace the continuous frequency response by a discrete Fourier spectrum with a multitude of samples compared to the kernel size, depending on the smoothness of the ideal filter and the weight function. The number of samples in the Fourier domain grows exponentially with the dimensionality and becomes a bottleneck concerning memory requirements.

In this paper we propose a method that avoids the discretization of the frequency space and makes filter optimization feasible in higher dimensions than the standard approach. The result is no longer depending on the choice of the sampling grid and it remains exact even if the weighting function is singular in the origin. The resulting improper integrals are efficiently computed using Gauss-Jacobi quadrature.

Keywords: Localized kernels, filter optimization, Gauss-Jacobi quadrature.

1 Introduction

A convolution kernel is termed optimal if its frequency response minimizes a chosen distance measure with respect to an ideal filter in the frequency space. State-of-the-art approaches replace the continuous frequency space by a discrete one with a multitude of samples compared to the kernel size, depending on how smooth the ideal filter and the weight function are [1,6,7]. We propose to use continuous formulations of the weighted distance measure, of the relative frequency error, and of the basic optimization problem in §2. Hence, the distance measure does not depend on the sampling of the Fourier space any longer. The basic optimization problem can be expressed by a linear system of equations $A\mathbf{f} = \mathbf{b}$. The entries of A and $\mathbf{b}$ are determined by improper integrals. In §3, it is shown that these integrals can be computed precisely by the means of Gauss-Jacobi quadrature. The numerical experiments of §4 compare some kernels obtained by the continuous and by the discrete approach as defined in [6]. Estimates of the memory requirements and of the number of floating points operations for both methods for d dimensions finish this section. Results in this paper are given without proof. All proofs are provided in the supplementary material.

R. Mester and M. Felsberg (Eds.): DAGM 2011, LNCS 6835, pp. 91–100, 2011.
© Springer-Verlag Berlin Heidelberg 2011

2   Filter Optimization: A Continuous Reformulation

Let d be the dimension of the spatial and the frequency space. Let the frequency response of an ideal filter F with bandwidth B, center frequency ρ_c, and filter direction $\mathbf{n} \in \Omega$, $|\mathbf{n}| = 1$, be defined on the cube $\Omega := [-\pi, \pi]^d$ by the radial symmetric factor $R_{B,c}(|\cdot|)$ and the directional factor $D_{\mathbf{n}}(\cdot)$ as follows [4]:

$$F(\mathbf{u}) := R_{B,c}(|\mathbf{u}|)\, D_{\mathbf{n}}(\mathbf{u}) \qquad \text{with} \qquad R_{B,c}(\rho) := \exp\left(-C_B(\ln \tfrac{\rho}{\rho_c})^2\right),$$

$$C_B := \tfrac{4}{B^2 \ln 2}, \qquad \text{and} \qquad D_{\mathbf{n}}(\mathbf{u}) := \begin{cases} \left(\tfrac{\mathbf{u}}{|\mathbf{u}|} \cdot \mathbf{n}\right)^2 & \text{if } \mathbf{u} \cdot \mathbf{n} > 0, \\ 0 & \text{otherwise.} \end{cases} \qquad (1)$$

Let a kernel be defined by n coefficients $f_k \in \mathbb{C}$, $1 \le k \le n$, assigned to the coordinates $\mathbf{x}_k$ of the local space. Then, its frequency response $\tilde{F}_{\mathbf{f}}(\mathbf{u})$ reads

$$\tilde{F}_{\mathbf{f}}(\mathbf{u}) := \sum_{k=1}^{n} f_k \exp(-i\, \mathbf{x}_k \cdot \mathbf{u}). \qquad (2)$$

Let $w : \Omega \to \mathbb{R}_{>0}$ be a positive weight function. Then, a distance measure is defined on the weighted frequency space $L_w^2(\Omega, \mathbb{C})$ by the weighted $L^2(\Omega)$-norm:

$$\|F - \tilde{F}_{\mathbf{f}}\|_{w,\Omega} := \left(\int_{\Omega} w(\mathbf{u}) \left| F(\mathbf{u}) - \tilde{F}_{\mathbf{f}}(\mathbf{u}) \right|^2 \, d\mathbf{u} \right)^{\frac{1}{2}}. \qquad (3)$$

Here, $|\cdot|$ denotes the absolute value $|z|$ of the complex number $z \in \mathbb{C}$. Using the norm $\|\cdot\|_{w,\Omega}$, we define the relative frequency error by

$$e_{\mathrm{rel}} := \|F - \tilde{F}_{\mathbf{f}}\|_{w,\Omega} \,/\, \|F\|_{w,\Omega}. \qquad (4)$$

The weight function w quantifies the significance of close approximation for different spatial or spatial-temporal frequencies. In conjunction with the weight w, note that a strict analog with the discrete distance used in computer vision [1,4,5,6] would suggest to define $\|\cdot\|_{w,\Omega}$ with the squared weight $w^2(\mathbf{u})$ instead of $w(\mathbf{u})$ in (3). We decided to take the unsquared w as this is consistent with literature dealing with weighted Lebesgue spaces and orthogonal polynomials [2,8]. Using the above definition, we can now write the optimization problem (OP): Determine $\mathbf{f} := (f_j)_{1 \le j \le N} \in \mathbb{C}^N$, so that $\mathcal{A}(\mathbf{f}) := \|F - \tilde{F}_{\mathbf{f}}\|_{w,\Omega}^2$ becomes minimal. The existence and uniqueness of $\mathbf{f}$ follows since $\mathcal{A}$ is a strongly convex functional lower-bounded by 0 on $\mathbb{C}^N$.

Although the squared absolute value $|z|^2 = \bar{z}z$ used in (3) is not a holomorphic function, one can differentiate $\mathcal{A}$ from (OP) with respect to the real and the imaginary components of the coefficient vector $\mathbf{f}$ using standard calculus and reassemble the real and the imaginary parts as follows:

Proposition 1. *Let $\frac{\partial}{\partial \Re \mathbf{f}}$ and $\frac{\partial}{\partial \Im \mathbf{f}}$ be the gradient with respect to the real and imaginary components of $\mathbf{f}$, respectively. Then there holds*

$$\left(\frac{\partial}{\partial \Re \mathbf{f}} + i\frac{\partial}{\partial \Im \mathbf{f}}\right) \mathcal{A}(\mathbf{f}) = \left(-2 \int_{\Omega} w(u)\, e^{i\, \mathbf{x}_k \cdot \mathbf{u}} \left(F(\mathbf{u}) - \tilde{F}_{\mathbf{f}}(\mathbf{u})\right) d\mathbf{u}\right)_{1 \le k \le N}. \qquad (5)$$

If $\mathbf{f}$ solves (OP), then $\left(\frac{\partial}{\partial \Re \mathbf{f}} + i\frac{\partial}{\partial \Im \mathbf{f}}\right)\mathcal{A}(\mathbf{f}) = \mathbf{0}$.

Eq. 5 can be rewritten as the linear system of equation $A\mathbf{f} = \mathbf{b}$ with the matrix $A := \big(a_{jk}\big)_{\substack{1 \le j \le N \\ 1 \le k \le N}} \in \mathbb{R}^{N \times N}$ and the right hand side $\mathbf{b} := \big(b_k\big)_{1 \le k \le N} \in \mathbb{C}^N$ where the entries a_{jk} and b_k are given by

$$a_{jk} := \int_\Omega 2w(\mathbf{u}) \cos\big((\mathbf{x}_k - \mathbf{x}_j) \cdot \mathbf{u}\big)\,d\mathbf{u}\,, \quad b_k := \int_\Omega w(\mathbf{u}) \exp(i\mathbf{x}_k \cdot \mathbf{u})F(\mathbf{u})d\mathbf{u}. \quad (6)$$

The following two corollaries characterize the linear system $A\mathbf{f} = \mathbf{b}$.

Corollary 1. *Let the weight w be fixed and $F_\mathbf{n}$ only dependent on $\mathbf{n}$ (see (1)). The vector components b_k of $\mathbf{b}$ from (6) depend only on $\mathbf{x} = \mathbf{x}_k$. Therefore, we write $b_{\mathbf{x},\mathbf{n}}$ as a short hand. If $\mathbf{n}$ is assumed fixed, we write $b_\mathbf{x}$.*

Let $\Omega_\mathbf{n} := \{\mathbf{u} \in \Omega \mid \mathbf{u} \cdot \mathbf{n} > 0\}$ be the half of Ω which elements lie on the same side of the hyper-plane $\mathbf{u} \cdot \mathbf{n} = 0$ with the filter direction vector $\mathbf{n}$ (see Figure 1 (right)). According to the definition of $F(\mathbf{u})$ by (1), one obtains

$$b_\mathbf{x} = b_{\mathbf{x},\mathbf{n}} = \int_{\Omega_\mathbf{n}} w(\mathbf{u})\ \exp(i\mathbf{x} \cdot \mathbf{u})\ R_{B,c}(|\mathbf{u}|)\ (\tfrac{\mathbf{u}}{|\mathbf{u}|} \cdot \mathbf{n})^2\ d\mathbf{u}\,.$$

Furthermore, one gets $b_{-\mathbf{x}} = \mathrm{conj}(b_\mathbf{x})$ and $b_{\mathbf{x},-\mathbf{n}} = \mathrm{conj}(b_{\mathbf{x},\mathbf{n}})$.

Corollary 2. *As the a_{jk} entries of A from (6) depend only on $\Delta\mathbf{x} = \mathbf{x}_k - \mathbf{x}_j$, we write $a_{\Delta\mathbf{x}} := a_{jk}$ as a short hand. For $\mathbf{x}$ sampled equidistantly in each dimension, A is a symmetric positive definite real-valued Toeplitz matrix.*

3   Numerical Quadrature of Improper Integrals

The statements of §2 assumed only $w(\mathbf{u}) > 0$ for all $\mathbf{u} \in \Omega$. The energy of normal images is usually concentrated around the frequency $\mathbf{u} = \mathbf{0}$ and decreases as $|\mathbf{u}|$ increases. The class of weight functions defined in the following corollary has been proven useful in practice and can be extended to more general weight functions known in filter design (cf. [5,6]) straight forwardly.

Corollary 3 (Boundedness of the integrals). *Let w be defined by $w(\mathbf{u}) := |\mathbf{u}|^{-2\beta}$ for $\beta \ge 0$. Then the matrix entries $a_{\Delta\mathbf{x}}$ are bounded for all $\mathbf{x} \in \mathbb{R}^d$, if and only if $\beta < \frac{d}{2}$.*

We consider the special case of the matrix entry $a_0 = \int_0^\pi u^{-2\beta}\,du = \frac{1}{1-2\beta}\pi^{1-2\beta}$ from Corollary 2 to explain the need of a numerical quadrature that takes care of the singularity at 0. Using equidistant sampling, a_0 is approximated by the sum $\hat{a}_0 := \frac{\pi}{n} \sum_{j=1}^n \big(\frac{2j-1}{2n}\pi\big)^{-2\beta}$. In Figure 1 (left) we plotted the relative error $(a_0 - \hat{a}_0)/a_0$ of this approximation versus the number of samples n using a double logarithmic scale of the axes. The solid and the dashed line of the plot show the upper and the lower limit of the convergence rate. With this it becomes clear that integration by equidistant sampling is not feasible because one needs millions of function evaluations. Therefore, we look for a quadrature which takes into account the singularity of the integrand. G. Szegö already showed the basics for such schemes in his book "Orthogonal polynomials" in 1938 [8, Chapter XV].

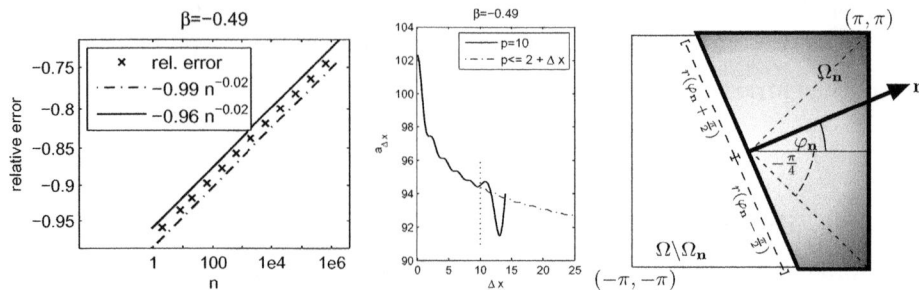

Fig. 1. Left: Computation of a_0 by equidistant sampling of $u^{-2\beta}$ for $\beta = 0.49$ with n points. The relative error $(a_0 - \hat{a}_0)/a_0$ decreases with $\mathcal{O}(n^{-0.02})$. Middle: Computation of $a_{\Delta x}$ for $\Delta x \in [0, 25]$ using the Gauss-Jacobi quadrature; $(a_{\Delta x} - \tilde{a}_{\Delta x})/a_{\Delta x} \leq 10^{-6}$ for all Δx if $p = 2 + \lceil \Delta x \rceil$ quadrature abscissae are used. Right: Integration over $\Omega_{\mathbf{n}}$.

3.1   The One-Dimensional Case

The integration domain $\Omega_{\mathbf{n}}$ must be considered for $\mathbf{n} = \pm 1$ in the one-dimensional case. As $b_{x,-1} = \mathrm{conj}(b_{x,1})$, it suffices to analyze Ω_1. The integrals

$$a_{\Delta x} = \int_0^\pi 2u^{-2\beta} \cos(\Delta x\, u)\; \mathrm{d}u \;\; \text{and} \;\; b_{x,1} = \int_0^\pi u^{-2\beta} \exp(i\, xu) R_{B,c}(u)\; \mathrm{d}u\,, \quad (7)$$

needed for A and b from (6) contain a singularity at 0. By the theory of orthogonal polynomials (cf. [8]) there exist polynomials J_p^γ of degree p for $\gamma > -1$ with $J_p^\gamma(\pi) = 1$ which are orthogonal to each other with respect to the scalar product $\langle \cdot, \cdot \rangle_\gamma$ given by $\langle f, g \rangle_\gamma := \int_0^\pi \zeta^\gamma f(\zeta) g(\zeta)\, \mathrm{d}\zeta$. We recall two basic properties that characterize these polynomials.

1. For any positive integer p, the zeros of J_p^γ are distinct real numbers $\zeta_i^{\gamma,p} \in (0, \pi)$, $1 \leq i \leq p$, called weighted quadrature points.
2. *Gauss-Jacobi quadrature.* There exist positive weight factors $\omega_i^{\gamma,p}$, $1 \leq i \leq p$, such that

$$\int_0^\pi \zeta^\gamma f(\zeta)\; \mathrm{d}\zeta = \sum_{i=1}^p \omega_i^{\gamma,p} f(\zeta_i^{\gamma,p}) \quad (8)$$

for all polynomials $f \in \mathbb{P}_{2p-1}((0, \pi))$.

The quadrature points $\zeta_i^{\gamma,p}$ and the weight factors $\omega_i^{\gamma,p}$ can be computed efficiently by solving an eigenvalue problem using the Givens-Householder algorithm (see [3, §5.3], [2, Remark 4.2] for the numerical scheme). The strength of the Gauss-Jacobi quadrature becomes clear by (8): p quadrature points are sufficient to compute ζ^γ weighted integrals of polynomials of degree $\leq 2p - 1$.

The drawback of the quadrature according to (8) is, roughly spoken, that the convergence for non-polynomial f depends on the boundedness of the derivatives of f. Bernardi and Maday gave a deep analysis of the approximation properties of the Gauss-Jacobi quadrature for non-polynomial f using weighted Sobolev spaces in [2]. In the supplementary material, this analysis is adapted to $a_{\Delta \mathbf{x}}$ and $b_{\mathbf{x}}$ to prove the following propositions.

Let $a_{\Delta x}$ and $b_{x,1}$ be approximated by (in accordance with (8))

$$\tilde{a}_{\Delta x} := 2 \sum_{j=1}^{p} \omega_j^{-2\beta,p} \cos(\Delta x \zeta_j^{-2\beta,p}) \quad \text{and} \quad \tilde{b}_{x,1} := \sum_{j=1}^{p} \omega_j^{-2\beta,p} \exp(i\, x \zeta_j^{-2\beta,p}) . \quad (9)$$

Proposition 2. *Let $\beta \in [0, \frac{1}{2})$. Furthermore, let $a_{\Delta x}$ and $\tilde{a}_{\Delta x}$ be given by (7) and (9), respectively. Then, there exist constants c_1 and c_2 such that the error $e := |a_{\Delta x} - \tilde{a}_{\Delta x}|$ may be estimated by*

$$e \le c_1(|\Delta x| + 1)\, p^{-1} \quad and \quad e \le c_2(|\Delta x|^2 + |\Delta x| + 1)\, p^{-2} .$$

Proposition 3. *Let $B \in [0.1, 3]$ be the bandwidth used in the definition of $R_{B,c}$, and let $b_{x,1}$ and $\tilde{b}_{x,1}$ be given by (7) and (9), respectively. Then, there exist constants c_3 and c_4 such that the error $e_w := |b_{x,1} - \tilde{b}_{x,1}|$ of the Gauss-Jaboci quadrature with respect to the weight function $\zeta^{-2\beta}$ may be estimated by*

$$e_w \le c_3(|x| + 1)\, B^{-1/2}\, p^{-1} \quad and \quad e_w \le c_4(|x|^2 + |x| + 1)\, B^{-3/2}\, p^{-2} .$$

Propositions 2 and 3 are limits for the errors of the Gauss-Jacobi quadrature applied to the improper integrals occuring in the filter optimization. Figure 1 (middle) documents how the weighted integration works for the computation of $a_{\Delta x}$ for $\Delta x \in [0, 25]$ using the Gaussian-Jacobi quadrature with the p abscissae $\zeta_j^{-2\beta,p}$ for the weight $|u|^{-2\beta}$ with $\beta = -0.49$. For $p = \lceil \Delta x \rceil + 2$ the relative error of $\tilde{a}_{\Delta x}$ against the exact value $a_{\Delta x}$ is less 10^{-6}. Even the step-like dependence of the exact $a_{\Delta x}$ from Δx is already caught with this number of points.

Due to Figure 1 (left) there holds $|a_0 - \hat{a}_0|/a_0 \approx 0.96n^{-0.02}$. Therefore, more than 10^{688} function evaluations are required to compete with $\tilde{a}_0$.

Using only $p = 10$ abscissae shows that the weighted quadrature collapses for $\Delta x > 9$. Let $\lceil y \rceil := \min\{k \in \mathbb{N} \,|\, k \ge y\}$. Numerical experiments like that presented in Figure 1 (middle) indicate that already $\lceil |\Delta x| \rceil + 2$ and $\lceil |x| \rceil + 5$ abscissae suffice to approximate the integrals of $a_{\Delta x}$ and $b_{x,1}$, respectively, so that the relative errors are smaller than 10^{-6}. These numbers are consistent with the following idea: The quality of the quadrature (8) depends on how good the interpolating polynom of degree $2p - 1$ approximates the integrand. If one conjectures that $\cos(|\Delta x|)$ can be approximated well by a polynomial of degree $2\lceil |\Delta x| \rceil + 1$, then $p = \lceil |\Delta x| \rceil + 2$ is a feasible number of quadrature points.

3.2   The Two-Dimensional Case

Due to Corollaries 1 and 2 the computation of $b_{\mathbf{x},\mathbf{n}}$ and $a_{\Delta \mathbf{x}}$ demands the integration over the half square $\Omega_{\mathbf{n}}$ (see Figure 1 (right)). Let $w(\mathbf{u})\hat{h}(\mathbf{u})$ be a short hand for the integrands given by corollaries. At the beginning we assume $|\varphi_{\mathbf{n}}| \le \frac{\pi}{4}$ for ease of presentation, i.e., there exists an intersection point of the right edge of the square Ω and the line $\{\lambda \mathbf{n} \,|\, \lambda \in \mathbb{R}\}$. As can be seen in Figure 1 (right), using the polar coordinates (ρ, φ) with $\mathbf{u} = (\rho \cos \varphi, \rho \cos \varphi)^T$ one may rewrite

$$\int_{\Omega_\mathbf{n}} w(u)\,\hat{h}(\mathbf{u})\,\mathrm{d}\mathbf{u} = \int_{\varphi_\mathbf{n}-\frac{\pi}{2}}^{-\frac{\pi}{4}} H(\varphi)\,\mathrm{d}\varphi + \int_{-\frac{\pi}{4}}^{\frac{\pi}{4}} H(\varphi)\,\mathrm{d}\varphi + \int_{\frac{\pi}{4}}^{\varphi_\mathbf{n}+\frac{\pi}{2}} H(\varphi)\,\mathrm{d}\varphi \quad (10)$$

with the interior integrals $H(\varphi) := \int_0^{r(\varphi)} \rho^{1-2\beta}\,h(\rho,\varphi)\,\mathrm{d}\rho$, $\varphi \in [0, 2\pi]$, in both cases. Here, h is well-defined by $h(\rho,\varphi) := \hat{h}(\mathbf{u})$ and the upper limit $r(\varphi)$ of the interior integrals is given by $r(\varphi) := \frac{\pi}{\cos\varphi}$ for $|\varphi| \le \frac{\pi}{4}$ and by $r(\varphi) := \frac{\pi}{|\sin\varphi|}$ for $\frac{1}{4}\pi \le |\varphi| \le \frac{3}{4}\pi$. The integration over $\Omega_\mathbf{n}$ for the general situation $\varphi_\mathbf{n} \in [\pi, \pi]$ is yielded by a shift argument: Let $\varphi_s = \frac{\sigma}{2}\pi$, if $\frac{1}{4}\pi \le \varphi_\mathbf{n} \le \frac{3}{4}\pi$, $\sigma \in \{-1, 1\}$, and let $\varphi_s = \pi$, if $\frac{3}{4}\pi < |\varphi_\mathbf{n}| \le \pi$. Then, we obtain $\int_{\Omega_\mathbf{n}} \hat{h}(\mathbf{u})\,\mathrm{d}\mathbf{u}$ by the substitution of the integrand $h(\rho,\varphi)$ in the right hand side of (10) with $h(\rho, \varphi + \varphi_s)$. The quadrature rule given by (8) can be adapted from the integration interval $(0, \pi)$ to the interval $I_\varphi := (0, r(\varphi))$ by a scaling of the abscissae $\zeta_j^{\gamma,p}$ and of the weights $\omega_j^{\gamma,p}$. Noting these adapted abscissae and weights by $\zeta_j^{\gamma,p,\varphi}$ and $\omega_j^{\gamma,p,\varphi}$, respectively, the interior integrals are obtained by

$$H(\varphi) \approx \tilde{H}(\varphi) := \sum_{j=1}^p \omega_j^{1-2\beta,p,\varphi}\,h\left(\zeta_j^{1-2\beta,p,\varphi}\right).$$

Note that the weight $\rho^{1-2\beta}$ in (10) does not contain a singularity as long as $0 \le \beta \le \frac{1}{2}$. In this case a normal Gaussian quadrature would be sufficient for the numerical evaluation of $H(\varphi)$. But the abscissae and the weights of the Gauss-Jacobi quadrature can also be calculated for weight functions ζ^γ with positive γ. As $H(\varphi)$ becomes an improper integral for $\frac{1}{2} < \beta < 1$, the numerical quadrature must account for the singularity in this case. The outer integrals $\int_{\Phi_a}^{\Phi_b} H(\varphi)\,\mathrm{d}\varphi$, $-\frac{3}{4}\pi \le \Phi_a \le \Phi_b \le \frac{3}{4}\pi$, used in (10) do not contain any singularities and their derivatives with respect to φ are good-natured. Therefore, a normal Gaussian quadrature scaled to the interval $[\Phi_a, \Phi_b]$ with p_{out} points will work well:

$$\int_{\Phi_a}^{\Phi_b} H(\varphi)\,\mathrm{d}\varphi \approx \frac{1}{2}(\Phi_b - \Phi_a)\sum_{k=1}^{p_{out}} \omega_k^{0,p_{out},[\Phi_a,\Phi_b]}\,\tilde{H}\left(\zeta_k^{0,p_{out},[\Phi_a,\Phi_b]}\right).$$

3.3   The Three and Four Dimensional Cases

Let $w(\mathbf{u})\,\hat{h}(\mathbf{u})$ be a short hand for the integrands given by (6) again. The computation of $b_{\mathbf{x},\mathbf{n}}$ and $a_{\Delta\mathbf{x}}$ asks for the integration of the volume integral $\int_{\Omega_\mathbf{n}} w(\mathbf{u})\,\hat{h}(\mathbf{u})$. Analogously to the two-dimensional approach presented in (10), one can use multidimensional polar coordinates $(\rho, \varphi_1, \ldots \varphi_{d-1})$, $d \in \{3, 4\}$, and write $h(\rho, \varphi_1, \ldots \varphi_{d-1}) := \hat{h}(\mathbf{u})$ for the integrand.

Let $\Omega_{\mathbf{e}_i}$, $i \in \{1, \ldots, d\}$ be the half cubes defined by using the definition of $\Omega_\mathbf{n}$ with the unit coordinate vectors $\mathbf{e}_i$ for $\mathbf{n}$. The cumbersome task of parameterizing $\Omega_\mathbf{n}$ in polar coordinates can be avoided by noting the the equivalent formulations

$$a_{\Delta\mathbf{x}} = \int_{\Omega_{\mathbf{e}_k}} 2\,w(u)\,\cos(\Delta\mathbf{x}\cdot\mathbf{u})\,\mathrm{d}\mathbf{u} \qquad \text{and}$$

$$b_{\mathbf{x},\mathbf{n}} = \int_{\Omega_{\mathbf{e}_k}} w(\mathbf{u})\,(\cos(\mathbf{x}\cdot\mathbf{u}) + i\,\sigma(\mathbf{u}\cdot\mathbf{n})\sin(\mathbf{x}\cdot\mathbf{u}))\,R_{B,c}(|\mathbf{u}|)\left(\tfrac{\mathbf{u}}{|\mathbf{u}|}\cdot\mathbf{n}\right)^2\,\mathrm{d}\mathbf{u}$$

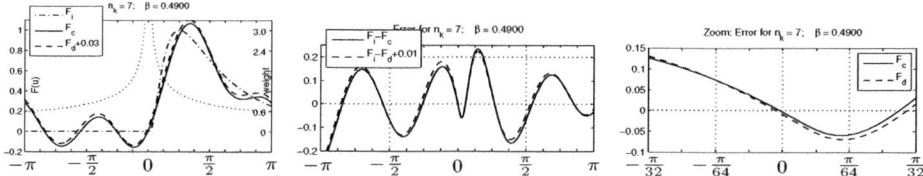

Fig. 2. Frequency responses F_c and F_d of the optimized kernels and the corresponding errors

with the sign function σ defined by $\sigma(y) := 1$ for $y \geq 0$ and $\sigma(y) := -1$ else. Nevertheless, the domain Ω_{e_i} must be divided into subdomains analogously to the 2d case, but more complicated, because the Gauss-Jacobi quadrature rule demands integrands with bounded higher derivatives. The details of this segmentation will be documented in a forthcoming technical documentation.

4 Numerical Experiments

4.1 Continuous versus Discrete Fourier Space Optimization

Let the ideal filter F_i be given by (1) with bandwidth $B = 2\sqrt{2}$, center frequency $\rho_c = \frac{\pi}{4}$, and direction $\mathbf{n} = 1$. We computed the optimized kernels of size $n = 7$ with respect to the weight function $w(u) = (u^{-\beta}+0.05)^2$, $\beta = 0.49$, using the continuous reformulation and using the discrete approach presented in [6]. F_i and the frequency responses F_c and F_d corresponding to the continuous and to the discrete optimization, respectively, are plotted in Figure 2 (left). The Fourier space was discretized using $N = 3n$ uniformly distributed samples. As F_c and F_d are almost identical, F_d is shifted shifted upwardly by $+0.03$ for reason of presentation. The weight function is plotted as the dotted curve with respect to the scale given on the right axis. The plot in the center of Figure 2 shows the frequency errors $F_i - F_c$ and $F_i - F_d$. Here, $F_i - F_d$ shifted upwardly by $+0.01$. The zoom of these errors presented in the rightmost plot

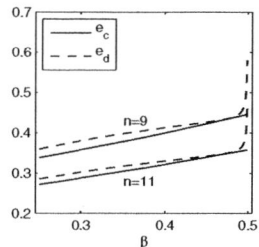

Fig. 3. Relative frequency errors for kernels of size $n=9$, $n=11$

of the figure makes it clear that the continuous optimization reflects better on the singularity of the weight function than the discrete approach. There holds $w(u) \geq 19$ for $u \in [-\frac{\pi}{64}, \frac{\pi}{64}]$, i.e., the errors are amplified here. In Figure 3 the two optimization approaches are compared by plotting the relative frequency errors for the continuous and the discrete errors, e_c and e_d, respectively, for varying $\beta \in [-0.25, 0.499]$ using the same ideal filter F_i. The error measure used is defined by (4). Again, we used $3n$ samples for the discretization of the Fourier space.

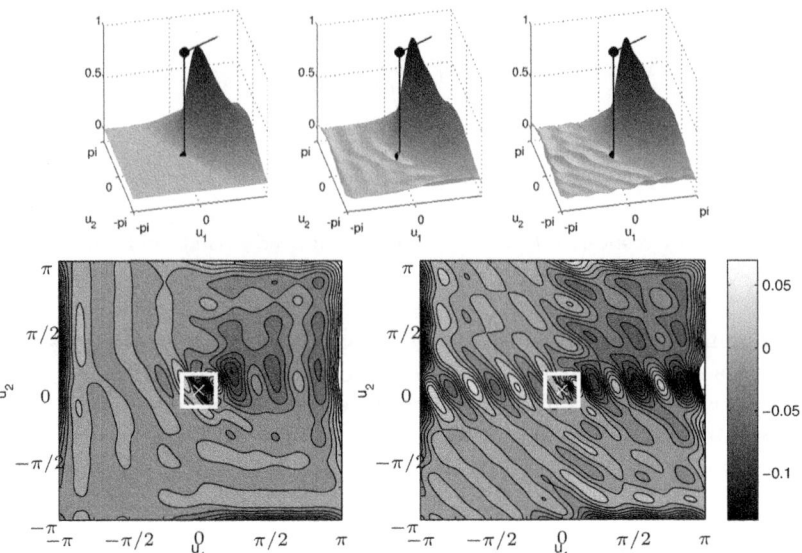

Fig. 4. Top row: Surface plots of the ideal frequency F_i (left) and of the frequency responses F_{w_1} (middle), F_{w_2} (right). Bottom row: Contour plots of frequency errors $F_i - F_{w_1}$ (left) and $F_i - F_{w_2}$ (right).

4.2   A Two-Dimensional Example

Let the ideal filter F_i be given by (1) with bandwidth $B = 2\sqrt{2}$, center frequency $\rho_c = \frac{\pi}{4}$, and direction $\mathbf{n} = (\cos\frac{\pi}{6}, \sin\frac{\pi}{6})^T$ (see the top left surface plot of Figure 4, the short line directing from the z-axis pictures the filter direction). Using the continuous formulation, we computed the optimized kernels of size 13×13 with respect to the weight functions $w_1 \equiv 1$ and $w_2(u) = (u^{-\beta} + 0.05)^2$, $\beta = 0.99$. The corresponding frequency responses F_{w_1} and F_{w_2} are visualized by the top middle and the top right surface plot of Figure 4.

In the bottom row of Figure 4 the pointwise frequency error $F_i - F_{w_j}$, $j \in \{1,2\}$, is shown by contour plots (left: w_1; right: w_2). A comparison of both plots makes it clear that the error is pushed away from the center by the singularity of the weight function w_2.

It was not possible to discriminate between the kernels obtained by continuous and by discrete optimization by visual inspection of the frequency response. A comparison of the relative frequency errors showed that the result of the continous optimization is less than 1 % more precise than the discrete approach when $(3 \cdot 13)^2$ samples are employed in contrast to $(13 + 2)^2$ quadrature points.

4.3   Computational Costs

Timings. Using the example of §4.2 for increasing kernel sizes $n \times n$, $n \in \{1, \dots, 69\}$, we measured the time t_c needed by the continuous approach and

Table 1. Time and memory requirements

Approach	Costs	1d	2d	3d	4d
discrete	real var.	$4n^2$	$36n^4$	$108n^6$	$324n^8$
continuous	real var.	n	n^2	n^3	n^4
discrete	flops	$\mathcal{O}(n^2 \log n)$	$\mathcal{O}(2n^4 \log n)$	$\mathcal{O}(3n^6 \log n)$	$\mathcal{O}(4n^8 \log n)$
continuous	flops	$\mathcal{O}(n)$	$\mathcal{O}(n^2)$	$\mathcal{O}(n^3)$	$\mathcal{O}(n^4)$

the time t_d needed by the discrete approach as presented in [6] in seconds. Figure 5 shows a double logarithmic plot of these timings. The solid line $10^{-3}n^3$ and the dashed line $10^{-7}n^6$ visualize the growth rates of the costs. A detailed timing of the discrete approach shows that the bottlenecks of the implementation following [6] are the assembling of a matrix B of size $n^2 \times (3n)^2$ and the computation of the products which contain B as a factor like $B^H W^2 B$. Here, B is the complex valued matrix which describes the linear mapping of the discrete local space into the discrete Fourier space and W is the real valued diagonal matrix corresponding to the discretization of the weight function. Assuming that efficient matrix multiplication algorithms are employed for the computation of $B^H W^2 B$, the costs for this multiplications will grow with $\mathcal{O}(2n^4 \log n)$.

The bottleneck of the implementation following the continuous approach is also the assembly of the matrix $A \in \mathbb{R}^{n^2 \times n^2}$ from (6). But our implementation uses that A is a symmetric Toeplitz matrix (see Corollary 2). Therefore, it suffices to compute n^2 matrix entries instead of $n^2 \cdot n^2$ and to store these in a lookup matrix L. With this, A can be simply assembled by copying the entries of L to the right positions. Neglecting the band structure of A, results in squaring the computation time, i.e., it increases the costs from $\mathcal{O}(n^3)$ to $\mathcal{O}(n)^6$. Furthermore, we note that there is no need to compute any matrix-matrix products containing A.

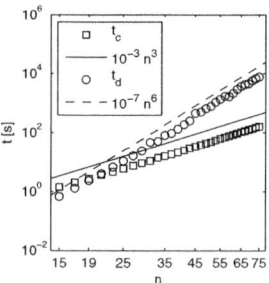

Fig. 5. Timings [s] of the filter optimization for square shaped 2d kernels

Memory requirements. The implementation following [6] needs two matrices with the dimensions of B at least: one for B and one for the results of matrix-matrix products with B. Counting a complex valued variable as two real valued variables, this means that we have to store not less than $2 \cdot 2 \cdot (3n)^2 \cdot n^2$ variables.

Using the band structure of A, there is no need to store A at all. As A is symmetric positive definite, we can take advantage from the preconditioned conjugate gradient algorithm which solves $A\mathbf{f} = \mathbf{b}$ iteratively. Therewith, it is sufficient to implement the product $A\mathbf{f}$ as a function which depends on L and $\mathbf{f}$. So, only the real valued matrix L with n^2 variables must be stored.

Estimates for d dimensions. Now, let n be the size of the kernel in each direction. Then the estimate of costs for the timing and the memory requirements can be generalized from two to d dimensions as presented in Table 1. Let us assume that we want to optimize a 4d kernel with 7 coefficients in each direction. If the computations are done with real valued double precision variables (8 Byte), we need 15 GByte at least to store the matrices of the discrete implementation in contrast to 20 kByte necessary for the lookup matrix L.

5   Conclusions

A novel approach for the optimization of d dimensional convolution kernels has been presented that avoids the discretization of the frequency response. Therewith, a weighted distance measure and relative frequency error have been defined that do not depend on the sampling density of the Fourier space any longer. The continuous approach yields similar kernels to the discrete method, but measurements of the relative frequency error show that the continuous approach behaves slightly better in case of strong singularities.

The continuous optimization avoids the storage and the multiplication of big matrices. As the linear system of the proposed approach is determined by a symmetric positive definite Toeplitz matrix, it can be solved by the preconditioned gradient method. The matrix can be replaced by a function which calculates the matrix-vector product. Compared to the discrete approach, the continuous method only needs a square root of the floating point operations. Therefore, it is better suited for filter optimization in high dimensions.

References

1. Austvoll, I.: Filter banks, wavelets, and frames with applications in computer vision and image processing (A review). In: Bigun, J., Gustavsson, T. (eds.) SCIA 2003. LNCS, vol. 2749, pp. 495–506. Springer, Heidelberg (2003)
2. Bernardi, C., Maday, Y.: Spectral methods. In: Handbook of Numerical Analysis, vol. V, pp. 209–485. North-Holland, Amsterdam (1997)
3. Gil, A., Segura, J., Temme, N.M.: Numerical methods for special functions, p. 417. SIAM. xiv, Philadelphia (2007)
4. Granlund, G.H., Knutsson, H.: Signal Processing for Computer Vision. Kluwer Academic Publishers, Dordrecht (1995)
5. Knutsson, H., Andersson, M.: Loglets: Generalized quadrature and phase for local spatio-temporal structure estimation. In: Bigun, J., Gustavsson, T. (eds.) SCIA 2003. LNCS, vol. 2749, pp. 741–748. Springer, Heidelberg (2003)
6. Knutsson, H., Andersson, M., Wiklund, J.: Advanced Filter Design. In: Proceedings of the 11th Scandinavian Conference on Image Analysis, SCIA, pp. 185–193 (1999)
7. Svensson, B., Andersson, M., Smedby, Ö., Knutsson, H.: Efficient 3-D Adaptive Filtering for Medical Image Enhancement. In: IEEE International Symposium on Biomedical Imaging, ISBI 2006, Arlington, USA, pp. 996–999, April 6-9 (2006)
8. Szegö, G.: Orthogonal polynomials, 4th edn., vol. XXIII. American Mathematical Society, Providence (1975); AMS, Colloq. Publ.

Real Time Head Pose Estimation from Consumer Depth Cameras

Gabriele Fanelli[1], Thibaut Weise[2], Juergen Gall[1], and Luc Van Gool[1,3]

[1] ETH Zurich, Switzerland
[2] EPFL Lausanne, Switzerland
[3] KU Leuven, Belgium
{fanelli,gall,vangool}@vision.ee.ethz.ch, thibaut.weise@epfl.ch

Abstract. We present a system for estimating location and orientation of a person's head, from depth data acquired by a low quality device. Our approach is based on discriminative random regression forests: ensembles of random trees trained by splitting each node so as to simultaneously reduce the entropy of the class labels distribution and the variance of the head position and orientation. We evaluate three different approaches to jointly take classification and regression performance into account during training. For evaluation, we acquired a new dataset and propose a method for its automatic annotation.

1 Introduction

Head pose estimation is a key element of human behavior analysis. For this reason, many applications would benefit from automatic and robust head pose estimation systems. While 2D video presents ambiguities hard to resolve in real time, systems relying on 3D data have shown very good results [5,10]. Such approaches, however, use bulky 3D scanners like [22] and are not useful for consumer products or mobile applications like robots. Today, cheap depth cameras exist, even though they provide much lower quality data.

We present an approach for real time 3D head pose estimation robust to the poor signal-to-noise ratio of current consumer depth cameras. The method is inspired by the recent work of [10] that uses random regression forests [9] to estimate the 3D head pose in real time from high quality depth data. It basically learns a mapping between simple depth features and real-valued parameters such as 3D head position and rotation angles. The system achieves very good performance and is robust to occlusions but it assumes that the face is the sole object in the field of view. We extend the regression forests such that they discriminate depth patches that belong to a head (*classification*) and use only those patches to predict the pose (*regression*), jointly solving the classification and regression problems. In our experiments, we evaluate several schemes that can be used to optimize both the discriminative power as well as the regression accuracy of such a random forest. In order to deal with the characteristic noise level of the sensor, we cannot rely on synthetic data as in [10], but we have to acquire real training examples, i.e., faces captured with a similar sensor. We

R. Mester and M. Felsberg (Eds.): DAGM 2011, LNCS 6835, pp. 101–110, 2011.
© Springer-Verlag Berlin Heidelberg 2011

therefore recorded several subjects and their head movements, annotating the data by tracking each sequence using a personalized template.

Our system works on a frame-by-frame basis, needs no initialization, and runs in real time. In our experiments, we show that it can handle large pose changes and variations such as facial hair and partial occlusions.

2   Related Work

The literature contains several works on head pose estimation, which can be conveniently divided depending on whether they use 2D images or depth data.

Among the algorithms based on 2D images, we can further distinguish between appearance-based methods, which analyze the whole face region, and feature-based methods, which rely on the localization of specific facial features, e.g., the eyes. Examples of appearance-based methods are [13] and [17], where the head pose space is discretized and separate detectors are learned for each segment. Statistical generative models, e.g., active appearance models [8] and their variations [7,19,2], are very popular in the face analysis field, but are rarely employed for head pose estimation. Feature-based methods are limited by their need to either have the same facial features visible across different poses, or define pose-dependent features [24,16]. In general, all 2D image-based methods suffer from several problems, in particular changes in illumination and identity, and rather textureless regions of the face.

With the recent increasing availability of depth-sensing technologies, a few notable works have shown the usefulness of the depth for solving the problem of head pose estimation, either as unique cue [5,10], or in combination with 2D image data [6,20]. Breitenstein et al. [5] developed a real time system capable of handling large head pose variations. Using high quality depth data, the method relies on the assumption that the nose is visible. Real time performance is achieved by using the parallel processing power of a GPU. The approach proposed in [10] also relies on high quality depth data, but uses random regression forests [9] to estimate the head pose, reaching real time performance without the aid of parallel computations on the GPU and without assuming any particular facial feature to be visible. While both [10] and [5] consider the case where the head is the only object present in the field of view, we deal with depth images where other parts of the body might be visible and therefore need to discriminate which image patches belong to the head and which don't.

Random forests [4] and their variants are very popular in computer vision [18,11,9,14,12] for their capability of handling large training sets, fast execution time, and high generalization power. In [18,11], random forests have been combined with the concept of Hough transform for object detection and action recognition. These methods use two objective functions for optimizing the classification and the Hough voting properties of the random forests. While Gall et al. [11] randomly select which measure to optimize at each node of the trees, Okada [18] proposes a joint objective function defined as a weighted sum of the classification and regression measures. In this work, we evaluate several schemes

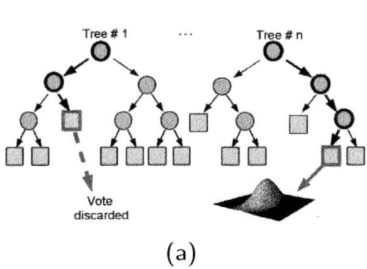 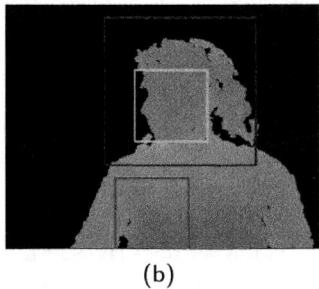

(a)   (b)

Fig. 1. Simple example of Discriminative Regression Forest a): A patch is sent down to two trees, ending up in a non-head leaf in the first case, thus not producing a vote, and in a head leaf in the second case, extracting the multivariate Gaussian distribution stored at the leaf. In b), one training depth image is shown. The blue bounding box enclosing the head specifies where to sample positive (green - inside) and negative patches (red - outside).

for integrating two different objective functions including linear weighting [18] and random selection [11].

3 Discriminative Random Regression Forests for Head Pose Estimation

Decision trees [3] are powerful tools capable of splitting a hard problem into simpler ones, solvable with trivial predictors, and thus achieving highly non-linear mappings. Each node in a tree performs a test, the result of which directs a data sample towards one of the children nodes. The tests at the nodes are chosen in order to cluster the training data as to allow good predictions using simple models. Such models are computed and stored at the leaves, based on the clusters of annotated data which reach them during training.

Forests of randomly trained trees generalize much better and are less sensitive to overfitting than decision trees taken separately [4]. Randomness is introduced in the training process, either in the set of training examples provided to each tree, in the set of tests available for optimization at each node, or in both.

When the task at hand involves both classification and regression, we call Discriminative Random Regression Forests (DRRF) an ensemble of trees which allows to simultaneously separate test data into whether they represent part of the object of interest and, only in the positive cases, vote for the desired real valued variables. A simple DRRF is shown in Figure 1(a): The tests at the nodes lead a sample to a leaf, where it is classified. Only if classified positively, the sample retrieves a Gaussian distribution computed at training time and stored at the leaf, which is used to cast a vote in a multidimensional continuous space.

Our goal is to estimate the 3D position of a head and its orientation from low-quality depth images acquired using a commercial, low-cost sensor. Unlike in [10], the head is not the only part of the person visible in the image, therefore the need to classify image patches before letting them vote for the head pose.

3.1   Training

Assuming a set of depth images is available, together with labels indicating head locations and orientations, we randomly select patches of fixed size from the region of the image containing the head as positives samples, and from outside the head region as negatives. Figure 1(b) shows one of the training images we used (acquisition and annotation is explained in Section 4), with the head region marked in blue, and examples of a positive and negative patch drawn in green, respectively red.

A tree T in the forest $\mathcal{T} = \{T_t\}$ is constructed from the set of patches $\{\mathcal{P}_i = (\mathcal{I}_i, c_i, \boldsymbol{\theta}_i)\}$ sampled from the training images. $\mathcal{I}_i$ are the depth patches and $c_i \in \{0, 1\}$ are the class labels. The vector $\boldsymbol{\theta}_i = \{\theta_x, \theta_y, \theta_z, \theta_{ya}, \theta_{pi}, \theta_{ro}\}$ contains the offset between the 3D point falling on the patch's center and the head center location, and the Euler rotation angles describing the head orientation. As in [10], we define the binary test at a non-leaf node as $t_{F_1, F_2, \tau}(\mathcal{I})$:

$$|F_1|^{-1} \sum_{q \in F_1} I(\boldsymbol{q}) - |F_2|^{-1} \sum_{q \in F_2} I(\boldsymbol{q}) > \tau, \tag{1}$$

where F_1 and F_2 are rectangular, asymmetric regions defined within the patch and τ is a threshold. Such tests can be efficiently evaluated using integral images.

During training, for each non-leaf node starting from the root, we generate a large pool of binary tests $\{t^k\}$ by randomly choosing F_1, F_2, and τ. The test which maximizes a specific optimization function is picked; the data is then split using the selected test and the process iterates until a leaf is created when either the maximum tree depth is reached, or less than a certain number of patches are left. Leaves store two kinds of information: The ratio of positive patches that reached them during training $p(c = 1|\mathcal{P})$ and the multivariate Gaussian distribution computed from the pose parameters of the positive patches.

For the problem at hand, we need trees able to both classify a patch as belonging to a head or not and cast precise votes into the spaces spanned by 3D head locations and orientations. This is the main difference with [10], where the face is assumed to cover most of the image and thus only a regression measure is used. We thus evaluate the goodness of a split using a classification measure $U_C(\{\mathcal{P}|t^k\})$ and a regression measure $U_R(\{\mathcal{P}|t^k\})$: The former tends to separate the patches at each node seeking to maximize the discriminative power of the tree, the latter favors regression accuracy.

Similar to [11], we employ a classification measure which, when maximized, tends to separate the patches so that class uncertainty for a split is minimized:

$$U_C(\{\mathcal{P}|t^k\}) = \frac{|\mathcal{P}_L| \cdot \sum_c p(c|\mathcal{P}_L) ln(p(c|\mathcal{P}_L)) + |\mathcal{P}_R| \cdot \sum_c p(c|\mathcal{P}_R) ln(p(c|\mathcal{P}_R))}{|\mathcal{P}_L| + |\mathcal{P}_R|},$$

$$\tag{2}$$

where $p(c|\mathcal{P})$ is the ratio of patches belonging to class $c \in \{0, 1\}$ in the set $\mathcal{P}$.

For what concerns regression, we use the information gain defined by [9]:

$$U_R\big(\{\mathcal{P}\,|t^k\,\}\big) = H(\mathcal{P}) - (w_L H(\mathcal{P}_L) + w_R H(\mathcal{P}_R)), \tag{3}$$

where $H(\mathcal{P})$ is the differential entropy of the set $\mathcal{P}$ and $w_{i=L,R}$ is the ratio of patches sent to each child node.

Our labels (the vectors $\boldsymbol{\theta}$) are modeled as realizations of a multivariate Gaussian, i.e., $p(\boldsymbol{\theta}|L) = \mathcal{N}(\boldsymbol{\theta}; \overline{\boldsymbol{\theta}}, \boldsymbol{\Sigma})$. Moreover, as in [10], we assume the covariance matrix to be block-diagonal, i.e., we allow covariance only among offset vectors and among head rotation angles, but not between the two. For these reasons, we can rewrite eq. (3) as:

$$U_R\big(\{\mathcal{P}\,|t^k\,\}\big) = \log\left(|\boldsymbol{\Sigma}^v| + |\boldsymbol{\Sigma}^a|\right) - \sum_{i=\{L,R\}} w_i \log\left(|\boldsymbol{\Sigma}_i^v| + |\boldsymbol{\Sigma}_i^a|\right), \tag{4}$$

where $\boldsymbol{\Sigma}^v$ and $\boldsymbol{\Sigma}^a$ are the covariance matrices of the offsets and rotation angles (the two diagonal blocks in $\boldsymbol{\Sigma}$). Maximizing Eq. (4) minimizes the determinants of these covariance matrices, thus decreasing regression uncertainty.

The two measures (2) and (4) can be combined in different ways, and we investigate three different approaches. While the method [11] randomly chooses between classification and regression at each node, the method [18] uses a weighted sum of the two measures, defined as:

$$\arg\max_k \left(U_C + \alpha \max\big(p(c=1|\,\mathcal{P}) - t_p, 0\big) U_R\right). \tag{5}$$

In the above equation, $p(c=1|\,\mathcal{P})$ represents the ratio of positive samples contained in the set, or purity, t_p is an activation threshold, and α a constant weight. When maximizing (5), the optimization is steered by the classification term alone until the purity of positive patches reaches the threshold t_p. From that point on, the regression term starts to play an ever important role.

We propose a third way to combine the two measures by removing the activation threshold from (5) and using as weight an exponential function:

$$\arg\max_k \left(U_C + (1.0 - e^{-\frac{d}{\lambda}})U_R\right), \tag{6}$$

where d is the depth of the node. In this way, the regression measure is given increasingly higher weight as we descend towards the leaves, with the parameter λ specifying the steepness of the change.

3.2   Head Pose Estimation

For estimating the head pose from a depth image, we densely extract patches from the image and pass them through the forest. The tests at the nodes guide each patch all the way to a leaf L, but not all leaves are to be considered for regression; only if $p(c=1|\,\mathcal{P}) = 1$ and $trace\,(\boldsymbol{\Sigma}) < max_v$, with max_v an empirical value for the maximum allowed variance, the Gaussian $p(\boldsymbol{\theta})$ is taken into account. As in [10], a stride in the sampling of the patches can be introduced

Fig. 2. Some head pose estimation results. Starting from the left, two successfull estimations, one failure, and one image with the camera placed on the side, showing the single votes. In particular, the blue, smaller spheres are all votes returned by the forest, while the larger, red spheres are the votes selected for the final estimation.

in order to find the desired compromise between speed and accuracy of the estimate. To be able to handle multiple heads and remove outliers, we perform a bottom-up clustering step: All votes within a certain distance to each other (the average head diameter) are grouped, resulting in big clusters around the heads present in the image. We subsequently run 10 mean shift iterations (using a spherical kernel with a fraction of the average head diameter as radius), in order to better localize the centroid of the clusters. Then, similarly to [9], we select only a percentage of the remaining votes, starting from the ones with smallest uncertainty: if more votes than a threshold are left, we declare a head detected. The Gaussians left at this point are summed, giving us another multivariate Gaussian distribution whose mean is the estimate of the head pose and whose covariance represents its confidence.

Figure 2 shows some processed frames. The green cylinder encodes both the estimated head center and direction of the face. The first two images show success cases, the third one is a failure case, while the last one shows a scan from a side view, revealing the colored votes clustering around the head center. The small blue spheres are all the votes returned by the forest (the means of the Gaussians stored at the leaves reached by the test patches), while the larger, red spheres represent the votes which were selected to produce the final result.

4   Data Acquisition and Labeling

For training and testing our algorithms, we acquired a database of head poses captured with a Kinect sensor. The dataset contains 24 sequences of 20 different people (14 men and 6 women, 4 wearing glasses) recorded while sitting about 1 meter away from the sensor. The subjects were asked to rotate their heads trying to span all possible ranges of angles their head is capable of. Because the depth data needs to be labeled with the 3D head pose of the users for training and evaluation, we processed the data off-line with a template-based head tracker, as illustrated in Fig. 3. To build the template, each user was asked to turn the head left and right starting from the frontal position. The face was detected using [21] and the scans registered and integrated into one 3D point cloud as described by [23]. A 3D morphable model [2] with subsequent graph-based non-rigid ICP [15] was used to adapt a generic face template to the

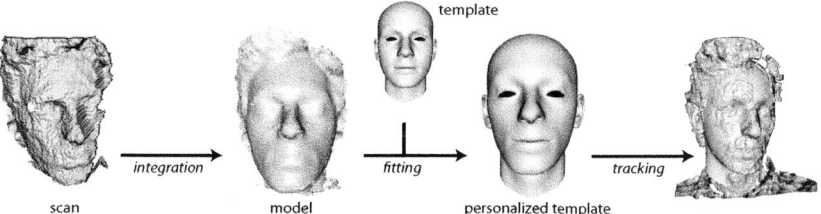

Fig. 3. Automatic pose labeling: A user turns the head in front of the depth sensor, the scans are integrated into a point cloud model and a generic template is fit to it. The personalized template is used for accurate rigid tracking.

point cloud. This resulted in a template representing the shape of the head. Thanks to such personalized template, each subject's sequence of head rotations was tracked using ICP [1], resulting in a pose estimate for each frame. Although this method does not provide perfect estimates of the pose, we found that the mean translation and rotation errors were around 1 mm and 1 degree respectively. Note that the personalized face model is only needed for processing the training data, our head pose estimation system does not assume any initialization phase.

The final database contains roughly 15K frames, annotated with head center locations and rotation angles. The rotations of the heads range between around $\pm 75\,^{\circ}$ for yaw, $\pm 60\,^{\circ}$ for pitch, and $\pm 50\,^{\circ}$ for roll.

5 Experiments

For evaluation, we divided the database into a training and test set of respectively 18 and 2 subjects. In order to compare the weighting schemes described in Section 3.1, we trained each forest using exactly the same patches. We fixed the following parameters: patch size (100x100 pixels), maximum size of the sub-patches F_1 and F_2 (40x40), maximum tree depth (15), minimum number of patches required for a split (20), number of tests generated at each node (20K), and number of positive and negative patches to be extracted from each image (10). Depending on the method used to combine the classification and regression measures, additional parameters might be needed. For the linear weighting approach, we set the α and t_p as suggested by [18], namely to 1.0 and 0.8. In the interleaved setting [11], each measure is chosen with uniform probability, except at the two lowest depth levels of the trees where the regression measure is used. For the exponential weighting function based on the tree depth, we used λ equal to 2, 5, and 10. For testing, we use the following settings: a 5 pixels stride, maximum leaf variance $max_v = 1500$, radius of the spherical kernel for clustering r_c equal to the average head diameter, and mean shift kernel radius $r_{ms} = r_c/6$.

Results are plotted in Fig. 4 and Fig. 5. All experiments were conducted by building 7 trees, each on 3000 sample images. In Fig. 4(a), the accuracy

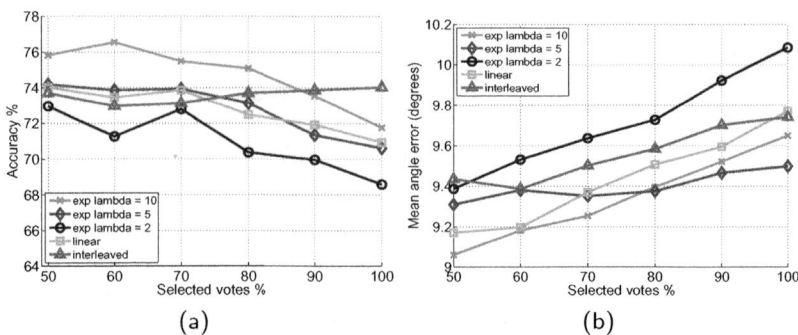

Fig. 4. Accuracy (a) of the tested methods as a function of the percentage of votes selected for each cluster; success is defined when the head estimation error is below 10mm and the thresholds for the direction estimation error is set to 15 degrees. The plots in (b) show the average angle errors again as a function of the percentage of selected votes. It can be noted that the evaluated methods perform rather similarly and the differences are small.

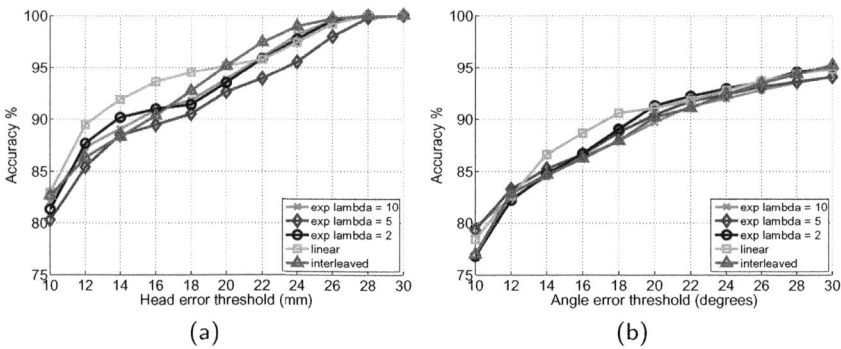

Fig. 5. Accuracy of the head center estimation error (a), respectively of the angle error (b) of the tested methods. The curves are plotted for different values of the threshold defining success. All methods show similar performance.

of all methods changes as function of the percentage of leaves to be retained during the last step of the regression, as explained in Section 3.2. Success means that the detected head center was within 10mm from the ground truth location, and the angle error (L2 norm of the Euler angles) below 10°. All methods appear to behave similarly, but we note a slightly higher accuracy for an exponential weight and a 60% of the votes retained. Fig. 4(b) shows the average angular error of the estimate, again plotted with respect to the percentage of retained votes. Again, the differences between the weighting schemes are very small, as can be seen also in the plots of Figs. 5 (a) and (b), showing the accuracy of the head center estimation error, respectively of the angle error, for different values of the threshold defining success.

Table 1. Mean and standard deviation of the errors for the 3D head localization task and the individual rotation angles as a function of the stride parameter, together with missed detection rates and average processing time. The values are computed by 5-fold cross validation on the entire dataset.

Stride	Head error	Yaw error	Pitch error	Roll error	Missed detections	Time
4	$14.7 \pm 22.5mm$	$9.2 \pm 13.7°$	$8.5 \pm 10.1°$	$8.0 \pm 8.3°$	1.0%	$87.5ms$
6	$14.5 \pm 22.1mm$	$9.1 \pm 13.6°$	$8.5 \pm 9.9°$	$8.0 \pm 8.3°$	1.5%	$24.6ms$
8	$14.1 \pm 20.2mm$	$9.0 \pm 13.2°$	$8.4 \pm 9.6°$	$8.0 \pm 8.3°$	2.1%	$11.8ms$
10	$14.6 \pm 22.3mm$	$8.9 \pm 13.0°$	$8.5 \pm 9.9°$	$7.9 \pm 8.3°$	2.3%	$7.7ms$

As a last experiment, we chose the exponentially decreasing weighting of the measures, defined by Equation (6), with λ set to 5. We then ran a 5-fold cross-validation on the full dataset. We trained 7 trees for each fold, each on 3000 depth images. The results are given in Table 1, where mean and standard deviation of the head localization, yaw, pitch and roll errors are shown together with the percentage of missed detections and the average time necessary to process an image, depending on the stride parameter. It can be noted that the system performs beyond real time already for a stride of 6 (needing only 25ms to process a frame on a 2.67GHz Intel Core i7 CPU), still maintaining a small number of wrong detections and low errors.

6 Conclusions

We presented a system for real time head detection and head pose estimation from low quality depth data captured with a cheap device. We use a discriminative random regression forest, which classifies depth image patches between head and the rest of the body and which performs a regression in the continuous spaces of head positions and orientations. The trees making up the forest are trained in order to jointly optimize their classification and regression power by maximizing two separate measures. Two existing methods were presented for combining such measures and a third weighting scheme was introduced which favors the regression measure as an exponential function of the node depth. In our experiments, we compared the proposed methods and observed similar performances in terms of accuracy. In order to train and test our algorithms, we collected and labelled a new dataset using a Kinect sensor, containing several subjects and large variations in head rotations.

Acknowledgments. The authors acknowledge financial support from the EU projects RADHAR (FP7-ICT-248873) and TANGO (FP7-ICT-249858) and from the SNF project Vision-supported Speech-based Human Machine Interaction (200021-130224).

References

1. Besl, P.J., McKay, N.D.: A method for registration of 3-d shapes. IEEE TPAMI 14(2), 239–256 (1992)
2. Blanz, V., Vetter, T.: A morphable model for the synthesis of 3d faces. In: SIGGRAPH 1999, pp. 187–194 (1999)
3. Breiman, L., Friedman, J., Olshen, R., Stone, C.: Classification and Regression Trees. Wadsworth and Brooks, Monterey (1984)
4. Breiman, L.: Random forests. Machine Learning 45(1), 5–32 (2001)
5. Breitenstein, M.D., Kuettel, D., Weise, T., Van Gool, L., Pfister, H.: Real-time face pose estimation from single range images. In: CVPR, pp. 1–8 (2008)
6. Cai, Q., Gallup, D., Zhang, C., Zhang, Z.: 3d deformable face tracking with a commodity depth camera. In: Daniilidis, K., Maragos, P., Paragios, N. (eds.) ECCV 2010. LNCS, vol. 6316, pp. 229–242. Springer, Heidelberg (2010)
7. Cootes, T.F., Wheeler, G.V., Walker, K.N., Taylor, C.J.: View-based active appearance models. Image and Vision Computing 20(9-10), 657–664 (2002)
8. Cootes, T.F., Edwards, G.J., Taylor, C.J.: Active appearance models. IEEE TPAMI 23, 681–685 (2001)
9. Criminisi, A., Shotton, J., Robertson, D., Konukoglu, E.: Regression forests for efficient anatomy detection and localization in ct studies. In: Recognition Techniques and Applications in Medical Imaging, pp. 106–117 (2010)
10. Fanelli, G., Gall, J., Van Gool, L.: Real time head pose estimation with random regression forests. In: CVPR, pp. 617–624 (2011)
11. Gall, J., Yao, A., Razavi, N., Van Gool, L., Lempitsky, V.: Hough forests for object detection, tracking, and action recognition. IEEE TPAMI (2011)
12. Huang, C., Ding, X., Fang, C.: Head pose estimation based on random forests for multiclass classification. In: Ünay, D., Çataltepe, Z., Aksoy, S. (eds.) ICPR 2010. LNCS, vol. 6388, pp. 934–937. Springer, Heidelberg (2010)
13. Jones, M., Viola, P.: Fast multi-view face detection. Tech. Rep. TR2003-096, Mitsubishi Electric Research Laboratories (2003)
14. Lepetit, V., Fua, P.: Keypoint recognition using randomized trees. IEEE TPAMI 28, 1465–1479 (2006)
15. Li, H., Adams, B., Guibas, L.J., Pauly, M.: Robust single-view geometry and motion reconstruction. ACM Trans. Graph. 28(5) (2009)
16. Matsumoto, Y., Zelinsky, A.: An algorithm for real-time stereo vision implementation of head pose and gaze direction measurement. In: Aut. Face and Gesture Rec., pp. 499–504 (2000)
17. Morency, L.-P., Sundberg, P., Darrell, T.: Pose estimation using 3d view-based eigenspaces. In: Aut. Face and Gesture Rec., pp. 45–52 (2003)
18. Okada, R.: Discriminative generalized hough transform for object dectection. In: ICCV, pp. 2000–2005 (2009)
19. Ramnath, K., Koterba, S., Xiao, J., Hu, C., Matthews, I., Baker, S., Cohn, J., Kanade, T.: Multi-view aam fitting and construction. IJCV 76, 183–204 (2008)
20. Seemann, E., Nickel, K., Stiefelhagen, R.: Head pose estimation using stereo vision for human-robot interaction. Aut. Face and Gesture Rec., pp. 626–631 (2004)
21. Viola, P., Jones, M.: Robust real-time face detection. IJCV 57(2), 137–154 (2004)
22. Weise, T., Leibe, B., Van Gool, L.: Fast 3d scanning with automatic motion compensation. In: CVPR, pp. 1–8 (2007)
23. Weise, T., Wismer, T., Leibe, B., Van Gool, L.: In-hand scanning with online loop closure. In: 3DIM 2009, pp. 1630–1637 (2009)
24. Yang, R., Zhang, Z.: Model-based head pose tracking with stereovision. In: Aut. Face and Gesture Rec., pp. 255–260 (2002)

Putting MAP Back on the Map

Patrick Pletscher[1], Sebastian Nowozin[2],
Pushmeet Kohli[2], and Carsten Rother[2]

[1] ETH Zurich, Switzerland
[2] Microsoft Research Cambridge, UK

Abstract. Conditional Random Fields (CRFs) are popular models in computer vision for solving labeling problems such as image denoising. This paper tackles the rarely addressed but important problem of learning the full form of the potential functions of pairwise CRFs. We examine two popular learning techniques, maximum likelihood estimation and maximum margin training. The main focus of the paper is on models such as pairwise CRFs, that are simplistic (misspecified) and do not fit the data well. We empirically demonstrate that for misspecified models maximum-margin training with MAP prediction is superior to maximum likelihood estimation with any other prediction method. Additionally we examine the common belief that MLE is better at producing predictions matching image statistics.

1 Introduction

Many computer vision tasks can be cast as an image labeling problem. Applications include semantic image segmentation [8], background-foreground segmentation [14] or image denoising [18,16]. Structured models such as Markov Random Fields and Conditional Random Fields have been successfully applied in this context and shown in practice to outperform other methods. These models combine local evidence, dependencies between neighboring pixels and possibly global cues for specifying the probability of a labeling. The usage of a structured model requires *learning* and *inference* (prediction). Learning consists of estimating the parameters of the model (i.e., the potentials) from labeled training data, while inference is the task of predicting a labeling for a given image.

Inference has received a lot of attention in recent years, the dominant approach being maximum-a-posteriori (MAP) inference, for which several efficient and accurate approximate algorithms have been developed [2,6]. On the other hand, learning is still predominantly done by either hand-tuning the parameters or performing a grid-search over a number of settings. This work considers the relation between learning and inference for image labeling using a structured model. Two approaches are discussed here. The classical approach estimates the parameters w of the posterior distribution $P(y|x, w)$ of a label y given an image x using maximum likelihood. It predicts the label according to Bayesian decision theory, which requires the specification of a suitable loss function Δ. Depending on the loss function, different prediction functions are obtained, such

R. Mester and M. Felsberg (Eds.): DAGM 2011, LNCS 6835, pp. 111–121, 2011.

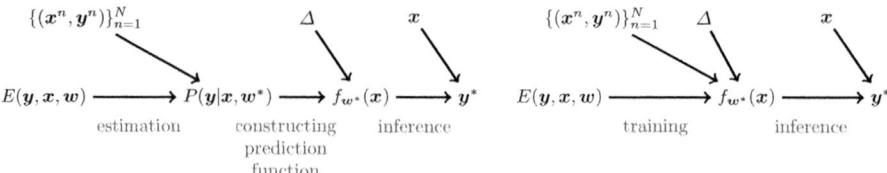

Fig. 1. The two learning and prediction approaches. Left: The classical approach first estimates a posterior $P(\boldsymbol{y}|\boldsymbol{x}, \boldsymbol{w}^*)$ from training data and incorporates the loss Δ at test-time to infer the optimal label. Right: The alternative approach directly trains a classifier for a specific loss and skips the distributional estimation step.

as MAP, maximum marginal or minimum mean squared error (MMSE). Expected risk minimization is the second approach, it directly trains a prediction function which already incorporates the loss. Training and inference in these two paradigms is visualized in Fig. 1. The first approach is known to be superior in the ideal case where the model accurately describes the underlying image acquisition process and sufficient amount of training data is given such that the parameters can be correctly estimated.

The primary contribution of this paper is to show that there exist practical situations in which the direct learning of a prediction function yields better performance. We show that such settings arise when the assumed model does not fully capture the dependencies in the data, a situation referred to as *misspecification* [20]. This is an important insight for computer vision applications since the data generating process is rather complicated and thus often inaccurately modeled. As a second contribution we show that it is possible to learn the full potentials of pairwise structured models even for relatively large state spaces such as in image denoising applications. We conclude that through appropriate training, efficient MAP inference can perform on par with more complex prediction functions such as MMSE. In particular, we also demonstrate that MAP is as good at reproducing image statistics as MMSE. Another goal of this work is to review important facts about prediction and learning for image labeling problems, which we feel are not well-known in the computer vision community.

2   The Image Labeling Problem

Most structured models for image labeling problems can be expressed as an *energy function* of a labeling $\boldsymbol{y}$, an image $\boldsymbol{x}$ and parameters $\boldsymbol{w}$ of the form

$$E(\boldsymbol{y}, \boldsymbol{x}, \boldsymbol{w}) = \sum_{t \in \mathcal{T}} \sum_{c \in \mathcal{C}_t} \psi_\alpha(\boldsymbol{y}_c, \boldsymbol{x}, \boldsymbol{w}^t). \tag{1}$$

The model factorizes into cliques which are assumed to be grouped into sets (templates) t that share the same parameter $\boldsymbol{w}^t$. y_i is assumed to be in the set $\{0, \ldots, K-1\}$, leading to a total of K^M possible labelings. Here M denotes the number of sites for which a label is predicted. The CRF assumes that the posterior of a labeling for an observed image is given by the Gibbs distribution

$$P(\boldsymbol{y}|\boldsymbol{x},\boldsymbol{w}) = \frac{1}{Z(\boldsymbol{x},\boldsymbol{w})}\exp(-E(\boldsymbol{y},\boldsymbol{x},\boldsymbol{w})), \qquad (2)$$

with partition sum $Z(\boldsymbol{x},\boldsymbol{w}) = \sum_{\boldsymbol{y}'}\exp(-E(\boldsymbol{y}',\boldsymbol{x},\boldsymbol{w}))$. In the context of structured models it is usually assumed that the model depends linearly on the parameters [5, Section 4.4.1.2], which we also do here. To make this linear dependence explicit, the energy in (1) is rewritten as $E(\boldsymbol{y},\boldsymbol{x},\boldsymbol{w}) = -\langle\boldsymbol{w},\boldsymbol{s}(\boldsymbol{x},\boldsymbol{y})\rangle$. Here $\boldsymbol{s}(\boldsymbol{x},\boldsymbol{y})$ denotes the sufficient statistics which counts using indicator functions the different configurations of the cliques in (1). We will discuss an example of such a sufficient statistics in more detail in the next section.

2.1   Image Denoising

In this work we discuss as a running example the problem of image denoising. Given an observed noisy image the goal is to reconstruct the original noise-free image. For this task we consider a simple pairwise CRF to illustrate all the concepts. The labeling $\boldsymbol{y}$ in this context is the reconstruction of the original image and $\boldsymbol{x}$ denotes the noisy observation. The energy is assumed to be

$$E(\boldsymbol{y},\boldsymbol{x},\boldsymbol{w}) = -\sum_{i\in\mathcal{V}}w^u_{|y_i-x_i|} - \sum_{(i,j)\in\mathcal{E}}w^p_{|y_i-y_j|}, \qquad (3)$$

where the graph $\mathcal{G} = (\mathcal{V},\mathcal{E})$ is the standard 4-neighborhood grid commonly used in computer vision. The potentials have one parameter for each possible outcome of the unary and pairwise term, respectively. This results in a total of $2K$ parameters. We denote by w^u_j the j-th component of the unary parameter $\boldsymbol{w}^u$ and similarly for $\boldsymbol{w}^p$ the pairwise parameter. For this simple image denoising model the sufficient statistics $\boldsymbol{s}(\boldsymbol{x},\boldsymbol{y}) = [\boldsymbol{s}^u(\boldsymbol{x},\boldsymbol{y})^\mathsf{T},\boldsymbol{s}^p(\boldsymbol{y})^\mathsf{T}]^\mathsf{T}$ are thus given by

$$s^u_k(\boldsymbol{x},\boldsymbol{y}) = \sum_{i\in\mathcal{V}}\delta_k(|x_i-y_i|), \quad s^p_k(\boldsymbol{y}) = \sum_{(i,j)\in\mathcal{E}}\delta_k(|y_i-y_j|).$$

Here $\delta_k(z)$ denotes the Kronecker delta function which evaluates to one if $z = k$ and to zero otherwise. For image denoising the state space of the variables y_i is typically quite large, for example $K = 256$ for a grayscale image.

2.2   Learning and Prediction

Most image labeling applications come with some form of labeled training data on which a parameter $\boldsymbol{w}^*$ is learned according to some objective. We will discuss maximum margin learning and maximum likelihood estimation. Having determined $\boldsymbol{w}^*$, the inference task considers predicting the optimal labeling $\boldsymbol{y}^*$ for an observed image. There exist several approaches for this, which we will discuss in § 4. The most popular prediction function is the MAP inference which can be understood as maximizing the posterior distribution in a CRF

$$\boldsymbol{y}^* = \operatorname*{argmin}_{\boldsymbol{y}} E(\boldsymbol{y},\boldsymbol{x},\boldsymbol{w}^*) = \operatorname*{argmax}_{\boldsymbol{y}}\langle\boldsymbol{w}^*,\boldsymbol{s}(\boldsymbol{x},\boldsymbol{y})\rangle.$$

Its popularity stems from the fact that efficient MAP inference algorithms such as graph-cut or TRW-S exist. Strictly speaking, the MAP interpretation of a labeling having minimal energy is only valid if the associated Gibbs distribution leads to reasonable posterior estimates, i.e., the parameter is estimated with the distributional aspect in mind. Here we use MAP to refer to finding the minimum energy labeling regardless of whether (2) accurately describes the posterior.

3   Related Work

Early work on learning the potentials for low-level vision from data dates back to the mid '90s [22]. With the advance of structured models in machine learning, more sophisticated techniques for estimating the parameters have also evolved in computer vision. [7] trains a CRF for the tasks of binary image denoising and the detection of man-made structures. More recently, principled discriminative training has gained popularity in high-level vision applications, such as semantic segmentation [11] and object recognition [4]. In the context of low-level vision problems, learning has been done in stereo vision [17] and image denoising. In denoising, the application considered in our work, the Fields-of-Experts (FoEs) model [13] is a popular continuous, generative model with higher-order factors (e.g., of size 3×3). In the original work, Roth and Black train the model using contrastive divergence, an approximate maximum likelihood learning approach, and finally perform MAP inference at test time. Better results can be obtained [16] by a training approach tailored towards the MAP prediction. Finally, [18] demonstrates improved accuracy when using contrastive divergence learning and MMSE instead of MAP inference. They find that their predictions better match the image statistics observed in natural images.

Our work sheds some light on these findings [18] and shows that MAP, while inferior to MMSE in theory for an ideal setting, in practice can still outperform MMSE. This is attributed to the fact that models are often misspecified and approximate maximum likelihood approaches, such as maximum pseudo-likelihood, lead to inaccurate parameter estimates. Experiments are shown for the pairwise model in § 2.1 which differs in several aspects to the FoE model. First, unlike the FoE model, it is a discrete model. This allows us to learn the full shape of the potential without any prior assumptions on the form. In contrast, such assumptions are needed in the FoE model as it is a continuous model whose potentials are functions parametrized by a small set of shape parameters. Second, maximum likelihood and maximum margin training for our model is convex, this is not the case for the FoE due to modeling assumptions. The convexity has the advantage that our learning approach does not get stuck in local minima.

4   Optimal Prediction

Assuming that one is given the true posterior $P(\boldsymbol{y}|\boldsymbol{x})$ (note in particular that we distinguish this from a model posterior $P(\boldsymbol{y}|\boldsymbol{x}, \boldsymbol{w}^*)$) we now consider the prediction task. In this context the loss $\Delta(\boldsymbol{y}', \boldsymbol{y})$ specifies the error/loss incurred when predicting the label $\boldsymbol{y}'$ if $\boldsymbol{y}$ would be the true label. The loss is application dependent and can be thought of as the error measure used in many computer vision benchmarks: For semantic image segmentation this might be given by the pixelwise accuracy, whereas for image denoising the pixelwise squared distance of prediction and ground-truth might be used. According to Bayesian decision theory [12, Theorem 2.3.2] the optimal prediction minimizes the expected risk:

$$\boldsymbol{y}^* = \operatorname*{argmin}_{\boldsymbol{y}'} \mathbb{E}_{P(\boldsymbol{y}|\boldsymbol{x})}[\Delta(\boldsymbol{y}', \boldsymbol{y})] = \operatorname*{argmin}_{\boldsymbol{y}'} \sum_{\boldsymbol{y}} \Delta(\boldsymbol{y}', \boldsymbol{y}) P(\boldsymbol{y}|\boldsymbol{x}). \qquad (4)$$

Next, we relate several prediction functions to their implied loss function. The loss is assumed to be non-negative and zero for the ground-truth labeling.

Zero-one error. The zero-one error is given by $\Delta(\boldsymbol{y}', \boldsymbol{y}) = 1 - \delta_{\boldsymbol{y}}(\boldsymbol{y}')$. Here we extend the Kronecker delta function to several variables. This loss treats all labels $\boldsymbol{y}'$ with $\boldsymbol{y}' \neq \boldsymbol{y}$ in the same way by assigning a loss of one to them. A labeling of an image with only one pixel different from the ground-truth is assigned the same loss as a label that is different in every pixel. If the zero-one loss is used in (4), then one identifies the MAP prediction rule $\boldsymbol{y}^* = \operatorname{argmax}_{\boldsymbol{y}} P(\boldsymbol{y}|\boldsymbol{x})$. As most evaluation metrics are not as aggressive as the zero-one error discussed here, it is clear that this is not the best loss term for most labeling tasks.

Mean pixel-wise error. The mean pixelwise error is given by $\Delta(\boldsymbol{y}', \boldsymbol{y}) = \frac{1}{|\mathcal{V}|} \sum_{i \in \mathcal{V}} (1 - \delta_{y_i}(y_i'))$. When inserting this loss into the Bayes predictor we end up with the max-marginal prediction rule $y_i^* = \operatorname{argmax}_{y_i} P(y_i|\boldsymbol{x}) \ \forall i \in \mathcal{V}$. Here $P(y_i|\boldsymbol{x})$ denotes the marginal for the i-th pixel.

Mean squared error. The mean squared error (MSE) $\Delta(\boldsymbol{y}', \boldsymbol{y}) = \frac{1}{\mathcal{V}} \sum_{i \in \mathcal{V}} (y_i - y_i')^2$ is a sensible choice if there exists an order on the labels, as for example in image denoising. Optimal prediction is achieved by $y_i^* = \mathbb{E}_{P(y_i|\boldsymbol{x})}[y_i] \ \forall i \in \mathcal{V}$. Thus, taking the mean of the individual variable posterior distribution minimizes the mean squared error. This predictor is referred to as minimum mean squared error (MMSE). For discrete variables one can round the expectation.

The underlying assumption in this section was that the true posterior distribution $P(\boldsymbol{y}|\boldsymbol{x})$ is known. In practice this posterior is modeled by the CRF distribution $P(\boldsymbol{y}|\boldsymbol{x}, \boldsymbol{w}^*)$ which in many scenarios in computer vision does not accurately model the true posterior. There might exist several reasons for this: First, not enough data might be available to estimate all the parameters accurately. Second, an improper estimation technique could be used for $\boldsymbol{w}^*$. Third, the model might not model all the dependencies in the data. As we will show, if a model posterior distribution $P(\boldsymbol{y}|\boldsymbol{x}, \boldsymbol{w}^*)$ does not match the true $P(\boldsymbol{y}|\boldsymbol{x})$, optimality of the schemes above is no longer guaranteed.

5   Learning

In this section we consider learning the optimal parameters $\boldsymbol{w}^*$ of a structured model for a given training set $\mathcal{D} = \{(\boldsymbol{x}^n, \boldsymbol{y}^n)\}_{n=1}^N$. We focus on maximum likelihood estimation (MLE) and maximum margin (MM) learning. As MLE is generally intractable we also consider the maximum pseudo-likelihood.

5.1 Maximum Likelihood and Maximum Pseudo-likelihood

MLE of the parameters for a given training set corresponds to finding the parameter with the largest likelihood given the observed data. To prevent overfitting, an L_2 regularizer is often included:

$$\boldsymbol{w}^{mle} = \operatorname*{argmin}_{\boldsymbol{w}} -\frac{1}{N}\sum_{n=1}^{N} \log P(\boldsymbol{y}^n|\boldsymbol{x}^n,\boldsymbol{w}) + \frac{\lambda}{2}\|\boldsymbol{w}\|^2. \tag{5}$$

In general, no closed form solution for the convex MLE objective exists and thus iterative methods are employed. To evaluate the function value and the gradient, the partition sum and the marginals need to be computed. For loopy graphs these computations are generally intractable and one resorts to approximations. A tractable alternative is given by the maximum pseudo-likelihood estimate [1] (MPLE) which replaces $\log P(\boldsymbol{y}^n|\boldsymbol{x}^n,\boldsymbol{w})$ by $\sum_{i\in\mathcal{V}}\log P(y_i^n|\boldsymbol{y}_{\mathcal{N}(i)}^n,\boldsymbol{x}^n,\boldsymbol{w})$. Here $\mathcal{N}(i)$ denotes the Markov blanket of a variable i and $\boldsymbol{y}_{\mathcal{N}(i)}$ all the variables in the Markov blanket. Conditioning on the ground-truth label of the neighboring variables makes the partition sum collapse to a sum over the different states of variable y_i, which has linear complexity. Interestingly, the MPLE has the desirable property that for enough data it converges to the MLE.

5.2 Maximum Margin

Instead of taking the detour of first estimating a posterior and subsequently constructing a predictor by incorporating a loss, one can directly train a linear predictor $f_{\boldsymbol{w}}(\boldsymbol{x}) = \operatorname{argmax}_{\boldsymbol{y}}\langle\boldsymbol{w},\boldsymbol{s}(\boldsymbol{x},\boldsymbol{y})\rangle$. This predictor can be trained using a particular loss function $\Delta(\boldsymbol{y}',\boldsymbol{y})$. Max-margin training (or equivalently the structured SVM) [19] considers the following training objective

$$\boldsymbol{w}^{mm} = \operatorname*{argmin}_{\boldsymbol{w}} \frac{\lambda}{2}\|\boldsymbol{w}\|^2 + \frac{1}{N}\sum_{n=1}^{N}\max_{\boldsymbol{y}'}\left[\langle\boldsymbol{w},\boldsymbol{s}(\boldsymbol{x}^n,\boldsymbol{y}')-\boldsymbol{s}(\boldsymbol{x}^n,\boldsymbol{y}^n)\rangle+\Delta(\boldsymbol{y}',\boldsymbol{y}^n)\right]. \tag{6}$$

For computer vision max-margin training has several advantages when compared to MLE. First, inference reduces to a standard MAP problem, and thus neither marginals nor the partition sum need to be computed. Second, it directly incorporates a loss in training and is expected to work well for this particular loss, even if the model is not expressive enough. However, for the ideal setting, the Bayes predictor in (4) is superior to MAP trained using max-margin, as it is more expressive. Most training algorithms for max-margin work by successively generating maximally violated constraints and repetitively solving the quadratic programming problem in (6). Generation of the constraints reduces to the MAP problem for the loss augmented model which incorporates the loss $\Delta(\boldsymbol{y}',\boldsymbol{y}^n)$.

5.3   Insights on Statistic Matching

It is widely known that the image statistics of natural images have a heavy tailed distribution [15]. This is conjectured to be an important property that most computer vision systems still fail to model. The image statistic of an image is obtained by applying linear filters to the image and building histograms of the resulting responses. For a pairwise gradient filter the histogram obtained is equivalent to the sufficient statistics $s^p(y)$ of our pairwise image denoising model. For the task of image

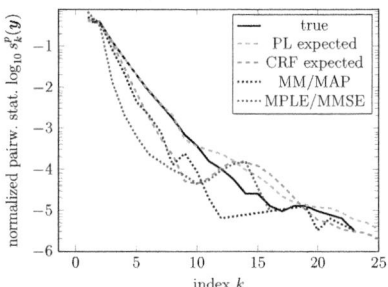

Fig. 2. Pairwise image statistics on logarithmic scale, see text for remarks

denoising, [18] observes that the MAP prediction of the FoE model trained using maximum likelihood, exhibit poor image statistics. The authors propose MMSE prediction as an alternative resulting in better image statistics. The discussion in § 4 shows that the *superior performance of MMSE can be explained by the loss being more suitable for the image denoising task.* The improved image statistics come only as a byproduct. MMSE in itself is not better at reproducing natural image statistics. If predictions should explicitly show the heavy tails observed in natural image statistics, then this property has to be either included in the model as in [21], or in the prediction function using an appropriate loss. If no regularization is included in the objective in (5) then MLE can be understood as matching the empirical distribution in training by the expected sufficient statistics under the model distribution $P(y|x^n, w^{mle})$:

$$\frac{1}{N}\sum_{n=1}^{N} \mathbb{E}_{P(y|x^n, w^{mle})}[s(x^n, y)] = \frac{1}{N}\sum_{n=1}^{N} s(x^n, y^n).$$

This follows from the derivative of (5). A similar expectation matching is identified for MPLE. However, this *does not guarantee that the sufficient statistics of the predicted labelings also match the observed training image statistics.* This behaviour is demonstrated in Fig. 2 for the image denoising application described in more detail in § 6.2. Here we train on one image (32 gray levels) and predict a labeling for the same image. The expected statistics using the simplified model assumed by pseudo-likelihood $P(y|y^1, x^1, w^{mple}) = \prod_i P(y_i|y^1_{\mathcal{N}_i}, x^1, w^{mple})$ (shown as 'PL expected'), are very close to the ground truth statistics (shown as 'true'). Smaller inaccuries are due to sampling. The expected statistics of the CRF model $P(y|x^1, w^{mple})$ (shown as 'CRF expected'), would coincide with the true statistics if exact MLE could be performed. This also illustrates the deficiencies of the pseudo-likelihood approximation for a small dataset. Neither the labeling predicted by MAP trained using max-margin (shown as 'MM/MAP'), nor the labeling predicted by MMSE learned using maximum likelihood (shown as 'MPLE/MMSE'), agree with the true statistics. Expected statistics are obtained using Gibbs sampling of labelings y and averaging $s(x^1, y)$ over the sampled y.

6   Experiments

In this section we demonstrate the practical implications of the concepts discussed for the simple pairwise CRF model in § 2.1.

6.1   Synthetic Data

Here we study the properties of maximum pseudo-likelihood estimation and max-margin learning on synthetic data. The synthetic nature of the dataset allows us to study the consistency property of the MPLE for large datasets. In this experiment we add structured noise to the labels to simulate a case where the model is misspecified, i.e., the relation-

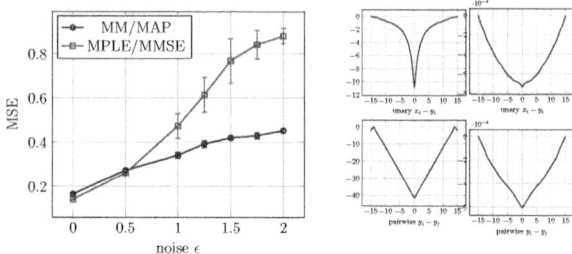

Fig. 3. Results of the synthetic experiment. Left: for increasing levels of misspecification MPLE trained MMSE becomes worse than max-margin trained MAP. Right: Learned potentials for $\epsilon = 2$ (MPLE left, MM right, unary top, pairwise bottom).

ship between x and y cannot be captured by the assumed posterior $P(y|x, w)$. The dataset $\mathcal{D} = \{(x^n, y^n)\}_{n=1}^N$ is generated as follows: For a given image x^n, a label y^n is sampled according to $y^n \sim P(y|x^n, w^{true})$ using a Gibbs sampler. The image x^n itself is generated by adding i.i.d. noise to a fixed image x^0 and rounding the values to integers within the domain $\{0, \ldots, K - 1\}$, here for $K = 16$. For the weights w^{true} we assume $w^{true,u} = -K/[1, 2, \ldots, K]^\mathsf{T}$ and $w^{true,p} = -3 \cdot [0, 2, \ldots, K - 1]^\mathsf{T}$. To study the influence of misspecification the labels are perturbed. This is an important scenario to study, as most computer vision models are still far from accurately describing the real world situation. Having a parameter estimation and prediction approach that is robust to misspecification is thus important in practice. To simulate the misspecification, the labels y^n are not sampled from the model in (3), but rather from a model which also includes a 4-neighborhood dependency to the pixel two pixels away (left, right, up, down). The weights of these interactions are chosen to be $w^{true,p,long} = -3\epsilon \cdot [0, 1, \ldots, K - 1]^\mathsf{T}$. Parameter estimation is done using the dataset $\mathcal{D}_\epsilon = \{(x^n, y^n)\}_{n=1}^N$ for the model in (3). As ϵ is increased, the model does not match the true data generating posterior anymore. To evaluate the methods we learn a parameter and report the MSE of predictions on held out test data. The results are averaged over five datasets. As we are primarily interested in the sensitivity of the estimation techniques to model misspecification, a relatively large training set of size $N = 500$ is used. In Fig. 3 the MSE of the different methods is shown.

The max-margin learning combined with MAP prediction leads to smaller MSE values than MPLE based learning with MMSE. This is in agreement with our intuition: max-margin learning directly considers the prediction function and should therefore be more robust to misspecifications. In the non-misspecified setting likelihood based learning combined with MMSE inference performed better. While the experiment was carried out using pseudo-likelihood, we conjecture that the same problem is also present in maximum likelihood estimation as we also performed an experiment that showed that MPLE converged for $\epsilon = 0$.

6.2   Image Denoising

We consider the real world task of image denoising, an active field of research. The state of the art methods can broadly be grouped into modifications of the Fields-of-Experts framework [18,16,13] and sparse coding approaches [9,3]. The image denoising experiment was performed on the images from the Berkeley image segmentation dataset [10]. The same train/test set split as in [18] was used. The images are reduced to grayscale values and i.i.d. Gaussian noise with $\sigma = 25$ is added. The resulting pixel values are rounded to integers in $\{0, \ldots, 255\}$. Furthermore, the image and the noisy version thereof are further discretized to 64 labels to obtain the label y and the input image x.

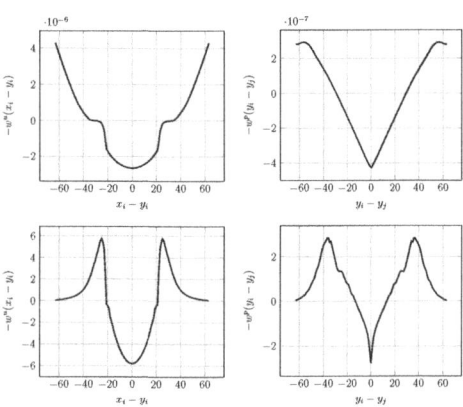

Fig. 4. Learned unary (left) and pairwise (right) potentials. Top: result for max-margin learning. Bottom: weights estimated by maximum pseudo-likelihood.

Maximum margin and MPLE training are performed on the 40 training examples. The resulting learned weights are shown in Fig. 4. We trained on the full images as opposed to only on smaller subpatches, as it is often done for contrastive divergence. We observe that the learned weights for the MM learning are much smaller. The pairwise potential is almost linear and the unary potential has a roughly quadratic shape with truncation areas. The potentials trained by MPLE differ substantially and show a much more varying shape.

As it is standard for image denoising problems we use the peak signal-to-noise ratio (PSNR) for comparison of the different methods. The test set consisted of 68 images. Comparing the results of the different approaches in Table 1, we see that max-margin training combined with MAP prediction leads to a lower MSE and PSNR than maximum pseudo-likelihood estimation followed by MMSE prediction. For comparison we also show

Table 1. Image denoising test results of the different methods. For MSE smaller is better, for PSNR higher is better.

method	standard model		with BM3D	
	MSE	PSNR	MSE	PSNR
MM/MAP	**8.65**	**27.05**	**6.86**	**28.23**
MPLE/MAP	17.42	24.30	13.31	25.5
MPLE/MMSE	10.04	26.65	8.47	27.54
BM3D only	-	-	6.95	28.19

noisy image,20.29dB   original image   MM/MAP,26.03dB   MPLE/MMSE,25.44dB   MPLE/MAP,23.11dB

Fig. 5. MAP can outperform MMSE if trained with maximum margin. In the (cropped) image above we observe that MM/MAP better preserves the fine structure on the rock. MAP prediction with the MPLE estimate leads to substantially worse results.

the results obtained using the BM3D algorithm [3], considered state-of-the-art. For BM3D we used the full 256 level grayscale images and discretized the result to 64 levels. We also trained our pairwise model with BM3D predictions as a secondary unary feature. The MAP labeling obtained using MM training result in a small improvement over BM3D.

Unlike in the synthetic experiment, we can not give a final conclusion on why MMSE performs worse: it could be either the inaccurate approximation made by pseudo-likelihood or as the model is simplistic, that misspecification becomes a problem as in the synthetic experiment. However, the image denoising experiment shows that in practice if trained appropriately, MAP can lead to accurate predictions on par with MMSE. *Unless the full image zero-one loss is desired as an evaluation criteria, MAP should not be used in combination with maximum likelihood learning.* We

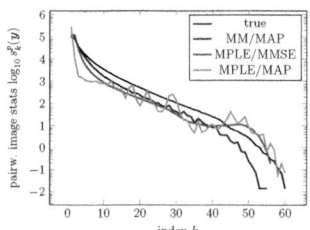

Fig. 6. Aggregated pairwise image statistics on the test images. MPLE/MMSE and MM/MAP result in similar statistics.

visualize the test set image statistics in Fig. 6. One observes that for the pairwise statistics the MM/MAP predictions show a very similar behavior as the MPLE/MMSE solutions. MM/MAP seems to be a bit closer to the true image statistics for the more often occurring configurations. An example of the predictions is shown in Fig. 5.

7   Conclusions

This paper gives a general review of learning and inference for structured models. For image denoising we found that if appropriately trained, MAP is competitive with MMSE, the optimal prediction in theory. We explain this by misspecifications of the model and the approximations needed in order for maximum likelihood learning to become tractable. MAP, with many efficient inference algorithms readily available, is therefore back on the road map of computer vision. Our investigations also show that there exist scenarios where MMSE can outperform MAP. As models become more accurate, these differences might get more pronounced in the future. However, we suspect that better approximate maximum likelihood approaches are needed for MMSE to substantially outperform MAP in practice.

Acknowledgments. PP was supported in parts by the Swiss National Science Foundation (SNF) under grant number 200021-117946.

References

1. Besag, J.: Statistical analysis of non-lattice data. The Statistician (1975)
2. Boykov, Y.: Fast approximate energy minimization via graph cuts. PAMI (2001)
3. Dabov, K., Foi, A., Katkovnik, V., Egiazarian, K.: Image denoising by sparse 3-D transform-domain collaborative filtering. IEEE TIP 16(8), 2080–2095 (2007)
4. Felzenszwalb, P.F., Girshick, R.B., McAllester, D., Ramanan, D.: Object detection with discriminatively trained part-based models. PAMI 32(9), 1627–1645 (2010)
5. Koller, D., Friedman, N.: Probabilistic Graphical Models. MIT Press, Cambridge (2009)
6. Kolmogorov, V.: Convergent tree-reweighted message passing for energy minimization. PAMI 28(10) (2006)
7. Kumar, S., Hebert, M.: Discriminative Random Fields. IJCV 68(2), 179–201 (2006)
8. Ladicky, L., Russell, C., Kohli, P., Torr, P.H.S.: Associative hierarchical CRFs for object class image segmentation. In: ICCV 2009 (2009)
9. Mairal, J., Bach, F., Ponce, J., Sapiro, G.: Online Learning for Matrix Factorization and Sparse Coding. JMLR 11, 19–60 (2010)
10. Martin, D., Fowlkes, C., Tal, D., Malik, J.: A database of human segmented natural images. In: ICCV 2001 (2001)
11. Nowozin, S., Gehler, P.V., Lampert, C.H.: On parameter learning in CRF-based approaches to object class image segmentation. In: Daniilidis, K., Maragos, P., Paragios, N. (eds.) ECCV 2010. LNCS, vol. 6316, pp. 98–111. Springer, Heidelberg (2010)
12. Robert, C.P.: The Bayesian Choice. From decision Theoretic Foundations to Computational Implementation. Springer, Heidelberg (2001)
13. Roth, S., Black, M.J.: Fields of Experts. IJCV (2008)
14. Rother, C., Kolomogorov, V., Blake, A.: GrabCut Interactive Foreground Extraction using Iterated Graph Cuts. TOG 23(3), 309–314 (2004)
15. Ruderman, D.: The statistics of natural images. Comp. in Neural Systems (1994)
16. Samuel, K.G.G., Tappen, M.F.: Learning Optimized MAP Estimates in Continuously-Valued MRF Models. In: CVPR 2009 (2009)
17. Scharstein, D.: Learning Conditional Random Fields for Stereo. In: CVPR 2007 (2007)
18. Schmidt, U., Gao, Q., Roth, S.: A Generative Perspective on MRFs in Low-Level Vision. In: CVPR 2010 (2010)
19. Taskar, Guestrin, Koller: Max-Margin Markov Networks. In: NIPS 2003 (2003)
20. White, H.: Maximum-likelihood estimation of misspecified models. Econom. (1982)
21. Woodford, O.J., Rother, C., Kolmogorov, V.: A Global Perspective on MAP Inference for Low-Level Vision. In: ICCV 2009 (2009)
22. Zhu, S., Mumford, D.: Prior learning and Gibbs reaction-diffusion. In: PAMI 1997 (1997)

Pose-Consistent 3D Shape Segmentation Based on a Quantum Mechanical Feature Descriptor

Mathieu Aubry[1,2], Ulrich Schlickewei[1], and Daniel Cremers[1]

[1] Department of Computer Science, TU München
[2] Adobe Systems Inc., Cambridge, MA

Abstract. We propose a novel method for pose-consistent segmentation of non-rigid $3D$ shapes into visually meaningful parts. The key idea is to study the shape in the framework of quantum mechanics and to group points on the surface which have similar probability of presence for quantum mechanical particles. For each point on an object's surface these probabilities are encoded by a feature vector, the Wave Kernel Signature (WKS). Mathematically, the WKS is an expression in the eigenfunctions of the Laplace–Beltrami operator of the surface. It characterizes the relation of surface points to the remaining surface at various spatial scales. Gaussian mixture clustering in the feature space spanned by the WKS signature for shapes in several poses leads to a grouping of surface points into different and meaningful segments. This enables us to perform consistent and robust segmentation of new versions of the shape.

Experimental results demonstrate that the detected subdivision agrees with the human notion of shape decomposition (separating hands, arms, legs and head from the torso for example). We show that the method is robust to data perturbed by various kinds of noise. Finally we illustrate the usefulness of a pose-consistent segmentation for the purpose of shape retrieval.

1 Introduction

Research in cognitive science suggests that human shape understanding is based on a decomposition of the shape in smaller parts [7]. Inspired by this insight, many algorithms in three-dimensional shape analysis rely on a segmentation of the objects' surface in meaningful parts.

Such a segmentation can be the building block of shape retrieval techniques where an object is recognized as the sum of its parts [23,24,12]. Other interesting applications include CAD, reverse engineering and medical image analysis [1], texture mapping [10] and texture superresolution [6].

In this work we propose a method for automatically determining visually meaningful, pose-consistent segmentations of non-rigid $3D$ shapes. Our approach builds upon a quantum mechanical feature descriptor and upon Gaussian mixture clustering in the feature space over several articulations of a shape.

R. Mester and M. Felsberg (Eds.): DAGM 2011, LNCS 6835, pp. 122–131, 2011.

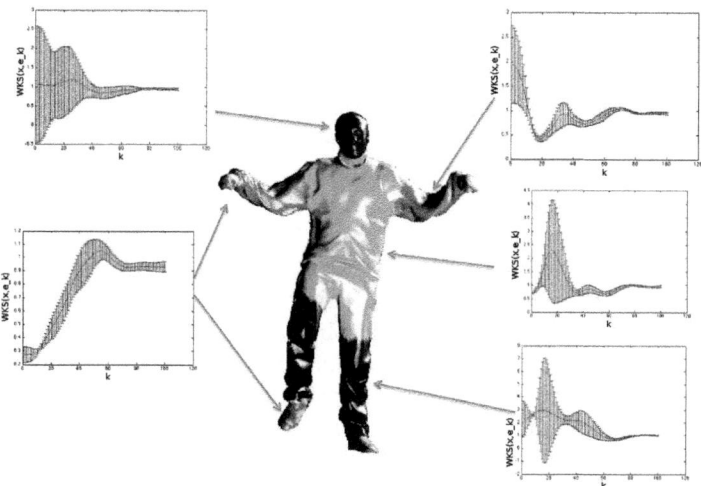

Fig. 1. The basic idea of our segmentation is to group those points in which quantum particles of different energy levels have similar probabilities to be measured. The clustering is achieved with an Expectation-Maximization using a Gaussian mixture distribution. Thus, any cluster is described by a mean descriptor and its variance.

1.1 Related Work

Shape segmentation is a classical problem in shape analysis. For recent surveys on existing methods we refer the reader to [17,1,3].

The problem of *pose-consistent segmentation of shapes* has only recently become to the focus of researchers. The task consists in extracting a meaningful partitioning of a shape which identifies the segments consistently over several poses of the shape.

Following the intuition that meaningful shape parts should be rigid, some approaches cluster points whose movement through the different poses is approximately described by the same Euclidean motion. The works [2,8,16] fall in this category. Of course, these methods depend on a precomputed correspondence between the articulated shapes which is computationally a very demanding problem.

Other methods employ local feature descriptors and group points with similar signatures. In [24], Toldo et al. cluster convex regions of similar curvature using normalized graph cuts. This approach is inspired by the minima rule in cognitive science. Because the principal curvatures are not isometry-invariant, pose-consistency is not theoretically granted. Indeed, typically the intrinsic distances on a shape do not change significantly from one pose to another, which make isometric deformations a good mathematical model for shape articulations. Shapira et al. [18] use the Shape Diameter Function (SDF) for clustering. The SDF measures at each point the diameter of the shape in inward-normal direction and therefore captures volumetric information on the shape's surface. Again, the SDF is not isometry-invariant whence the segmentation results are not guaranteed to be pose-invariant.

A class of very powerful, isometry-invariant tools for shape analysis rely on the study of the spectrum of the Laplace–Beltrami operator. Our approach belongs to this class. In the geometry processing community, these ideas first appeared in the work [9] of Lévy. Rustamov [15] introduced the Global Point Signature which encodes all local and global information about a point on the shape's surface. Very nice shape segmentation results where shown as an application. However, because the signs and the ordering of the Laplace eigenfunctions can flip from one articulation to another, it is not easy to identify segments over different poses. Reuter [14] proposed a watershed-based segmentation employing a single, user-selected Laplace eigenfunction. Robustness is ensured by persistence-based denoising of the basins. In order to identify labels over different poses, Reuter proposes to align the eigenfunctions of different shapes by comparing persistence diagrams. In [19], Sharma et al. use a constrained spectral clustering approach to segment a single deformable shape. The constraints enforce certain pairs of points to belong to the same segment or to belong to different segments and are given by user input. Label transfer to different shape poses is achieved by registering the shapes. Again, this step involves reordering and sign-flipping of the Laplace eigenfunctions.

To overcome the sign and ordering problem, Sun et al. [22] introduced a very nice, physically motivated feature descriptor, the Heat Kernel Signature (HKS) which encodes the heat dissipation process on the surface. They showed that the HKS contains all information to characterize points uniquely. While the HKS proved to be the current state-of-the-art feature descriptor [5], it has several draw-backs. First of all, the natural parametrization domain for the HKS is time which does not have an intrinsic meaning for a shape. Secondly, due to the exponential decay in diffusion processes, the HKS mixes local and global scales in an intransparent way. In contrast to this, our quantum mechanical feature descriptor, the WKS, is parametrized on the energy domain which has by means of eigenenergies an intrinsic interpretation for a shape. Furthermore, different scales are clearly separated by the WKS.

A persistence-based segmentation technique using the HKS was presented by Skraba et al. [20]. Similarly to Reuter's work, this method is based upon the watershed approach using the HKS function for a user-fixed value of the time t. This value determines whether more local or global features should guide the segmentation.

1.2   Contribution

In this work we present a novel approach for automatically finding pose-consistent segmentations of $3D$ shapes. Our work builds upon a quantum mechanical feature descriptor, the Wave Kernel Signature (WKS). A segmentation is computed in two steps: In a learning step we use several different poses of a shape to build clusters of points for which the probability to find quantum mechanical particles at different energy levels is similar. In the segmentation step, new poses of the shape are partitioned by sorting each point in the most likely cluster. The main contributions can be summarized as follows.

– We show how to incorporate the framework of Quantum Mechanics to pose-consistent shape segmentation. By grouping points in which particles over different energy levels have similar probabilities to be measured, we exploit global as well as local shape information in the segmentation process.
– Our method inherently guarantees consistent transfer of labels to different shape poses, without the need of computationally expensive shape registrations.
– Relying on a clustering in the feature space, our method is easily implemented and fully automatic.

Experimental results show that our segmentation results agree with the human intuition, that labels are consistently carried over to new poses and that our method can cope with perturbed data. Finally, we illustrate the usefulness of meaningful shape decompositions with an experiment on shape retrieval.

2   The Wave Kernel Signature – A Quantum Mechanical Feature Descriptor

In this section we describe a quantum mechanical feature descriptor, the WKS, which assigns with each point on an object's surface a vector in $\mathbb{R}^M$. This vector encodes the probability to measure particles of different energy levels in the point. After a brief review of the dynamics of quantum particles on surfaces in 2.1, we give the definition of WKS in 2.2. In 2.3 we outline why WKS is useful for shape analysis, and in particular why it is more convenient than the previously defined HKS. For a more detailed study of the WKS we refer the reader to [4].

2.1   Quantum Particles on Surfaces

A quantum mechanical particle moving on a closed, differentiable surface $X \subset \mathbb{R}^3$ is completely described by its wave function $\psi(x,t) : X \times \mathbb{R}_{>0} \to \mathbb{C}$. This function solves Schrödinger's equation

$$i\frac{\partial \psi}{\partial t}(x,t) = -\Delta_X \psi(x,t), \tag{1}$$

where Δ_X is the Laplace–Beltrami operator of X. While the wave function itself does not have an easy intuitive explanation, for fixed $t > 0$ its squared norm $|\psi(x,t)|^2 : X \to \mathbb{R}$ is the probability density function of the position of the particle at time t.

We now focus on the following physical experiment: Consider a quantum particle on X. Assume that we measure approximately at time $t = 0$ the energy E of this particle and that subsequently we want to determine its position at time $t > 0$. Since we did only an approximate measurement, the state of the particle is a superposition of eigenstates. Mathematically, the eigenstates and eigenenergies are given by the orthonormal eigenfunctions $\phi_0, \phi_1, \phi_2, \ldots$ and by the corresponding eigenvalues $0 = E_0 > -E_1 \geq -E_2 \geq \ldots$ of the Laplace–Beltrami operator Δ_X. We call $f_E^2(E_k)$ the probability of our particle to be in the state corresponding to E_k. Assume now that the eigenvalues E_k are pairwise distinct which is the case with probability 1. For our particle with energy distribution f_E^2 (hence allowing for uncertainty in the energy), its wave function is given by

$$\psi_E(x,t) = \sum_{k \geq 0} f_E(E_k) \exp\left(-iE_k t\right) \phi_k(x). \qquad (2)$$

Using that the functions $\exp\left(-iE_k t\right)_{k \geq 0}$ are orthogonal for the L^2-norm, the average probability that the particle is measured in a point $x \in X$, is computed as

$$\lim_{T \to \infty} \frac{1}{T} \int_0^T |\psi_E(x,t)|^2 dt = \sum_{k \geq 0} f_E(E_k)^2 \phi_k(x)^2. \qquad (3)$$

2.2   The Wave Kernel Signature

Now we work out how to use the above insights to design a feature descriptor for shape analysis. For this, it remains to choose the energy distributions f_E^2.

Recall that we aim for a segmentation of shapes undergoing strong pose changes, which correspond mathematically to near-isometric deformations. Therefore we have to optimize our descriptor for robustness to small non-isometric deformations. A perturbation-theoretical analysis which we leave out here due to the lack of space shows that the eigenenergies of a shape under articulation can be modeled as log-normally distributed random variables. More details on this can be found in [4].

This leads us to choose f_E in (3) as a Gaussian distribution in the logarithmic energy $e = \log(E)$ for f_E and we define the Wave Kernel Signature at a point x as

$$\text{WKS}(x, \cdot) : \mathbb{R} \to \mathbb{R}, \quad e \mapsto \frac{1}{C_e} \sum_{k \geq 0} \exp\left(-\frac{(e - \log(E_k))^2}{2\sigma^2}\right) \phi_k^2(x), \qquad (4)$$

where $C_e = \sum_{k \geq 0} \exp\left(-\frac{(e - \log(E_k))^2}{2\sigma^2}\right)$.

2.3   Comparison of WKS and HKS

The eigenfunctions of the Laplace–Beltrami operator on X can be seen as a generalization of the classical Fourier basis. In this interpretation, eigenvalues play the role of frequencies. Consider a point on a surface as a signal by means of its delta function. Both, the Heat Kernel Signature (HKS) [22] which is defined by

$$\text{HKS}(x,t) = \sum_{k \geq 0} \exp(-E_k t) \phi_k^2(x) \qquad (5)$$

and WKS defined by equation (4) are symmetric expressions in the squared Fourier coefficients. Note that the Laplace eigenfunctions depend on the choice of a basis: even in the case of non-repeated Laplace eigenvalues there is a sign ambiguity. Luckily, HKS and WKS are independent of the choice of an orthonormal basis of eigenfunctions. Both descriptors characterize points up to non-rigid motion (cf. [22,4]).

The difference between HKS and WKS lies in the way Fourier coefficients are filtered. HKS can be seen as a collection of low-pass filters parametrized over the time t. The higher t, the more high frequencies are suppressed. In contrast, WKS is a collection of smoothed delta filters in the Fourier domain. The precise form of these smoothed delta filters is chosen in such a way that robustness to pose changes is granted as outlined in Section 2.2.

Thereby, WKS should allow for more precise localization of features of points in the frequency domain and thus for a higher precision in recognizing corresponding points. For a thorough experimental comparison of HKS and WKS confirming this heuristic we refer the reader to [4].

3   Learning Pose-Invariant Shape Segmentation

Assume now that we are given a shape in several different poses. Our segmentation aims at grouping points in which quantum particles at different energy levels have similar probabilities to be detected. We build clusters in the following way:

- Pick a subset of training poses which are used for learning the clusters. Typically we used 3-5 training poses.
- Compute the WKS for all points of all training shapes, leading to a point cloud in $\mathbb{R}^M$, where M is the number of evaluation energies of the WKS (which is 100 in all our experiments).
- Fit a Gaussian mixture model with K clusters to these training signatures. The computation was done using the EM algorithm initialized by K-means.

Once the learning step is completed, we can segment both the training poses and new poses by assigning with each point the label of the cluster, on which its WKS has the highest score in the Gaussian mixture distribution.

Of course, we could also use other clustering schemes, leading to similar results. In some cases, we found that imposing the same variance to all the Gaussians of the mixture can lead to slightly more robust results. Indeed, this is a simple way to avoid overfitting: if some scale is very consistent in a cluster, the variance for the corresponding Gaussian at this scale will be so small that a slight change at this scale in a test shape will attribute the points to another cluster. A shared variance will avoid that kind of effects.

4   Experimental Results

4.1   Computational Details

For computing the WKS on triangle meshes, we discretized the Laplacian using the cotan scheme introduced by Pinkall and Polthier [13]. Boundaries were

Fig. 2. Fully unsupervised segmentation of $3D$ shapes: for different shape classes and for different numbers of clusters, our segmentation algorithm is able recognize semantically meaningful parts and to transfer correctly labels through strong pose-deformations. The left and the middle column show segmentations of shapes from the training set, while the right column visualizes the segmentation of new poses. The shapes are courtesy of [25,5,21].

treated with Neumann conditions. We computed the first $N = 300$ eigenvalues and evaluated the WKS at $M = 100$ values of e ranging from $e_{\min} = \log(E_1)$ to $e_{\max} = \frac{\log(E_N)}{1.02}$ with linear increment $\delta = \frac{e_{\max}-e_{\min}}{M}$. The variance was set to $\sigma = 7\delta$. All these values were fixed in all our experiments.

4.2 Segmentation Results

Figure 2 shows results of segmentations of different shapes in several poses for a varying number of clusters. Notice that the labels, visualized by colors, are automatically transferred correctly to the different articulations and that they are naturally spatially consistent.

4.3 Robustness

To test the robustness of our segmentation, we used the data of the SHREC 2010 benchmark [5]. This dataset contains different shapes undergoing a large variety

Fig. 3. Robustness of the segmentation results tested on shapes from the SHREC 2010 robustness dataset [5]. On the top, one shape from the training set and at the bottom test shapes with different perturbations. From the left to the right: topology, holes, and shot noise.

| query shape | 0.7457 | 0.6662 | 0.3850 | -0.0881 |

Fig. 4. Shape segmentation applied to shape retrieval on the SHREC 2010 dataset [11]. The four columns on the right show representatives of four shape classes. For each shape class a Gaussian mixture distribution was computed as outlined in Section 3. The resulting segmentations are color encoded. The log-likelihood of the query shape (leftmost column) with respect to these distributions is displayed below each class.

of poses and of different kinds of perturbations such as topological changes, noise or holes. The method proves stable to such data as can be seen in Figure 3 where some results are visualized.

4.4 Shape Retrieval

As an application of our pose-invariant shape segmentation framework we show an experiment on shape retrieval on the dataset of the SHREC 2010 non-rigid shape retrieval contest [11]. This dataset consists of 10 shape classes each of which contains 20 different shape poses. We choose 5 training shapes from each class and learn a segmentation of these training shapes. As a result of this learning step, we dispose of a Gaussian mixture probability distribution for each shape class. Given a query shape from the database which was not included in the learning process, we compute its WKS at all points and evaluated the negative log-likelihoods of the Gaussian mixtures. The query shape is sorted to the shape class with the maximal log-likelihood. In Figure 4 we visualize the resulting log-likelihood of a query shape for four different shape classes.

On the 150 query shapes we achieved 72% of correct assignments which is a proof of concept that our part decomposition of shapes is of high informative value for shape recognition.

5 Conclusion

We proposed a novel method for fully unsupervised, pose-consistent $3D$ shape segmentation which arises from a Quantum Mechanical analysis of shapes. By grouping those points in which quantum particles of different energy levels have similar probabilities to be detected, we get an unsupervised partitioning of the shape. Label transfer to different poses is granted by construction without the need of user input or of computationally expensive shape registrations. Interestingly, the computed part decomposition of shapes is consistent with human notions of shape decomposition (torso, head, arms, legs, etc). Finally, we demonstrate that such a segmentation can be efficiently used for shape retrieval.

References

1. Agathos, A., Pratikakis, I., Perantonis, S., Sapidis, N., Azariadis, P.: 3D mesh segmentation methodologies for CAD applications. Computer-Aided Design and Applications 4(6), 827–841 (2007)
2. Anguelov, D., Koller, D., Pang, H.C., Srinivasan, P., Thrun, S.: Recovering articulated object models from 3d range data. In: UAI, pp. 18–26 (2004)
3. Attene, M., Katz, S., Mortara, M., Patané, G., Spagnuolo, M., Tal, A.: Mesh segmentation-a comparative study. In: Shape Modelling International (SMI). IEEE Computer Society, Los Alamitos (2006)
4. Aubry, M., Schlickewei, U., Cremers, D.: The Wave Kernel Signature - A Quantum Mechanical Approach to Shape Analyis. Tech. rep., TU München, Germany (June 2011)
5. Bronstein, A., Bronstein, M., Bustos, B., Castellani, U., Crisani, M., Falcidieno, B., Guibas, L., Kokkinos, I., Murino, V., Ovsjanikov, M., et al.: SHREC 2010: robust feature detection and description benchmark. In: Proc. 3DOR (2010)
6. Goldluecke, B., Cremers, D.: Superresolution texture maps for multiview reconstruction. In: IEEE International Conference on Computer Vision (ICCV), Kyoto, Japan (2009)
7. Hoffman, D.: Visual intelligence: How we create what we see. WW Norton and Company, New York (2000)
8. James, D., Twigg, C.: Skinning mesh animations. ACM Transactions on Graphics (SIGGRAPH 2005) 24(3) (August 2005)
9. Lévy, B.: Laplace-Beltrami Eigenfunctions Towards an Algorithm That "Understands" Geometry. In: Proc. Int. Conf. on Shape Modeling and Applications, p. 13. IEEE, Los Alamitos (2006)

10. Lévy, B., Petitjean, S., Ray, N., Maillot, J.: Least squares conformal maps for automatic texture atlas generation. ACM Transactions on Graphics 21(3), 362–371 (2002)
11. Lian, Z., Godil, A., Fabry, T., Furuya, T., Hermans, J., Ohbuchi, R., Shu, C., Smeets, D., Suetens, P., Vandermeulen, D., et al.: SHREC 2010 Track: Non-rigid 3D Shape Retrieval. In: Eurographics 3DOR (2010)
12. Ovsjanikov, M., Bronstein, A., Bronstein, M., Guibas, L.: Shape Google: a computer vision approach to invariant shape retrieval. In: Proc. NORDIA, vol. 1(2) (2009)
13. Pinkall, U., Polthier, K.: Computing discrete minimal surfaces and their conjugates. Experimental Mathematics 2(1), 15–36 (1993)
14. Reuter, M.: Hierarchical shape segmentation and registration via topological features of laplace-beltrami eigenfunctions. International Journal of Computer Vision
15. Rustamov, R.: Laplace-Beltrami eigenfunctions for deformation invariant shape representation. In: SGP, pp. 225–233. Eurographics (2007)
16. Schaefer, S., Yuksel, C.: Example-based skeleton extraction. In: Symposium on Geometry Processing, pp. 153–162 (2007)
17. Shamir, A.: A survey on mesh segmentation techniques. Computer Graphics Forum 27, 1539–1556 (2008)
18. Shapira, L., Shalom, S., Shamir, A., Cohen-Or, D., Zhang, H.: Contextual part analogies in 3d objects. International Journal of Computer Vision 89(2-3), 309–326 (2010)
19. Sharma, A., von Lavante, E., Horaud, R.: Learning shape segmentation using constrained spectral clustering and probabilistic label transfer. In: Daniilidis, K., Maragos, P., Paragios, N. (eds.) ECCV 2010. LNCS, vol. 6315, pp. 743–756. Springer, Heidelberg (2010)
20. Skraba, P., Ovsjanikov, M., Chazal, F., Guibas, L.: Persistence-based segmentation of deformable shapes. In: NORDIA, pp. 45–52. IEEE, Los Alamitos (2010)
21. Sumner, R., Popović, J.: Deformation transfer for triangle meshes. ACM Transactions on Graphics (TOG) 23(3), 399–405 (2004)
22. Sun, J., Ovsjanikov, M., Guibas, L.: A Concise and Provably Informative Multi-Scale Signature Based on Heat Diffusion. Computer Graphics Forum 28(5), 1383–1392 (2009)
23. Tal, A., Zuckerberger, E.: Mesh retrieval by components. In: GRAPP, pp. 142–149 (2006)
24. Toldo, R., Castellani, U., Fusiello, A.: Visual vocabulary signature for 3D object retrieval and partial matching. In: Proc. 3dOR, vol. 8, pp. 21–28 (2009)
25. Vlasic, D., Baran, I., Matusik, W., Popović, J.: Articulated mesh animation from multi-view silhouettes. In: ACM SIGGRAPH 2008 papers, pp. 1–9. ACM, New York (2008)

Multiple Instance Boosting for
Face Recognition in Videos

Paul Wohlhart, Martin Köstinger, Peter M. Roth, and Horst Bischof

Institute for Computer Graphics and Vision
Graz University of Technology, Austria
{wohlhart,koestinger,pmroth,bischof}@icg.tugraz.at

Abstract. For face recognition from video streams often cues such as transcripts, subtitles or on-screen text are available. This information could be very valuable for improving the recognition performance. However, frequently this data can not be associated directly with just one of the visible faces. To overcome this limitations and to exploit valuable information, we define the task as a multiple instance learning (MIL) problem. We formulate a robust loss function that describes our problem and incorporates ambiguous and unreliable information sources and optimize it using Gradient Boosting. A new definition of the posterior probability of a bag, based on the L_p-norm, improves the ability to deal with varying bag sizes over existing formulations. The benefits of the approach are demonstrated for face recognition in videos on a publicly available benchmark dataset. In fact, we show that exploring new information sources can drastically improve the classification results. Additionally, we show its competitive performance on standard machine learning datasets.

1 Introduction

TV and video-sharing websites constantly provide large amounts of digital video data. This data could be an extremely valuable and important source of information, that today remains mostly unexplored. In fact, since most of the video data is only indexed by some meta-data and not by its content, it is inaccessible to goal-oriented search. Manual annotation is laborious or even infeasible at large scale, thus, to allow for a more efficient search and retrieval, methods for automatic interpretation of the visual content are needed.

In this paper, we address the problem of fully automated identification of people in videos, where we have to carry out the following steps: First, detecting people's faces and tracking them throughout a scene. Second, automatically extracting as much information as possible about the persons' identities from associated information sources, such as the audio track (speech recognition), subtitles, the transcript, on-screen text, or electronic program guide (EPG) data. Third, using the gathered data to learn to re-identify them in different contexts, only based on their visual appearance.

This problem was recently tackled by several authors [3,4,7,8,17,18]. Everingham *et al.* [7,8] label exemplars by visual speaker detection. The name of

R. Mester and M. Felsberg (Eds.): DAGM 2011, LNCS 6835, pp. 132–141, 2011.

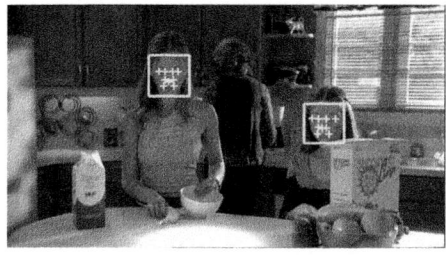 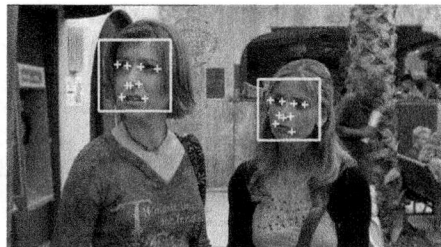

(a) Buffy, Dawn, Joice   (b) Willow, Buffy

Fig. 1. Face recognition in videos: Often valuable information cannot be assigned unambiguously to exactly one person. For instance we know from the video transcript that a character is present in a scene, but the corresponding face is unknown.

the speaker is obtained by automatically aligning the timing information of the subtitles with the naming information from the transcript. However, due to the nearest neighbor classification label noise is propagated. Thus, the method cannot recover from labeling errors. The work of Sivic *et al.* [18] replaces the nearest neighbor framework by multiple kernel classification. The base kernels operate on the min-min distance between HOG blocks. Therefore, the optimized combination coefficients describe the relative importance of the individual blocks for classification. Nevertheless, it is not possible to integrate cues providing information that can not be assigned unambiguously to one single instance. Ramanan *et al.* [17] use a multitude of inference cues to obtain face clusters. Different cues apply to different time scales. However, the system requires manual user interaction to label an initial set of face clusters.

Thus, these methods require either manual labeling or cannot make use of information that applies to multiple instances. However, this is a reasonable scenario when learning from videos and associated sources. For instance, as illustrated in Figure 1, we know from textual cues that a specific character should be present in one scene of a movie. But we do not know to which of the currently visible faces this information corresponds. The goal of this paper is to make use of information which cannot be disambiguated. Additionally, we have to ensure robustness, *i.e.*, since the information extraction procedure is not completely reliable, we have to inherently deal with noisy and uncertain labels. We meet these requirements by formulating the task as a Multiple Instance Learning (MIL) problem.

In particular, for that purpose we adopt Gradient Boosting. Compared to other methods Gradient Boosting has the advantage that any loss function that fits the task can be used, as long as it is differentiable, thus providing a very general optimization framework. In our case we build on the Logit-loss function – to ensure the required robustness – and further incorporate the MIL constraints. The approach is similar to the one of Viola *et al.* [19], however, their formulation implicitly assumes that all bags in the training data are more or less of the same size and essentially not too big. To overcome this limitation, we define a new formulation of the posterior probability of a bag, approximating more directly the original definition of MIL, which is better suited for our task. Additionally, we generalize the framework such that arbitrary learning algorithms can be used to form the weak hypotheses.

In the following, we first introduce our new Gradient Boosting based MIL algorithm and then give an experimental evaluation on both, standard benchmark datasets as well as on a publicly available face recognition dataset.

2   MIL - Boosting

In a supervised learning scenario the training data is given in the form of a set $\mathcal{D} = \{(\mathbf{x}_1, y_1), \ldots, (\mathbf{x}_N, y_N)\}$, where $\mathbf{x}_i \in \mathbb{R}^d$ is a sample and $y_i \in \mathcal{Y} = \{-1, +1\}$ its corresponding binary label. However, in practice, it is often hard or even impossible to assign a label to all samples. But it is rather easy to specify a group of data samples for which it can be ensured that at least one instance carries the label, which leads to Multiple Instance Learning (MIL) [6]. In MIL the data is provided in form of labeled bags $\mathcal{D}_{\mathrm{mil}} = \{(\mathcal{B}_1^l, y_1), \ldots, (\mathcal{B}_N^l, y_N)\}$, where $\mathcal{B}_i = \{\mathbf{x}_{i1}, \ldots, \mathbf{x}_{iN_{B_i}}\}$, $\mathbf{x}_{ij} \in \mathbb{R}^d$, is a bag containing N_{B_i} samples and $y_i \in \mathcal{Y}$ its binary label. A bag is defined to be positive if *at least one* instance in the bag is positive, whereas accordingly for a negative bag all instances have to be negative. Building on these ideas, in the following, we will derive a new formulation for MIL which is based on Gradient Boosting.

2.1   Gradient Boosting

In general, the goal of Boosting is to estimate a strong classifier $F(\mathbf{x})$ as a linear combination of weak classifiers $f_t(\mathbf{x})$ such that the the expected classification error is minimized:

$$F(\mathbf{x}) = \sum_{t=1}^{T} \alpha_t f_t(\mathbf{x}) \ . \tag{1}$$

In particular, Gradient Boosting aims to find a strong classifier $F^*(\mathbf{x})$ by solving the following optimization problem:

$$F^*(\mathbf{x}) = \arg\min_{F(\mathbf{x})} \mathcal{L}(\mathcal{D}; F(\mathbf{x})) \ , \tag{2}$$

where $\mathcal{L}(\mathcal{D}; F(\mathbf{x}))$ is a *loss function* measuring the performance of the classifier by giving penalties for misclassified training examples.

Gradient Boosting iteratively estimates the function $F^*(\mathbf{x})$ by greedily constructing base functions $f_t(\mathbf{x})$ (weak learners) based on the preceding $f_1(\mathbf{x}), \ldots, f_{t-1}(\mathbf{x})$. This is accomplished by taking the derivative of the loss function with respect to the current strong classifier's output for each training sample and constructing the new $f_t(\mathbf{x})$ such as to produce outputs that approximate the inverse direction of this gradient (*i.e.*, reduce the residuals):

$$f_t(\mathbf{x}) = \underset{f(\mathbf{x})}{\arg\max} \left\langle -\left\{ \frac{\partial \mathcal{L}(\mathcal{D}; F)}{\partial F(\mathbf{x}_1)}, \ldots, \frac{\partial \mathcal{L}(\mathcal{D}; F)}{\partial F(\mathbf{x}_N)} \right\}, \{f(\mathbf{x}_1), \ldots, f(\mathbf{x}_N)\} \right\rangle \quad (3)$$

$$= \underset{f(\mathbf{x})}{\arg\max} - \sum_{i=1}^{N} \frac{\partial \mathcal{L}(\mathcal{D}; F)}{\partial F(\mathbf{x}_i)} f(\mathbf{x}_i) . \quad (4)$$

Finally, when the new $f_t(\mathbf{x})$ is found, the best weight α_t is determined by a line search.

2.2   Loss Functions

The main advantage of Gradient Boosting over other Boosting variants is the flexibility of choosing a loss function that suites the task to be solved. Several different losses have been proposed in the literature (Exponential [10], Logit [11], Savage [16]), mainly differing in the way how misclassified samples are punished, mainly influencing the robustness of the method against label noise. Since the Logit loss has shown to be a considerable trade-off between robustness and performance we build our algorithm on it. Thus, in the following we derive a Gradient Boosting variant using a Logit loss, which can then easily be extended by incorporating the Multiple Instance Learning constraints in Section 2.3.

The Logit loss of a classifier $F(\mathbf{x})$ over a dataset $\mathcal{D}$ is defined as

$$\mathcal{L}(\mathcal{D}; F(\mathbf{x})) = \sum_{i=1}^{N} \log\left(1 + e^{-y_i F(\mathbf{x}_i)}\right) = -\sum_{i=1}^{N} \log\left(\frac{1}{1 + e^{-y_i F(\mathbf{x}_i)}}\right) . \quad (5)$$

Thus, taking the logistic regression of the strong classifier's output $F(\mathbf{x})$, let

$$P(y = z | \mathbf{x}_i) = \frac{1}{1 + e^{-z F(\mathbf{x}_i)}} \quad (6)$$

be the predicted probability that an instance $\mathbf{x}$ is assigned the label $z \in \mathcal{Y}$. Then, we can interpret Eq. (5) as the cross entropy of the labels and the instance probabilities reported by the classifier:

$$\mathcal{L}(\mathcal{D}; F(\mathbf{x})) = -\sum_{i=1}^{N} \sum_{z \in \mathcal{Y}} [z = y_i] \log\left(P(y = z | \mathbf{x}_i)\right) , \quad (7)$$

where $[\cdot]$ is the Iverson bracket.

With this loss the optimization for the weak learners in Eq. (4) becomes

$$f_t(\mathbf{x}) = \underset{f(\mathbf{x})}{\arg\max} \sum_{i=1}^{N} \sum_{z \in \mathcal{Y}} [z = y_i] \frac{\partial \log P(y = z | \mathbf{x}_i)}{\partial F(\mathbf{x}_i)} f(\mathbf{x}_i) . \quad (8)$$

Thus, we are looking for a new $f_t(\mathbf{x})$ whose output approximates the derivative of the log of the instance probabilities, which we denote as

$$a_i(z) = \frac{\partial \log P(y=z|\mathbf{x}_i)}{\partial F(\mathbf{x}_i)} . \tag{9}$$

Generally, existing learning algorithms are not designed to solve Eq. (8). However, we can define a weight w_i for each training sample as

$$\forall \mathbf{x}_i \in \mathcal{D}: \quad w_i = |a_i(y_i)| . \tag{10}$$

Thus, we are very flexible and can use any learning algorithm that can handle training data with (importance-)weighted samples to construct a new weak learner approximating the gradient.

2.3   Solving MIL with Gradient Boosting

In order to solve the MIL problem we define a new loss function over the bags

$$\mathcal{L}(\mathcal{D}_{\text{mil}}; F(\mathbf{x})) = -\sum_{i=1}^{N} \sum_{z \in \mathcal{Y}} [z = y_i] \log(P(y=z|\mathcal{B}_i)) , \tag{11}$$

where $P(y=1|\mathcal{B}_i)$ is the bag posterior. Following the definition of MIL, the bag posterior is defined over the probabilities of its instances as

$$P(y=1|\mathcal{B}_i) = \max_j P(y=1|\mathbf{x}_{ij}) . \tag{12}$$

However, this measure is not differentiable, thus, approximations have to be used. For instance, Viola et al. [19] proposed to use noisy-or [15] as the bag posterior model:

$$P_{\text{NOR}}(y=1|\mathcal{B}_i) = 1 - \prod_{j=1}^{N_{\mathcal{B}_i}} (1 - P(y=1|\mathbf{x}_{ij})) . \tag{13}$$

The main disadvantage of the noisy-or formulation is that the size of the bag (number of instances) substantially influences the outcome. For example, if all instances in a bag have a very low probability, it is still assigned a high posterior probability if the number of instances is large. This is especially unfavorable if the size of the bags varies strongly within the training data, as it is the case in our task.

Therefore, we propose to use a more direct approximation to the max operation in Eq. (12), by making use of the L_p-norm:

$$P_{L_p}(y=1|\mathcal{B}_i) = \left(\sum_{j=1}^{N_{\mathcal{B}_i}} P(y=1|\mathbf{x}_{ij})^p \right)^{1/p} . \tag{14}$$

For large values of p this well approximates the max operation and as $p \rightarrow \infty$ even converges to it. Thus, according to Eq. (8), the optimization for generating the next weak learner is given by

$$f_t(\mathbf{x}) = \underset{f(\mathbf{x})}{\arg\max} \sum_{i=1}^{N} \sum_{z \in \mathcal{Y}} [z = y_i] \sum_{j=1}^{N_{\mathcal{B}_i}} \frac{\partial \log P(y = z | \mathcal{B}_i)}{\partial F(\mathbf{x}_{ij})} f(\mathbf{x}_{ij}) . \qquad (15)$$

Again, we can derive the weights for each instance by

$$\forall (\mathcal{B}_i, y_i) \in \mathcal{D}_{\text{mil}}, \forall \mathbf{x}_{ij} \in \mathcal{B}_i : \quad w_{ij} = |a_{ij}(y_i)| , \qquad (16)$$

where, in contrast to Eq. (9), the $a_{ij}(z)$ are now defined on bag level:

$$a_{ij}(z) = \frac{\partial \log P(y = z | \mathcal{B}_i)}{\partial F(\mathbf{x}_{ij})} . \qquad (17)$$

In our case, the derivation of Eq. (14) is given by

$$a_{ij}^{L_p}(z) = \frac{\hat{z} - P(y = 1 | \mathcal{B}_i)}{1 - P(y = 1 | \mathcal{B}_i)} (1 - P(y = 1 | \mathbf{x}_{ij})) \frac{P(y = 1 | \mathbf{x}_{ij})^p}{\sum_{k=1}^{N_{\mathcal{B}_i}} P(y = 1 | \mathbf{x}_{ik})^p} , \qquad (18)$$

where $\hat{z} = (z + 1)/2$. The bigger we choose p the better the approximation. As $p \rightarrow \infty$, we get

$$\tilde{a}_{ij}^{L_\infty}(z) = (\hat{z} - P(y = 1 | \mathcal{B}_i)) \left[P(y = 1 | \mathbf{x}_{ij}) = \max_k P(y = 1 | \mathbf{x}_{ik}) \right] / N_{\mathcal{B}_i, \max} , \qquad (19)$$

where $N_{\mathcal{B}_i, \max} = |\{j | P(y = 1 | \mathbf{x}_{ij}) = \max_k P(y = 1 | \mathbf{x}_{ik})\}|$ is the number of instances in bag $\mathcal{B}_i$ having the highest probability. Note that $\tilde{a}_{ij}^{L_\infty}$ is not necessarily the analytical derivative of P_{L_∞}, since the series of P_{L_p} converges pointwise, but not uniform. Nevertheless, we use it since it gives the best approximation for the weights w_{ij} and it is easy to compute.

3   Benchmark Datasets

Before showing results for the actual task, i.e., face recognition, we would like to give a broad quantitative comparison to other methods. In particular, we evaluate the proposed MILBoost using the P_{L_p} bag posterior model on the well known and frequently used CBIR machine learning database [1] with its three multiple instance datasets *Tiger*, *Fox* and *Elephant* as well as on the two Musk datasets [6]. Here, as well as in the other experiments, the weak learners used are probabilistic decision stumps, which test one feature of a sample against a threshold and report a probability of begin positive, estimated from the training data, on either side. The mean areas under the ROC curves over 10 individual 10-fold cross validation runs are reported in Table 1.[1]

---

[1] Note that for mi-SVM and MI-SVM there are three different versions depending on the kernel (linear, poly, rbf) and we report the best one for each class.

On Musk, MILBoost is in the range of state-of-the-art algorithms, although it does not reach the performance of certain specialized methods. However, MIL-Boost with the noisy-or bag posterior model, to the best of our knowledge, delivers the best results reported so far for the Tiger and Elephant classes of the CBIR dataset. Our P_{L_p} bag posterior model also produces very good results on those two classes and considerably outperforms noisy-or on the difficult Fox dataset. Note also, that its theoretical advantage of being able to handle variably sized bags does not apply for these datasets, since the bags are of equal size.

Table 1. Results of various MIL algorithms on the standard MIL datasets CBIR and Musk1&2. MILBoost outperforms all other methods on CBIR, with MILBoost L_p producing the best overall performance. The best performance for each dataset is marked in bold, second best in italics.

	Tiger	Elephant	Fox	Musk1	Musk2
sbMIL [2]	82.95	88.58	*69.78*	*91.78*	87.40
NSK [13]	79.07	82.94	64.01	85.61	**90.78**
MI-SVM [1]	84.00	81.40	59.40	81.50	86.30
mi-SVM [1]	78.90	82.20	58.20	87.40	83.60
MI-CRF [5]	78.90	82.20	58.20	77.90	84.30
PPMM [20]	80.20	82.00	60.30	**95.60**	81.20
MICA [12]	82.00	82.50	62.00	84.40	*90.50*
ALP-SVM [14]	86.00	83.50	66.00	86.30	86.20
MILBoost n-or	**91.70**	**93.43**	65.72	81.98	81.92
MILBoost L_p	*89.79*	*91.82*	**71.80**	81.98	81.87

4   Face Recognition from Videos

In the following we demonstrate our method for face recognition from associated information sources on the publicly available part of the *Buffy* dataset proposed by Everingham *et al.* [7][2]. It consists of 27504 individual frontal face detections and additionally provides face descriptions and face tracks. Faces are described by normalized pixel patches extracted at salient facial feature points, which are localized by a Pictorial Structures model [9]. Within a shot face detections (in individual frames) are grouped into face tracks by motion information. Hence, the task is to assign the correct cast name to each of the 516 face tracks. The cast list of the ground truth annotation consists of 11 named entities, the class *other* and *false positive* of the detection process. For each cast member we train a one-vs.-all classifier.

To automatically obtain training labels, we exploit information sources closely associated to the video, namely transcript and subtitles, both containing the dialogs. The transcript additionally provides naming information and embraces scenes with a textual description of what is happening. From the transcript we extract the coarse scene structure. Further, to augment the transcript with the

---

[2] The more recent "Buffy" dataset [18] is not publicly available.

timing information it is aligned with the subtitles by dynamic time warping. Thus, we now know who is speaking when but neither if the speaker is visible or to which face the current utterance belongs.

We use these cues to compose training bags. A bag consists of one or more face tracks and an associated label. First, we form *speaker bags*. To judge if a person is speaking we observe the optical flow [21] around the mouth region. Tracks identified as speaking are assigned the label of the current speaker from the augmented transcript. Second, we define *scene bags* that contain all face tracks present in a scene. The idea is to decide if a certain character is likely to appear in a particular scene or not, dependent on the number of spoken text chunks. To finally test the labeling performance, each face track forms a singleton bag. Testing is done standalone based on pure face appearance and does not need additional information.

Compliant with previous work we measure the performance in a *refusal to predict* style. By taking the difference of the leading two classifier scores a confidence is obtained. Further, we rank and threshold the confidences. In that sense, recall means the percentage of face tracks which have a higher confidence than the current threshold and thus are labeled. Precision means the ratio of correctly labeled samples. We first report the performances of the different models for the bag posterior probabilities on this task. The comparison is shown in Table 2, where it can be seen that, as expected, P_{L_p} outperforms P_{NOR} over most levels of recall, especially for higher recall values. Thus, for the succeeding experiments we just use the P_{L_p} bag posterior.

Table 2. Performance comparison of the different models for the posterior probability of a bag. P_{L_p} outperforms P_{NOR} over most levels of recall.

Recall	50%	60%	70%	80%	90%	100%
P_{L_p}	91,5%	**90,9%**	**88,7%**	**86,3%**	**81,8%**	**77,7%**
P_{NOR}	91,5%	90,6%	86,5%	83,9%	78,5%	73,8%

Next, in Figure 2 we compare our method with previous work [7,8]. Everingham *et al.* proposed to classify each track based on the min-min distance to the tracks labeled by the speaker detection. The min-min distance $d_f(F_i, F_j)$ between two face tracks F_i and F_j is defined as:

$$d_f(F_i, F_j) = \min_{f_i \in F_i} \min_{f_j \in F_j} \|f_i - f_j\|, \tag{20}$$

where $f_i \in F_i$ and $f_j \in F_j$ are face descriptions. This method is denoted as NN. For comparison, we also include the original curve from [7]. Please note that this method makes use of additional clothing descriptors and a different speaker detection, not provided with the published dataset. As reference we also state the performance of labeling all face tracks with the cast name appearing most frequently in the transcript (Prior on *Buffy*). Further, also the performance of using the aligned subtitles to propose a name is reported.

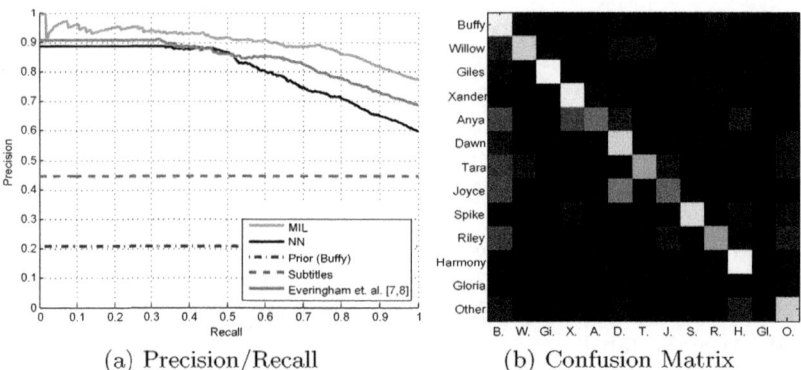

(a) Precision/Recall   (b) Confusion Matrix

Fig. 2. Buffy dataset: (a) MIL-L_p clearly outperforms the baseline (NN) over all levels of recall. Subtitles describe further baseline methods, see text for details. (b) The associated confusion matrix.

With the speaker detection we can label 33.4% of the tracks with a precison of 89.0%. Please note that the baseline method provides no means for ranking the tracks detected as *speaking*. Therefore, the curve is constant for the first levels of recall. Due to the nearest neighbor classification the baseline method has no real chance to recover from labeling errors. Label noise propagates directly into the classification. If the method is required to label all face tracks a precision of 60.1% is reached. MIL clearly outperforms the baseline method over all levels of recall. At 100% recall the precision is 77.7%. This is an improvement of 17.6% over the baseline. Indeed, the method even delivers a higher precision than the speaker detection up to a recall level of 65%. It labels nearly twice as many face tracks with an accuracy of 89%. This shows clearly the ability of MIL to recover from labeling errors.

5   Conclusion

In this work we presented the task of face recognition in weakly labeled videos as Multiple Instance Learning problem. We formulated the MIL concept in a probabilistic loss function and optimized it in a Gradient Boosting framework. The new formulation of the posterior probabilities of the bags using the L_p-norm allows us to better deal with bags of varying size, as the comparison with noisy-or confirmed. The evaluation on standard machine learning data shows excellent results for the learning algorithm. Further, the task of face recognition in videos verified that it is able to benefit from ambiguous and even noisy data. This can be attributed to the design of the loss function, based on Logit. It gives penalties for misclassifying training samples, but does not exaggerate the influence of very wrong classifications to avoid over-fitting to potentially noisy labels.

Acknowledgments. The work was supported by the FFG projects MDL (818800) and SECRET (821690) under the Austrian Security Research Programme KI-RAS.

References

1. Andrews, S., Tsochantaridis, I., Hofmann, T.: Support vector machines for multiple-instance learning. In: NIPS (2003)
2. Bunescu, R.C., Mooney, R.J.: Multiple instance learning for sparse positive bags. In: Proc. ICML (2007)
3. Cour, T., Sapp, B., Jordan, C., Taskar, B.: Learning from ambiguously labeled images. In: Proc. CVPR (2009)
4. Cour, T., Sapp, B., Nagle, A., Taskar, B.: Talking pictures: Temporal grouping and dialog-supervised person recognition. In: Proc. CVPR (2010)
5. Deselaers, T., Ferrari, V.: A conditional random field for multiple-instance learning. In: Proc. ICML (2010)
6. Dietterich, T.G., Lathrop, R.H., Lozano-Pérez, T.: Solving the multiple instance problem with axis-parallel rectangles. Artificial Intelligence 89(1–2), 31–71 (1997)
7. Everingham, M., Sivic, J., Zisserman, A.: Hello! My name is.. Buffy – automatic naming of characters in TV video. In: Proc. BMVC (2006)
8. Everingham, M., Sivic, J., Zisserman, A.: Taking the bite out of automatic naming of characters in TV video. Image and Vision Computing 27(5) (2009)
9. Felzenszwalb, P.F., Huttenlocher, D.P.: Pictorial structures for object recognition. Intern. Journal of Computer Vision 61, 55–79 (2005)
10. Freund, Y., Shapire, R.E.: Experiments with a new boosting algorithm. In: Proc. ICML (1996)
11. Friedman, J., Hastie, T., Tibshirani., R.: Additive logistic regression: a statistical view of boosting. The Annals of Statistics 28(2), 337–374 (2000)
12. Fung, G., Rosales, R., Krishnapuram, B.: Learning rankings via convex hull separation. In: Advances NIPS (2006)
13. Gärtner, T., Flach, P.A., Kowalczyk, A., Smola, A.J.: Multi–instance kernels. In: Proc. ICML (2002)
14. Gehler, P.V., Chapelle, O.: Deterministic annealing for multiple-instance learning. In: Proc. Int. Conf. on Artificial Intelligence and Statistics (2007)
15. Maron, O., Lozano-Pérez, T.: A framework for multiple-instance learning. In: Advances NIPS (1998)
16. Masnadi-Shirazi, H., Vasconcelos, N.: On the design of loss functions for classification: theory, robustness to outliers, and SavageBoost. In: Advances NIPS (2009)
17. Ramanan, D., Baker, S., Kakade, S.: Leveraging archival video for building face datasets. In: Proc. ICCV (2007)
18. Sivic, J., Everingham, M., Zisserman, A.: Who are you? – learning person specific classifiers from video. In: Proc. CVPR (2009)
19. Viola, P., Platt, J., Zhang, C.: Multiple instance boosting for object detection. In: Advances NIPS (2006)
20. Wang, H.Y., Yang, Q., Zha, H.: Adaptive p-posterior mixture-model kernels for multiple instance learning. In: Proc. ICML (2008)
21. Werlberger, M., Trobin, W., Pock, T., Wedel, A., Cremers, D., Bischof, H.: Anisotropic Huber-L1 optical flow. In: Proc. BMVC (2009)

SHOG - Spherical HOG Descriptors for Rotation Invariant 3D Object Detection

Henrik Skibbe[1,3], Marco Reisert[2], and Hans Burkhardt[1,3]

[1] Department of Computer Science, University of Freiburg, Germany
[2] Dept. of Diagnostic Radiology, Medical Physics,
University Medical Center, Freiburg
[3] Center for Biological Signalling Studies (BIOSS), University of Freiburg
skibbe@informatik.uni-freiburg.de, marco.reisert@uniklinik-freiburg.de

Abstract. We present a method for densely computing local spherical histograms of oriented gradients (SHOG) in volumetric images. The descriptors are based on the continuous representation of the orientation histograms in the harmonic domain, which we compute very efficiently via spherical tensor products and the Fast Fourier Transformation. Building upon these local spherical histogram representations, we utilize the Harmonic Filter to create a generic rotation invariant object detection system that benefits from both the highly discriminative representation of local image patches in terms of histograms of oriented gradients and an adaptable trainable voting scheme that forms the filter. We exemplarily demonstrate the effectiveness of such dense spherical 3D descriptors in a detection task on biological 3D images. In a direct comparison to existing approaches, our new filter reveals superior performance.

1 Introduction

The rapid development of imaging techniques has led to a dramatic increase in the amount of volumetric image data that need to be processed. Especially in the field of biomedical imaging the third dimension becomes more and more important as it enables studying organisms in their natural constellation. Objects and organisms are sought to be located and analyzed in any number, at every position, and in every orientation. This means, that volumetric data yields not only more demanding constraints regarding computational efficiency, but also the interrelationship of neighboring intensity values becomes more complex. One of the most relevant issues is to cope with 3D rotation.

In this paper, we aim at creating filters based on the information of local gradient histograms that offer a robust, dense and rotation invariant object detection in volumetric images. For this we transfer the widely used HOG [2] features to the third dimension and show how to represent them in terms of so-called spherical tensors. Upon this representation we are capable to benefit from the simple rotation behavior of spherical tensors which enables the usage of Harmonic Filters [4,8]. This leads to a trainable 3D object and landmark detection system (figure 1) that benefits from both highly characteristic gradient orientation histograms and a memory and computational efficient trainable filter framework.

R. Mester and M. Felsberg (Eds.): DAGM 2011, LNCS 6835, pp. 142–151, 2011.

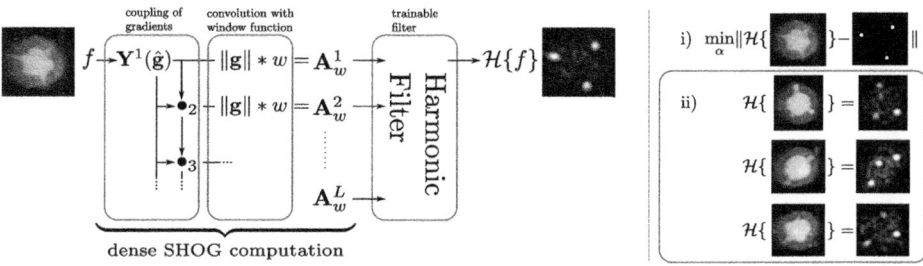

Fig. 1. Aiming at 3D landmark-detection: Above the flow diagram of the trainable SHOG-Filter. We first compute the spherical gradient image of an input image and split it into its spherical orientation field $\mathbf{Y}^1(\hat{\mathbf{g}}) : \mathbb{R}^3 \to S^2$ and its magnitude image $\|\mathbf{g}\| : \mathbb{R}^3 \to \mathbb{R}$. Then the continuous spherical histograms of oriented gradients (SHOG) are computed densely in the whole image in a recursive manner. We get an expansion of the histograms in terms of vector-valued coefficients $\mathbf{A}_w^\ell$. We finally use a trainable filter framework (Harmonic Filter) that learns a non-linear combination of the SHOG coefficients $\mathbf{A}_w^\ell$ such that a filter response is only given at the desired landmark positions. Moreover, all responses on the remaining positions are suppressed. Thanks to the continuous representation and the design of the coefficients $\mathbf{A}_w^\ell$ in combination with the Harmonic Filter, the filter response rotates smoothly with respect to the orientation of the landmarks without additional computational costs.
SHOG-Filter training and application: i) Optimizing the filter parameter α. For this a binary label image is required. ii) The filter can now be applied to further objects.

Mathematical Notation: We write vectors $\mathbf{v} \in \mathbb{C}^n$ in bold letters. We denote the complex conjugate of $\mathbf{v}$ by $\overline{\mathbf{v}}$ and the transpose of $\mathbf{v}$ by $\mathbf{v}^T$. We consider unit-length vectors $\mathbf{n} = (x, y, z)^T \in \mathbb{R}^3$, $\|\mathbf{n}\| = 1$ w.l.o.g as points on the unit-sphere which we denote by $\mathbf{n} \in S_2$. We equivalently can represent $\mathbf{n}$ in spherical coordinates (θ, ϕ), where $\theta = \arccos(z)$ and $\phi = \operatorname{atan2}(y, x)$ (see figure 2). We denote complex numbers by i, with $i^2 = -1$ and denote the convolution by $*$.

2   SHOG - Spherical Histograms of Oriented Gradients

Local descriptors based on orientation histograms, such as SIFT [3] and HOG [2], have revolutionized detection and matching in natural 2D images. Recently in particular HOG found its way in many applications because it can be computed efficiently and shows excellent performance. One step toward the third dimension HOG based features have been used for describing 3D mesh models [7,1]. What we propose here is a direct extension to volumetric images, where we aim at densely computing HOG at every image position. In contrast to 2D where a histogram is build upon gradient directions in a local neighborhood with respect to one angle (figure 2 a)), we must consider two angles for the 3D case (figure 2 b)). Hence the resulting histogram can be considered to be a histogram on the 2-sphere (unit-sphere in 3D). We call the 3D representation of a HOG spherical HOG, or shortly SHOG. It is worth noting that the literature discriminates

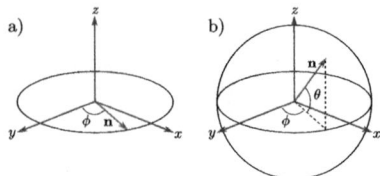

Fig. 2. In 3D the gradient direction is described by two angles thus a histogram of oriented gradients (HOG) can be considered as function on the sphere

between R-HOG (rectangular spatial window) and C-HOG (circular, isotropic window). Since the rotation of objects plays an important role in our framework, we only consider the latter one. Given an image $f : \mathbb{R}^3 \to \mathbb{R}$. We denote a dense field of SHOG descriptors defined over the whole image domain as SHOG$\{f\}$: $\mathbb{R}^3 \times S_2 \to \mathbb{R}$, where S_2 denotes the unit-sphere. For capturing only the structure in a voxel's surrounding a window function $w : \mathbb{R}^3 \to \mathbb{R}$ is required. Such a window function is e.g. the 3D Gaussian function. We compute a local SHOG at position $\mathbf{x}$ by collecting all magnitudes of gradients within the window function w contributing to orientation $\mathbf{n}$ according to the continuous distribution function

$$\text{SHOG}\{f\}_w(\mathbf{x}, \mathbf{n}) = \int_{\mathbf{r} \in \mathbb{R}^3} \|\mathbf{g}(\mathbf{r})\| \delta_{\mathbf{n}}^2(\hat{\mathbf{g}}(\mathbf{r})) w(\mathbf{x} - \mathbf{r}) d\mathbf{r} \quad , \tag{1}$$

where $\mathbf{g} : \mathbb{R}^3 \to \mathbb{R}^3$, $\mathbf{g} = \nabla f$ is the gradient field of the volumetric image f, $\hat{\mathbf{g}} := \mathbf{g}/\|\mathbf{g}\|$, $\hat{\mathbf{g}} : \mathbb{R}^3 \to S_2$ the gradient orientation field and $\mathbf{n} \in S_2$ is the current histogram entry (the direction) taken into account. $\delta_{\mathbf{n}}^2 : S_2 \to \mathbb{R}$ denotes the Dirac delta function on the unit sphere (see figure 5) that selects those gradients out of $\mathbf{g}$ with orientation $\mathbf{n}$. A direct extension to the 2D HOG descriptor would require discrete sampling of the orientation space which is trivial in 2D, but in general a non-trivial task in 3D. An equidistant discretization would require an equidistant sampling of the sphere which in general can not be solved explicitly (known as Thomson problem [10]). To overcome this problem we propose to keep the histogram continuous and realize the "binning" in frequency domain instead. Due to this reason we gain the following advantages: First, no interpolation is required because our SHOG descriptor is based on the true continuous distribution function. Furthermore, if the window function is isotropic, the descriptor rotates with respect to rotation of its underlying data without leading to any discretization artifacts in the histogram. This plays a very important role when aiming at detecting objects in volumetric images at any position and in any orientation using the Harmonic Filter framework.

SHOG Decomposition: The Racah normalized spherical harmonic functions[6] $Y_m^\ell : S_2 \to \mathbb{C}$ build a complete orthogonal basis for functions on the unit sphere $f : S_2 \to \mathbb{C}$. Similar to the Cartesian Fourier basis, spherical harmonics represent the different frequency components of spherical functions. We always have $2\ell + 1$ functions $Y_{m=\{-\ell,\cdots,\ell\}}^\ell : S_2 \to \mathbb{C}$ representing a basis function of frequency ℓ, which can be arranged in a vector-valued function $\mathbf{Y}^\ell : S_2 \to \mathbb{C}^{2\ell+1}$.

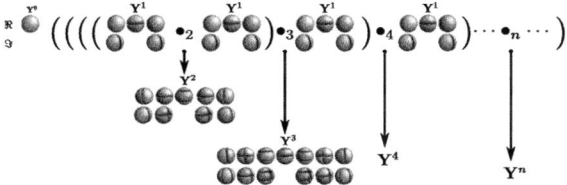

Fig. 3. Key property of $\bullet_\ell$ and $\mathbf{Y}$: higher order spherical harmonics $\mathbf{Y}^{\ell+1}$ can be obtained by element-wise coupling of spherical tensor fields $\mathbf{Y}^\ell$ with $\mathbf{Y}^1$

Since a SHOG is a function on the sphere we can represent $\mathrm{SHOG}_w(\mathbf{x})$ in terms of the orthogonal basis functions $\mathbf{Y}^\ell$, namely

$$\mathrm{SHOG}\{f\}_w(\mathbf{x}, \mathbf{n}) = \sum_{\ell=0}^{\infty} \left(\mathbf{A}_w^\ell(\mathbf{x})\right)^T \mathbf{Y}^\ell(\mathbf{n}) \quad , \tag{2}$$

where $\mathbf{A}_w^\ell(\mathbf{x}) \in \mathbb{C}^{2\ell+1}$ are the vector valued expansion coefficients completely representing the SHOG at image position $\mathbf{x}$ in the spherical harmonic domain.

We identify the coefficients $\mathbf{A}_w^\ell(\mathbf{x})$ by plugging the spherical expansion of the Dirac delta function (figure 5) into eq. (2):

$$\mathrm{SHOG}\{f\}_w(\mathbf{x}, \mathbf{n}) := \int_{\mathbf{r} \in \mathbb{R}^3} \|\mathbf{g}(\mathbf{r})\| \delta_{\mathbf{n}}^2(\hat{\mathbf{g}}(\mathbf{r})) w(\mathbf{x} - \mathbf{r}) d\mathbf{r}$$

$$= \sum_{\ell=0}^{\infty} \int (2\ell+1) \|\mathbf{g}(\mathbf{r})\| (\overline{\mathbf{Y}^\ell}(\hat{\mathbf{g}}(\mathbf{r})))^T w(\mathbf{x} - \mathbf{r}) d\mathbf{r} \mathbf{Y}^\ell(\mathbf{n})$$

$$= \sum_{\ell=0}^{\infty} (2\ell+1) \underbrace{\left(\left(\|\mathbf{g}\| (\overline{\mathbf{Y}^\ell}(\hat{\mathbf{g}}))^T\right) * w\right)(\mathbf{x})}_{=\mathbf{A}_w^\ell(\mathbf{x}) \in \mathbb{C}^{2\ell+1}} \mathbf{Y}^\ell(\mathbf{n}) = \sum_{\ell=0}^{\infty} \left(\mathbf{A}_w^\ell(\mathbf{x})\right)^T \mathbf{Y}^\ell(\mathbf{n}) . \tag{3}$$

For a fast computation of SHOG we utilize so-called spherical tensor products $\bullet_\ell : \mathbb{C}^{2\ell_1+1} \times \mathbb{C}^{2\ell_2+1} \rightarrow \mathbb{C}^{2\ell+1}$ [4] which can be used for coupling *spherical tensors*

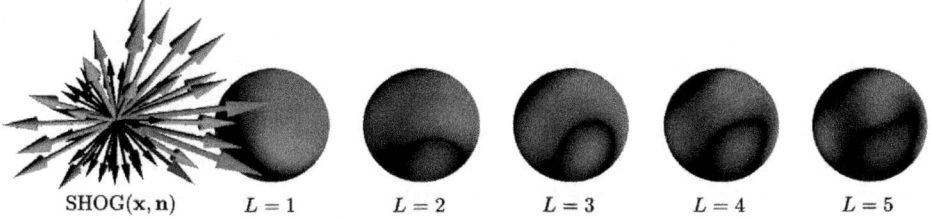

SHOG(x, n) $L=1$ $L=2$ $L=3$ $L=4$ $L=5$

Fig. 4. The most left image shows a quantized SHOG. A band limited expansion in terms of spherical harmonics offers a smooth rotation with the underlying data and a memory efficient representation (here for $\ell \leq 5$).

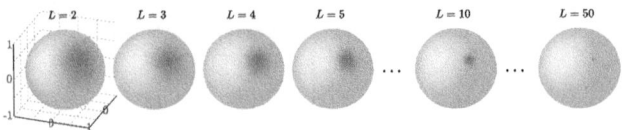

Fig. 5. Band limited expansion of the Dirac delta $\delta_n^2 : S_2 \to \mathbb{R}$ on the unit-sphere: $\delta_n^2(\mathbf{n}') := \sum_{\ell=0}^{\infty}(2\ell+1)(\overline{\mathbf{Y}^\ell}(\mathbf{n}'))^T \mathbf{Y}^\ell(\mathbf{n})$. For our experiments we use $\ell \leq 5$.

associated with different *orders* ℓ_1, ℓ_2 to form new tensors of higher or lower order ℓ i.e. in our scenario here for (point-wise) coupling different functions $\mathbf{Y}^\ell$ or for coupling the expansion coefficients $\mathbf{A}_w^\ell$ of SHOG$_w$. Most important, we can use $\bullet_\ell$ for recursively deriving spherical harmonics of order $\ell + 1$ by coupling two spherical harmonics of order ℓ and 1 with $\mathbf{Y}^{\ell+1} = \mathbf{Y}^\ell \bullet_{\ell+1} \mathbf{Y}^1$ for $\ell \geq 1$. In Fig. 3 we illustrate how higher order spherical harmonics can be computed recursively. Utilizing this property we gain a recursive rule with which we avoid an explicit, expensive computation of $\mathbf{Y}^\ell(\hat{\mathbf{g}})$, namely

$$\mathbf{Y}^{\ell+1}(\hat{\mathbf{g}}) = \mathbf{Y}^\ell(\hat{\mathbf{g}}) \bullet_{\ell+1} \mathbf{Y}^1(\hat{\mathbf{g}}) \quad . \tag{4}$$

Moreover, it turns out that $\|\mathbf{g}\|\mathbf{Y}^1(\hat{\mathbf{g}}) = (\frac{1}{\sqrt{2}}(\frac{\partial f}{\partial x} - i\frac{\partial f}{\partial y}), \frac{\partial f}{\partial z}, -\frac{1}{\sqrt{2}}(\frac{\partial f}{\partial x} + i\frac{\partial f}{\partial y}))^T$ is just the spherical gradient of f which we compute in an initial step. The remaining computations are just the convolutions with the window function w that can be realized very efficiently by utilizing the Fast Fourier Transform.

Object Detection in 3D - SHOG Features for Harmonic Filters: The Harmonic Filter [4,8] is a nonlinear polynomial filter that is designed for detecting arbitrary structures in volumetric images. The most important characteristic of this filter is a trainable voting scheme. The scheme comprises local image features to train a voting function such that the filter responses only to certain structures while responses to all remaining structures in the image are suppressed. This is achieved in an initial training step where the voting scheme is learned by providing a reference image together with a binary-valued label image (see our introductory example in figure 1). The local features of the original Harmonic Filter are the spherical derivatives of the 3D Gaussian encoding the intensity values of a voxel's surrounding in some kind of Taylor expansion coefficients. These features are then combined in a weighted, non-linear way. These weights are the free parameters that are optimized during the training step. Because of the spherical representation of the derivatives the features show a special, very simple rotation behavior depending on the rotation state of the underlying data. The filter comprises the rotation state of the features to steer the voting function wherefore the filter response itself rotates smoothly with respect to the underlying data. Hence structures like objects or landmarks can be detected in any orientation. Since the spherical expansion coefficients $\mathbf{A}_w^\ell$ of the SHOG obey the same rotation behavior like the expansion coefficients of the spherical Gaussian derivatives in the original filter we propose to simply replace

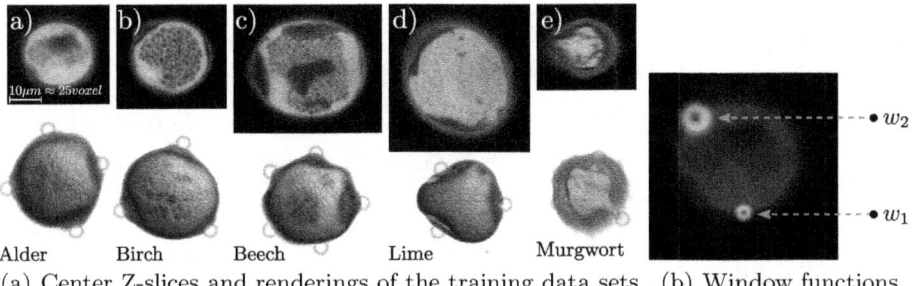

(a) Center Z-slices and renderings of the training data sets   (b) Window functions

Fig. 6. Our Database: Alder pollen (4 porates for training, 56 for testing), Birch pollen (3 train, 42 test), Beech pollen (4 train, 65 test), Lime pollen (3 train, 42 test), Murgwort pollen (3 train, 42 test). **Figure b)** illustrates the size and shape of the two window functions that we use in our experiments (two nested smoothed spheres).

the Gaussian derivatives by SHOG in the Harmonic Filter framework. In addition to a non-linear combination of all expansion coefficients $\mathbf{A}_w^\ell$ we propose to additionally compute and combine coefficients derived from different window functions w_n (an angular cross-correlation of different local SHOG). The expansion coefficients of the voting function of the Harmonic Filter (eq. (6) in [4]) are now

$$\mathbf{V}^\ell(\mathbf{x}) := \sum_{\substack{|\ell_1-\ell_2|\leq\ell\leq\ell_1+\ell_2 \\ \ell_1+\ell_2+\ell \text{ even} \\ \ell_1,\ell_2,\ell\leq N \\ n,m}} \alpha_{\ell_1,\ell_2,\ell}^{n,m} \underbrace{\left(\mathbf{A}_{w_n}^{\ell_1}(\mathbf{x}) \bullet_\ell \mathbf{A}_{w_m}^{\ell_2}(\mathbf{x})\right)}_{\substack{\text{non-linear combination} \\ \text{of coefficients}}} \quad ; \tag{5}$$

$\alpha_{\ell_1,\ell_2,\ell}^{n,m} \in \mathbb{R}$ are the new weighting parameters that are learned in a training step.

3   Experiments

For evaluating the performance of the SHOG-filter we aim at detecting landmarks in volumetric confocal recordings of airborne pollen. In particular we aim at detecting porates in 5 different kinds of pollen species [5], namely (see figure 6) Alder, Birch, Beech, Lime and Murgwort pollen. Each dataset consists of 15 volumetric images where the porates have been manually labeled by an expert for training and evaluation. Note that the number of porates varies between but also within the different species. The image sizes for the Alder, Birch and Murgwort pollen are about 80^3 voxels. For the Beech and Lime pollen we have about 110^3 and 120^3, respectively. One voxel corresponds to $0.4\mu m$.

Apart from our SHOG-Filter, we consider two other trainable filters, namely the original Harmonic Filter [4] and the Bessel Filter [9]. For all filters the experimental setup is as follows: We conduct 5 different experiments based on the different pollen datasets. For each experiment we use one single dataset for training. The training sets are depicted in figure 6 (the labels for training are marked

Table 1. a) Filter parameters in our Experiments. The filter parameters are given in voxel size (voxel size $\approx 0.4\mu m$). **b)** Performance on the Birch dataset when using different normalization strategies.

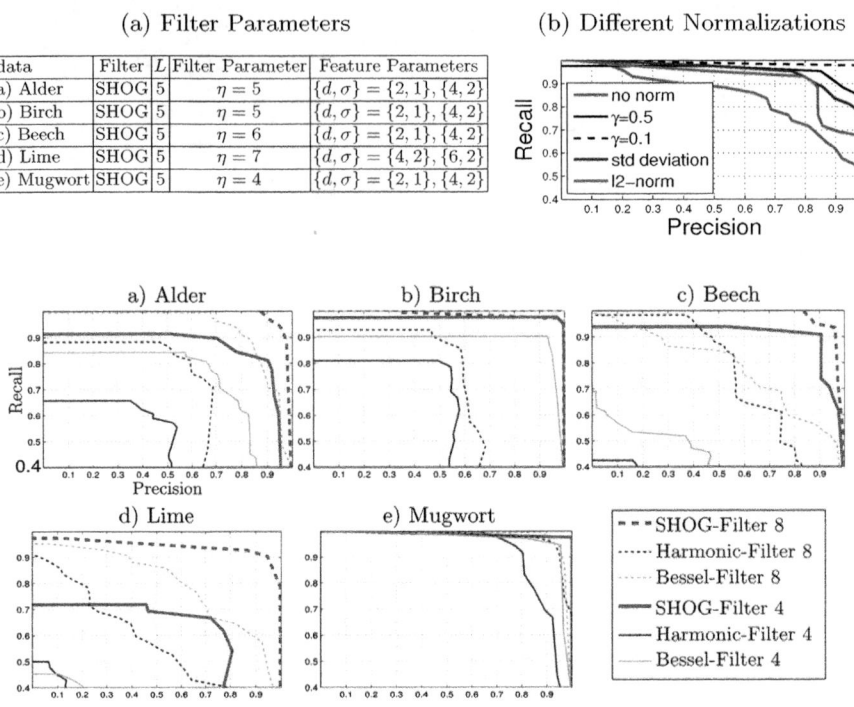

(a) Filter Parameters

data	Filter	L	Filter Parameter	Feature Parameters
a) Alder	SHOG	5	$\eta = 5$	$\{d, \sigma\} = \{2, 1\}, \{4, 2\}$
b) Birch	SHOG	5	$\eta = 5$	$\{d, \sigma\} = \{2, 1\}, \{4, 2\}$
c) Beech	SHOG	5	$\eta = 6$	$\{d, \sigma\} = \{2, 1\}, \{4, 2\}$
d) Lime	SHOG	5	$\eta = 7$	$\{d, \sigma\} = \{4, 2\}, \{6, 2\}$
e) Mugwort	SHOG	5	$\eta = 4$	$\{d, \sigma\} = \{2, 1\}, \{4, 2\}$

(b) Different Normalizations

Fig. 7. The PR-curves are showing the performance of our SHOG-Filter compared to two existing state-of-the-art approaches for all 5 datasets. The dashed lines show the performance when tolerating an 8-voxel displacement to the ground-truth. The straight line shows the performance when only tolerating a 4-voxel displacement. We additionally show the maximum intensity projections of the raw filter responses of the SHOG-Filter in figure 8, clearly emphasizing its superior performance.

by a red circle). In this step the filters optimize their parameter (least square fit) such that the filter response is most similar to the labeling. The filters are then applied to the remaining datasets for evaluation.

For all filters some parameters must be set manually. For finding the optimal parameters we follow the way proposed in [9]. The optimization is done by varying the parameters during several training steps until the Euclidean distance of the filter responses to the training label-images cannot be further reduced significantly. For the SHOG-Filter we must determine the following parameters: A filter degree $L \in \mathbb{N}$ that limits the number of expansion coefficients of the SHOG filter $\mathbf{A}_w^\ell, \ell \leq L$. Furthermore, for the Harmonic Filter framework we need to set the parameter η that steers the size of a Gaussian window that restricts

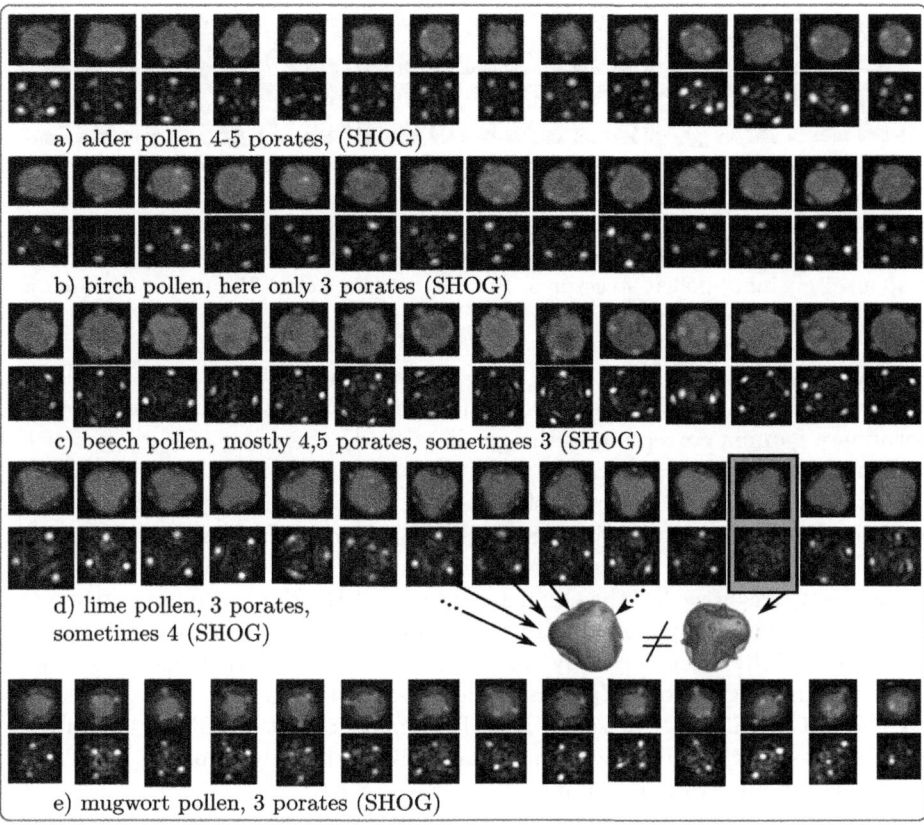

Fig. 8. Detection of airborne-pollen porates in 5 different datasets (see figure 6). We show the maximum intensity projection (MIP) of the raw filter responds of the SHOG-Filter together with the MIP of the detections (colored images) after thresholding (local maxima, threshold selected with respect to the ERR). The SHOG-Filter clearly only response to the porates. Furthermore, the SHOG-Filter didn't respond to a pollen that has accidentally found its way into the database (red mark).

the SHOG features that can contribute to a local filter response. We finally must define one or more window function w for the SHOG itself. We observed that for the given data two nested Gaussian windowed spheres $w(\mathbf{r}, d, \sigma) := e^{\frac{-(\|\mathbf{r}\|-d)^2}{2\sigma^2}}$ lead to the best performance. We exemplarily illustrate the size and shape of the window functions we use for Alder datasets in figure 6(b). The parameters for all SHOG-Filters are summarized in table 1(a).

The gradient magnitude highly varies over a wide range due to variations in illuminations and in particular in volumetric biomedical images due to absorption and occlusion effects. Similar to [2] we observed that unnormalized gradients lead to poor performance. See figure 1(b) for results on the Birch dataset corresponding to different normalization methods. Normalizing SHOG with respect to the standard deviation of the local intensity values [4] increases the performance

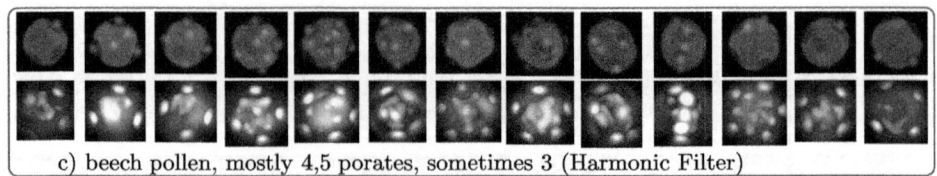

c) beech pollen, mostly 4,5 porates, sometimes 3 (Harmonic Filter)

Fig. 9. Detection of a Harmonic Filter for the Beech dataset (compare to figure 8 c)). The Harmonic Filter detects the porates. However, we where not able to avoid responses on inner-pollen structures. Similar for the Bessel Filter on the Lime and Beech dataset.

significantly. However, we achieve the best performance when almost neglecting the gradient magnitude and only considering the gradient orientation by performing a gamma correction of the gradient field, whereas $\mathbf{g}_\gamma = \|\mathbf{g}\|^\gamma \hat{\mathbf{g}}$. For our experiments we use $\gamma = 0.1$.

Figure 7 lists the PR graphs showing the performance of the filters in all 5 experiments for both tolerating a 8 voxel ($\approx 3.27\mu m$) displacement to the ground truth and tolerating only a more strict 4 voxel ($\approx 1.64\mu m$) displacement. For a better comparison we list the equal error rate (EER) for all experiments in table 1(a). We additionally show qualitative results of the SHOG-Filter in figure 8. The SHOG-Filter produces only clear responses at the correct porate positions. All remaining regions of the pollen are successfully suppressed. Moreover, thanks to the SHOG-Filter we detected a pollen that accidentally found its way into the database. The structure of the porates differ strongly from the training set and thus the filter didn't respond at all (figure 8 d)).

In figure 9 we expemplarily show detections on the Beech dataset corresponding to the Harmonic Filter. Here we can observe that the Harmonic Filter clearly can detect the porates but produces a lot of false positive detections within the pollen. Similar for the remaining pollen species having high variations within the pollen. We observed similar problems for the Bessel Filter. We were not able to suppress responses on the inner structures of the Beech and Lime pollen while still getting clear responses at porate positions. The main difference of the SHOG-Filter is that the gamma normalized SHOG features are mainly comprising the gradient orientations. Thus SHOG is very robust against non-linear, local illumination and contrast changes. In contrast, the Bessel and Harmonic Filters are both indirectly encoding the gradient magnitudes in their features and thus are sensitive to non-linear illumination changes and noise.

4   Conclusions

In this paper, we have presented a way to efficiently compute dense spherical HOG (SHOG) descriptors in volumetric images. Upon theses descriptors we extended the Harmonic Filter to comprise the SHOG features instead of simple Gaussian derivatives to benefit from both a dense, robust and discriminative description in terms of gradient histograms and the trainable voting scheme of the Harmonic Filter which can be realized in a very computational and memory efficient way.

We have shown the superior detection performance of our filter compared to previous state-of-the-art trainable 3D filters. These results are very promising in connection with the growing importance of volumetric data especially in the life sciences. In order to foster further research and experiments, we will provide public executables for using the proposed filter upon acceptance of this paper.

Acknowledgment. This study was supported by the Excellence Initiative of the German Federal and State Governments (EXC 294).

References

1. Buch, N., Orwell, J., Velastin, S.: 3d extended histogram of oriented gradients (3dhog) for classification of road users in urban scenes. In: BMVC 2009, London, UK (2009)
2. Dalal, N., Triggs, B.: Histograms of oriented gradients for human detection. In: Proc. of the CVPR 2009, pp. 886–893 (2005)
3. Lowe, D.G.: Distinctive image features from scale-invariant keypoints. Int. J. Comput. Vision 60(2), 91–110 (2004)
4. Reisert, M., Burkhardt, H.: Harmonic filters for generic feature detection in 3D. In: Denzler, J., Notni, G., Süße, H. (eds.) Pattern Recognition. LNCS, vol. 5748, pp. 131–140. Springer, Heidelberg (2009)
5. Ronneberger, O., Wang, Q., Burkhardt, H.: 3D invariants with high robustness to local deformations for automated pollen recognition. In: Hamprecht, F.A., Schnörr, C., Jähne, B. (eds.) DAGM 2007. LNCS, vol. 4713, pp. 425–435. Springer, Heidelberg (2007)
6. Rose, M.: Elementary Theory of Angular Momentum. Dover Publications, New York (1995)
7. Scherer, M., Walter, M., Schreck, T.: Histograms of oriented gradients for 3d object retrieval. In: Proceedings of the WSCG 2010, Plzen, Czech Republic, pp. 41–48 (2010)
8. Schlachter, M., Reisert, M., Herz, C., Schluermann, F., Lassmann, S., Werner, M., Burkhardt, H., Ronneberger, O.: Harmonic filters for 3d multi-channel data: Rotation invariant detection of mitoses in colorectal cancer. IEEE Transactions on Medical Imaging 29(8), 1485–1495 (2010)
9. Skibbe, H., Reisert, M., Ronneberger, O., Burkhardt, H.: Spherical Bessel filter for 3D object detection. In: Proc. of the 8th ISBI, Chicago,Illinois, USA (April 2011)
10. Thomson, J.J.: On the structure of the atom: an investigation of the stability and periods of oscillation of a number of corpuscles arranged at equal intervals around the circumference of a circle; with application of the results to the theory of atomic structure. Philosophical Magazine Series 67(39), 237–265 (1904)

Pick Your Neighborhood – Improving Labels and Neighborhood Structure for Label Propagation

Sandra Ebert[1,2], Mario Fritz[1], and Bernt Schiele[1]

[1] MPI Informatics, Saarbrucken
[2] TU Darmstadt

Abstract. Graph-based methods are very popular in semi-supervised learning due to their well founded theoretical background, intuitive interpretation of local neighborhood structure, and strong performance on a wide range of challenging learning problems. However, the success of these methods is highly dependent on the pre-existing neighborhood structure in the data used to construct the graph. In this paper, we use metric learning to improve this critical step by increasing the precision of the nearest neighbors and building our graph in this new metric space. We show that learning of neighborhood relations before constructing the graph consistently improves performance of two label propagation schemes on three different datasets – achieving the best performance reported on Caltech 101 to date. Furthermore, we question the predominant random draw of labels and advocate the importance of the choice of labeled examples. Orthogonal to active learning schemes, we investigate how domain knowledge can substantially increase performance in these semi-supervised learning settings.

1 Introduction

Object recognition and scene classification are frequently addressed in computer vision and state-of-the-art methods are dominated by purely supervised learning methods [8,7]. Yet, there is common agreement that unlabeled data conveys important information of the global data distribution as well as the structure of the classes themselves. Nevertheless, we rarely find approaches successfully tapping into both types of sources that would be able to challenge the best supervised approaches. In a previous investigation, we show that the success of such methods critically depends on the neighborhood relations in the data [4]. This strongly suggests that learning should start before a neighborhood structure is imposed on the data points in order to surpass the inherent limitations of traditional semi-supervised learning schemes.

One might argue that with the availability of crowd sourcing services like Mechanical Turk the value of unlabeled data has shrunken and will ultimately loose its significance. Evidently, there has been a big impact on the vision community as data and labels seem now available in abundance. But recent data collection efforts at those large scales have their own set of problems due to labeling errors and ambiguities [21]. Also adding label information in an unstructured manner

R. Mester and M. Felsberg (Eds.): DAGM 2011, LNCS 6835, pp. 152–162, 2011.

will lead to redundant information yielding an inefficient learning scheme. While active learning has provided useful insights and improvements in this area, the role of domain knowledge has gone largely overlooked.

Contributions: This paper is concerned with the question of how to make better use of the provided labels already in the early stages of popular semi-supervised learning methods. Therefore, our first main contribution is to employ a metric learning approach to improve the graph construction which leads to a consistent improvement in performance. As second main contribution, we propose methods of querying more informative labels based on domain knowledge that are complimentary to traditional active learning settings. Our semi-supervised learning schemes deliver consistent improvements across 3 dataset and show state-of-the-art performance on Caltech-101.

2   Related Work

Graph-based methods are a popular choice for semi-supervised learning (SSL) as they are well understood and easy to implement. The way they exploit neighborhood structure is intuitive and the computational demands are usually moderate. One of the key issue of these methods is the construction of the graph. But this critical aspect is often neglected [24] and meaningful neighborhood relations as well as a class structure is assumed to be encoded in the distances of the raw feature space. We have shown in a recent study [4] that for visual categories those assumptions cannot be taken for granted and that the quality of the graph is in fact highly correlated with performance. Thus it is surprising how little attention graph construction [19,13] has received in comparison to various algorithmic contributions [22,23]. In [19], the authors uses the neighboring data points to reconstruct each data point from its neighbors. In [13], they propose a method to balance a graph such that dominant nodes are weighted down. All those methods do not use the information which are contained in the labels itself and they are all based on the limiting assumption that the initial feature representation is sufficient for immediate graph construction.

In contrast, metric learning learns a representation better suited to the task at hand. The proposed methods essentially differ in the parameterization of the learned metric (including regularizers and constraints) and optimization procedures. Some methods learn a Mahalanobis distance [3,14,17,9] often with pairwise constraints, while other approaches maximize the inter-class distance by a large margin approach [20]. Although, there are other works combining SSL with some feature transformation [10,18,16], this work tightly interleaves a metric learning scheme with label propagation. We use [3] and the follow-up work [14] that show impressive improvements for Caltech 101. Beside the success, it is scalable to large problems in particular in a high dimensional space and it guarantees convergence to the global maximum.

3   Improving Neighborhood Structure for SSL

As motivated above, we use metric learning [3] to improve our neighborhood structure and apply a graph-based label propagation algorithm [22] on top of this new metric space. Both methods are briefly explained in the following. As shown in sec. 5 the proposed combination of these two techniques leads to improved results over either technique alone, outperforming previously published results e.g. for Caltech 101 using the same underlying image representation [14].

Information theoretic metric learning (ITML): [3] optimizes the Mahalanobis distance between each point pair $x_i, x_j \in \mathbb{R}^d$

$$d_A(x_i, x_j) = (x_i - x_j)^T A(x_i - x_j) \tag{1}$$

Eq. (1) reduces to a simple euclidean distance if $A = I$. To learn matrix A, the algorithm minimizes the logdet divergence between a matrix A and an initial matrix A_0 with respect to pairwise similarity and dissimilarity constraints:

$$
\begin{aligned}
\min \ & D_{ld}(A, A_0) \\
s.t. \ & d_A(x_i, x_j) \le b_u \quad (i,j) \in \mathcal{S} \\
& d_A(x_i, x_j) \ge b_l \quad (i,j) \in \mathcal{D}
\end{aligned}
\tag{2}
$$

b_u and b_l are upper and lower bound of similarity and dissimilarity constraints. $\mathcal{S}$ and $\mathcal{D}$ are sets of similarity and dissimilarity constraints based on the labeled data. To make this optimization feasible, a slack parameter γ is introduced to control the trade-off between satisfying the constraints and minimizing $D_{ld}(A, A_0)$. The larger γ the more constraints are ignored. The optimization is done by repeatedly Bregman projections of a single constraint per iteration.

One benefit of this optimization scheme is the efficient kernelization with $K = X^T A X$. A proof can be found in [3]. The kernel version has several advantages. The run time depends only on the number of constraints n_c and not on the dimensions d that is critical in a high dimensional space. We can subsample the number of constraints such that $n_c \ll d$ which reduces the costs from $O(d^2)$ to $O(n_c^2)$. Finally, we can easily compute the at most violated constraint per iteration since only matrix additions ($K_{ii} + K_{jj} - 2K_{ij}$) is required and no complex multiplications as in eq. (1) leading to faster convergence.

Label propagation (LP): We use the common and robust method by [22]. Given a labeled set $\{(x_1, y_1), ..., (x_l, y_l)\}$ and an unlabeled set $\{x_{l+1}, ..., x_{l+u}\}$ with $n = l + u$ data $x_i \in \mathbb{R}^d$ and l labels $y_i \in \mathcal{L} = \{1, ..., c\}$, we build a k-nearest

neighbor graph $\hat{P}_{ij} = \begin{cases} 1 & \text{if } d_A(x_i, x_j) \text{ is one of the smallest } k \text{ distances of } i \\ 0 & \text{otherwise} \end{cases}$

that is symmetric, e.g., $P_{ij} = max(\hat{P}_{ij}, \hat{P}_{ji})$, and weighted with a Gaussian kernel $W_{ij} = P_{ij} \exp\left(\frac{-d_A(x_i, x_j)}{2\sigma^2}\right)$. Based on this graph a normalized graph Laplacian

$S = I - D^{-1/2} W D^{-1/2}$ with $D_{ij} = \begin{cases} \sum_j W_{ij} & \text{if } i = j \\ 0 & \text{otherwise} \end{cases}$ is built.

Fig. 1. Left: ETH, middle: C-PASCAL (column 5-8), and right: Caltech 101

For the learning, we split our multi-class problem into c binary problems and get a prediction vector for each class by an iterative procedure

$$Y_m^{(t+1)} = \alpha S Y_m^{(t)} + (1 - \alpha) Y_m^{(0)} \tag{3}$$

with $1 \leq m \leq c$ and Y_m^* the limit of this sequence. Parameter $\alpha \in (0, 1]$ controls the overwriting of the original labels. The final prediction is obtained by $\hat{Y} = \text{argmax}_{1 \leq m \leq c} Y_m^*$.

4   Datasets and Representation

We analyze three datasets with increasing number of object classes and different difficulty. Some of the images are shown in Fig. 1.

ETH-80 (ETH) [15] contains 3,280 images divided in 8 object classes and 10 instances per class. Each instance is photographed from 41 viewpoints in front of a uniform background.

We propose Cropped PASCAL (C-PASCAL) in [4] where we use the bounding box annotations of the PASCAL VOC challenge 2008 training set [5] to extract the objects such that classification can be evaluated in a multi-class setting. The resulting data set contains 4,450 images of aligned objects from 20 classes but with varying object poses, challenging appearances, background clutter, and truncation. For the data representation of both datasets, we also use a HOG [2] representation with cells of 8×8 pixels.

Caltech 101 [6] is a dataset with 9,144 images and 101 object classes. Objects are located in the middle of the image, but there is still background clutter and a large intra-class variability. As a representation we use the same kernel as in [12] (obtained from the authors), which uses an average of four kernels: two kernels based on the geometric blur descriptor, Pyramid Match Kernel (PMK) and the Spatial PMK using SIFT features [11].

5   Evaluation of Metric Learning for Label Propagation

In this section, we show first the performance on all three datasets and compare our results with the k-nearest neighbors results (KNN) given by [14]. Next, we give some insight in the learned metric and the resulting neighborhood structure. Based on these observations, we propose a new propagation scheme – *Interleaved*

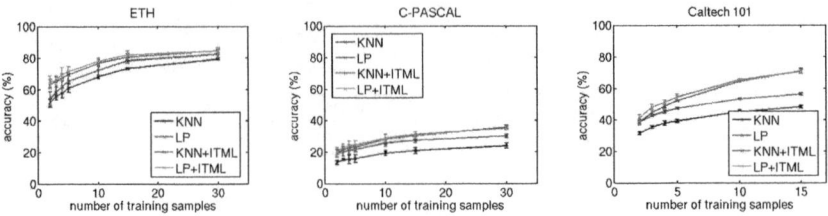

Fig. 2. Overall accuracy for different number of training samples. left: ETH, middle: C-PASCAL, and right: Caltech 101.

Metric Learning and Propagation (IMLP) – by continuously adding unlabeled data. Finally, we show results on Caltech 101 that outperform the state-of-the-art for 5 training samples.

Metric learning for label propagation: In all experiments, we use the kernelized version of ITML with a gaussian kernel. Only for ETH we report plain metric learning as we didn't observe any increased performance. Parameter σ for the kernel and the slack parameter γ are set empirically. For the number of nearest neighbor k we choose always the best for each algorithm. All experiments were repeated 5 times with random splits. In table 1, results for k nearest neighbor classifier before (KNN) and after (KNN+ITML) metric learning, and label propagation before (LP) and after (LP+ITML) are shown for 5 training samples per class. First, KNN+ITML (col. 3) is always better than KNN (col. 2). Moreover, there is an increase from 39.1% to 52.2% for Caltech 101. Second, LP (col. 4) is consistently improved by LP+ITML (col. 5), i.e., for Caltech 101 from 47.1% to 54.5%. Finally, all LP+ITML results are better than KNN+ITML due to the additional information from the unlabeled data. This leads to an improvement of 2.3% for Caltech 101 in comparison to [14]. The same observation holds true when we vary the number of training examples as in fig. 2. The light blue curve (LP+ITML) is for all 3 datasets above all other curves. It is noteworthy to mention that both LP curves are above all KNN results for ETH.

Discussion and analysis: In fact, the precision of our neighborhood structure increases. This is also illustrated in fig. 3 for C-PASCAL. The first nearest neighbors of a query image (1st col.) are shown before ITML (first row) and after ITML (second row). True positives are outlined with green. Indeed, training examples of a class are pushed close together. But ITML tends to overfit to the training samples. This is more obvious when we split the quality of k nearest

Table 1. Overall accuracy for all datasets and 5 training samples

dataset	KNN	KNN+ITML	LP	LP+ITML
ETH	61.0 ± 2.6	69.3 ± 0.8	65.3 ± 4.7	71.4 ± 3.0
C-PASCAL	15.8 ± 2.6	23.0 ± 1.6	21.5 ± 1.6	24.2 ± 2.7
Caltech 101	39.1 ± 1.1	52.2 ± 0.5	47.1 ± 0.6	54.5 ± 1.7

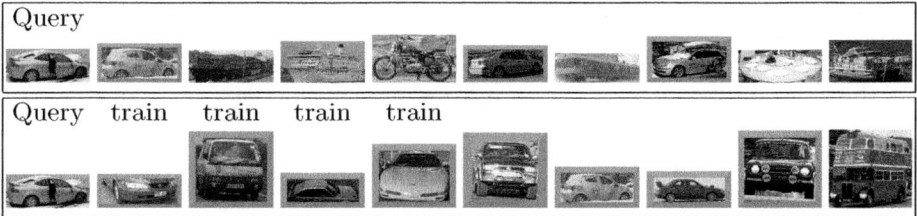

Fig. 3. First nearest neighbors of a query image (1st column) of C-PASCAL. Top: before ITML and bottom: after ITML. True positives are outlined with green and training samples are marked with "train".

neighbors into labeled (NN_L) and unlabeled (NN_U) quality, i.e., the number of true positives within the k nearest neighbors. Fig. 4 shows these qualities for different number of neighbors k. In particular for C-PASCAL and Caltech 101, where we use a Gaussian kernel, NN_L increases up to $95\% - 100\%$ for $k = 1$ while the effect on NN_U is substantially smaller.

Interleaved Metric Learning and Propagation (IMLP): Based on this observation, we address the lack of generalization by incorporating few predictions from unlabeled data. We propose an iterative procedure with interleaved metric learning and label propagation. This improves incrementally the nearest neighbor precision with the condition that the manifold structure given by the unlabeled data is taken into account. The resulting procedure is as follows:

1. metric learning to get kernel K
2. label propagation with kernel K to obtain predictions $\hat{Y}$ of unlabeled data
3. choose $m = m + n_s$ data points x_i such that $|\tilde{y}_1| \geq ... \geq |\tilde{y}_i| \geq |\tilde{y}_{i+1}| \geq ... \geq |\tilde{y}_m|$ with $\tilde{Y} = \max_{1 \leq j \leq c} Y_j^*$ and $l < i <= u$
4. construct new sets of similarities $\mathcal{S}$ and dissimilarities $\mathcal{D}$ from l labels and m predicted labels, and go to step 1.

Table 2 shows results for Caltech 101, 5 training samples, and $n_s = 200$. We improve our results of LP+ITML to 58.7% that goes beyond existing best known numbers of 56.9% by Boiman[1] and 54.2% by Gehler[8]. Also, the performance of KNN+ITML increases to 59.1%. The better performance in comparison to LP+ITML can be explained by incorporating more structure from unlabeled data. Finally, we also get a small improvement for C-PASCAL even though not as much as for Caltech 101 due to lower prediction quality, and almost no improvement for ETH.

6   Selection of Training Data Based on Domain Knowledge

While the previous section was concerned with algorithmic improvements, we now want to shift the focus to the importance of selecting good training examples for semi-supervised learning algorithms. As those methods tend to operate in a regime where only a few labels are available, a random strategy can easily pick

Table 2. Overall accuracy for Caltech 101 and 5 training samples on our original setting and with predictions

dataset	KNN+ITML	LP+ITML
original	52.2 ± 0.5	54.5 ± 1.7
with predictions	59.1 ± 0.7	58.7 ± 0.8

a set of atypical examples or simply provide poor coverage of the class and/or viewpoint variation. We illustrate these issues in fig. 5, where we provide a more detailed analysis for the class "car" from our C-PASCAL experiment. The first column shows the best random draw w.r.t. average precision (PASCAL VOC criteria) of the retrieved unlabeled examples. We observe a good coverage of intra-class variation and view-points. The next column shows the worst draw. Atypical examples, less viewpoint variation, and truncation have lead to a drop in precision from 28.6% to 13.7%! Next we selected 5 prototypical examples by hand to convey our domain knowledge of cars, which results in a performance of 22.4%, right in between the best and worst results of a random draw. To take a step towards an automated approach, we also seek prototypical examples in a statistical sense by finding modes in the distribution of the car examples. Please note that this is best-case type analysis as we are finding the modes for the cars isolated from the other classes. However, this leads to a performance of 35% which is over 6% better than the best random draw we have and over 20% better than the worst one. This large margin emphasizes the potential of selecting appropriate labeled examples opposed to a random draw. The last two columns represent draws from a method we are going to present in this section, that almost recover the best-case performance.

In the following, we address the sampling process in an unsupervised manner by using graph properties. The results on all 3 datasets show an improvement for both precision and robustness. In the last experiment, we look at ETH where we use the viewpoint information to obtain better distributed and more representative training examples.

Towards indentifying prototypical instances: In our first experiment, we build a graph based on our kernels and use the intrinsic graph structure to identify highly connected nodes or nodes with a high weight. The intuition behind is that

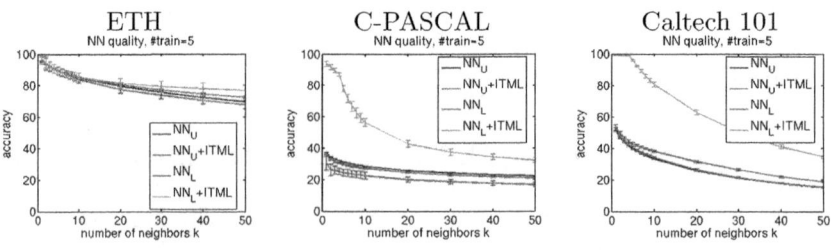

Fig. 4. Nearest neighbor quality splitted into labeled and unlabeled quality

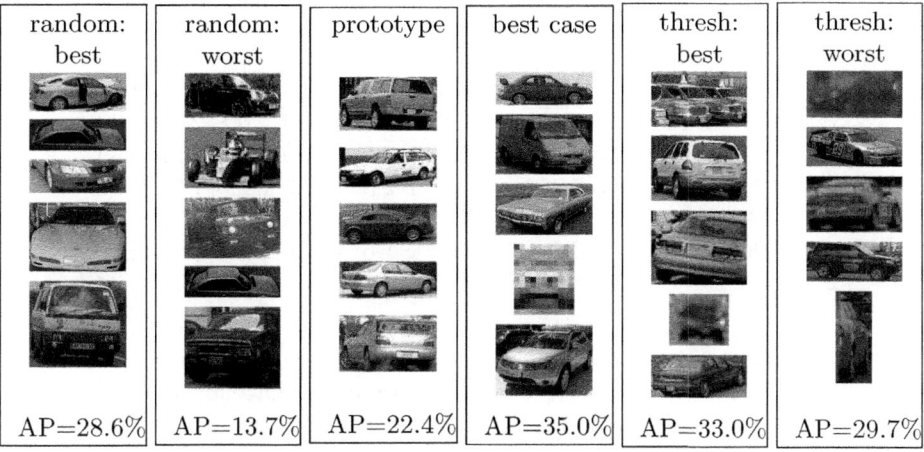

random: best	random: worst	prototype	best case	thresh: best	thresh: worst
AP=28.6%	AP=13.7%	AP=22.4%	AP=35.0%	AP=33.0%	AP=29.7%

Fig. 5. Training samples of C-PASCAL: random best and worst seed (column 1-2), prototypical selection, and best case estimation (4th column), and with threshold on the graph structure for best and worst seed (column 5-6). AP is the average precision for this class calculated by the PASCAL VOC criteria.

representative images for a class are usually well integrated in the graph and form almost a clique with other similar images, e.g., these nodes have many edges ($\gg k$) with high weights. Our goal is to find such key images. To eliminate images that have many neighbors but only with low weights, we normalize this term by the number of edges:

$$\frac{\sum_i W_{ij}}{\sum_i P_{ij}} > thresh \tag{4}$$

We set *thresh* in our experiments to 0.6. For C-PASCAL, this reduces the number of possible selected images from 222 on average to 136 images per class.

Table 3. Overall accuracy of different sampling methods – random sampling, with threshold, and a best case estimate – for 5 training samples

dataset	sampling	KNN	KNN+ITML	LP	LP+ITML
ETH	random	61.0 ± 2.6	65.3 ± 4.7	69.3 ± 0.8	71.3 ± 3.0
	threshold	63.8 ± 2.0	67.4 ± 1.0	72.9 ± 2.8	73.0 ± 3.3
	best case	68.5	73.5	81.1	82.6
C-PASCAL	random	15.8 ± 2.6	21.5 ± 1.6	23.0 ± 1.6	24.2 ± 2.7
	threshold	19.0 ± 1.1	23.5 ± 1.0	24.7 ± 1.9	25.6 ± 2.0
	best case	30.1	30.4	36.2	36.4
Caltech 101	random	39.1 ± 1.1	47.1 ± 0.6	52.2 ± 0.5	54.5 ± 1.7
	threshold	40.3 ± 0.6	47.3 ± 1.1	53.3 ± 1.2	55.5 ± 0.9
	best case	45.7	53.9	57.9	59.9

Table 4. Overall accuracy of ETH for different viewpoint sampling methods in comparison to our random baseline (first line)

long.	width	KNN	KNN+ITML	LP	LP+ITML
random	random	61.0 ± 2.6	65.3 ± 4.7	69.3 ± 0.8	71.3 ± 3.0
$90°$	$360°/5$	64.0 ± 2.2	65.5 ± 3.5	74.9 ± 2.6	74.2 ± 3.6
$68° - 90°$		63.7 ± 2.8	66.2 ± 2.3	73.9 ± 2.5	74.4 ± 3.1
$45° - 90°$		65.4 ± 2.3	68.3 ± 2.7	73.3 ± 1.7	75.2 ± 2.4
$35° - 90°$		64.3 ± 1.9	68.2 ± 1.5	73.6 ± 2.2	**76.5 ± 2.0**
$22° - 90°$		62.2 ± 3.5	67.1 ± 3.1	69.8 ± 3.1	71.8 ± 3.6

Table 3 shows the performance with and without thresholding for all three datasets (row 1-2) and 5 training examples. Again, we have an improvement for all datasets. For C-PASCAL, we increase the performance of LP+ITML from 24.2% to 25.6% while decreasing the standard deviation from 2.7% to 2.0%. Fig. 5 shows the according training samples for the best and the worst seed in the last two columns. It stands out that the average precision (AP) of the worst seed of thresholded sampling is higher with 29.7% than the best random sampling AP with 28.6%.

To get an idea what we can achieve in an almost best case scenario, we build a graph with $k = 50$, and calculate for each node the number of correct neighbors. We apply k-means clustering for each class to get 5 clusters. Finally, we choose for each cluster the image with the highest nearest neighbor accuracy. This procedure ensures both class coverage and high precision. The results are shown in table 3 last row and the corresponding training examples for C-PASCAL are in fig. 5 (col. 4). It is obvious that there is a huge potential in selecting the "right" training samples. While we improve the performance of LP+ITML of C-PASCAL from 24.2% to 36.4%, we also increase the difference to KNN+ITML from 2.7% to 6% that suggests a large unused potential in the underlying structure.

Towards indentifying prototypical viewpoints: For our second experiment, we use domain knowledge in terms of viewpoint information. Each object in ETH is captured from 41 different viewpoints with varying degrees on both the longitudinal axis from $0°$ to $90°$ and the width axis with $360°$. We split the width axis with $360°$ into 5 parts and sample one example from each of these areas. Additional, we increase the radius on the longitudinal axis starting from $90°$ to $22°$. The larger the range the more objects from above are sampled.

In Table 4 are the results in comparison to our random baseline (first line). All sampling methods based on domain knowledge (row 2-6) lead to a higher performance and a lower standard deviation in comparison to the baseline with 71.3% that contains many images photographed from above. Our best result for LP+ITML with viewpoint information is 76.5%.

7   Conclusion

In this work, we use metric learning to enhance our nearest neighborhood structure that is key for graph-based algorithms and their performance. We show a consistent and significant improvement on three different datasets, and give insights into the learned metric space. We propose a second label propagation scheme – Interleaved Metric Learning and Propagation (IMLP) – that leads to the best published performance on Caltech 101 to date. Finally, we use domain knowledge to sample training data for the semi-supervised framework, and point out the potential in comparison to the common random sampling strategy.

In future work, we intend to make this approach scalable to large image collections like ImageNet since we have not yet exploited all information contained in massive data sets. It would also be interesting to explore other domain-specific or structure knowledge to get better and more representative training samples that require less supervision.

References

1. Boiman, O., Shechtman, E., Irani, M.: In defense of Nearest-Neighbor based image classification. In: CVPR (2008)
2. Dalal, N., Triggs, B.: Histograms of Oriented Gradients for Human Detection. In: CVPR (2005)
3. Davis, J.V., Kulis, B., Jain, P., Sra, S., Dhillon, I.S.: Information-theoretic metric learning. In: ICML (2007)
4. Ebert, S., Larlus, D., Schiele, B.: Extracting structures in image collections for object recognition. In: Daniilidis, K., Maragos, P., Paragios, N. (eds.) ECCV 2010. LNCS, vol. 6311, pp. 720–733. Springer, Heidelberg (2010)
5. Everingham, M., Van Gool, L., Williams, C.K.: The PASCAL VOC (2008)
6. Fei-Fei, L., Fergus, R., Perona, P.: One-shot learning of object categories. PAMI 28(4), 594–611 (2006)
7. Felzenszwalb, P.F., Girshick, R.B., McAllester, D., Ramanan, D.: Object detection with discriminatively trained part-based models. PAMI 32, 1627–1645 (2010)
8. Gehler, P., Nowozin, S.: On feature combination for multiclass object classification. In: ICCV (2009)
9. Goldberger, J., Roweis, S., Hinton, G., Salakhutdinov, R.: Neighbourhood components analysis. In: NIPS (2005)
10. Grabner, H., Leistner, C., Bischof, H.: Semi-supervised on-line boosting for robust tracking. In: Forsyth, D., Torr, P., Zisserman, A. (eds.) ECCV 2008, Part I. LNCS, vol. 5302, pp. 234–247. Springer, Heidelberg (2008)
11. Grauman, K., Darrell, T.: The Pyramid Match Kernel: Discriminative Classification with Sets of Image Features. In: ICCV (2005)
12. Jain, P., Kapoor, A.: Active learning for large multi-class problems. In: CVPR (2009)
13. Jebara, T., Wang, J., Chang, S.F.: Graph construction and b -matching for semi-supervised learning. In: ICML (2009)
14. Kulis, B., Jain, P., Grauman, K.: Fast Similarity Search for Learned Metrics. PAMI 31(12), 2143–2157 (2009)

15. Leibe, B., Schiele, B.: Analyzing Appearance and Contour Based Methods for Object Categorization. In: CVPR (2003)
16. Lu, Z., Jain, P., Dhillon, I.S.: Geometry-aware metric learning. In: ICML (2009)
17. Saenko, K., Kulis, B., Fritz, M., Darrell, T.: Adapting visual category models to new domains. In: Daniilidis, K., Maragos, P., Paragios, N. (eds.) ECCV 2010. LNCS, vol. 6314, pp. 213–226. Springer, Heidelberg (2010)
18. Teramoto, R.: Prediction of Alzheimer's diagnosis using semi-supervised distance metric learning with label propagation. Comp. Biol. and Chem. 32(6), 438–441 (2008)
19. Wang, F., Zhang, C.: Label propagation through linear neighborhoods. KDE 20(1), 55–67 (2008)
20. Weinberger, K.Q., Saul, L.K.: Distance Metric Learning for Large Margin Nearest Neighbor Classification. JMLR 10, 207–244 (2009)
21. Welinder, P., Branson, S., Belongie, S., Perona, P.: The multidimensional wisdom of crowds. In: NIPS (2010)
22. Zhou, D., Schölkopf, B., Bousquet, O., Lal, T.N., Weston, J.: Learning with Local and Global Consistency. In: NIPS (2004)
23. Zhu, X., Lafferty, J.: Harmonic mixtures: combining mixture models and graph-based methods for inductive and scalable semi-supervised learning. In: ICML (2005)
24. Zhu, X.: Semi-supervised learning literature survey. Tech. rep., University of Wisconsin-Madison (2006)

People Tracking Algorithm for Human Height Mounted Cameras

Vladimir Kononov, Vadim Konushin, and Anton Konushin

Graphics & Media Lab, Moscow State University
{vkononov,vadim,ktosh}@graphics.cs.msu.ru

Abstract. We present a new people tracking method for human height mounted camera, e.g. the one attached near information or advertising stand. We use state-of-the-art particle filter approach and improve it by explicitly modeling of object visibility which makes the method able to cope with difficult object overlapping. We employ our own method based on online-boosting classifiers to resolve occlusions and show that it is well suited for tracking multiple objects. In addition to training an online-classifier which is updated each frame we propose to store object appearance and update it with a certain lag. It helps to correctly handle situations when a person enters the scene while another one leaves it at the same time. We demonstrate the perfomance of our algorithm and advantages of our contributions on our own video dataset.

1 Introduction

Person tracking is a well-studied problem in computer vision. During the last decades many methods and approaches have been proposed in this field. One of the main applications of such methods is video surveillance in security and sport translations. It determines some common scenarios which are considered in many methods. In these scenarios camera is mounted high above the ground and is remote from the tracked objects. We consider another scenario where camera is attached to an information stand, 1-2 meters above the ground and watches people who pass in front of it, look at it or come close to it. Such scenario arises in a number of applications, e.g. information and advertising stands.

The concerned scenario differs from standard security applications or sport translations (Fig. 1). First, bottom parts of people and the ground are not visible. This complicates an estimation of trajectories in 3D. Also it makes standard people detection algorithms unreliable. Second, people are often occluded by each other for a long time, which is not as common in scenarios with higher located cameras. It means that tracking in this scenario implies multi-target tracking with a lot of occlusions among targets. Third, objects occupy large part of a frame. It causes problems with proper handling of objects, entering and leaving the scene. Fourth, objects tend to stop and look at camera. Along with almost 1D trajectories it reduces reliability of motion models. Fifth, algorithm should be able to react almost instantly because of its usage in information

R. Mester and M. Felsberg (Eds.): DAGM 2011, LNCS 6835, pp. 163–172, 2011.
© Springer-Verlag Berlin Heidelberg 2011

Fig. 1. Tracking scenarios: (left) - example from PETS sequences, (center) - frame from soccer match video, (right) - the proposed scenario

stands. That means, the algorithm cannot use global optimization schemes, but is restricted to employ frame-by-frame basis.

We propose a novel method for tracking people in such scenario. Our method processes video frame by frame and is based on a widespread and acknowledged particle filter framework. We improve it by explicitly modeling of object visibility state. It helps to correctly track people even after long-term occlusions. To distinguish objects from each other we employ online-boosting for training object appearance models. We improve this method by training a classifier using 'one target against every other' approach rather than 'one target against all other'. It improves distinguishing objects in crowded scenes. Finally, we propose to store object appearances with a certain update lag in order to determine its rapid changes. This is very often caused by simultaneous enter of one person and leaving of another. Our method is able to perform tracking correctly in these difficult situations.

We tested our algorithm on our own collection of 29 videos of the concerned scenario. The results show a good performance of the proposed method and the advantages of our contributions.

The rest of the paper is organized as follows. The related work is discussed in Section 2. The proposed method is described in Section 3. Our video database and the experimental results are discussed in Section 4. Section 5 concludes the paper.

2   Related Work

For object tracking tasks a lot of algorithms has been proposed starting from following a manually marked object against complex background to video surveillance of huge amount of people in airports [20].

Multi-target tracking consists of algorithms which focus on tracking several or many objects simultaneously. They need to solve problems that are not typical for other tracking approaches. These problems are distinguishing objects one from another, resolving occlusions between objects, processing of objects entering and leaving the scene.

Some algorithms rely on global optimization to resolve multi-target ambiguities. Classical approaches such as JPDAF [6] and MHT [18] are very time-consuming, because the search space of these methods grows exponentially with the number of targets and time steps. Other approaches employ a mixture of greedy schemes and dynamic programming to overcome the problem [1][2][15]. In [14] authors use similar approache to find reliable parts of trajectories. Then their method tries to stitch derived tracklets together. Global optimization algorithms showed good results. But they consider a whole video sequence and therefore cannot work in online applications in the original form without modifications.

In order to work online tracking algorithms should stick to frame-by-frame basis [3][4]. The most prominent methods of this type use Particle Filter approach [3][17][19]. Algorithms either model all objects in the scene with one set of particles [8] or use independent sets for each object. The former approach leads to exponentially growing number of particles or to lowering approximation accuracy with the number of objects. Meanwhile use of independent set of particles for each object leads to problems with resolving occlusions.

Different approaches are used to resolve occlusions: motion estimation, learning objects appearance models and 3D modeling by use of two or several cameras [11][16]. While some of these approaches might be very helpful, they are not always available. For example, in our scenario we can not use several cameras.

Some algorithms perform tracking in scenarios similar to the concerned one. In [12] objects are represented as mixtures of 5D Gaussians without training any object-specific classifiers. Also authors use euristic approach for finding new people in a frame and don't properly handle their leaving. In [9] authors use a particle filter framework but they use one appearance model for all objects. That means that their algorithm can find objects in the scene but cannot distinguish them properly.

Although many algorithms such as [3] show good quality in different video sequences, they do not explicitly model occlusions. This can lead to possible loss of objects. We propose to explicitly model occluded object state to overcome this problem.

3   Approach

3.1   Background Subtraction

In this paper we consider a scenario in which camera is mounted on 1-2 meter height, and does not see the ground. This fact makes an estimation of object 3D position very hard. A special upper-body detector can be used as in [5]. But it is suited only for frontal people, so we use background subtraction method. This step should not be time-consuming, so we use simple background modeling with Gaussian distribution in each pixel. We use short background videos for initialization. Then we retrieve foreground masks frame-by-frame pixel-by-pixel. Foreground pixels are post-processed with simple morphological operations and final foreground mask is obtained.

We employ the fact that all people in our scenario are cut by the bottom of the frame. After background subtraction step we find all sufficiently big blobs in a frame. These blobs restrain possible positions of objects, i.e. no object can be

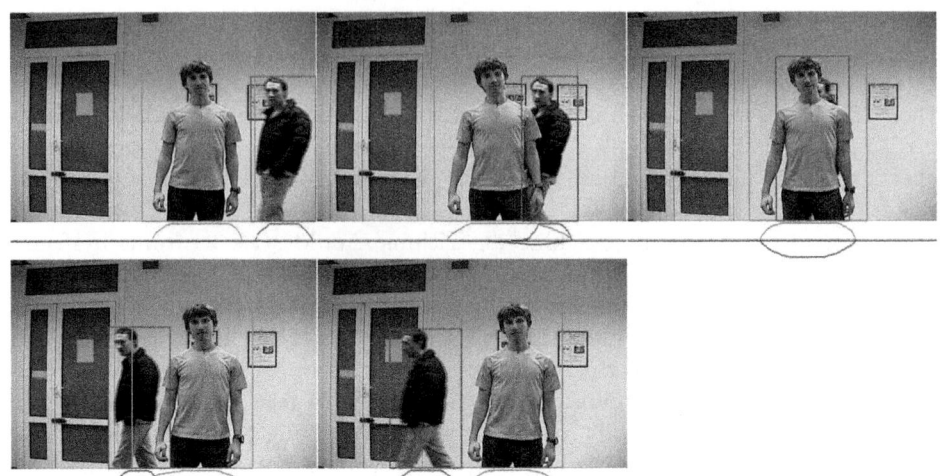

Fig. 2. Example of a simple occlusion handling. Graphics under frames show a distribution of current particle filter set. The parts of graphics above the line correspond to visible particles and vise versa.

outside the blobs. In order to correctly model objects, which are only partially inside the scene, we add two invisible blobs: one to the right and one to the left of a frame.

3.2   Particle Filter

We use a first-order Markov process in order to model object states during tracking. Within this context Particle Filter(PF) approach models probability distribution of object states as a weighted set of particles.

$$p(S) = \sum_{i=1}^{N} w^i \delta(S - s^i), where \sum_{i=1}^{N} w^i = 1. \tag{1}$$

Here w^i are weight coefficients, s^i are particles and N is their number.

PF also known in literature as Bootsrap Filter and Condensation algorithm [10], allows to predict object state in a new frame based on a current set of particles, and to estimate the likelihood of each particle based on a new frame. The main advantage of Particle Filter approach is its ability to model a huge variety of possible distributions, while other approaches are not so powerful. For example, another popular approach Kalman Filter (KF) works only if both prediction and observation models can be modeled with Gaussian distributions.

Classical PF approach uses particles consisting of object position and velocity information. In our case object positions can be modeled in 1D. Bottom of each object is the frame bottom line in our scenario, and object height can be defined by foreground mask. This leads to the following particle structure

Fig. 3. Example of object loss when particles don't have visibility label

$s = (x, wd, v, l)$, where x is a center of object's bounding box, wd is its width, and v is an object's speed. The last component l is a binary label which shows whether we consider this particle visible or occluded. This component comprises our contribution to classical particle structure. Label l (we named it visibility label) helps in describing current situation more carefully. Now particles have an option to become occluded by changing their visibility label instead of obligatory following some visible objects. Explicit modeling of visibility state makes it possible not only to estimate probable positions of objects but also to assess if the object is occluded by another one.

During a prediction step particle states are updated based on motion model:

$$\begin{cases} x_t = x_{t-1} + v_{t-1} + \mathcal{N}(0, \delta_x), \\ wd_t = wd_{t-1} + \mathcal{N}(0, \delta_{wd}), \\ v_t = v_{t-1} * (1 - \beta) + \beta * (x_t - x_{t-1}) + \mathcal{N}(0, \delta_v) \end{cases} \quad (2)$$

Visibility label change is modeled with Bernoulli distribution:

$$P(l_t|l_{t-1}) = l_{t-1} * (1 - \alpha) + \alpha * l_t \quad (3)$$

We use α equal to 0.2 in our experiments. Thereby during each prediction step some pixels change their visibility label.

Fig. 2 shows an example of tracking 2 people. The importance of our contribution is shown in Fig. 3 where tracking is performed by baseline PF framework without explicit visibility modeling. During complex occlusion blue object particles lose the tracked person. This is not the case with visibility label (Fig. 6). During the same occlusion blue object particles change their visibility labels and divide between two blobs. After reappearing of the person after occlusion, particles find him and continue tracking.

3.3 Appearance Model

During an estimation step each particle is assigned with a weight coefficient according to the observation model:

$$w_t^i \propto p(z_t|s_t^i) \quad (4)$$

Here z_t is an observation in frame t. As in [3] for likelihood modeling of a particle, we use online boosting classifier similar to [7]. We use color and texture histogram bin values as features. Positive examples are derived from the object appearances and negative examples are derived from the other targets. But as opposed to [3] we train online classifiers 'one target against every other' rather than 'one target against all other'.

In [7] mean bin values are used to train a classifier. This is sufficiently good approach when there are just two targets. But in case of several targets, their mean histogram bin values might not correspond to actual object appearances. That is why we propose to train binary online boosting classifiers. Our approach is based on the fact that two objects can be efficiently distinguished by [7] method. So for each object we trained *M-1* binary classifiers, where M is equal to the total number of objects in the scene. Each binary classifier estimates the likelihood of the observation model as if there were just two objects. The output of the overall classifier is set to the minimum of binary classifiers outputs. This means that the overall classifier gives positive answer only if observed data are more similar to the current object than to any other target in the scene.

We use RGB 4x4x4 histograms and LBP 256-bin histograms to create object appearance model. We update this model each frame for objects which are not involved in any occlusions. The classifier output is scaled to [0; 1] segment. [0; 0.5) values correspond to negative classifier answers, while (0.5; 1] - to positive ones. If a particle is occluded (i.e. its visibility label is false) or its position is outside the frame then its likelihood is set equal to 0.5.

$$\begin{cases} p(z_t|s_t^i) = \min_{k \neq j} BinaryClassifier_{(j,k)}(z_t, s_t^i), & l_t^i = true \\ p(z_t|s_t^i) = 0.5, & l_t^i = false \end{cases} \quad (5)$$

3.4   Processing of Entries and Leavings

Each blob in a frame can contain several objects. If a blob does not contain any objects, it is initialized with a new one. The leaving of an object from the scene is detected if the following conditions are true:

- Sum of weights of particles outside the frame should be more than the specified threshold
- Particles inside the frame are mainly occluded ($l = false$)
- At least K frames have passed since some object particle weight is outside the frame

In a simple case, when a person comes to the boundary alone and then goes away, all its particles migrate outside the scene. But in our scenario there are a lot of cases when two persons simultaneously approach frame boundary and one occludes another. In this case we cannot say precisely whether the person is outside or just occluded by another one. The proposed algorithm turns on the timer for the person who might have left. If a person doesn't appear for several frames then we stop tracking it. Otherwise if it reappears we continue to track it and turn off the timer. Example of processing a leaving person is shown in Fig. 4.

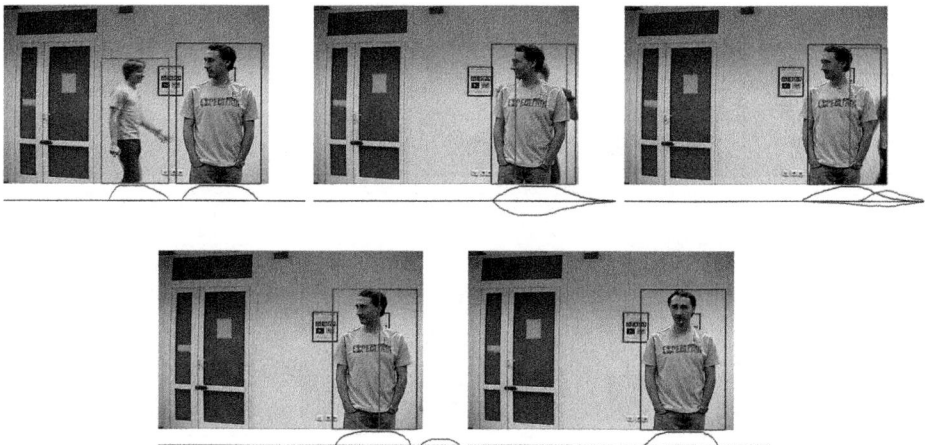

Fig. 4. Handling person leaving the scene: note that in bottom left frame the person has already left but the algorithm is not sure and keeps two hypotheses where person can be: either behind the other one, or outside the frame

Another frequent case in our scenario is an entrance of one person while another person is leaving at the same time in the same part of a frame. In this case PF tends to retrain and start tracking the new person. This causes ID switch mistake. To overcome this problem we keep object appearance for the last L frames. If object appearance differs much from itself L frames ago, while no other objects is nearby and the object is near a boundary, then we create a new object with current appearance and set the existing object appearance to its previous appearance. This allows to correctly process cases when a new object appears in front of or behind existing one, no matter whether existing object is leaving the scene or just standing near its boundary. Fig. 5 shows the advantage of our method in such case.

4 Experiments

We were unable to find well-recognized video sequence databases containing videos of the proposed scenario. So we created our own database using a simple camera. We made 29 indoor videos consisting of 174 to 877 frames and 2 to 13 people.

We provided ground-truth labeling for each video sequence in a semi-automatic mode. We manually drew bounding boxes every Pth frame (usually $P = 10$). Then ground-truth in intermediate frames was obtained by linear interpolation.

We implemented the proposed method in Matlab. We compared it with the baseline method, i.e. PF framework with online-boosting classifiers for resolving occlusions. In the baseline method we used 'one target against all other' online-boosting approach. We tested full version and baseline method along with

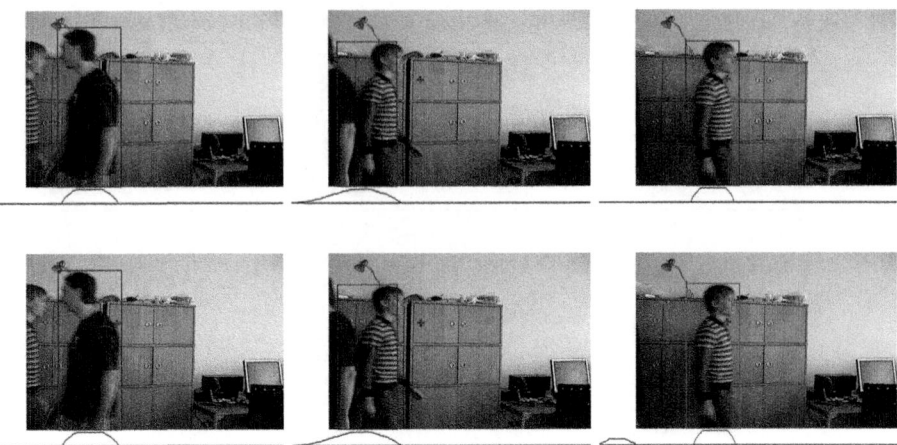

Fig. 5. Example of tracking with processing of simultaneous entering and leaving objects (bottom row), and without it (top row)

modifications which comprise our contributions. They are the use of visibility label (VL), 'one target against every other' online-boosting approach (OTAEO) and storing of object appearances with a certain update lag for determining an object entrance during leaving of another object (SAUL). We used the same parameters for all video sequences.

We have met the problem of matching between output and ground-truth results which is non-trivial, and was mentioned in [14]. We implemented automatic method based on Hungarian algorithm [13] to perform the matching. For the evaluation we use standard metrics such as ID switches, Fragments, Recall and Precision in terms of [14]. We use PASCAL VOC criterion (intersection over union) to determine whether output and ground-truth match. The results can be seen in Table 1.

It appears that in easy sequences where there are no long-term occlusions involving many people our contributions do not help much. Moreover they are not necessary; tracking problem can be solved without them. However in difficult examples our contributions help to improve the overall performance. This can be seen by evident difference in ID switches and Fragments metrics. The example of

Table 1. Experimental results of our algorithm

Algorithm type	IDS	Frag	Recall	Precision
Baseline	21	17	86%	87%
Baseline + [VL]	14	10	87%	88%
Baseline + [VL] + [OTAEO]	13	4	90%	90%
Baseline + [VL] + [OTAEO] + [SAUL]	8	3	90%	91%

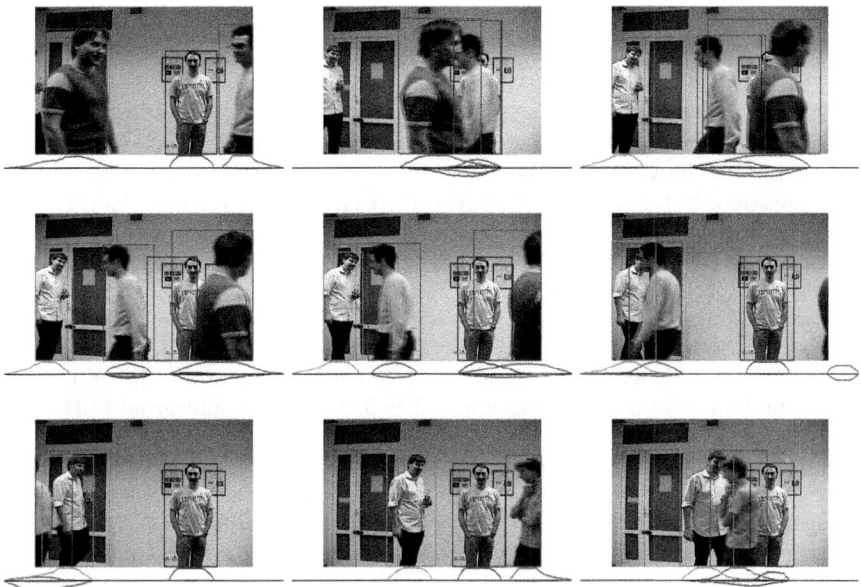

Fig. 6. Example of tracking in a sequence with many occlusions

the proposed algorithm tracking result in a complex video can be seen in Fig. 6. Supplemental materials with some other results can be found on our website: http://graphics.cs.msu.ru/en/projects/hmc-people-tracking/.

5 Conclusion

We have proposed a new method for tracking people in case in which a camera is mounted on a human height. We have made our own video database and compared our proposed method with a baseline particle filter framework with online learning of object appearance. Our experiments a good performance of our method along with the importance of our contribution. The key factors for this performance are: (1) explicit modeling of occlusion state, (2) using 'one target against every other' online boosting scheme rather than 'one target against all other', (3) storing object appearance with a certain update lag to resolve simultaneous entrance-leaving ambiguities.

Although we consider only specific scenario we believe that our ideas can be very helpful for improving performance in other types of multi-target tracking problems.

Acknowledgements. The work was partially supported by Russian Foundation for Basic Research, project N. 11-01-00957-a and the federal target program Scientific and scientific-pedagogical personnel of innovative Russia in 2009-2013, contract N. 14.740.11.0356.

References

1. Andriyenko, A., Schindler, K.: Globally optimal multi-target tracking on a hexagonal lattice. In: Daniilidis, K., Maragos, P., Paragios, N. (eds.) ECCV 2010. LNCS, vol. 6311, pp. 466–479. Springer, Heidelberg (2010)
2. Berclaz, J., Fleuret, F., Fua, F.: Robust people tracking with global trajectory optimization. In: CVPR (2006)
3. Breitenstein, M.D., Reichlin, F., Leibe, B., Koller-Meier, E., Van Gool, L.: Robust tracking-by-detection using a detector confidence particle filter. In: ICCV (2009)
4. Bugeau, A., Perez, P.: Track and cut: simultaneous tracking and segmentation of multiple objects with graph cuts. ACM J. on Image and Video Processing (2008)
5. Ferrari, V., Marin-Jimenez, M., Zisserman, A.: Progressive search space reduction for human pose estimation. In: CVPR (2008)
6. Fortmann, T., Shalom, Y.B., Scheffe, M.: Sonar tracking of multiple targets using joint probabilistic data association. IEEE J. Oceanic Engineering 8(3), 173–184 (1983)
7. Grabner, H., Bischof, H.: On-line boosting and vision. In: CVPR (2006)
8. Hue, C., Le Cadre, J.P., Perez, P.: Sequential monte carlo methods for multiple target tracking and data fusion. IEEE Tr. Signal Processing 50(1), 309–325 (2002)
9. Isard, M., MacCormick, J.: Bramble: a bayesian multiple-blob tracker. In: ICCV (2001)
10. Isard, M., Blake, A.: Condensation - conditional density propagation for visual tracking. International Journal of Computer Vision 29, 5–28 (1998)
11. Kang, J., Cohen, I., Medioni, G.: Tracking people in crowded scenes across multiple cameras. In: ACCV (2004)
12. Khan, S., Shah, M.: Tracking people in presence of occlusion. In: ACCV (2000)
13. Kuhn, H.: The hungarian method for solving the assignment problem. Naval Research Logistics Quart. 2, 83–97 (1955)
14. Li, Y., Huang, C., Nevatia, R.: Learning to associate: Hybridboosted multi-target tracker for crowded scene. In: CVPR (2009)
15. Li, Z., Yuan, L., Nevatia, R.: Global data association for multi-object tracking using network flows. In: CVPR (2008)
16. Mitzel, D., Horbert, E., Ess, A., Leibe, B.: Multi-person tracking with sparse detection and continuous segmentation. In: Daniilidis, K., Maragos, P., Paragios, N. (eds.) ECCV 2010. LNCS, vol. 6311, pp. 397–410. Springer, Heidelberg (2010)
17. Okuma, K., Taleghani, A., de Freitas, N., Little, J.J., Lowe, D.G.: A boosted particle filter: Multitarget detection and tracking. In: Pajdla, T., Matas, J(G.) (eds.) ECCV 2004. LNCS, vol. 3021, pp. 28–39. Springer, Heidelberg (2004)
18. Reid, D.: An algorithm for tracking multiple targets. IEEE Trans. Automatic Control 24(6), 843–854 (1979)
19. Song, B., Jeng, T.-Y., Staudt, E., Roy-Chowdhury, A.K.: A stochastic graph evolution framework for robust multi-target tracking. In: Daniilidis, K., Maragos, P., Paragios, N. (eds.) ECCV 2010. LNCS, vol. 6311, pp. 605–619. Springer, Heidelberg (2010)
20. Yilmaz, A., Javed, O., Shah, M.: Object tracking: A survey. ACM J. Computing Surveys 38(4) (2006)

Multi-person Localization and Track Assignment in Overlapping Camera Views

Martijn Liem[1] and Dariu M. Gavrila[1,2]

[1] Intelligent Systems Lab, Fac. of Science, Univ. of Amsterdam, The Netherlands
[2] Environment Perception, Group Research, Daimler AG, Ulm, Germany

Abstract. The assignment of multiple person tracks to a set of candidate person locations in overlapping camera views is potentially computationaly intractable, as observables might depend upon visibility order, and thus upon the decision which of the candidate locations represent actual persons and which do not. In this paper, we present an approximate assignment method which consists of two stages. In a hypothesis generation stage, the similarity between track and measurement is based on a subset of observables (appearance, motion) that is independent of the classification of candidate locations. This allows the computation of the K-best assignment in low polynomial time by standard graph matching methods. In a subsequent hypothesis verification stage, the known person positions associated with the K-best solutions are used to define the full set of observables, which are used to compute the maximum likelihood assignment. We demonstrate that our method outperforms the state-of-the-art on a complex outdoor dataset.

1 Introduction

We are interested in tracking a handful of persons in dynamic, uncontrolled environments using overlapping cameras[1]. Cost and logistics typically limit the number of cameras that can be used, as well as their viewpoints. We aim for methods that can cope with as few as three surrounding cameras and diagonal viewing directions that maximize overlap area (as opposed to ceiling-mounted cameras with a bird-eye's view). The considered set-up makes it difficult to establish individual feature correspondences across camera views, furthermore, inter-person occlusion can be considerable. We aim for robustness by performing detection and tracking based on a 3D scene reconstruction, obtained by volume carving [14]. A main challenge is to establish correct object correspondence across multiple views. Matching different objects together across multiple views leads to erroneous 3D objects, so-called 'ghosts' (see Figure 1).

2 Previous Work

Person tracking has been studied extensively. Due to space limitations, we restrict ourselves to work using overlapping cameras that aims to recover multi-

---

[1] This research received funding under EC's FP7/2007-2013 under grant agreement nr. 218197 (ADABTS).

R. Mester and M. Felsberg (Eds.): DAGM 2011, LNCS 6835, pp. 173–183, 2011.

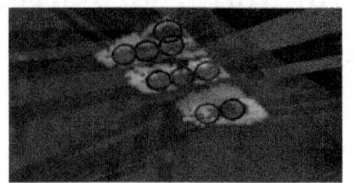 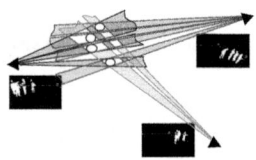

Fig. 1. (left: real-world, right: schematic) Volume carving [14] projects foregrounds for all cameras into a 3D space, 'carving out' potential persons (left: red areas, right: red bounded, white areas). Splitting these into individual potential person measurements results in superfluous objects caused by incorrect correspondences ('ghosts' or artifacts, black ellipses (left), unmarked white areas (right)) and actual persons (blue ellipses).

person location. See Table 1 for an overview that highlights the way person localization and track assignment is performed - our primary paper scope. These approaches can thereafter be embedded in a state estimation framework, either recursive (Kalman [1][8][12], particle filtering) or in batch mode (Viterbi-style MAP estimation [6], graph-cut space-time segmentation [9] or otherwise [4,10]).

Apart from the various ways correspondence and localization is performed the main point to note from Table 1 is that multi-person localization and track assignment is performed in a decoupled manner. This means that person localization does not take advantage of motion and appearance cues associated with active tracks; only *after* person position has been determined are the latter cues incorporated for track assignment [6]. This approach faces difficulties in disambiguating tracks in close proximity. Therefore, in this paper, we pursue person localization and track assignment jointly. A similar concept was proposed in [10] in a single view context. However, only pairwise object interactions were taken into account while leaving out the dependency between the perceived object appearance and the selected hypotheses. Here, we consider an instantiation specific to multi-view tracking, and we propose a novel two-stage joint estimation procedure to handle the potentially unfavorable (exponential) complexity.

3   Multi-person Track Assignment

To treat person localization and track assignment jointly, we formulate the problem as an edge selection task on a bipartite graph $G = (X, Z, E)$ with vertex sets X and Z and edges E. Given m measurements of potential persons (see figure 1), n currently existing tracks, p possible track creations and r possible track terminations, each set contains $v = \max(n, m) + \max(p, r) + 1$ vertices. Vertex set $X = \{x_1 \ldots x_n, \pi_1 \ldots \pi_p, \gamma_1 \ldots \gamma_{v-n-p}\}$ contains vertices x_i for existing person tracks, π_i for the generation of new person tracks, and γ_i for the generation of a false positives ('ghosts'). Vertex set $Z = \{z_1, \ldots, z_m, \omega_1, \ldots \omega_r, \delta_1 \ldots \delta_{v-m-r}\}$ contains vertices z_j for measurements, ω_j corresponding to terminated tracks, and δ_j to represent erroneous (i.e. noise) measurements. The bipartite graph has

Table 1. Overview of multi-person localization and track assignment using overlapping cameras (CA: Number of cameras, NP: Number of persons)

Method	CA	NP	Localization	Track Assignment
Arsić [1]	4	5	foreground segmentation, multi-plane homography, basic false pos. reduction	quadratic programming: position + appearance (SIFT)
Berclaz [2]	4	5	person classifier, prob. occupancy map	-
Calderara [4]	4	3	homography, epipolar constraints, appearance based	-
Eshel [5]	9	21	homography, intensity corr., false pos. reduction only during tracking	position + appearance
Fleuret [6]	4	4-6	foreground segmentation, probabilistic occupancy map	foreground segmentation + position + appearance (color hist.)
Hu [7]	2-3	4	foreground segmentation, principal axis, homography	position
Kang [8]	2	5	foreground segmentation, homography	multi-hypothesis (JPDA): 2D and 3D position + appearance (color descr.)
Khan [9]	4	9	foreground likelihood homography	space-time segmentation
Liem [11]	3	4	foreground segmentation, volume carving, no false positive reduction	nearest neighbor: position + appearance (color hist.)
Mittal [12]	4-16	3-6	color matching of epipole segments	position, velocity
Yang [15]	8	8	foreground segmentation volume carving basic false positive reduction	-
This method	3	2-4	joint person localization and assignment: foreground segm., volume carving + appearance (color hist.) + position Hungarian method and combinatoric approach	

edges E such that: (1) all edges $e \in E$ connect vertices from X and Z: $e \in X \times Z$, (2) vertices within X and Z have degree one (i.e. are connected by one edge) and (3) E does not contain edges connecting a vertex π_i to ω_j.
The set E can be divided into subsets E^C, E^N, E^D, and E^G, containing

- $\langle x_i, z_j \rangle \in E^C$: z_j is the person assigned to continued track x_i,
- $\langle \pi_i, z_j \rangle \in E^N$: z_j is a person which should be assigned to a new track,
- $\langle x_i, \omega_j \rangle \in E^D$: track x_i can be deleted,
- all other edges $\in E^G$: involving 'ghosts'.

Furthermore, we set $p = r = 1$, thus allowing the addition/removal of only one person track per frame. At a framerate of 20 Hz, this means that 20 persons could be added or removed every second. We also ensure that X and Z have at least one vertex γ_i and δ_j by setting $v = max(n, m) + 2$ in our experiments.

3.1   Likelihood Formulation

A set of features O is derived from the measurements. This set consists of the foreground image regions O^{FG}, the position on the ground plane O^{Pos} and appearance O^{App} of (possible) persons. For a given set of edges in the bipartite graph, we model the probability of observing these features:

$$p(O|E) = p(O^{Pos}|E)\, p(O^{FG}|E)\, p(O^{App}|E). \tag{1}$$

The probability distribution over the positions of measurements only depends on the position of the assigned tracks, or the position where a new track is created or removed.

$$p(O^{Pos}|E) = \prod_{e_k \in E^C} p(O_k^{Pos,C}|e_k) \times \prod_{e_k \in E^N} p(O_k^{Pos,N}|e_k) \times \prod_{e_k \in E^D} p(O_k^{Pos,D}|e_k) \times p_{nPos}^{|E^G|}$$

(2)

$O_k^{Pos,C}$ denotes the deviation between predicted location of a track and the position of a measurement on the ground plane. $O_k^{Pos,N}$ denotes the measured position of a new track on the ground plane. $O_k^{Pos,D}$ denotes the disappearance of a measurement. p_{nPos} is a penalty factor, given by the likelihood at the particular distance where $p(O^{Pos}|E^G) = p(O^{Pos}|E^C)$. Note that $p(O_k^{Pos,C}|E) = p(O_k^{Pos,C}|e_k)$ and $p(O_k^{Pos,N}|E) = p(O_k^{Pos,N}|e_k)$ (i.e. $p(O_k^{Pos,N}|e_k)$ does not depend on any $e \in E \setminus e_k$).

We expect that tracked persons explain the observed foreground regions O^{FG} in each camera view. Following [6], the foreground observation probability in a camera c is $p(O_c^{FG}|E) = \frac{1}{Z}e^{-\Psi(B_c,A_c(E))}$, where $A_c(E)$ denotes the synthetic image obtained by putting rectangles at locations corresponding to z_j for which $e_k \in E^C \cup E^N$ (i.e. the union of the corresponding rectangles), B_c is the segmented foreground region, and $\Psi(B_c, A_c(E))$ the fraction of the foreground correctly segmented (c.f. [6]). Averaging over all C cameras results in

$$p(O^{FG}|E) = \frac{1}{C}\sum_{c=1}^{C} p(O_c^{FG}|E) = \frac{1}{C}\sum_{c=1}^{C} \frac{1}{Z}e^{-\Psi(B_c,A_c(E))}.$$

(3)

If all z_j are outside the field of view of camera c, $p(O^{FG}|E)$ is not computable (since $\Psi(B_c, A_c(E))$ contains a division by $|A_c(E)|$). For these cases, a good value for $\frac{A_c(E) \oplus B_c}{A_c(E)}$ in $\Psi(B_c, A_c(E))$, with $\oplus$ the per-pixel exclusive or, was experimentally found to be 1.5. This value is also used for computing the penalty term p_{nFG}, used when the foreground likelihood is not computable (e.g. for E^D).

Appearances are represented as three RGB color histograms ($10 \times 10 \times 10$ bins): for the legs, arms/torso and head/shoulders, respectively. Splitting the appearance vertically allows us to use and update appearance features, even if a person is partially occluded. Spatial occlusion information, based on detected persons in E, is taken into account when sampling the images and updating the tracked appearance. Histograms are taken from each camera viewpoint and averaged over the different viewpoints:

$$p(O^{App}|E) = \prod_{e_k \in E^C} \left[p(O_k^{App}|E) \right] \times p_{nApp}^{|E \setminus E^C|}$$

with

$$p(O_k^{App}|E) = \frac{1}{C}\sum_{c=1}^{C} p(O_{k,c}^{App}|E).$$

(4)

where $O_{k,c}^{App}$ is the Hellinger distance [3] (equal to $\sqrt{1 - BC}$, with BC being the Bhattacharyya Coefficient) between the appearance of measurement k in camera

c and the known appearances of the tracks in E^C. The factor p_{nApp} compensates for the lack of appearance information for objects not linked to existing tracks, represented by the point where $p(O^{App}|E^G) = p(O^{App}|E^C)$. Distributions $O_{ij}^{Pos,C}|e_k$ and $O_{ij}^{App}|e_k$, are determined experimentally on a separate validation set. Values for these distributions are aggregated across C different camera views. See also section 4.1.

3.2   Likelihood Optimization

A brute-force approach to finding the most likely set of edges E for (1) would quickly become intractable due to the combinatorial nature of the assignment problem, especially when there are many measurements. Instead, the idea is to only compute the full likelihood on K preselected probable solutions, after which the most likely one is selected as our final estimate. Preselection is achieved by approximating $p(O|E)$ as a function $\hat{p}(O|E)$ that can be written as a product of independent edge likelihoods. An extended version of the Hungarian algorithm [13] finds the top K most likely solutions for $\hat{p}(O|E)$ in the bipartite graph by expressing it as a max-sum problem which can be solved in low polynomial time.

Since (3) and (4) contain terms dependent on the complete assignment E (e.g. due to occlusion), the conditional probabilities $p(O_{k,c}^{App}|E)$ and $p(O_k^{FG}|E)$ are replaced by approximations $\hat{p}(O_{k,c}^{App}|E)$ and $\hat{p}(O_k^{FG}|E)$ respectively where the likelihood of each edge is independent of the other edges.

Instead of taking possible occlusion of people into account, as was the case in (3), $\hat{p}(O^{FG}|E)$ approximates the foreground probability by computing it independently for assigned tracks:

$$\hat{p}(O^{FG}|E) = \prod_{e_k \in E^{cont,new}} \hat{p}(O_k^{FG}|e_k) \times p_{nFG}^{|E \setminus \{E^C \cup E^N\}|}$$

with

$$\hat{p}(O_k^{FG}|e_k) = \frac{1}{C} \sum_{c=1}^{C} \frac{1}{Z} e^{-\Psi(B_c, A_c(e_k))}. \tag{5}$$

Approximation $\hat{p}(O_{k,c}^{App}|E)$ only includes the appearance of measurements k in those camera views $\mathbf{C}^k$ where the appearances are *guaranteed* not to be occluded, such that dependency on E can be dropped:

$$\hat{p}(O_{k,c}^{App}|E) = \begin{cases} p(O_{k,c}^{App}|e_k) & \text{iff } c \text{ in } \mathbf{C}^k \\ p_{nApp} & \text{otherwise} \end{cases} \tag{6}$$

Now (1) is approximated as:

$$\hat{p}(O|E) = \prod_{e_k \in E^C} p(O_k^{Pos,C}|e_k)\hat{p}(O_k^{FG}|e_k)\hat{p}(O_k^{App}|e_k) \times \prod_{e_k \in E^N} p(O_k^{Pos,N}|e_k)\hat{p}(O_k^{FG}|e_k) \; p_{nApp}$$

$$\times \prod_{e_k \in E^D} p(O_k^{Pos,D}|e_k) \; p_{nFG} \; p_{nApp} \times \prod_{e_k \in E^G} p_{nPos} \; p_{nFG} \; p_{nApp}, \tag{7}$$

which contains a term for each edge independent of the other edges. Using this expression we preselect the K solutions with the Hungarian method.

4   Experiments

4.1   Setup

Experiments were performed in a complex, outdoor setting. On a train station platform, 2 to 4 actors engaged in various activities. The background is dynamic (trains are passing by, bystanders are walking around) and lighting conditions change continuously. Ten sequences were used, with about 5300 multi-view frames (avg. distance between center points of closest persons is 1.6 m, std. dev. is 1.2 m). For the purpose of evaluation, we only considered the area visible in all three cameras, see Figure 2(left). Ground truth (torso position) was created by manual labeling.

Proposed Method. Space volume carving is used to 'reconstruct' a 3D representation of the objects in the scene, making use of foreground segmented images. All objects are projected onto the ground plane where only those having sufficient vertical mass to represent a person are kept. An object is detected as a possible person when the area of its top-down projection has at least half the size of an average person. Preliminary tests on our data have shown that on average a person has a top-down silhouette approximated by the area of a circle with a 40 cm diameter. The number of possible persons within one object is determined to be the number of times this 'average person' fits into the detected object. The EM algorithm is used to find the most likely positions of multiple persons in objects larger than one person. It is adapted in such a way that it fits an equally sized ellipse for each person, each ellipse having an aspect ratio of 2:3 representing the average human shape seen from top-down.

Parameterizing the likelihood $p(O_k^{Pos,C}|e_k)$ is done by an exponential distribution using $\lambda = 1/0.03$ (estimated by measuring distances between people in a validation set). The steep descent of such a distribution makes high values unlikely, which de facto puts a bound on the distance a person can travel between 2 frames (0.05 seconds). Approximating the distance distribution of non-person objects $p(O^{Pos}|E^G)$ is optimal using a log-normal distribution $\ln \mathcal{N}(0.22, 0.05)$. The largest allowable distance between two objects, still being classified as persons is set at the distance where $p(O^{Pos,C}|E^C) = p(O^{Pos}|E^G)$, which is 0.2 m. This results in a maximum movement speed of about 14 km/h.

Distribution $p(O^{App}|E^C)$ and $p(O^{App}|E^G)$ are described as log-normal distributions having parameter settings $\ln \mathcal{N}(-2.2, 0.6)$ and $\ln \mathcal{N}(-1.0, 0.5)$ respectively. Since the Hellinger distance takes on values between 0 (complete match) and 1 (no match at all), the range of these functions is limited. For the penalty term $p_{nApp}^{|E \setminus E^C|}$, a Hellinger distance of 0.3 is used, representing a likelihood of 0.5.

Finally, $p(O_k^{Pos,N}|e_k)$ and $p(O_k^{Pos,D}|e_k)$ are defined using an inverted distance map (figure 2, right) based on the boundaries of the scene's visible area (figure 2, left). This map assigns high likelihood to person creations and deletions at the borders of the scene and decreases the likelihood according to the distance from the nearest edge. For the penalty term p_{nPos}, a value of 10^{-4} is found to be reasonable.

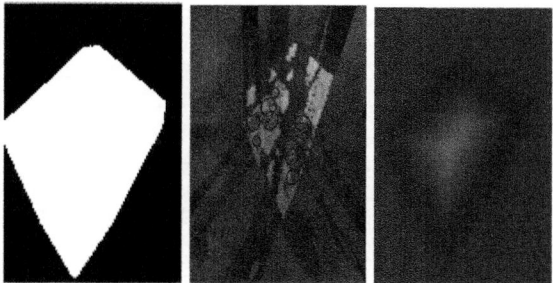

Fig. 2. (left) Area of interest on the ground plane, covered by 3 cameras and used for tracking and detection. (middle) Scene top-down view (similar to figure 1, left) (right) Distance map for determining addition/removal likelihood. Blue: high likelihood, red: low likelihood.

Comparison Method. We compare our proposed algorithm with the Probability Occupancy Map (POM) algorithm, a state-of-the-art method for which the software was kindly made available by the authors of [6]. This system uses the foreground segmented images as returned by our system as input. For each item on a predefined list of discretized ground plane positions, the POM algorithm returns the likelihood that a person is present at that location. In [6] the ground plane was discretized using a regular grid of size 20 cm. We increased the resolution to 10 cm to compensate for binning effects; this improved performance, especially at low positional error tolerance. Computing the person presence likelihood is done based on the amount of segmented foreground inside a fixed-size Region of Interest (ROI), positioned on each ground plane location. These ROI are represented by boxes of 2 m high and 70 cm wide, projected in each camera. These proportions roughly correspond to those provided in the software by [6] and have been verified to work well in preliminary experiments.

Due to the large grid (9100 locations) and the large number of detections in the neighborhood of a person at the selected likelihood threshold (see next section), computing a match between all persons at t and all detections at $t+1$ would be very costly. In order to keep things manageable, Non-Maxima Suppression (NMS) is used to keep only the most likely person positions in a 3×3 grid neighborhood. Matching is done by evaluating $p(O^{Pos}|E)p(O^{App}|E)$ for all combinations of accepted detections at t and $t+1$. The term $p(O^{FG}|E)$ from (1) is left out of this equation since it is already embedded in the initial POM results [6].

4.2 Evaluation

Detections. Both the proposed and POM method have a main parameter that controls the number of candidate person locations that are detected. For our method, this is the minimum vertical mass, for the POM method, this is a threshold on person likelihood at a grid position. In order to find comparable values for the later evaluation of track assignment and tracking, we computed

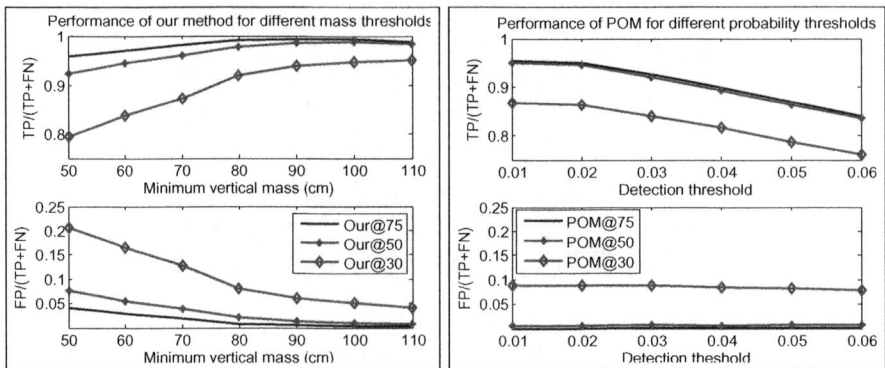

Fig. 3. (left) Our detection performance for different minimum allowed vertical mass (right) POM detection performance for different detection thresholds. Lower threshold values for POM could not be tested since the resulting increase in the number of detections causes computational issues. Both figures show multiple maximum allowable GT to detection distances (30 cm, 50 cm and 75 cm).

their effect on the True Positives (TP), False Positives (FP) and False Negatives (FN). See figure 3. Based on this, we selected a minimum vertical mass threshold of 90 cm for our method, and a likelihood threshold of 0.01 for the POM method.

Preselection. The quality of the proposed preselection (Section 3.2) is tested on a separate validation set (around 10^4 frames, eight scenarios). A cumulative plot of the fraction of frames where the correct solution occurs within the first x solutions is given in figure 4 (left). A solution is deemed correct when all Ground Truth (GT) persons are localized in the scene with a maximum distance error of 75 cm and there are no false positives. The results were computed incrementally, i.e. persons detected at time t are based on the result found at $t-1$, which in turn depended on result at $t-2$, etc. (no filtering is performed). The cases where the correct solution was not present among the top-100 ranked solutions are mostly caused by errors in foreground segmentation (this does not necessarily mean that the system loses track from that point on; a tracker might still recuperate). From these experiments, 40 is determined to be a good cut-off point for the number of hypotheses maintained after preselection.

Person Localization and Track Assignment. Performance evaluation is done for both methods on a frame-to-frame basis, i.e. new detections at $t+1$ are matched to GT person positions from t. This allows us to focus on the person localization and track assignment capability. For a fair comparison, POM detections are used as the input of our system, replacing volume carving. Cylinders of 70 cm diameter and 2 m high (equal to the ROI used by POM, section 4.1) are generated in the voxelspace at the locations of POM's detections. Person detection is done using our two-stage estimation process on this POM-generated voxelspace. Figure 4 (right, dotted lines) shows the performance of our method

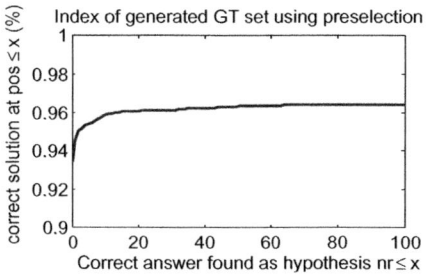
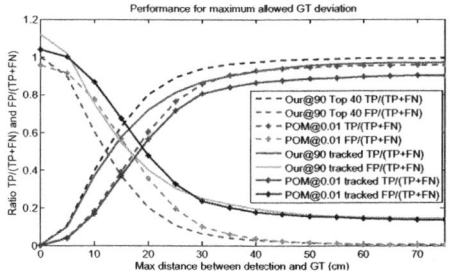

Fig. 4. (left) Percentage of cases that the correct solution is among the top x of solutions produced. (right) Detection and tracking performance of our method and the POM method, given a maximum allowable error between the GT positions and the detected positions.

as well as the POM method, given different maximum allowable errors between the GT and the detections. Our method outperforms POM for any of the tested maximum GT error distances (higher TP, lower FP). This is especially the case for positional tolerances below 30 cm, where the grid-based nature of POM leads to binning artifacts. Even at the highest allowable GT error of 75 cm, our method still has a TP rate about 4% above POM. This is due to a combination of the close proximity of the people in certain parts of the scenes (up to 25 cm) and their occlusion by other people. If people are positioned so that it is no longer possible to segment the foreground regions of different people in any view, POM is unable to detect all individual persons (as described in [6]).

Tracking. Although the focus of the current paper is on person localization and track assignment, we also embed the results of both methods in a standard Kalman Filter (KF) framework, to compare results at the tracking level. We use a KF with a constant velocity model; the assignments of measurements are now made with respect to the KF predictions. We use a gating distance of 1.5 m to search for measurements from the locations corresponding to predictions. We require a track to be of certain duration, before it is considered active. Similarly, visible tracks are discontinued after a certain time during when no measurements are assigned. Both durations are set to 20 frames in the experiments. See Figure 4 (right, solid lines). As can be expected, the number of FP rises and the number of TP declines, when compared to the detection results (figure 4, right, dotted lines) which use GT data at time t. Nevertheless, the proposed method maintains its advantage versus the baseline POM method. Results can be seen in Figure 5.

Computational cost. of both methods was assessed on a comparatively difficult 4-person sequences of 620 frames. Processing involved a single core Xeon 3 GHz system with 3 GB RAM. The POM detection method required about 7.5 s per frame, while our volume reconstruction took 3 s (both C++). The subsequent two-stage track assignment required 3 s per frame, for both localization approaches. This was reduced to 1.1 s when using 10 instead of 40 candidate assignments from preselection. All frames had a resolution of 752×560 pixels.

Fig. 5. Tracking sequences from four scenarios, one triplet of three time instances per scenario. Each triplet shows one of the three camera perspectives. Clockwise: (1) Four people starting a fight. (2) Three people argue. (3) People meet, hug and leave the scene. (4) people pass each other.

5   Conclusion

We presented an efficient two-step method for the joint person localization and track assignment in the context of a multi-view, multi-person tracking system. The proposed person localization approach, based on volume carving, outperformed a baseline POM localization method. This holds in particular for the cases where people stand close together so that their projections are merged in the camera foregrounds. The POM method would converge onto the center of the cluster as the most likely person location; non-maxima suppression would discard the rest. Our system deals with this problem adequately.

References

1. Arsic, D., Hristov, E., Lehment, N., et al.: Applying multi layer homography for multi camera person tracking. In: ICDSC (2008)
2. Berclaz, J., Fleuret, F., Fua, P.: Principled detection-by-classification from multiple views. In: Proc. of CVTA (2008)
3. Bishop, C.: Pattern Recognition and Machine Learning. Springer, Heidelberg (2006)
4. Calderara, S., Cucchiara, R., Prati, A.: Bayesian-competitive consistent labeling for people surveillance. IEEE Trans. on PAMI 30(2), 354–360 (2008)
5. Eshel, R., Moses, Y.: Homography based multiple camera detection and tracking of people in a dense crowd. In: Proc. of the IEEE CVPR, pp. 1–8 (2008)
6. Fleuret, F., Berclaz, J., Lengagne, R., et al.: Multicamera people tracking with a probabilistic occupancy map. IEEE Trans. on PAMI 30(2), 267–282 (2008)
7. Hu, W., Hu, M., Zhou, X., et al.: Principal axis-based correspondence between multiple cameras for people tracking. IEEE Trans. on PAMI 28(4), 663–671 (2006)
8. Kang, J., Cohen, I., Medioni, G., et al.: Tracking people in crowded scenes across multiple cameras. In: Proc. of the ACCV (2004)
9. Khan, S., Shah, M.: Tracking multiple occluding people by localizing on multiple scene points. IEEE Trans. on PAMI 31(3), 505–519 (2009)

10. Leibe, B., Schindler, K., et al.: Coupled object detection and tracking from static cameras and moving vehicles. IEEE Trans. on PAMI 30(10), 1683–1698 (2008)
11. Liem, M., Gavrila, D.M.: Multi-person tracking with overlapping cameras in complex, dynamic environments. In: Proc. of the BMVC (2009)
12. Mittal, A., Davis, L.: M2 tracker: a multi-view approach to segmenting and tracking people in a cluttered scene. IJCV 51(3), 189–293 (2003)
13. Murty, K.: An algorithm for ranking all the assignments in order of increasing cost. Operations Research 16(3), 682–687 (1968)
14. Szeliski, R.: Rapid octree construction from image sequences. CVGIP 58(1), 23 (1993)
15. Yang, D., Gonzalez-Banos, H., et al.: Counting people in crowds with a real-time network of simple image sensors. In: Proc. of the IEEE ICCV, pp. 122–129 (2003)

Relaxed Exponential Kernels
for Unsupervised Learning

Karim Abou-Moustafa[1], Mohak Shah[2],
Fernando De La Torre[3], and Frank Ferrie[1]

[1] Dept. of Electrical and Computer Engineering
Centre of Intelligent Machines, McGill University,
3480 University street, Montréal, QC, H3A 2A7, Canada
{karimt,ferrie}@cim.mcgill.ca
[2] Accenture Technology Labs.
161 N. Clark street Chicago, IL, 60601, U.S.A
mohak.shah@gmail.com
[3] The Robotics Institute, Carnegie Mellon Unviersity,
5000 Forbes Avenue, Pittsburg, PA 15213, U.S.A
ftorre@cs.cmu.edu

Abstract. Many unsupervised learning algorithms make use of kernels that rely on the Euclidean distance between two samples. However, the Euclidean distance is optimal for Gaussian distributed data. In this paper, we relax the global Gaussian assumption made by the Euclidean distance, and propose a locale Gaussian modelling for the immediate neighbourhood of the samples, resulting in an augmented data space formed by the parameters of the local Gaussians. To this end, we propose a convolution kernel for the augmented data space. The factorisable nature of this kernel allows us to introduce (semi)-metrics for this space, which further derives relaxed versions of known kernels for this space. We present empirical results to validate the utility of the proposed localized approach in the context of spectral clustering. The key result of this paper is that this approach that combines the local Gaussian model with measures that adhere to metric properties, yields much better performance in different spectral clustering tasks.

1 Introduction

Many unsupervised learning algorithms rely on the exponential kernel K_E, and the Gaussian kernel K_G to measure the similarity between two input vectors[1] $\mathbf{x}, \mathbf{y} \in \mathbb{R}^p$. The Euclidean distance in K_E and K_G, however, has two implicit assumptions on the data under consideration. First, by expanding the squared norm $\|\mathbf{x} - \mathbf{y}\|^2$ to $(\mathbf{x} - \mathbf{y})^\top \mathbf{I}(\mathbf{x} - \mathbf{y})$, where $\mathbf{I}$ is the identity matrix, one directly

---

[1] **Notations:** Bold small letters $\mathbf{x}, \mathbf{y}$ are vectors. Bold capital letters $\mathbf{A}, \mathbf{B}$ are matrices. Calligraphic and double bold capital letters $\mathcal{X}, \mathcal{Y}, \mathbb{X}, \mathbb{Y}$ denote sets and/or spaces. Positive definite (PD) and positive semi-definite (PSD) matrices are denoted by $\mathbf{A} \succ 0$ and $\mathbf{A} \succeq 0$ respectively.

R. Mester and M. Felsberg (Eds.): DAGM 2011, LNCS 6835, pp. 184–195, 2011.

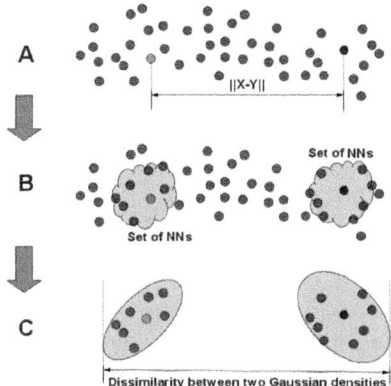

Fig. 1. (A) The exponential kernel K_E relies on the Euclidean distance between X (green) and Y (blue). (B) The local Gaussian assumption considers the few nearest neighbours (NNs) around X and Y, and then each set of NNs is modelled as a Gaussian distribution as in (C). The proposed relaxed kernels will rely on the dissimilarity (or difference) between the two Gaussian distributions instead of the Euclidean distance between X and Y.

obtains a special case of the generalized quadratic distance (GQD) $d(\mathbf{x}, \mathbf{y}; \mathbf{A}) = \sqrt{(\mathbf{x} - \mathbf{y})^{\top} \mathbf{A}(\mathbf{x} - \mathbf{y})}$, where $\mathbf{A}$ is a symmetric PD matrix. From a statistical vantage point, the Euclidean distance is the optimal metric if the data is generated from a spherical Gaussian distribution with unit variances – *the spherical assumption* – which is a hard to attain natural setting in real world data sets.

Second, the GQD has an inherent limitation for which the matrix $\mathbf{A}$ is constrained to be globally defined over the whole input space, which enforces the global Gaussian assumption of the data, or *the ellipsoidal assumption*. Besides that this constraint on $\mathbf{A}$ is restrictive, the ellipsoidal assumption is unjustified since a large Gaussian distribution with a full covariance matrix, does not yield a faithful modelling for the true empirical density of the data. In turn, this affects the relative distances between the samples, which finally affects the similarity evaluated by K_E and K_G.

In this paper, we propose to relax the constraint that enforces the global Gaussian assumption on the data. That is, as depicted in Figure (1), instead of being globally defined over all the data set, the Gaussian assumption is allowed to only hold in a local neighbourhood around each sample $\mathbf{x}_i \in \mathcal{X} \subseteq \mathbb{R}^p$, where $\mathcal{X}$ is the input space. Note that the local Gaussian assumption, does not impose any constraints nor assumptions on the global data distribution. The local Gaussian assumption, however, associates with each $\mathbf{x}_i$ a symmetric PD matrix $\mathbf{A}_i$, which is the covariance matrix of the local Gaussian distribution centered at $\mathbf{x}_i$. In turn, this changes the structure of the data from the simple set of vectors $D = \{\mathbf{x}_i\}_{i=1}^{n} \subseteq \mathcal{X}$, to a new *augmented data set* $D_A = \{(\mathbf{x}_i, \mathbf{A}_i)\}_{i=1}^{n} \subseteq \mathbb{X}$ of the 2-tuples $(\mathbf{x}_i, \mathbf{A}_i)$. Note that all $\mathbf{A}_i$'s are defined in an unsupervised manner.

To this end, we propose a convolution kernel $K_{\mathbb{X}}$ [17] that measures the similarity between the inputs $(\mathbf{x}_i, \mathbf{A}_i)$ and $(\mathbf{x}_j, \mathbf{A}_j)$. The kernel $K_{\mathbb{X}}$ is an exponential function of a dissimilarity measure for the 2-tuples $(\mathbf{x}_i, \mathbf{A}_i)$. Due to the factorizable nature of $K_{\mathbb{X}}$, it turns that $K_{\mathbb{X}}$ derives a set of metrics and semi-metrics on the augmented space $\mathbb{X}$, which further derive a set of relaxed kernels for $\mathbb{X}$. Interestingly, these (semi-)metrics are based on divergence measures of probability distributions, and the Riemannian metric for symmetric PD matrices [15]. Moreover, we show that using the exponential function in $K_{\mathbb{X}}$, the space $\mathbb{X}$ is isometrically embeddable into a Hilbert space $\mathcal{H}$ [16].

Preliminaries. In order to make the paper self-contained, we find it necessary to introduce the following definitions. A metric space is an ordered pair $(\mathcal{M}, d)$ where $\mathcal{M}$ is a non-empty set, and d is a distance function, or a metric, defined as $d : \mathcal{M} \times \mathcal{M} \mapsto \mathbb{R}$, and $\forall\, a, b, c \in \mathcal{M}$, the following Axioms hold: (1) $d(a, b) \geq 0$, (2) $d(a, a) = 0$, (3) $d(a, b) = 0$ iff $a = b$, (4) symmetry $d(a, b) = d(b, a)$, and (5) the triangle inequality $d(a, c) \leq d(a, b) + d(b, c)$. A semi-metric distance satisfies Axioms (1), (2) and (4) only. That is, the triangle inequality need not hold for semi-metrics, and $d(a, b)$ can be zero for $a \neq b$. For instance, $\|\mathbf{x} - \mathbf{y}\|_2$ in K_E is a metric, but $\|\mathbf{x} - \mathbf{y}\|_2^2$ in K_G is a semi-metric. Similarly for the GQD, $d^2(\mathbf{x}, \mathbf{y}; \mathbf{A})$ is a semi-metric, and if $\mathbf{A}$ is not strictly PD, then $d(\mathbf{x}, \mathbf{y}; \mathbf{A})$ is also a semi-metric. Note that the definition of a metric space is independent from whether $\mathcal{M}$ is equipped with an inner product or not.

Axioms (1) & (2) produce the positive semi–definiteness (PSD) of d, and hence metrics and semi-metrics are both PSD. Note that this PSD property is only valid for metrics and semi-metrics due to their Axiomitic definition above, and can not be generalized to other PSD function as defined in the following.

A necessary and sufficient condition to guarantee that a symmetric similarity function K is a kernel function over $\mathcal{X}$, is that K should be PSD[2]. This ensures the existence of a mapping $\phi : \mathcal{X} \mapsto \mathcal{H}$, where $\mathcal{H}$ is a Hilbert space called the feature space, in which K turns into an inner product: $K(\mathbf{x}_i, \mathbf{x}_j) = \langle \phi(\mathbf{x}_i), \phi(\mathbf{x}_j) \rangle$.

The family of p–dimensional Gaussian distributions is denoted by $\mathbb{G}_p$, and for $\mathcal{G} \in \mathbb{G}_p$, it is defined as:

$$\mathcal{G}(\mathbf{x}; \boldsymbol{\mu}, \boldsymbol{\Sigma}) = (2\pi)^{-\frac{p}{2}} |\boldsymbol{\Sigma}|^{-\frac{1}{2}} \exp\{-\tfrac{1}{2}(\mathbf{x} - \boldsymbol{\mu})^{\top} \boldsymbol{\Sigma}^{-1}(\mathbf{x} - \boldsymbol{\mu})\},$$

where $|\cdot|$ is the determinant, $\mathbf{x}, \boldsymbol{\mu} \in \mathbb{R}^p$, $\boldsymbol{\Sigma} \in \mathbb{S}_{++}^{p \times p}$, and $\mathbb{S}_{++}^{p \times p}$ is the manifold of symmetric PD matrices.

2   The Local Gaussian Assumption

Our proposal for relaxing the constraint on matrix $\mathbf{A}$ in the GQD is equivalent to relaxing the global Gaussian assumption on the data to be only valid in a small neighbourhood around each sample $\mathbf{x}_i \in \mathcal{X}$. Note that this mild assumption

---

[2] For the set $\mathcal{X}$ and for any set of real numbers $a_1, \ldots, a_n$, the function K must satisfy the following: $\sum_{i=1}^{n} \sum_{j=1}^{n} a_i a_j K(\mathbf{x}_i, \mathbf{x}_j) \geq 0$.

on the local distribution around each $\mathbf{x}_i$ does not impose any constraints nor assumptions on the global data distribution. To realize the local Gaussian assumption, each $\mathbf{x}_i$ is associated with a symmetric matrix $\mathbf{A}_i \succ 0$ defined as:

$$\mathbf{A}_i = \frac{1}{m-1} \sum_{\mathbf{x}^j \in \mathcal{N}_i}^{m} (\mathbf{x}^j - \mathbf{x}_i)(\mathbf{x}^j - \mathbf{x}_i)^\top + \gamma \mathbf{I} , \tag{1}$$

where $\mathbf{x}^j \in \mathcal{X}$, $\mathcal{N}_i = \{\mathbf{x}^j\}_{j=1}^m$ is the set of m nearest neighbours (NNs) to $\mathbf{x}_i$, and $0 < \gamma \in \mathbb{R}$ is a regularization parameter. The regularization here is necessary to avoid the expected rank deficiencies in $\mathbf{A}_i$'s, which are due to the small number of NNs considered around $\mathbf{x}_i$, together with the high dimensionality of the data[3], and hence, this helps avoid over-fitting and outlier reliance. The definition of $\mathbf{A}_i$ in (1) is simply the average variance–covariance matrix between $\mathbf{x}_i$ and its m NNs. Hence, the local Gaussian assumption, depicted in Figure (1), can be seen as anchoring a Gaussian density $\mathcal{G}_i(\boldsymbol{\mu}_i, \boldsymbol{\Sigma}_i)$ at point $\mathbf{x}_i$, where its mean $\boldsymbol{\mu}_i \equiv \mathbf{x}_i$ and its covariance matrix $\boldsymbol{\Sigma}_i \equiv \mathbf{A}_i$. The local Gaussian assumption can be taken further and extended in the spirit of manifold Parzen windows [18] by including $\mathbf{x}_i$ in $\mathcal{N}_i$, and define $\boldsymbol{\mu}_i$ and $\boldsymbol{\Sigma}_i$ as follows:

$$\boldsymbol{\mu}_i \equiv \hat{\boldsymbol{\mu}}_i = \frac{1}{m+1} \sum_{\mathbf{x}^j \in \mathcal{N}_i} \mathbf{x}^j, \quad \text{and} \tag{2}$$

$$\boldsymbol{\Sigma}_i \equiv \hat{\boldsymbol{\Sigma}}_i = \frac{1}{m} \sum_{\mathbf{x}^j \in \mathcal{N}_i} (\mathbf{x}^j - \hat{\boldsymbol{\mu}}_i)(\mathbf{x}^j - \hat{\boldsymbol{\mu}}_i)^\top + \gamma \mathbf{I} . \tag{3}$$

This can be seen as a local smoothing for the data, combined with local feature extraction by means of a generative model, where the features are the parameters $\hat{\boldsymbol{\mu}}_i$ and $\hat{\boldsymbol{\Sigma}}_i$ for each $\mathbf{x}_i \in \mathcal{X}$. Note that $\mathbf{A}_i$ and $\hat{\boldsymbol{\Sigma}}_i$ are defined in an unsupervised manner, however when auxiliary information is available in the form of labels or side information, they can be defined in a supervised or a semi–supervised manner.

The result of the local Gaussian assumption introduces a new component $\mathbf{A}_i$ for each $\mathbf{x}_i \in \mathcal{X}$ which changes the structure of the input data from the set of vectors $D = \{\mathbf{x}_i\}_{i=1}^n$ to an augmented data set $D_A = \{(\mathbf{x}_i, \mathbf{A}_i)\}_{i=1}^n \subseteq \mathbb{X}$ of 2-tuples $(\mathbf{x}_i, \mathbf{A}_i)$. This change in the data structure, in turn, requires a change in K_E and K_G which can only operate on the first element of the 2-tuples $(\mathbf{x}_i, \mathbf{A}_i)$ – elements in $\mathbb{R}^p$ – and not the symmetric matrix $\mathbf{A}_i \succ 0$.

Note that the augmented space $\mathbb{X}$ implicitly represents the parameters for the set of local Gaussians $\mathscr{G} = \{\mathcal{G}_i(\boldsymbol{\mu}_i, \boldsymbol{\Sigma}_i)\}_{i=1}^n$, which will be referred to as *the dual perspective* for $\mathbb{X}$. In order to avoid any future confusion in the notations, this will be the default definition for $\mathbb{X}$, where implicitly, $(\boldsymbol{\mu}_i, \boldsymbol{\Sigma}_i) \equiv (\mathbf{x}_i, \mathbf{A}_i)$, or $(\boldsymbol{\mu}_i, \boldsymbol{\Sigma}_i) \equiv (\hat{\boldsymbol{\mu}}_i, \hat{\boldsymbol{\Sigma}}_i)$.

---

[3] Note that γ is unique for all $\mathbf{A}_i$'s.

3   A Convolution Kernel for the Space $\mathbb{X}$

The framework of convolution kernels suggests that a possible kernel for the space $\mathbb{X}$ can have the following structure [17]:

$$K_{\mathbb{X}}\{(\boldsymbol{\mu}_i, \boldsymbol{\Sigma}_i), (\boldsymbol{\mu}_j, \boldsymbol{\Sigma}_j)\} = K_{\mu}(\boldsymbol{\mu}_i, \boldsymbol{\mu}_j)K_{\Sigma}(\boldsymbol{\Sigma}_i, \boldsymbol{\Sigma}_j),$$

where K_{μ} and K_{Σ} are symmetric PSD kernels, which yields that $K_{\mathbb{X}}$ is symmetric and PSD as well. Our approach for defining K_{μ} and K_{Σ} is based on the definition of K_E, which is an exponential function of the Euclidean distance between its two inputs. Due to the PSD and symmetry properties of (semi-)metrics (Axioms (1), (2), & (3)), it follows that K_E is symmetric and PSD. This result is due to Theorem (4) in [16] which states that:

Theorem 1. *The most general positive function $f(x)$ which is bounded away from zero and whose positive powers $[f(x)]^{\alpha}$, $\alpha > 0$, are PSD is of the form: $f(x) = \exp\{c + \psi(x)\}$, where $\psi(x)$ is PSD and $c \in \mathbb{R}$.*

If $\psi(\boldsymbol{\mu}_i - \boldsymbol{\mu}_j) = \|\boldsymbol{\mu}_i - \boldsymbol{\mu}_j\|$, $\sigma > 0$, and $c = -\frac{2}{\sigma}\|\boldsymbol{\mu}_i - \boldsymbol{\mu}_j\|$, it follows from Theorem (3.1) that K_E is PSD. This discussion suggests that, if $d_{\mu}(\cdot, \cdot)$ and $d_{\Sigma}(\cdot, \cdot)$ is (semi-)metric for $\{\boldsymbol{\mu}_i\}_{i=1}^n$ and $\{\boldsymbol{\Sigma}_i\}_{i=1}^n$ respectively, then K_{μ} and K_{Σ} can be defined as:

$$K_{\mu}(\boldsymbol{\mu}_i, \boldsymbol{\mu}_j) = \exp\left\{-\tfrac{1}{\sigma}d_{\mu}(\boldsymbol{\mu}_i, \boldsymbol{\mu}_j)\right\},$$
$$K_{\Sigma}(\boldsymbol{\Sigma}_i, \boldsymbol{\Sigma}_j) = \exp\left\{-\tfrac{1}{\sigma}d_{\Sigma}(\boldsymbol{\Sigma}_i, \boldsymbol{\Sigma}_j)\right\}, \text{ and hence}$$
$$K_{\mathbb{X}} = \exp\left\{-\tfrac{1}{\sigma}[d_{\mu} + d_{\Sigma}]\right\}, \tag{4}$$

where $\sigma > 0$, and $[d_{\mu} + d_{\Sigma}]$ is a (semi-)metric for the augmented space $\mathbb{X}$. In Section (4), it will be shown that, in general, d_{μ} is the GQD between $\boldsymbol{\mu}_i$ and $\boldsymbol{\mu}_j$, while d_{Σ} is a (semi-)metric for symmetric PD covariance matrices.

3.1   Isometric Embedding in a Hilbert Space $\mathcal{H}$

An interesting property of the exponential function in K_E and K_G is its ability to perform an isometric embedding for $(\mathbb{R}^p, \|\cdot\|_2)$ and $(\mathbb{R}^p, \|\cdot\|_2^2)$ into a Hilbert space $\mathcal{H}$. This result is due to Theorems (1) in [16] which states that:

Theorem 2. *A necessary and sufficient condition that a separable space $\mathcal{S}$ with a semi-metric distance d, be isometrically embeddable in $\mathcal{H}$, is that the function $\exp\{-\alpha d^2\}$, $\alpha > 0$, be PSD in $\mathcal{S}$.*

Moreover, if d is a metric, then the triangle inequality is preserved through the embedding, and the new space becomes a metric space[4]. Therefore, if d_{μ} and d_{Σ} are metrics (or semi-metrics) for $\{\boldsymbol{\mu}_i\}_{i=1}^n$ and $\{\boldsymbol{\Sigma}_i\}_{i=1}^n$ respectively, then by Theorem (3.1), $K_{\mu} \succeq 0$ and $K_{\Sigma} \succeq 0$, and by Theorem (3.2), $(\{\boldsymbol{\mu}_i\}_{i=1}^n, d_{\mu})$, $(\{\boldsymbol{\Sigma}_i\}_{i=1}^n, d_{\Sigma})$ and $(\mathbb{X}, [d_{\mu} + d_{\Sigma}])$ are isometrically embeddable in $\mathcal{H}$.

---

[4] See footnote in [16, p. 525].

Theorem (2) in [16], which we do not state here due to space limitations, is similar to Theorem (3.2), however it addresses the particular case of spaces with m real numbers, denoted by $\mathcal{S}_m$, and equipped with a norm function $\varphi(\mathbf{x})$, $\mathbf{x} \in \mathcal{S}_m$, and a distance function $\varphi(\mathbf{x} - \mathbf{x}')^{\frac{1}{2}}$. This theorem will be used instead of Theorem (3.2), when the Riemannian metric for symmetric PD matrices is introduced.

4   Kernels for Probability Distributions

To derive d_μ and d_Σ, our discussion begins from the dual perspective for $\mathbb{X}$, or the set $\mathscr{G} = \{\mathcal{G}_i(\boldsymbol{\mu}_i, \boldsymbol{\Sigma}_i)\}_{i=1}^n$, and the definition of K_E as an exponential function of the Euclidean distance between its input vectors. The fundamental difference here is that the elements of interests are not the vectors $\mathbf{x}_i, \mathbf{x}_j \in \mathbb{R}^p$, but rather two Gaussian distributions $\mathcal{G}_i, \mathcal{G}_j \in \mathbb{G}_p$, with $\boldsymbol{\mu}_i \neq \boldsymbol{\mu}_j$ and $\boldsymbol{\Sigma}_i \neq \boldsymbol{\Sigma}_j$. It follows that the Euclidean distance describing the difference between $\mathbf{x}_i$ and $\mathbf{x}_j$ needs to be replaced with a dissimilarity measure for probability distributions, and this measure should be at least a semi-metric in order to guarantee that the resulting kernel is PSD, according to Theorem (3.2).

A natural measure for the dissimilarity between probability distributions is the divergence, which by definition according to [1] and [3] is not a metric. To see this, let $\mathcal{P}$ be a family of probability distributions, and let $P_1, P_2 \in \mathcal{P}$ be defined over the same domain of events $\mathcal{E}$, then the divergence of P_2 from P_1 is:

$$\text{div}(P_1, P_2) = \mathbb{E}_{p_1}\{C(\phi)\} = \int_{\mathcal{E}} p_1(x)C(\phi(x))dx, \tag{5}$$

where $\text{div}(P_1, P_2) \in [0, \infty)$, p_1, p_2 are the probability density functions of P_1 and P_2 respectively, $\phi(x) = p_1(x)/p_2(x)$ is the likelihood ratio, and C is a continuous convex function on $(0, \infty)$. Note that by definition, $\text{div}(P_1, P_2) \geq 0$, and equality only holds when $P_1 = P_2$ [1]. This is equivalent to Axioms (1) & (2) of a metric, and hence $\text{div}(P_1, P_2)$ is PSD. The divergence as defined in Equation (5), is not symmetric[5], since $\text{div}(P_1, P_2) \neq \text{div}(P_2, P_1)$. However, a possible symmetrization for the divergence can be as : $\text{sdiv}(P_1, P_2) = \text{div}(P_1, P_2) + \text{div}(P_2, P_1)$, where sdiv preserves all the properties of a divergence as postulated by Ali–Silvey and Csiszar. Hence, sdiv is symmetric and PSD – a semi-metric – and a possible kernel for P_1 and P_2 can be defined as:

$$K_{\mathcal{P}}(P_1, P_2) = \exp\{-\tfrac{1}{\sigma}\text{sdiv}(P_1, P_2)\}, \ \sigma > 0. \tag{6}$$

Using Theorems (3.1) and (3.2), $K_{\mathcal{P}}$ is symmetric and PSD, and $(\mathcal{P}, \text{sdiv})$ is isometrically embeddable in $\mathcal{H}$. Note that $K_{\mathcal{P}}$ is in the same spirit of the exponential kernel K_E as explained above. In addition, $K_{\mathcal{P}}$ is valid for any symmetric divergence measure from the class of Ali–Silvey or f–divergence [3], and hence it is valid for any probability distribution. It is also important to note that the kernel $K_{\mathcal{P}}$ is not the only kernel for probability distributions, and other kernels were proposed in the work of [6,4,11].

---

[5] Depending on the choice of $C(\cdot)$ in (5) and its parametrization, one can derive symmetric divergence measures, see [1] for examples.

4.1   The Case of Gaussian Densities

We now consider the particular case of Gaussian densities under some classical symmetric divergence measures such as the symmetric KL divergence, or Jeffreys divergence d_J, the Bhattacharyya divergence d_B, and the Hellinger distance d_H. For $\mathcal{G}_1, \mathcal{G}_2 \in \mathbb{G}_p$, Jeffreys divergence d_J can be expressed as:

$$d_J(\mathcal{G}_1, \mathcal{G}_2) = \tfrac{1}{2}\mathbf{u}^\top \boldsymbol{\Psi} \mathbf{u} + \tfrac{1}{2}\mathrm{tr}\{\boldsymbol{\Sigma}_1^{-1}\boldsymbol{\Sigma}_2 + \boldsymbol{\Sigma}_2^{-1}\boldsymbol{\Sigma}_1\} - p, \tag{7}$$

where $\boldsymbol{\Psi} = (\boldsymbol{\Sigma}_1^{-1} + \boldsymbol{\Sigma}_2^{-1})$, and $\mathbf{u} = (\boldsymbol{\mu}_1 - \boldsymbol{\mu}_2)$. The Bhattacharyya divergence d_B and the Hellinger distance d_H are both derived from the Bhattacharyya coefficient ρ, which is a measure of similarity between probability distributions:

$$\rho(\mathcal{G}_1, \mathcal{G}_2) = |\boldsymbol{\Gamma}|^{-\frac{1}{2}}|\boldsymbol{\Sigma}_1|^{\frac{1}{4}}|\boldsymbol{\Sigma}_2|^{\frac{1}{4}}\exp\{-\tfrac{1}{8}\mathbf{u}^\top \boldsymbol{\Gamma}^{-1}\mathbf{u}\},$$

where $\boldsymbol{\Gamma} = (\tfrac{1}{2}\boldsymbol{\Sigma}_1 + \tfrac{1}{2}\boldsymbol{\Sigma}_2)$. The Hellinger distance can be obtained from ρ as $d_H(\mathcal{G}_1, \mathcal{G}_2) = \sqrt{2[1 - \rho(\mathcal{G}_1, \mathcal{G}_2)]}$, while $d_B(\mathcal{G}_1, \mathcal{G}_2) = \log[\rho(\mathcal{G}_1, \mathcal{G}_2)]$ is defined as:

$$d_B(\mathcal{G}_1, \mathcal{G}_2) = \tfrac{1}{8}\mathbf{u}^\top \boldsymbol{\Gamma}^{-1}\mathbf{u} + \tfrac{1}{2}\ln\left\{\frac{|\boldsymbol{\Gamma}|}{|\boldsymbol{\Sigma}_1|^{\frac{1}{2}}|\boldsymbol{\Sigma}_2|^{\frac{1}{2}}}\right\}. \tag{8}$$

Kullback [9] notes that d_J is positive and symmetric but violates the triangle inequality. Similarly, Kailath [7] notes that d_B is positive and symmetric but violates the triangle inequality, while d_H meets all metric Axioms. Using the kernel definition in (6), it is straight forward to define the following kernels:

$$K_J(\mathcal{G}_1, \mathcal{G}_2) = \exp\{-\tfrac{1}{\sigma}d_J(\mathcal{G}_1, \mathcal{G}_2)\}, \ \sigma > 0, \tag{9}$$

$$K_H(\mathcal{G}_1, \mathcal{G}_2) = \exp\{-\tfrac{1}{\sigma}d_H(\mathcal{G}_1, \mathcal{G}_2)\}, \ \sigma > 0, \ \text{and} \tag{10}$$

$$K_B(\mathcal{G}_1, \mathcal{G}_2) = \exp\{d_B(\mathcal{G}_1, \mathcal{G}_2)\} = \rho(\mathcal{G}_1, \mathcal{G}_2). \tag{11}$$

We note that [8] have proposed the Bhatacharyya kernel $\rho(\mathcal{G}_1, \mathcal{G}_2)$ and confirm that it is PSD through the product probability kernel (PPK). In contrary, [12] have proposed the KL kernel $K_J(\mathcal{G}_1, \mathcal{G}_2)$ and claim, without justification, that it is not PSD. Since d_J and d_B are semi-metrics, and d_H is a metric, then using Theorems (3.1) and (3.2), K_J, K_H and K_B are symmetric and PSD kernels, and $(\mathbb{X}, d_J)$, $(\mathbb{X}, d_B)$, and $(\mathbb{X}, d_H)$ are isometrically embeddable in $\mathcal{H}$.

4.2   A Close Look at d_J and d_B

Kullback [9, pp. 6,7] describes $d_J(\mathcal{G}_1, \mathcal{G}_2)$ in Equation (7) as a sum of two components, one due to the difference in means weighted by the covariance matrices (the first term), and the other due to the difference in variances and covariances (the second term). Note that this explanation is also valid for $d_B(\mathcal{G}_1, \mathcal{G}_2)$ in Equation (8). Recalling $K_{\mathbb{X}}$ from Equation (4), then d_μ and d_Σ can be characterized as follows. The first term in Equations (7) and (8) is equivalent to the GQD, up to a constant and a square root – hence both terms are semi-metrics. If $\boldsymbol{\Sigma}_1 = \boldsymbol{\Sigma}_2 = \boldsymbol{\Sigma}$, then:

$$\left.\begin{array}{l} d_J(\mathcal{G}_1, \mathcal{G}_2) = \mathbf{u}^\top \boldsymbol{\Psi} \mathbf{u}, \\ d_B(\mathcal{G}_1, \mathcal{G}_2) = \mathbf{u}^\top \boldsymbol{\Gamma}^{-1}\mathbf{u}. \end{array}\right\} d_\mu \tag{12}$$

The second term in Equations (7) and (8) is a discrepancy measure between two covariance matrices that is independent from $\boldsymbol{\mu}_1$ and $\boldsymbol{\mu}_2$. If $\boldsymbol{\mu}_1 = \boldsymbol{\mu}_2 = \boldsymbol{\mu}$ then:

$$\left.\begin{array}{l} d_J(\mathcal{G}_1, \mathcal{G}_2) = \text{tr}\{\boldsymbol{\Sigma}_1^{-1}\boldsymbol{\Sigma}_2 + \boldsymbol{\Sigma}_2^{-1}\boldsymbol{\Sigma}_1\} - p, \\ d_B(\mathcal{G}_1, \mathcal{G}_2) = \ln\left\{|\boldsymbol{\Gamma}||\boldsymbol{\Sigma}_1|^{-\frac{1}{2}}|\boldsymbol{\Sigma}_2|^{-\frac{1}{2}}\right\}, \end{array}\right\} d_\Sigma \tag{13}$$

which define two dissimilarity measures between $\boldsymbol{\Sigma}_1$ and $\boldsymbol{\Sigma}_2$, and both measures are semi-metrics.

4.3   A Metric for Symmetric PD Matrices

The factorisable nature of $K_\mathbb{X}$, and the decomposition of $d_J(\mathcal{G}_1, \mathcal{G}_2)$ and $d_B(\mathcal{G}_1, \mathcal{G}_2)$ into two difference components, where the second term is independent from $\boldsymbol{\mu}_1$ and $\boldsymbol{\mu}_2$, allows us to introduce a metric for symmetric PD matrices that can be used instead of the semi-metrics in Equation (13).

A symmetric PD matrix is a geometric object, and the space of all symmetric PD matrices, denoted by $\mathbb{S}_{++}^{p \times p}$, is a differentiable manifold in which each point $\mathbf{A} \in \mathbb{S}_{++}^{p \times p}$ has a tangent space $\mathcal{T}_\mathbf{A}(\mathbb{S}_{++}^{p \times p})$ that is endowed with an inner product, or a Riemmanian metric $\langle \cdot, \cdot \rangle_\mathbf{A}$, on the elements of the tangent space. The dimensionality of $\mathbb{S}_{++}^{p \times p}$ and its tangent space is $p(p+1)/2$. Due to the inner product $\langle \cdot, \cdot \rangle_\mathbf{A}$, the tangent space for $\mathbb{S}_{++}^{p \times p}$ is a finite dimensional Euclidean space.

The Riemannian metric, by default, respects the geometry of $\mathbb{S}_{++}^{p \times p}$, which is unlike the semi-metrics in (13) that are just derived from the divergence measures $d_J(\mathcal{G}_1, \mathcal{G}_2)$ and $d_B(\mathcal{G}_1, \mathcal{G}_2)$, and unaware of the geometry of $\mathbb{S}_{++}^{p \times p}$. If $d_\mathcal{R}$ is the Riemannian metric for $\mathbb{S}_{++}^{p \times p}$, then d_Σ in Equation (4) can be replaced with $d_\mathcal{R}$, and hence $K_\mathbb{X}$ can be redefined as follows:

$$K_\mathbb{X} = K_\mu(\boldsymbol{\mu}_1, \boldsymbol{\mu}_2) K_\mathcal{R}(\boldsymbol{\Sigma}_1, \boldsymbol{\Sigma}_2), \tag{14}$$

$$= \exp\{-\tfrac{1}{\sigma}d_\mu\}\exp\{-\tfrac{1}{\sigma}d_\mathcal{R}\},$$

$$= \exp\{-\tfrac{1}{\sigma}[d_\mu + d_\mathcal{R}]\}, \ \sigma > 0. \tag{15}$$

where $d_\mathcal{R}$ is the distance between the two matrices $\{\boldsymbol{\Sigma}_1, \boldsymbol{\Sigma}_2 \in \mathbb{S}_{++}^{d \times d}\}$ defined as :

$$d_\mathcal{R}(\boldsymbol{\Sigma}_1, \boldsymbol{\Sigma}_2) = \text{tr}\{\ln^2 \boldsymbol{\Lambda}(\boldsymbol{\Sigma}_1, \boldsymbol{\Sigma}_2)\}^{\frac{1}{2}}, \tag{16}$$

and $\boldsymbol{\Lambda}(\boldsymbol{\Sigma}_1, \boldsymbol{\Sigma}_2) = \text{diag}(\lambda_1, \ldots, \lambda_d)$ is the solution of a generalized eigenvalue problem (GEP): $\boldsymbol{\Sigma}_1\mathbf{V} = \boldsymbol{\Lambda}\boldsymbol{\Sigma}_2\mathbf{V}$. The metric $d_\mathcal{R}$ was first derived by C. Rao [15], and latter analyzed by Atkinson and Mitchel [2] [6], while independently derived by Förstner and Moonen in [5]. Note that $d_\mathcal{R}$ is invariant to inversion and to affine transformations of the coordinate system. Since $d_\mathcal{R}$ is induced by a norm on $\mathcal{T}(\mathbb{S}_{++}^{p \times p})$, then using Theorem (3.1) and Theorem(2) in [16], $K_\mathcal{R}$ is PSD, and $(\mathcal{T}_\mathbf{A}(\mathbb{S}_{++}^{p \times p}), d_\mathcal{R})$ is isometrically embeddable in $\mathcal{H}$, for all $\mathbf{A} \in \mathbb{S}_{++}^{p \times p}$.

---

[6] See their affiliated references.

5   Relaxed Kernels for the Augmented Space $\mathbb{X}$

Besides the Jeffreys kernel K_J, the Hellinger kernel K_H, and the Bhattacharyya kernel K_B in Equations (9), (10) and (11) respectively, we define two new kernels for the space $\mathbb{X}$ based on the metric $d_{\mathcal{R}}$:

$$K_{J\mathcal{R}}(\mathcal{G}_1, \mathcal{G}_2) = \exp\{-\tfrac{1}{\sigma} d_{J\mathcal{R}}(\mathcal{G}_1, \mathcal{G}_2)\}, \quad \text{and} \tag{17}$$

$$K_{B\mathcal{R}}(\mathcal{G}_1, \mathcal{G}_2) = \exp\{-\tfrac{1}{\sigma} d_{B\mathcal{R}}(\mathcal{G}_1, \mathcal{G}_2)\}, \quad \text{where} \tag{18}$$

$$d_{J\mathcal{R}}(\mathcal{G}_1, \mathcal{G}_2) = (\mathbf{u}^\top \boldsymbol{\Psi} \mathbf{u})^{\frac{1}{2}} + d_{\mathcal{R}}(\boldsymbol{\Sigma}_1, \boldsymbol{\Sigma}_2),$$

$$d_{B\mathcal{R}}(\mathcal{G}_1, \mathcal{G}_2) = (\mathbf{u}^\top \boldsymbol{\Gamma}^{-1} \mathbf{u})^{\frac{1}{2}} + d_{\mathcal{R}}(\boldsymbol{\Sigma}_1, \boldsymbol{\Sigma}_2),$$

$$\boldsymbol{\Psi} \succ 0, \quad \boldsymbol{\Gamma}^{-1} \succ 0, \quad \text{and} \quad \sigma > 0.$$

The positive definiteness of $\boldsymbol{\Psi}$ and $\boldsymbol{\Gamma}^{-1}$, and the square root on the quadratic terms of $d_{J\mathcal{R}}$ and $d_{B\mathcal{R}}$, assure that the quadratic terms are metrics. If $\boldsymbol{\mu}_1 = \boldsymbol{\mu}_2 = \boldsymbol{\mu}$, then $d_{J\mathcal{R}}$ and $d_{B\mathcal{R}}$ will yield the Riemannian metric $d_{\mathcal{R}}$, and hence, $K_{J\mathcal{R}}$ and $K_{B\mathcal{R}}$ will be equal to $K_{\mathcal{R}}$. If $\boldsymbol{\Sigma}_1 = \boldsymbol{\Sigma}_2 = \boldsymbol{\Sigma}$, then $d_{J\mathcal{R}}$ and $d_{B\mathcal{R}}$ will yield the GQD. If $\boldsymbol{\Sigma} = \mathbf{I}$, the GQD will be equal to the Euclidean distance, and $K_{J\mathcal{R}}$ and $K_{B\mathcal{R}}$ will yield the original exponential kernel K_E.

Similar to K_E and K_G, the relaxed kernels K_J, K_H, K_B, $K_{J\mathcal{R}}$ and $K_{B\mathcal{R}}$ rely on the distance between the 2-tuples $(\boldsymbol{\mu}_1, \boldsymbol{\Sigma}_1)$ and $(\boldsymbol{\mu}_2, \boldsymbol{\Sigma}_2)$. Moreover, they all provide an isometric embedding for the space $\mathbb{X}$, and the difference between these embeddings is due the metric or semi-metric defining each kernel. While d_J and d_B are semi-metrics, d_H, $d_{J\mathcal{R}}$ and $d_{B\mathcal{R}}$ are metrics. Since Axioms (3) & (5) do not hold for semi-metrics, it follows that d_J and d_B will not preserve the relative geometry between the elements in $\mathbb{R}^p$, and that between the elements in $\mathbb{S}_{++}^{p \times p}$. Although d_H is a metric, it relies on a semi-metric for covariances matrices, which is not the case for $d_{J\mathcal{R}}$ and $d_{B\mathcal{R}}$.

6   Related Work

Our research work parallels a stream of ideas that consider distances (or similarities) between two subspaces, tangent spaces, or sets of vectors, instead of the direct distance (or similarity) between points. In the context of learning over sets of vectors (SOV's), [19] propose a general learning approach within the kernel framework. For two SOV's, their kernel is based on the principal angles between two subspaces, each spanned by one of the two SOV's. In [8], each SOV is a bag of pixels representing one image. Each SOV is modelled as a Gaussian distribution, and the Bhattacharyya kernel K_B is used with SVMs to classify the images. Similarly, in [12] each SOV is a bag of features representing one multimedia object (an image or an audio signal), and modelled as Gaussian distribution. However, instead of K_B, they use the KL kernel K_J with SVMs to classify the multimedia objects.

Table 1. Specifications of the data sets used in the experiments. The number of classes, samples, and attributes are denoted by c, n, and p respectively.

Data set	c	n	p	Data set	c	n	p
Balance	3	625	4	NewThyroid	3	215	5
Bupa	2	345	6	Pima	2	768	8
Glass	6	214	9	Segment	7	2310	18
Iris	3	150	4	Sonar	2	208	60
Lymphography	4	148	18	WDBC	2	569	30
Monks–1	2	556	6	Wine	3	178	13
Monks–2	2	601	6	Yeast	10	1484	6
Monks–3	2	554	6				

7   Experimental Results

We validate the proposed relaxed kernels in the context of unsupervised learning using spectral clustering (SC) algorithms. Here we compare the performance of 1) the standard k-means algorithm, 2) SC according to the version of [14]–as described in [10]–using the exponential kernel K_E, and 3) SC over the augmented space $\mathbb{X}$ using four (4) different kernels: the KL kernel K_J [12], the Bhattacharyya kernel K_B [8], the Hellinger kernel K_H, and the proposed kernel K_{BR}. Although our experiments included K_{JR} as well, we found that the results of K_{JR} and K_{BR} are very close to each other, and hence we show only the results for K_{BR}. This shows that the main difference between d_J and d_B are the semi-metrics for covariance matrices in Equation (13). The parameter σ for K_E, K_J, K_B, K_H and K_{BR} was selected using a simple quantile based approach[7]. In all our experiments, the regularization parameter $\gamma = 1$. Although we do not focus on selecting the *best* γ values, it nevertheless shows that, under this uniform γ assumption, the local Gaussian assumption typically shows significantly better results.

All algorithms were run on 15 data sets from the UCI machine learning repository [13], shown in Table (1). Clustering accuracy was measured using the Hungarian score of [20][8]. The performance of each algorithm was averaged over 30 runs with different initializations. Since the number of classes of the UCI data sets is given, we assumed that the number of clusters is known. Before proceeding to the results, it is important to emphasize that selecting the best parameter values for k, σ, γ and the number of clusters, is largely a model selection issue, and hence, it should not be confounded with verification of the effectiveness of the local Gaussian modelling premise.

Columns two and three in Table (2) show the results for k-Means and SC with K_E on the original data set $\mathcal{X}$. Columns four to seven in Table (2) show the results of SC over the augmented data set $D_A = \{(\hat{\boldsymbol{\mu}}_i, \hat{\boldsymbol{\Sigma}}_i)\}_{i=1}^n$ with the 4 different relaxed kernels. Due to space limitaitons, we do not show the results for SC over the augmented data set $D_A = \{(\mathbf{x}_i, \mathbf{A}_i)\}_{i=1}^n$. It can be seen that

---
[7] The approach was suggested in Alex Smola's blog: http://blog.smola.org/page/2
[8] See [20] for more details.

Table 2. Clustering accuracy for k-Means, SC with K_E, and SC over $D_A = \{(\hat{\mu}_i, \hat{\Sigma}_i)\}_{i=1}^{n}$ with K_J, K_B, K_H, and $K_{B\mathcal{R}}$

Data set	k-Means	K_E	K_J	K_B	K_H	$K_{B\mathcal{R}}$
Balance	51.1 (3.2)	53.6 (4.5)	60.0 (3.4)	61.2 (3.5)	60.3 (0.2)	**64.9 (4.9)**
Bupa	55.1 (0.1)	57.1 (0.2)	62.9 (0.1)	62.3 (0.18)	61.1 (0.07)	**64.3 (0.18)**
Glass	51.3 (3.4)	50.8 (2.0)	52.5 (2.8)	52.4 (3.3)	52.2 (2.9)	**53.8 (4.6)**
Iris	84.5 (12.0)	93.5 (7.1)	93.1 (18.1)	**94.4 (9.2)**	93.4 (5.4)	93.3 (10.4)
Lymphography	48.0 (6.1)	52.5 (5.7)	65.9 (2.1)	**69.6 (2.9)**	67.6 (5.3)	65.0 (6.0)
Monks–1	64.6 (5.4)	66.4 (0.1)	62.0 (2.1)	62.7 (1.0)	67.6 (0.02)	**69.4 (0.04)**
Monks–2	51.6 (2.0)	53.1 (3.0)	65.3 (0.1)	65.3 (0.02)	65.4 (1.7)	**65.7 (0.1)**
Monks–3	63.4 (4.2)	65.7 (0.1)	**79.9 (0.02)**	**79.9 (0.02)**	**79.9 (0.02)**	79.9 (0.02)
NewThyroid	78.0 (9.7)	75.8 (0.1)	79.9 (1.5)	80.3 (0.4)	86.5 (3.2)	**91.1 (2.5)**
Pima	66.0 (0.1)	64.7 (0.2)	**68.2 (0.1)**	67.8 (0.16)	67.9 (0.02)	67.5 (0.05)
Segment	51.5 (8.1)	65.4 (5.1)	62.7 (13.7)	62.9 (6.5)	67.7 (3.6)	**69.1 (5.7)**
Sonar	54.5 (0.7)	54.8 (4.2)	63.2 (3.1)	**64.2 (2.4)**	63.1 (2.1)	64.3 (2.4)
WDBC	85.4 (0.1)	84.0 (0.1)	92.7 (5.4)	93.6 (0.08)	94.2 (0.1)	**95.6 (0.1)**
Wine	67.8 (5.1)	67.8 (7.0)	**90.4 (4.9)**	88.1 (8.9)	88.7 (0.3)	88.2 (6.3)
Yeast	34.2 (1.3)	42.7 (2.8)	**46.9 (1.8)**	45.5 (1.8)	45.0 (2.2)	45.4 (2.5)

for most of the cases, the performance of SC over the augmented data sets outperforms the standard SC and the k-Means algorithms. More specifically, the performance of SC over $D_A = \{(\hat{\mu}_i, \hat{\Sigma}_i)\}_{i=1}^{n}$, is consistently better than k-Means and the standard SC, which is due to the smoothing included in defining the 2-tuple $(\hat{\mu}_i, \hat{\Sigma}_i)$. In terms of kernels over $D_A = \{(\hat{\mu}_i, \hat{\Sigma}_i)\}_{i=1}^{n}$, K_H and $K_{B\mathcal{R}}$ are usually better than K_J and K_B, and at least, very close to their performance. This emphasizes the role of the (semi-)metric defining each kernel.

8   Conclusion

We relax the global Gaussian assumption of the Euclidean distance in the exponential kernel K_E. The relaxation anchors a Gaussian distribution on the local neighbourhood of each point in the data set, resulting in the augmented data space $\mathbb{X}$. Based on convolution kernels, divergence measures of probability distributions, and Riemannian metrics for symmetric PD matrices, we propose a set of kernels for the space $\mathbb{X}$, and show using preliminary experiments that the local Gaussian assumption significantly outperforms the global one. Since all our approach described here is unsupervised, a main future research direction is to investigate the usefulness of this approach in supervised and semi-supervised learning tasks.

References

1. Ali, S.M., Silvey, S.D.: A general class of coefficients of divergence of one distribution from another. J. of the Royal Statistical Society. Series B 28(1), 131–142 (1966)
2. Atkinson, C., Mitchell, A.F.S.: Rao's distance measure. The Indian J. of Statistics, Series A 43(3), 345–365 (1945)

3. Csiszár, I.: Information–type measures of difference of probability distributions and indirect observations. Studia Scientiarium Mathematicarum Hungarica 2, 299–318 (1967)
4. Cuturi, M., Fukumizu, K., Vert, J.-P.: Semigroup kernels on measures. JMLR 6, 1169–1198 (2005)
5. Förstner, W., Moonen, B.: A metric for covariance matrices. Tech. rep., Dept. of Geodesy and Geo–Informatics, Stuttgart University (1999)
6. Hein, M., bousquet, O.: Hilbertian metrics and positive definite kernels on probability measures. In: Proc. of AISTATS, pp. 136–143 (2005)
7. Kailath, T.: The divergence and Bhattacharyya distance measures in signal selection. IEEE Trans. on Communication Technology 15(1), 52–60 (1967)
8. Kondor, R., Jebara, T.: A kernel between sets of vectors. In: ACM Proc. of ICML 2003 (2003)
9. Kullback, S.: Information Theory and Statistics – Dover Edition. Dover, New York (1997)
10. Luxburg, U.v.: A tutotrial on spectral clustering. Tech. Rep. TR–149, Max Plank Institute for Biological Cybernetics (2006)
11. Martins, A., Smith, N., Xing, E., Aguiar, P., Figueiredo, M.: Nonextensive information theoretic kernels on measures. JMLR 10, 935–975 (2009)
12. Moreno, P., Ho, P., Vasconcelos, N.: A Kullback–Leibler divergence based kernel for svm classification in multimedia applications. In: NIPS, vol. 16 (2003)
13. Newman, D., Hettich, S., Blake, C., Merz, C.: UCI Repository of Machine Learning Databases (1998), www.ics.uci.edu/~mlearn/MLRepository.html
14. Ng, A., Jordan, M., Weiss, Y.: On spectral clustering: Analysis and an algorithm. In: NIPS, vol. 14, pp. 849–856. MIT Press, Cambridge (2002)
15. Rao, C.R.: Information and the accuracy attainable in the estimation of statistical parameters. Bull. Calcutta Math. Soc. (58), 326–337 (1945)
16. Schoenberg, I.: Metric spaces and positive definite functions. Trans. of the American Mathematical Society 44(3), 522–536 (1938)
17. Shawe-Taylor, J., Cristianini, N.: Kernel Methods for Pattern Analysis. Cambridge University Press, Cambridge (2004)
18. Vincent, P., Bengio, Y.: Manifold Parzen windows. In: NIPS, vol. 15, pp. 825–832. MIT Press, Cambridge (2003)
19. Wolf, L., Shashua, A.: Learning over sets using kernel principal angles. JMLR 4, 913–931 (2003)
20. Zha, H., Ding, C., Gu, M., He, X., Simon, H.: Spectral relaxation for k–means clustering. In: NIPS, vol. 13. MIT Press, Cambridge (2001)

Using Landmarks as a Deformation Prior for Hybrid Image Registration

Marcel Lüthi, Christoph Jud, and Thomas Vetter

Computer Science Department
University of Basel, Switzerland
{marcel.luethi,christoph.jud,thomas.vetter}@unibas.ch

Abstract. Hybrid registration schemes are a powerful alternative to fully automatic registration algorithms. Current methods for hybrid registration either include the landmark information as a hard constraint, which is too rigid and leads to difficult optimization problems, or as a soft-constraint, which introduces a difficult to tune parameter for the landmark accuracy. In this paper we model the deformations as a Gaussian process and regard the landmarks as additional information on the admissible deformations. Using Gaussian process regression, we integrate the landmarks directly into the deformation prior. This leads to a new, probabilistic regularization term that penalizes deformations that do not agree with the modeled landmark uncertainty. It thus provides a middle ground between the two aforementioned approaches, without sharing their disadvantages. Our approach works for a large class of different deformation priors and leads to a known optimization problem in a Reproducing Kernel Hilbert Space.

1 Introduction

The problem of establishing point-to-point correspondence between two images is central to computer vision and medical image analysis. It is usually addressed using image registration methods, which aim to find a mapping such that each point in a reference image is mapped to its corresponding point in the target image. Formally, the registration problem can be defined as follows: Given a reference and target image $I_R, I_T : \Omega \to \mathbb{R}$ find the deformation field $u : \Omega \to \mathbb{R}^d$ from a class of admissible deformations that optimally aligns the warped reference image $I_R(x + u(x))$ with the target $I_T(x)$. This problem is usually formulated as a minimization problem of the functional

$$J[u] := \mathcal{D}_I[I_T, I_R, u] + \lambda \mathcal{R}[u] \tag{1}$$

where $\mathcal{D}_I$ is a similarity measure for the images, $\mathcal{R}$ a regularization term that penalizes non-smooth solutions and λ a regularization parameter. In cases where the images are noisy or corrupted, minimizing (1) may not lead to the desired correspondence. Hybrid registration schemes have shown to be a powerful alternative for such cases. These schemes let the user specify a set of corresponding landmark points $L_R, L_T \subset \Omega$ for the reference and the target image.

R. Mester and M. Felsberg (Eds.): DAGM 2011, LNCS 6835, pp. 196–205, 2011.

Various different methods for integrating these landmarks are known. They broadly fall into two classes. The first class of methods integrate the landmarks as a hard constraint [9,5,3,2]. The resulting problem is to find a deformation field that minimizes (1), but subject to additional landmark constraints:

$$J'[u] = \mathcal{D}_I[I_T, I_R, u] + \lambda \mathcal{R}[u] \quad s.t. \quad \mathcal{D}_{LM}[L_R, L_T, u] \leq \varepsilon, \tag{2}$$

where $\mathcal{D}_{LM}$ measure the landmark distance. Most such methods require a perfect interpolation of the landmarks (i.e. $\varepsilon = 0$ in (2)) [5,3,2]. The resulting optimization problem is a difficult numerical problem. To the best of our knowledge, solutions have only been presented for the case of the thin-plate spline model. The second class of methods do not strictly enforce the landmark constraint, but add it as a penalty into (1) [14,13,6,8]. This leads to the minimization problem of the functional

$$J''[u] = \mathcal{D}_I[I_T, I_R, u] + \eta \mathcal{D}_{LM}[L_T, L_R, u] + \lambda \mathcal{R}[u], \tag{3}$$

where η is an additional parameter. This approach has the advantage that the optimization problem is easier to handle and its integration into existing registration schemes is straight-forward. Moreover, we argue that it is more natural to treat the landmarks as a soft constraint as they are usually only approximately known. The main problem with this formulation is that it treats the landmark and regularization term independently, even though landmarks clearly provide a-priori information about the deformations. The regularization parameters λ and η become mutually dependent, which makes parameter tuning difficult.

In this paper we propose a formulation of hybrid registration that combines both approaches, by integrating the landmark information into the regularization term in (1). The uncertainty of the landmarks positions σ is the only additional parameter that we introduce. Its value is at least approximately known from the experimental setup. If we set $\sigma = 0$, our solution matches the landmark points perfectly, whereas for $\sigma > 0$ an approximate solution is achieved. The main idea is to model the admissible deformations as a (vector-valued) Gaussian process $u \sim \mathcal{GP}(0, k)$. Its covariance function k determines the regularization properties of the deformation field. Landmark registration becomes the problem of Gaussian process regression [10], where the displacement at the landmark points are our observations. Gaussian process regression does not only provide us with a MAP solution for the landmark registration problem, but yields the full posterior distribution $p(u|L_T, L_R)$. This distribution is again a Gaussian process $\mathcal{GP}(\mu_{LM}, k_{LM})$, whose parameters are known in closed form. Its covariance function k_{LM} spans a Reproducing Kernel Hilbert Space (RKHS), whose associated norm $\|\cdot\|_{k_{LM}}$ penalizes functions according to the posterior probability $p(u|L_T, L_R)$. Thus, it is an ideal regularization term for the registration problem (1) and leads to a hybrid scheme. The resulting formulation of the registration problem has recently been addressed by Schölkopf et al. [13]. They proposed a general solution strategy that can be applied to any covariance function. Yet in contrast to our work, they do not include the landmarks into the covariance function, but model them as a soft constraint as in (3).

Unlike most previous approaches for hybrid registration, which have been formulated for a fixed deformation model such as the thin-plate splines [5,3,9], elastic body splines [17] or B-splines [14,8], our approach works for any valid (i.e. positive definite) covariance function. In particular it includes the deformation models that arise from Green's functions of regularization operators, which have been proposed for hybrid registration in [2].

We present experiments for a simple toy example and a 2D X-ray image of the hand. Although our current implementation does not allow us to register large images, our results clearly illustrate the benefits of our approach. Our experiments show that while different covariance functions lead to different regularization properties, the parameter σ that models the landmark accuracy keeps its intuitive meaning. Furthermore we illustrate that the ability to model the landmark inaccuracies is important to obtain good registration results.

2   Background

The core idea of our method is to use Gaussian process regression to obtain a deformation prior that implicitly incorporates the landmark term. In this section we briefly review Gaussian processes and their application to regression.

2.1   Gaussian Processes

Stochastic processes allow us to define a probability distribution over a function space. Formally, a stochastic process is a collection of random variables $f(x), x \in \Omega$ where Ω is an index set. A Gaussian process is a stochastic process with the property that for any finite number of observations, $x_1, \ldots, x_n \in \Omega$ the values $f(x_1), \ldots, f(x_n)$ are jointly normally distributed [10]. A Gaussian process is completely defined by its mean $\mu : \Omega \to \mathbb{R}$ and a covariance function $k : \Omega \times \Omega \to \mathbb{R}$. We write $\mathcal{GP}(\mu, k)$ to specify a Gaussian process. To simplify the discussion, we consider here only Gaussian processes $\mathcal{GP}(0, k)$ with zero mean. The extension to the general case is, however, straight-forward.

The covariance function $k(x, y)$ specifies for each pair of points x, y their covariance $E[f(x)f(y)]$. By specifying a covariance function we define which functions are likely under the given process. Many known covariance functions require that nearby values are strongly correlated, which leads to that they effectively favor smooth functions. Indeed, many covariance functions arise as Greens functions of common regularization operators [16]. Covariance functions are also often referred to as kernels, and we will use the terms interchangeably.

Vector-valued Gaussian Processes. To be able to use Gaussian process for modeling deformation fields, the above concepts need to be generalized to the case in which each random variable $u(x)$ is a d dimensional random vector. The covariance function becomes matrix valued $k(x, y) : \Omega \times \Omega \to \mathbb{R}^{d \times d}$, with $k(x, y) = E[u(x)u(y)^T]$. It can be shown that the vector-valued case can be reduced to the scalar case. Thus all known results for real-valued Gaussian processes carry over to this more general setting. We refer to the article by Hein et al. for further details [4].

A useful class of covariance functions for the vector valued case arise from the scalar valued covariance functions. Let $A \in \mathbb{R}^{d \times d}$ be a symmetric, positive definite matrix and l a real valued covariance function. It can be shown that the matrix valued function k with entries k_{ij} defined by

$$k_{ij}(x, y) = A_{ij} l(x, y), \tag{4}$$

is a valid covariance function [7]. The entry A_{ij} determines the correlation between the i-th and j-th output component. In cases where we do not have any a-priori knowledge about their correlation, we can choose $A = \mathcal{I}_d$ as the identity. In this case each dimension is considered as independent.

2.2   Gaussian Process Regression

Assume that we are given an i.i.d. sample $S = \{(x_1, y_1,), \ldots, (x_n, y_n)\} \subset \Omega \times \mathbb{R}^d$ and let $u \in \mathcal{GP}(0, k)$ be a vector valued Gaussian process with $k : \Omega \times \Omega \to \mathbb{R}^{d \times d}$. Gaussian process regression lets us infer the distribution $p(u|S)$. We assume that $y \sim \mathcal{N}(u(x), \sigma^2 \mathcal{I}_d)$. This means, instead of observing the actual values $u(x)$ we observe noisy instances y thereof. The likelihood of the data is given as $p(S|u)) = \prod_{i=1}^{n} \mathcal{N}(u(x_i), \sigma^2 \mathcal{I}_d)$. Under this assumption the posterior distribution $p(u|S) \propto p(u)p(S|u)$ is known in closed form [10]. It is again a Gaussian process $\mathcal{GP}(\mu_p, k_p)$ and its parameters are

$$\mu_p(x) = K_X(x)^T (K_{XX} + \sigma^2 \mathcal{I})^{-1} Y \tag{5}$$
$$k_p(x, x') = k(x, x') - K_X(x)^T (K_{XX} + \sigma^2 \mathcal{I})^{-1} K_X(x'). \tag{6}$$

Here, we defined $K_X(x) = (k(x, x_i))_{i=1}^{n} \in \mathbb{R}^{nd \times d}$, $K_{XX} = (k(x_i, x_j))_{i,j=1}^{n} \in \mathbb{R}^{nd \times nd}$ and $Y = (y_1, \ldots, y_n)^T \in \mathbb{R}^{nd}$. Note that K_X and K_{XX} consist of sub-matrices of size $d \times d$.

Under this posterior distribution, only functions that agree with the given sample S are likely observations. This is illustrated in Figure 1. Figure 1a shows random samples from a one-dimensional prior distribution where we used the Gaussian covariance function, defined by $k(x, x') = \exp(-\|x - x'\|^2)$. Figure 1b shows the corresponding posterior distribution after the sample has been observed.

3   Hybrid Registration Using a Landmark Prior

In this section we show how Gaussian process regression yields a solution of the landmark registration problem, and how the resulting posterior process can be used as a regularization term. Furthermore, we outline a generic procedure how the resulting registration functional can be solved.

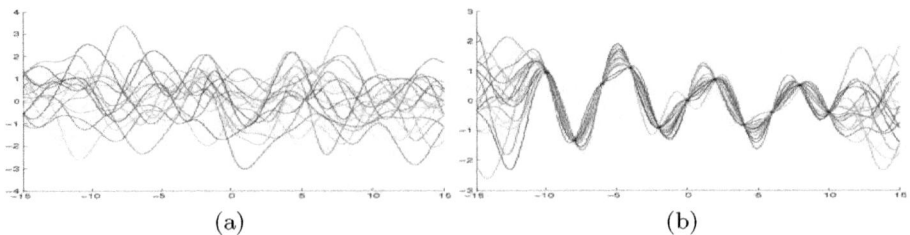

(a)   (b)

Fig. 1. (a) Random samples from a Gaussian process. (b) Random samples from the posterior process, after a number of points have been observed. Only functions that agree with the observations are likely to be observed.

3.1 Landmark Registration

Let $u \sim \mathcal{GP}(0, k)$ be a vector valued Gaussian process with covariance function $k : \Omega \times \Omega \to \mathbb{R}^{d \times d}$ that defines our prior assumptions about the possible deformations. Usually, we choose k, such that the Gausssian process favours smooth deformation fields. Further let $L_R = \{l_R^1, \ldots, l_R^n)\}$ and $L_T = \{l_T^1, \ldots, l_T^n)\}$ be the given landmarks. These landmarks provide us with known deformation at the landmark points

$$L = \{(l_R^1, l_T^1 - l_R^1), \ldots, (l_R^n, l_T^n - l_R^n)\} =: \{(l_R^1, y_1), \ldots, (l_R^n, y_n)\},$$

and thus we have a sample set S on which we can apply Gaussian process regression. The likelihood function is given by

$$p(L|u) = \prod_{i=1}^{N} \mathcal{N}(u(x_i), \sigma^2 \mathcal{I}_d),$$

and corresponds to our assumption that the inaccuracies of the landmarks can be modeled as independent Gaussian noise. We know from Section 2 that the posterior $p(u|L) \propto p(u)p(L|u)$ is under these assumptions again a Gaussian process $p(u|L) \sim \mathcal{GP}(\mu_{LM}, k_{LM})$, whose parameters are known in closed form and are defined by (5). This posterior distribution thus defines a distribution over deformation fields which incorporates the landmark constraints. Its mean deformation μ_{LM} is the MAP solution to the landmark registration problem and provides an optimal trade-off between our a-priori information about the deformation field and the landmark constraints.

3.2 Combined Landmark and Image Registration

Our starting point for combining the landmark prior with image registration is the probabilistic formulation of the registration problem by Christenson et al. [1]. They pointed out that the registration problem (1) can be interpreted as the following MAP estimation problem:

$$\arg\max_{u} p(u)p(I_T|I_R, u), \tag{7}$$

where $p(u) \propto \exp(-\mathcal{R}[u])$ is a Gaussian process prior over the admissible deformation fields and $p(I_T|I_R, u) \propto \exp(\lambda^{-1}\mathcal{D}[I_R, I_T, u])$ is the likelihood. Given the displacements from the landmarks L, it is natural to reformulate (7) as

$$\arg\max_u p(u|L)p(I_T|I_R, u) \tag{8}$$

and to choose $p(u|L) \sim \mathcal{GP}(\mu_{LM}, k_{LM})$ using the closed form solution derived in the previous section.

To solve (8) we exploit the well known fact that finding the MAP solution of a Gaussian process model corresponds to solving minimization problem in the Reproducing Kernel Hilbert Space (RKHS) $\mathcal{F}_k$ defined by the covariance function k (see e.g. Wahba [16]). In the following discussion we chose the sum of squared differences as a distance measure:

$$\mathcal{D}[I_T, I_R, u] = \int_\Omega [I_T(x) - I_R(x + u(x))]^2 \, dx. \tag{9}$$

The problem corresponding to (8) becomes

$$\arg\min_{u \in \mathcal{F}_k} \|u\|_{k_{LM}}^2 + \lambda^{-1} \int_\Omega [I_T(x) - I_R(x + \mu_{LM}(x) + u(x))]^2 \, dx. \tag{10}$$

where $\|\cdot\|_{k_{LM}}$ denotes the RKHS norm. Treating the registration problem as a minimization problem in a RKHS is the starting point of a recent paper by Schölkopf et al. [13]. We briefly sketch the approach and refer to the original paper for further details. The idea is to approximate the integral in (9) by uniformly sampling N points from Ω and solve the discretized problem:

$$u^* = \arg\min_{u \in \mathcal{F}_k} \lambda\|u\|_{k_{LM}}^2 + \frac{1}{N}\sum_{i=1}^N [I_T(x_i) - I_R(x_i + \mu_{LM}(x_i) + u(x_i))]^2 \tag{11}$$

The generalized representer theorem [12] asserts that the optimal solution u^* is given as a finite linear combination of the covariance functions k_{LM}

$$u^*(x) = \sum_{i=1}^N k_{LM}(x, x_i)\alpha_i^*, \tag{12}$$

where $\alpha_i^* \in \mathbb{R}^d$ is a vector of optimal coefficients for each output dimension. The optimal coefficients $(\alpha_1^*, \ldots, \alpha_n^*)$ can be found by plugging (12) into (11) to obtain a finite dimensional minimization problem

$$\arg\min_{\alpha_1,\ldots,\alpha_N} \lambda \sum_{i,j}^N \alpha_i^T k_{LM}(x_i, x_j)\alpha_j + \frac{1}{N}\sum_{i=1}^N [I_T(x_i) - I_R(x_i + \mu_{LM}(x_i) + \sum_{j=1}^N k_{LM}(x_j, x_i)\alpha_j)]^2. \tag{13}$$

This problem can be solved using any standard optimization scheme.

3.3   A Note on the Implementation

The above approach provides us with a general method to find the MAP solution to (8) for the case when the prior $p(u)$ is a Gaussian process. This is a extremely general formulation and includes many different registration schemes as a special case. This generality comes at the price that each optimization step requires the evaluation of the covariance function in a double sum over N points. For most real images N is too large for this to be feasible. Schölkopf et al. [13] proposed to use compactly supported covariance functions. The matrix $K_{XX} = (k_{LM}(x_i, x_j))_{i,j=1}^{N}$ becomes sparse and needs to be computed only once. The double sums in (13) can be replaced by matrix-vector multiplications. Using a straight-forward implementation of this approach, we can register an 128×128 image in about 15 minutes on a standard PC (single core). For the registration of 3D images this approach remains infeasible. To be able to solve (8) more efficiently, some of the generality might have to be sacrificed and the solution scheme targeted to special covariance functions.

4   Results

In this section we illustrate our method on a toy example and a X-ray image. We choose the following covariance functions: The (cubic) B-spline, defined by

$$k_b(x, x') := \sum_{l \in \mathbb{Z}^2} \beta_\otimes(x - l)\beta_\otimes(x' - l) \tag{14}$$

where $\beta_\otimes$ are tensor product B-splines defined for $x \in \mathbb{R}^2$ as $\beta_\otimes(x) = \beta_3(x_1)\beta_3(x_2)$ and β_3 in turn is the cubic B-spline basis function [15]. Further, the Wu's functions defined by [11]

$$k_{0,0}(x, x') := k_{0,0}(r) = \max(0, (1 - r))$$

where $r = \|(x - x')\|^2/s$ and s determines the support of the kernel and finally the Wu's function defined by

$$k_{2,1}(x, x') := k_{2,1}(r) = \max(0, (1 - r))^4(4 + 16r + 12r^2 + 3r^3).$$

To obtain the corresponding matrix valued functions, we multiply the covariance function by the identity matrix $\mathcal{I}_2$ (Cf. Section 2.1). Thus, we effectively treat each output dimension as independent. We keep the regularization parameter λ, as well as the parameters of the covariance functions constant in all the examples.

Figure 2 shows the result for the toy example. A proper registration solution would match all the corners onto each other. Using only a standard smoothness prior the registration method will not be able to find the right correspondences. Figure 2c shows the result for the B-spline covariance function when the landmarks are ignored. By forcing the landmarks point to match exactly (i.e. setting $\sigma = 0$), we can enforce a correct solution (Figure 2, (d)-(f)).

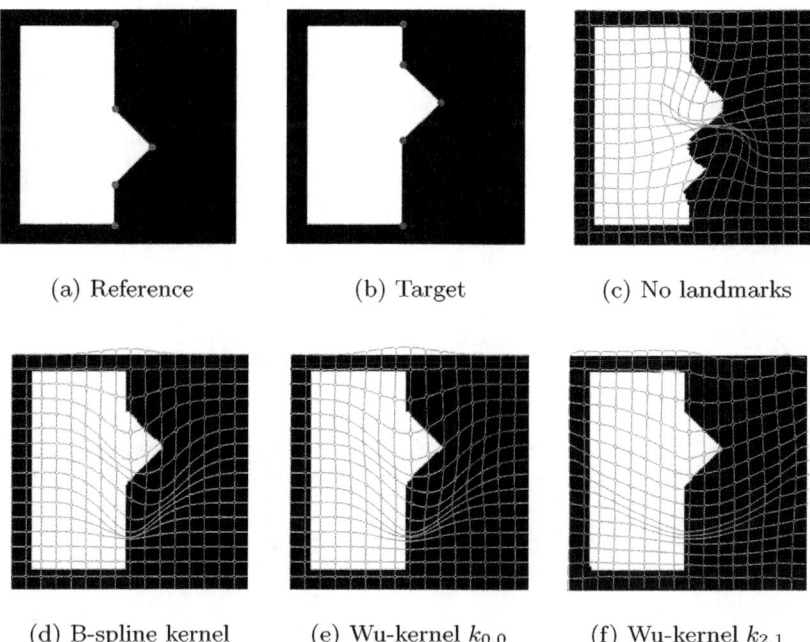

| (a) Reference | (b) Target | (c) No landmarks |

| (d) B-spline kernel | (e) Wu-kernel $k_{0,0}$ | (f) Wu-kernel $k_{2,1}$ |

Fig. 2. A toy example: The goal is to transform the reference (a) onto the target (b). (c) shows a result using the B-spline kernel without landmarks. Using the landmarks we can enforce the desired matching of the corners (d)-(f). From the deformed grids we see that the deformation fields differ for different covariance functions, even though the registration result looks the same.

We see that the result looks the same in 2d-2f, but the actual deformations (as shown by the grid) strongly depend on the chosen covariance functions. In our second example we illustrate the influence of the landmark accuracy on the solution. Figure 3a and 3b show the target and reference image together with the correct landmarks. Using these landmarks, we obtain the registration result depicted in Figure 3c. We then add Gaussian noise with a standard deviation of 5mm onto the landmarks position (Figure 3d). Forcing the landmarks to perfectly match, by setting $\sigma = 0$mm, leads to the result shown in Figure 3e. A much better solution is obtained if we model the landmark inaccuracy correctly by setting $\sigma = 5$mm (Figure 3f).

5   Conclusion

We have presented a novel formulation of hybrid registration. In contrast to previous approaches, we proposed to integrate the landmark information directly into the deformation prior. This avoids a new trade-off parameter, but still allows us to control how accurately the landmarks should be matched. Furthermore,

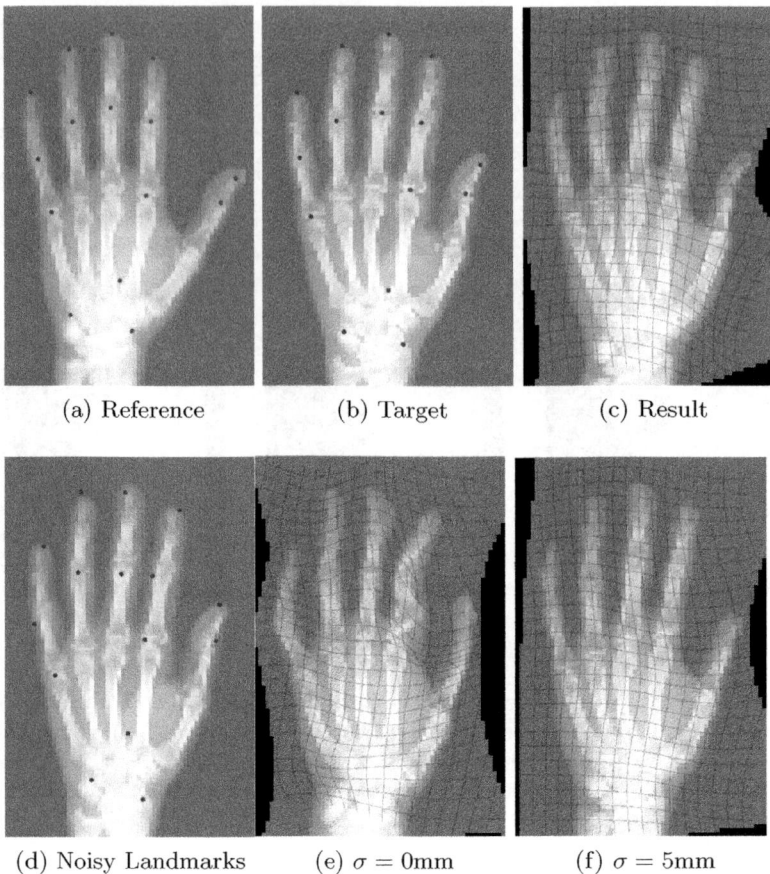

(a) Reference   (b) Target   (c) Result

(d) Noisy Landmarks   (e) $\sigma = 0$mm   (f) $\sigma = 5$mm

Fig. 3. Two X-ray images of hands ((a), (b)) are registered. (c) shows the solution using the Wu kernel $k_{2,1}$. In (d) we add noise to the landmark positions. (e) shows the solution when a perfect match ($\sigma = 0$mm) is enforced. Correctly modeling the noise on the landmarks greatly improves the result (f).

the regularization term has a natural probabilistic interpretation as the posterior $p(u|L_T, L_R)$ of the deformations u given the landmarks. Our results illustrated that we can both enforce a perfect match of the landmark points, and allow for an approximate matching. Further, we showed that by using different covariance functions, different regularization properties can be obtained, which makes this approach more versatile than previous formulations. The use of compact covariance functions makes the method practical for the registration of 2D images of moderate size. However, it is still not feasible at this point to use it for the registration of 3D images. Devising an efficient scheme for special classes of covariance functions, such that 3D hybrid registration becomes possible is an interesting challenge, which we will address in future work.

Acknowledgements. We thank our colleague, Brian Amberg, for insightful discussions regarding this work. This work has been supported by the COME/NCCR research network of the Swiss National Science Foundation.

References

1. Christensen, G.E., Miller, M.I., Vannier, M.W., Grenander, U.: Individualizing neuro-anatomical atlases using a massively parallel computer. Computer 29(1), 32–38 (1996)
2. Fischer, B., Modersitzki, J.: Combination of automatic non-rigid and landmark based registration: the best of both worlds. Medical Imaging, 1037–1048 (2003)
3. Haber, E., Heldmann, S., Modersitzki, J.: A Scale-Space approach to landmark constrained image registration. Scale Space and Variational Methods in Computer Vision, 612–623 (2009)
4. Hein, M., Bousquet, O.: Kernels, associated structures and generalizations. Max-Planck-Institut fuer biologische Kybernetik, Technical Report (2004)
5. Johnson, H.J., Christensen, G.E.: Consistent landmark and intensity-based image registration. IEEE Transactions on Medical Imaging 21(5), 450–461 (2002)
6. Lu, H., Cattin, P., Reyes, M.: A hybrid multimodal non-rigid registration of MR images based on diffeomorphic demons. In: International Conference of the IEEE Engineering in Medicine and Biology Society, pp. 5951–5954 (2010)
7. Micchelli, C.A., Pontil, M.: On learning vector-valued functions. Neural Computation 17(1), 177–204 (2005)
8. Papademetris, X., Jackowski, A.P., Schultz, R.T., Staib, L.H., Duncan, J.S.: Integrated intensity and point-feature nonrigid registration. In: Barillot, C., Haynor, D.R., Hellier, P. (eds.) MICCAI 2004. LNCS, vol. 3216, pp. 763–770. Springer, Heidelberg (2004)
9. Papenberg, N., Olesch, J., Lange, T., Schlag, P.M., Fischer, B.: Landmark constrained non-parametric image registration with isotropic tolerances. Bildverarbeitung für die Medizin 2009, 122–126 (2009)
10. Rasmussen, C.E., Williams, C.K.: Gaussian processes for machine learning. Springer, Heidelberg (2006)
11. Schaback, R.: Creating surfaces from scattered data using radial basis functions. Mathematical Methods for Curves and Surfaces, 477–496 (1995)
12. Schölkopf, B., Herbrich, R., Smola, A.: A generalized representer theorem. In: Computational Learning Theory, pp. 416–426 (2001)
13. Schölkopf, B., Steinke, F., Blanz, V.: Object correspondence as a machine learning problem. In: ICML 2005: Proceedings of the 22nd International Conference on Machine Learning, pp. 776–783. ACM Press, New York (2005)
14. Sorzano, C.O.S., Thevenaz, P., Unser, M.: Elastic registration of biological images using vector-spline regularization. IEEE Transactions on Biomedical Engineering 52(4), 652–663 (2005)
15. Unser, M.: Splines: A perfect fit for signal and image processing. IEEE Signal Processing Magazine 16(6), 22–38 (1999)
16. Wahba, G.: Spline models for observational data. Society for Industrial Mathematics (1990)
17. Wörz, S., Rohr, K.: Hybrid spline-based elastic image registration using analytic solutions of the navier equation. Bildverarbeitung für die Medizin 2007, 151–155 (2007)

Improving Denoising Algorithms via a Multi-scale Meta-procedure

Harold Christopher Burger and Stefan Harmeling

Max Planck Institute for Intelligent Systems, Tübingen, Germany

Abstract. Many state-of-the-art denoising algorithms focus on recovering high-frequency details in noisy images. However, images corrupted by large amounts of noise are also degraded in the lower frequencies. Thus properly handling all frequency bands allows us to better denoise in such regimes. To improve existing denoising algorithms we propose a meta-procedure that applies existing denoising algorithms across different scales and combines the resulting images into a single denoised image. With a comprehensive evaluation we show that the performance of many state-of-the-art denoising algorithms can be improved.

1 Introduction

The problem of removing noise from natural images has been extensively studied, so methods to denoise natural images are numerous and diverse. [4] classifies denoising algorithms into three categories: The first class of algorithms rely on smoothing parts of the noisy image [12,16,14] with the aim of "smoothing out" the noise while preserving image details. The second class of denoising algorithms exploit learned image statistics. A natural image model is typically learned on a noise-free training set (such as the Berkeley segmentation dataset) and then exploited to denoise images [11,17,5]. In some cases, denoising might involve the careful shrinkage of coefficients. For example [13,1,8,9] involve shrinkage of wavelet coefficients. Other methods denoise small images patches by representing them as sparse linear combinations of elements of a learned dictionary [3,7,6]. The third class of algorithms exploits the fact that different patches in the same image are often similar in appearance [2,4].

Denoising algorithms are usually evaluated on their ability to remove additive white Gaussian noise (AWGN). Standard test images exist for this purpose. The most popular performance measure is arguably the peak signal to noise ratio (PSNR), which is related to the mean squared error (MSE).

Hypothesis: We speculate that most denoising algorithms focus on removing noise on the higher frequencies and thus are often best suited for recovering fine-scale information. Wiener filtering, bilateral filtering [14], but also the fields of experts approach [11] rely on relatively small filters to denoise images. The small size of these filters causes these approaches to ignore larger-scale information. Denoising approaches based on dictionaries such as [3] typically decompose the

R. Mester and M. Felsberg (Eds.): DAGM 2011, LNCS 6835, pp. 206–215, 2011.

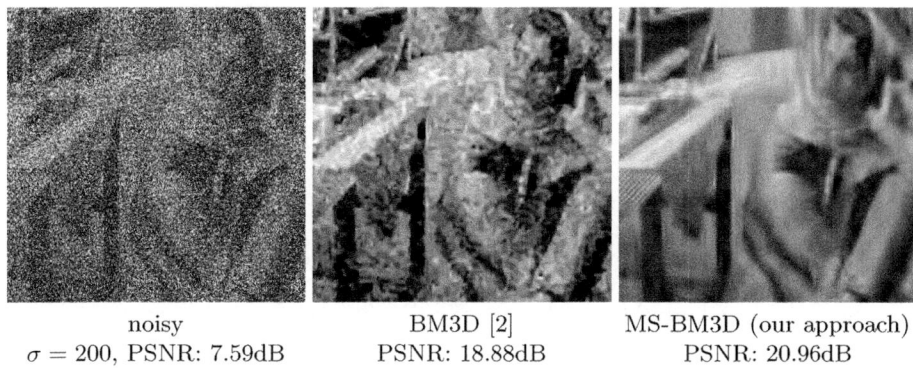

noisy	BM3D [2]	MS-BM3D (our approach)
$\sigma = 200$, PSNR: 7.59dB	PSNR: 18.88dB	PSNR: 20.96dB

Fig. 1. In high noise settings, our approach improves the results achieved with BM3D

image into small patches and then denoise the patches separately and independently. Larger-scale structure is lost when the image is decomposed into small patches. So we hypothesize that many denoising algorithms can be improved by employing a multi-scale approach.

Assumption: Our approach assumes that the statistics of natural images are invariant to changes in spatial scale. An intuitive justification for this assumption is that scenes are about equally likely to be viewed from different distances. This assumption has been successfully exploited by others [9].

Contributions: We present a meta-procedure than can be used in combination with existing denoising methods, yet often improves the results. We choose algorithms from all three categories to show that our procedure is versatile. We evaluate the PSNR on a set of 13 standard test images with varying amounts of added noise. In most cases, we use commonly available implementations of these algorithms.

Related work: Besides the denoising method mentioned above, there is a procedure that is relatively similar to ours. In [4], the authors introduce the "stochastic denoising" procedure and propose an extension (called "multi-pass denoising") in order to handle "larger-scale" noise (i.e. noise that is not uncorrelated across neighboring pixels). The extension is similar to our meta-procedure in that in addition to the original image, a single down-sampled version is denoised. The down-sampled denoised image is up-sampled and combined with the denoised image of the original size. Different from our method is that the authors combine the images using a pixel-specific linear blend between the two images. The ratio of the blend is controlled by the gradient of the image at that pixel. No quantitative evaluation was provided in [4], but we include it in our evaluation. [10] also considers a multiscale approach for image denoising by thresholding coefficients in different frequency bands.

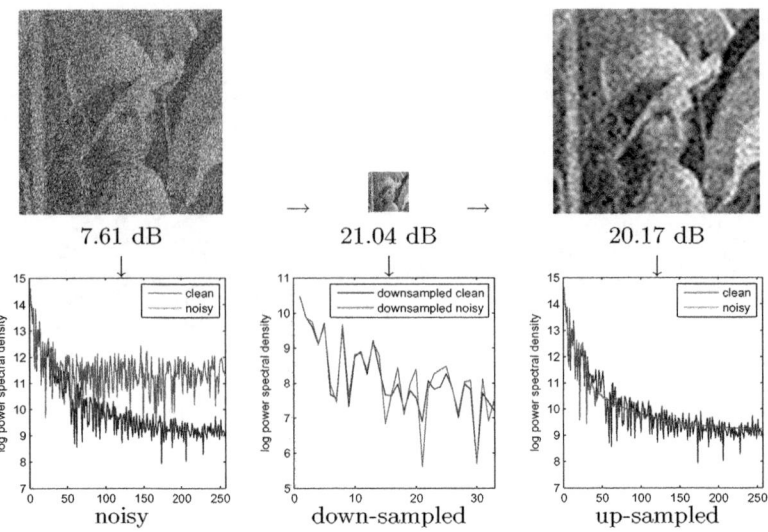

Fig. 2. Noisy Lena becomes less noisy by down- and up-sampling (top row) with power spectra (bottom row)

2   Down-Scaling Has a Denoising Effect

When an image that has been corrupted with AWGN is down-scaled, the image becomes more recognisable. The effect is illustrated in Fig. 2: adding a large amount of Gaussian noise leaves the "Lena" image barely recognisable (upper left). Nonetheless, the down-scaled version (upper middle) seems to contain much less noise.

Down-scaling an image effectively averages neighboring pixel values, causing the uncorrelated values of the noise to become smaller. Since neighboring pixels in natural images are often highly correlated, the down-scaling process is not that damaging to the image information. Another explanation is that natural images have the most energy in the low frequencies whereas AWGN is uniformly spread over the whole spectrum. Down-sampling an image keeps mainly the low frequencies, which are precisely the frequencies where the image information is strongest (bottom row in Fig. 2). Nonetheless, if the amount of noise is very large, frequencies in the middle of the spectrum are also affected, so the image information in lower frequencies should also be denoised.

3   How to Denoise Lower Frequencies

We imagine a hypothetical scenario in which we wish to recover the low frequencies of a noisy image as best as possible. To evaluate how well we recovered the low frequencies, we compare the resulting image to a down-scaled version of the ground truth image. We compare two approaches:

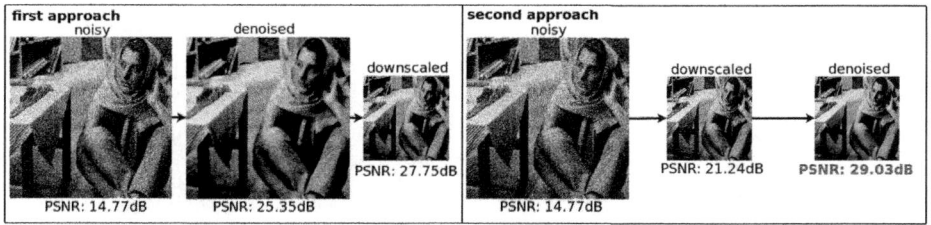

Fig. 3. Which approach better recovers the low frequencies? First down-scaling, then denoising is better than the other way around when the noise is strong

1. First denoise, then down-scale the result.
2. First down-scale, then denoise.

Which approach is better? In the first approach, the denoising algorithm has more information available, while in the second approach the denoising algorithm is applied to the down-sampled version. Denoising a down-scaled image should be an easier task, which would suggest that the second approach is better. If the second approach achieves better results, we could conclude that denoising algorithms are not good at recovering large-scale (i.e. low frequency) information, confirming the hypothesis we advanced in the introduction.

Fig. 3 compares the two approaches using KSVD as the denoising procedure. Comparing the achieved PSNRs we see that the second approach is preferable to the first. This effect also holds for other denoising algorithm for a variety of different noise settings (see supplementary material for details).

Thus we can conclude that if we wish to recover low-frequency information with a denoising algorithm that is not designed to recover low frequencies, downscaling the image might help. Effectively the down-scaling transforms the low-frequency information into high-frequency information which can be accessed by the denoising algorithm. In the following we show how this insight can be exploited with a multi-scale procedure such that the high-frequencies are recovered from the given noisy image, while we get the low frequencies from a down-scaled version of it.

4   Multi-scale Denoising

We propose a meta-procedure that relies on denoising not only the original noisy image, but also down-scaled versions of that image. This meta-procedure is formulated such that it can be combined with any existing denoising algorithm. The last step of our procedure consists in combining the denoised images at the different scales. The combination is motivated by Laplacian pyramids. Fig. 4 summarizes our method graphically.

We will denote by $d_\alpha(x)$ a procedure that down-samples the image x by the factor α. Similarly, we denote by $u_\alpha(x)$ the procedure that up-samples the image x by the factor α. In practice, we applied Matlab's `imresize` function with the Lanczos-3 kernel. Other kernels do not lead to significantly different results.

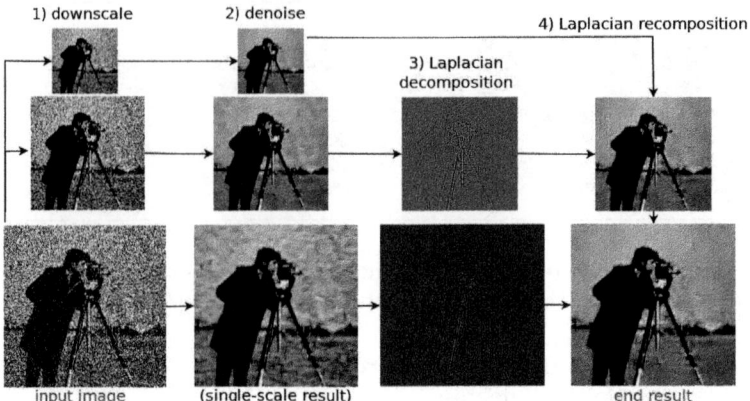

Fig. 4. Our procedure denoises a noisy image at different scales and then combines these images similarly to Laplacian pyramids

Note that resizing is a linear operator which can be represented as a matrix D. The covariance matrix of downsampled Gaussian noise is proportional to DD^T which is approximately the identity matrix for most resampling kernels (e.g. Lanczos). This fact implies that the AWGN assumption also holds for downsampled images.

Denoising at different scales. As parameters to our procedure we initially choose a denoising algorithm and scaling factors $\alpha_1, \ldots, \alpha_n$ (sorted in ascending order). Given a noisy image x_0, we create n down-sampled versions $x_1, \ldots, x_n$,

$$x_1 = d_{\alpha_1}(x_0); \quad \cdots \quad x_n = d_{\alpha_n}(x_0). \tag{1}$$

The images $x_0, \ldots, x_n$ are subsequently denoised using the same denoising procedure:

$$y_0 = \text{denoise}(x_0); \quad \cdots \quad y_n = \text{denoise}(x_n). \tag{2}$$

Next we combine the $n + 1$ denoised images $y_0, \ldots, y_n$ in a Laplacian-pyramid fashion to obtain the best possible denoised image z_0 (which will have the same size as the input image x_0).

Recombining the images on the different scales. For this we decompose the image y_i into low and high frequency components l_i and h_i:

$$l_i = d_{\alpha_i/\alpha_j}(y_i) \qquad\qquad h_i = y_i - u_{\alpha_j/\alpha_i}(l_i). \tag{3}$$

Next, the low frequency information l_i is discarded and replaced by y_{i+1}, which has the same size as l_i. We do so because y_{i+1} contains more accurate low-frequency information. Combining y_{i+1} and h_i we obtain a reconstruction z_i at level i:

$$z_i = h_i + u_{\alpha_j/\alpha_i}(y_{i+1}) \tag{4}$$

which combines the best of y_i and y_{i+1}, i.e. the high frequencies of y_i and the low frequencies from y_{i+1}.

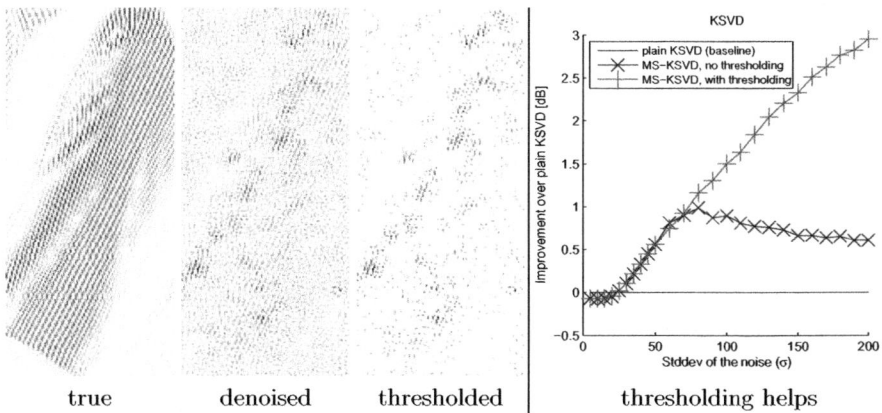

| true | denoised | thresholded | thresholding helps |

Fig. 5. Left: high frequencies of the clean image (lower-right corner of "Barbara"). Center: high frequency image of the denoised image (recovered from noisy image with $\sigma = 100$). The image contains mostly noise, but Barbara's pants are discernible. Right: thresholded high frequency image. Structure from the pants is kept. Panel on the right shows that thresholding helps.

As common for Laplacian pyramids, we start the multi-scale reconstruction with the two smallest images y_{n-1} and y_n and proceed through all scales until we reconstruct the image z_0 which is the denoising result of our method.

Shrinking high frequency coefficients. The right panel in Fig. 5 shows the benefit of using the proposed multi-scale meta-procedure with two scales in combination with the KSVD denoising algorithm. At noise levels above $\sigma = 25$, the meta-procedure (MS-KSVD, no thresholding, line '—x—') improves the results over the plain denoising algorithm (solid line). At first, the improvement grows with growing noisiness. However, when the noise becomes very strong, this effect is reversed: The multi-scale meta-procedure helps less and less. This effect is due to the fact that the high-frequency components z_i are beneficial in lower noise settings, but detrimental at higher noise levels. At very high noise levels, the denoising algorithm becomes incompetent at recovering high-frequencies. A possible solution to the problem is to attenuate the values in the high-frequency image z_i in such a way as to keep only the strongest components. We replace Eq. (4) by:

$$z_i = \mathcal{T}(h_i, \lambda) + u_{\alpha_j/\alpha_i}(y_j) , \tag{5}$$

where $\mathcal{T}(h_i, \lambda)$ is the hard-thresholding operator with threshold λ. Other attenuation methods lead to similar results.

The three images on the left of Fig. 5 show the effect of the hard-thresholding operator on a high-frequency image: The smaller values in the high-frequency are mostly due to errors in the denoising procedure and are successfully removed by the thresholding operation. The larger values however are unlikely to be due to errors in the denoising procedure and are therefore kept.

5   Experimental Evaluation and Results

Our meta-procedure is sensitive to the threshold parameter λ as well as to the sizes and numbers of scales used in the Laplacian pyramid. We tuned those hyperparameters for each considered denoising algorithm and for each noise level σ on a training set of 20 images from the Berkeley segmentation training dataset, see supplementary material. The smallest number of scales is 1 (no multi-scale approach) and the largest is 4. The scale sizes we chose are $(1/2)^k$ with $0 \leq k \leq 3$. This corresponds to repeatedly down-scaling by a factor of two.

As the test set, we used the 13 standard gray-scale images commonly known as: "Barbara", "Boat", "Cameraman", "Couple", "Fingerprint", "Flintstones", "Hill", "House", "Baboon", "F16", "Lena", "Man" and "Peppers" (see supplementary material for images).

We applied our meta-procedure to nine state-of-the-art denoising algorithms whose implementations are commonly available. (1) Wiener filtering using Matlab's `wiener2` function with the default neighborhood size of 3. (2) Bilateral filtering [14][1] with three hyper-parameters that need to be set. Empirically, we found 10 to be a good value for the half-size of the Gaussian bilateral filter window. We chose $\sigma_1 = 3$ and set σ_2 between 10^{-4} and 2.2 depending on the noisiness of the image. (3) Bayesian least-squares Gaussian scale mixtures (BLS-GSM) [9][2], (4) Stochastic denoising [4][3], (5) Block-matching 3D (BM3D) [2][4], (6) Fields of Experts (FoE) [11][5], (7) Basis roation fields of experts (BRFoE) [17][6], and (8) Total variation denoising (TV) [12][7] all have implementations publicly available online. We used the default parameters for all methods except for FoE, where we were able to improve results over the publicly available implementation by adapting the number of iterations to the amount of noise in the image. We used our own implementation for (9) KSVD [3]. We found 10 iterations for training the dictionary to be sufficient.

Improvements for varying noise levels. Fig. 6 reports for various noise levels σ the difference between the results obtained in the single scale setting (denoted "baseline . . . ") compared to our multi-scale meta-procedure (denoted "MS-. . . "). We also included results obtained with the "multi-pass" procedure proposed in [4] (denoted "Estrada-. . . "). The integer values from one to four along the line of our multi-scale procedure ("—x—") indicate the number of scales applied.

When the noise level is low, in most cases our multi-scale meta-procedure does not improve the results of the baseline algorithm. In fact, the results are in those cases identical to the baseline algorithm. This happens when our multi-scale

---

[1] http://www.mathworks.com/matlabcentral/fileexchange/12191

[2] http://decsai.ugr.es/~javier/denoise/software/

[3] http://www.cs.utoronto.ca/~strider/Denoise/

[4] http://www.cs.tut.fi/~foi/GCF-BM3D/index.html#ref_software

[5] http://www.gris.informatik.tu-darmstadt.de/~sroth/research/foe/index.html

[6] http://www.cs.huji.ac.il/~yweiss/BRFOE.zip

[7] http://visl.technion.ac.il/~gilboa/PDE-filt/tv_denoising.html

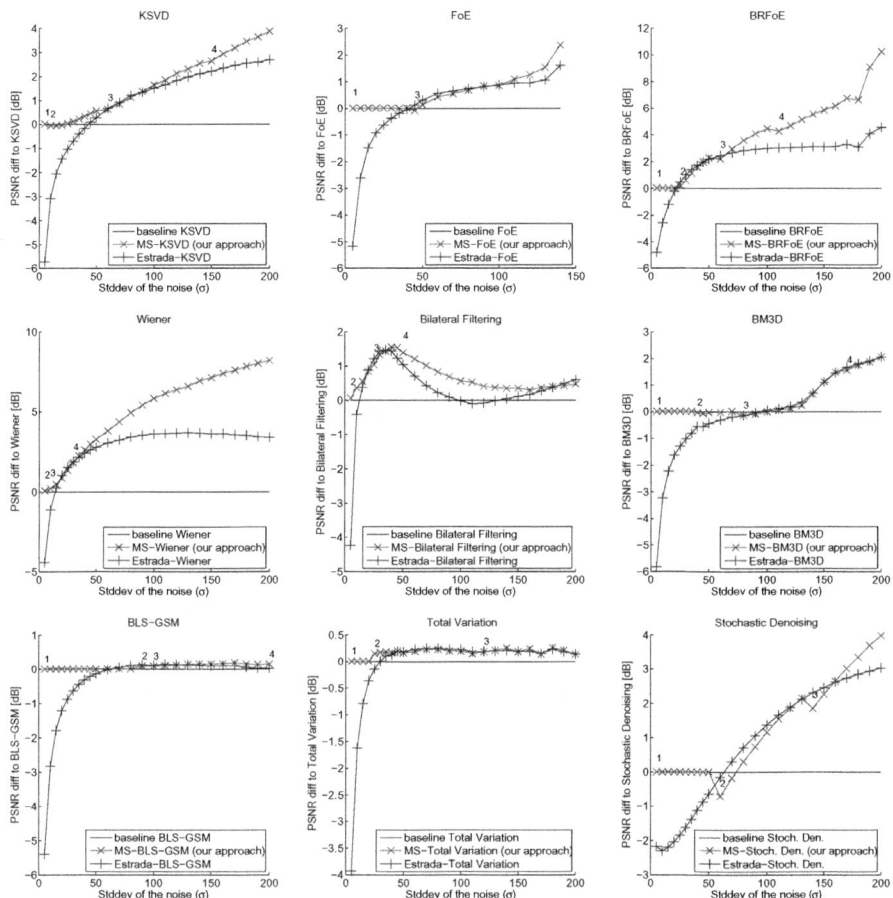

Fig. 6. Improvements achieved by combining our meta-procedure with nine different denoising algorithms. Results are averaged over 13 test images.

approach employs only the original scale (leading to the original denoising algorithm), indicating that in those noise regimes, it was not beneficial to use more scales in the training set.

The largest improvement achieved with our multi-scale meta-procedure occurs when the noise becomes stronger, which corrupts the low frequencies more and more. The improvement is particularly dramatic for Wiener and BRFoE (more than 8dB), which are patch-based methods that ignore the lower frequencies. Also KSVD is a method that is based on small patches, which also makes it blind to low frequencies, explaining the improvements obtained. However, some algorithms cannot be improved, such as BLS-GSM and Total Variation. This can be explained by the fact that BLS-GSM is a wavelet method and therefore already a multi-scale algorithm. So we see that a limitation of our meta-procedure is that it is only useful to apply it to denoising methods which are not already considering lower frequencies.

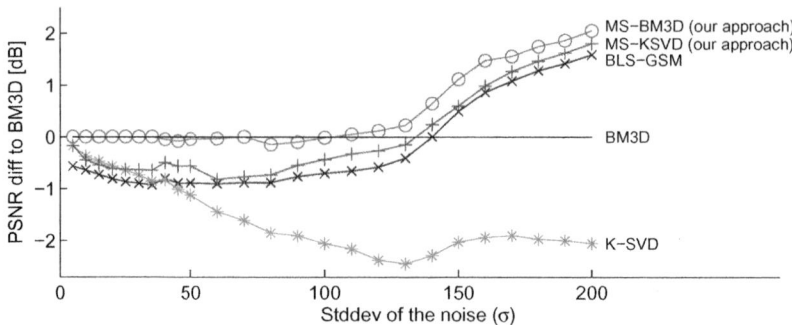

Fig. 7. The overall best methods compared to the baseline BM3D. For high noise setting our multi-scale approach applied to BM3D leads to the best results.

Note that our proposed meta-procedure outperforms the procedure by Estrada et al. [4] in almost all cases. Furthermore, our approach almost never deteriorates the denoising results, which sometimes happens for Estrada's method, especially when the noise is low. The improvements are reported in terms of PSNR, but we observed similar improvements in the structural similarity index [15] (see supplementary material).

KSVD vs. BLS-GSM revisited. In [3], the KSVD denoising algorithm is compared to BLS-GSM, described in [9]. It was noted that on the images "Peppers", "House" and "Barbara", KSVD outperforms BLS-GSM as long as the noise is below $\sigma = 50$. When the noise level is increased, BLS-GSM outperforms KSVD. We repeat the experiment on our images, but this time also report the results achieved with the multi-scale extension applied to KSVD (Fig. 7). We indeed observe that baseline KSVD outperforms BLS-GSM when the noise is low. However, the multi-scale version of KSVD outperforms BLS-GSM on all noise settings, see Fig. 7.

Multi-scale KSVD vs. BM3D. BM3D is often considered to be the best denoising algorithm currently available, even though Fig. 7 shows that for high noise levels BLS-GSM is superior. Also the multi-scale extensions of KSVD is better when the noise is very high.

Multi-scale BM3D vs. all others. Our multi-scale extension combined with BM3D delivers results that outperform all other denoising algorithms especially on the high noise levels, see Fig. 7.

6   Conclusion

For high noise levels, not only the high frequencies but also the low frequencies are corrupted. However, most image denoising algorithms are not always good at recovering low-frequency information. To improve such algorithms we devised a strategy to improve the denoising results using a multi-scale approach.

In comprehensive experiments we have shown that several state-of-the-art image denoising algorithms can be improved using this approach. Even though BM3D is arguably one of the best currently existing denoising algorithms, our method was able to improve its results on images that have been corrupted by high noise levels.

References

1. Chang, S., Yu, B., Vetterli, M.: Adaptive wavelet thresholding for image denoising and compression. IEEE Transactions on Image Processing 9(9), 1532–1546 (2002)
2. Dabov, K., Foi, A., Katkovnik, V., Egiazarian, K.: Image denoising by sparse 3-D transform-domain collaborative filtering. IEEE Transactions on Image Processing 16(8), 2080–2095 (2007)
3. Elad, M., Aharon, M.: Image denoising via sparse and redundant representations over learned dictionaries. IEEE Transactions on Image Processing 15(12), 3736–3745 (2006)
4. Estrada, F., Fleet, D., Jepson, A.: Stochastic image denoising. In: Proceedings of the British Machine Vision Conference, BMVC (2009)
5. Jain, V., Seung, H.: Natural image denoising with convolutional networks. Advances in Neural Information Processing Systems (NIPS) 21, 769–776 (2009)
6. Mairal, J., Bach, F., Ponce, J., Sapiro, G., Zisserman, A.: Non-local sparse models for image restoration. In: IEEE 12th International Conference on Computer Vision (ICCV). pp. 2272–2279 (2009)
7. Mairal, J., Elad, M., Sapiro, G., et al.: Sparse representation for color image restoration. IEEE Transactions on Image Processing 17(1), 53 (2008)
8. Pizurica, A., Philips, W., Lemahieu, I., Acheroy, M.: A joint inter- and intrascale statistical model for Bayesian wavelet based image denoising. IEEE Transactions on Image Processing 11(5), 545–557 (2002)
9. Portilla, J., Strela, V., Wainwright, M., Simoncelli, E.: Image denoising using scale mixtures of Gaussians in the wavelet domain. IEEE Transactions on Image processing 12(11), 1338–1351 (2003)
10. Rajashekar, U., Simoncelli, E.: Multiscale denoising of photographic images. In: The Essential Guide To Image Processing, pp. 241–261. Academic Press, London (2009)
11. Roth, S., Black, M.: Fields of experts. International Journal of Computer Vision 82(2), 205–229 (2009)
12. Rudin, L., Osher, S., Fatemi, E.: Nonlinear total variation based noise removal algorithms. Physica D: Nonlinear Phenomena 60(1-4), 259–268 (1992)
13. Simoncelli, E., Adelson, E.: Noise removal via Bayesian wavelet coring. In: Proceedings of International Conference on Image Processing (ICIP), pp. 379–382 (1996)
14. Tomasi, C., Manduchi, R.: Bilateral filtering for gray and color images. In: Proceedings of the Sixth International Conference on Computer Vision (ICCV), pp. 839–846 (1998)
15. Wang, Z., Bovik, A., Sheikh, H., Simoncelli, E.: Image quality assessment: From error visibility to structural similarity. IEEE Transactions on Image Processing 13(4), 600–612 (2004)
16. Weickert, J.: Anisotropic diffusion in image processing. ECMI Series. Teubner-Verlag, Stuttgart (1998)
17. Weiss, Y., Freeman, W.: What makes a good model of natural images? In: Proceedings of the IEEE Conference on Computer Vision and Pattern Recognition, CVPR 2007, pp. 1–8 (2007)

Assessment of Visibility Quality in Adverse Weather and Illumination Conditions

Andrzej Śluzek[1] and Mariusz Paradowski[2]

[1] Khalifa University, Abu Dhabi
andrzej.sluzek@gmail.com
[2] Institute of Informatics, Wroclaw University of Technology
mariusz.paradowski@pwr.wroc.pl

Abstract. A framework for the automatic detection of dangerously deteriorating visibility (e.g. due to bad weather and/or poor illumination conditions) is presented. The method employs image matching techniques for tracking similar fragments in video-frames captured by a forward-looking camera. The visibility is considered low when performances of visual tracking deteriorate and/or its continuity is lost either temporarily (i.e. a sudden burst of light, a splash of water) or more permanently. Two variants of the tracking algorithm are considered, i.e. the topological approach (more important) and the geometric one. Using the most difficult examples of DAGM2011 Challenge dataset (e.g. *Snow*, *Rain* and *Light-sabre* clips) it is demonstrated that the visibility quality can be numerically estimated, and the most severe cases (when even the human eye can hardly recognize the scene components) are represented by zero (or near-zero) values. The paper also briefly discusses the implementation issues (based on a previously developed similar real-time application) and directions of future works.

1 Introduction

Vision-based navigation in adverse conditions is one of the most challenging issues in building (semi-)intelligent vehicles. Even in relatively good conditions and within partially structured environments (e.g. driving cars on roads with marked lanes) only narrowly-defined problems can be more or less robustly handled using purely visual approaches (lane tracking, e.g. [1,2], detection and tracking individual vehicles, e.g. [3,4], recognition of road signs, e.g. [5,6], etc.). However, to the best of our knowledge, there are no attempts to address the most general question of machine vision in vehicular applications, i.e. whether the existing conditions are good enough to apply vision techniques or whether alternative sensing techniques (if available) should be used instead. From the pragmatic perspective, the conditions can be considered acceptable if the visual contents can be robustly tracked in the stream of camera-captured data (e.g. in a sequence of video-frames). Of course, such conditions may not be good enough to successfully apply a particular algorithm, but most probably *no* vision-based algorithm can be used if the visibility conditions are too adverse.

R. Mester and M. Felsberg (Eds.): DAGM 2011, LNCS 6835, pp. 216–225, 2011.
© Springer-Verlag Berlin Heidelberg 2011

This paper presents a general methodology to estimate the quality of visual data captured from a forward-looking moving camera (i.e. it assesses the current visibility conditions). No models of roads (e.g. lane marks, dividers, etc.), infrastructure (e.g. road signs, traffic lights, etc.) or vehicles are used so that the method can be instrumental in any typical road conditions and scenarios. Using the principles of image fragment matching (recently reported in a few papers) we propose to measure the visibility quality by estimating how smoothly similar fragments of the captured scenes can be tracked in sequences of video-frames. Various categories of visibility quality can be defined. In general, the visibility is considered acceptable when sufficiently large similar fragments of scenes can be tracked over a number of subsequent frames. Thus, we can identify cases of temporary visibility disruptions (e.g. caused by sudden flashes of illumination, splashes of water, etc.) and cases of more permanent visibility disruptions (e.g. periods of heavy precipitation, dense fog, etc.). Two numerical measures are proposed to distinguish between the categories and to evaluate current conditions within a category.

Section 2 of the paper briefly overviews state-of-the-art in keypoint-based image matching techniques. In Section 3, we discuss how the image matching techniques can be used to automatically assess the road visibility conditions. Exemplary results obtained using a selection of the most challenging DAGM2011 Challenge videos are presented in Section 4. The concluding Section 5 focuses on the future directions of the presented work.

2   Principles of Keypoint-Based Fragment Matching

Keypoint matching is considered one of the most universal tools for detecting local correspondences between similar but not necessarily identical visual data. Various keypoint detectors and descriptors have been proposed, but from large numbers of published papers it can claimed that affine-invariant detectors proposed in [7] are satisfactorily robust and stable for a wide range of applications. Correspondingly, SIFT features, [8], and their derivatives are a well established standard for keypoint descriptors. Therefore, this combination of detectors and descriptors is used throughout this paper, although any other keypoint detectors and descriptors can be alternatively used in all presented algorithms.

Similarities between images or their fragments can be established by detecting sets of correspondingly matched keypoint pairs which satisfy the required configuration constraints. Affine transformations are typically used to model similarities between rigid objects (assuming additionally that perspective distortions are negligibly small). Currently, the method proposed in [9] (where similar fragments are detected in a pair of images as local maxima in the histogram of affine transformations build between triangles of matched keypoints from both images) seems to be the most general approach in detecting locally planar similar objects/fragments/scenes in images of diversified and unpredictable contents. In this approach, similar (near-duplicate) fragments are represented by convex hulls of keypoints contributing to such maxima. Fig. 1 provides examples

Fig. 1. Detection of (almost) planar near-duplicate fragments in exemplary pairs of images from diversified domains

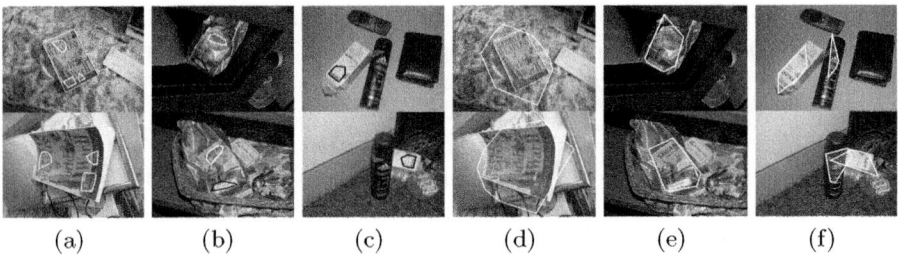

(a)   (b)   (c)   (d)   (e)   (f)

Fig. 2. Comparison between near-duplicates detected by the affine method (a, b, c) and by the topological approach (d, e, f) in images containing deformable and non-planar components

of near-duplicate detection in a wide range of domains (indoor scenes, face authentication, landscapes, detection of small similar objects on unpredictable backgrounds, etc.).

In case of deformable objects (and/or strong perspective deformations) the affine-based matching can be too rigid so that we use alternative topological constraints proposed in [10]. Using these constraints, groups of similar keypoint pairs defining near-duplicates in the compared images are identified as connected sub-graphs of the topological graph built over pairs of matched keypoints. Convex hulls of such groups of keypoints are considered estimates of detected near-duplicates. The extracted near-duplicates are generally larger than their affine counterparts (by incorporating distorted and non-planar similar fragments of matched images). Moreover, in case of similar objects on different backgrounds, parts of the backgrounds can also be included (if they are topologically consistent with some fragments of the other background). Exemplary results obtained by the affine and topological approached are compared in Fig. 2.

3   From Image Matching to Visibility Conditions

From the perspective of traffic applications, good visibility can be informally defined as conditions when objects and components of the observed moving world can be smoothly and unobtrusively tracked by standard visual means (i.e. human eyes or forward-looking cameras). It can be argued, therefore, that matches between contents of frames captured by a video-camera can be a feasible model of the visibility quality.

Four aspects of image matching in the context of visibility assessment in traffic applications should be highlighted:

- Keypoint-based image matching is possible only if keypoints are detected. Since keypoints generally represent locations with the most prominent variations of image gradients, a small number (or lack) of keypoints usually indicates foggy, rainy or otherwise difficult conditions limiting the visibility of scene details. Even though very few keypoints can be found in highly uniform areas as well (e.g. very smooth roads, cloudless sky, etc.) such areas seldom occupy the most important parts of typical views in traffic scenarios.
- Neighboring frames of video-streams are usually highly similar (i.e. many consistently located keypoint matches can be found) even if the visibility is poor (see Fig. 3). Thus, for a proper evaluation of visibility conditions, well separated (e.g. by 5 or 10 frames) views should be compared. In such pairs of frames, groups of consistently matched keypoints usually represent the same objects while random visual artifacts formed by precipitation or bursts of illumination are not matched.
- Geometric distortions between forward-view frames can be only partially modeled by affine transformations (mostly distant parts of the view and/or central fragments of the frames). Fragments located closer to the vehicles are subject to strong perspective distortions (non-affine mappings). Moreover, even within affine-related areas there could be fragments (e.g. other moving vehicles) related by different affine mappings so that multiple near-duplicates can be detected. Therefore, we should consider both the topological approach (to identify as large near-duplicates as possible) and the affine technique (to prospectively obtain more accurate estimates of the scene geometry).
- The critical visual data are usually located in the central sections of captured frames (excluding their lower parts which typically show just the road surface in front of the vehicle). Thus, near-duplicate fragments detected in these areas should be considered more important than near-duplicates in other parts of frames.

Based on the above observations, we propose a method of the quantitative visibility assessment (primarily for traffic applications, but suitable for other domains as well). Since the method is based on near-duplicate detection, no models of the environment or its components are needed. Assuming availability of a forward-looking video-camera, the method incorporates the following operations:

1. Select the time increment T for frame matching. In the conducted experiments on DAGM2011 Challenge videos, we use $T = 10$frames (0.4sec for 25Hz camera), i.e. frame F_N is matched to frame F_{N+10}. In practice, T can be adaptively adjusted by taking into account the camera frame rate and the current speed of the vehicle (see also Section 5).

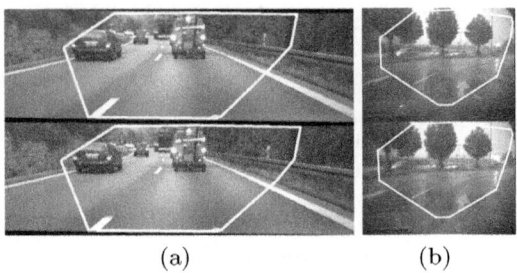

$$(a) \hspace{4cm} (b)$$

Fig. 3. Near-duplicates detected in neighboring frames captured in good (a) and poor (b) weather. In both cases, large near-duplicates are detected in spite of very different visibility conditions.

2. In the video-stream, identify near-duplicates in pairs of frames (F_0, F_T), (F_T, F_{2T}), (F_{2T}, F_{3T}), etc. Topological near-duplicates are considered the main result, but affine near-duplicates can be detected as well for specialized applications or further analysis of road conditions. Let D_N^{N+T} be the near-duplicate found in F_N matched with F_{N+T}, and D_{N+T}^N be its counterpart in F_{N+T}. In order to reduce the noise of moving wipers (see Fig. 4) and other similar effects, it is recommended to match at each step frames (F_N, F_{N+T}), (F_N, F_{N+T+1}), (F_{N+1}, F_{N+T}) and (F_{N+1}, F_{N+T+1}) instead of frames (F_N, F_{N+T}) only, and to use the largest detected near-duplicates as D_N^{N+T} and D_{N+T}^N results.

3. Define the *region of interest* R in the captured video. Typically, R occupies the central part of frames; it can be adaptively shifted and/or resized depending on the specific needs of applications.

4. For F_N frame, calculate the current *visibility quality* VQ using

$$VQ(N) = \frac{\|R \cap D_N^{N-T}\|}{\|R\|}. \tag{1}$$

Subsequently, the current *visibility continuity* VC is estimated using

$$VC(N) = \frac{\|D_{N-T}^{N-2T} \cap D_{N-T}^N \cap R\|}{\|D_{N-T}^{N-2T} \cap R\|}, \tag{2}$$

unless $\|D_{N-T}^{N-2T} \cap R\| = 0$ ($VC(N) = 0$ in such cases by definition). Note that the $VC(N)$ value is obtained from the near-duplicates found in F_{N-T} frame.

Informally, VQ indicates how much of the visual data from the previous frame can be recognized within the *region of interest* of the current frame, while VC estimates the overlaps between the matching similar fragments in a sequence of three frames (i.e. tracking continuity). Fig. 5 illustrates how the above definitions are applied to exemplary frames (frames F_{N-T} and F_N are shown). Visibility at

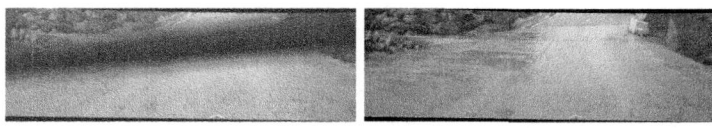

Fig. 4. Two neighboring frames with and without the noise of a moving wiper

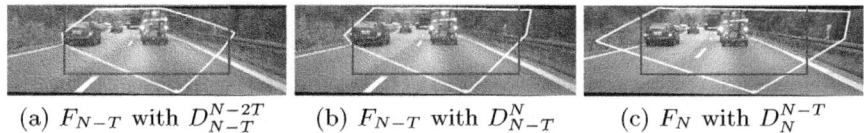

(a) F_{N-T} with D_{N-T}^{N-2T} (b) F_{N-T} with D_{N-T}^{N} (c) F_N with D_N^{N-T}

Fig. 5. Visibility quality estimates from exemplary frames F_{N-T} and F_N: $VQ(N) = 93.05\%$, $VC(N) = 86.96\%$. The size of interest region R is defined arbitrarily.

these images is good and both quality measures are correspondingly high. More results are presented in the next section to confirm that VQ and VC values consistently agree with the subjective evaluation of visibility quality.

4   Experimental Result

The proposed method has been tested using clips provided in DAGM2011 Challenge (mainly the most difficult examples, e.g. *Snow, Rain* and *Light-sabre* clips). The goal is to verify whether the correlation between VQ and VC measures and the subjective assessment of visibility actually exists. The following Figs 6 to 9 contain exemplary sequences of images separated (subject to the remark in Step 2 of Section 3) by $T = 10$ frames. Shapes of the interest region R have been defined arbitrarily, mainly based on aspect ratio of the videos. Each image in the sequences contains two copies of F_N frame with either D_N^{N-10} (top) or D_N^{N+10} (bottom) near-duplicate shown (the terminal frames are obviously displayed only once). Thus, the values of VQ correspond to the coverage of ROI's by near-duplicate in the top half-images, while the overlaps between near-duplicates from top and bottom half-images visually represent the values of VC.

5   Future Works and Conclusions

The paper presents only the feasibility study of the proposed method. Thus, further researches are needed to fully implement the method and to integrate it with the actual vehicular systems. In our opinion, three problems should be investigated in particular.

- **Real-time implementation.** The paper does not discuss details of the real-time implementation although this is obviously the ultimate objective. A similar real-time webcam-based application has been reported in [11]. In this

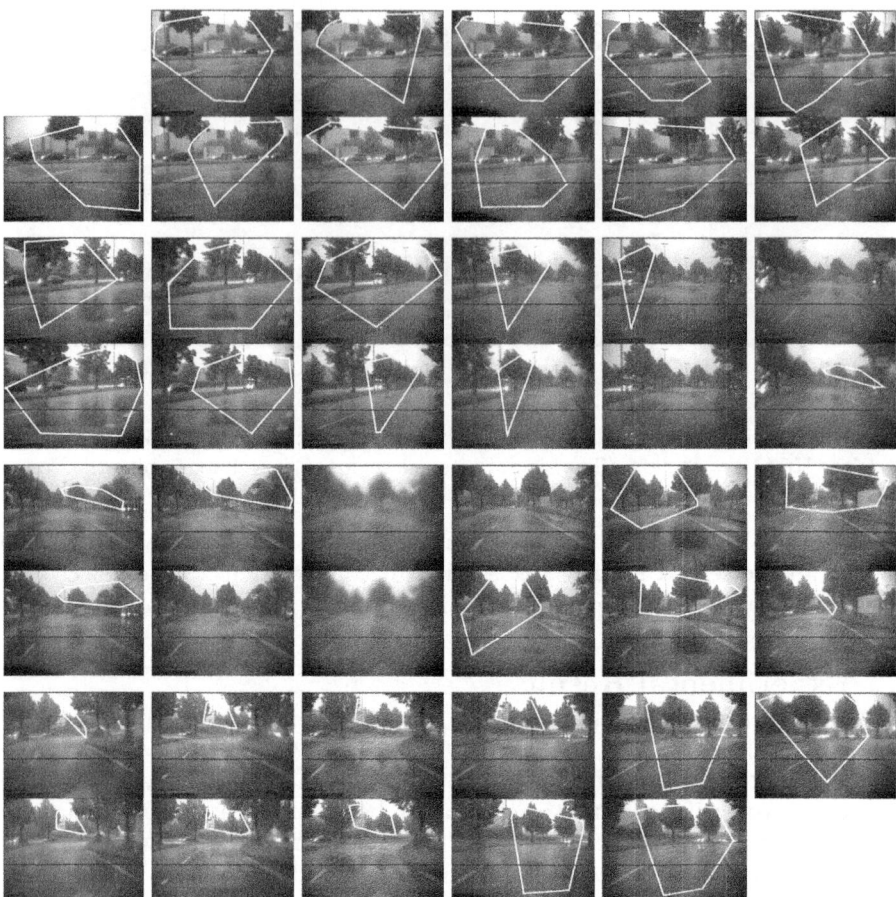

Fig. 6. Visibility changes during *Rain* video-clip. Initially, the visibility is acceptable, then it deteriorates and eventually improves again. The sequences of VQ and VC measures are: $VQ = \{65.3\%, 54.9\%, 66.5\%, 43.2\%, 59.5\%, 50.1\%, 59.7\%, 63.7\%, 25.4\%,$ $14.3\%, 0\%, 8.3\%, 22.6\%, 0\%, 0\%, 36.0\%, 40.3\%, 2.6\%, 7.4\%, 12.4\%, 11.6\%, 46.2\%,$ $54.6\%\}$ and $VC = \{57.2\%, 87.4\%, 59.6\%, 84.2\%, 50.8\%, 73.5\%, 72.7\%, 35.1\%, 50.7\%,$ $0\%, 0\%, 72.9\%, 0\%, 0\%, 0\%, 53.2\%, 5.7\%, 80.7\%, 84.1\%, 72.1\%, 57.5\%, 91.7\%\}$.

application, an input frame can be memorized as the reference image, and its content is subsequently tracked (using the topological approach) in the following frames. However, we cannot apply the same methodology because of certain simplifying assumptions, which render it unsuitable for our problem (e.g. real-time implemented SURF detector and descriptor are used; they are computationally more efficient, but reported inferior to SIFT). Nevertheless, we believe that by reducing the effective frame-capturing rate (frames of interests are separated by intervals of T frames) more computational resources can be released to apply in real time more advanced algorithms of keypoint detection, description and matching.

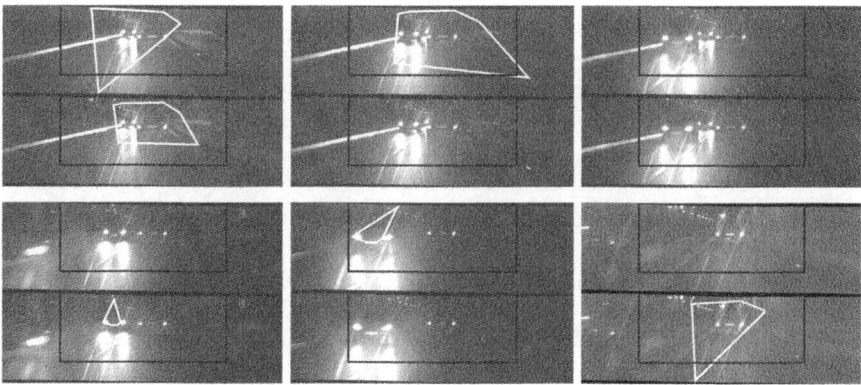

Fig. 7. A period of very poor visibility in *Light-sabre* video-clip. $VQ = \{34.2\%, 49.3\%, 0\%, 0\%, 5.4\%, 0\%\}$ and $VC = \{51.0\%, 0\%, 0\%, 0\%, 0\%, 0\%\}$.

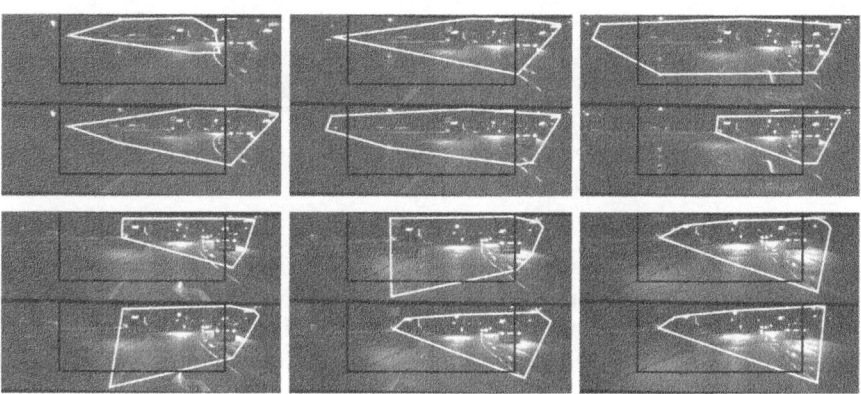

Fig. 8. A period of relatively good visibility in *Light-sabre* video-clip. $VQ = \{32.6\%, 49.6\%, 78.6\%, 31.5\%, 68.4\%, 51.9\%\}$ and $VC = \{85.5\%, 98.4\%, 33.4\%, 99.5\%, 56.9\%, 99.8\%\}$.

- **Statistical analysis.** Currently, only a limited number of videos have been used in the experiments. More data are needed to, first, conduct a thorough analysis of the method's performances and, secondly, to establish statistical relations between the subjective impression of visibility and numerical characteristics (e.g. thresholds, fluctuations, etc.) of VQ and VC measures.
- **Visibility-based speed control.** It has been shown in Fig. 3 that even in poor visibility conditions large near-duplicates are found if the scenes are almost identical (e.g. neighboring frames or frames captured with longer intervals from a slow-moving vehicle). Thus, the values of VQ and VC can be

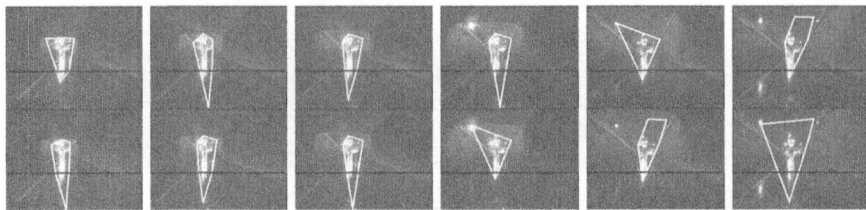

Fig. 9. Good visibility within the central part of the view only (*Snow* video-clip). Although the VQ values are low (i.e. $VQ = \{8.5\%, 6.5\%, 6.8\%, 7.5\%, 11.8\%, 11.3\%\}$) the continuity is very high ($VC = \{80.9\%, 93.8\%, 97.7\%, 79.3\%, 53.1\%, 95.6\%\}$).

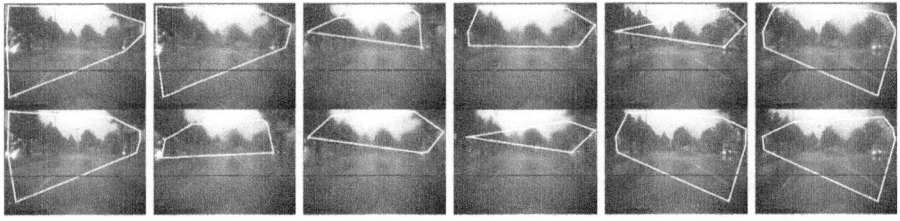

Fig. 10. VQ and VC improvement by reducing the inter-frame interval T (which emulates the vehicle speed reduction)

prospectively improved by speed reduction. If the "safe visibility" threshold values can be established for VQ and VC (as suggested in the previous paragraph) the corresponding speed-control mechanism could be proposed. When unsafe visibility conditions are numerically estimated, the vehicle's velocity should be reduced until the values of VQ and VC exceed the thresholds (using the same inter-frame interval T, of course). Since alternative video-clips of the same roads in the same conditions captured from a slower vehicle are not available, we have emulated lower speeds by using shorter intervals T. Fig. 10 shows the results for one of the most difficult sections in Fig. 6 (i.e. the end of Row 2) by using $T = 2$. The visibility measures clearly improve (although, objectively, the conditions remain the same). These numerical improvements are, in our opinion, justified. They can be interpreted as indicators that at lower speeds the human vision has to handle less visual changes, i.e. it can do it more efficiently.

Altogether, it can be concluded that the paper (although presenting only the preliminary results of the proposed method) suggests a new approach to the vision-based solutions for traffic applications and, thus, opens novel perspectives in such applications.

References

1. Apostoloff, N., Zelinsky, A.: Robust vision-based lane tracking using multiple cues and particle filtering. In: Proc. of IEEE Symp. on Intelligent Vehicles, pp. 558–563 (2003)
2. McCall, J.C., Trivedi, M.M.: Video-based lane estimation and tracking for driver assistance: Survey, system, and evaluation. IEEE Transactions on Intelligent Transportation Systems 7, 20–37 (2006)
3. Betke, M., Haritaoglu, E., Davis, L.S.: Real-time multiple vehicle detection and tracking from a moving vehicle. Machine Vision and Applications 12, 69–83 (2000)
4. Fossati, A., Schonmann, P., Fua, P.: Real-time vehicle tracking for driving assistance. Machine Vision and Applications 22, 439–448 (2011)
5. de la Escalera, A., Armingol, J.M., Mata, M.: Traffic sign recognition and analysis for intelligent vehicles. Image and Vision Computing 21, 247–258 (2003)
6. Broggi, A., Cerri, P., Medici, P., Porta, P.P., Ghisio, G.: Real time road signs recognition. In: Proc. of IEEE Symp. on Intelligent Vehicles, pp. 981–986 (2007)
7. Mikolajczyk, K., Schmid, C.: Scale and affine invariant interest point detectors. International Journal of Computer Vision 60, 63–86 (2004)
8. Lowe, D.G.: Distinctive image features from scale-invariant keypoints. International Journal of Computer Vision 60, 91–110 (2004)
9. Paradowski, M., Śluzek, A.: Local Keypoints and Global Affine Geometry: Triangles and Ellipses for Image Fragment Matching. In: Kwaśnicka, H., Jain, L.C. (eds.) Innovations in Intelligent Image Analysis. SCI, vol. 339, pp. 195–224. Springer, Heidelberg (2011)
10. Paradowski, M., Śluzek, A.: Keypoint-based detection of near-duplicate image fragments using image geometry and topology. In: Bolc, L., Tadeusiewicz, R., Chmielewski, L.J., Wojciechowski, K. (eds.) ICCVG 2010. LNCS, vol. 6375, pp. 175–182. Springer, Heidelberg (2010)
11. Śluzek, A., Paradowski, M.: Real-time retrieval of near-duplicate fragments in images and video-clips. In: Blanc-Talon, J., Bone, D., Philips, W., Popescu, D., Scheunders, P. (eds.) ACIVS 2010, Part I. LNCS, vol. 6474, pp. 18–29. Springer, Heidelberg (2010)

Robust Point Matching in HDRI through Estimation of Illumination Distribution

Yan Cui, Alain Pagani, and Didier Stricker

DFKI, Augmented Vision
Kaiserslautern University, Germany

Abstract. High Dynamic Range Images provide a more detailed information and their use in Computer Vision tasks is therefore desirable.
However, the illumination distribution over the image often makes this
kind of images difficult to use with common vision algorithms. In particular, the highlights and shadow parts in a HDR image are difficult to
analyze in a standard way. In this paper, we propose a method to solve
this problem by applying a preliminary step where we precisely compute
the illumination distribution in the image. Having access to the illumination distribution allows us to subtract the highlights and shadows from
the original image, yielding a material color image. This material color
image can be used as input for standard computer vision algorithms, like
the SIFT point matching algorithm and its variants.

1 Introduction

While High Dynamic Range Images (HDRI) representing the real word's range
of luminance are commonly used in the Computer Graphics community, their use
in machine vision tasks (e.g. Registration and Identification) is not widespread
in the Computer Vision community. HDRI can measure a high radiance and
illumination range for the real world scenes, thus providing more information
than the low dynamic range images (LDRI). Many applications, such as image-
based lighting [6], and BRDF measurement [14] require access to the whole
dynamic range of a scene. In this paper, we present a method to use HDR images
for computer vision tasks by estimating the illumination distribution first and
applying a suitable tone-mapping method for computer analysis. We apply this
concept to the matching problem, yielding a SIFT [16] method for the HDRI.

Illumination distribution estimation is an important task for the computer
vision. The appearance of objects depends greatly on illumination conditions.
Since substantial image variation can result from shading, shadows and highlights, there has been much research on dealing with such lighting effects for a
LDRI [3] [15] [13], but not much for HDRI [23]. Because of the significant effect
of lighting, it is often helpful to know the lighting conditions of a scene so that
an image can be more accurately analyzed. Recovery of illumination conditions
is also important for computer graphics applications, such as inserting correctly
shaded virtual objects into augmented reality systems [22] and lighting reproduction for compositing actors into video footage [7]. While these graphics methods

R. Mester and M. Felsberg (Eds.): DAGM 2011, LNCS 6835, pp. 226–235, 2011.

introduce special devices into a scene to capture the lighting distribution, estimation of illumination in image has proven to be a challenge. In this paper, we do not only estimate light source position (like e.g. [23]), but we provide the illumination distribution as a Gaussian Mixture Model (GMM) over the image for each different exposure layer in the HDR image.

The development of techniques for HDRI capture and synthesis have made tone-mapping an important problem in computer graphics [9]. The fundamental problem is how to map the large range of intensities found in an HDRI into the limited range generated by a conventional display device. There are three main taxonomies of tone-mapping operators. A primary distinction is whether an operator is global or local. Global operators apply a single mapping function to all pixels of the image, whereas local operators modify the mapping depending on the characteristics of different parts of the image. A second important distinction is between empirical and perceptually based operators. A third distinction is between static and dynamic operators. In this paper we suggest to use a new tone-mapping method, more suited to computer vision tasks, and to get a "material color" of the scene or the object without the illumination interference.In all feature extraction methods, the invariance with respect to imaging conditions represents the biggest challenge. More specifically, the local extracted features should be invariant with respect to geometrical variations, such as translation, rotation, scaling, and affine transformations. Furthermore, these features should be invariant with respect to photometric variations such as illumination direction, intensity, colors, and highlights. SIFT [16] [17] has been proven to be the most robust among the local invariant feature descriptors with respect to different geometrical changes [20]. However, due to the color constancy problem, a lot of geometrical invariant approaches avoid dealing with illumination problem. Therefore, illumination invariance is a crucial problem which has to be solved for local features. While some researchers already focused on the color constancy problem [2] [19], some attempts to make use of the color information inside the SIFT descriptors have been proposed [5] [4] [10] [1]. In this paper, we solve the illumination invariance problem for the HDR images, using result of our illumination distribution estimation.

The paper provides three main contributions to the HDR image processing research. First, we show that it is possible to estimate the illumination distributions in each exposure layer of HDRI with a Gaussian Mixture Model. Second, we propose a new tone-mapping algorithm which is more suitable for the computer analyzing through material color recovery. Third, as an application, we show that the SIFT algorithm using the tone-mapped images performs better in terms of robustness and number of matches.

The remainder of the paper is organized as follows: We first present illumination distribution with GMM in Sect. 2. In Sect. 3, we explain how to estimate the GMM parameters in HDRI. We show how to recover the shadow and highlight parts position in the image from the illumination distribution result in Sect. 4. Finally, the SIFT method for HDRI and the results is presented in Sect. 5. We conclude in Sect. 6 with directions for future work.

2   Illumination Distribution with GMM

We can assume that the illumination distribution in the 2D image is a Gaussian mixture model (GMM) for several light sources. For a single light source, we assume that the illumination distribution is a Gaussian model as Eq. (1)

$$e(\boldsymbol{x}) = p(\boldsymbol{x}|\,\theta) = \frac{1}{\sqrt{2\pi}\sigma} \exp\left(-\frac{(\boldsymbol{x}-\boldsymbol{\mu})^T(\boldsymbol{x}-\boldsymbol{\mu})}{2\sigma^2}\right) \qquad (1)$$

In the Eq. (1), $\boldsymbol{x}$ is the 2d image position, $\boldsymbol{\mu}$ is the light source position, σ stands for the light intensity and the distribution property, and we assume that σ is same for the two direction, but different for each exposure layer in the multi-exposure sequence of the HDRI. There are 11 exposure layers created from one light source HDRI, as shown in Fig. 1a, the exposure times varied by powers of two between f-stops from $\frac{1}{32}$ to 32. Fig. 1b shows the Gaussian illumination distribution results for each exposure layer with the method in Sect. 3, the light source position $\boldsymbol{\mu}$ is not changed, the variance σ increases from layer to layer.

Then we can assume that the GMM model for more than one light sources, as the Eq. (2)

$$e(\boldsymbol{x}) = \sum_{k=1}^{K} \rho_k * p(\boldsymbol{x}|\,\theta_k) \quad with \quad \boldsymbol{x}|\,\theta_k \propto N(\boldsymbol{\mu}_k, \sigma_k) \qquad (2)$$

In the Eq. (2), ρ_k is the mixture weight for the light source k, we assume that ρ_k are same for the different exposure layer to the same light source. Fig. 1c shows one exposure layer created from a two light sources HDRI, Fig. 1d expresses the Gaussian distribution result as the method in Sect. 3.

Our hypothesis is that illumination can be estimated as a GMM for different exposure layers.

3   Illumination Distribution in HDRI

In this section we show how to estimate the GMM parameters for the illumination distribution in each exposure layer. The input of our algorithm is a HDRI. We first create a multi-exposure durations sequence with normal global tone-mapping method. Equivalently, the input can be a number of digitized photographs taken from the same point with different known exposure durations t_j. Using diffuse body reflection Lambertian model [11]:

$$E_i = e(i)R_\infty(\lambda, i) \qquad (3)$$

In the Eq. (3), where i denotes the position at the imaging plane and λ the wavelength. Further, $E(\lambda, i)$ denotes the illumination spectrum, the material reflectivity is denoted by $R_\infty(\lambda, i)$, for this part, it's the property of the material, we call it "material color", which is used in the feature extraction in Sect. 5.

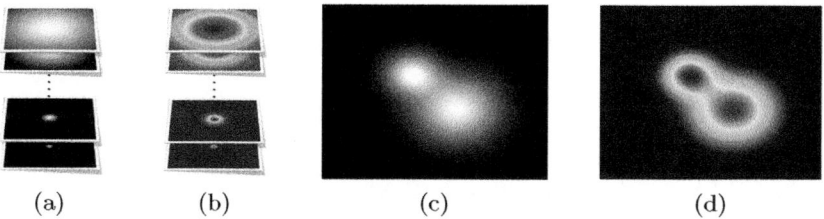

Fig. 1. (a) A multi-exposure sequence of HDRI with one light source. (b) Gaussian distribution results for (a); (c) One HDRI exposure layer with two light sources. (d) Gaussian distribution results for (c).

For different exposure time layer j, as [8], we can get:

$$M_{ij} = e(i)R_\infty (\lambda, i) \, t_j \qquad (4)$$

As presented in Sect. 2, we can estimate the $e(i)$ part as GMM for the illumination distribution. Taking the GMM $e(i)$ to the Eq. (4), the final illumination distribution function for each pixel in each layer:

$$M_{ij} = \left(\sum_{k=1}^{K} \rho_k * p(i \mid \theta_{k,j}) \right) R_\infty (\lambda, i, j) \, t_j \qquad (5)$$

Finally, the "material color" $R_\infty (\lambda, i, j)$ part for each pixel can be expressed:

$$R_\infty (\lambda, i, j) = M_{ij} / \left(\sum_{k=1}^{K} \rho_k * p(i \mid \theta_{k,j}) t_j \right) \qquad (6)$$

For each exposure layer j, we can assume that the "material color" $R_\infty (\lambda, i, j)$ part is the same. We define the energy function:

$$E(\rho_k, \theta_{k,j}) = \sum_{j=1}^{L-1} \sum_{i=1}^{N} \left(\frac{M_{ij+1}}{\sum\limits_{k=1}^{K} \rho_k p(i \mid \theta_{k,j+1}) t_{j+1}} - \frac{M_{ij}}{\sum\limits_{k=1}^{K} \rho_k p(i \mid \theta_{k,j}) t_j} \right)^2 \qquad (7)$$

In Eq. (7), L stands for the number of different exposure duration layers, N is the number of pixels, and K is the number of the light source for each layer. We assume that the light intensity σ in θ are different, but the light position μ in θ and the light intensity weight ρ are same for each layer. We use iterative Expectation Maximization (EM) procedure to find a solution to minimize the energy function Eq. (7). Because $\sum\limits_{k=1}^{K} \rho_k p(i \mid \theta_{k,j}) t_j \neq 0$ for each pixel in every layer, then energy function turns to:

$$E(\rho_k, \theta_{k,j}) = \sum_{k=1}^{K} \sum_{j=1}^{L-1} \sum_{i=1}^{N} \rho_k \left(p(i \mid \theta_{k,j}) t_j M_{ij+1} - p(i \mid \theta_{k,j+1}) t_{j+1} M_{ij} \right)^2 \qquad (8)$$

With the EM algorithm, we can get the Q function:

$$Q(\rho,\theta) = \sum_{k=1}^{K} \sum_{j=1}^{L-1} \sum_{i=1}^{N} \rho_k^{old} \left(\ln(p(i|\theta_{k,j})t_j M_{ij+1}) - \ln(p(i|\theta_{k,j+1})t_{j+1}M_{ij}) \right) \quad (9)$$

$$\rho_k^{old} = \frac{\sum_{j=1}^{L-1}\sum_{i=1}^{N} (\ln(p(i|\theta_{k,j})t_j M_{ij+1}) - \ln(p(i|\theta_{k,j+1})t_{j+1}M_{ij}))}{\sum_{k=1}^{K}\sum_{j=1}^{L-1}\sum_{i=1}^{N} (\ln(p(i|\theta_{k,j})t_j M_{ij+1}) - \ln(p(i|\theta_{k,j+1})t_{j+1}M_{ij}))} \quad (10)$$

We set the initial value $\rho_k^{old} = 1$. During the minimization-step, we can estimate $\sigma_{k,j}$ to maximum Q function. Then during expectation-step, we estimate the new ρ_k for each alternative light source position. If the weight $\rho_k < T_{light}$ (T_{light} is a threshold defined by user), we consider this pixel is not the light source position, and assign 0 to this weight ρ_k directly. For the experiments, we set $T_{light} = 4.0$.

The above EM procedure converges to a local minimum of the Eq. (7). Please note that the variances $\sigma_{k,j}$ are continuously recomputed, they're increasing from low exposure layer to high exposure layer, which is similar to an annealing procedure in which support of the Gaussians is reduced when assignment 0 to this weight ρ_k.

The first result are shown in Fig. 1b for one light source and Fig. 1d for two light sources. For these two experiments, the lights and the scene are controled strictly, the exposure times varied by powers of two between f-stops from $\frac{1}{32}$ to 32. K is the alternative light sources, considering as the whole image size 1...N. We can see the illumination changed for one light source in Fig. 1b, and the illumination distribution for two light source in Fig. 1d.

In order to make the EM convergence fast, the initial light area can be calculated firstly, then the alternative light source number K in the energy function becomes smaller than the whole image size. For the initial light area detection for HDRI, there are known methods to solve this problem [23] [12]. However, for our case, we need not to estimate the light source accurately. We can get the initial light source from the low exposure time layer with a threshold. In the low exposure time layer, the light densities are low, and if the pixel value is bigger than a threshold, we can consider it as the initial alternative light position. When the energy function is minimized with EM algorithm step by step, an accurate light source position will be determined by the weight parameters ρ_k.

We test our approach for natural environments and complex light conditions in two scenes: Church and Studio.

For the Church scene, a number of digitized photographs are taken from the same point with different known exposure durations, there are 16 photographs of a church taken at 1-stop increments from 1/1000 sec to 30 sec. Fig. 4 shows 5 samples from the sequence, the exposure times are 0.0146, 0.1172, 0.4688, 1.8750, 30.0 sec. The sun is directly behind the rightmost stained glass window, making it especially bright. The initial light source is given by exposure 0.1172 layer, as Fig. 2a. The final illumination distribution for these layers results are shown in Fig. 5. The algorithm can detect three main light sources, window on the top of

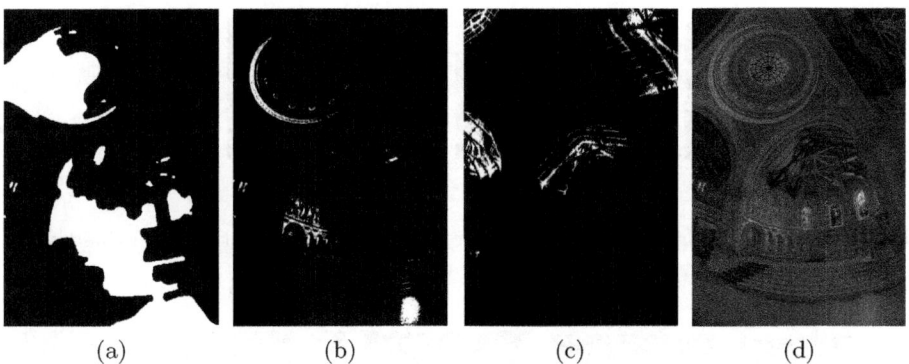

(a)   (b)   (c)   (d)

Fig. 2. (a)Initial light sources for EM procedure. (b) Highlight and (c) Shadow area for church of exposure time 1.8750 sec layer. (d) "Material color".

the church and three windows in the middle of the church. As the exposure time increase, the illumination distribution is changed, but the light source position is not changed. The light intensity is increasing layer to layer.

For the Studio scene, we can created 11 exposure layers by normal global tone-mapping method, the exposure time increments from $-11EV$ to $2EV$. As Fig. 6 shows 5 samples from the sequence, the exposure times are $-10, -8, -1.5, 0, 1.5$ EV. The sun is outside the glass window, making it especially bright. The initial light source is given by exposure $-10EV$ layer, as Fig. 3a. The final illumination distribution for these layers results are shown in Fig. 7. The algorithm can detect the light sources from outside of the window and the lamp inside the room.

From the experiments, our algorithm not only can detect the point light sources as the Fig. 1b and Fig. 1d, but also can detect the plane light source as the natural case, as Fig. 5 and Fig. 7. Once we have computed the illumination distribution information, we can compute highlight parts and shadow parts in the image, as described in the Sect. 4.

4   Shadow and Highlight Parts in HDRI

In this section, the shadow, highlight parts and the "material color" images are calculated by the illumination distribution results in Sect. 3. In Eq. (4), $e(i)$ is the light sources distribution, in the real environment image, we can assume that there is another light source (ambient light) that distributes evenly in the 2D image. For our experiments, the ambient light A is constant, $A = 0.001$. We can then derive the "material color" for each layer:

$$R_\infty\left(\lambda, i, j\right) = M_{ij}/\left((e(i) + A)\, t_j\right) \tag{11}$$

For each layer, we define two thresholds T_{up} and T_{below}, If the "material color" $R_\infty\left(\lambda, i, j\right) > T_{up}$, consider this area as the highlight part for this layer, the highlight part are not included the light source positions. Similarly, if the "material color" $R_\infty\left(\lambda, i, j\right) < T_{below}$, we consider this area as the shadow part

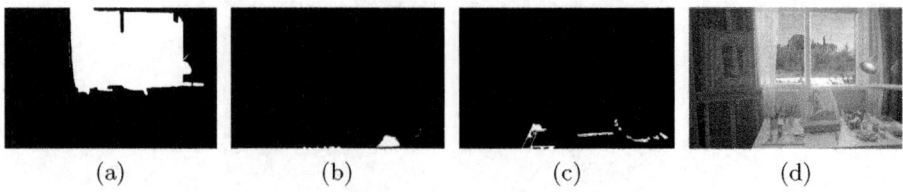

(a)   (b)   (c)   (d)

Fig. 3. (a)Initial light sources for EM procedure. (b) Highlight and (c) Shadow area for Studio of exposure 0 EV layer. (d)"Material color".

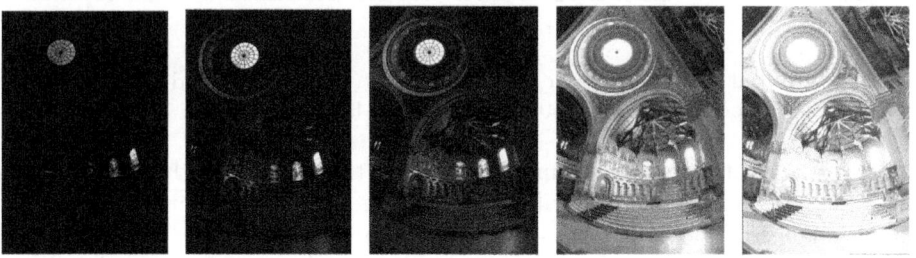

Fig. 4. Church, exposure times sequence 0.0146, 0.1172, 0.4688, 1.8750, 30.0 sec

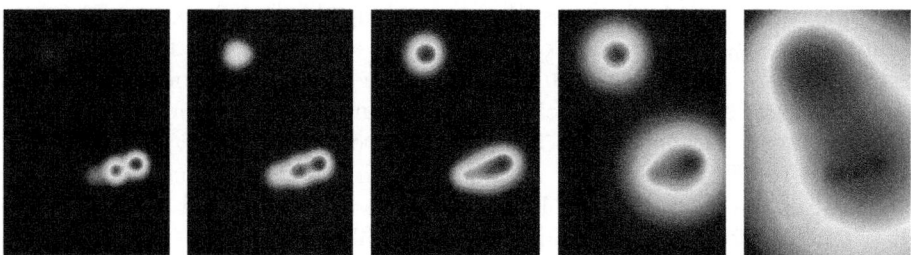

Fig. 5. Church, illumination distribution results for the image layers above

Fig. 6. Studio, exposure times sequence −10, −8, −1.5, 0, 1.5 EV

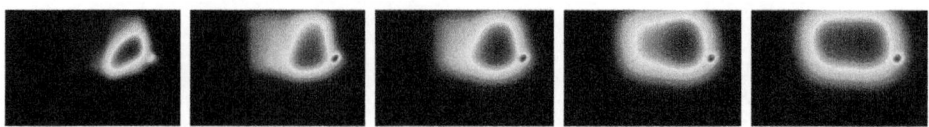

Fig. 7. Studio, illumination distribution results for the image layers above

for this layer. For the experiments, we set $T_{up} = 240$ and $T_{below} = 20$. The highlight parts and shadow parts for the church exposure time 1.8750 sec layer are shown in Fig. 2b 2c; The result for the studio exposure $0EV$ is shown in Fig. 3b 3c.

Furthermore, the "material color" can be determined by $R_\infty (\lambda, i, j)$ in multi-exposure layers $j = 1...L$:

$$R_\infty (\lambda, i) = \left(\sum_{j=1}^{L} w(j) R_\infty (\lambda, i, j) \right) / \sum_{j=1}^{L} w(j) \qquad (12)$$

Because the information in the middle exposure time layers are more reliable, the weight parameters $w(j)$ are assigned as 1-D Gaussian distribution, $w(j)$ are small for the lower and higher exposure time, and large for the middle exposure time in the sequence. We can consider this step as a tone-mapping procedure. It is worth noting that, different from the usual tone-mapping methods that try to produce a pleasant visual effect, our tone mapped results are more suitable for the computer analysis. We test the image feature extraction and corresponding problem with SIFT with our tone-mapping algorithm in Sect. 5. The final "material color" image results are shown in Fig. 2d of church image and Fig. 3d of studio image. There is no highlight area in the final image.

5   Point Matching in HDR Images and Results

In this section we will calculate the corresponding points with SIFT method for two HDRI for a same scene and a same object. As Sect. 4, the "material color" image can be calculated from one HDRI, without highlight area. Then the corresponding invariant features can be detected for two HDRI. We use the PC-SIFT method [5], which is motivated by perception-based color space, instead of using the gray value as the input image, the PC-SIFT approach builds the SIFT descriptors in 3 channel color space, is more robust than the normal SIFT with respect to color and photometrical variations.

The main stages using local invariant features are interest points detection, descriptor building and descriptor matching. Interest points should be selected so that they achieve the maximum possible repeatability under different photometric and geometric imaging conditions. As discussed in Sect. 3, our SIFT is based on "material color" image, which is illumination invariance. In the same time, the extrema in Laplacian pyramid, which is approximated by difference-of-Gaussian for the input image in different scales, has been proven to be the most robust interest points detector to geometrical changes [20] [4].

The experiment results are shown below. First, we test an object feature with two different views, for each view, there are 12 exposure duration from $\frac{1}{60}$sec to 0.4sec. In Fig. 8a shows the $\frac{1}{8}$sec layer and the PC-SIFT result. The "material color" and the PC-SIFT results are shown in Fig. 8b, from which we can notice there is no highlight and shadow part on the object. Meanwhile the SIFT can find the corresponding points without the light interference.

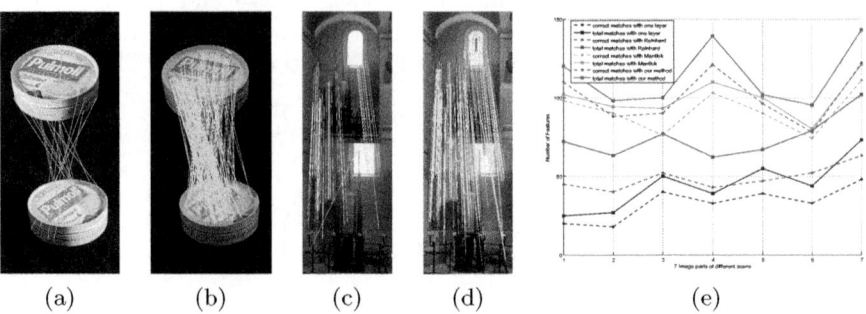

(a)   (b)   (c)   (d)   (e)

Fig. 8. (a) One exposure time 1/8 sec and (b) 0.8EV layer of 12 multi-exposure and PC-SIFT result, (b)(d) The "material color" and PC-SIFT result. (e)Total matches and correct matches of different tone-mapping methods.

Second, we test a scene with two different views HDRI, 14 exposure layers are created by normal tone-mapping method from −3EV to 9EV, In Fig. 8c, shows the 0.8EV layer and the PC-SIFT result. The "material color" and the PC-SIFT results are shown in Fig. 8d, there is not enough information to clear the shadow part, because the shadow parts exist in each exposure layer. For the SIFT result, our algorithm can detect the corresponding without the light source factor, finding the correct corresponding near the window part. Further, the shadow part can be extracted, as Fig. 2c shows, if we do not like the corresponding points in the shadow area, they can be cleaned away.

Finally, we compare our method (red line) to the other tone-mapping algorithm, global tone-mapping filter Reinhard [21] (blue line), local filter Mantiuk [18] (green line) and one exposure LDR image layer (black line) in Fig. 8e, the dotted lines show the correct matches, and the solid lines show the total matches for the 7 image paris of different scenes. As the result show, our method can detect more matches and find more correct matches.

6   Conclusions

In this paper, we presented a robust point matching approach for HDR images. Our method is based on a robust estimation of the illumination distribution in the 2D image using a Gaussian Mixture Model. The parameters of the GMM are recovered directly from the HDRI with EM-algorithm. With the estimated illumination distribution in the 2D image, we can compute the highlight parts, shadow parts and "material color" image, which is suitable for many computer vision tasks. We show that we can successfully apply this method to the point matching problem, using SIFT as underlying method. Our results show that a better matching is achieved in terms of robustness and number of matches.

Acknowledgment. This work has been partially funded by the project CAPTURE (01IW09001).

References

1. Abdel-Hakim, A.E., Farag, A.A.: Csift: A sift descriptor with color invariant characteristics. In: 2006 IEEE CVPR, vol. 2, pp. 1978–1983 (2006)
2. Brainard, D., Freeman, W.: Bayesian color constancy. The Journal of Optical Society of America 14, 1393–1411 (1997)
3. Brooks, M.J., Horn, B.K.P.: Shape and Source from Shading. In: Shape from shading, pp. 53–68. MIT Press, Cambridge (1989)
4. Brown, M., Lowe, D.G.: Invariant features from interest point groups. In: British Machine Vision Conference, pp. 656–665 (2002)
5. Cui, Y., Pagani, A., Stricker, D.: Sift in perception-based color space. In: IEEE 17th International Conference on Image Processing (ICIP), pp. 3909–3912 (2010)
6. Debevec, P.: Rendering synthetic objects into real scenes: bridging traditional and image-based graphics with global illumination and high dynamic range photography. In: ACM SIGGRAPH 2008, New York, NY, USA, pp. 32:1–32:10 (2008)
7. Debevec, P., Wenger, A., Tchou, C., Gardner, A., Waese, J., Hawkins, T.: A lighting reproduction approach to live-action compositing. ACM Trans. 21, 547–556 (2002)
8. Debevec, P.E., Malik, J.: Recovering high dynamic range radiance maps from photographs. In: SIGGRAPH 1997, New York, NY, USA, pp. 369–378 (1997)
9. Devlin, K., Chalmers, A., Wilkie, A., Purgathofer, W.: Star: Tone reproduction and physically based spectral rendering. In: dcwp (ed.) State of the Art Reports, Eurographics 2002, pp. 101–123. The Eurographics Association (September 2002)
10. Farag, A., Abdel-Hakim, A.E.: Detection, categorization and recognition of road signs for autonomous navigation. In: ACIVS 2004, pp. 125–130 (2004)
11. Judd, D.B., Wyszecki, G.: Color in Business, Science, and Industry, New York
12. Krawczyk, G., Mantiuk, R., Myszkowski, K., Seidel, H.P.: Lightness perception inspired tone mapping. In: Proceedings of the 1st Symposium on Applied Perception in Graphics and Visualization, pp. 172–172. ACM, New York (2004)
13. Lalonde, J.-F., Efros, A.A., Narasimhan, S.G.: Estimating natural illumination from a single outdoor image. In: IEEE ICCV (2009)
14. Lensch, H.P.A., Kautz, J., Goesele, M., Heidrich, W., Seidel, H.P.: Image-based reconstruction of spatial appearance and geometric detail. ACM Trans. Graph. 22, 234–257 (2003)
15. Li, Y., Lin, S., Lu, H., yeung Shum, H.: Multiple-cue illumination estimation in textured scenes. In: IEEE Proc. 9th ICCV, pp. 1366–1373 (2003)
16. Lowe, D.G.: Object recognition from local scale-invariant features. In: Computer Vision, vol. 2, pp. 1150–1157 (1999)
17. Lowe, D.G.: Distinctive image features from scale-invariant keypoints. Int. J. Comput. Vision 60(2), 91–110 (2004)
18. Mantiuk, R., Myszkowski, K., Seidel, H.P.: A perceptual framework for contrast processing of high dynamic range images (2005)
19. D'Zmura, M., Lennie, P.: Mechanisms of color constancy. The Journal of Optical Society of America 3, 1662–1672 (1986)
20. Mikolajczyk, K., Schmid, C.: A performance evaluation of local descriptors. IEEE Transactions on PAMI 27(10), 1615–1630 (2005)
21. Reinhard, E., Stark, M., Shirley, P., Ferwerda, J.: Photographic tone reproduction for digital images. In: PROC. OF SIGGRAPH 2002, pp. 267–276. ACM Press, New York (2002)
22. Sato, I., Sato, Y., Katsushi, I.: Acquiring a radiance distribution to superimpose virtual objects onto a real scene (1999)
23. Yoo, J.D., Cho, J.H., Kim, H.M., Park, K.S., Lee, S.J., Lee, K.H.: Light source estimation using segmented hdr images. In: SIGGRAPH 2007. ACM, NY (2007)

Illumination-Robust Dense Optical Flow Using Census Signatures

Thomas Müller[1,2], Clemens Rabe[1], Jens Rannacher[1],
Uwe Franke[1], and Rudolf Mester[2]

[1] Daimler Research, Sindelfingen
[2] Goethe-Universität Frankfurt am Main

Abstract. Vision-based motion perception builds primarily on the concept of optical flow. Modern optical flow approaches suffer from several shortcomings, especially in real, non-ideal scenarios such as traffic scenes. Non-constant illumination conditions in consecutive frames of the input image sequence are among these shortcomings. We propose and evaluate the application of intrinsically illumination-invariant census transforms within a dense state-of-the-art variational optical flow computation scheme. Our technique improves robustness against illumination changes, caused either by altering physical illumination or camera parameter adjustments. Since census signatures can be implemented quite efficiently, the resulting optical flow fields can be computed in real-time.

1 Introduction

1.1 Dense Optical Flow in Real Scenes

Reliable motion estimation in real-time is a key task for a variety of applications, e.g., in robotics or automotive driver assistance. While many new variants of dense variational optical flow algorithms have been proposed in recent years, they have focused mainly on accuracy under ideal conditions—which is benchmarked on the Middlebury optical flow data set [1]—rather than on robustness in practical applications.

Algorithms for optical flow estimation in real scenes under non-ideal conditions still suffer from the following issues in particular: non-constant illumination conditions in consecutive frames, large displacements (some improvements have been made here in recent years, e.g., [2]), weakly textured areas, and model violations such as transparency or reflections. In this work, we focus on the first topic and provide a new optical flow technique to cope with non-constant illumination conditions, caused either by physical illumination changes (including shadows) or by unanticipated and unknown adjustments of the camera parameters (e.g. the exposure time).

1.2 Related Work

Since most variation-based optical flow algorithms exploit the brightness constancy constraint in consecutive frames, they are not stable under changing

R. Mester and M. Felsberg (Eds.): DAGM 2011, LNCS 6835, pp. 236–245, 2011.

illumination conditions. During the last three decades, since Horn and Schunck [8] introduced their dense optical flow model, several approaches have been proposed to overcome this illumination sensitivity.

One might first think of a simple global mean-and-variance equalization to overcome the illumination sensibility. Although this can help remove global illumination offsets and can compensate the gain of a global transition function, the approach has some drawbacks. First, the device-dependent transition functions which map the incident light energy at the sensor elements to electronic signals are often non-linear. Second, changes of the mean intensity of the image can also result from real changes of the scene rather than the illumination (think of a big dark truck moving into the scene in front of the observer) and a mean-and-variance equalization would lead to incorrect results. Last, even a more generalized histogram adaptation approach could not cope with local changes of the physical illumination of a scene.

In [14], based on the improved model from [15], the authors propose the pre-processing of the original images with an ROF[10] denoising scheme (computed according to [4]) and take the difference to the original images as the new input. This structure/texture decomposition leads to slightly better results than the application of a simple Gauss-based high-pass band filter, which also yields some illumination-change resistance and is computationally more efficient. The shortcoming of an ROF denoising based high-pass filtering of the input images is two-fold: even when a pyramid scheme is used, the structure-texture decomposition leads to problems with larger displacements and an ROF denoising is computationally still quite expensive.

A qualitatively different approach is proposed in [5], where an additional scalar function is estimated together with the optical flow field in a joint optimization process. This function is then expected to cover all illumination inconsistencies. Since this function must be very smooth on the image domain, good results require many iterations. This eliminated the real-time capability in our implementation. An interesting and completely different approach for color images was presented in [9], where the authors use the constancy of a set of photometric invariances from color space in a variational scheme. The use of an advanced data term for illumination robustness in variational optical flow is mentioned in [12], where the normalized cross correlation is used as residual and leads to robustness against multiplicative illumination changes.

2   Dense Motion Estimation

Given two image functions $I_{\{1,2\}} : \Omega \rightarrow \mathbb{R}^+$ on the image domain $\Omega \subset \mathbb{R}^2$, the optical flow is defined as the apparent motion of the pixels from I_1 to I_2. Neglecting transparency or reflections, the projected motion of the objects of the real world onto the two-dimensional image plane is an element of the set of possible optical flow fields (ambiguities in the optical flow arise when there are textureless areas in the image sequence).

A reasonable optical flow field $u : \Omega \to \mathbb{R}^2$ is received by solving

$$\arg\min_{u} \{\lambda E_{\mathrm{D}}\,[u] + E_{\mathrm{S}}\,[u]\} \,, \tag{1}$$

with a m.a.p. expectation maximization in mind. The data term

$$E_{\mathrm{D}}\,[u] = \int_{\Omega} \Psi\,(\rho\,(x, u\,(x)))\;\mathrm{d}x \tag{2}$$

consists of a norm $\Psi : \mathbb{R} \to \mathbb{R}^+$ and the residual function $\rho : \Omega \times \mathbb{R}^2 \to \mathbb{R}$. The exact form of ρ can vary and determines the behavior under illumination changes as we will show in the next section. The regularizing smoothness term E_{S} helps to provide the most probable solution for Eq. (1), given our model conception in the exact form of E_{S}. Since, per definition, the regularizing smoothness term is independent of the input data $I_{\{1,2\}}$, it is not in the remainder of this paper.

2.1   A General Numerical Solution Scheme

Following the algorithm proposed in [15], we use the coupling term $E_{\mathrm{C}}\,[u, v] = (1/2\theta) \cdot \int_{\Omega} (u\,(x) - v\,(x))^2 \;\mathrm{d}x$ with the coupling constant θ to separate the optical flow functional Eq. (1) into two parts, which are then solved iteratively. Given the result of the previous computation step in v, the first part

$$\arg\min_{u} \{\lambda E_{\mathrm{D}}\,[u] + E_{\mathrm{C}}\,[u, v]\} \tag{3}$$

contains the data term and can be solved pointwise. Having the result of (3) in u, the second part

$$\arg\min_{v} \{E_{\mathrm{C}}\,[u, v] + E_{\mathrm{S}}\,[v]\} \tag{4}$$

contains the regularization and is solved depending on the exact form of E_{S}. The iterative solution of Eqs. (3) and (4) is performed until the desired accuracy is achieved or a fixed number of iterations have been executed. As proposed in [14], this iterative scheme is combined with median filtering for robustness and a pyramid scheme to cope with larger displacements.

2.1.1   Solving the Data Part for Arbitrary Residuals. Taking a closer look at the solution of the data part Eq. (3) allows describing a general straightforward gradient-descent solution scheme. This can be applied later for special forms of ρ and Ψ, especially for illumination-robust ones. Linearizing the residual ρ around the start value v in the second argument yields

$$\rho\,(x, u) \approx \tilde{\rho}\,(x, u) = \rho\,(x, v) + \nabla^{\top}\rho\,(x, v) \cdot (u - v) \,. \tag{5}$$

With the notation $(u_1, u_2)^{\top} \equiv u\,(x)$ and solving for $i \in \{1, 2\}$

$$0 = \frac{\partial}{\partial u_i} \{\lambda E_{\mathrm{D}}\,[u]\,(x) + E_{\mathrm{C}}\,[u, v]\,(x)\}$$

establishes the gradient descent step. Noting $u \equiv u(x), v \equiv v(x), (\rho_1, \rho_2)^\top \equiv \nabla \rho(x, v)$ leads to

$$0 = \lambda f \cdot \tilde{\rho}(x, u) \cdot \rho_i + \frac{1}{\theta}(u_i - v_i) \tag{6}$$

with the factor f depending on the exact form of the norm Ψ and computed by $f \equiv \Psi'(\rho(x, v))/\rho(x, v)$. Since Eq. (6) is linear in u_i, it is possible to formulate a linear equation system $\mathbf{A} \cdot u = b$ with

$$\mathbf{A} = \begin{pmatrix} \frac{1}{\theta} + \lambda f \rho_1^2 & \lambda f \rho_1 \rho_2 \\ \lambda f \rho_1 \rho_2 & \frac{1}{\theta} + \lambda f \rho_2^2 \end{pmatrix}$$

and

$$b = \frac{1}{\theta} v - \lambda f \cdot \nabla \rho(x, v) \cdot R$$

with $R = \rho(x, v) - \nabla^\top \rho(x, v) \cdot v$ and solve it with respect to u by a standard algorithm.

2.1.2 Special Data Terms in the Literature. In the classical approach by Horn and Schunck [8], we have $\rho(x, u) = I_2(x + u) - I_1(x)$, the well-known brightness constancy constraint $\tilde{\rho}(x, u) = \nabla I(x) \cdot u + I_t(x)$ (with $I_t(x) = I_2(x) - I_1(x)$), $\Psi(\rho) = \rho^2$ and $f = 2$. Approximating $\Psi(\rho) = |\rho|$ with $\Psi \approx \sqrt{\rho^2 + \epsilon}, \epsilon \ll 1$ in the outlier-robust TV-L^1 model by Zach and Pock [15] leads to $f = 1/\Psi(\rho)$. Many other models known from literature (e.g. the photometric invariant model in [9] or the dense Lucas-Kanade approach in [3]) can also be solved by this scheme. The following, we will use $\Psi = \sqrt{\rho^2 + \epsilon}, \epsilon \ll 1$ for our own approach.

3 Illumination-Invariant Motion Estimation

3.1 Illumination Robustness with Local Compensation of the Mean

The numerical framework sketched in the previous section used the residual function ρ which in [8] or [15] corresponds to the grey-value constancy. Using more sophisticated residuals, such as

$$\rho(x, u) = \sum_{i=1}^{n} \left| I_2(x + y_i + u) - \bar{I}_2(x + u) - I_1(x + y_i) + \bar{I}_1(x) \right|^d \tag{7}$$

with $\bar{I}_{\{1,2\}}(x) = 1/n \cdot \sum_{i=1}^{n} I_{\{1,2\}}(x + y_i)$ as the mean grey value and the fixed list of points $(y_1, y_2, \ldots, y_n)^\top \in \mathbb{R}^{n \times 2}, n \in \mathbb{N}$ around the origin, is a first step towards illumination robustness. The pointwise compensation by the local mean leads to an invariance of the results against local offsets of the illumination. In some cases, this is already sufficient to establish an effective protection against erroneous flow vectors due to the change of illumination conditions. The application of the residual in Eq. (7) is similar to a high pass filtering, which is performed in [14] by a structure-texture decomposition based on the ROF model. The special cases are the zero mean sum of absolute differences (ZSAD) for $d = 1$ and the zero mean squared sum of differences (ZSSD) for $d = 2$, which can both be easily implemented using the numerical scheme presented in the previous section and which are evaluated in the experimental part (Section 4).

3.2   Illumination Model

Before presenting more illumination-robust variants of the residual ρ, first a closer look at the illumination process. The image intensity field $I : \Omega \to \mathbb{R}^+$ of our input images at a point in time is the result of this process. It can be modeled by

$$I(\boldsymbol{x}) = T(J(c(\boldsymbol{x}), \boldsymbol{x})) \tag{8}$$

with the intrinsic, physical color field $c : \Omega \to \mathbb{R}^+$, the physical illumination (which here includes all atmospheric effects, noise etc.) $J : \mathbb{R}^+ \times \Omega \to \mathbb{R}^+$ and the device-specific generally time-dependent and unknown but always monotonic transition function $T : \mathbb{R}^+ \to \mathbb{R}^+$. The physical illumination J varies slowly in the space domain (apart from shadow and object edges) and it is monotonic in its first argument for a fixed point $\boldsymbol{x}$. This leads to the conclusion that data terms of the optical flow functional not relying on the exact grey-values or ratios, but rather on their ordering, lead to the most robust results under non-constant illumination conditions. In other words, though T and J are widely arbitrary and time-dependent, apart from shadow and object edges, their monotonicity can be relied upon.

3.3   Illumination-Invariant Census Based Residuals

How can we profit from the monotonicity of the functions T and J from Eq. (8) which constitute the illumination process? It is necessary to look at the ordering of the grey-values rather than their exact values, differences or ratios. Exactly this is provided by census transforms. Census signatures for sparse optical flow computation have already been used in [11], where they were used to efficiently compute large displacements.

The census transform maps to every pixel $\boldsymbol{x}$ of the image plane Ω one signature vector, $\boldsymbol{s}_t : \Omega \to \{0,1\}^n$, $n \in \mathbb{N}, t \in \{1,2\}$, which is defined as

$$s_{t,i}(\boldsymbol{x}) = [I_t(\boldsymbol{x} + \boldsymbol{y}_i) - I_t(\boldsymbol{x}) + \epsilon \geq 0] , \tag{9}$$

with $i \in [1,n]$ given the fixed list of points $(\boldsymbol{y}_1, \boldsymbol{y}_2, \ldots, \boldsymbol{y}_n)^\top \in \mathbb{R}^{n \times 2}$ near the origin and a small $\epsilon \in \mathbb{R}$. The brackets $[X]$ in Eq. (9) indicate whether the statement X is true ($[X] = 1$, the pixel at $\boldsymbol{x} + \boldsymbol{y}_i$ is clearly brighter than the pixel at $\boldsymbol{x}$) or false ($[X] = 0$, the pixel at $\boldsymbol{x} + \boldsymbol{y}_i$ is darker than or similar to the pixel at $\boldsymbol{x}$). Our implementation uses points in the direct neighborhood of the origin. Depending on the chosen patch size r, the first r rectangles of pixels around the origin are considered, so that $n = (2r + 1)^2 - 1$. Our evaluation used a 3×3 ($n = 8$) and a 5×5 ($n = 24$) patch size variant of the census transform.

In the classical case, the residual ρ is based on the grey value difference between two corresponding points of the consecutive images. We will now introduce a residual function which is based on the similarity of the census signatures of the two corresponding points. We propose to use the Hamming distance

$$\rho\left(\boldsymbol{x}, \boldsymbol{u}\right) = \sum_{i=1}^{n} \left[s_{2,i}\left(\boldsymbol{x} + \boldsymbol{u}\right) \neq s_{1,i}\left(\boldsymbol{x}\right)\right] \tag{10}$$

which is zero if and only if $s_1\left(\boldsymbol{x}\right) = s_2\left(\boldsymbol{x} + \boldsymbol{u}\right)$ and which is n if every component of s_1 is different to corresponding component of s_2. The Hamming distance based on the signature vectors has the nice property that it is inherently invariant under arbitrary changes of the device specific transition function T (since T is monotonic), and it is also invariant under most changes of the physical illumination J (since J is piecewise slowly varying on the space domain), if the point does not lie on an illumination edge; the illumination process does not affect the value of the Hamming distance $\rho\left(\boldsymbol{x}, \boldsymbol{u}\right)$.

The best choice for the parameter ϵ in Eq. (9) depends on the noise level of the image. Note that the residual function ρ has to be smooth in the second argument (the displacement $\boldsymbol{u}$) to be used in the iterative gradient descent scheme described in Sec. 2.1. While this turns out to be also the case for the Hamming distance in Eq. (10) (we use linear interpolation of the grey values at non-integer image positions for s_2), the smoothness of ρ is further promoted by the small offset ϵ when dealing with image noise. A ternary variant, where equality between the values $I_t\left(\boldsymbol{x} + \boldsymbol{y}_i\right)$ and $I_t\left(\boldsymbol{x}\right)$ is treated as a third case, provides more information and can also be applied.

4 Results

4.1 Evaluation of a Synthetic Scene from the Middlebury Data Set

Testing the illumination-robustness on the Grove2 sequence from the Middlebury optical flow data set [1], for which the ground-truth optical flow $\boldsymbol{u}_{\mathrm{GT}} : \Omega \rightarrow \mathbb{R}^2$ is available, provides a reproducible quantitative evaluation of the method proposed here. Considering the optical flow field between the frames 10 and 11 with the corresponding images I_{10} and I_{11} and varying the γ value of I_{11} from $\gamma = 1$ to $\gamma = 4$ results in the modified images $I_{11,\gamma}$ with $I_{11,\gamma}\left(\boldsymbol{x}\right) = 255 \cdot \left(I_{11}\left(\boldsymbol{x}\right)/255\right)^{\gamma}$. For a variety of optical flow methods, the average endpoint error of the flow field, $1/\left|\Omega\right| \cdot \int_{\Omega} \left|\boldsymbol{u}\left(\boldsymbol{x}\right) - \boldsymbol{u}_{\mathrm{GT}}\left(\boldsymbol{x}\right)\right| \mathrm{d}\boldsymbol{x}$, is computed for every γ in the range $[1, 4]$.

Though it can be seen in the table of Fig. 1 that the census-based approaches are slightly outperformed by the grey-value-based TV-L^1 approach from [13] for $\gamma = 1$ (no illumination change), the graph on the left shows that when increasing the γ value, one approach after another—apart from the census based methods—becomes unstable and fails to provide correct flow results. The illumination robustness of the census based methods is only affected by discretization effects of the γ correction.

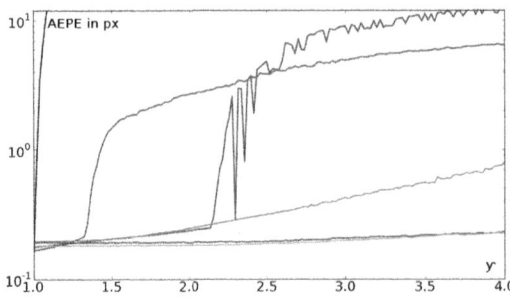

AEPE in px	$\gamma = 1$	$\gamma = 2$	$\gamma = 4$
TV-L^1	0.150	89.6	106
TV-L^1+S/T	0.165	2.69	6.46
Illumination term	0.175	0.236	13.4
ZSAD	0.193	0.246	0.780
3×3 Census	0.191	0.189	0.231
5×5 Census	0.179	0.180	0.227

Fig. 1. Evaluation of the `Grove2` sequence from the Middlebury optical flow dataset from frame 10 to 11. Frame 10 is γ-corrected with $1 \leq \gamma \leq 4$. Left: Average endpoint error, blue: TV-L^1 optical flow without structure/texture decomposition; green: TV-L^1 with structure/texture decomposition, both from [14]; red: optical flow with joint illumination term estimation [5]; cyan: ZSAD based optical flow; magenta: 3×3 census based optical flow; yellow: 5×5 census based optical flow. Right: Exemplary quantitative results.

4.2   Real Scenes

4.2.1   Example: Buggy Scene. Two different real image sequences are qualitatively explored using the proposed methods. In the first example, we again perform an artificial gamma adjustment on two input images of a city scene (first image $\gamma = 0.9$, second $\gamma = 0.8$) and compare the flow results of the several algorithms. The results in Fig. 2 are now descussed in detail.

In the second row of Fig. 2, the result of the TV-L^1 approach from [14], applied on the two differently γ-adjusted input images (top row), is shown. Clearly, the illumination difference between the two input images makes it impossible for the grey-value based algorithm to provide correct flow fields. In contrast, the structure/texture decomposition on the right hand side allows for illumination robustness in this case. The joint computation of an additional illumination term, already mentioned in Sec. 1.2 from [5], also solves the problem (third row, right) but leads to a loss of details in the flow field. Note for example the fast moving foot of the woman in the right part of the image which is merged with the environment, or consider the absence of the umbrella.

There are two main aspects when reviewing the census result: First, even without structure/texture precomputation or computation of an additional illumination term, both variants of census based optical flow are indeed inherently illumination-invariant. Second, the resulting flow fields are more detailed than the ones received from approaches known from literature: the fast moving foot can be clearly observed when using census signatures. In addition, the underestimation of the flow vectors on the turning car known from the approaches above vanishes almost completely. Note that census signatures are patch-based and are therefore suffering from one major drawback: the loss of resolution in the result. As seen in Fig. 2, a patch structure is clearly visible in the resulting optical flow field.

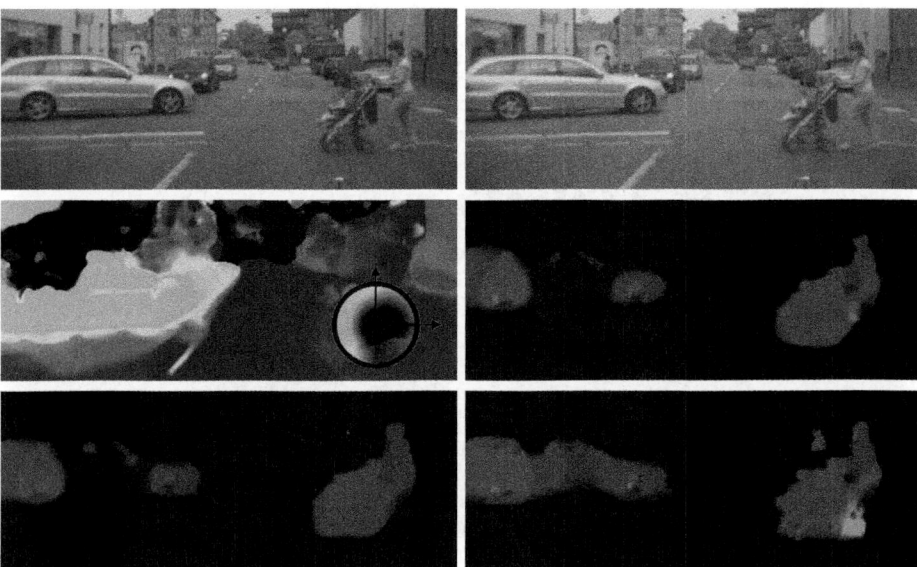

Fig. 2. Comparison of flow results of a typical traffic scene. Top row: The two differently gamma adjusted input images (note that the right one has a slightly lower gamma value). Second row: TV-L^1 optical flow from [14] without (left, color encoding: color indicates direction, intensity indicates magnitude) and with structure/texture decomposition (right). Third row, left: image intensity based optical flow with joint illumination term computation from [5]. Right: binary 3×3 census based optical flow (left) without illumination term or structure/texture decomposition.

4.2.2   Example: Highway Scene. We also explore the results on a second traffic scene taken on a highway [6] which is very challenging for flow estimation. In addition to illumination changes, large flow vectors, large weakly textured regions, and aliasing effects occur. As a consequence, even with constant illumination between two frames, standard optical flow methods (see Fig. 3, third row, left) only yield partially reasonable flow fields (note that we would expect a rainbow-like structure on the highway surface). During the sequence, the camera system is exposed to very different illumination conditions which change abruptly. This causes the device-internal transfer function to change as well in a wide range. Results of several optical flow methods are presented in Fig. 3. No artificial gamma adjustment is performed for this sequence.

We were not able to receive reasonable flow results with standard approaches like the TV-L^1 from [14] with (third row, left) or without structure/texture decomposition (second row, right). However, the joint estimation of an illumination field [5] (third row, right) was able to detect the moving car on the left and the car in front of the camera which is correctly colored black, since it is nearly constantly moving with the same velocity in the focus of expansion. Both census approaches (bottom row) are apparently able to detect the correct motion, if the corresponding image region is sufficiently textured.

Fig. 3. Comparison of flow results from a very challenging highway scene [6], frame 108 to 109. Top row: The two differently exposed input images (note the different illumination). Second row, left: TV-L^1 flow from [14] without structure/texture decomposition of the previous frame (107 to 108), without illumination changes for reference; right: TV-L^1 optical flow from [14] without structure/texture decomposition. Third row: TV-L^1 optical flow with structure/texture decomposition from [14] (left), image intensity based flow with joint illumination term computation from [5] (right). Bottom row: binary census based optical flow (left), ternary census optical flow (right), both from Sec. 3. Color encoding as in Fig. 2.

5   Conclusion

This work proposed a new technique for optical flow computation coping with illumination changes often occurring in real scenes such as traffic scenarios. A variety of different residual functions can be used in a general numerical solution scheme for optical flow. Profiting from the monotonicity of the illumination process, illumination-invariant residuals can be constructed when considering the grey value ordering rather than their exact differences. Hamming distances, based on several different census signatures, replace the simple grey value constancy constraint from classical optical flow approaches. In the second part, results from the proposed novel technique are compared to those based on work known from literature. The application of census signatures in dense variational optical flow leads to the best results both on synthetic and real traffic scenes during illumination changes. While census signatures may have their shortcomings when used as single correspondence measures, they generally seem to provide very robust results when applied in a regularized global optimization scheme (see also the application of census transforms in stereo vision [7]). Future work will combine the census based optical flow computation method with large displacement support using feature correspondences and extended regularizing models to make it possible to apply dense motion estimation in real scenarios, e.g. in traffic scenes for driver assistance systems.

References

1. Baker, S., Scharstein, D., Lewis, J., Roth, S., Black, M., Szeliski, R.: A database and evaluation methodology for optical flow. International Journal of Computer Vision 92(1), 1–31 (2011)
2. Brox, T., Bregler, C., Malik, J.: Large displacement optical flow. In: IEEE International Conference on Computer Vision and Pattern Recognition, Miami Beach, Florida, USA (2009)
3. Bruhn, A., Weickert, J., Schnörr, C.: Lucas/Kanade meets Horn/Schunck: Combining local and global optic flow methods. International Journal of Computer Vision 61(3), 211–231 (2005)
4. Chambolle, A.: An algorithm for total variation minimization and applications. Journal of Mathematical Imaging and Vision 20(1-2), 89–97 (2004)
5. Chambolle, A., Pock, T.: A first-order primal-dual algorithm for convex problems with applications to imaging (2010),
   http://hal.archives-ouvertes.fr/hal-00490826/en/
6. Friedrich, H., Rabe, C., Mester, R.: DAGM 2011 AVCC website (2011),
   http://www.dagm2011.org/adverse-vision-conditions-challenge.html
7. Hirschmüller, H., Gehrig, S.: Stereo matching in the presence of sub-pixel calibration errors. In: IEEE Conference on Computer Vision and Pattern Recognition (2009)
8. Horn, B.K.P., Schunck, B.G.: Determining optical flow. Artificial Intelligence 17, 185–203 (1981)
9. Mileva, Y., Bruhn, A., Weickert, J.: Illumination-robust variational optical flow with photometric invariants. In: Hamprecht, F.A., Schnörr, C., Jähne, B. (eds.) DAGM 2007. LNCS, vol. 4713, pp. 152–162. Springer, Heidelberg (2007)
10. Rudin, L.I., Osher, S., Fatemi, E.: Nonlinear total variation based noise removal algorithms. Physica D 60, 259–268 (1992)
11. Stein, F.J.: Efficient computation of optical flow using the census transform. In: Rasmussen, C.E., Bülthoff, H.H., Schölkopf, B., Giese, M.A. (eds.) DAGM 2004. LNCS, vol. 3175, pp. 79–86. Springer, Heidelberg (2004)
12. Steinbrücker, F., Pock, T., Cremers, D.: Advanced data terms for variational optic flow estimation. In: Vision, Modelling, and Visualization Workshop, Braunschweig, Germany (2009)
13. Wedel, A., Meissner, A., Rabe, C., Franke, U., Cremers, D.: Detection and segmentation of independently moving objects from dense scene flow. In: Energy Minimization Methods in Computer Vision and Pattern Recognition (2009)
14. Wedel, A., Pock, T., Zach, C., Bischof, H., Cremers, D.: An improved algorithm for TV-L1 optical flow. In: Cremers, D., Rosenhahn, B., Yuille, A.L., Schmidt, F.R. (eds.) Statistical and Geometrical Approaches to Visual Motion Analysis. LNCS, vol. 5604, pp. 23–45. Springer, Heidelberg (2009)
15. Zach, C., Pock, T., Bischof, H.: A duality based approach for realtime TV-L1 optical flow. In: Hamprecht, F.A., Schnörr, C., Jähne, B. (eds.) DAGM 2007. LNCS, vol. 4713, pp. 214–223. Springer, Heidelberg (2007)

Efficient Stereo and Optical Flow with Robust Similarity Measures

Christian Unger[1,2], Eric Wahl[1], and Slobodan Ilic[2]

[1] BMW Group, München, Germany
[2] Technische Universität München, Germany
firstname.lastname@bmw.de, firstname.lastname@in.tum.de

Abstract. In this paper we address the problem of dense stereo matching and computation of optical flow. We propose a generalized dense correspondence computation algorithm, so that stereo matching and optical flow can be performed robustly and efficiently at the same time. We particularly target automotive applications and tested our method on real sequences from cameras mounted on vehicles.

We performed an extensive evaluation of our method using different similarity measures and focused mainly on difficult real-world sequences with abrupt exposure changes. We did also evaluations on Middlebury data sets and provide many qualitative results on real images, some of which are provided by the adverse vision conditions challenge of the conference.

1 Introduction

Dense stereo matching and the computation of optical flow in real-time are important for many computer vision tasks. In automotive applications very useful driver assistance systems can be realized based on this information – collision avoidance maneuvering, preventive pedestrian protection, longitudinal vehicle control or camera-based parking slot detection – are just some examples.

Many of those automotive applications rely on real-time stereo and optical flow. Therefore, in this paper, we focus on dense stereo, motion-stereo and optical flow that can be applied in real-time to challenging real-world sequences acquired by cameras integrated into vehicles. Since dense matching is very demanding in terms of processing power, we focus on highly efficient methods, but still try to maintain reasonable quality. In practice, stereo matching and in particular motion-stereo becomes difficult under sudden exposure or illumination changes (e.g. in garages), low-light scenarios, different weather conditions (rain, snow, etc.) or due to glare light effects. Standard block matching techniques that are fast usually use very simple similarity measures and exhibit lots of artifacts in such realistic scenarios. On the other hand robust similarity measures are better and may be used to improve results in such situations. However, the computational burden often prohibits their usage in real-time systems. A more generic and complicated problem than stereo is optical flow. It helps determining the motion of moving objects and has to face similar challenges as ordinary

R. Mester and M. Felsberg (Eds.): DAGM 2011, LNCS 6835, pp. 246–255, 2011.

stereo. However, while for stereo the epipolar geometry can be used to constrain possible matches to epipolar lines, in optical flow a large rectangular search region must be considered instead. This usually results in a high computational overhead. Therefore, the formulation of a highly efficient and robust approach based on block matching is much more difficult than for stereo.

In this paper we propose a generalized dense correspondence computation algorithm, so that stereo matching and optical flow can be performed robustly and efficiently at the same time. We generalize and extend the concepts of the efficient disparity computation approach given in [18], which was originally designed for highly efficient disparity retrieval. There, stereo matching is performed iteratively by alternating minimization and propagation phases at every pixel. We significantly increase the correspondence search range to a two dimensional area and, although based on window-based block matching, still maintain a surprisingly high efficiency. Consequently, our approach can be applied not only to stereo, but also to optical flow.

We demonstrate the effectiveness on challenging real-world and Middlebury data sets and the results underline a significant improvement in running times, while quality is not sacrificed.

In the rest of the paper, we will first review related work and explain briefly the ideas in [18], then present our method and finally show an exhaustive experimental evaluation.

2   Related Work

Traditional *correlation-based* or *local methods* [4, 8] can be implemented very efficiently [15,19,3] and are still widely used in many real-time applications. The main assumption of these approaches is that all pixels in the matching region originate from co-planar or even fronto-parallel scene points. This assumption is often violated in real world scenarios and results in inaccurate object boundaries [8,17]. Some techniques have been introduced to improve the quality [21,12,8], but are often quite time consuming or have limited effect.

In global methods the stereo problem is formulated as an energy minimization problem and is solved using standard optimization techniques like in [3,1,17,7, 9,5,20,14,13]. These approaches usually achieve much better visual and quantitative quality, but are also computationally quite expensive. Several attempts have been made to improve their running times using GPUs [1,16]. However, such hardware is not available on many mobile platforms or vehicles.

Among the global methods, semi-global matching [7,6] is known to be the most efficient approach and also comes with a reasonable quality. However, real-time processing requires specialized hardware [6] or enormous processing power and much memory. From this prospect, a generalization of semi-global matching from stereo towards optical flow is infeasible due to the increased amount of memory and number of cost function evaluations.

By contrast, in this paper, we demonstrate both memory and computationally efficient stereo and optical flow using robust cost measures.

3   Background

In [18] an efficient dense stereo matching algorithm was presented, which does not rely on an exhaustive search technique. Unlike related correlation based methods no a-priori maximum disparity is required. In their approach matching is done by a localized minimization technique at every pixel and uses SAD. Since the maximal disparity is not known, only neighboring disparity values are checked. The one which decreases the dissimilarity is retained. However, this procedure might be confused by local minima. Therefore a propagation step was introduced where the dissimilarity is also checked using the larger neighborhood, i.e for the larger disparity values. This allows jumping over some local minima and when done in several iterations may converge to the global minimum. It is evident that the pixel dissimilarity is evaluated in every iteration and at every pixel. However, the efficiency and quality was still higher than the one of traditional real-time correlation methods based on using integral images. This can be explained by very few cost function evaluations.

4   Method

These properties of [18] motivated us to use this method and to extend it. We first use robust similarity measures and later generalize it to the optical flow problem. Since the algorithm of [18] does not rely on box filtering or integral images [19] our goal is to preserve as much efficiency as possible, even though using complex cost functions.

4.1   Robust Similarity Measures

The convergence of [18] is mainly based on the use of matching costs which are aggregated over a support region (e.g. a square window). Therefore, we argue that the use of normalized cross-correlation (NCC) or Census Transform (CT) [22] is possible as long as matching windows are used. We chose to use the following robust cost functions.

Normalized Cross-Correlation (NCC).

$$E_{NCC} = \frac{\sum\sum (I_L(\mathbf{p}) - \bar{I}_L)(I_R(\mathbf{q}) - \bar{I}_R)}{\sigma_L \sigma_R} \tag{1}$$

with I_L and I_R being the left and right images, $\bar{I}_L$ and $\bar{I}_R$ being average pixel intensities in the correlation window computed as $\bar{I}_L = \sum\sum \frac{I_L(\mathbf{p})}{N}$ where $N = (w+1)^2$ and w is the window size. $\sigma_{I_L}^2 = \sum\sum (I_L(\mathbf{p}) - \bar{I}_L)^2$ is the variance of the image intensities in the defined correlation window. I_R, $\bar{I}_R$ and σ_{I_R} are computed analogously.

Census Transform (CT). The Census filter computes a bit string for every image pixel. Every bit encodes a specific pixel of the local window centered around a pixel of interest. The bit is set to one if the pixel has a lower intensity than the pixel of interest. Later, the pixel-wise matching cost is defined as the Hamming distance of pairwise bit strings. In practice, we sum these Hamming distances over a small support region.

4.2   Optical Flow

For optical flow, we generalize the approach presented in [18], by modifying the individual processing steps. For every pixel location $\mathbf{p} = (x, y)^T$ we search for a flow vector $\mathbf{f} = (u, v)^T$, where u and v are the displacements in x- and y-direction. For the dissimilarity E of image pixels, we use matching costs based on SAD E_{SAD}, NCC E_{NCC}, or Census transform E_{CT}. The two-dimensional flow vectors are stored in a flow field $\mathcal{F}(\mathbf{p})$.

Optimization Procedure. One of the central ideas of the method is that at every pixel location, a steepest descent is performed. This means that at every pixel, the flow vector is modified using the *minimization* step. However, the minimization will stop at local, suboptimal minima. To alleviate this problem, a *propagation* is introduced, so that at every pixel, the flow vectors of adjacent pixels are evaluated.

Minimization Step. Let the current flow vector at $\mathbf{p}$ be $\mathbf{f}_0 = \mathcal{F}(\mathbf{p}) = (u_0, v_0)^T$ (which is $(0, 0)^T$ directly after initialization). The mapping for the iteration is then given as:

$$\mathbf{f}_{n+1} = (u_{n+1}, v_{n+1})^T := \mathrm{argmin}_{\mathbf{f} \in M} E(\mathbf{p}, \mathbf{f}) \tag{2}$$

with the modified vectors

$$M := \left\{ \begin{pmatrix} u_n + i \\ v_n + j \end{pmatrix} \middle| \, i, j \in \{-1, 0, 1\}, i^2 + j^2 \leq 1 \right\} \tag{3}$$

Please note that we do not include diagonal steps in M, because it improves the efficiency and the result is not notably affected. If $\mathbf{f}_{n+1} = \mathbf{f}_n$ the iteration is stopped and the flow field is updated.

Propagation Step. In the propagation at every pixel, the flow vectors from surrounding pixels are evaluated and the flow field is updated:

$$\mathcal{F}(\mathbf{p}) \mapsto \mathrm{argmin}_{\mathbf{f} \in N(\mathbf{p})} E(\mathbf{p}, \mathbf{f}) \tag{4}$$

with the neighboring flow vectors $N(\mathbf{p})$ (with $\mathcal{F}(\mathbf{p}) \in N(\mathbf{p})$). At this step, flow vectors may be spread through their local neighborhood. In practice, we alternate minimization and propagation steps for a few iterations until convergence is achieved (2-3 repetitions from experience).

Hierarchical Iteration. In the original formulation, the image pyramid was created only by scaling the horizontal dimension to reduce ambiguity in texture-less regions. In case of optical flow, where we search also along the vertical axis, we scale both dimensions.

We start the matching at the lowest resolution. In every pyramid level, we perform the optimization procedure, which computes an estimated flow field. At next resolution, the optimization uses the upscaled flow field from the previous resolution as a starting point (in the beginning, all flow vectors are set to $(0,0)^T$):

$$\mathcal{F}^{(k+1)}(2x + i, 2y + j) = 2\mathcal{F}^{(k)}(x, y) \quad \text{with } i, j \in \{0, 1\} \tag{5}$$

5   Results

In this section we present our experiments with dense stereo and optical flow methods applied to a number of real sequences and Middlebury data sets for quantitative results.

5.1   Robust Stereo Matching

Quantitative evaluation. In our experiments with the Middlebury data set *Art* from [10] we performed stereo matching using image pairs with different combinations of exposures or illuminations similar to [10]. The main result depicted in the graphs of Fig. 1 is that the tested cost measures are less effective for different illuminations than for exposure changes. The matching error depends on the amount of the illumination change between the image pair. On the contrary, the exposure change has less influence on the error variation. The Census Transform is very effective in this case and shows only slight variations between the combinations. It is interesting that in many cases local matching can keep up with semi-global matching and was in two cases even better. However, also SGM could be improved by Census Transform if more processing time is spent.

Qualitative evaluation. We performed tests on real world sequences provided by the 2011 DAGM Adverse Vision Conditions Challenge and imagery from our vehicle. In particular, we present results on the sequences *Exposure Changes* (see Fig. 2), *Groundplane Violation* (see Fig. 3) and a motion-stereo video from our application (see Fig. 4), because there are interesting differences noticeable. For the *Motion-Stereo* example we picked a very challenging data with incident sunlight. In practice, our sequences feature glare light effects, frequent exposure changes, specular reflections and specular highlights.

In Fig. 2 (*Exposure Changes*), Fig. 3 (*Groundplane Violation*) and Fig. 4 (*Motion-Stereo*) we show a comparison of traditional matching algorithms and our matching method with different similarity measures. As expected, Census Transform performs in overall better than the other similarity measures, and surprisingly, SAD performs also quite well in combination with a x-Sobel operator. The quality when using NCC is relatively bad, which might be explained by

Illumination 1 Illumination 2 Illumination 3 Exposure 1 Exposure 2 Exposure 3

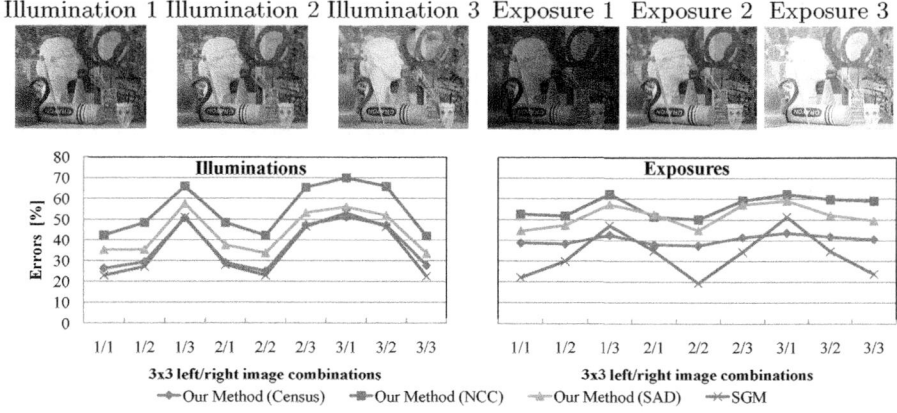

Fig. 1. Results on the stereo dataset *Art* for different exposures and illuminations. The x-axis denotes the different exposure/illumination combinations.

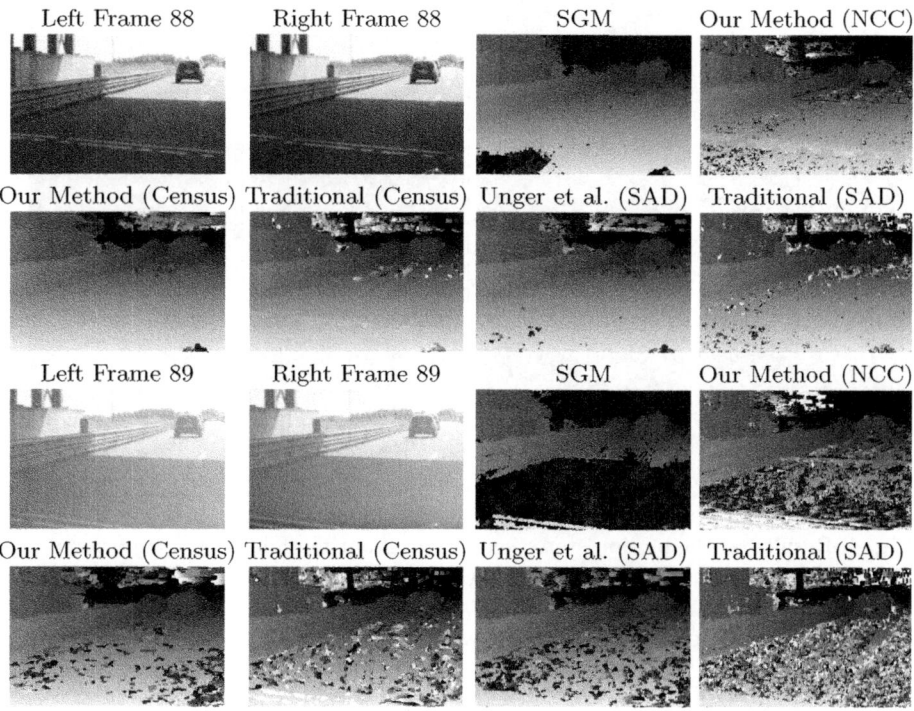

Fig. 2. Results on the sequence *Exposure Changes*

a high sensitivity in homogeneous regions. The semi-global method of [7] produces relatively good results, but in some difficult situations the density of the disparity maps is reduced in homogeneous regions (see Fig. 2 frame 89, Fig. 3 and Fig. 4).

Fig. 3. Results on the sequence *Groundplane Violation*

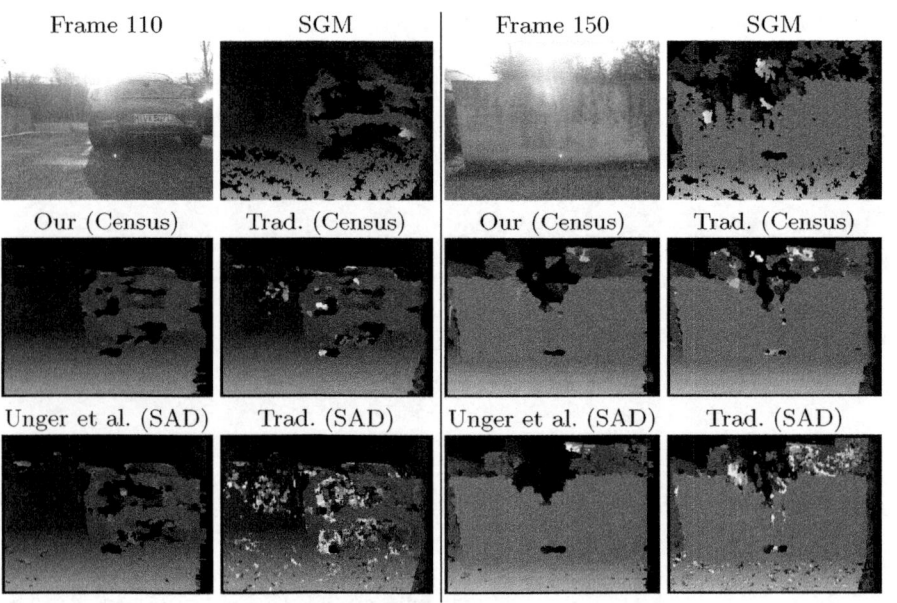

Fig. 4. Results on the motion-stereo sequences of our method (Our), traditional block matching (Trad.), semi-global matching (SGM) and the method of Unger et al.

5.2 Efficient Dense Optical Flow

We performed tests on the challenging real image sequences *Large Displacement* and *Exposure Changes* also provided by the 2011 DAGM AVCC and show results in Fig. 5. In *Large Displacement*, the vehicle in front (entering from the left) drives with a higher velocity than the cars in the background (which move from right to left). The sequence *Exposure Changes* is a video from a forward looking camera on a forward moving vehicle, where a sudden change in exposure takes place between frames 90 and 91. Our method with Census Transform shows again the best overall result, but also the SAD cost measure works surprisingly

Large Displacement, Frames 200–202   *Exposure Changes*, Frames 90, 91

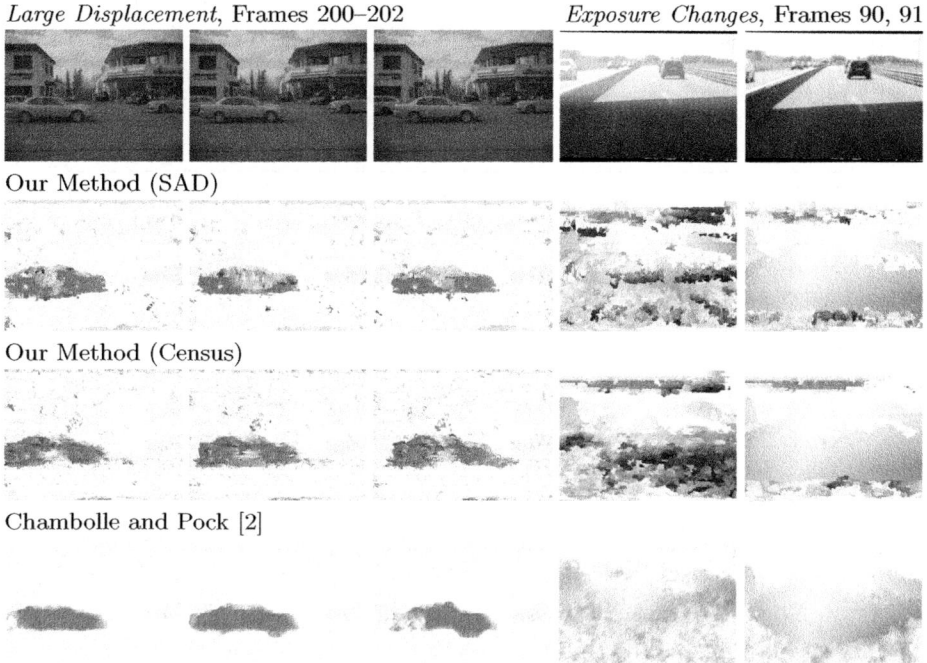

Our Method (SAD)

Our Method (Census)

Chambolle and Pock [2]

Fig. 5. Results on the sequences *Large Displacement* (flow fields were computed for frame pairs (200, 201), (201, 202) and (202, 203)) and *Exposure Changes* (frame pairs (90, 91) and (91, 92)). The image on the right denotes the color-coding of the computed flow vectors. **Please note that this figure is best viewed in color.**

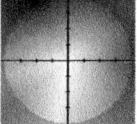

well on images that were previously filtered with a Sobel filter in x direction. We do not include the results of the Horn and Schunck algorithm [11], because it recovered only very localized motion. TV-L1 of [2] works relatively well, but is highly sensitive to exposure changes. Due to this reason we use Sobel-filtered images, but in this case the smoothness is negatively affected by image noise. At dramatic changes of the exposure time, none of the methods succeeded.

5.3 Efficiency

Table 1 shows the execution times in milliseconds of our single-threaded implementations on a standard Intel E8200 CPU and underlines the high efficiency of our methods. We tested stereo matching on images with a resolution of 1024x334 and a maximum disparity of 48 (for traditional methods that require an a-priori specification). Optical flow methods were also tested on 640x481 images and flow vectors with displacements of at most 30 pixels in each direction (the timings of [2] are not comparable, because their Matlab implementation took minutes and a GPU version reported as real-time [2] is of course not comparable to a

Table 1. The execution times of the different methods in milliseconds. Stereo matching was tested on images with a resolution of 1024x334 and a maximum disparity of 48 was used for methods that require it a-priori. Optical flow was tested on 640x481 images and flow vectors with displacements of at most 30 pixels in each direction. We also performed tests on images scaled to one third of their original size.

Method	Stereo 1024x334	Flow 640x481	Flow 213x160
SGM	536	-	-
Unger et al. (SAD)	129	-	-
Our Method (SAD)	-	466	52
Our Method (Census)	403	1763	167
Our Method (NCC)	560	1812	179
Trad. Block Matching (SAD)	263	39744	641
Trad. Block Matching (Census)	2313	162769	2029
Trad. Block Matching (NCC)	2691	140648	1913
Horn and Schunk [11]	-	313	34
Chambolle and Pock [2]	-	N/A	N/A

CPU implementation). We also performed tests with down-scaled images (third of their original size). The timings underline the high efficiency of our proposed optical flow formulation which demonstrates that with small images it is possible to compute dense optical flow with large displacements in real-time on commodity hardware, even with robust cost measures. On higher resolutions, the performance gap to traditional block matching is extremely big: our proposal is up to 90 times faster due to our efficient search algorithm and the hierarchical setup.

6 Conclusion

We presented a generalized framework for dense stereo matching and optical flow which can be computed efficiently and robustly at the same time. We tested our method on a number of real world sequences and provided quantitative results on Middlebury data sets. The comparison of different similarity measures showed that robust ones, like census transform, are usually the best choice. However, in some situations traditional measures like SAD perform also quite well. The main strengths of our framework are its efficiency, which is maintained even when using more demanding robust measures, and its genericity, since complex problems like optical flow can be addressed, and its good results, obtained on very challenging real world data.

Acknowledgements. We would like to thank Daniel Scharstein and Richard Szeliski for providing stereo images with ground truth data. This work is supported by the BMW Group.

References

1. Brunton, A., Shu, C., Roth, G.: Belief propagation on the gpu for stereo vision. In: Canadian Conference on Computer and Robot Vision, pp. 76–81 (2006)
2. Chambolle, A., Pock, T.: A first-order primal-dual algorithm for convex problems with applications to imaging. Tech. rep., Graz University of Technology (2010)
3. Di Stefano, L., Marchionni, M., Mattoccia, S.: A fast area-based stereo matching algorithm. Image and Vision Computing 22(12), 983–1005 (2004)
4. Faugeras, O., Hotz, B., Mathieu, H., Viéville, T., Zhang, Z., Fua, P., Théron, E., Moll, L., Berry, G., Vuillemin, J., Bertin, P., Proy, C.: Real time correlation-based stereo: algorithm, implementations and applications. Tech. Rep. RR-2013, INRIA (1993)
5. Felzenszwalb, P.F., Huttenlocher, D.P.: Efficient belief propagation for early vision. Int. J. Comput. Vis. 70(1), 41–54 (2006)
6. Gehrig, S.K., Eberli, F., Meyer, T.: A real-time low-power stereo vision engine using semi-global matching. In: Fritz, M., Schiele, B., Piater, J.H. (eds.) ICVS 2009. LNCS, vol. 5815, pp. 134–143. Springer, Heidelberg (2009)
7. Hirschmuller, H.: Accurate and efficient stereo processing by semi-global matching and mutual information. In: CVPR, pp. 807–814 (2005)
8. Hirschmüller, H., Innocent, P.R., Garibaldi, J.: Real-time correlation-based stereo vision with reduced border errors. IJCV 47(1-3), 229–246 (2002)
9. Hirschmüller, H., Scharstein, D.: Evaluation of cost functions for stereo matching. In: CVPR, pp. 1–8 (2007)
10. Hirschmüller, H., Scharstein, D.: Evaluation of stereo matching costs on images with radiometric differences. TPAMI 31(9), 1582–1599 (2009)
11. Horn, B.K.P., Schunck, B.G.: Determining optical flow. Artif. Intell. 17(1-3), 185–203 (1981)
12. Hosni, A., Bleyer, M., Gelautz, M., Rhemann, C.: Local stereo matching using geodesic support weights. In: ICIP (2009)
13. Klaus, A., Sormann, M., Karner, K.: Segment-based stereo matching using belief propagation and a self-adapting dissimilarity measure. In: ICPR, pp. 15–18 (2006)
14. van der Mark, W., Gavrila, D.M.: Real-time dense stereo for intelligent vehicles. IEEE Trans. Intell. Transport. Syst. 7(1), 38–50 (2006)
15. Mühlmann, K., Maier, D., Hesser, J., Männer, R.: Calculating dense disparity maps from color stereo images, an efficient implementation. IJCV 47(1-3), 79–88 (2002)
16. Rosenberg, I.D., Davidson, P.L., Muller, C.M.R., Han, J.Y.: Real-time stereo vision using semi-global matching on programmable graphics hardware. In: SIGGRAPH 2006 Sketches (2006)
17. Scharstein, D., Szeliski, R., Zabih, R.: A taxonomy and evaluation of dense two-frame stereo correspondence algorithms. Int. J. Comput. Vis. 47, 7–42 (2002)
18. Unger, C., Benhimane, S., Wahl, E., Navab, N.: Efficient disparity computation without maximum disparity for real-time stereo vision. In: BMVC (2009)
19. Veksler, O.: Fast variable window for stereo correspondence using integral images. In: CVPR, pp. 556–561 (2003)
20. Wang, L., Liao, M., Gong, M., Yang, R., Nister, D.: High-quality real-time stereo using adaptive cost aggregation and dynamic programming. In: Proc. Int. Symp. 3D Data Proc., Vis., and Transm (3DPVT), pp. 798–805 (2006)
21. Yoon, K.-J., Kweon, I.-S.: Locally adaptive support-weight approach for visual correspondence search. In: CVPR, pp. 924–931 (2005)
22. Zabih, R., Woodfill, J.: Non-parametric local transforms for computing visual correspondence. In: Eklundh, J.-O. (ed.) ECCV 1994. LNCS, vol. 801, pp. 151–158. Springer, Heidelberg (1994)

Shape- and Pose-Invariant Correspondences Using Probabilistic Geodesic Surface Embedding

Aggeliki Tsoli[1] and Michael J. Black[2]

[1] Brown University, Providence, RI, USA
[2] Max Planck Institute for Intelligent Systems, Tübingen, Germany
aggeliki@cs.brown.edu, black@is.mpg.de

Abstract. Correspondence between non-rigid deformable 3D objects provides a foundation for object matching and retrieval, recognition, and 3D alignment. Establishing 3D correspondence is challenging when there are non-rigid deformations or articulations between instances of a class. We present a method for automatically finding such correspondences that deals with significant variations in *pose, shape* and *resolution* between pairs of objects. We represent objects as triangular meshes and consider normalized geodesic distances as representing their intrinsic characteristics. Geodesic distances are invariant to pose variations and nearly invariant to shape variations when properly normalized. The proposed method registers two objects by optimizing a joint probabilistic model over a subset of vertex pairs between the objects. The model enforces preservation of geodesic distances between corresponding vertex pairs and inference is performed using loopy belief propagation in a hierarchical scheme. Additionally our method prefers solutions in which local shape information is consistent at matching vertices. We quantitatively evaluate our method and show that is is more accurate than a state of the art method.

1   Introduction

Finding correspondences between non-rigid 3D deformable objects is a critical task for many applications. Examples include object recognition and retrieval, shape deformation and morphing, 3D surface registration, *etc.* By defining correspondences using a structure preservation criterion, we can assess the similarity between two objects based on the amount of structure distortion. For applications involving search for similar 3D object models, it may be critical to have a measure of similarity that is invariant to common variations within a class (e.g. body pose and identity variation). Additionally, mesh alignment, for example of laser scans of human bodies, typically employs surface registration methods like ICP [3], [15] which require an initial set of correspondences. Here we describe a fully automated method for obtaining such correspondences between meshes that vary in shape, pose, and resolution.

Although the problem of establishing correspondences among rigid objects has been addressed in the literature adequately, finding correspondences between non-rigid deformable objects is still a challenge. Variations in pose and shape change the local geometry of the object's surface increasing the likelihood

R. Mester and M. Felsberg (Eds.): DAGM 2011, LNCS 6835, pp. 256–265, 2011.

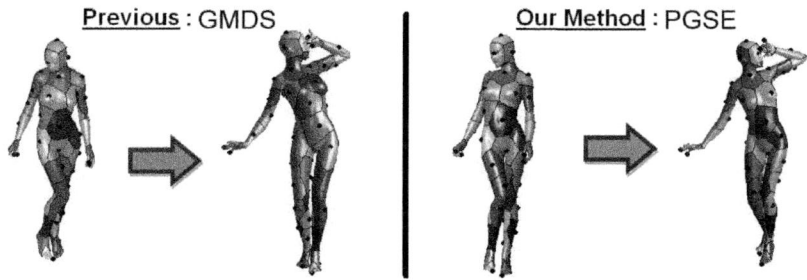

Fig. 1. Local optima in a combinatorial optimization problem for matching objects varying in pose and shape. Previous work, Generalized Multi-Dimensional Scaling (GMDS) [5], relies only on the preservation of geodesic distances and can yield non-meaningful correspondences; e.g. the chest of the body in the left pose is mapped to the back of the body in the right pose (corresponding regions are shown with the same color). Our method, Probabilistic Geodesic Surface Embedding (PGSE), achieves more intuitive results by combining geodesic distances with local surface descriptors in a coarse-to-fine probabilistic optimization framework.

of a false match. In addition, matching two objects entails solving a combinatorial problem in the exponential space of possible pairwise correspondences. Such an optimization may get stuck in local optima resulting in non-meaningful correspondences. Figure 1 shows an example of non-meaningful correspondences produced by related work, Generalized Multi-Dimensional Scaling (GMDS) [5], where the chest is mapped to the back of the human model and vice versa. This effect is significantly diminished using our method, Probabilistic Geodesic Surface Embedding (PGSE).

Previous methods for matching nonrigid deformable objects with significant variation in pose aim at providing global consistency of correspondences by preserving intrinsic properties of the objects. Usually these methods find deformation-invariant representations of the objects and match the objects in the representation domain. Examples include the use of geodesic distances [5], diffusion distances [6] or representations in the Möbius domain [13].

Although preservation of the intrinsic properties of the objects may be sufficient to assess their similarity, intrinsic-only matching criteria are oblivious to object self-symmetries and may yield non-meaningful correspondences. To overcome this weakness, previous work has explored the use of local surface properties and/or costs of surface deformation. Previous local surfaces properties are either geometric or based on the intrinsic characteristics of the shape or both. For instance, the work in [2] uses oriented histograms describing the distribution of points in local neighborhoods along the object surface (spin images [11]). Dubrovina *et al.* [7] use a local surface descriptor based on the eigenvalues of the Laplace-Beltrami operator which is related to the flow in the mesh representation of the object. Wang *et al.* [16] use descriptors based on curvature and surface normals targeted towards a specific class of surfaces (brain surfaces). Efforts that also take into account object deformation include [10], [18].

Most previous work considers pose variations of the same object. To the best of our knowledge, only the work in [18] considers variations in shape, but the objects to be matched do not have significant differences in pose. We are concerned with finding correspondences among objects of the same category varying in shape, pose, and resolution. Extending previous approaches for global matching, we rely on preserving normalized geodesic distances to account for the additional variation in shape. We also employ a probabilistic framework for optimization similar to the one in [2]. We enforce stricter geodesic preservation constraints and use alternative local surface descriptors that are invariant to shape, pose, and resolution variations.

Our main contributions can be summarized as follows:

- A method for finding surface point correspondences of a non-rigid object undergoing significant deformation due to *pose* and *shape* variation.
- A method for finding surface point correspondences between objects differing in global/local *resolution* and triangulation, containing up to a small proportion of holes.
- Correspondence search that effectively explores the space of possible correspondences and is more robust to local optima than previous work. It relies on a discriminative probabilistic model that preserves properties related to geodesic distances and uses loopy belief propagation (LBP) for inference.

2   Probabilistic Geodesic Surface Embedding

We consider the problem of finding correspondences between two triangular meshes, a model mesh X and a data mesh Z. The *model mesh* $X = (V^X, E^X)$ is a complete surface consisting of a set of vertices $V^X = (x_1, \ldots, x_{N^X})$ and a set of edges E^X. The *data mesh* $Z = (V^Z, E^Z)$ may contain a modest number of holes (missing data); the vertices and edges are $V^Z = (z_1, \ldots, z_{N^Z})$ and E^Z respectively. Typically the data and model meshes differ in shape, pose, and resolution. Each data mesh vertex $z_k, k = 1, \ldots, N^Z$ is associated with a *correspondence variable* $c_k \in \{1, \ldots, N^X\}$ that specifies the model mesh vertex it corresponds to. The task of finding correspondences is one of estimating the most likely set of all correspondence variables $C = (c_1, \ldots, c_{N^Z})$ given a specific pair of model and data meshes X, Z.

2.1   Probabilistic Model

We cast the problem of finding correspondences as one of finding the most likely embedding of the data mesh Z into the model mesh X encoded as an assignment to all correspondence variables $C = (c_1, \ldots, c_{N^Z})$. More specifically we take a discriminative approach where our goal is to find a configuration of C that maximizes the distribution $p(C|X, Z)$ over all correspondence variables conditioned on a pair of mesh instances X, Z. Writing this distribution as an undirected graphical model, we get the Conditional Random Field (CRF) model depicted in Figure 2. Each latent variable node in the model denotes the correspondence

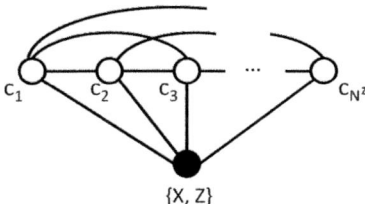

{X, Z}

Fig. 2. Conditional Random Field (CRF) model for finding correspondences. The observed variable in the model is a pair of a model mesh $X = (V^X, E^X)$ and a data mesh $Z = (V^Z, E^Z)$. The latent variables are the correspondence variables $C = (c_1, \ldots, c_{N^Z})$ of all data mesh vertices. Edges in the model between latent and observed variables favor correspondences that preserve the intrinsic properties of the data mesh vertices. Geodesic constraints between all possible pairs of correspondence variables are enforced through the edges between latent variables.

variable c_k of vertex z_k, $k = 1, \ldots, N^Z$, in the data mesh. The observed variable is a pair of model and data meshes X, Z.

We *approximate* the conditional distribution of the correspondence variables using potential functions, ψ, linking all *pairs* of latent variables and unary potentials, ϕ, linking each latent variable with the data. Formally we approximate the conditional distribution as: $p(C|X, Z) \propto \prod_k \phi(c_k, X, Z) \prod_{k,l} \psi(c_k, c_l, X, Z)$.

The main idea behind our approach is that the geodesic distances between points in the data mesh Z should be the same as the geodesic distances between the corresponding points in the model mesh X. Our method searches for correspondences that satisfy this property. At the same time we want to preserve in the embedding the intrinsic geodesic properties (geodesic signature) of the data mesh vertices. All the abovementioned constraints are enforced using the potentials described below.

Pairwise geodesic potential $\psi(c_k, c_l, X, Z)$: We consider normalized geodesic distances as the invariant used to match meshes that deform non-rigidly due to changes in shape and pose. We calculate exact geodesic distances using the the Fast Marching method described in [12]. For each pair of data mesh vertices z_k, z_l, we define a potential function $\psi(c_k, c_l, X, Z)$ that constrains the pair of correspondences c_k, c_l in the model mesh X to be geodesically consistent with vertices z_k, z_l in the data mesh Z. Let $M = (V, E)$ be a mesh with vertices V and edges E and $h : V \times V \to \Re$ be a geodesic distance function. Then $h(j, m; M)$ represents the normalized geodesic distance between two vertices j and m in mesh M. The normalization is done by dividing the geodesic distance by the maximum geodesic distance over all pairs of vertices in M. The geodesic potential between a pair of data mesh vertices z_k, z_l is defined as

$$\psi(c_k, c_l, X, Z) = N(h(c_k, c_l; X); h(k, l; Z), \sigma_{kl}^2) \tag{1}$$

where σ_{kl} is a user defined parameter; here $\sigma_{kl} = 0.1 \cdot h(k, l; Z)$.

Geodesic signature potential $\phi(c_k, X, Z)$: We encode a potential that enforces that corresponding vertices c_k in the model mesh have similar intrinsic properties as those in the data mesh z_k. Our goal is to distinguish spatially different areas in the model and data meshes as much as possible. The intrinsic property we use is the mean normalized geodesic distance of vertex z_k over all possible vertices in the data mesh (geodesic signature). The resulting potential can be written as

$$\phi(c_k, X, Z) = N(g(c_k; X); g(k; Z), \sigma_k^2) \tag{2}$$

where $g(j; M = (V, E)) = \frac{1}{|V|} \sum_{m \in V} h(j, m; M)$ is the mean normalized geodesic distance from j to all other vertices m in the mesh M and σ_k is a user defined parameter. The use of geodesic signatures is important because it biases the embedding of the data mesh to the model mesh to match spatially similar areas between the meshes. In practice we observe that this also improves convergence of the optimization procedure described below.

2.2 Inference

Our goal is to find an assignment of the correspondence variables that maximizes the probability $p(C|X, Z)$ as represented by the graphical model. Exact inference is computationally infeasible due to the large number of variables and loops in the graph. Instead we use max-product *loopy belief propagation* (LBP) [17] for approximate inference. Running LBP until convergence yields a set of probabilities over model mesh vertices for each correspondence variable c_k. We compute the optimal correspondence for each data mesh vertex z_k as the model mesh vertex that maximizes the probability distribution of the correspondence variable c_k.

Our inference scheme is performed in two rounds as shown in Figure 3. In the first round, the data mesh is sampled at a coarse level (Figure 3 (a)) using the farthest point sampling method [8]. In a similar way, the model mesh is sampled at a coarse level (Figure 3 (b)) and an initial set of correspondences is obtained using LBP. In the second round, the initial correspondences are refined by restricting the domain for each correspondence variable to be geodesically close to the solution of the first round of inference (Figure 3 (d)). Here we restrict the search to vertices with a geodesic distance up to $1/2$ the average geodesic distance between nearby samples in the model mesh. The complexity of each round is $O(K^2 L^2)$ where K is the number of samples in the data mesh and L the number of corresponding samples in the model mesh.

3 Results

3.1 Data

We evaluate our algorithm on triangular meshes from the TOSCA nonrigid world database [4] and human bodies generated using the SCAPE model [1]. All the objects are represented as triangular meshes and they are simplified to have

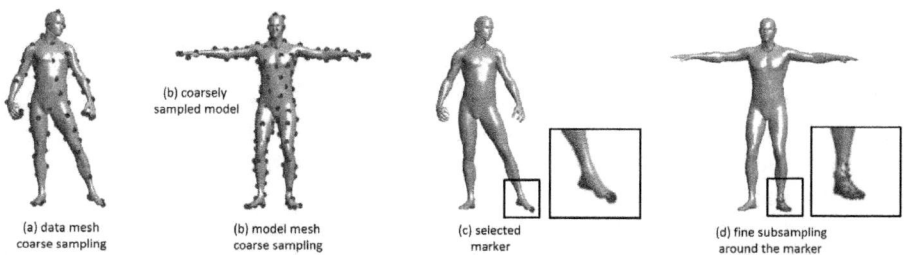

Fig. 3. Illustration of the sampling process during the inference procedure. In the first round, a data mesh and a model mesh are sampled at a coarse level. A coarse sampling of the data mesh to e.g. 75 markers (a) and a coarse sampling of the model mesh to e.g. 150 samples (b) produce an initial set of correspondences. In the second round, for each individual marker in the data mesh (c), the domain of possible correspondences is obtained from finer sampling around the solution found in the first round (d).

2000-4000 vertices to aid comparison with related work. For each pair of meshes we find correspondences of 75-100 surface points. For the following experiments our method requires around 5GB of RAM per pair of meshes. The running time is approximately 1h on a 2.66GHz Intel Xeon processor.

3.2   Evaluation

The meshes we use do not come with any ground truth information about correspondences between their vertices. Typical error metrics in this case measure the degree that geodesic distances are preserved between the data mesh and the model mesh. However, preservation of geodesic distances does not ensure that the correspondences are qualitatively meaningful. The smaller the number of markers used and the larger the number of self-symmetries in the object, the larger the number of possible correspondence configurations with geodesic distances similar to the geodesic distances between data mesh markers. We find that comparing Voronoi regions around the markers and their optimal correspondences provides a more intuitive measure than comparing the degree in which geodesic distances have been preserved. Similar Voronoi regions between the data and model meshes also lead to similar geodesic distances among markers and their optimal correspondences. The opposite is not necessarily true. Comparing Voronoi regions does not only include how well the geodesic distances are preserved, but also how similar the neighborhoods around markers and their optimal correspondences are.

Let $v_s(i)$ be the area of the Voronoi region around marker i and $v_m(c_i^*)$ the area of the Voronoi region around the optimal correspondence c_i^* of marker i in the model. We define the following error metric, T_e, representing the average change in the Voronoi area over all markers and their correspondences.

$$T_e = \frac{1}{|U|} \sum_{i \in U} \left| \frac{v_s(i) - v_m(c_i^*)}{v_s(i)} \right| \tag{3}$$

where U is the set of markers in the data mesh.

Correspondences in Meshes with Same Topology. We compare our method, PGSE, to the GMDS method presented in [5] using triangular meshes of the same topology. For each object in the TOSCA nonrigid world database, we find correspondences to the canonical object of the category it belongs to. For the SCAPE bodies, we find correspondences between the mean SCAPE body in the canonical pose as defined in the CAESAR dataset [14] and SCAPE bodies varying in pose, shape, and pose and shape together.

Figure 4(a) illustrates the correspondences found with GMDS and PGSE. Evaluating the correspondences using the error metric defined above, we get the error plots shown in Figures 4(b, c, d). For the parameterized bodies generated using the SCAPE model, we sort the results based on pose or shape variation. Pose variation is measured as the average joint angle deviation from the joint angle configuration in the canonical pose. It is weighted by the percentage of mesh vertices each joint controls and it is measured in radians. Shape variation is measured based on the L2-norm of the shape coefficients in the SCAPE model. Given the variety of categories in the TOSCA nonrigid world database, we present only summary statistics of the error over the database. For the case of PGSE, the average T_e error is 0.1410 with standard deviation 0.1059. For the case of GMDS, the average T_e error is 0.2799 with standard deviation 0.1564.

In all cases we see that the error increases as we vary the pose or the shape. Although not reported with error metrics, GMDS performs better on average at preserving geodesic distances; this is not surprising as the GMDS method minimizes exactly this error. In contrast, our method combines the preservation of geodesic distances with local shape matching constraints. Our approach, PGSE, performs better in terms of the maximum discrepancy in geodesic distances between pairs of markers and their correspondences. Evaluating the correspondences using the T_e error (Figure 4), we see that PGSE performs better in all cases. Statistical significance values for the errors per dataset are shown in Table 4(e). Changing the pose yields a bigger increase in the mean error than changing the shape. Changing both shape and pose yields the biggest increase in error as expected.

Correspondences in Meshes with Different Topology. Next we evaluate the effects of changing the global and local resolution of the triangulated meshes used above. We use QSLIM [9] to change the global resolution of the meshes generated based on the SCAPE model and we observe an almost uniform reduction in resolution across the surface of the SCAPE bodies. In this case, we find no significant difference in performance between GMDS and PGSE as a function of mesh resolution.

Often one wants to align an artist-generated template mesh with higher-resolution meshes created by a laser scanner or other structured light system. In this case the meshes have very different topology and resolution. Consequently we find correspondences between the SCAPE bodies varying in shape and pose as above and a custom made template mesh shown as the right mesh in Figure 5 (a). This template mesh exhibits significant differences in local resolution and topology compared with the SCAPE bodies. We are unable to quantitatively evaluate GMDS because in most cases the markers collapse to the same vertex

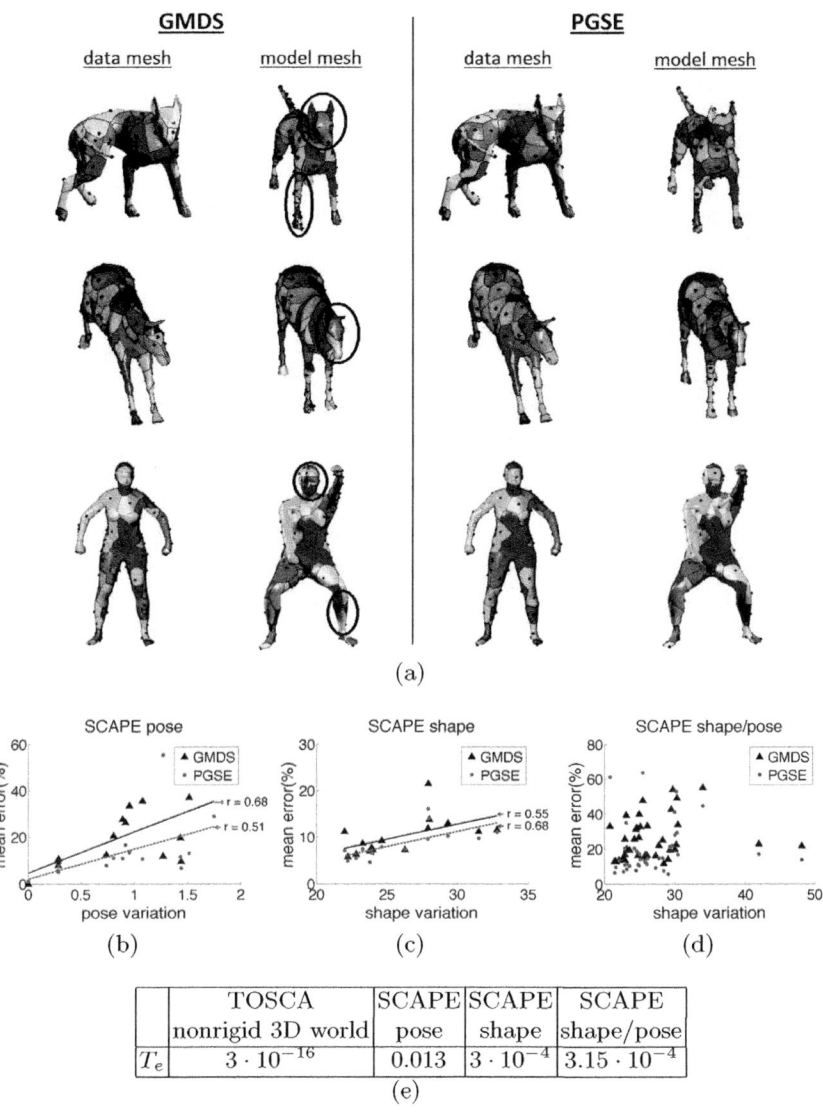

Fig. 4. (a) Visual correspondences between meshes in the TOSCA nonrigid world database and SCAPE bodies varying in pose and/or shape. Corresponding areas are shown with the same color. Areas where our method, PGSE, performs better than GMDS are circled. Note that correspondences are defined up to intrinsic symmetries in the meshes. (b) Mean Voronoi error plot for the SCAPE bodies varying in pose, (c) shape, and (d) pose and shape. The data points in figures (c,d) are ordered based on shape variation. Table (e) shows the results of the Wilcoxon signed rank test on the errors induced by the GMDS, PGSE correspondences. All the p-values displayed in the table are below the default significance level of 5%.

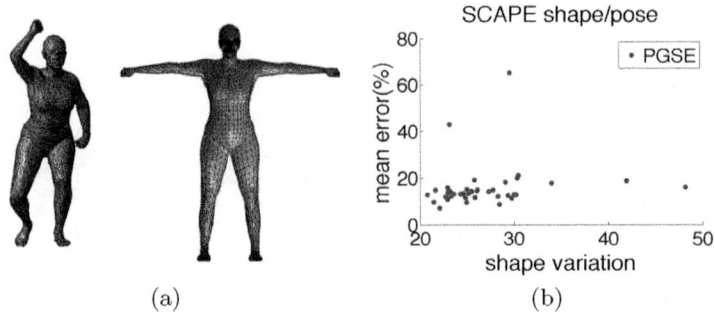

(a)   (b)

Fig. 5. (a) An example pair of meshes with significant differences in local resolution and mesh topology: a SCAPE body and our template mesh. (b) Mean Voronoi-based error for correspondences between the SCAPE bodies varying in shape & pose and the template. To simplify visualization the SCAPE bodies are ordered only based on shape variation. A Voronoi-based error cannot be defined for the case of GMDS due to markers collapsing at the same vertex.

on the data mesh surface resulting in Voronoi regions with zero area. In contrast, we observe that even large differences in local resolution between the surface of the data and model meshes does not influence the performance of our algorithm (the error in Figure 5 (b) is similar to the error in Figure 4 (d)) .

4   Conclusions

We present a method that finds correspondences between non-rigid articulated objects varying in pose, shape, and global or local resolution. Our method preserves pairwise normalized geodesic distances between a pair of objects as well as local surface properties also based on geodesic distances. We show improved correspondence over previous work on widely varying mesh models. Additionally using the SCAPE model we are able to separately evaluate accuracy as a function of pose, shape, and resolution variation. We also define a Voronoi-based error measure that better measures correspondences that are intuitively "good." Future work involves making our method robust to noisy surfaces as well as surfaces with missing information. Learning the parameters of our CRF model from training data is another direction for future work.

Acknowledgements. This work was supported by the Office of Naval Research under contract W911QY-10-C-0172.

References

1. Anguelov, D., Srinivasan, P., Koller, D., Thrun, S., Rodgers, J., Davis, J.: Scape: shape completion and animation of people. ACM Transactions on Graphics (TOG) 24(3), 408–416 (2005)
2. Anguelov, D., Srinivasan, P., Pang, H., Koller, D., Thrun, S., Davis, J.: The correlated correspondence algorithm for unsupervised registration of nonrigid surfaces. In: Advances in Neural Information Processing Systems 17: Proceedings of the 2004 Conference, p. 33. The MIT Press, Cambridge (2005)

3. Besl, P., McKay, N.: A method for registration of 3-D shapes. IEEE Transactions on Pattern Analysis and Machine Intelligence, 239–256 (1992)
4. Bronstein, A., Bronstein, M., Bronstein, M., Kimmel, R.: Numerical geometry of non-rigid shapes. Springer-Verlag New York Inc., Secaucus (2008)
5. Bronstein, A., Bronstein, M., Kimmel, R.: Generalized Multidimensional Scaling: a framework for isometry-invariant partial surface matching. Proceedings of the National Academy of Sciences of the United States of America 103(5), 1168 (2006)
6. Bronstein, A., Bronstein, M., Kimmel, R., Mahmoudi, M., Sapiro, G.: A Gromov-Hausdorff framework with diffusion geometry for topologically-robust non-rigid shape matching. International Journal of Computer Vision 89(2), 266–286 (2010)
7. Dubrovina, A., Kimmel, R.: Matching shapes by eigendecomposition of the Laplace-Beltrami operator. In: Proc. 3DPVT, vol. 2 (2010)
8. Eldar, Y., Lindenbaum, M., Porat, M., Zeevi, Y.Y.: The farthest point strategy for progressive image sampling. IEEE Transactions on Image Processing 6(9), 1305–1315 (2002)
9. Garland, M., Heckbert, P.: Surface simplification using quadric error metrics. In: Proceedings of the 24th Annual Conference on Computer Graphics and Interactive Techniques, pp. 209–216. ACM Press/Addison-Wesley Publishing Co. (1997)
10. Huang, Q., Adams, B., Wicke, M., Guibas, L.: Non-rigid registration under isometric deformations. In: Proceedings of the Symposium on Geometry Processing, pp. 1449–1457. Eurographics Association (2008)
11. Johnson, A.E., Hebert, M.: Using spin images for efficient object recognition in cluttered 3D scenes. IEEE Transactions on Pattern Analysis and Machine Intelligence 21(5), 433–449 (2002)
12. Kimmel, R., Sethian, J.: Computing geodesic paths on manifolds. Proceedings of the National Academy of Sciences of the United States of America 95(15), 8431 (1998)
13. Lipman, Y., Funkhouser, T.: Möbius voting for surface correspondence. ACM Transactions on Graphics (TOG) 28(3), 1–12 (2009)
14. Robinette, K., Daanen, H., Paquet, E.: The caesar project: a 3-d surface anthropometry survey. In: Proceedings of Second International Conference on 3-D Digital Imaging and Modeling, pp. 380–386. IEEE, Los Alamitos (1999)
15. Rusinkiewicz, S., Levoy, M.: Efficient variants of the ICP algorithm. In: 3dim, p. 145. IEEE Computer Society, Los Alamitos (2001)
16. Wang, Y., Peterson, B., Staib, L.: 3d brain surface matching based on geodesics and local geometry. Computer Vision and Image Understanding 89(2-3), 252–271 (2003)
17. Yedidia, J., Freeman, W., Weiss, Y.: Understanding Belief Propagation and its generalizations. Exploring Artificial Intelligence in the New Millennium 8, 236–239 (2003)
18. Zhang, H., Sheffer, A., Cohen-Or, D., Zhou, Q., Van Kaick, O., Tagliasacchi, A.: Deformation-Driven Shape Correspondence. In: Computer Graphics Forum, vol. 27, pp. 1431–1439. Wiley Online Library, Chichester (2008)

Dense 3D Reconstruction of Symmetric Scenes from a Single Image

Kevin Köser, Christopher Zach, and Marc Pollefeys

Computer Vision and Geometry Group, ETH Zürich
Universitätsstrasse 6, 8092 Zürich, Switzerland
{kevin.koeser,chzach,marc.pollefeys}@inf.ethz.ch

Abstract. A system is presented that takes a single image as an input (e.g. showing the interior of St.Peter's Basilica) and automatically detects an arbitrarily oriented symmetry plane in 3D space. Given this symmetry plane a second camera is hallucinated that serves as a virtual second image for dense 3D reconstruction, where the point of view for reconstruction can be chosen on the symmetry plane. This naturally creates a symmetry in the matching costs for dense stereo. Alternatively, we also show how to enforce the 3D symmetry in dense depth estimation for the original image. The two representations are qualitatively compared on several real world images, that also validate our fully automatic approach for dense single image reconstruction.

1 Introduction

Symmetry is a key design principle in man-made structures and it is also frequently present in nature. Quite some effort has been spent to detect or exploit symmetry in computer vision (e.g. [6,11,14,4,20,9,2,3]). Unlike previous researchers, in this contribution we investigate how 3D symmetry can be exploited to *automatically* obtain a *dense* three-dimensional perception of some scene from a single image, in particular when the scene is symmetric with respect to some virtual symmetry plane. The intuition is that when the observer is not exactly in this symmetry plane, then each object and its symmetric counterpart are seen from a (slightly) different perspective. These two different perspectives onto essentially the same thing can be exploited as in standard two-view stereo to obtain a dense, three-dimensional model (see fig. 1). The key steps are essentially comparable to structure from motion [13], however we run the whole pipeline on a single image, where we assume the intrinsic camera parameters to be known beforehand: Within-image feature matching, robust estimation of autoepipolar geometry and symmetry plane followed by dense depth estimation. Our key contributions are a novel, straight-forward 3D formulation of the single image symmetry scenario which is analog to multi-image structure from motion, a single-texture plane-sweep for a symmetric viewpoint to create a cost volume, and enforcing 3D symmetry in the global optimization by equality constraints in the minimum-surface formulation. The next section will relate this contribution to previous work, before the following sections detail the steps of the approach.

R. Mester and M. Felsberg (Eds.): DAGM 2011, LNCS 6835, pp. 266–275, 2011.
© Springer-Verlag Berlin Heidelberg 2011

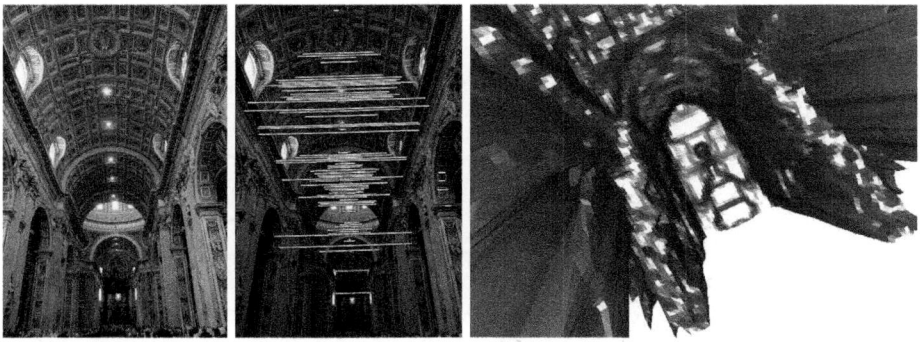

Fig. 1. From left to right: Input image taken at St.Peter's Basilica, detected symmetry (lines connecting features), some rendered oblique view of a very coarse, untextured but shaded model, reconstructed from the single image

2   Previous Work

Previous work related to this contribution can roughly be divided into two categories. The first category describes the general ideas of symmetry exploitation and uses interactive techniques like clicking correspondences or works on restricted scenarios. Gordon [6] seems to be the first to have described the idea of shape from symmetry, later Mitsumoto et al. consider mirrors [11]. Much later, also [4] considers symmetric scene geometry but seems to be unaware of Gordon's work. In terms of dense reconstruction, Shimshoni et al. show interesting results on reconstructing textureless, lambertian objects [14], but they assume a weak perspective camera, horizontal symmetry and a single light source. Their iterative approach starts from a rough estimate of the light source and symmetry plane to optimize normals and scene parameters using shape-from-shading. In other works, geometric relations using planar mirrors have been considered (e.g. [5]) or silhouette-based reconstruction therein [20].

The second category of approaches is concerned about automatic *detection* of symmetry. Here, with the advances of automatic matching, feature-based estimation of planar homologies present in symmetry and repetition (e.g. [15]) became possible, also with non-fronto-parallel planes. In terms of 2D symmetry, Loy and Eklundh [9], observed that SIFT features[8] can either be extracted on mirrored regions or that the SIFT descriptor itself can be rearranged for in-image matching to find mirrored features. Detection was then extended by Cornelius et al. [2,3] to planar but non-frontal scenes. Wu et al. [16] detected and reconstruct repetitions on rectified planar facades with relief structures. For more details on computational symmetry, we refer to the recent survey paper by Liu et al. [17].

In general, we observe that there is no fully automatic approach to reconstruct a dense, textured 3D model from a single image showing a symmetric scene, which we show in this contribution. Furthermore, we give a novel, clear derivation of the geometry of the symmetric scene which nicely shows the duality of interpreting an image point as being the projection of a reflected point

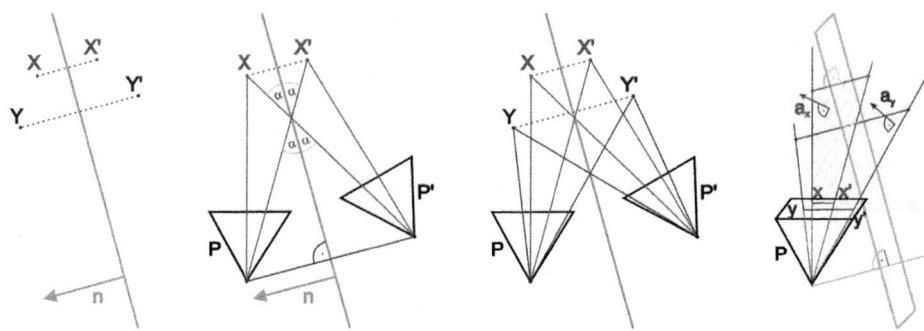

Fig. 2. Left: Reflection of points on a plane with normal n according to equation 2. Center images: dual interpretation of mirrored point and mirrored camera of equation 3. Right: normal constraint of eq.6: the normal n must lie in all backprojection planes of symmetry correspondences.

in one camera or the projection of the original point in a "reflected" camera. Finally, we obtain a dense reconstruction that particularly enforces consistent depth for symmetric points. Posing the depth estimation as a labeling problem, we show how to integrate symmetry as equality constraints into a voxel-based (continuous) minimum-cut. The symmetry of the scene allows to compute depth with respect to a central view on the symmetry plane or for the original image, where we compare advantages and drawbacks for both solutions.

3   Symmetric Scene Geometry

In this contribution we focus on symmetric scenes, i.e. scenes with a global symmetry plane so that for each point X on one side of the plane there is a corresponding 3D point X' on the opposite side of the plane.

It is easy to see that the image X'_e of a Euclidian 3D point X_e given a mirror plane with normal n through the origin can be obtained by

$$X'_e = X_e - 2(n^\mathsf{T} X_e)n = \left(I_3 - 2nn^\mathsf{T}\right) X_e \qquad (1)$$

Now consider that the symmetry plane can have an arbitrary position (not necessarily going through the origin, but by passing it at distance d) and it is expressed in homogeneous coordinates as $\pi = \left(n^\mathsf{T} \quad - d\right)$. A reflection by this plane (see figure 2, left image) can then be written linearly in homogeneous coordinates as

$$X' = \underbrace{\begin{pmatrix} I_3 - 2nn^\mathsf{T} & -2dn \\ 0_3^\mathsf{T} & 1 \end{pmatrix}}_{M_\pi} X \qquad (2)$$

Here, M_π is a projective transformation that encodes the mirroring.

Consider now a (intrinsically calibrated) camera observing the point $\mathbf{X}$ at image position $\mathbf{x} \simeq \mathsf{P}\mathbf{X}$, where we assume P being the canonic camera at the origin and looking into positive z-direction (cf. to [7]): $\mathsf{P} = (I_3 \; \mathbf{0}_3)$. It will observe the mirrored point $\mathbf{X}'$ at $\mathbf{x}' \simeq \mathsf{P}\mathbf{X}'$, which can also be written using M_π as

$$\mathbf{x}' \simeq \overbrace{\mathsf{P} \cdot \mathsf{M}_\pi}^{\mathsf{P}'} \cdot \underbrace{\mathbf{X}}_{\mathbf{X}'} \tag{3}$$

This equation shows a duality of possible interpretations: M can be absorbed into the projection matrix, defining a new camera that observes an image with $\mathbf{x}$ and $\mathbf{x}'$ swapped, or, M can be absorbed into the point to project the mirrored point (see figure 2, center images). In case we absorb it into the mirrored camera we obtain the 3×4 projection matrix

$$\mathsf{P}' = \mathsf{P}\mathsf{M}_\pi = (I_3 \; \mathbf{0}_3) \begin{pmatrix} I_3 - 2\boldsymbol{n}\boldsymbol{n}^\mathsf{T} & -2d\boldsymbol{n} \\ \mathbf{0}_3^\mathsf{T} & 1 \end{pmatrix} = \begin{pmatrix} \underbrace{I_3 - 2\boldsymbol{n}\boldsymbol{n}^\mathsf{T}}_{\mathsf{S}} & -2d\boldsymbol{n} \end{pmatrix} \tag{4}$$

Please note that S is an orthogonal 3×3-matrix with determinant -1 (not a rotation matrix), however P' is still a valid projection matrix. If we compute the essential matrix between P' and P (or between the image and itself) we obtain

$$\mathsf{E} \simeq [\boldsymbol{n}]_\times \left(I_3 - 2\boldsymbol{n}\boldsymbol{n}^\mathsf{T}\right) \simeq [\boldsymbol{n}]_\times \tag{5}$$

which is *autoepipolar* [7].

4   Estimating the Symmetry Plane

Obtaining Correspondences. Since the goal is to recover the symmetry plane in three-dimensional scenes, local regions and their symmetric counterparts may look significantly different. In fact, since perspective effects and illumination differences may appear (depending on the distance of the camera to the symmetry plane and depending on illumination and scene normals), this is a wide-baseline matching problem. Similar to previous authors, who were looking for symmetry only in 2D[9] or on planes [3,2], we exploit the fact that local affine features (cf. to [10] for an overview) locally compensate for perspective effects. Since classical shape + dominant orientation normalization (cf. to [8]) does not allow for general affine transformation but only for those with positive determinant (reflections are not compensated by this), for each feature we explicitly extract also a mirrored descriptor as proposed by [9][1]. Then we find within image correspondences between mirrored and non-mirrored descriptors according to proximity in descriptor space.

---

[1] If speed is not a concern, just mirroring the whole image along any direction, extracting features and re-assigning descriptors to the coordinates in the original image is sufficient.

Symmetry Plane Normal. By definition we know that the line connecting a point X and its symmetric counterpart X' is in direction of the symmetry plane normal (as long as X is not on the symmetry plane and thus identical to X'). The plane that is spanned by the camera center and the two viewing rays to the two 3D points contains also this line and consequently the symmetry plane's normal vector must lie in this plane (compare figure 2, right image). Let $(\mathbf{x}, \mathbf{x}')$ be a pair of corresponding (symmetric) features. Then

$$\underbrace{\left([\mathbf{x}']_\times \mathbf{x}\right)^\mathsf{T}}_{\mathbf{a_x}} \boldsymbol{n} = 0 \tag{6}$$

If we use a second correspondence $(\mathbf{y}, \mathbf{y}')$ then the analogue constraint must hold and consequently $\boldsymbol{n}$ has to lie in the null space of the matrix composed of the rows $\mathbf{a}_i$:

$$\begin{pmatrix} \mathbf{a_x} \\ \mathbf{a_y} \end{pmatrix} \boldsymbol{n} = 0 \tag{7}$$

Obviously, $\boldsymbol{n} \simeq \mathbf{a_x} \times \mathbf{a_y}$ fulfills this equation. This is a minimal solution to the 3D symmetry normal from 2 points, which is essentially the same as estimating the epipole for autoepipolar matrices or a vanishing point from images of parallel line segments (cf. to [7]). Please note that this is similar in spirit to [3], however we explicitly write it down for 3D scenes.

Since points on the symmetry plane do not provide constraints, we reject all correspondences with less than 10% image width displacement and apply 2-point RANSAC with the above minimal solver to estimate the symmetry plane normal. Afterwards we apply maximum likelihood estimation for the normal as common also for standard vanishing point estimation approaches [7].

Camera Geometry. Since we are aiming at dense stereo, some baseline is required to reconstruct the scene geometry. We will now construct a second virtual camera to perform the stereo. Assume for now that the original image has not been taken from exactly inside the symmetry plane. Then, since image-based reconstructions are only up to scale, we can define the baseline of our to cameras to be 2. However, since $\boldsymbol{n}$ and $-\boldsymbol{n}$ are projectively equivalent, there are still two options for the second camera center that need to be resolved, e.g. by checking in which of the configurations the correspondences are in front of the cameras.

As explained in equation 4, we know that a camera with the projection matrix P' would observe an image with coordinates of $\mathbf{x}$ and $\mathbf{x}'$ swapped. This camera can be converted to a more intuitive right-handed representation by multiplying the projection matrix by -1, subsequent $\mathsf{K}, R, \boldsymbol{C}$-decomposition (this camera is then looking away) and appropriate rotation, e.g. to obtain a rectified standard stereo setup. However, we decided for a more direct approach and use the (left-handed) P' directly in plane-sweep stereo.

We observe that the proposed approach fails in case the camera center is on the symmetry plane, which corresponds to the case of no baseline in standard stereo. Being close to the symmetry plane means only small baseline and potentially only a few measurable disparity steps.

5 Dense Depth Estimation

Dense Stereo and Plane-Sweep. Beside using a rectified configuration for dense stereo computation, there are two natural choices for the reference frame used to represent the depth map. Both approaches are based on the plane-sweep methodology. Note that the image to use for the mirrored view is exactly the original image, since symmetric 3D points are treated as the same 3D point by construction. Thus, no additional image has to be synthesized for the mirrored camera.

The first option is to utilize a virtual view between the original and the mirrored camera residing on the mirror plane (see Fig. 3(a)). A fronto-parallel plane sweep approach for stereo with respect to this central view is similar to computational stereo after image rectification, but in this setting both matching images are moving in horizontal direction. This setup has a few advantages, but one major disadvantage. First, by using a symmetric matching score (i.e. symmetric with respect to swapping image patches), and if a symmetric smoothness term is utilized, then the result depth map is naturally symmetric without explicit enforcement. Second, the central view configuration usually minimizes the perspective distortion when using larger aggregation windows for the matching score, since the plane of symmetry is often orthogonal to the surface of manmade objects. Thus, fronto-parallel planes with respect to the central camera tend to be aligned with surface elements leading to better matching scores. The disadvantage of the central reference view configuration is, that there is no fixed reference image unaffected by the current depth hypothesis, and therefore one pixel (or patch) e.g. in the left (original) image may match several pixels/patches in the mirrored view. This leads to noticeable artefacts induced especially by textureless regions (see Fig. 4(b) and (c)).

The other natural configuration uses the original camera as reference view, and the mirrored camera as matching image (see Fig. 3(b)). The symmetry of the 3D geometry induced by the resulting depth map is lost, and must be explicitly

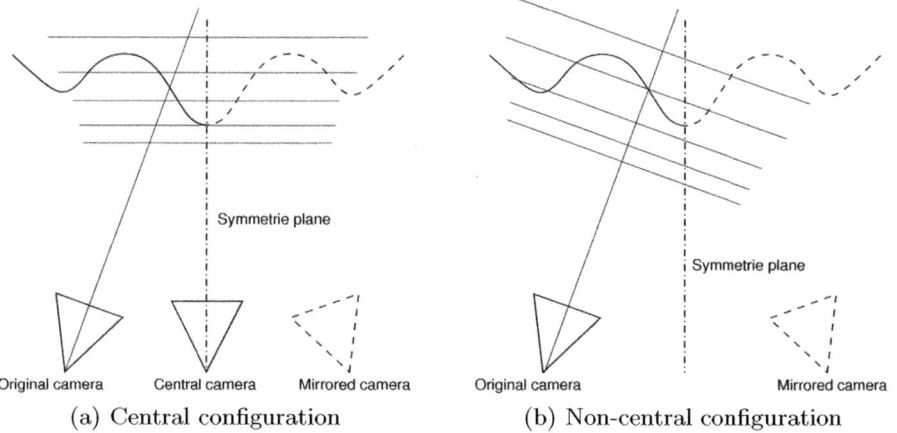

(a) Central configuration   (b) Non-central configuration

Fig. 3. The two setups used for dense depth estimation via plane sweep

enforced if desired. Since in this configuration the symmetry requirement of the reconstructed object cannot easily be formulated in terms of the resulting depth map, global methods for depth map computation are difficult to extend with symmetry constraints. We utilize the globally optimal stereo method based on finding the minimum-cost surface separating a near plane from a far plane in 3D [1,12,18]. In the following section we describe, how 3D symmetry constraints can be incorporated into a class of global stereo methods.

Global Stereo with Symmetry Constraints. The basic model for globally optimal stereo is

$$E(u) = \int_{\Omega \times \mathcal{L}} \phi(\nabla u) \, dx \, dl,$$

where $u : \Omega \times \mathcal{L} \to \{0,1\}$ represents the sublevel function of the desired label assignment $\Lambda : \Omega \to \mathcal{L}$. ϕ is a family of positively 1-homogeneous functions implicitly indexed by grid positions $(x,l) \in \Omega \times \mathcal{L}$. In order to avoid the trivial solution $u \equiv 0$ we fix the boundaries, $u(x,0) = 0$ and $u(x,L) = 1$.

Each grid position (x,l) (i.e. a camera ray with an associated depth label) corresponds to a point X in 3D space. Thus, u can be interpreted as 3D occupancy function whether a voxel corresponding to (x,l) is filled $(u(x,l) = 1)$ or empty $(u(x,l) = 0)$. Knowing that the object to be modeled is symmetric with respect to a mirror plane $n^\top X = 1$, implies that both 3D locations X and its reflection $X' = (I - 2nn^\top)X + 2n$ are either occupied or empty, i.e. have the same state. The constraints can be translated to a set of equality constraints for corresponding locations in the domain $\Omega \times \mathcal{L}$, $u(x,l) = u(x',l')$ for $((x,l),(x',l')) \in C$. Here C is a set of corresponding locations within the viewing frustum.

Overall the depth labeling task can be written as (after relaxing the binary constraint $u(x) \in \{0,1\}$ to $u(x) \in [0,1]$)

$$E(u) = \int_{\Omega \times \mathcal{L}} \phi(\nabla u) \, dx \, dl,$$

subject to $u(x,l) \in [0,1]$, $u(x,0) = 0$, $u(x,L) = 1$, and $u(x,l) = u(x',l')$ for $((x,l),(x',l')) \in C$. This is a non-smooth convex problem. On a discrete grid and with ϕ being a weighted L^1 norm this can be solved with a graph cut method [1]. The additional equality constraints can be enforced by infinite links between the respective nodes in the graph (and therefore both sites have to be on the same side of the cut). Using similar arguments as in [19] it can be shown that u attains essentially binary values also in the case of general positively 1-homogeneous functions ϕ.

Implementation Details. We utilize the L^1 difference between 5×5 pixel patches of Sobel-filtered images as our image matching score. Consequently, pixel brightness differences due to shading effects are largely addressed by this choice of the similarity function. We increase the robustness of the matching score by truncating its value to a maximum of 5 (with respect to normalized pixel

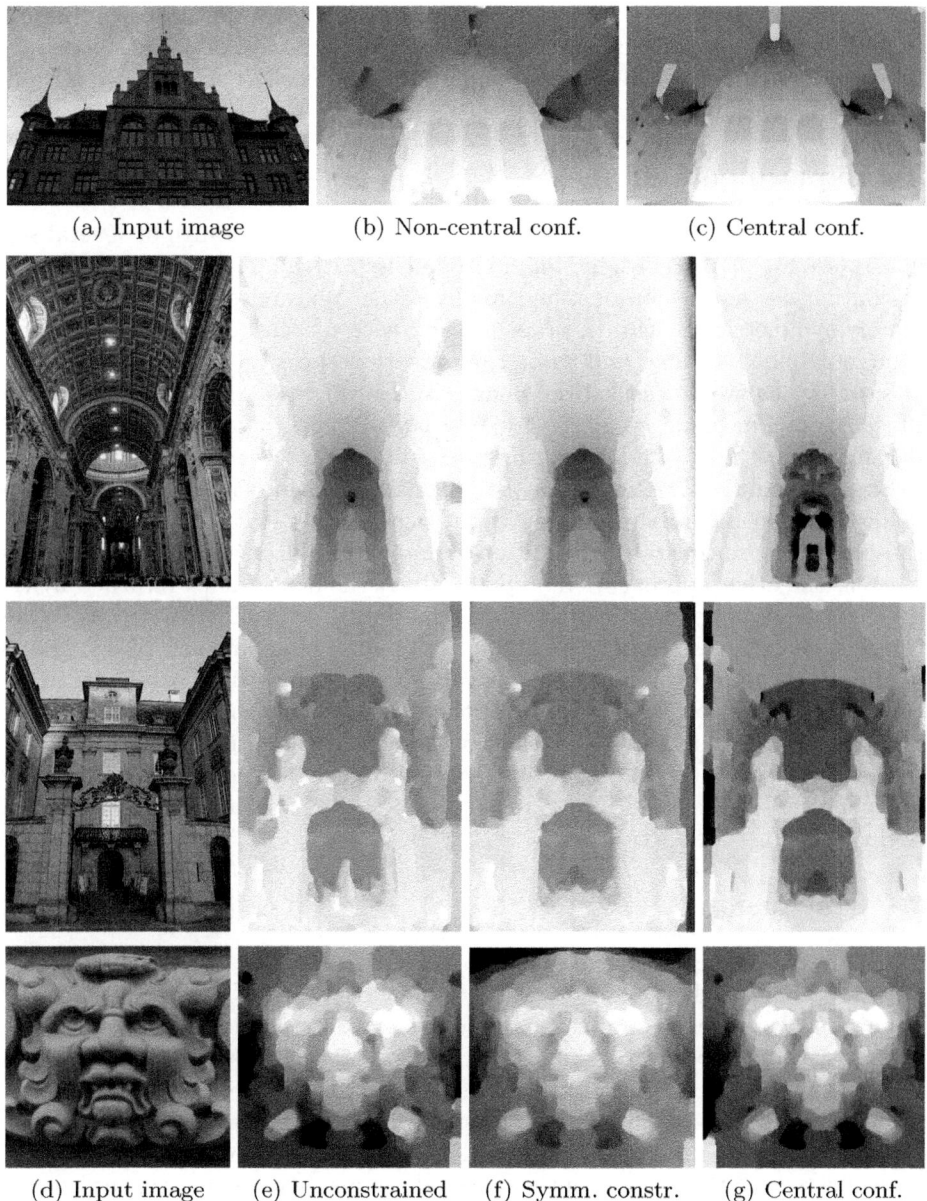

(a) Input image   (b) Non-central conf.   (c) Central conf.

(d) Input image   (e) Unconstrained   (f) Symm. constr.   (g) Central conf.

Fig. 4. Results for our datasets. First row: while the central configuration naturally leads to symmetric depth maps, some artefacts induced by textureless regions are visible (see the apexes of the towers in (b) and (c)). Bottom rows: input images (d) and depth maps obtained for the non-central configuration without explicit symmetry constraints (e), with symmetry constraints (f), and for the central configuration (g).

intensities in $[0, 1]$). This is very helpful to limit the influence of non-symmetric high-frequency textures on the overall result. Global optimization to obtain a smooth depth map is based on a primal-dual gradient method. Spatial smoothness is enforced by utilizing the isotropic total variation. The final depth value (potentially at subpixel accuracy) is extracted from u as the 0.5-isolevel.

6   Experiments

We evaluated our approach on a set of real images from a range of several scenarios (see Fig. 4): facades, indoor environments with a large depth range, depth discontinuities and occlusions, and finally rather textureless and only approximately symmetric objects. In order to cope with inaccuracies of the estimated symmetry plane normal, and to be robust with respect to texture asymmetries at small scales, we downsized the images to quarter resolution (of originally 3-6 MegaPixel). The plane sweep method evaluates 120 depth values, and the weight parameter for the data fidelity term is set to 5.

Since a quantitative evaluation is difficult due to missing ground truth, we qualitatively compare the different approaches. First it can be observed that the global but unconstrained solution does not produce symmetric 3D scenes, whereas the other approaches do. Qualitatively the depth maps returned by the different dense stereo methods are similar, although they differ in details. While the central approach seems to be attractive because of its intrinsic 2D symmetry of the depth map, we noticed that it can introduce undesired artefacts: in the central configuration a single pixel of the original view can be consistent with different depth hypotheses and thus be assigned to multiple depths. Objects with small depth variations and concave environments are clearly most suitable for symmetry-based single view reconstruction, due to the absense of strong occlusions (Fig. 4, first two rows).

7   Conclusion

After anaylzing the underlying 3D geometry, we have presented a novel automatic approach to densely reconstruct a symmetric scene from a single image. In particular we suggested and compared different representations of the 3D scene (depth with respect to a virtual central view or with respect to the original camera), and enforced the reconstructed scene to be symmetric by equality constraints between corresponding 3D locations in a minimal surface formulation.

Future work might exploit multiple local symmetries, and could also investigate in detecting the support of the detected symmetry in the image, i.e. separate symmetric and non-symmetric scene elements.

References

1. Boykov, Y., Veksler, O., Zabih, R.: Markov random fields with efficient approximations. In: Proc. CVPR, pp. 648–655 (1998)
2. Cornelius, H., Loy, G.: Detecting bilateral symmetry in perspective. In: Proceedings of the 2006 CVPR-Workshop on POCV, p. 191 (2006)

3. Cornelius, H., Perďoch, M., Matas, J., Loy, G.: Efficient symmetry detection using local affine frames. In: Ersbøll, B.K., Pedersen, K.S. (eds.) SCIA 2007. LNCS, vol. 4522, pp. 152–161. Springer, Heidelberg (2007)
4. Francois, A., Medioni, G., Waupotitsch, R.: Reconstructing mirror symmetric scenes from a single view using 2-view stereo geometry. In: Proceedings of 16th International Conference on Pattern Recognition, vol. 4, pp. 12–16 (2002)
5. Fujiyama, S., Sakaue, F., Sato, J.: Multiple view geometries for mirrors and cameras. In: Proceedings of ICPR, pp. 45–48 (2010)
6. Gordon, G.: Shape from symmetry. In: Proc. of SPIE, Intelligent Robots and Computer Vision VIII: Algorithms and Techniques, vol. 1192 (1989)
7. Hartley, R., Zissermann, A.: Multiple View Geometry in Computer Vision, 2nd edn. Cambridge University Press, Cambridge (2004)
8. Lowe, D.G.: Distinctive Image Features from Scale-Invariant Keypoints. International Journal of Computer Vision 60(2), 91–110 (2004)
9. Loy, G., Eklundh, J.-O.: Detecting symmetry and symmetric constellations of features. In: Leonardis, A., Bischof, H., Pinz, A. (eds.) ECCV 2006. LNCS, vol. 3952, pp. 508–521. Springer, Heidelberg (2006)
10. Mikolajczyk, K., Tuytelaars, T., Schmid, C., Zisserman, A., Matas, J., Schaffalitzky, F., Kadir, T., Van Gool, L.: A Comparison of Affine Region Detectors. International Journal of Computer Vision 65(1-2), 43–72 (2005)
11. Mitsumoto, H., Tamura, S., Okazaki, K., Kajimi, N., Fukui, Y.: 3-d reconstruction using mirror images based on a plane symmetry recovering method. IEEE Transact. on Pattern Analysis and Machine Intelligence 14(9), 941–946 (1992)
12. Pock, T., Schoenemann, T., Graber, G., Cremers, D., Bischof, H.: A convex formulation of continuous multi-label problems. In: Forsyth, D., Torr, P., Zisserman, A. (eds.) ECCV 2008, Part III. LNCS, vol. 5304, pp. 792–805. Springer, Heidelberg (2008)
13. Pollefeys, M., Van Gool, L., Vergauwen, M., Verbiest, F., Cornelis, K., Tops, J., Koch, R.: Visual modeling with a hand-held camera. IJCV 59, 207–232 (2004)
14. Shimshoni, I., Moses, Y., Lindenbaum, M.: Shape reconstruction of 3d bilaterally symmetric surfaces. In: Int. Conf. Image Analysis and Processing, pp. 76–81 (1999)
15. Tuytelaars, T., Turina, A., Gool, L.V.: Non-Combinatorial Detection of Regular Repetitions under Perspective Skew. IEEE Trans. PAMI 25(4), 418–432 (2003)
16. Wu, C., Frahm, J.-M., Pollefeys, M.: Repetition-based dense single-view reconstruction. In: IEEE Conference on Computer Vision and Pattern Recognition (2011)
17. Yanxi, L., Hagit Hel-Or, C.S.K., Gool, L.V.: Computational symmetry in computer vision and computer graphics. Foundations and Trends in Computer Graphics and Vision 5(1-2), 1–195 (2010)
18. Zach, C., Niethammer, M., Frahm, J.M.: Continuous maximal flows and Wulff shapes: Application to MRFs. In: Proc. CVPR, pp. 1911–1918 (2009)
19. Zach, C., Shan, L., Niethammer, M.: Globally optimal finsler active contours. In: Denzler, J., Notni, G., Süße, H. (eds.) Pattern Recognition. LNCS, vol. 5748, pp. 552–561. Springer, Heidelberg (2009)
20. Zhong, H., Sze, W.F., Hung, Y.S.: Reconstruction from plane mirror reflection. In: Proceedings of ICPR 2006, vol. 1, pp. 715–718 (2006)

Fingerprints for Machines – Characterization and Optical Identification of Grinding Imprints

Ralf Dragon[1], Tobias Mörke[2], Bodo Rosenhahn[1], and Jörn Ostermann[1]

[1] Institut für Informationsverarbeitung
{dragon,rosenhahn,ostermann}@tnt.uni-hannover.de
[2] Institute of Production Engineering and Machine Tools
moerke@ifw.uni-hannover.de
Leibniz Universität Hannover, Germany

Abstract. The profile of a 10 mm wide and 1 μm deep grinding imprint is as unique as a human fingerprint. To utilize this for fingerprinting mechanical components, a robust and strong characterization has to be used. We propose a feature-based approach, in which features of a 1D profile are detected and described in its 2D space-frequency representation. We show that the approach is robust on depth maps as well as intensity images of grinding imprints. To estimate the probability of misclassification, we derive a model and learn its parameters. With this model we demonstrate that our characterization has a false positive rate of approximately 10^{-20} which is as strong as a human fingerprint.

1 Introduction

For more than one century, many mechanical components are manufactured interchangeable. This allowed mass production with enhanced quality at lower costs. However interchangeable parts are usually indistinguishable and thus not identifiable. This leads to problems with product plagiarism and the determination of origin of a component. Labeling components is often not a suitable approach as labels may get lost, copied or change functional properties of a component. Thus, the variation of inherent material properties is used for fingerprinting in various fields, e.g. *chemical fingerprints* [10] for marking medicine

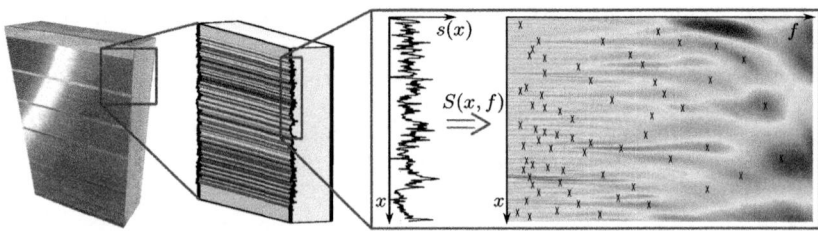

Fig. 1. Approach: Profile $s(x)$ of a grinding imprint image is obtained and characteristic features are extracted in the space-frequency domain $S(x,f)$

R. Mester and M. Felsberg (Eds.): DAGM 2011, LNCS 6835, pp. 276–285, 2011.

or *Physical Unclonable Functions* [14] for the identification of computer chips. In this work, grinding imprints are characterized for fingerprinting mechanical components (cf. Fig. 1). They are created by a grinding wheel which is shifted in grinding direction. The imprints here have a width of 10 mm and a depth standard deviation of $\sigma \approx 0.8 \, \mu$m. To enforce statistically independent fingerprints, the grinding wheel is straightened before an imprint is created, which means that several layers of abrasive materials are removed from its surface.

In this paper, we derive the framework to extract, to characterize and to verify such imprints in order to identify components. There are four requirements for the characterization. It should be (a) independent to geometric variations of the imprint such as a shift or a scale, as a a highly-precise alignment of extracted data should not be necessary, (b) robust to a few but maybe strong local perturbations, and (c) unique like a human fingerprint. As we want to allow that the characterization is computed from depth maps as well as from intensity images, the characterization should also be (d) independent from a non-linear scale in depth. In our approach, the characteristic feature constellation is learned in the space-frequency domain of the imprint profile. Our contributions are

- the detection of features of a 1D grinding profile in the 2D continuous wavelet space
- the characterization and matching of profiles using feature locations and descriptions, and
- the analysis of the strength of our fingerprint characterization with respect to false positive detection and surface perturbation.

By this, we demonstrate that our approach allows identification as secure as if a human fingerprint was analyzed.

1.1   Related Works

Historically, fingerprints are characterized by the constellation of *minutiae* which are ridge properties like crossings, bifurcations, dots and endings. The strength of a fingerprint is due to the fact that the constellation of the minutiae is unique. The probability of a false positive classification with only 12 correspondences is that low ($\approx 10^{-20}$) that it is sufficient as evidence in court [11].

In our approach we follow the idea of detecting minutiae. As the analyzed imprint does not contain explicit patterns like ridge crossings, we use an approach inspired by feature-based image analysis, where generalized salient features are detected. These features may be maxima in the DoG scale space [6], anisotropic blobs [9], homogeneous regions [8] or maxima of local entropy [5]. Then, analog to the minutiae type, a descriptor is built which usually is an affine and illumination invariant representation of the local image contents. To verify the constellation of matching descriptors, usually an affine or projective transformation is fitted to the correspondences using RANSAC [2]. However, grinding imprints are not suitable for feature-based approaches as they vary slowly in the grinding direction and abruptly orthogonal to it. This means that an imprint is better characterized using its 1D profile. Thus, we focus on features of grinding imprint profiles.

Traditionally, grinding imprints are characterized according to ISO 25178, which describes the rules and procedures for the assessment of surface texture. However, such global surface texture parameters such as the root mean square height of the surface S_q or the maximum height of the surface S_z can neither be used to distinguish nor to describe surfaces robustly.

Further, methods of statistical texture analysis could be used to characterize an imprint. E.g. in [13], the maxima locations of an entropy measure over different orders and scales is used as characteristic *fingerprint image*. But as the relevant information is contained in one dimension, statistical methods for signal analysis in one dimension seem more adequate.

The differences between audio data and grinding profiles are the statistical signal properties –grinding profile samples are highly transient– and the number of samples –a profile consist only of 3200 samples whereas audio data usually of 10 s or more at 44 kHz. Most approaches tackle audio fingerprinting as a pattern recognition problem where feature vectors are to be classified. These are usually *regularly* sampled from the distribution of spectral coefficients like Fourier Coefficients, Mel Frequency Cepstral Coefficients or Wavelet Coefficients. For a broad overview we refer to [1]. In contrast to this, we decided to *detect* specific salient positions in the space-frequency domain and describe them locally. This has the advantage that signals with change in scale or with partial differences are better comparable.

A similar idea has recently been introduced for audio indexing [15]. They analyze the *Short Time Fourier Transform* (STFT) spectrogram and use customary SIFT [6] features for its description. However as imprint profiles are more transient than audio data, the STFT is not a stable characterization. Further SIFT is not a suitable approach for describing features as rotation invariance is not desirable. Nonetheless, in Experiment 4.4, we use this method for a comparison with our proposed approach.

There exist many applications in which the continuous wavelet transformation [7] (CWT) is used to compare 1D data. In [3], CWTs of two time series are multiplied to analyze the correlation between different climatic effects. The same method is applied in [12] to analyze economic relationships. However to the best of our knowledge, besides [15], there is no approach in which salient features in the space-frequency domain are detected and compared.

The outline of this paper is as follows: In Section 2, our feature-based profile characterization approach is explained. We derive an estimate on the probability of falsely matching two profiles in Section 3. We evaluate the properties of the approach in experiments in Section 4. A conclusion is given in Section 5.

2   Feature-Based Profile Characterization

2.1   Detection

First, the profile $s(x)$ is extracted from the 2D depth map or intensity image $d(x,y)$ of the imprint (cf. Fig. 1). We assume that x is the dimension orthogonal to the grinding. To cancel out noise and outliers, $s(x)$ is built by averaging over n_y image rows around $y = y_0$:

$$s(x) = \frac{1}{n_y} \sum_{y=y_0-n_y/2}^{y_0+n_y/2} d(x,y)\,. \tag{1}$$

$s(x)$ is transformed to the space-frequency domain $S(x,f)$ using the continuous wavelet transform [7] (CWT) with the wavelet $\phi_{x,f}(\xi)$:

$$S(x,f) = \int_{-\infty}^{\infty} s(\xi) \cdot \phi_{x,f}(\xi)\, d\xi\,. \tag{2}$$

ϕ is parametrized by x and f, where x is the translation the wavelet is centered around and f is the dominant frequency in the power density spectrum of $\phi_{x,f}$. To cover a wide range of frequencies, the frequency is sampled logarithmically between $\lambda_0 = s_c/2$ and $\lambda_1 = s_x/2$, where s_x is the profile length and s_c the expected diameter of the imprint of one grain, which is $125\,\mu m$ here.

Like the filter response of every linear system, for a constant f, $S(x,f)$ denotes a local estimate of the cross correlation (cf. (2)) of the profile at position x and the wavelet. Peaks in S at (x_m, f_m) indicate a high correlation between the local neighborhood of $s(x_m)$ and ϕ_{x_m, f_m}. The distribution of peaks (cf. Fig. 1) is specific for each profile and fulfills requirement (b) as local changes do not change the global distribution (cf. Fig. 2).

Wavelets are useful here to obtain sharp-edged and stable peaks in $S(x,f)$. In principle, an arbitrary real-valued wavelet could be used. On the one hand, sharp-peaked wavelet distributions are better locatable in x and f. Thus, a wavelet should be shaped like a profile. On the other hand, peaks should occur at different frequencies f, so the wavelet should be generic enough. We empirically chose the Daubechies wavelet [7] of order 4 as it matches both criteria, but we did not do extensive evaluation of different wavelets.

As feature location, local maxima are chosen as they are locatable most precisely and robustly under perturbation. The candidate m with coordinates (x_m, f_m) is found using non-maximum suppression on $|S(x,f)|$. Then region R_m is determined which describes the extents of feature m. In order to be scale invariant, its extents are proportional to the wavelet wavelength $\lambda_m = f_m^{-1}$. In spatial direction, the extent is $x = x_m \pm \lambda_m/2$. Similarly, in frequency direction it is chosen such that $f^{-1} = \lambda_m \pm \lambda_m/2$. Thus, the borders of R_m are

$$x = [x_m - \lambda_m/2; x_m + \lambda_m/2]\,, \quad f = [2/3 f_m; 2 f_m]\,. \tag{3}$$

2.2   Description

To avoid clusters in the profile characterization, all candidates j are discarded, if their detected location (x_j, f_j) falls into the region of another candidate i with higher absolute value in S:

$$|S(x_j, f_j)| < |S(x_i, f_i)| \quad \vee \quad (x_j, f_j) \in R_i\,. \tag{4}$$

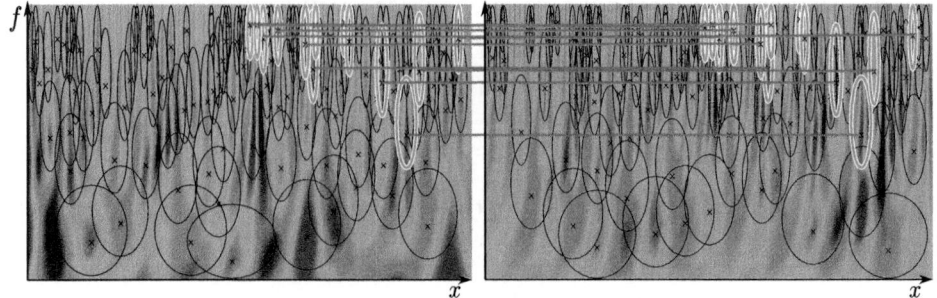

Fig. 2. Detected (black ellipses) and matching (green ellipses) features in the continuous wavelet space $S(x,f)$ between two profiles with partially similar local (right half) but different global structure (lower half)

For all remaining candidates m, a descriptor $\boldsymbol{D}_m$ is built by sampling R_m in equal intervals. In this work, we sample 3 frequencies with 9 samples each resulting in a descriptor length of 27. Next, the descriptor is normalized, such that $\mathrm{E}[\boldsymbol{D}_m] = 0$ and $\|\boldsymbol{D}_m\| = 1$. As a scaling or a depth shift of the profile has no influence on the descriptor, requirement (d) is achieved. Finally, we have a list of feature locations $(x_m, f_m = 1/\lambda_m)$ with one descriptor $\boldsymbol{D}_m$ for each feature.

2.3   Comparison

In this Section, we explain how the characterizations of two profiles $s^{(1)}$ and $s^{(2)}$ are compared. First, all correspondence candidates (i,j) are found whose descriptors $\boldsymbol{D}_i^{(1)}$ and $\boldsymbol{D}_j^{(2)}$ are similar under the cosine metric:

$$\cos(\angle(\boldsymbol{D}_i^{(1)}, \boldsymbol{D}_j^{(2)})) = \frac{\langle \boldsymbol{D}_i^{(1)}, \boldsymbol{D}_j^{(2)} \rangle}{\|\boldsymbol{D}_i^{(1)}\| \cdot \|\boldsymbol{D}_j^{(2)}\|} = \langle \boldsymbol{D}_i^{(1)}, \boldsymbol{D}_j^{(2)} \rangle > d_t, \tag{5}$$

where d_t is a threshold set to 0.9 here.

Next, the spatial constellation of all candidates is verified. It is assumed that profile $s^{(1)}$ and $s^{(2)}$ spatially differ by a shift Δ_x and a wavelength ratio Δ_λ. Thus, the constellation of all correspondence pairs (i,j) must fulfill

$$\boldsymbol{l}_j^{(2)} = \begin{bmatrix} x_j^{(2)} \\ \lambda_j^{(2)} \end{bmatrix} = \Delta_\lambda \cdot \begin{bmatrix} x_i^{(1)} + \Delta_x \\ \lambda_i^{(1)} \end{bmatrix} = \Delta_\lambda \cdot (\boldsymbol{l}_i^{(1)} + \boldsymbol{\Delta}_x). \tag{6}$$

The two unknowns can be estimated from one correspondence pair. They are optimized by minimizing the squared symmetric Euclidean distance

$$e_{i,j}^2 = \frac{1}{2}|\boldsymbol{l}_j^{(2)} - \Delta_\lambda \cdot (\boldsymbol{l}_i^{(1)} + \boldsymbol{\Delta}_x)|^2 + \frac{1}{2}|\boldsymbol{l}_i^{(1)} - \boldsymbol{l}_j^{(2)}/\Delta_\lambda - \boldsymbol{\Delta}_x|^2 \tag{7}$$

over all candidates (i,j) using RANSAC [2]. Outliers are detected if $e_{i,j}$ is bigger than an error radius r, which is set to 6 samples here. After this, correspondences with the same geometric constellation have been found.

3   False Positive Profile Matches

In this section, we derive a model on the probability $p_{\mathrm{fp,prof}}$ of wrongly matching two profiles of different components. We assume that the classification is based on the numbers of correspondences k.

For each possible correspondence, there are two criteria in order to be regarded as inlier: According to Section 2.3, first the descriptors have to match. We call the probability of one false descriptor match $p_{\mathrm{fp,desc}}$. Second, a correspondence has to fulfill spatial constraints with a probability of p_{cstl} in order to be considered as inlier to RANSAC. Assuming statistical independence, the probability of fulfilling both constraints for a random correspondence inlier is

$$p_{\mathrm{ri}} = p_{\mathrm{fp,desc}} \cdot p_{\mathrm{cstl}} \,. \tag{8}$$

If there are n_1 features detected in the first profile and n_2 in the second, there may be $n = n_1 n_2$ correspondences. Assuming $n \gg k$, the probability of exactly k inliers meeting the inlier criteria out of n correspondences can be expressed using the binomial distribution

$$B(k,n,p_{\mathrm{ri}}) = \binom{n}{k} \cdot p_{\mathrm{ri}}^k \cdot (1 - p_{\mathrm{ri}})^{n-k} \,. \tag{9}$$

However, one of the k correspondences always fulfills the RANSAC motion model as this model is derived from it. This correspondence matches with $p_{\mathrm{fp,desc}}$ and there may be n_2 possible motions derived from it. So the probability of obtaining exactly k correspondences is

$$p_{\mathrm{k,prof}}(k) = 1 - (1 - p_{\mathrm{fp,desc}} \cdot B(k-1,n-1,p_{\mathrm{ri}}))^{n_2} \,, k \geq 2 \,. \tag{10}$$

Thus, the distribution of two independent profiles to match using a threshold of k filtered correspondences is

$$p_{\mathrm{fp,prof}}(k) = \sum_{i=k}^{n} p_{\mathrm{k,prof}}(i), k \geq 2 \,. \tag{11}$$

4   Experiments

4.1   Evaluation of False Positive Detections

We use the model from Section 3 in order to determine the probability of two independent fingerprints to match. The profiles are extracted from depth images taken with a confocal white light microscope which uses *depth from focus* [4]. Its lateral sampling distance is 3.1 μm, so there are 3200 samples for the 10 mm wide profile. The a priori probabilities $p_{\mathrm{fp,desc}}$ and p_{cstl} from Eq. (8) are estimated from depth images of 45 different grinding imprints. Of each depth image $d^{(i)}$, two profiles $s_1^{(i)}$ and $s_2^{(i)}$ are taken of each at a distance of 1 mm. All descriptors from $s_1^{(i)}$ are compared with all descriptors from $s_2^{(j)}$. As the descriptors should

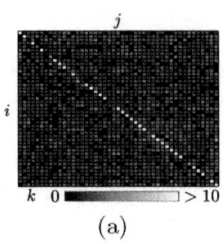
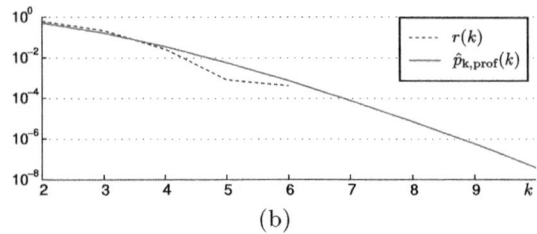

(a)   (b)

Fig. 3. (a) Confusion matrix C with number of matches $C(i,j) = k$ between profile $d_1^{(i)}$ and $d_2^{(j)}$. (b) Probability for two different fingerprints having exactly k correspondences: $\hat{p}_{k,\text{prof}}(k)$ vs. normalized histogram $r(k)$ from C.

only match, if $i = j$ and if their position is not altered, we get an estimate for $p_{\text{fp},\text{desc}}$ by counting false positive correspondences n_{fp} versus true negative correspondences n_{tn}. Regarding p_{cstl}, which is the probability for a random RANSAC inlier, we compare the inlier area s_i with the area of possible feature locations s_p. As nearly all mismatches from the descriptor matching occur at small frequency differences, we chose to compare the areas in the 1D space domain and not in the 2D space-frequency domain:

$$\hat{p}_{\text{fp},\text{desc}} = \frac{n_{\text{fp}}}{n_{\text{tn}} + n_{\text{fp}}} = 1.54\%, \quad \hat{p}_{\text{cstl}} = \frac{s_i}{s_p} = \frac{2r}{s_p} = 0.48\%. \quad (12)$$

In Fig. 3a, the confusion matrix $C(i,j)$ with the number of correspondences k between $d_1^{(i)}$ and $d_2^{(j)}$ is displayed. For enhanced visibility, C is scaled between $k = 0$ and $k = 10$. Please note that true positives on the diagonal have a higher expected match count of $E[C(i,i)] = 26$. For $i \neq j$, only up to $k = 6$ false correspondences occurred with $E[C(i,j)] = 1.9$. The normalized histogram $r(k)$ of $C(i,j) = k$ is displayed in Fig. 3b. It is visible that our estimate $\hat{p}_{k,\text{prof}}(k)$ follows $r(k)$. To compare the strength of our approach to natural fingerprints, we extrapolate using $\hat{p}_{k,\text{prof}}(k)$ up to $k = 19$, which is a reasonable value as classification border as the expected true positive match count is significantly higher. We receive a profile false detection probability of $\hat{p}_{\text{fp},\text{prof}}(k = 19) \approx 10^{-20}$. Thus, we have shown that such grinding imprints are as strong as human fingerprints for identification.

4.2   Corrosion

In this experiment, we analyze the influence of corrosion to the redetection of an imprint. Salt spray corrosion tests (DIN EN ISO 9227) were used to artificially age the component: 1.5 ml/h of a 5% NaCl salt solution are sprayed onto the surface for a certain duration τ of aging. Afterward, the surface is acid cleaned. From the surface views in Fig. 4, it can be seen, that two different effects occur: continuous perturbation of the surface, and the complete destruction of local spots which is best visible for $\tau = 19$ h. We compare the number of correspondences k between original and corroded imprint over τ in Fig. 5.

Fig. 4. Corrosion on the grinding imprint after aging for a time span τ

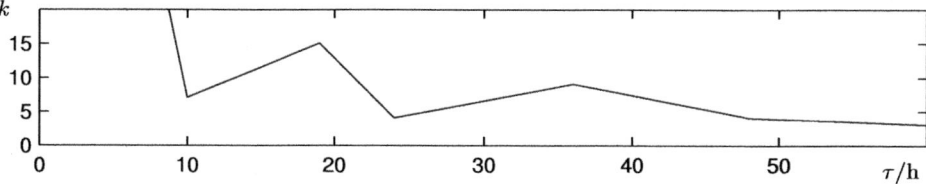

Fig. 5. Number of correspondences k after aging for time span τ

It can be seen that the outcomes are lowering unsteadily, which is a result of local destruction. However k is still significantly higher than for different imprints as our representation allows partial matches in space and frequency. This can be observed in Fig. 2, in which the correspondences between original and a corrosion of $\tau = 19$ h are displayed.

4.3 Optical Fingerprint Comparison

In this experiment, we will demonstrate that the here-presented approach is able to identify imprints obtained from the plain image intensities. As input, we use diffusely-illuminated images from the same imprint which were taken with a customary camera at a resolution of 1000×1000 pel^2. In contrast to Experiment 4.1, we focus on a high detection rate here for an optical on-line comparison, as a positive detection could be verified by a depth map if a low false detection rate is needed. Thus, we set the correspondence threshold to $k = 10$, which is reasonable as the number of samples is only one third compared to depth profiles. Apart from this, only d_t from (5) was adopted to 0.8.

In Fig. 6a, images from the same profile with varying brightness, camera pose (up to 10% shift) and scaling (up to 30% zoom) were taken. Similar to Experiment 4.1, we match every profile $s_1^{(i)}$ obtained from the upper image half to every profile $s_2^{(j)}$ from the lower half. In Fig. 6b, the number of correspondences between i and j is displayed. In total, we receive a detection rate of 44%, which is very good for this challenging task. If we fix the pose and only vary the illumination, we even get 77% detection rate.

4.4 Comparison to SIFT Matching

We now compare our results to the approach of [15], in which customary SIFT features are used on an audio signal STFT spectrogram. We use the provided

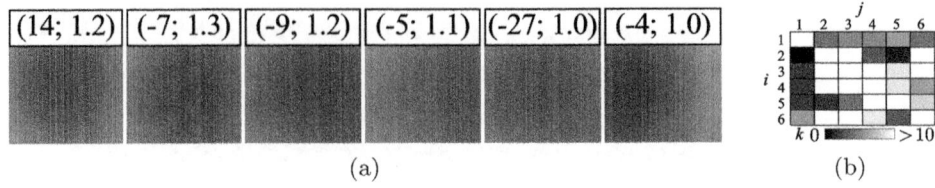

(a) | (b)

Fig. 6. (a) Intensity images $d^{(i)}$ with varying camera pose and estimates of $(\Delta_x/\text{pel}; \Delta_f)$ for profile $s_1^{(i)}$ with respect to profile $s_2^{(6)}$ with smallest zoom. (b) Confusion matrix with number of matches between $s_1^{(i)}$ and $s_2^{(j)}$.

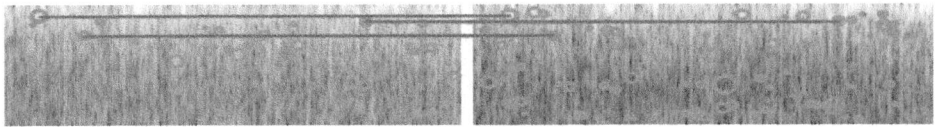

Fig. 7. Depth profile spectrograms of the same surface. Unlike the data of [15], there is no coarse structure which could be used for SIFT matches (Cf. Fig. 2).

parameters and input the depth profiles from Experiment 4.1 instead of audio data. As the signal length is much shorter (3200 samples compared to 441000 for a 10 s block) and as the profiles are more transient than audio signals, we chose a window length of 32 samples to obtain the spectrogram. Feature extraction and comparison was carried out as described in [15].

In Fig. 7, spectrograms from two measurements $s_1^{(i)}$ and $s_2^{(i)}$ of the same depth profile are displayed. It can be seen that there are only 3 correspondences detected, which is one of the best results of this method. In total, if profile $s_1^{(i)}$ is matched with itself, an average of 84 correspondences were found, if it is matched with the second measurement $s_2^{(i)}$ at 1 mm distance, this value drops to 0.36 (for different profiles $s_1^{(i)}$ and $s_2^{(j)}$, it is 0.03). This shows that the spectrogram is not suitable to robustly and uniquely describe transient profiles.

5   Summary and Conclusion

In this paper we have shown an approach to extract and compare robust and precise characterizations of grinding imprints. It is based on features obtained from the continuous wavelet transformation. This allows a shift and scale invariant characterization of the profile. For the comparison of two fingerprints, the number of corresponding features with consistent geometric constellation is used and compared with a threshold k. In experiments we have shown that the approach is robust to perturbations like corrosion. We have shown that a similar approach which uses an STFT spectrogram in combination with SIFT is not suited for this data. We further have demonstrated that our approach works on intensity images as well as on depth maps, even under variation of illumination and pose. To estimate the strength of the proposed approach, a model on the false positive detection probability $\hat{p}_{\mathrm{fp,prof}}(k)$ was derived and its parameters trained. This model indicates that a reasonable amount of $k \geq 19$ matches leads to as few false positive detections as if human fingerprints were compared.

Acknowledgments. This work was funded by the DFG within the Collaborative Research Centre 653. We thank the Institute of Materials Science of the Leibniz Universität Hannover for their support of artificially aging components. Further we thank the author of the RANSAC implementation [16] that we used.

References

1. Cano, P., Batlle, E., Kalker, T., Haitsma, J.: A review of audio finger printing. The Journal of VLSI Signal Processing 41, 271–284 (2005)
2. Fischler, M.A., Bolles, R.C.: Random sample consensus: a paradigm for model fitting with applications to image analysis and automated cartography. CACM 24, 381–395 (1981)
3. Grinsted, A., Moore, J.C., Jevrejeva, S.: Application of the cross wavelet transform and wavelet coherence to geophysical time series. Nonlinear Processes in Geophysics 11(5/6), 561–566 (2004)
4. Grossmann, P.: Depth from focus. Pattern Recognition Letters 5(1), 63–69 (1987)
5. Kadir, T., Zisserman, A., Brady, M.: An affine invariant salient region detector. In: Pajdla, T., Matas, J(G.) (eds.) ECCV 2004. LNCS, vol. 3021, pp. 228–241. Springer, Heidelberg (2004)
6. Lowe, D.G.: Distinctive image features from scale-invariant keypoints. International Journal of Computer Vision 60, 91–110 (2004)
7. Mallat, S.: A wavelet tour of signal processing– The Sparse Way. Elsevier, Amsterdam (2009)
8. Matas, J., Chum, O., Urban, M., Pajdla, T.: Robust wide-baseline stereo from maximally stable extremal regions. Image and Vision Computing (2004)
9. Mikolajcyk, K., Schmid, C.: An affine invariant interest point detector. In: Proc. ICCV (2002)
10. Murphy, B., Morrison, R.D. (eds.): Introduction to environmental forensics, 2nd edn. Academic Press, London (2007)
11. Pankanti, S., Prabhakar, S., Jain, A.K.: On the individuality of fingerprints. Transactions on Pattern Analysis and Machine Intelligence 24, 1010–1025 (2001)
12. Rua, A.: Measuring comovement in the time-frequency space. Journal of Macroeconomics 32(2), 685–691 (2010)
13. Sporring, J., Weickert, J.: Information measures in scale-spaces. Transactions on Information Theory 45(3), 1051–1058 (1999)
14. Tuyls, P., Guajardo, J., Batina, L., Kerins, T.: Anti-counterfeiting. In: Tuyls, P., Skoric, B., Kevenaar, T. (eds.) Security with Noisy Data, pp. 293–312. Springer, London (2007)
15. Zhu, B., Li, W., Wang, Z., Xue, X.: A novel audio fingerprinting method robust to time scale modification and pitch shifting. In: Proc. ACM International Conference on Multimedia, pp. 987–990 (October 2010)
16. Zuliani, M.: Ransac toolbox for matlab (November 2008), http://www.mathworks.com/matlabcentral/fileexchange/18555

Efficient and Robust Alignment of Unsynchronized Video Sequences

Georgios D. Evangelidis[1] and Christian Bauckhage[2]

[1] Department of Computer Engineering & Informatics,
University of Patras, Rio-Patras, 26500, Greece
[2] Fraunhofer IAIS, Schloss Birlinghoven, St. Augustin, Germany

Abstract. This paper addresses the problem of aligning two unsynchronized video sequences. We present a novel approach that allows for temporal and spatial alignment of similar videos captured from independently moving cameras. The goal is to synchronize two videos of a scene such that changes between the videos can be detected automatically. This aims at applications in driver assistance or surveillance systems but we also envision applications in map building. Our approach is novel in that it adapts an efficient information retrieval framework to a computer vision problem. In addition, we extend the recent ECC image-alignment algorithm to the temporal dimension in order to improve spatial registration and enable synchro refinement. Experiments with traffic videos recorded by in-vehicle cameras demonstrate the efficiency of the proposed method and verify its effectiveness with respect to spatio-temporal alignment accuracy.

1 Introduction

Video alignment requires matching scene points in both space and time. Given two or more video sequences, the goal is to find correspondences between projections of the same scene point in a time-coherence framework so that frames from the different videos can be registered.

Most related contributions either assume stationary cameras or consider settings of jointly moving cameras in a fixed relative orientation [2,9,14]. With the exception of [9], these works also consider a linear model for temporal displacements between videos. Independently moving cameras have been studied either in the context of a constant temporal offset between sequences (overlap in time) [13] or of a dynamic time shift (no overlap in time) [3,10]. Since the latter poses difficult problems when moving cameras accelerate irregularly, related contributions assumed nearly coincident camera trajectories or the availability of metadata such as GPS coordinates [3,10]. While most approaches to video synchronization attempt to align trajectories of interest points [2,9,13,14], other methods rely on spatial intensity information [2,3,10]. To establish the geometry between synchronized frames, models such as 2D homographies [2], fundamental matrices [2,9], 3D rotations [3], or affine projections [14] have been used.

In this paper we consider independently moving un-calibrated cameras whose trajectories are similar. In particular, we consider in-vehicle cameras that are mounted behind the windshield and record everyday street scenes. We aim at aligning videos that are recorded on *different days* from within different vehicles driving the same route and

R. Mester and M. Felsberg (Eds.): DAGM 2011, LNCS 6835, pp. 286–295, 2011.

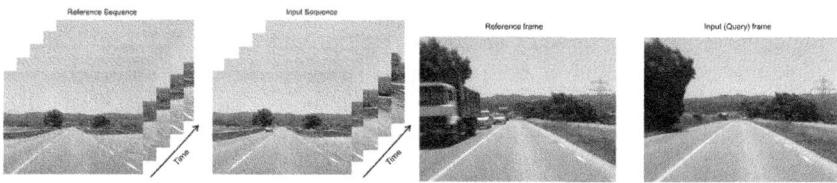

Fig. 1. *Top*: An example of two video sequences [3]. Due to non-overlapping capture times, different moving objects appear in the sequences. *Bottom*: Examples of corresponding frames with noticeably different scene content.

following approximately the same lane (see Fig.1). In this scenario, velocity and acceleration of the cameras naturally vary and the corresponding temporal mapping is highly non-linear. Unlike previous works, the method we propose in this paper can even deal with backward motion of cameras. It is fast enough to allow for online application and the recorded 3D scene is not required to be static.

Our scenario is closely related to [3,10], yet, we consider completely different algorithmic approach: we treat video synchronization as an information retrieval problem where we apply highly efficient low-level descriptors and efficient subsequent matching steps. As our video data sets are captured at sensibly different times, the first recorded sequence can be preprocessed and indexed before the second sequence becomes available for analysis. This mimics a recent trend in computer vision where computations are pushed back to an off-line task in order to accelerate online procedures [6,12]. In our case, pre-processing focuses on efficiently storing the frames of the first sequence in a database, indexing the database, and structuring the index appropriately. This way we can handle the subsequent synchronization problem by means of querying the database for content that is similar to a given frame in the second video sequence. Having thus obtained a rough synchronization, we then address the spatial registration between synchronized frame and the problem of subframe correction and propose a space-time extension of the recently introduced ECC algorithm [4].

Our presentation proceeds as follows: Next, we formalize the video alignment problem. Section 3 casts video synchronization as an information retrieval problem and Section 4 presents our extension of the ECC algorithm to the space-time dimension. In Section 5, we discuss efficiency and, in Section 6, we evaluate our approach on real world sequences. Finally, Section 7 concludes this contribution.

2   Problem Formulation

Suppose we are given two image sequences $S_r = I_r(\hat{\mathbf{x}})$ and $S_q = I_q(\mathbf{x})$, where the first is a reference and the second is a query sequence and $\hat{\mathbf{x}} = [\hat{x}, \hat{y}, \hat{t}]^t$, $\mathbf{x} = [x, y, t]^t$ denote space-time points. The goal of video alignment is to match space-time points in the two sequences. We are interested in a spatio-temporal mapping $W(\mathbf{x}; \mathbf{p})$ where $\mathbf{p}$ is a space-time parameter vector, such that $\hat{\mathbf{x}} = W(\mathbf{x}; \mathbf{p})$. Following [2], we define the mapping model as $W(\mathbf{x}; \mathbf{p}) = [W_s([x,y]^t; \mathbf{p}_s)^t, W_t(t, \mathbf{p}_t)]^t$ where $W_s()$ is the spatial- and $W_t()$ is the time-warp parameterized by $\mathbf{p}_s$ and $\mathbf{p}_t$ respectively, and $\mathbf{p} = [\mathbf{p}_s^t, \mathbf{p}_t^t]^t$. For independently moving cameras, both parameter vectors $\mathbf{p}_s$ and $\mathbf{p}_t$ vary along S_q. Yet, in the case of irregular and backward motion, both vectors must be re-estimated for all query frames.

In order to efficiently handle such cases, we propose a new approach to video synchronization that can also be viewed as an initialization scheme for the spatio-temporal alignment. Let us suppose that the time mapping is roughly expressed through a finite discrete-time signal $T : \mathbb{N} \rightarrow \mathbb{N}$, such that $t' = T(t)$ and t' is close to $\hat{t}$. Towards the goal of finding *integer* values $T(t)$ for all time indices t, we consider this signal to be the outcome of an information retrieval step. More specifically, we consider the whole set of reference frames as a *database* of images and all input frames as *query* frames. Then, by querying the database with an input frame assigned to time index t_0, we retrieve the corresponding frame assigned to time index $t_0' = T(t_0)$.

Given the pair $(t_0, T(t_0))$ we adopt a *time-local* spatio-temporal model $W()$, which permits us not only to spatially align synchronized frames, but to refine the time alignment result, thus providing subframe accuracy. Note that this model does not imply a short-time sequence-to-sequence alignment but an image-to-sequence, or better *frame-to-subframe*, alignment. Given a query frame $I_q(x, y, t_0)$ and the mapped pair $(t_0, T(t_0))$, we are looking for a *spatio-temporally warped* image (subframe) from the short-time sequence $I_r(\hat{x}, \hat{y}, T(t_0) \pm \mu)$, where μ is a small integer so that a predefined error criterion between corresponding frames is satisfied. As a result, we obtain subframe accuracy without using expensive spatio-temporal manifold computations [2]. This is due to the space-time extension in parameter-domain only. Next, we discuss how to determine the time-mapping $T()$ and the spatio-temporal model $W()$.

3   An IR Approach to Video Synchronization

We adopt an information retrieval approach to deal with the video synchronization problem. This allows us to preprocess the reference data *without any knowledge of the query sequence* and to devise an efficient synchronization step. Similar to modern information retrieval methods [8,12] we apply inverted index lists and weighted voting scores in order to improve the reliability of the retrieval process.

Although most retrieval works in computer vision society rely on multidimensional descriptors [7,12], our scenario permits the use of short-length descriptors. In order to *describe* image patches we apply a geometric hashing method introduced in [6] for astrometry. Specifically, let us assume that we have applied an interest point detector [11] in an image and the locations of the interest points are available. Then we consider quadruples of nearby interest points to characterize local image structures.

Suppose a quadruple (*quad*) of interest points $\bar{\mathbf{x}}_i = [\bar{x}_i, \bar{y}_i]^t, i = \{a, b, c, d,\}$ as shown in Figure 2. $\bar{\mathbf{x}}_a, \bar{\mathbf{x}}_b$ are the *control points* which are defined by the most widely separated pair of points. By s we denote the distance (*diameter*) between control points; φ denotes the *orientation* of the diameter vector and $\mathbf{c}$ denotes the *centroid* of the quad. That is

$$s = \|\bar{\mathbf{x}}_a - \bar{\mathbf{x}}_b\|, \quad \varphi = \tan^{-1}\frac{\bar{y}_b - \bar{y}_a}{\bar{x}_b - \bar{x}_a}, \quad \mathbf{c} = \frac{1}{4}\sum_i \bar{\mathbf{x}}_i, \quad (1\text{a-c})$$

where $\|\cdot\|$ denotes the Euclidean distance. We then consider a local coordinate system oriented and centered with respect to the control points $\bar{\mathbf{x}}_a, \bar{\mathbf{x}}_b$, so that their locations

Fig. 2. (a) Geometric hashing using a quad structure; (b) query frame with extracted Harris points; (c) and (d) valid quads of the query and corresponding reference frame; red dots are quad centers

coincide with $(0,0)$ and $(1,1)$, respectively. This allows for *hashing* the remaining points $\bar{\mathbf{x}}_c, \bar{\mathbf{x}}_d$ in the local coordinate system through their new coordinates (x'_c, y'_c), (x'_d, y'_d). Accordingly, any quad of nearby features can be coded using a length-four hash-code (x'_c, y'_c, x'_d, y'_d). In other words, each quad is represented as a 4D point space and similar quads correspond to nearby points in this space. Similar to [6], we only consider quads where the points $\bar{\mathbf{x}}_c, \bar{\mathbf{x}}_d$ lie inside a circle of diameter s. Any different order of points in pairs $(\bar{\mathbf{x}}_a, \bar{\mathbf{x}}_b)$ and $(\bar{\mathbf{x}}_c, \bar{\mathbf{x}}_d)$ creates a different symmetry which can be easily resolved [6].

This novel local descriptor is translation-, scale-, and rotation invariant which is required to match quads between frames. Also, small localization errors from interest point detection entail only small displacements of the hash code in the 4D feature space.

3.1 Indexing, Structure, and Retrieval

Once the reference sequence is available, we store each frame $I_r(\hat{x}, \hat{y}, \hat{i}_n)$ as an image I_n in a database where $n = 1, 2, \cdots, N$. We apply an interest point detector (e.g. Harris) to all images, extract all valid quads and assign to the jth quad of the nth image its hash code $q_{nj} = (x'_c, y'_c, x'_d, y'_d)_{nj}$, where $j = 1, 2, \cdots, J_n$. Since the discriminative power of the quad descriptor is low, we do not apply vector quantization [12] but keep working with continuous hash-codes. In addition, the short-length descriptor allows us to store all hash-codes q_{nj} and create an inverted index list assigning to every record its reference set $R_{nj} = \{n, \mathbf{c}_{nj}, s_{nj}, \varphi_{nj}\}$.

Given a query quad, we do not search for the nearest neighbor but look for similar quads inside a range. This implies a *range search* problem and in order to quickly answer a query we apply a kD-tree structure ($k = 4$). Searching for a corresponding frame to a query frame can then be cast as a voting approach. Given a query image and its quads $q_k, k = 1, 2, \cdots, K$, we query the database with all q_k and any quad q_{nj} which is ε-close to q_k votes for the nth image. By initializing all image scores v_n to 0, we increase the score of each retrieved image by $v_n \leftarrow v_n + f(q_k, q_{nj})$, where

$$f(q_k, q_{nj}) = \begin{cases} w_n & \text{if} \quad \|q_k - q_{nj}\| < \varepsilon \\ 0 & \text{otherwise.} \end{cases} \qquad (2)$$

The weights w_n could be chosen to be the *terms frequency - inverse document frequency* (TF-IDF) scores used in text retrieval [8]. However, since quads correspond to continuous

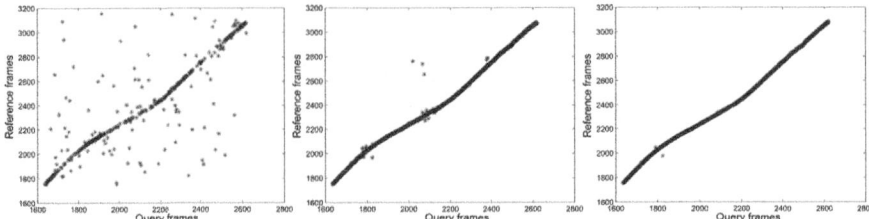

Fig. 3. Frame synchronization for the *Rural* sequence [3] based on pure retrieval results (*left*), after enforcing spatio-temporal consistency with $R_0 = 50$ (*middle*) and after additionally enforcing rotation consistency constraints with $|\varphi_k - \varphi_{nj}| < \pi/12$ (*right*)

vectors and thus are unique with high probability, the TF factor does not add to the precision. The IDF factor, on the other hand, improves the retrieval precision since quads that appear in a similar form in many images are not indicative of image content. Hence, we choose $w_n = log\frac{N}{N_k}$, where N_k is the number of the retrieved images after querying q_k.

3.2 Spatio-temporal Coherence

In order to reject false positive matches before voting, we enforce a spatio-temporal coherence constraint which agrees with our basic assumption that the trajectories of two cameras are approximately coincident. Since we would like to retrieve that frame which has been captured from the closest point to the viewpoint of the query frame, it is justified to not allow matches between far apart quads. Therefore, for correspondence, we require a quad in the database image to be inside a circular region whose center coincides with the centroid of the query quad, i.e. $\|c_k - c_{nj}\| < R_0$. Due to large overlaps between images this constraint favors both spatial and temporal coherence.

We can also enforce additional constraints like scale- and rotation-consistency by enabling appropriate coarse coherence measures for s and φ respectively. However, we found such constraints not to be as vital as the spatio-temporal one. Fig 3 shows the synchronization result before and after enabling constraints.

4   Spatial Alignment and Synchro Refinement

The above rough video synchronization step results in a sequence $T : \text{IN} \to \text{IN}$ and matched frames $(t, T(t))$. Ideally, however, synchronization would yield a sequence $T : \text{IN} \to \text{IR}_+$ providing subframe accuracy. To further refine synchronization results and to spatially align synchronized frames, we extend a recent, robust image alignment algorithm [4].

The Enhanced Correlation Coefficient (ECC) scheme as reported in [4] supposes that $I_q(x, y, t_0)$ is the template image and $I_r(\hat{x}, \hat{y}, T(t_0))$ is the input image that must be warped towards the alignment. If $A = \{x_m | m = 1, 2, \ldots, M\}$ is the set of space-time points of the query image, ECC then determines the corresponding set $\hat{A} = \{\hat{x}_m | \hat{x}_m = W(x_m; p), m = 1, 2, \ldots, M\}$ in the other sequence. This requires to explicitly define the spatio-temporal mapping $W()$. Although the fundamental matrix would apply to our scenario, its use only characterizes pixel motions up to an epipolar line and entails extra effort for computing dense correspondences [5]. Moreover, estimating the fundamental matrix is susceptible to errors and moving cameras may increase this uncertainty. Therefore, we approximate the spatial motion using a 2D homography model. Incorporating only temporal shifts for the time warping and using homogeneous spatial coordinates, we can write the space-time model as

$$
\begin{bmatrix} \tilde{x} \\ \tilde{y} \\ \tilde{w} \\ \hat{t} \end{bmatrix} = \begin{bmatrix} h_1 & h_2 & h_3 & 0 \\ h_4 & h_5 & h_6 & 0 \\ h_7 & h_8 & 1 & 0 \\ 0 & 0 & \tau & 1 \end{bmatrix} \begin{bmatrix} \hat{x} \\ \hat{y} \\ 1 \\ t_0 \end{bmatrix} ,
\tag{3}
$$

where $x = \tilde{x}/\tilde{w}$, $y = \tilde{y}/\tilde{w}$, $\mathbf{p}_s = [h_1, \ldots, h_8]^t$ and $\mathbf{p}_t = \tau$, being τ appropriately initialized via the synchronization task.

ECC alignment aims at estimating the optimal parameter vector such that the correlation coefficient between the query image and the *warped* retrieved image is maximized. Stacking the intensities of the points contained in A and $\hat{A}$ we form the vector $\mathbf{i}_q = [I_q(\mathbf{x}_1), I_q(\mathbf{x}_2), \cdots, I_q(\mathbf{x}_M)]^t$ and the warped vector $\mathbf{i}_p = [I_r(\hat{\mathbf{x}}_1), I_r(\hat{\mathbf{x}}_2), \cdots, I_r(\hat{\mathbf{x}}_M)]^t$, and let $\bar{\mathbf{i}}_q$ and $\bar{\mathbf{i}}_p$ be their zero mean counterparts. Then, the objective function that must be maximized is the *enhanced correlation coefficient* defined as

$$
\rho(\mathbf{p}) = \frac{\bar{\mathbf{i}}_q^t \bar{\mathbf{i}}_p}{\|\bar{\mathbf{i}}_q\| \, \|\bar{\mathbf{i}}_p\|} .
\tag{4}
$$

In order to solve the maximization problem, we assume similar to [4] that a nominal parameter vector $\tilde{\mathbf{p}}$ is known, such that $\mathbf{p} = \tilde{\mathbf{p}} + \Delta\mathbf{p}$. Then, using a first order Taylor expansion on $\bar{\mathbf{i}}_p$, the ECC function amounts to

$$
\rho(\Delta\mathbf{p}; \tilde{\mathbf{p}}) = \frac{\bar{\mathbf{i}}_q^t [\bar{\mathbf{i}}_{\tilde{\mathbf{p}}} + J_{\tilde{\mathbf{p}}} \Delta\mathbf{p}]}{\|\bar{\mathbf{i}}_q\| \sqrt{\|\bar{\mathbf{i}}_{\tilde{\mathbf{p}}}\|^2 + 2\bar{\mathbf{i}}_{\tilde{\mathbf{p}}}^t J_{\tilde{\mathbf{p}}} \Delta\mathbf{p} + \Delta\mathbf{p}^t J_{\tilde{\mathbf{p}}}^t J_{\tilde{\mathbf{p}}} \Delta\mathbf{p}}} ,
\tag{5}
$$

where $J_{\tilde{\mathbf{p}}}$ is the Jacobian of the vector $\bar{\mathbf{i}}_p$ with respect to parameters evaluated at $\tilde{\mathbf{p}}$. However, our extension requires the redefinition of this matrix. Its size is $M \times 9$ and the mth row is formed by the product $\nabla I_r^t J_W$ where $\nabla I_r = [\frac{\partial I_r}{\partial \hat{x}}, \frac{\partial I_r}{\partial \hat{y}}, \frac{\partial I_r}{\partial \hat{t}}]^t$ is the spatio-temporal gradient of image I_r evaluated at point $W(\mathbf{x}_m; \tilde{\mathbf{p}})$ and J_W is the Jacobian of the transformation in (3) evaluated at $\tilde{\mathbf{p}}$. Note that both spatial and temporal gradients build on first-order central differences of smoothed intensities. As far as J_W is concerned, based on (3) we have

$$
J_W = \begin{bmatrix} \frac{\partial W_s}{\partial \mathbf{p}_s} & \mathbf{0} \\ \mathbf{0}_{1 \times 8} & \frac{\partial W_t}{\partial \tau} \end{bmatrix} = \frac{1}{\tilde{w}} \begin{bmatrix} \hat{x} & \hat{y} & 1 & 0 & 0 & 0 & -\hat{x}x & -\hat{x}y & 0 \\ 0 & 0 & 0 & \hat{x} & \hat{y} & 1 & -\hat{y}x & -\hat{y}y & 0 \\ 0 & 0 & 0 & 0 & 0 & 0 & 0 & 0 & \tilde{w} \end{bmatrix} .
\tag{6}
$$

Despite the non-linearity of the function $\rho(\Delta\mathbf{p}; \tilde{\mathbf{p}})$, its maximization results in the following closed form solution

$$
\Delta\mathbf{p} = (J_{\tilde{\mathbf{p}}}^t J_{\tilde{\mathbf{p}}})^{-1} J_{\tilde{\mathbf{p}}}^t \{\lambda \bar{\mathbf{i}}_q - \bar{\mathbf{i}}_{\tilde{\mathbf{p}}}\} ,
\tag{7}
$$

(a)	(b)	(c)	(d)

Fig. 4. (a) A query frame and (b) the best retrieved frame; (c) the space-time alignment after 2 and (d) after 10 iterations; differences between frames are indicated in lawn-green and hot-pink

with λ being given by

$$\lambda = \frac{\bar{\mathbf{i}}_{\bar{\mathbf{p}}}^t (I_M - P_J) \bar{\mathbf{i}}_{\bar{\mathbf{p}}}}{\bar{\mathbf{i}}_q^t (I_M - P_J) \bar{\mathbf{i}}_{\bar{\mathbf{p}}}} , \qquad (8)$$

where I_M is the identity matrix and $P_J = J_{\bar{\mathbf{p}}} (J_{\bar{\mathbf{p}}}^t J_{\bar{\mathbf{p}}})^{-1} J_{\bar{\mathbf{p}}}^t$ is a projection operator.

By translating this solution into an iterative scheme $\mathbf{p}^{\{i\}} = \mathbf{p}^{\{i-1\}} + \Delta\mathbf{p}^{\{i\}}$, we can approximate the solution of the highly non-linear problem of maximizing the function in (4). This yields the optimum parameter vector for dense spatio-temporal correspondences of subpixel and subframe accuracy. The complexity per iteration of this scheme can be shown to be $O(M\eta^2)$, where η is the number of parameters [4]. Figure 4 shows an example of the resulting spatio-temporal alignment.

5   Efficiency

An important characteristic of our proposed framework is that we can exploit the sequential nature of video data which implies a *coarse* time-consistency for synchronizing successive frames. We thus propose to split the database of frames into β subsets of successive frames and use a separate kD-tree for the quads of each subset. For a regular split (Fig.5 *left*), we would need to investigate two adjacent subtrees whenever the current results are inside a transition area. To avoid this, we allow overlap between adjacent subtrees in the forest (Fig.5 *right*). This way, we need to query only one sub-tree and have to change the tree index if the current retrieval results are above a threshold (e.g. the median of the overlap area).

For range search problems, querying a 4D-tree structure requires $O(n^{\frac{3}{4}} + \kappa)$ where n is the number of points and κ is the number of neighbors within range [1]. Adopting the above splitting method, the query time reduces to $O((n/\beta)^{\frac{3}{4}} + \kappa/\beta)$, which accelerates the synchronization process without affecting its precision. For spatial alignment, we can apply a pyramid based scheme [2] which not only accelerates the alignment algorithm but also compensates for large displacements. Additionally, since gradient-based alignment schemes mainly rely on high frequent parts of a signal, we ignore low-frequency pixels and aggregate only those pixels around key points. Taking into account the complexity $O(M\eta^2)$, where $M \gg \eta$, the computational burden of spatio-temporal alignment drastically reduces via these two modifications.

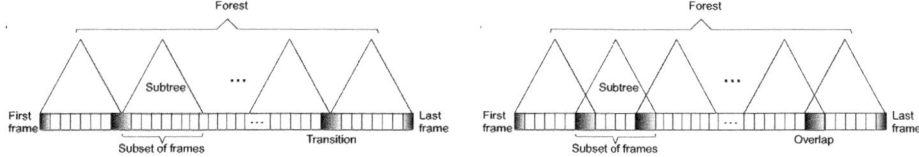

Fig. 5. Subtrees of quads that belong to subsets of reference frames. Regular split (*left*) and split with overlap (*right*).

6 Results

Following the methodology of [3], we evaluate the accuracy of the proposed synchronization method via the resulting synchronization error. As we adopt an IR approach, we compare our method with the recently proposed SIFT-flow algorithm [7] and the method presented in [3]. SIFT-flow estimates temporal alignments by histogram matching whereas spatial correspondences result from a pixel-based flow algorithm. The work in [3] models synchronization as a MAP inference problem in a Bayesian network and considers the common least-squares framework for spatial registration.

We experiment with three real-world video sequences recorded from within moving vehicles at different times, namely the *Backroad*, the *Campus* and the *Highway* sequences [3]. Each dataset shows footage from *accelerating and decelerating* cars. Ground truth is available in form of lower and upper bounds of synchronization indices. If the sequence $f_t(t)$ represents any synchronization result and $L(t)$ and $U(t)$ are the sequences of the lower and upper bounds respectively, the synchronization error is

$$e(f_t(t)) = \begin{cases} 0 & \text{if } L(t) \leq f_t(t) \leq U(t) \\ \min\{|f_t(t) - L(t)|, |f_t(t) - U(t)|\} & \text{otherwise} \end{cases}. \quad (9)$$

The resolution of sequences is 540×720 pixels in space and 1500 frames on average in time. The interest point detector we used is the Harris detector as described in [11]. We also tested other detectors, but our results were in accordance with the results of [11] verifying the favorable repeatability of Harris detector. Each subtree of the forest structure (Fig.5 *left*) efficiently stored the descriptors of 250 successive frames, being the overlap equal to 20 frames. Based on equation (2) we considered a tolerance threshold with $\varepsilon = 0.07$ while retrieval results were re-ranked by the space-time coherence constraint with $R_0 = 50$ pixels (the latter should be defined with respect to the video resolution). Finally, ECC run within a coarse-to-fine framework in spatial domain only, using a 4-level gaussian pyramid and running 5 iterations per level.

Table 6 shows the performance of the methods in terms of the synchronization error, i.e. the percentage of values where $e(f_t(t)) > \delta$. We provide results for $\delta = 0$ and $\delta = 1$ to indicate the error variance. We observe that the proposed method performs better for *Highway* dataset since the vehicle follows an almost straight road with high velocity; the latter leads to fewer reference frames as candidate matches to a query. Moreover, the low error variance favors the refinement, as ECC cannot cancel out strong synchronization errors. In other words, even if the quad-based alignment returns false positives, what seems to be important is the distribution of errors, being their concentration around

Table 1. Synchronization Error (%)

	Backroad		Campus		Highway		Average	
	$\delta = 0$	$\delta = 1$	$\delta = 0$	$\delta = 1$	$\delta = 0$	$\delta = 1$	$\delta = 0$	$\delta = 1$
Quad-based	29.4	15.4	26.4	13.5	25.3	8.7	**27.0**	**12.5**
Quad-based-ECC	25.4	8.4	23.8	11.4	8.3	2.9	**19.1**	**7.5**
Diego *et al.* [3]	37.4	31.9	17.7	9.17	32.6	27.7	**29.2**	**22.9**
SIFT-flow [7]	27.7	13.6	18.5	11.7	25.7	12.9	**23.9**	**12.7**

Fig. 6. (*Top*) Alignment results and (*bottom*) pixel-wise differences after alignment by applying (*left*) the proposed approach, (*middle*) SIFT-flow and (*right*) the method in [3]

zero particularly desired. On the other hand, in *Campus* and *Backroad* sequences there appear near-camera "objects" and road turns; the former affects the quad-based alignment while the latter gives rise to homography uncertainties. The SIFT-flow method provides slightly higher error scores while it obviously requires many more operations due to the descriptor's size (a 128-dimensional vector). Still, our method also exhibits better performance than the method in [3] which actually incorporates GPS data.

Figure 6 illustrates change detection results obtained from the three approaches. The proposed method detects scene changes with higher accuracy. SIFT-flow seems to be affected by the presence of moving cars and creates artifacts and truncated objects. The method in [3] performs poorly. As far as the complexity is concerned, the average synchronization time of the proposed method is **0.22 sec** per frame (Matlab implementation on a 3GHz Pentium) and the space-time alignment requires **1.12 sec**. As a result, we envision online execution of the proposed algorithm in a GPU-based environment. The retrieval time of the SIFT-based histogram matching is 9.46 sec per frame, while SIFT-flow re-ranks the top-5 list in terms of the flow energy and register the frames in 160.5 sec (5×32.1). The method in [3] compares each input image to all reference images and the comparison is meaningless.

Please refer to **http://xanthippi.ceid.upatras.gr/people/evangelidis/DAGM2011/** for alignment videos of the real sequences.

7   Conclusions

A novel method for video alignment with applications in change detection was pre-sented. This method enables the spatio-temporal alignment of similar videos captured from independently moving cameras. We proposed an efficient method adopted from information retrieval that applies short-length descriptors of frame content for video synchronization and a spatio-temporal alignment scheme for accurate change detection between synchronized frames. We experimented with a series of real world traffic videos captured from within moving vehicles. Our results verified both the efficiency and the effectiveness of the proposed method. Although we aim at driver assistance and security scenarios, the proposed framework obviously also applies to problems such as automated 3D map building or visual odometry.

Acknowledgements. This work has been funded by ERCIM. We also thank the ADAS group of the Computer Vision Center of Barcelona (Spain) for video data sharing and Ferran Diego for discussion.

References

1. de Berg, M., van Kreveld, M., Overmars, M., Schwarzkopf, O.: Computational Geometry: Algorithms and Applications, 2nd edn. Springer, Heidelberg (2000)
2. Caspi, Y., Irani, M.: Spatio-temporal alignment of sequences. IEEE Trans. Pattern Analysis and Machine Intelligence 24(11), 1409–1424 (2002)
3. Diego, F., Ponsa, D., Serrat, J., Lopez, A.M.: Video alignment for change detection. IEEE Trans Image Processing PP(99) (2010) (preprint)
4. Evangelidis, G.D., Psarakis, E.Z.: Parametric image alignment using enhanced correlation coefficient maximization. IEEE Trans. Pattern Analysis and Machine Intelligence 30(10), 1858–1865 (2008)
5. Hartley, R.I., Zisserman, A.: Multiple View Geometry in Computer Vision, 2nd edn. Cambridge University Press, Cambridge (2004)
6. Lang, D., Hogg, D.W., Mierle, K., Blanton, M., Roweis, S.: Astrometry.net: Blind astrometric calibration of arbitrary astronomical images. The Astronomical J. 37, 1782–2800 (2010)
7. Liu, C., Yuen, J., Torralba, A., Sivic, J., Freeman, W.T.: SIFT flow: Dense correspondence across different scenes. In: Forsyth, D., Torr, P., Zisserman, A. (eds.) ECCV 2008, Part III. LNCS, vol. 5304, pp. 28–42. Springer, Heidelberg (2008)
8. Manning, C.D., Raghavan, P., Schütze, H.: Introduction to Information Retrieval. Cambridge University Press, Cambridge (2008)
9. Rao, C., Gritai, A., Shah, M., Syeda-Mahmood, T.: View-invariant alignment and matching of video sequences. In: Proc. ICCV (2003)
10. Sand, P., Teller, S.: Video matching. ACM Trans. Graphics 22(3), 592–599 (2004)
11. Schmid, C., Mohr, R., Bauckhage, C.: Evaluation of interest point detectors. Int. J. Computer Vision 37(2), 151–172 (2000)
12. Sivic, J., Zisserman, A.: Efficient visual search of videos cast as text retrieval. IEEE Trans. Pattern Analysis and Machine Intelligence 31(4), 591–606 (2009)
13. Tuytelaars, T., Gool, L.C.: Synchronizing video sequences. In: Proc. CVPR (2004)
14. Wolf, L., Zomet, A.: Wide baseline matching between unsynchronized video sequences. Int. J. Computer Vision 68(1), 43–52 (2006)

Time-Consistent Foreground Segmentation of Dynamic Content from Color and Depth Video

Anatol Frick*, Markus Franke, and Reinhard Koch

Christian-Albrechts-University Kiel,
Computer Science Department,
Hermann-Rodewald-Str. 3, 24118 Kiel, Germany
{africk,mfranke,rk}@mip.informatik.uni-kiel.de

Abstract. This paper introduces an approach for automatic foreground extraction from videos utilizing depth information from time of flight(ToF) cameras. We give a clear definition of background and foreground based on 3D scene geometry and provide means of foreground extraction based on one-dimensional histograms in 3D space. Further a refinement step based on hierarchical grab-cut segmentation in a video volume with incorporated time constraints is proposed. Our approach is able to extract time-consistent foreground objects even for a moving camera and for dynamic scene content, but is limited to indoor scenarios.

1 Introduction

Accurate separation of foreground from background in video sequences plays an important role in many applications, like virtual studios, TV and 3DTV production, teleconferencing or video surveillance and is a difficult task, which has been extensively studied over twenty years. The approaches found in the literature can be roughly divided into two categories: interactive and automatic.

Interactive approaches [14,2,11] require some sort of user input, for example a trimap, consisting of definitive foreground, definitive background and uncertainty region. While high quality results can be achieved, processing long video sequences becomes a time-consuming operation. Using user input for selected keyframes only [10], reduces the complexity, but the amount of required user interaction still remains high and the quality decreases with the number keyframes. Automatic approaches try to perform foreground segmentation without any user input. A common technique here is to perform background subtraction based on color similarity with known background of uniform color distribution [16]. While very accurate results can be achieved, a special setup with controlled lighting conditions is required. Another category of automatic approaches try to detect foreground based on motion in combination with contrast and color cues [17,5]. Such approaches however, are limited to stationary cameras and dynamic content

---

* This work was partially funded by the "Zukunftsprogramm Schleswig-Holstein (2007-2013)" with funds from the European Commission (EFRE) and Land Schleswig-Holstein, Germany, as part of the Initiative KoSSE, project 122-09-048.

R. Mester and M. Felsberg (Eds.): DAGM 2011, LNCS 6835, pp. 296–305, 2011.

and are unable to detect still objects. Recently, many researchers are investigating the use of additional cues, like depth or infrared illumination, for foreground extraction [1,18,9,13,4].

In [1] authors use a 3D model, constructed in an offline phase to perform foreground extraction based on depth comparison. They achieve good separation of foreground in real - time but the need of a 3D model makes the system inflexible. In [19,4,18] authors use a simple thresholding technique on depth (infrared) image to initially identify the foreground and perform additional refinements steps in later processing. While this may be suitable for some scenes, it will certainly fail in presence of slanted surfaces like floor or ceiling. In [19] authors use a graph cut technique to optimize initial segmentation results similar to our approach, but segment each frame separately which can lead to temporal inconsistencies. In [9] authors use a standard stereo system and combine disparity estimation with color and contrast cues. However, only objects in the front layer are extracted, what maybe not enough for some applications.

This paper introduces automatic foreground extraction for videos in indoor scenarios utilizing depth information from ToF cameras. In the approach depth from two ToF cameras is transformed to the view of a color camera and used to perform initial foreground extraction based on surface normal and histogram thresholding. Afterwards a hierarchical automated grab-cut segmentation is performed to refine the results over a batch of images simultaneously incorporating temporal constraints to insure temporal consistency without any user interaction.

2   Data Acquisition and Preprocessing

For the data acquisition we use the system from [7]. It consists of 5 CCD cameras and 2 ToF cameras. Figure 1 shows a picture of the camera system. For the foreground extraction only the reference color camera C_5 (1920 × 1080 px.) and the two ToF cameras (200 × 200 px) T_1 left and T_2 right from the reference camera, which measure depth per pixel through correlation of emitted and reflected infrared light, are used. The ToF cameras provide reliable depth information but are limited to 7.5 meters. For more information on ToF cameras refer to [8]. Before data aquistion, all cameras are calibrated using a joint method described in [15]. After data acquisition, the ToF depth images are transformed to the view

Fig. 1. From left to right: Camera system, color image from the reference camera, transformed depth image

of the reference camera, using 3D mesh warping technique from [7,1]. Figure 1 shows the transformed depth from the view of the reference camera. Black areas are caused by occlusion regions not seen by the depth cameras. After data acquisition and pre-processing we have a video sequence in form of color images and corresponding depth images from the view of the reference camera.

3   Separation of Foreground and Background

Separation of foreground and background is an important task for many applications. However the question of what is considered to be the foreground and what the background is application specific and can't be answered in general. Many applications, for example in TV or 3DTV, are concerned with foreground extraction in indoor scenarios, where all objects inside a room a considered as foreground, and room walls, ceiling and floor as background. Therefore, we assume that the scene is confined to a room. Under this assumption we define the outer boundaries of the room, like floor, walls or ceiling to be the background and consider the interior as the foreground.

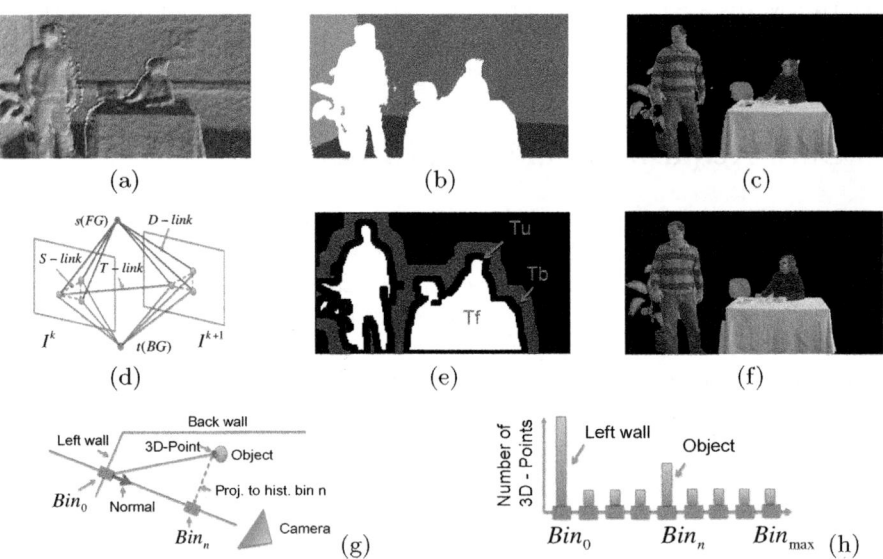

Fig. 2. (a) Normals after initial estimation with PCA (11×11 window), color coded; (b) normals for the pixel in the most outer histogram bin after refinement, color coded; (c) original image without background; (d) schematic representation of 3D graph; (e) trimap generated from image in (c): black pixel are not considered for segmentation; (f) final segmentation result; (g) a schematic representation of a room with objects, and normal for the left wall; (h) histogram built in the direction of the normal; Bin_0 is the most outer bin in the scene for this direction and contains all wall points

3.1   Foreground Extraction Based on Directed Histograms

The idea to use one thresholding plane to separate foreground from the background based on depth or infrared images is not new [19,4,18]. However, in presence of slanted surfaces like walls, floor or ceiling, to do the separation with only one plane is difficult and in some cases impossible. In order to overcome these limitations we developed a method, which uses multiple thresholding planes, fitted to bounding walls, which are positioned in the scene automatically.

Initial estimation of the plane orientation
In a first step we estimate a normal for each point in the depth image. This is done by projecting each neighbor point in a window around the current point in 3D space and by applying principal component analysis (PCA). PCA is applied by calculating the covariance matrix from the given point cloud and by performing singular value decomposition.The calculated eigenvector with the smallest eigenvalue is then the plane normal in least squares sense. Figure 2 (a) shows the results from the normal estimation through the PCA.

In a second step we apply a clustering method from [12] to get a discrete set of normals as the first estimates for the thresholding plane orientations. The method performs iterative splitting of the clusters orthogonal to their greatest variance axis. The clustering is performed hierarchically, starting with one cluster constructed from all image points and proceeding to split a cluster with the biggest variance until a maximal cluster number is reached. To determine the optimal cluster number adaptively, we stop the splitting if no cluster with variance over a certain threshold exist. The main idea behind the clustering is to reduce the set of candidates for later processing.

Robust orientation estimation
After the initial normal estimation we have a discrete set of normals representing initial orientations for the thresholding planes. To increase robustness in our refinement process, we order the normals in decreasing order based on the size of the corresponding clusters (biggest cluster first). Following steps are then performed iteratively for each normal in the set:

- First, the normal is oriented to point to the inside of the room, and a histogram is calculated in the direction of the normal, by projecting all 3D data points from ToF data to the line defined by the normal. By orienting the normal inwards, we assure that the first bin (Bin_0) in the histogram is the most outer bin in the scene (see figure 2 (g) and (h)). The bin size of the histogram is defined by the user and was set in our experiments to 20 cm, to increase robustness against errors in depth measurement.
- Second, from the first histogram bin a new plane orientation is estimated based on RANSAC [6]. All points in the bin are then classified in inliers and outliers based on predefined threshold for distance from the plane and an optimal fitting plane is calculated for the inliers using principal component analysis. The refined normal is set to the normal of the estimated fitting plane and a new iteration starts.

The number of iterations in the refinement process is defined by the user and was fixed in our experiments to 3. After the iterative refinement all 3D points in the first bin are projected to the fitting plane in first bin from the last iteration. Figure 2 (b) shows the normal vectors for the pixel corresponding to the 3D points in the first bin for each refined normal. The pixel colored white correspond to the 3D points, which are not lying in the first bin of any normal and are foreground candidates.

Final thresholding

The final thresholding is performed by construction of a directed histogram for each refined thresholding plane orientation (refined normal in the discrete set) and by placing the thresholding plane after the first histogram bin. All pixel in the depth image, corresponding to 3D points in the first bin are removed from the image (all points in the outer hull of the scene point cloud, see figure 2 (g) and (h)).

3.2   Grab-Cut Segmentation in a Video Volume

Due to the ToF depth measurement errors and big resolution change during the transformation of depth to the view of the reference camera some artifacts appear in the thresholded image after initial foreground extraction (see figure 2 (c)). In order to reduce these artifacts, we apply time-consistent color segmentation step based on grab - cut algorithm [14], extended to a video volume.

Similar to the grab - cut algorithm for one color image, we use trimaps to divide an image in definitive foreground, definitive background and uncertainty region. We use gaussian color mixture models to represent foreground and background, but build and update these models for a batch of images simultaneously. To achieve the temporal consistency we construct a 3D graph from all images in a batch, connecting pixel in different images through temporal edges. To handle the complexity we operate on the image pyramid and include only pixel in the uncertainty region, as well as their direct neighbors in definitive foreground and background in graph construction. In the following we describe our refinement scheme in more detail.

Automatic Trimap generation

For the trimap generation we convert each thresholded image to a binary image. After that morphological operations, erosion and dilation, are performed. Let E^k be the k-th binary image after erosion and D^k the k-th binary image after dilation and DD^k the binary image after dilation applied to D^k. The definitive foreground for the k-th batch image is then defined as $T_f^k = E^k$, uncertainty region as $T_u^k = D^k - E^k$ and definitive background as $T_b^k = DD^k - D^k$. The trimap for bacth image k is defined as $T^k = T_u^k \cup T_f^k \cup T_b^k$. Additionally a reduced trimap is defined, as $\overline{T}^k = T_u^k \cup \{p^k \in (T_b^k \cup T_f^k) | \exists q^k \in T_u^k \text{ with } dist(q^k, p^k) \leq \sqrt{2}\}$. The number of erosion and dilation operations defines the size of T_u^k, T_f^k and T_b^k in the trimap. Figure 2 (e) shows the generated trimap for the thresholded image from figure 2 (c).

Hierarchical segmentation scheme

To reduce computational complexity we build an image pyramid of N levels, whereby in each next level the resolution of the image from the previous level is reduced by a factor of 2. All images in a level are processed in batches of size $|B|$ as follows. For each batch B:

1. A trimap is created for each image.
2. Using the definitive foreground and definitive background from all trimaps in the batch two gaussian mixture color models are created, one for the foreground GM_f and one for the background GM_b. To create a gaussian mixture model, we use the clustering method from [12] with a specified variance threshold as a stopping criterium (as described in section 3). The clusters calculated by the clustering algorithm are used to determine individual gaussian components of a gaussian mixture model. By using a variance threshold as a stopping criterium, we are able to determine the number of clusters and hence the number of gaussian components automatically, instead of setting it to a fixed number specified by the user as in [14].
3. A 3D graph in a video volume is constructed similar to [10] and a graph - cut segmentation technique [2] is applied to classify all pixel in the unknown regions T_u^k ($k = 0, ..., |B|$) as foreground or background. The classification of pixel is stored in a map A, with $A[p^k] = FG$ if the pixel p^k from the k-th batch image is classified as foreground and $A[p^k] = BG$ else.
4. The color models are updated based on the pixel classification A.
5. Steps 3 and 4 are repeated until a maximum number of iterations is reached.

We start processing with the lowest level N. For this level trimaps are generated from the thresholded images as described before. For each successive level we use the segmentation results from the previous level to create more accurate trimap. For the level N the size of the uncertainty region is specified once for the whole sequence (each trimap has the same uncertainty size) and has to be chosen appropriate to compensate for errors due to imperfect depth measurements. For the successive levels the width of the uncertainty region is fixed, to compensate for errors due to up-sampling.

Graph cut segmentation

The classification of pixel in a video volume (batch B) in foreground and background can be formulated as a binary labeling problem on the map A and expressed in the form of the following energy functional

$$F_A = \sum_{p^k \in \bigcup_{k=0}^{|B|} \overline{T}^k} D(p^k) + \sum_{\{p^k, q^k\} \in E_S} \lambda_S S_A(p^k, q^k) + \sum_{\{p^j, q^k\} \in E_T} \lambda_T T_A(p^j, q^k) \quad (1)$$

E_S defines spatial 8-neighborhood for each image $I^k \in B$

$$E_S = \{\{p^k, q^k\} | p^k, q^k \in \overline{T}^k \wedge dist(p^k, q^k) \leq \sqrt{2}\} \quad (2)$$

E_T defines temporal neighborhood between two successive images $I^k, I^j \in B$.

$$E_T = \{\{p^j, q^k\} | p^j \in \overline{T}^j \wedge q^k \in \overline{T}^k \wedge (p^j \in T_u^j \vee q^k \in T_u^k) \wedge dist(p^j, q^j) \leq n\} \quad (3)$$

In other words, a pixel $p^j \in I^j$ is considered a temporal neighbor for a pixel $q^k \in I^k$, if the distance between pixel coordinates does not exceed a maximum distance n and either p^j or q^k belong to an uncertainty region. The size of the neighborhood is defined through the factor n. For simplicity the neighborhood is chosen as a rectangular window with the size $TN \times TN$ pixel.

$D(p^k)$ is a data cost term penalizing assignment of a pixel p^k to foreground or background based on similarity to the gaussian mixture models GM_f and GM_b.

$$D(p^k) = \begin{cases} -lnPr(p^k|GM_b), & \text{if } A[p^k] = BG \wedge p^k \in T_u^k \\ -lnPr(p^k|GM_f), & \text{if } A[p^k] = FG \wedge p^k \in T_u^k \\ 0, & \text{if } A[p^k] = FG \wedge p^k \in T_f^k; A[p^k] = BG \wedge p^k \in T_b^k \\ \infty, & \text{if } A[p^k] = FG \wedge p^k \in T_b^k; A[p^k] = BG \wedge p^k \in T_f^k \end{cases}$$
(4)

$S_A(p^k, q^k)$ is a spatial cost term penalizing the assignment of the neighbor pixel p^k, q^k to different labels and is defined as

$$S_A(p^k, q^k) = S(p^k, q^k)\frac{\delta(A[p^k], A[q^k])}{dist(p^k, q^k)}, \quad S(p^k, q^k) = \exp(-\frac{|I(p^k) - I(q^k)|^2}{2\sigma_S^2}),$$
(5)

where $\delta(A[p^k], A[q^k]) = 0$ if $A[p^k] = A[q^k]$ and 1 else.

$T_A(p^j, q^k)$ is a temporal cost term which should assure consistency between successive frames $I^k, I^j \in B$ and is defined as

$$T_A(p^j, q^k) = T(p^j, q^k)\delta(A[p^j], A[q^k]), \quad T(p^j, q^k) = \exp(-\frac{|I^j(p^j) - I^k(q^k)|^2}{2\sigma_T^2}).$$
(6)

The parameters λ_S and λ_T are weighting factors for the balance between different cost terms. The parameters σ_T^2 and σ_S^2 model spatial and temporal color variance. The energy functional F_A can be mapped on a 3D graph G and efficiently minimized using one of the max - flow / min-cut algorithms from the literature. We define G as $G = (V, E)$, with the node set $V = \bigcup_{k=0}^{|B|} \overline{T}^k \cup \{s, t\}$ and the edge set $E = E_D \cup E_S \cup E_T$, whereby s and t are two additional nodes representing background (t) and foreground (s). We define E_D as

$$E_D = \{\{s, p^k\}, \{t, p^k\} | p^k \in \bigcup_{k=0}^{|B|} \overline{T}^k\}$$
(7)

and set the capacity weights for an edge $e \in E$ to $S(e)$, if $e \in E_S$ and $T(e)$, if $e \in E_T$. For $e \in E_D$ we set the capacity weights for $p^k \in T_u^k$ to $-lnPr(p^k|GM_b)$, if $s \in e$ and $-lnPr(p^k|GM_f)$, if $t \in e$. For $p^k \in T_f^k$ the capacity weights are set to ∞, if $s \in e$ and 0, if $t \in e$ and for $p^k \in T_b^k$ to ∞, if $t \in e$ and 0, if $s \in e$. To minimize the functional a minimum cut is calculated on the graph G using the algorithm from [3], where minimum cut capacity is equivalent to the minimum of the functional F_A. Figure 2 (f) shows the segmentation result for the image from figure 1 and figure 2 (d) a schematic representation of the graph G.

Fig. 3. Results after initial thresholding (left) and after grab-cut refinement with temporal constraints (right)

4   Experimental Results

For the experimental evaluation we captured a sequence of 800 frames. After pre-processing, depth and color images were first scaled to the resolution of 960×540 px. to reduce computational complexity. For the initial foreground extraction, based on depth thresholding, the bin size in the orientation refinement step was set to 20 cm and the inlier threshold for RANSAC to 3 cm. The bin size for the last thresholding step was set to 10 cm. For some frames the bin size and inlier threshold had to be adjusted to compensate errors on image borders due to bad normal alignment, but no manual correction of thresholded images was necessary. Figure 3 (left) shows the result from image 296 after the initial thresholding step. For the grab - cut refinement we used 3 pyramid levels. The segmentation parameters like: T_u size $(s(T_u))$, λ_S, λ_T, batch size $|B|$ and temporal neighborhood size TN, were set for the whole sequence as follows: (level 3: $s(T_u) = 4$, $\lambda_S = 3$, $\lambda_T = 3$, $|B| = 100$, $TN = 7$), level 2 ($s(T_u) = 6$, $\lambda_S = 3$, $\lambda_T = 3$, $|B| = 30$, $TN = 13$) and level 1 ($s(T_u) = 6$, $\lambda_S = 30$, $\lambda_T = 10$, $|B| = 50$, $TN = 1$). Through our experiments we found out that longer batches provide in general better segmentation results due to more stable color models. The smoothness parameters λ_S and λ_T were determined experimentally. The size of the uncertainty region for the level 3 was also chosen experimentally to compensate for depth measurement errors. For the levels 2 and 1 it was fixed to 6 px., to compensate for errors due to up-sampling. The size of the temporal neighborhood in general should be chosen appropriately to compensate scene motion. However, to handle computational complexity and memory consumption, we chose TN for level 1 to be 1 pixel. To compensate possible errors due to motion, the spatial and temporal balance smoothness weights were chosen unequal: $\lambda_S = 30$ and $\lambda_T = 10$. For other levels TN was chosen appropriately to capture moderate movements of the standing person in the foreground. Figure 3 shows the results after the grab-cut refinement (right) in comparison to the results after the initial thresholding (left). Figure 4 shows some chosen frames from the sequence (top) together with the segmentation results (bottom). Notice that the camera was moved from right to left and back during the capturing. To

Fig. 4. Frames 0, 200, 430, 700 and corresponding segmentation results

evaluate the quality of the segmentation more thoroughly we segmented 11 successive images (286 − 296) manually. The results from automatic segmentation through the proposed approach were than compared to the manual segmentation results (see automatic results for 296 in figure 3 (right)). Without time edges the percentage of false classified pixel compared to manual segmentation is 1.97%, with time edges the number of false classified pixel decreases to 1.57%. While the difference is only about 0.4%, the flickering on the object borders decreases significantly.

5   Conclusion

We introduced an approach for automatic foreground - background separation in videos. One contribution of this paper is a clear definition of background based on one dimensional histograms in 3D space. The second contribution is an automatic segmentation scheme of the foreground objects in a video volume incorporating temporal constraints. Based on depth and color/contrast cues our approach is capable of handling dynamic scenes and moving camera, as shown in the experimental results. In our future work we plan to extend our approach to segmentation of individual objects in the scene, which could be extracted from the initial thresholded images based on further depth analysis. We will also investigate the alternatives to the trimap-controlled segmentation, as it can lead to errors in presence of thin structures and large depth errors.

References

1. Bartczak, B., Schiller, I., Beder, C., Koch, R.: Integration of a time-of-flight camera into a mixed reality system for handling dynamic scenes, moving viewpoints and occlusions in real-time. In: Proceedings of the 3DPVT Workshop (2008)
2. Boykov, Y., Funka-Lea, G.: Graph cuts and efficient nd image segmentation. International Journal of Computer Vision 70(2), 109–131 (2006)
3. Boykov, Y., Kolmogorov, V.: An experimental comparison of min-cut/max- flow algorithms for energy minimization in vision. IEEE Transactions on Pattern Analysis and Machine Intelligence 26(9), 1124–1137 (2004)

4. Crabb, R., Tracey, C., Puranik, A., Davis, J.: Real-time foreground segmentation via range and color imaging. In: IEEE Computer Society Conference on Computer Vision and Pattern Recognition Workshops, CVPRW 2008, pp. 1–5 (2008)
5. Criminisi, A., Cross, G., Blake, A., Kolmogorov, V.: Bilayer Segmentation of Live Video. In: IEEE Computer Society Conference on Computer Vision and Pattern Recognition, vol. 1, pp. 53–60 (2006)
6. Fischler, M., Bolles, R.: Random sample consensus: a paradigm for model fitting with applications to image analysis and automated cartography. Communications of the ACM 24(6), 381–395 (1981)
7. Frick, A., Bartczak, B., Koch, R.: Real-time preview for layered depth video in 3D-TV. In: Proceedings of SPIE 7724, 77240F (2010)
8. Kolb, A., Barth, E., Koch, R., Larsen, R.: Time-of-flight sensors in computer graphic. In: Eurographics 2009 - State of the Art Reports pp. 119–134 (2009)
9. Kolmogorov, V., Criminisi, A., Blake, A., Cross, G., Rother, C.: Bi-layer segmentation of binocular stereo video. In: IEEE Computer Society Conference on Computer Vision and Pattern Recognition, CVPR 2005, vol. 2, pp. 407–414 (2005)
10. Li, Y., Sun, J., Shum, H.: Video object cut and paste. ACM Transactions on Graphics (TOG) 24(3), 600 (2005)
11. Li, Y., Sun, J., Tang, C., Shum, H.: Lazy snapping. ACM Transactions on Graphics (TOG) 23(3), 303–308 (2004)
12. Orchard, M., Bouman, C.: Color quantization of images. IEEE Transactions on Signal Processing 39(12), 2677–2690 (1991)
13. Pham, V., Takahashi, K., Naemura, T.: Live video segmentation in dynamic backgrounds using thermal vision. Advances in Image and Video Technology, 143–154 (2009)
14. Rother, C., Kolmogorov, V., Blake, A.: Grabcut: Interactive foreground extraction using iterated graph cuts. ACM Transactions on Graphics 23, 309–314 (2004)
15. Schiller, I., Beder, C., Koch, R.: Calibration of A PMD-Camera using a Planar Calibration Pattern Together with a Multi-camera Setup. In: Proc. XXXVII Int'l Soc. for Photogrammetry (2008)
16. Smith, A., Blinn, J.: Blue screen matting. In: Proceedings of the 23rd Annual Conference on Computer Graphics and Interactive Techniques, pp. 259–268 (1996)
17. Sun, J., Zhang, W., Tang, X., Shum, H.-Y.: Background cut. In: Leonardis, A., Bischof, H., Pinz, A. (eds.) ECCV 2006. LNCS, vol. 3952, pp. 628–641. Springer, Heidelberg (2006)
18. Wang, O., Finger, J., Yang, Q., Davis, J., Yang, R.: Automatic Natural Video Matting with Depth. In: 15th Pacific Conference on Computer Graphics and Applications, PG 2007, pp. 469–472 (2007)
19. Wu, Q., Boulanger, P., Bischof, W.: Robust Real-Time Bi-Layer Video Segmentation Using Infrared Video. In: Canadian Conference on Computer and Robot Vision, CRV 2008, pp. 87–94 (2008)

Channel Coding for Joint
Colour and Depth Segmentation

Marcus Wallenberg[1], Michael Felsberg[1],
Per-Erik Forssén[1], and Babette Dellen[2]

[1] Linköping University, SE-581 83 Linköping, Sweden
{wallenberg,mfe,perfo}@isy.liu.se
[2] Institut de Robotica i Informatica Industrial (CSIC-UPC)
Llorens i Artigas 4-6, 08028 Barcelona, Spain

Abstract. Segmentation is an important preprocessing step in many applications. Compared to colour segmentation, fusion of colour and depth greatly improves the segmentation result. Such a fusion is easy to do by stacking measurements in different value dimensions, but there are better ways. In this paper we perform fusion using the channel representation, and demonstrate how a state-of-the-art segmentation algorithm can be modified to use channel values as inputs. We evaluate segmentation results on data collected using the Microsoft Kinect peripheral for Xbox 360, using the superparamagnetic clustering algorithm. Our experiments show that depth gradients are more useful than depth values for segmentation, and that channel coding both colour and depth gradients makes tuned parameter settings generalise better to novel images.

1 Introduction

Segmentation of a colour image into semantically meaningful regions is one of the oldest problems in computer vision. Purely colour-based segmentation is often problematic, due to colour changes on the surfaces of textured objects. It is thus often argued that without auxiliary information (such as prior knowledge obtained e.g. using object appearance learning) bottom up, image based segmentation is an ill-posed problem [15,11].

In contrast to colour regions, homogeneous regions obtained from depth segmentation are more likely to correspond to what we intuitively perceive as objects. The reason for this is that we categorise objects, mainly according to what actions we can perform on them [14,11]. An entity that is defined in 3D is more likely to be acted upon separately, than one that is defined only by colour. By fusing colour and depth we can however obtain an even better result, and here we investigate how to do so.

Our intended application is segmentation of individual leaves on growing plants, and we use data from the recently introduced Microsoft Kinect sensor[1]. As an operational problem definition, we make use of a set of hand-labelled images, where individual leaves have been assigned different labels.

---

[1] http://www.xbox.com/Kinect

R. Mester and M. Felsberg (Eds.): DAGM 2011, LNCS 6835, pp. 306–315, 2011.
© Springer-Verlag Berlin Heidelberg 2011

1.1 Related Work

Much work on fusion of colour and depth has been done over the years. Such work has either used custom made sensors, as e.g. in [4], or more recently, time-of-flight sensors [7,3,5]. Another large body of similar work is stereo rig segmentation [1,20]. Stereo rig research is however of a different nature, as the input is two RGB images, and thus best results are obtained when jointly estimating a segmentation and a depth map [20].

We use depth from structured light (the Kinect output), which gives us *quasi-dense* depth maps; values almost everywhere, but with thin missing-data shadows near occlusion boundaries.

Currently there exists no standard evaluation set for RGB+depth segmentation, instead only qualitative examples of success are shown, see e.g. [4,1,7,3]. In [20,5] only the depth map quality is evaluated. In colour image segmentation, good evaluation datasets exist, see e.g. [16], and these are of great use when selecting algorithms for particular applications. We have assembled a dataset with hand-labelled ground truth, and we use it to thoroughly verify the relative contributions of colour and depth, as well as the improvement offered by channel coding.

Our application is inspection and measurement of growing plants. As the scene is static, we cannot exploit either background modelling [7] or tracking [3]. Furthermore, purely colour-based segmentation is particularly brittle here, due to small reflectance variations, shadows, and in particular occlusions [6]. Segmentation for plant model registration is considered to be a hard problem that requires manual interaction even if colour and depth information is used [17].

We improve fusion of colour and spatial derivatives of depth, by using the channel representation [12]. By feeding the fused channel vectors to a state-of-the-art colour segmentation algorithm [2] we obtain a method that once tuned, will generalise well to new data.

2 Methods and Materials

2.1 The Microsoft Kinect

The Microsoft Kinect[1] is a peripheral device for the Xbox 360. It is used to obtain dense depth estimates using a structured light pattern. The device contains a colour camera, a *near-infrared* (NIR) camera and a laser projector, offset by a narrow baseline, see Fig. 1, **a, b**.

A structured light pattern is projected onto the scene, using a laser projector with a characteristic wavelength of 830 nm[2]. The structured light pattern is designed to have a negligible auto-correlation, and is imaged by the NIR camera. The displacement of the NIR camera relative to the laser projector allows the distance to objects in the scene to be computed using triangulation [18]. The device is capable of outputting RGB, NIR and depth images with 640×480

---

[2] http://openkinect.org/wiki

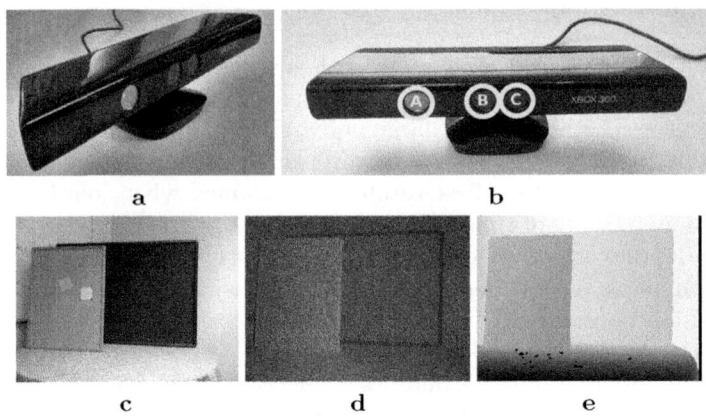

a   b

c   d   e

Fig. 1. The Kinect device: a, b (A) – laser projector, (B) – colour camera, (C) –
NIR camera; **Images from the Kinect: c** – RGB image from colour camera; **d** –
light pattern as imaged by NIR camera; **e** – resulting depth map

pixels at 30 frames per second (Fig. 1, c–e). Open source drivers in the form
of the libfreenect[3] library are available from the OpenKinect[4] community
and can be used to interface with the Kinect device. Approximate formulae for
converting the Kinect depth map to metric distances are also available[2].

We use the libfreenect[3] library to control the Kinect, and receive the colour
and depth video streams. The two streams need to be aligned, since the position,
orientation and *field of view* (FoV) of the cameras are different. We do this by first
estimating the intrinsic camera parameters of the two cameras, using the widely
used OpenCV[5] implementation of [22]. We then find the relative orientation and
translation between the cameras, by minimising the transfer error in the image
plane of the colour image, using manually selected corresponding points in the
colour and NIR images. We do this using the non-linear least squares solver
lsqnonlin in MATLAB.

Note that, as the Kinect cameras are rigidly mounted, the calibration described here only has to be performed once for each unit. In the following, we
thus consider the RGB image $\mathbf{f}(x, y)$, and the depth map $h(x, y)$, transferred to
the RGB camera as the input.

2.2   Fused Feature Vectors

The depth image $h(x, y)$ delivered by the Kinect is a) quantised and b) the
quantisation levels are proportional to the absolute depth. This implies that
segmentation based on the depth becomes more difficult if the respective part of
the scene is located further away from the camera. Due to the constant spatial

---

[3] https://github.com/OpenKinect/libfreenect

[4] http://openkinect.org

[5] http://opencv.willowgarage.com

accuracy in the NIR camera, this behaviour is sensible. However, for leaves that touch each other and which are at distances of approximately one meter, the segmentation will bleed out between neighbouring leaves if the segmentation is based on regularising the gradient of the depth image:

$$E_{\text{smooth}} = \rho(|\nabla h(x,y)|^2) \ , \tag{1}$$

where E_{smooth} is the regularising term and $\rho()$ is a monotonic function.

Touching leaves are unlikely to have identical surface normals. Therefore, we choose to regularise the differences in the gradients of the depth map instead:

$$E_{\text{smooth}} = \rho(|\nabla h_x(x,y)|^2 + |\nabla h_y(x,y)|^2) \ , \tag{2}$$

where $h_x(x,y) = \frac{\partial}{\partial x} h(x,y)$ and $h_y(x,y) = \frac{\partial}{\partial y} h(x,y)$.

Thus, we have three requirements for assigning image points to the same segment: similar colour ($\mathbf{f}(x,y)$), similar x-derivative of the depth image ($h_x(x,y)$), and similar y-derivative of the depth image ($h_y(x,y)$). In the ideal case, the feature vector used for segmentation, called $\mathbf{g}(x,y)$ in what follows, should represent $\mathbf{f}(x,y)$, $h_x(x,y)$, and $h_y(x,y)$. In the experiments below, five different variants of the feature vector will be used:

$$\mathbf{g}(x,y) = \mathbf{f}(x,y) \tag{3}$$

$$\mathbf{g}(x,y) = h(x,y) \tag{4}$$

$$\mathbf{g}(x,y) = \begin{bmatrix} h_x(x,y) \\ h_y(x,y) \\ \sqrt{h_x(x,y)^2 + h_y(x,y)^2} \end{bmatrix} \tag{5}$$

$$\mathbf{g}(x,y) = \begin{bmatrix} (1-\lambda)\mathbf{w}(\mathbf{f}(x,y); b_1) \\ \lambda\mathbf{w}(h_x(x,y); b_2) \\ \lambda\mathbf{w}(h_y(x,y); b_2) \end{bmatrix} \tag{6}$$

$$\mathbf{g}(x,y) = \begin{bmatrix} (1-\lambda)\mathbf{f}(x,y) \\ \lambda h_x(x,y) \\ \lambda h_y(x,y) \\ \lambda\sqrt{h_x(x,y)^2 + h_y(x,y)^2} \end{bmatrix} \tag{7}$$

where $\lambda > 0$ is a weight factor between colour and depth and $\mathbf{w}$ is the channel vector computed using the basis function b_j, cf. sect. 2.4. The respective feature vector $\mathbf{g}(x,y)$ is then spatially clustered using superparamagnetic clustering.

2.3   Superparamagnetic Clustering

In the image, each pixel is characterised by a feature vector $\mathbf{g}(x,y)$. Our goal is to to group the image pixels into spatially connected areas of similar feature values. This defines a pixel labelling problem, where a label has to be assigned to every pixel i, which we call l_i. To find this label configuration, we use the method of superparamagnetic clustering of data [2]. In this method, each pixel i is assigned a spin variable σ_i (not to be confused with the label l_i), which can take q different states. The spins interact with each other such that spins having a similar feature value have the tendency to align. Here, we only consider nearest neighbour coupling, i.e., two pixels are i and j with coordinates (x_i, y_i) and (x_j, y_j) are only interacting if $|(x_i - x_j)| \leq 1$ and $|(y_i - y_j)| \leq 1$.

The spin states configuration is then determined by a Potts energy function

$$E = -\sum_{\langle ij \rangle} J_{ij} \delta(\sigma_i, \sigma_j) \ , \tag{8}$$

with $J_{ij} = 1 - \triangle/\bar{\triangle}$ and $\triangle_{ij} = |\mathbf{g}_i - \mathbf{g}_j|$, where $\mathbf{g}_i$ and $\mathbf{g}_j$ are the feature vectors of the pixels i and j, respectively. The mean distance $\bar{\triangle}$ is obtained by averaging over all bonds and scaling with a factor h. The Kronecker δ function is defined as $\delta(a, b) = 1$ if $a = b$ and zero otherwise.

The model is a statistical model, so the probability $P(S)$ of a spin configuration S is determined by the Boltzmann distribution through $P(S) \propto \exp(-E/T)$, where T is the temperature of the system. This implies that the energy is the logarithm of the probability of the spin configuration and can thus also be viewed as the log posterior of a Markov Random Field [10].

The grouping problem is then solved by finding clusters of correlated spins in the low temperature equilibrium states of the energy function E, using a sigmoid of E as the link strength. The total number M of segments is then determined by counting the computed segments. It is usually different from the total number q of spin states, which is a parameter of the algorithm (here $q = 30$).

We solve this task by implementing a clustering algorithm. In a first step, "satisfied" bonds, i.e. bonds connecting pixels of identical spins $\sigma_i = \sigma_j$, are identified. Then, in a second step, the satisfied bonds are "frozen" with some probability P_{ij}. Pixels connected by frozen bonds define a cluster, which are updated by assigning the same value to all spins inside a cluster [19]. In the method of superparamagnetic clustering proposed by Blatt et al. [2] this is done independently for each cluster. The algorithm is controlled by the "temperature" parameter, and has been shown to deliver robust results over a large temperature range. After 100 iterations, clusters are used to define segments with labels l_i. As a consequence, two spins which are in the same spin state can carry different segment labels. This allows testing new spin combinations in the next iteration, while stabilising segments having similar feature values.

2.4   Channel Coding

Adding depth derivatives, $h_x(x, y)$, $h_y(x, y)$, and colour, $\mathbf{f}(x, y)$, as different components of a vector space (7) is not sensible due the different respective physical units. Instead, we will use smooth basis functions to generate probabilistic representations of colour and depth derivatives and combine those (6). The generated representations, called *channel representations* [12], are a special case of soft histograms, with the additional property that modes of the underlying density can be extracted with sub-bin accuracy [9].

Channel representations are also known as population codes [21]. They differ from GMMs and Parzen window (or kernel density) estimators, because positions of the basis functions are spread regularly across the domain. This has the advantage that signal processing methods can be used for manipulation, see e.g. [13] for the use of basis functions in the colour channels.

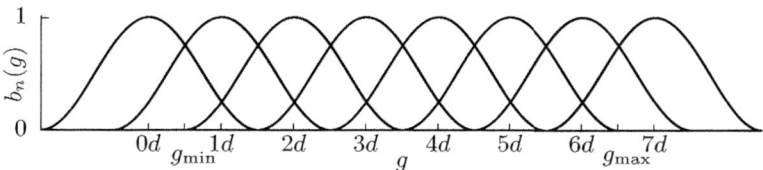

Fig. 2. Illustration of basis functions for $N = 8$. The basis functions are spaced with distance d and have a width of $3d$. The encoded values may lie between g_{min} and g_{max}.

Given a feature component g, the basis functions are located on a grid with spacing d. The used kernel function $b(g)$ are compact and overlapping. Throughout this paper they have a support of size $3d$, see Fig. 2. In the remainder of this paper, $\cos^2$ kernel functions [12] are used:

$$b(g) \triangleq \frac{2}{3d} \begin{cases} \cos^2(\frac{\pi g}{3d}) & |g| < \frac{3d}{2} \\ 0 & |g| \geq \frac{3d}{2} \end{cases} .$$ (9)

The range of g together with d determine the number of basis functions $N = (g_{max} - g_{min})/d + 2$. The grid index is $n \in \{0 \ldots N - 1\}$. Using (9), we obtain the *channel vector* $\mathbf{w} = [w_0, w_1, \ldots, w_{N-1}]^T$ from g using:

$$w_n(g; b) = b(g - nd - d/2 - g_{min}) .$$ (10)

Usually, several feature components from a local neighbourhood are pooled in each vector by local averaging of channel vectors.

The distance of channel vectors behaves like a sigmoid function of the corresponding feature distance: Large distances become saturated [9]. Statistically independent channel vectors can be concatenated, as is done in (6), and still result in sensible distance measures. The RGB vector might be interpreted as a channel vector of the spectral density with length $N = 3$ and the colour matching function as basis functions. Applying spatial averaging, the resolution of the channel vector is increased [8]. Channel encoding is denoted $\mathbf{w}(\mathbf{f}(x, y); b_1)$ in (6).

3   Experiments

3.1   Data Sets

Evaluation data consists of six pairs of images, each consisting of a colour image (640×480 pixels in 8-bit RGB), and an aligned depth map of equal resolution. An example of such an image pair is shown in figure 3. These image pairs (henceforth denoted *plant1* to *plant6*) were chosen to illustrate the challenges faced when performing segmentation based on colour and depth. The objective is to segment leaves on the plant from the background, and from each other. This causes problems when using colour-based segmentation due to the similarity in colour between one leaf and another. The complex structure with many occlusion boundaries where leaves overlap also causes problems for depth-based segmentation, as do the connections of leaves to one another.

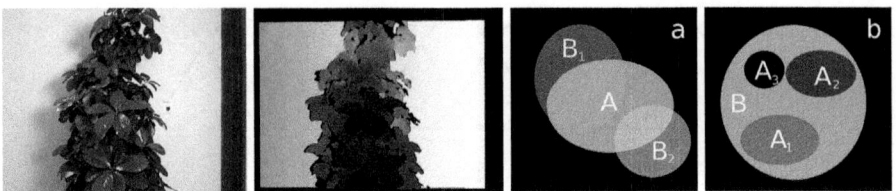

Fig. 3. Examples of evaluation images and segmentation evaluation. From left to right: Colour image and depth map for the *plant3* images. Illustrations (a) and (b) used to describe the segmentation evaluation procedure (see section 3.2).

3.2   Performance Evaluation

Performance evaluation was carried out using manually segmented ground-truth images. In these images, regions of the kind we wish to segment were manually separated and labelled. Examples of such images are shown in figure 5, first and third row. In [16], *precision* and *recall* measures are used to evaluate performance. While this is readily applicable to a binary problem, its generalisation to the multi-region segmentation case is not straightforward. We instead propose a *consensus score*, s, with which to score a particular segmentation of an image. The score s is computed as the sum of two terms, where one serves to reward coverage of ground truth segments and penalise over-segmentation, and the other serves to penalise under-segmentation and merging of ground-truth regions.

When calculating $s_{\mathbf{Y}}(X)$, X is the segment for which the score is calculated, and $\mathbf{Y} = \{Y_j\}_1^J$ are overlapping segments in the result being compared to. With regions as in figure 3(a) (with $X = A$ and $\mathbf{Y} = \{B_1, B_2\}$), A corresponds to a ground-truth segment, and B_1 and B_2 correspond to overlapping segmentation results. With $S(R)$ denoting the area of a particular segment, $s_{\mathbf{B}}(A)$ is:

$$s_{\mathbf{B}}(A) = \max_i \left(S(A \cap B_i) - \sum_{j \neq i} S(A \cap B_j) \right). \tag{11}$$

For the example in figure 3(a) we get $s_{\mathbf{B}}(A) = S(A \cap B_1) - S(A \cap B_2)$.

When all ground-truth segments in an image have been scored in this way, the roles of ground-truth and segmentation results are reversed. With regions as in figure 3(b), with B corresponding to a segment in the segmentation result, and A_1, A_2 and A_3 corresponding to ground-truth regions, $s_{\mathbf{A}}$ is calculated as in (11), which in this case means $s_{\mathbf{A}}(B) = S(B \cap A_1) - S(B \cap A_2) - S(B \cap A_3)$.

The final consensus score s is then the sum over all K ground-truth regions and all J segments as:

$$s = \frac{\sum_{k=1}^{K} s_{\mathbf{B}}(A_k) + \sum_{j=1}^{J} s_{\mathbf{A}}(B_j)}{2 \sum_{k=1}^{K} S(A_k)}, \tag{12}$$

where $\sum_{k=1}^{K} S(A_k)$ is the total area of ground-truth regions in an image (this produces a score in the range $-1 < s \leq 1$). Note that this method differs

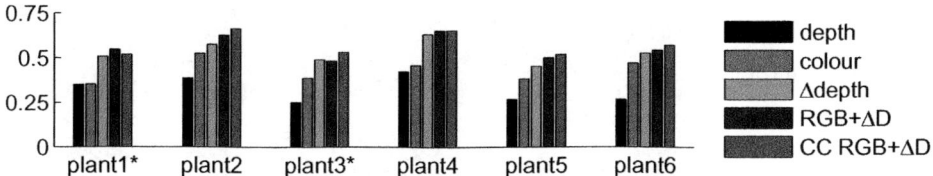

Fig. 4. Consensus scores on the *plant* data set. Images indicated with asterisks were used for parameter tuning of all methods. Note that although RGB+ΔD and channel coded RGB+ΔD have similar results on the tuning images, channel coded RGB+ΔD has a higher score on all evaluation images.

from [16]. Since we cannot evaluate results in areas not covered by ground truth data, these will not affect the resulting score (12). We also use the entire regions instead of comparing boundaries as our goal is coverage, rather than precise location of boundaries.

3.3   Tested Methods

The methods we evaluate all make use of superparamagnetic clustering, as described in section 2.3. The feature vectors used are those described in section 2.2. The depth map gradient was estimated using finite differences. A small amount of low-pass filtering (3×3 Gaussian kernel with $\sigma = 1.5$ px) was applied to each component of the feature vectors before clustering. This serves to reduce noise, and was found to improve the results for all tested methods.

For all methods, the temperature parameter was kept constant at $T = 0.05$. Scaling parameters were tuned by maximising consensus score on the *plant1* and *plant3* sets. For the methods using only colour or depth, the global scaling parameter was tuned individually for each method. In the cases when both depth and colour information was used, the global scale factor was optimised together with the relative weight λ for each method (see section 2.2, eq. (3) to (7)). The number of basis functions in channel coding was $N = 6$ for colour and $N = 7$ for each of $h_x(x,y)$ and $h_y(x,y)$ (resulting in a total of 20 channels).

3.4   Results

Results of the evaluation procedure are shown in figures 4 (consensus scores) and 5 (segmented images). Purely colour- and depth-based segmentation performs worst, as can be expected given the nature of the data. Depth gradient-based segmentation (Δdepth) performs better than either of these two. The concatenation of RGB colour and depth gradient (RGB + ΔD) performs well overall, but seems to show a slight tendency toward overfitting. The channel-coded variant (CC RGB + ΔD) shows similar results on the training data, but generalises better to the other image sets.

Ground truth 1–3

Result 1–3

Ground truth 4–6

Result 4–6

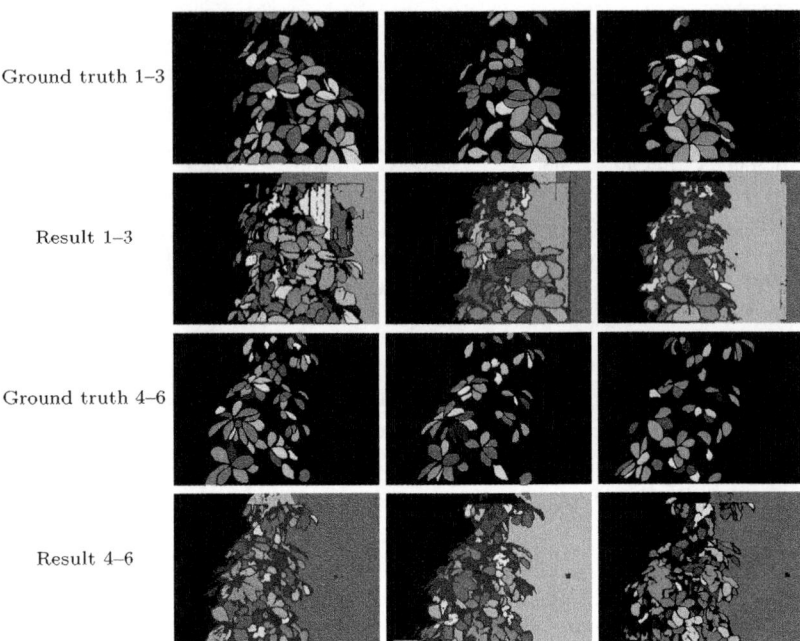

Fig. 5. Segmentation results on the *plant* data set, and corresponding ground truth

4 Conclusions

We have evaluated a method for joint colour and depth-based segmentation using data gathered with the Kinect. The results show that it is indeed possible to obtain better results by fusing colour and depth, than using either one in isolation. The greater robustness of the channel-based segmentation indicates that this is a suitable approach for fusing these measurement modalities. Our experimental setup with consensus score tuning on two of the image pairs, and evaluation on all pairs also demonstrates that the parameters found by tuning generalise well to new data. Future work will include exploring the use of other colour spaces, as well as other ways to represent the depth maps, before feeding them to the channel encoding procedure.

Acknowledgements. This work was supported by the EC's 7th Framework Programme (FP7/2007-2013), grant agreement 247947 (GARNICS), the Swedish Research Council through a grant for the project *Embodied Visual Object Recognition*, and by Linköping University. B. Dellen also acknowledges support from the Spanish Ministry for Science and Innovation via a Ramon y Cajal fellowship.

References

1. Björkman, M., Eklundh, J.-O.: Vision in the real world: Finding, attending and recognizing objects. Int. J. of Imag. Sys. and Technology 5(16), 189–209 (2006)
2. Blatt, M., Wiseman, S., Domany, E.: Superparametric clustering of data. Physical Review Letters 76(18) (1996)
3. Bleiweiss, A., Werman, M.: Fusing time-of-flight depth and color for real-time segmentation and tracking. In: Kolb, A., Koch, R. (eds.) Dyn3D 2009. LNCS, vol. 5742, pp. 58–69. Springer, Heidelberg (2009)
4. Boulanger, P.: Simultaneous segmentation of range and color images based on bayesian decision theory. In: Computer and Robot Vision, CRV 2004 (2004)
5. Dellen, B., Alenya, G., Torras, C.: Segmenting color images into surface patches by exploiting sparse depth data. In: WACV, pp. 591–598 (2011)
6. Walter, A., et al.: Dynamics of seedling growth acclimation towards altered light conditions can be quantified via GROWSCREEN. New Phytol. 174, 447–455 (2007)
7. Leens, J., Piérard, S., Barnich, O., Van Droogenbroeck, M., Wagner, J.-M.: Combining color, depth, and motion for video segmentation. In: Fritz, M., Schiele, B., Piater, J.H. (eds.) ICVS 2009. LNCS, vol. 5815, pp. 104–113. Springer, Heidelberg (2009)
8. Felsberg, M.: Incremental computation of feature hierarchies. In: Goesele, M., Roth, S., Kuijper, A., Schiele, B., Schindler, K. (eds.) Pattern Recognition. LNCS, vol. 6376, pp. 523–532. Springer, Heidelberg (2010)
9. Felsberg, M., Forssén, P.-E., Scharr, H.: Channel smoothing: Efficient robust smoothing of low-level signal features. IEEE TPAMI 28(2), 209–222 (2006)
10. Geman, S., Geman, D.: Stochastic relaxation, Gibbs distributions, and the Bayesian restoration of images. IEEE TPAMI 6, 721–741 (1984)
11. Granlund, G.H.: Does vision inevitably have to be active? In: SCIA 1999 (1999)
12. Granlund, G.H.: An associative perception-action structure using a localized space variant information representation. In: Sommer, G., Zeevi, Y.Y. (eds.) AFPAC 2000. LNCS, vol. 1888. Springer, Heidelberg (2000)
13. Kass, M., Solomon, J.: Smoothed local histogram filters. In: ACM SIGGRAPH 2010 papers, pages 100:1–100:10. ACM, New York (2010)
14. Lakoff, G.: Women, Fire, and Dangerous Things - what categories reveal about the mind. University of Chicago Press, Chicago (1987)
15. Leibe, B., Schiele, B.: Interleaved object categorization and segmentation. In: British Machine Vision Conference, pp. 759–768 (2003)
16. Martin, D.R., Fowlkes, C.C., Malik, J.: Learning to detect natural image boundaries using brightness and texture. In: Advances in Neural Information Processing Systems (NIPS 2002). MIT Press, Cambridge (2002)
17. Quan, L., Tan, P., Zeng, G., Yuan, L., Wang, J., Kang, S.B.: Image-based plant modeling. In: ACM SIGGRAPH 2006, New York, NY, USA, pp. 599–604 (2006)
18. Shpunt, A., Pesach, B.: Optical pattern projection. US Patent Application Publication, US 2010/0284082 A1 (November 2010)
19. Swendsen, R.H., Wang, S.: Nonuniversal critical dynamics in monte carlo simulations. Physical Review Letters 76(18), 86–88 (1987)
20. Taguchi, Y., et al.: Stereo reconstruction with mixed pixels using adaptive over-segmentation. In: CVPR (2008)
21. Zemel, R.S., Dayan, P., Pouget, A.: Probabilistic interpretation of population codes. Neural Computation 10(2), 403–430 (1998)
22. Zhang, Z.: A flexible new technique for camera calibration. IEEE Transactions on Pattern Analysis and Machine Intelligence 22, 1330–1334 (1998)

Simultaneous Interpolation and Deconvolution Model for the 3-D Reconstruction of Cell Images

Ahmed Elhayek[1], Martin Welk[2], and Joachim Weickert[3]

[1] Max Planck Institute for Computer Science
Stuhlsatzenhausweg 85, 66123 Saarbrücken, Germany
elhayek@mpi-inf.mpg.de
[2] University for Health Sciences, Medical Informatics and Technology
Eduard-Wallnöfer-Zentrum 1, 6060 Hall/Tyrol, Austria
martin.welk@umit.at
http://ibia.umit.at
[3] Mathematical Image Analysis Group
Campus E1.1, Saarland University, 66041 Saarbrücken, Germany
weickert@mia.uni-saarland.de
http://www.mia.uni-saarland.de

Abstract. Fluorescence microscopy methods are an important imaging technique in cell biology. Due to their depth sensitivity they allow a direct 3-D imaging. However, the resulting volume data sets are undersampled in depth, and the 2-D slices are blurred and noisy. Reconstructing the full 3-D information from these data is therefore a challenging task, and of high relevance for biological applications. We address this problem by combining deconvolution of the 3-D data set with interpolation of additional slices in an integrated variational approach. Our novel 3-D reconstruction model, Interpolating Robust and Regularised Richardson-Lucy reconstruction (IRRRL), merges the Robust and Regularised Richardson-Lucy deconvolution (RRRL) from [16] with variational interpolation. In this paper we develop the theoretical approach and its efficient numerical implementation using Fast Fourier Transform and a coarse-to-fine multiscale strategy. Experiments on confocal fluorescence microscopy data demonstrate the high restoration quality and computational efficiency of our approach.

1 Introduction

Imaging science and cell biology have been interwoven since the beginnings of both fields, when Robert Hooke discovered plant cells with the help of a microscope [9, Observ. XVIII]. In their continual symbiosis, virtually every advance in each of the two fields has been inherently linked with the progress of the other discipline. More than three centuries after Hooke, cell biology forms one of the keystones of today's life sciences, and it continues to pose exciting challenges for imaging science.

Three-dimensional imaging of intracellular structures in living cells is one of these problems. Its solution is of utmost importance for the understanding of life processes, or influences that interfere with these life processes. For example, nanoparticles play an increasing role in modern technology, but their inflammatory and toxicological effects in human cells are hardly understood. This drives the interest of researchers to study the effects of nanoparticles within cells. Tracing the transport of those tiny objects in a living cell is an important part of this research.

R. Mester and M. Felsberg (Eds.): DAGM 2011, LNCS 6835, pp. 316–325, 2011.
© Springer-Verlag Berlin Heidelberg 2011

While some well-established tools of 3-D imaging such as tomographic methods turn out impractical for imaging living specimens on the desired scale, one of the most promising approaches in current imaging that is compatible with the requirements of this application field are fluorescence microscopy techniques such as Confocal Laser Scanning Microscopy (CLSM) [12] or Stimulated Emission Depletion Microscopy (STED) [8]. Due to physical limitations, however, these methods have much lower resolution in depth direction than within a constant depth plane. Also, light contributions from out-of-focus planes cannot be completely suppressed. The low light intensities involved lead to Poisson noise.

One obtains therefore blurred and noisy data that are severely undersampled in depth direction. To make them suitable for further analysis in biological research, they need to be sharpened, denoised, and interpolated to approximately isotropic resolution. Since measured volumes range up to about $1600 \times 1600 \times 50$ voxels, computationally efficient algorithms are needed.

Related work. Deconvolution has been in the focus of image processing research for a long time. An early and still popular approach is the Richardson-Lucy algorithm [13,10]. Variational deconvolution methods have been introduced in the nineties [11]. The minimisation interpretation of Richardson-Lucy deconvolution [14] establishes a relation between both approaches that has been used to establish Richardson-Lucy type methods with regularisation [2], specifically in variational formulation [5,16]. Deconvolution of confocal microscopy images has been considered recently e.g. in [5,6].

Variational formulations for interpolation have been considered in [3,15]. A joint variational approach for (blind) deconvolution and interpolation of missing image information (inpainting) has been proposed in [4]. A variational framework for simultaneous deblurring and motion estimation has been proposed in [1].

Our contribution. To address the multiple degradation of fluorescence microscopy imagery of living cells, we propose a novel variational method for simultaneous deconvolution and interpolation in 3-D. By choosing as deconvolution component the modified Richardson-Lucy approach of the type of [5,16], we obtain an efficient fixed point iteration for minimisation.

Structure of the paper. In Section 2 we develop our joint variational deconvolution and interpolation approach, and derive the fixed point iteration for its optimisation. Its space-discrete numerical realisation is addressed in Section 3. Section 4 presents experimental results on confocal microscopy data to demonstrate the reconstruction quality and efficiency of the model. We end with conclusions in Section 5.

2   Joint Variational Interpolation and Deconvolution

In this section, we present our model for simultaneous interpolation and deconvolution. It combines variational interpolation methods [3,15] with the deconvolution model from [16]. The advantage of the latter is that it leads to a computationally efficient fixed point iteration similar to Richardson-Lucy deconvolution, called Robust and Regularised Richardson-Lucy deconvolution. Computational efficiency is crucial since we aim at reconstructing large fluorescence microscopy 3-D data sets.

2.1 Deconvolution Model

The deconvolution model from [16] is a modification of the popular Richardson-Lucy (RL) algorithm [10,13] which is also in broad use for fluorescence microscopy 3-D deconvolution, due to its simplicity and computational efficiency. Let the degraded image f, the sharp image u, and the point-spread-function (PSF) h be smooth functions over $\Omega = \mathbb{R}^3$ (or $\mathbb{R}^2$ for 2D images). Then RL generates a sequence of successively sharpened images $u^1, u^2, \ldots$ from the initial image $u^0 := f$ via the fixed point iteration

$$u^{k+1} = \left(h^* * \frac{f}{u^k * h} \right) \cdot u^k . \tag{1}$$

Here, we denote by h^* the adjoint of the PSF, $h^*(\boldsymbol{x}) := h(-\boldsymbol{x})$. In the case of a noise-free observed image (where $f = g * h$ is satisfied exactly), the multiplier $h^* * \frac{f}{g*h}$ equals 1. Thus, the sharp image g is a fixed point of (1) in this case.

The single parameter of this method is the number of iterations. With more iterations, the degree of sharpening increases, but at the same time the amount of regularisation sinks. In the presence of (even very low) noise the results will be dominated by amplified noise after some number of iterations.

The fixed point iteration (1) is associated with the minimisation of the functional

$$E_{f,h}[u] := \int_\Omega \left(u * h - f - f \ln \frac{u * h}{f} \right) \, \mathrm{d}\boldsymbol{x} \tag{2}$$

with respect to a *multiplicative* perturbation, thus slightly adapting the usual Euler-Lagrange formalism. This variational viewpoint allows to modify RL by introducing additional regularisers [5,16] that provide a more flexible means of structure-preserving or structure-enhancing regularisation than the original regularisation by stopping. Moreover, robust data terms can be introduced [16]. With both modifications and the abbreviation $r_f(v) := v - f - f \ln(v/f)$, the energy functional reads

$$E_{f,h}[u] = \int_\Omega \Phi\left(r_f(u * h)\right) + \alpha \, \Psi\left(|\nabla u|^2\right) \mathrm{d}\boldsymbol{x} \tag{3}$$

where both $\Phi, \Psi : \mathbb{R}^+ \to \mathbb{R}$ are increasing penalty functions, and the regularisation weight α should be chosen dependent on the noise level in the blurred image. The robust data term not only handles extreme noise, but also copes with imprecisions in the blur model and the PSF. Assuming multiplicative perturbation, one can derive from (3) an Euler-Lagrange equation and finally the fixed point iteration, cf. [16]

$$u^{k+1} = \frac{h^* * \left(\Phi'(r_f(u^k * h)) \left(\frac{f}{u^k*h} \right) \right) + \alpha \left[\mathrm{div}\left(\Psi'(|\nabla u^k|^2)\nabla u^k\right)\right]_+}{h^* * \Phi'(r_f(u^k * h)) - \alpha \left[\mathrm{div}\left(\Psi'(|\nabla u^k|^2)\nabla u^k\right)\right]_-} u^k \tag{4}$$

where $[z]_\pm := \frac{1}{2}(z \pm |z|)$. This iteration is called *robust and regularised Richardson-Lucy deconvolution (RRRL)*. It achieves an image restoration quality comparable to state-of-the-art variational deconvolution at a computational cost comparable to that of the original RL method, see [16].

2.2   Interpolation Model

In the interpolation part of our approach, we tie up to PDE models for interpolation and variational image regularisation as were formulated in [3,15].

Assume that image data is observed in the region $D \subset \Omega$ and is to be extended to the entire domain Ω. Taking into account that image data on D are also contaminated by noise, minimisation of the functional

$$E[u] = \frac{1}{2} \int_D |u - f|^2 \, d\boldsymbol{x} + \alpha \int_\Omega \Psi(|\nabla u|^2) \, d\boldsymbol{x} \tag{5}$$

performs simultaneous interpolation and denoising, see [3] with total variation regulariser $\Psi(s^2) = |s|$. The use of a non-quadratic penaliser Ψ ensures that edges are preserved. For $D = \Omega$, variational denoising is recovered.

2.3   Joint Model

To achieve simultaneous interpolation and deconvolution, we proceed in a similar manner as in [4] where a blind deconvolution approach with quadratic penalisation in the data term was combined with TV inpainting. We replace the simple data term of (5) with the deconvolution data term from (3) but evaluate it on the observed domain D only as in (5). The regulariser is inherited from (5) and acts therefore throughout Ω. We aim therefore at minimising the functional

$$E[u] = \int_D \underbrace{\Phi\left(r_f(u * h)\right)}_{\text{data}} \, d\boldsymbol{x} + \alpha \int_\Omega \underbrace{\Psi(|\nabla u|^2)}_{\text{smoothness}} \, d\boldsymbol{x} \ . \tag{6}$$

Similar as before, the data term herein suppresses deviations from the blur model in the observed image domain D by asymmetric penalisation of the reconstruction error. The smoothness term combines structure-preserving denoising in D with structure-preserving interpolation in $\Omega \setminus D$. One should, however, be aware that due to the convolutions also the direct influence of the data term is not limited to D. The regularisation weight $\alpha > 0$ balances the influence of the data and smoothness terms.

In order to compute the minimiser u, we derive again the Euler-Lagrange equation for a multiplicative perturbation. As in the case of RRRL, this proceeding not only allows to derive an efficient RL-style fixed point iteration but also ensures that the positivity of u is strictly preserved. Denoting by χ_D the characteristic function of D, the resulting equation reads

$$\left(h^* * \left(\chi_D \Phi'(r_f(u * h)) \left(1 - \frac{f}{u * h}\right)\right) - \alpha \operatorname{div}\left(\Psi'(|\nabla u|^2)\nabla u\right)\right) \cdot u = 0 \ , \tag{7}$$

from which we obtain the fixed point iteration

$$u^{k+1} = \frac{h^* * \left(\chi_D \Phi'(r_f(u^k * h)) \left(\frac{f}{u^k * h}\right)\right) + \alpha \left[\operatorname{div}\left(\Psi'(|\nabla u^k|^2)\nabla u^k\right)\right]_+}{h^* * (\chi_D \Phi'(r_f(u^k * h))) - \alpha \left[\operatorname{div}\left(\Psi'(|\nabla u^k|^2)\nabla u^k\right)\right]_-} u^k \ . \tag{8}$$

We will call this iteration *simultaneous interpolation and RRRL deconvolution (IRRRL)*. It converges to the steady-state much faster than gradient descent schemes, which are often used for conventional variational approaches, see [4] for simultaneous interpolation and deconvolution. This will make our method computationally more efficient than conventional approaches, while at the same time it achieves reconstruction quality comparable to those approaches.

We remark that classic RL deconvolution [10,13] as well as regularised RL [5], robust RL [16] and RRRL [16] are embedded as special cases in IRRRL. An extension to multi-channel image data is straightforward along the lines of [16]. For more details we refer to [7].

3   Numerical Aspects

To implement IRRRL for the reconstruction of 3-D images, a discretised version of (8) is required. In the discretisation of the data terms (i.e. the first term in the numerator and the first term denominator) at voxel (i, j, l) the expensive 3-D convolution operations are transferred to the Fourier domain. In order to use a Fast Fourier Transform (FFT) implementation for which image dimensions need to be powers of two, and to mitigate wraparound errors, images are extended by mirroring within a suitable stripe around the image domain. The Fourier strategy considerably improves the computational efficiency of our model over the direct implementation of the convolutions in the spatial domain. The characteristic function χ_D is implemented using a binary image.

For the diffusion term $D := \operatorname{div}(g \, \nabla u)$, we found that the discretisation method does not have a major effect on the performance of our model. Thus, we use the simplest discretisation based on central differences:

$$
\begin{aligned}
D_{i,j,l} \\
= \frac{1}{h_1} & \left(\frac{g_{i+1,j,l} + g_{i,j,l}}{2} \frac{u_{i+1,j,l} - u_{i,j,l}}{h_1} - \frac{g_{i,j,l} + g_{i-1,j,l}}{2} \frac{u_{i,j,l} - u_{i-1,j,l}}{h_1} \right) \\
+ \frac{1}{h_2} & \left(\frac{g_{i,j+1,l} + g_{i,j,l}}{2} \frac{u_{i,j+1,l} - u_{i,j,l}}{h_2} - \frac{g_{i,j,l} + g_{i,j-1,l}}{2} \frac{u_{i,j,l} - u_{i,j-1,l}}{h_2} \right) \\
+ \frac{1}{h_3} & \left(\frac{g_{i,j,l+1} + g_{i,j,l}}{2} \frac{u_{i,j,l+1} - u_{i,j,l}}{h_3} - \frac{g_{i,j,l} + g_{i,j,l-1}}{2} \frac{u_{i,j,l} - u_{i,j,l-1}}{h_3} \right) , \quad (9)
\end{aligned}
$$

where h_1, h_2, and h_3 are the spatial grid sizes in x, y, and z directions, respectively. The diffusivity $g = \Psi'(|\nabla u|^2)$ is discretised by

$$
g_{i,j,l} = \Psi' \left(\left(\frac{u_{i+1,j,l} - u_{i-1,j,l}}{2h_1} \right)^2 + \left(\frac{u_{i,j+1,l} - u_{i,j-1,l}}{2h_2} \right)^2 \right.
$$
$$
\left. + \left(\frac{u_{i,j,l+1} - u_{i,j,l-1}}{2h_3} \right)^2 \right) . \quad (10)
$$

In order to speed up the computation, we complement the scheme developed so far by a coarse-to-fine strategy. On each level (except the coarsest one), the result of

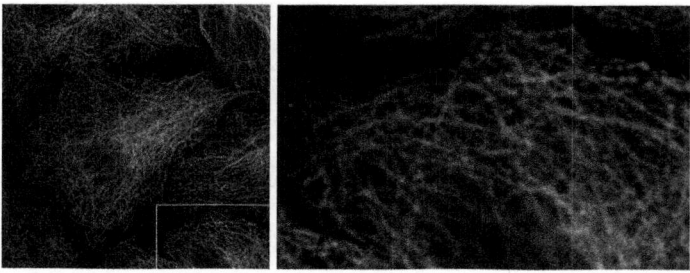

Fig. 1. Confocal microscopy 3-D image of the filament network of a cell. **(a) Left:** Slice 12 from the complete 3-D image ($1024 \times 1024 \times 24$ voxels). **(b) Right:** Corresponding slice from the clipped 3-D image (Dataset A, $376 \times 244 \times 24$ voxels).

the next coarser level serves as a fairly good initialisation, which makes the iteration converge considerably faster.

Since in our case interpolation is used to increase resolution in depth (z) direction, we implemented the coarse-to-fine approach as follows:

1. Downsample the 3-D image to a coarse scale in x, and y directions.
2. Apply the IRRRL fixed point iteration at the coarse version of the image.
3. Interpolate the solution of the coarse level and use it as an initialisation at the next finer scale.

In experiments on 3-D cell images the coarse-to-fine strategy boosts the computational efficiency of IRRRL by more than a factor 4.

4   Experimental Evaluation

In this section, we show experimental results based on real-world data to illustrate the benefits of the proposed simultaneous model. Note that all computations were performed in 3-D although only exemplary slices are displayed. In all models, we use as penalisation functions $\Phi(r) = 2\sqrt{r}$ in the data term, and the Charbonnier function $\Psi(s^2) = 2\lambda\sqrt{1 + s^2/\lambda^2} - 2\lambda$ in the smoothness term.

The data sets used in the experiment are confocal fluorescence microscopy 3-D images of the filament network of living cells. Images and 3-D PSFs were provided by the Nano-Cell Interactions group at the Leibniz Institute for New Materials (INM), Saarbrücken. The resolution of these data sets in z direction is significantly lower than in x and y directions. We aim therefore at deblurring these images and at the same time interpolating a number of additional slices (typically, 1–5 slices) between each pair of neighbouring slices in z direction, in order to compensate the unequal resolution and achieve approximately equal voxel dimensions in x, y, and z directions.

Due to the huge image dimensions, 3-D reconstruction of an entire data set was beyond the memory capacity of available PCs. The experiments presented here were therefore carried out on cutouts. Fig. 1(a), for example, shows Slice 12 of a confocal microscopy data set. Its central part represents the filament network of a complete cell,

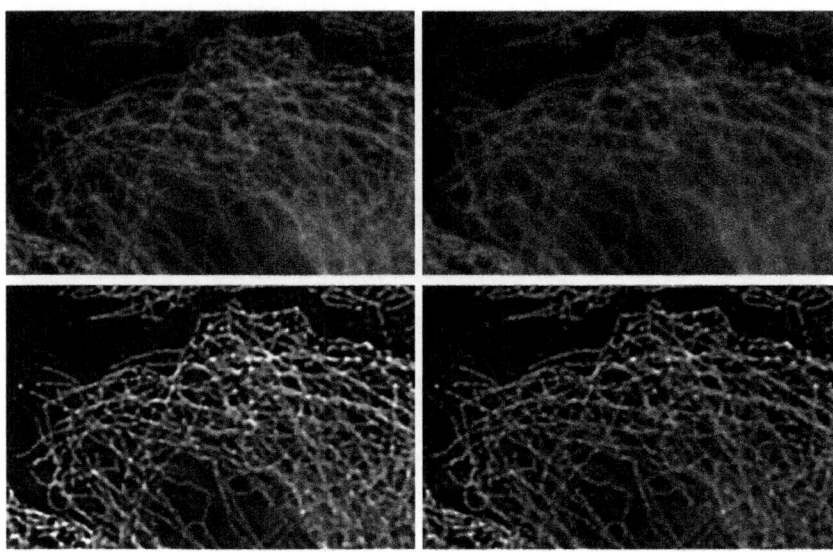

Fig. 2. 3-D reconstruction of Dataset A/2 by 100 iterations of IRRRL with Charbonnier regulariser, $\alpha = 0.002$. **(a) Top left:** Slice 8 of Dataset A/2. **(b) Top right:** Slice 9 of Dataset A/2. **(c) Bottom left:** Reconstruction of Slice 8. **(d) Bottom right:** One of the three slices interpolated between Slices 8 and 9.

while the outer parts belong to adjacent cells. For our experiments, the number of slices was retained but all slices were clipped as shown in Fig. 1(b). In the following, this clipped image will be called Dataset A.

In Dataset A, the voxel size is about 126 nm in depth and 62 nm within the constant depth planes. Interpolating a single slice between each pair of subsequent slices would actually suffice to make the voxel dimensions almost equal in x, y, and z directions. For a more informative test of the performance of our method, we remove the even-numbered slices from the data set. We will refer to this thinned dataset as Dataset A/2. To compensate for the thinning, each gap between slices of Dataset A/2 should be filled with three reconstructed slices. On one hand, this makes the problem considerably harder. On the other hand, it enables us to assess the reconstruction quality: Using sharpened versions of the retained slices from Dataset A as ground truth, we can quantify the reconstruction error of the second of three reconstructed slices. To this end, we use the average absolute error (AAE).

Fig. 2 illustrates the result of the first experiment. In (a) and (b) subsequent slices from Dataset A/2 are shown. The reconstruction of the slice in (a) is shown in (c). This demonstrates the deconvolution quality of IRRRL, since details in the processed slice (c) are much sharper than in the original slice (a). This makes it easier to track the filament network of the cell which is essential for microbiological applications like tracing nanoparticle transport in living cells. The interpolation effect of IRRRL is demonstrated in Subfigure (d) by one of the three slices interpolated between (a) and (b).

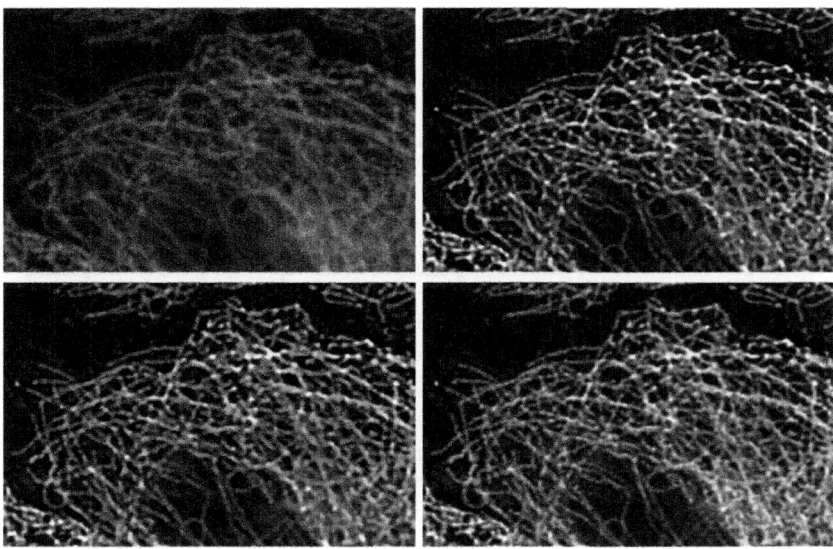

Fig. 3. Comparison with the sequential approach. **(a) Top left:** Slice 14 of Dataset A (not present in Dataset A/2). **(b) Top right:** Ground truth (Slice 14 after the preprocessing step). **(c) Bottom left:** Corresponding interpolated slice from IRRRL reconstruction of Dataset A/2. **(d) Bottom right:** Corresponding interpolated slice from sequential deconvolution and interpolation of Dataset A/2. Note particularly the unsatisfactory reconstruction in the lower right part.

In Fig. 3 we present further results together with a ground-truth comparison. Subfigure (a) shows one of the even-numbered slices of Dataset A which are removed in A/2. The sharpened version shown in Subfigure (b) is taken from an IRRRL reconstruction of the undecimated Dataset A. This slice forms the ground truth for our subsequent comparison. Figure 3(c) shows the second interpolated slice between slices 7 and 8 from our IRRRL reconstruction of the decimated Dataset A/2, which corresponds to Slice 14 of Dataset A. Indeed, the slices in (c) and (b) are not only visually similar, but also the AAE between them amounts to a low 4.55, confirming the good quality of the interpolation. For comparison, the AAE between the sharpened slices 7 and 8 is 16.83.

In our second experiment, we want to demonstrate the advantage of simultaneous interpolation and deconvolution over a *sequential approach* that deconvolves the data first, and then interpolates additional slices. We deconvolve therefore Dataset A/2 by RRRL and then interpolate the three missing slices using the variational interpolation model (5). The result is shown in Fig. 3(d). This image corresponds to the same slice as (b) and (c). The visual impression that the reconstruction quality of (d) is inferior to (c) is confirmed by the AAE of (d) vs. (b) which is 11.4.

A second example of reconstruction by IRRRL is shown in Fig. 4, based on a different dataset.

Finally, in order to illustrate the computational efficiency of IRRRL, we collect in Table 1 runtime measurements of IRRRL and a conventional variational approach for simultaneous deconvolution and interpolation.

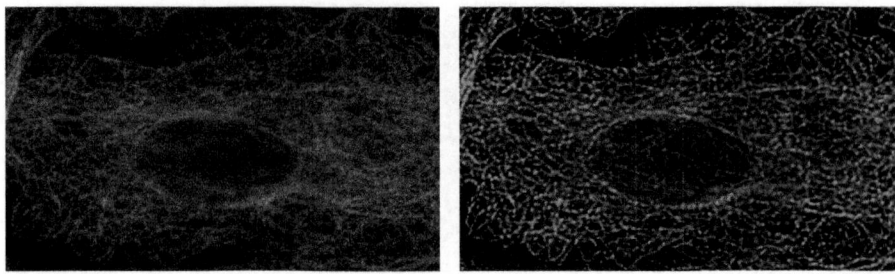

Fig. 4. 3-D reconstruction by IRRRL with Charbonnier regulariser, 100 iterations, $\alpha = 0.001$.
(a) Left: Slice 5 of a fluorescence microscopy data set (Dataset B, $486 \times 297 \times 22$ voxels). **(b)**
Right: Interpolated slice between slices 5 and 6.

Table 1. Approximate computational expense of the conventional variational simultaneous interpolation and deconvolution model and different implementations of the IRRRL model. Computation times refer to a single-threaded calculation on a Core2Duo CPU running at 2.00 GHz.

Implementation	Iterations	Computation time (m)	Reduction factor w.r.t. conventional implementation
conventional	500	6020	1
Spatial	100	1791	3.36
Fourier-spatial	100	135	44.59
Coarse-to-fine	20-20	33	182.42

We start with the conventional method. It consists essentially in a non-blind variant
of the functional from [4] being minimised by gradient descent. For reasonable reconstruction quality, 500 iterations are needed. A straightforward IRRRL implementation
speeds up the computation by a factor of more than three. Some increase in the computational cost of a single iteration is more than outbalanced by the reduction of the
iteration count to 100 for comparable reconstruction quality.

In both cases so far convolution was computed in the spatial domain. Since the confocal microscopy blur kernel has fairly large spatial dimensions, it is beneficial to use
instead an FFT-based convolution via the Fourier domain. In our example, this achieves
a speed-up factor of about thirteen. In a last step, we improve this method further by
introducing the coarse-to-fine strategy with just two scales, thereby increasing the speed
roughly to fourfold.

5   Conclusion and Future Work

We have developed an integrated variational approach for 3-D image deconvolution
and interpolation that does not only deliver reconstruction in high quality but also allows
efficient numerical implementation by means of a fixed point iteration similar to the
Richardson-Lucy algorithm. Further speed-up was achieved by transferring convolution
operations to the Fourier domain via FFT, and a coarse-to-fine strategy.

Future work will be directed to integrate this method with other image processing tools for 3-D confocal microscopy data into efficient software for cell biological research. Moreover, improvements of the model like edge-enhancing regularisers will be investigated. Concerning the implementation, 3-D image processing is highly demanding in terms of time and memory, so further algorithmic optimisation in both parameters is another topic of ongoing research.

References

1. Bar, L., Berkels, B., Rumpf, M., Sapiro, G.: A variational framework for simultaneous motion estimation and restoration of motion-blurred video. In: Proc. Eleventh International Conference on Computer Vision, Rio de Janeiro, Brazil (October 2007)
2. Bratsolis, E., Sigelle, M.: A spatial regularization method preserving local photometry for Richardson-Lucy restoration. Astronomy and Astrophysics 375(3), 1120–1128 (2001)
3. Chan, T.F., Shen, J.: Mathematical models for local nontexture inpaintings. SIAM Mathematics 62, 1019–1043 (2002)
4. Chan, T.F., Yip, A.M., Park, F.E.: Simultaneous total variation image inpainting and blind deconvolution. International Journal of Imaging Systems and Technology 15, 92–102 (2005)
5. Dey, N., Blanc-Feraud, L., Zimmer, C., Roux, P., Kam, Z., Olivo-Marin, J., Zerubia, J.: Richardson-Lucy algorithm with total variation regularization for 3D confocal microscope deconvolution. Microscopy Research and Technique 69(4), 260–266 (2006)
6. Dupé, F.X., Fadili, J., Starck, J.L.: Deconvolution of confocal microscopy images using proximal iteration and sparse representations. In: 5th IEEE International Symposium on Biomedical Imaging: From Nano to Macro, Paris, pp. 736–739 (2008)
7. Elhayek, A.: Simultaneous Interpolation and Deconvolution Approach to 3D Reconstruction of Cell Images. Master's thesis, Department of Mathematics and Computer Science, Saarland University, Saarbrücken (2011)
8. Hell, S.W., Wichmann, J.: Breaking the diffraction resolution limit by stimulated emission: stimulated-emission-depletion fluorescence microscopy. Optics Letters 19(11), 780–782 (1994)
9. Hooke, R.: Micrographia: or Some physiological descriptions of minute bodies made by magnifying glasses. J. Martyn and J. Allestry, London (1965)
10. Lucy, L.: An iterative technique for rectification of observed distributions. The Astronomical Journal 79(6), 745–765 (1974)
11. Osher, S., Rudin, L.: Total variation based image restoration with free local constraints. In: Proc. 1994 IEEE International Conference on Image Processing, Austin, Texas, pp. 31–35 (1994)
12. Pawley, J.B. (ed.): Handbook of Biological Confocal Microscopy, 3rd edn. Springer, Berlin (2006)
13. Richardson, W.H.: Bayesian-based iterative method of image restoration. Journal of the Optical Society of America 62, 55–59 (1972)
14. Snyder, D., Schulz, T.J., O'Sullivan, J.A.: Deblurring subject to nonnegativity constraints. IEEE Transactions on Image Processing 40(5), 1143–1150 (1992)
15. Weickert, J., Welk, M.: Tensor Field Interpolation with PDEs. In: Weickert, J., Hagen, H. (eds.) Visualization and Processing of Tensor Fields, pp. 315–325. Springer, Berlin (2006)
16. Welk, M.: Robust variational approaches to positivity-constrained image deconvolution. Tech. Rep. 261, Department of Mathematics, Saarland University, Saarbrücken, Germany (March 2010)

Steerable Deconvolution
Feature Detection as an Inverse Problem

Marco Reisert[1] and Henrik Skibbe[2]

[1] Department of Radiology, Medical Physics
University Medical Center Freiburg, Freiburg, Germany
[2] University of Freiburg, Computer Science Department,
79110 Freiburg i.Br., Germany
marco.reisert@uniklinik-freiburg.de

Abstract. Steerable filters are a common tool for feature detection in early vision. Typically, a steerable filter is used as a matched filter by rotating a template to achieve the highest correlation value. We propose to use the steerable filter bank in a different way: it is interpreted as a model of the image formation process. The filter maps a hidden 'orientation' image onto an observed intensity image. The goal is to estimate the hidden image from the given observation. As the problem is highly under-determined, prior knowledge has to be included. A simple and effective regularizer which can be used for edge, line and surface detection will be used. Further, an efficient implementation in terms of Circular Harmonics in the conjunction with the iterated use of local neighborhood operators is presented. It is also shown that a simultaneous modeling of different low-level features can improve the detection performance. Experiments show that our approach outperforms other existing methods for low-level feature detection.

1 Introduction

Steerable filters, introduced in [1], are a common tool in early vision and image analysis. The original idea was motivated by correlating a matched filter for different orientations to get an evidence for some local feature of interest. Applications of steerable filters are widespread, e.g. in local orientation analysis [2], texture modeling [3], 2D rotation invariant object recognition [4] and feature detection in 2D [5] and 3D [6]. Different frameworks make use steerable filters, for example, nonlinear anisotropic diffusion filters [7,8] smooth along local prominent direction which are obtained from a steerable filter, or, the tensor voting framework [9] uses steerable filters to establish orientation coherence to reliable detect local features.

The first main contribution of this work is to use the steerable filter bank in a different sense, but for the original purpose, to detect local oriented features. The steerable filter is interpreted as a generative model of image formation: an unknown orientation field is convolved with an orientable template to create the observed image, which is thereafter corrupted by additive noise. The goal is to estimate the orientation field given the noisy observation. This is the main difference to a conventional matched filter: an inverse problem is solved. In fact, we can interpret the solution as a MAP-estimate of the posterior distribution for the feature orientation profile. As the problem is highly

R. Mester and M. Felsberg (Eds.): DAGM 2011, LNCS 6835, pp. 326–335, 2011.

under-determined, we have to assume additional prior knowledge about the spatial organization of the template, which relates the approach to Markov random fields. We will adopt a principle which was already used in the context of processing of diffusion weighted MR-images [10,8]. The idea is quite simple: for instance, assume a line crosses a pixel $\mathbf{r}$ with direction $\mathbf{n}$, then it is very likely that the line will also cross pixel $\mathbf{r} + \epsilon\mathbf{n}$, where ϵ is a small real number. We will extend this idea to edges: if an edge crosses a voxel $\mathbf{r}$ with normal $\mathbf{n}$, then it is also reasonable to assume that edge is also present in the pixel $\mathbf{r} + \epsilon\mathbf{n}_\perp$ where $\mathbf{n}_\perp$ are the vectors perpendicular to $\mathbf{n}$. Our second main contribution is the efficient implementation of the proposed approach for arbitrary higher order kernels. The idea is based on a circular harmonic representation of the orientation fields. In this representation the iterated use of complex derivatives admits the efficient computation of the steerable filter, which is indispensable for solving the inverse problem. Necessarily the prior will also be formulated in terms of the circular basis system.

The experiments will show that the new approach is better than other state-of-the-art approaches for a line detection task. Moreover, it will also be shown that the simultaneous modeling of edge and line templates substantially improves the overall detection performance.

2   Steerable Deconvolution

In this section we present the central idea of our approach and give a rough impression of the optimization process which is involved. We denote vectors $\mathbf{r} \in \mathbb{R}^2$ in bold face. Variables in 'orientation'-space are denoted by normalized vectors $\mathbf{n} \in S_1$ on the unit circle. Images are just functions $y : \mathbb{R}^2 \mapsto \mathbb{R}$ which we also denote compactly in bold letters as $\mathbf{y}$ depending on the context. Orientation images are functions of type $x : \mathbb{R}^2 \times S_1 \mapsto \mathbb{R}$ whose second argument is associated with an orientation. For brevity we define $\mathbb{O}^2 := \mathbb{R}^2 \times S_1$. Linear operators acting on images are denoted by capital bold letters, e.g. $\mathbf{A}$. The adjungate is denoted by $\cdot^\top$ and the complex conjugate by $\overline{\cdot}$.

2.1   The Idea

A steerable filter is very similar to a matched filter, where a template patch, usually called kernel, is correlated for different orientations and position with an image y by

$$x(\mathbf{r}, \mathbf{n}) = \int_{\mathbb{R}^2} \overline{A}(\mathbf{r}', \mathbf{n}) y(\mathbf{r}' - \mathbf{r}) d\mathbf{r}'.$$

The steerable filter response is an orientation function $x : \mathbb{O}^2 \mapsto \mathbb{R}$ describing the correlation value of the image with the template $A : \mathbb{O}^2 \mapsto \mathbb{R}$. We write the filter kernel A here in a general way with two arguments: the second argument $\mathbf{n}$ determines the the direction in which the template is steered. Usually the kernel is of the form $A(\mathbf{r}, \mathbf{n}) = t(\mathbf{U_n}\mathbf{r})$ where t is the template patch and $\mathbf{U_n}$ a rotation matrix depending on the direction $\mathbf{n}$.

The above filter equation can be written compactly as $\mathbf{x} = \mathbf{A}^\top\mathbf{y}$, where $\mathbf{x}$ and $\mathbf{y}$ denote the images and $\mathbf{A}^\top$ describes the linear matching process with the steerable filter kernel A. Now, in these terms our approach can be formulated easily. The key idea is to use the operator $\mathbf{A}$ as a generative model of the image formation process. That is, the orientation image $\mathbf{x}$ is interpreted as the hidden variable of the system which is mapped by $\mathbf{A}$ onto the observed image $\mathbf{y}$. The goal is to estimate $\mathbf{x}$ given the observed image. The most simple approach to solve this problem is to assume independent distributed Gaussian noise on the observation and, hence, minimize the squared difference:

$$J(\mathbf{x}) = \|\mathbf{A}\mathbf{x} - \mathbf{y}\|^2$$

which is nothing else than a deconvolution of the image $\mathbf{y}$ with the kernel A. Note the difference to usual deconvolution problems: in our approach the image formation model maps an orientation image onto a scalar intensity image. The image formation renders the kernel $A(\mathbf{x}, \mathbf{n})$ into a scalar image $\mathbf{y}$ by superimposing the contributions from each position *and* orientation weighted by the underlying hidden orientation distribution $\mathbf{x}$.

2.2 Regularization

Obviously, the number of unknowns is much higher than the number known variables, thus, an additional regularization term is necessary. A simple and generally applicable one is a smoothness prior, that is, we have the additional term

$$R_{\mathrm{iso}}(\mathbf{x}) = \int_{\mathbb{O}^2} |\nabla x|^2 \, d\mathbf{r} d\mathbf{n},$$

where ∇ is the gradient operator with respect to the spatial coordinates $\mathbf{r} = (r_1, r_2)$. This regularizer penalizes large local deviations, which results in blurring across edges and lines, a well known problem with quadratic regularizers. In fact, in orientation space there is a regularizer that can prevent this effect while still being quadratic. Think of a line template $A(\mathbf{x}, \mathbf{n})$, where $\mathbf{n}$ is the direction of the line. In this scenario the regularizer

$$R_{\mathrm{fc}}(\mathbf{x}) = \int_{\mathbb{O}^2} (\mathbf{n}^\top \nabla x)^2 \, d\mathbf{r} d\mathbf{n},$$

blurs only along the lines but not across. This prior was already used in [10] in the context of High Angular Resolution Diffusion Imaging (HARDI) and can be motivated by a diffusion process [8] on orientation scores. There is a simple extension for edges: the direction is chosen perpendicular to the orientation of the edge, because we want to smooth along the edge and not across. In spite its simplicity, it is astonishing that a Gaussian prior (that is quadratic), which gives a linear system to solve, can preserve edges. Typically, anisotropic filters that preserve edges/lines depend nonlinearly on the image.

2.3 Probabilistic Interpretation and Optimization

The proposed approach has a natural statistical interpretation as a continuous Gauss Markov random field (GMRF). One can assume that the joint posterior probability density $p(\mathbf{x}|\mathbf{y})$ for the occurrence of a certain feature orientation intensity profile $\mathbf{x}$ is given by

$$p(\mathbf{x}|\mathbf{y}) \propto p(\mathbf{y}|\mathbf{x})p(\mathbf{x}) = \frac{1}{Z}e^{-\|\mathbf{A}\mathbf{x}-\mathbf{y}\|^2}e^{-\lambda\|\mathbf{n}^\top\nabla\mathbf{x}\|^2} \qquad (1)$$

The goal of minimizing the proposed objective is equivalent to finding the MAP-estimate. Note, that in this way it is also possible to interpret the classical steerable filter as a approximative MAP-estimate: choose the prior to be the usual mean-free Gaussian $p(\mathbf{x}) \propto e^{-\lambda\|\mathbf{x}\|^2}$, then, for large λ one has the approximation $\mathbf{x}_{MAP} = (\mathbf{A}^\top\mathbf{A} + \lambda I)^{-1}\mathbf{A}^\top\mathbf{y} \approx \mathbf{A}^\top\mathbf{y}$. Finding the MAP-estimate of the posterior in equation (1) is equivalent to the minimization of the objective

$$\mathbf{x}_{MAP} = \operatorname{argmin} I(\mathbf{x}) = \operatorname{argmin} (J(\mathbf{x}) + \lambda R(\mathbf{x})),$$

with regularization parameter $\lambda \in \mathbb{R}$. The necessary condition for $\mathbf{x}$ to be a minimum of I is that the variation of $I(\mathbf{x})$ vanishes. The computation of the variation follows standard variational calculus. Finally we obtain

$$\frac{d}{d\mathbf{x}}I = \mathbf{A}^\top\mathbf{A}\mathbf{x} - \mathbf{A}^\top\mathbf{y} + \lambda(\mathbf{n}^\top\nabla)^2\mathbf{x} = 0, \qquad (2)$$

where $\frac{d}{d\mathbf{x}}$ defines the functional derivative with respect to $x(\mathbf{r}, \mathbf{n})$. To solve this equation we will use the standard linear conjugate gradients algorithm. Therefore, one has to apply the operator $\mathbf{A}^\top\mathbf{A} + \lambda(\mathbf{n}^\top\nabla)^2$ several times. Its efficient implementation will be presented in the next section.

3   Complex Formulation

In this section we focus on the efficient implementation of the proposed idea for arbitrary higher order kernels, and, in particular, we look at one specific combined edge/ridge kernel, which admits an efficient formulation by local neighborhood operators. For a naive implementation of the general formulation the orientation variable $\mathbf{n}$ (which is actually just an angle) would be discretized in an equidistant manner. In this way, the optimization becomes computationally quite expensive. Imagine, in each iteration a matching of the filter kernel for lots of different orientation has to be applied (that is the operator $\mathbf{A}^\top$) and vice versa the kernel has to be rendered back (which is just an application of $\mathbf{A}$). For each orientation a direct convolution (usually by the FFT) has to be computed. The complexity of the regularizer is the same as for any standard anisotropic PDE-based smoothing process times the number the discrete directions involved. We want to point out a different way: the use of Fourier analysis combined with complex derivative operators. The idea is to represent all function with respect to their angular coordinate $\mathbf{n}$ in Fourier space, this was already done e.g. by [11] and is a common way to represent arbitrary shaped steerable filter templates.

3.1   Fourier Representation of the Steerable Convolution

The idea is to expand the function $x(\mathbf{r}, \mathbf{n})$ and the kernel $A(\mathbf{r}, \mathbf{n})$ locally in the Fourier basis with respect to the second coordinate $\mathbf{n}$, which we will replace by the angle ϕ:

$$x(\mathbf{r}, \phi) = \sum_{k=-L}^{L} b_k(\mathbf{r}) e^{ik\phi},$$

where L is the finite cut-off parameter. Thus, we have now represented x by a series of complex-valued 'expansion'-images $b_k(\mathbf{r})$. We do the same for the kernel A and denote the corresponding expansion images by $a_k(\mathbf{r})$. We first look how we take advantage from this during the computation of expression $\mathbf{A}^\top \mathbf{y}$ which appears in equation (2). Due to the linearity of the expansion and the correlation operations we have

$$(\mathbf{A}^\top \mathbf{y})(\mathbf{r}, \phi) = \sum_{k=-L}^{L} \underbrace{\left(\int \overline{a_k}(\mathbf{r}') y(\mathbf{r}' - \mathbf{r}) \right)}_{c_k(\mathbf{r})} e^{ik\phi}, \tag{3}$$

that is, the defined c_k are the Fourier expansion images of the 'orientation' function $\mathbf{A}^\top \mathbf{y}$. Thus, the application of $\mathbf{A}$ turns out to be a correlation of the individual expansion images a_k of the kernel with the image y. Typically, one can use a much lower number L of Fourier expansion images than discretized angle images, so this is already a step towards a lower computationally complexity. Now, look at the application of the operator $\mathbf{A}$:

$$(\mathbf{A}\mathbf{x})(\mathbf{r}) = \int_{\mathbb{R}^2 \times S_1} A(\mathbf{r} - \mathbf{r}', \mathbf{n}) x(\mathbf{r}', \mathbf{n}) \, d\mathbf{r}' d\mathbf{n}$$

Inserting the Fourier expansions and using the relation $\int_0^{2\pi} e^{i\phi k} = 2\pi \delta_k$ yields

$$(\mathbf{A}\mathbf{x})(\mathbf{r}) = \sum_{k=-L}^{L} \int_0^{\infty} a_{-k}(\mathbf{r} - \mathbf{r}') b_k(\mathbf{r}) d\mathbf{r}'. \tag{4}$$

That is, the application of $\mathbf{A}$ just convolves the expansion coefficients of the kernel a_k and the image b_{-k} pairwise and sums them all up. In this way, we have already gained a bit of computational performance, but still several explicit convolutions are involved. Before presenting a way of avoiding them, we want to introduce the Fourier representation of the above mentioned regularizer.

3.2   Regularizer in Fourier Representation

How does the directed diffusion generator $(\mathbf{n}^\top \nabla)^2$ of the proposed regularizer act on the Fourier representation of the orientation function x? To answer this question, it is convenient to introduce complex derivatives, which are defined by $\partial_z = \frac{1}{2}(\partial_1 - i\partial_2)$

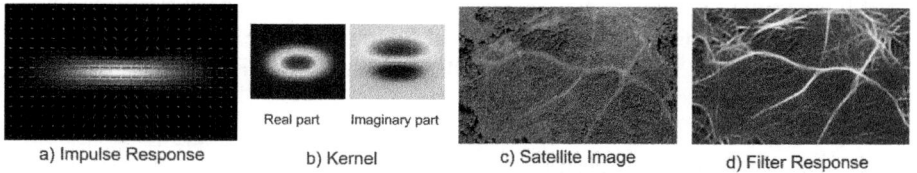

Real part   Imaginary part

a) Impulse Response   b) Kernel   c) Satellite Image   d) Filter Response

Fig. 1. a) impulse response of the regularizer for $L = 8$: the free action of the regularizer onto the pulse $x_k(\mathbf{r}) = \delta(\mathbf{r})e^{ik\theta}$ after several iterations ($\theta = 0$). b) the proposed kernel A_G: the real part contains the line, the imaginary part the edge template. c) a satellite image for demonstration of the filter. d) the maximal filter response of the satellite image with filter parameters $L = 8, \sigma = 8, \alpha = 12, \lambda = 5$.

and $\partial_{\bar{z}} = \frac{1}{2}(\partial_1 + i\partial_2)$, respectively, where ∂_1, ∂_2 are ordinary Cartesian derivatives. With their help one can write

$$4(\mathbf{n}^\top \nabla)^2 = (e^{i\phi}\partial_z + e^{-i\phi}\partial_{\bar{z}})^2 = e^{i2\phi}\partial_{zz} + 2\partial_{z\bar{z}} + e^{-i2\phi}\partial_{\bar{z}\bar{z}},$$

where $\mathbf{n}$ is just related to ϕ by $\mathbf{n} = (\cos(\phi), \sin(\phi))^\top$. To compute the action of $(\mathbf{n}^\top \nabla)^2$ on x in terms of the describing coefficients b_k we have to compute the orthogonal projection of $(\mathbf{n}^\top \nabla)^2 x(\mathbf{r}, \phi)$ onto the basis function $e^{ik\phi}$,

$$\frac{d}{db_k} R_{\text{fc}} = \frac{1}{2\pi} \int_0^{2\pi} (\mathbf{n}^\top \nabla)^2 x(\mathbf{r}, \phi) e^{-i\phi k} d\phi$$

Replacing the Cartesian derivative by the complex one and the function x by its Fourier expansion yields after some basic algebraic manipulations

$$\frac{d}{db_k} R_{\text{fc}} = \partial_{zz} b_{k-2} + 2\partial_{z\bar{z}} b_k + \partial_{\bar{z}\bar{z}} b_{k+2}. \tag{5}$$

Compared to the angle-discretized version the complexity per coefficient image b_k is a little bit more, but as described above there are much less images if one uses Fourier representation. In Figure 1 we show the impulse response of the regularizer by displaying the orientation maximas in gray scale together with the direction of the maximas in red.

If the regularizer is used in conjunction with edge templates, the only modification is to switch for the first and last term in equation (5) the sign. Actually, it is possible to neglect the differences for edges and ridges, if edge templates are made imaginary. An edge template $A^{\text{edge}}(\mathbf{r}, \mathbf{n})$ obviously fulfills $A^{\text{edge}}(\mathbf{r}, \mathbf{n}) = -A^{\text{edge}}(\mathbf{r}, -\mathbf{n})$, on the other hand a ridge kernel $A^{\text{ridge}}(\mathbf{r}, \mathbf{n}) = A^{\text{ridge}}(\mathbf{r}, -\mathbf{n})$. It is quite natural to combine both as follows $A(\mathbf{r}, \mathbf{n}) = A^{\text{ridge}}(\mathbf{r}, \mathbf{n}) + iA^{\text{edge}}(\mathbf{r}, \mathbf{n})$. Then, the combined kernel fulfills $A(\mathbf{r}, -\mathbf{n}) = \overline{A}(\mathbf{r}, -\mathbf{n})$ and the regularizer as given in equation (5) works for both types of templates simultaneously.

3.3   A Combined Edge/Ridge Kernel

It was already described how arbitrary steerable kernels $\mathbf{A}$ and $\mathbf{A}^\top$ can be computed by direct convolutions with their complex expansion images. In fact, this way might be still computationally expensive. There is actually an even cheaper way to do these operations: by repeated applications of local finite difference operators. If denote the angle between $\mathbf{n}$ and $\mathbf{r}$ by θ we can write the combined edge/ridge kernel described in [12] as

$$A_G(\mathbf{r}, \mathbf{n}) := \cosh\left(\frac{\alpha|\mathbf{r}|\sin(\theta)}{\sigma^2}\right) \exp\left(\frac{\alpha \mathbf{in}^\top \mathbf{r} - |\mathbf{r}|^2}{\sigma^2}\right)$$

$$= \sum_{k=0}^{\infty} \left(\frac{(-w)^k}{k!}\partial_{\bar{z}}^k + \frac{\overline{w}^k}{k!}\partial_z^k\right) e^{-|\mathbf{r}|^2/\sigma^2},$$

where $w \in \mathbb{C}$ is related to $\mathbf{n} = (\cos(\phi), \sin\phi)^\top$ and $\alpha \in \mathbb{R}$ just by $w = \alpha e^{i\phi}$. The kernel is similar to a gabor wavelet, but more local due to the additional hyperbolic cosine. In Figure 1b) we show real and imaginary part of the kernel. The real part contains a ridge template, while the imaginary part contains an edge template, and thus, the kernel is symmetric in the sense that $A_G(\mathbf{r}, \mathbf{n}) = \overline{A_G}(\mathbf{r}, -\mathbf{n})$, and the regularizer as given in equation (5) will work without any modification. To compute the correlation of this kernel for all possible rotation we have to determine the expansion images $a_k = \frac{1}{2\pi} \int A_G e^{-ik\phi} d\phi$, which are computed to

$$a_0 = 2e^{-|\mathbf{r}|^2}, \qquad a_k = \frac{(-\alpha)^k}{k!}\partial_{\bar{z}}^k e^{-|\mathbf{r}|^2/\sigma^2}, \qquad a_{-k} = \frac{\alpha^k}{k!}\partial_z^k e^{-|\mathbf{r}|^2/\sigma^2}$$

By using the fact that convolutions and differentiation commute we can now insert this into equation (3) and compute the integral $c_k(\mathbf{r})$ to

$$c_k = \frac{(-\alpha)^k}{k!}\partial_{\bar{z}}^k y^s \text{ and } c_{-k} = \frac{\alpha^k}{k!}\partial_z^k y^s \qquad (6)$$

where $y^s = y * e^{-|\mathbf{r}|^2/\sigma^2}$ is the Gaussian smoothed image y. On the other hand we have to evaluate the sum *and* the integral in equation (4). In fact, there is a similar way to do this:

$$y(\mathbf{r}) = \sum_{k=0}^{L} \frac{\alpha^k}{k!}\partial_{\bar{z}}^k b_k^s + \sum_{k=0}^{L} \frac{(-\alpha)^k}{k!}\partial_z^k b_{-k}^s \qquad (7)$$

where again $b_k^s = b_k * e^{-|\mathbf{r}|^2}$. In conclusion, we have shown that both operations $\mathbf{A}$ and $\mathbf{A}^\top$ can be computed for the proposed kernel by the help of complex partial derivatives. In the next section it will be shown that, actually, just $4L$ finite difference operations are needed to apply them.

In Algorithm 1 we give pseudo code of the implementation of the operator $(\mathbf{A}^\top \mathbf{A} + \lambda(\mathbf{n}^\top \nabla)^2)$. First the diffusion generator is computed (line 1), which is the direct implementation of equation (5). In line 2-5 the application of $\mathbf{A}$ is performed by following equation (7). In fact, there is very efficient scheme just needing $2L$ differentiations. The complex derivatives are implemented by central finite differences. In line 6 the only explicit convolution takes place, which simultaneously accomplishes those needed for $\mathbf{A}$ and $\mathbf{A}^\top$. Line 7 computes equation (6), again in an iterative and efficient way.

Finally, the above described operator is used with the common conjugate gradient (CG) algorithm for optimization. In the experiments we used 40 CG iterations.

Algorithm 1. $x_{new} = (A^\top A + \lambda (n^\top \nabla)^2)x$

Input: x in terms expansion images b_k
Output: x_{new} in terms of expansion images b_k^{new}

1: Compute the diffusion generator according to eq. (5)

$$b_k^{new} = \lambda(\partial_{zz}b_{k-2} + 2\partial_{z\bar{z}}b_k + \partial_{\bar{z}\bar{z}}b_{k+2}),$$

2: Let $y^+(\mathbf{r}) := 0$ and $y^-(\mathbf{r}) := 0$
3: **for** $k = L : -1 : 1$ **do**
4:     According to eq. (7) compute

$$y^+ := \frac{\alpha^k}{k!}b_k + \partial_{\bar{z}}y^+ \quad \text{and} \quad y^- := \frac{(-\alpha)^k}{k!}b_{-k} + \partial_z y^-$$

5: **end for**
6: Convolve $c_0 := (y^+ + y^-) * e^{-|\mathbf{r}|^2/(2\sigma^2)}$
7: According to eq. (6) compute for $k > 0$

$$c_k := \frac{-\alpha}{k}\partial_z c_{k-1} \quad \text{and} \quad c_{-k} := \frac{\alpha}{k}\partial_{\bar{z}}c_{-k+1}$$

8: Let $b_k^{new} := b_k^{new} + c_k$

4   Experiments

For a quantitative assessment a simulation is performed. The simulation was set up by drawing lines of width 3px and adding independent Gaussian noise with standards deviation of 1. The lines were drawn such that their curvature do not exceed $1/5(px)^{-1}$. For comparison we consider three other approaches: a steerable filter, anisotropic diffusion and tensor voting. The optimal steerable filter proposed in [5] was used, where the scale was optimized with respect to the area under the curve (AUC) of the ROC curve. To apply the anisotropic diffusion framework the following strategy was applied: the principal direction of the steerable filter is used to compute a diffusion tensor field. The diffusion tensor field is, then, used to blur the steerable filter response in an anisotropic way. The approach is based on the idea of coherence enhancing filtering of tensor valued functions [13,14,15]. The tensor voting idea is closely related to this strategy but makes use of a more sophisticated blurring kernel. Instead of using the diffusion equation to blur the image anisotropically (with a squeezed Gaussian) the tensor valued function is convolved with the kernel (we used Medioni's voting field, [16]) The advantage of this approach is the particular shape of the tensor valued convolution kernel (the voting function), which leads to constructive interference along the lines but to destructive inference orthogonal to them. For details we refer to [16]. The parameters of all three reference approaches were tuned with respect to the AUC criterion.

In Figure 2 steerable deconvolution (SD) is analyzed in terms of ROC curves. To determine the evidence map for a line occurence we search for each position $\mathbf{r}$ the angle ϕ which maximizes the deconvolution result $x_{MAP}(\mathbf{r}, \phi)$ (in case of the complex kernel

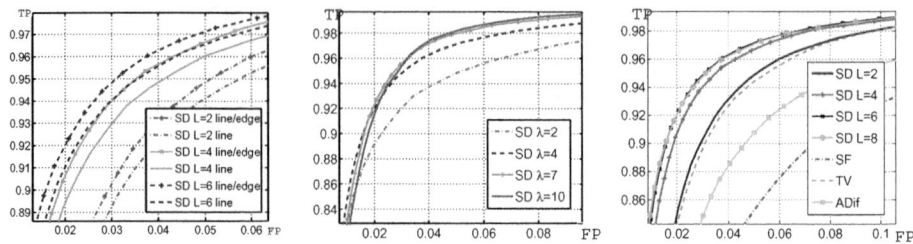

Fig. 2. ROC diagrams for simulated data with SNR=1. (left) Comparison of joint edge/line modeling versus sole line modeling for different values of L. (middle) Spherical deconvolution for different regularization parameters λ. (right) Comparison of steerable deconvolution ($\sigma = 2, \mu = 0.5, \lambda = 4$ SD), steerable filter (SF $\sigma = 3.5, \mu = 0$), tensor voting (TV) and anisotropic diffusion.

the real part of x_{MAP}). Figure 2a) compares the different usage of the kernel described in section 3.3. On the one hand we used the full complex kernel, that is, lines and edges are modeled simultaneously, and on the other hand only the real part (the line template) of the kernel is used for modeling. Note, that both approaches are not equivalent like for a matched filter approach. Despite the fact that the even (real) and the odd (imaginary) parts are orthogonal the deconvolution gives, due to its global nature, different results. One can observe in Figure 2a) that the joint modeling of lines and edges is able to significantly improve the detection performance regardless the expansion degree L of the kernel. The reasons are not so obvious. One may explain it by the fact that the edge template helps to absorb some of noise, which otherwise would enter the line response. In Figure 2b) we compare steerable deconvolution with the full complex kernel for different regularization parameters λ. Low λ leads to higher precision because the response is not so blurry. On the other hand higher λ gives much earlier high recall rates but suffers from false positive detections, due to the more blurry response. Finally, in Figure 2c) steerable deconvolution is compared to the three reference approaches: steerable filters (SF), tensor voting (TV) and anisotropic diffusion (ADiff). For an expansion degree of $L = 2$ the performance of SD is comparable to tensor voting, while for higher degrees SD significantly outperforms TV, SF ans ADiff. It is understandable that ADiff is slightly worse than TV because the TV-voting function incorporates the prior knowledge that we are looking for lines with a certain amount of curvature. One can further observe a saturation of the SD performance for $L = 8$.

5   Conclusion

In this paper we proposed to use a steerable filter bank as a generative model of image formation. Together with a special directed regularizer the approach can be interpreted as a continuous GMRF. We proposed an efficient implementation of the approach in terms of circular harmonics on complex local neighborhood operators. The synthetic experiments have shown that the approach outperforms existing line-detectors like steerable filter, tensor voting and anisotropic diffusion. The application of the proposed approach to real world applications remains subject to future work (see Figure 1 for an example on a satellite image).

References

1. Freeman, W.T., Adelson, E.H.: The design and use of steerable filters. IEEE Trans. Pattern Anal. Machine Intell. 13(9), 891–906 (1991)
2. Simoncelli, E.P., Farid, H.: Steerable wedge filters for local orientation analysis. IEEE Trans. Image Processing 5(9) (1996)
3. Portilla, J., Simoncelli, E.: A parametric texture model based on joint statistics of complex wavelet coefficients. Int'l Journal of Computer Vision 40(1), 49–71 (2000)
4. Ballard, D., Wixson, L.: Object recognition using steerable filters at multiple scales. In: Proceedings of IEEE Workshop on Qualitative Vision, pp. 2–10 (1993)
5. Jacob, M., Unser, M.: Design of steerable filters for feature detection using canny-like criteria. IEEE Trans. Pattern Anal. Machine Intell. 26(82), 1007–1019 (2004)
6. Aguet, F., Jacob, M., Unser, M.: Three-dimensional feature detection using optimal steerable filters. vol. 2, pp. II – 1158–61 (September 2005)
7. Weickert, J.: Anisotropic diffusion in image processing. Ph.D. dissertation, Universität Kaiserslautern (January 1996)
8. Duits, R., Franken, E.: Left-invariant diffusions on the space of positions and orientations and their application to crossing-preserving smoothing of hardi images. International Journal of Computer Vision 92, 231–264 (2011)
9. Mordohai, P.: Tensor Voting: A Perceptual Organization Approach to Computer Vision and Machine Learning. Morgan and Claypool (2006) ISBN-10: 1598291009
10. Reisert, M., Kiselev, V.: Fiber continuity: An anisotropic prior for odf estimation. IEEE Trans Med Imaging (in press, 2011)
11. Perona, P.: Deformable kernels for early vision. IEEE Trans. Pattern Anal. Machine Intell. 17(5), 488–499 (1995)
12. Reisert, M., Burkhardt, H.: Complex derivative filters. IEEE Trans. Image Processing 17(12), 2265–2274 (2008)
13. Weickert, J.: Coherence-enhancing diffusion filtering. International Journal of Computer Vision 31(2-3), 111–127 (1999)
14. Tschumperlé, D., Deriche, R., Faugeras, O.: Constrained flows of matrix-valued functions: Application to diffusion tensor regularization. In: Heyden, A., Sparr, G., Nielsen, M., Johansen, P. (eds.) ECCV 2002. LNCS, vol. 2350, pp. 251–265. Springer, Heidelberg (2002)
15. Burgeth, B., Didas, S., Weickert, J.: A General Structure Tensor Concept and Coherence-Enhancing Diffusion Filtering for Matrix Fields, pp. 305–323. Springer, Heidelberg (2009)
16. Guy, G., Medioni, G.: Inferring global perceptual contours from local features. International Journal of Computer Vision 20(1), 113–133 (1996)

Probabilistic Object Models
for Pose Estimation in 2D Images

Damien Teney[1] and Justus Piater[2]

[1] University of Liège, Belgium
`Damien.Teney@ULg.ac.at`
[2] University of Innsbruck, Austria
`Justus.Piater@UIBK.ac.at`

Abstract. We present a novel way of performing pose estimation of known objects in 2D images. We follow a probabilistic approach for modeling objects and representing the observations. These object models are suited to various types of observable visual features, and are demonstrated here with edge segments. Even imperfect models, learned from single stereo views of objects, can be used to infer the maximum-likelihood pose of the object in a novel scene, using a Metropolis-Hastings MCMC algorithm, given a single, calibrated 2D view of the scene. The probabilistic approach does not require explicit model-to-scene correspondences, allowing the system to handle objects without individually-identifiable features. We demonstrate the suitability of these object models to pose estimation in 2D images through qualitative and quantitative evaluations, as we show that the pose of textureless objects can be recovered in scenes with clutter and occlusion.

1 Introduction

Estimating the 3D pose of a known object in a scene has many applications in different domains, such as robotic interaction and grasping [1,6,13], augmented reality [7,9,19] and the tracking of objects [11]. The observations of such a scene can sometimes be provided as a 3D reconstruction of the scene [4], e.g. through stereo vision [5]. However, in many scenarios, stereo reconstructions are unavailable or unreliable, due to resource limitations or to imaging conditions such as a lack of scene texture.

This paper addresses the use of a single, monocular image as the source of scene observations. Some methods in this context were proposed to make use of the appearance of the object as a whole [6,13,15]. These so-called *appearance-based* methods however suffer from the need of a large number of training views. The state-of-the-art methods in the domain rather rely on matching characteristic, local features between the observations of the scene and a stored, 3D model of the object [1,7,17]. This approach, although efficient with textured objects or otherwise matchable features, would fail when considering non-textured objects, or visual features that cannot be as precisely located as the texture patches or geometric features used in the classical methods. Hsiao et al.'s method [8] seeks

R. Mester and M. Felsberg (Eds.): DAGM 2011, LNCS 6835, pp. 336–345, 2011.

to better handle multiple possible correspondences between the model and scene features, but still requires a large fraction of exact matches to work efficiently.

The proposed method follows a similar approach to the aforementioned references for modeling the object as a 3D set of observable features, but it is different in the sense that few assumptions are made about the type of features used, and in that it does not rely on establishing specific matches between features of the model and features of the observed scene. For this purpose, we represent both the object model and the 2D observations of a scene as probabilistic distributions of visual features. The model is built from 3D observations that can be provided by any external, independent system. One of the main interests of the proposed method, in addition to the genericity of the underlying principles, is its ability to effectively handle non-textured objects. The general method itself does not make particular assumptions about the type of features used, except that they must have a given, although not necessarily exact, position in space, and they must be potentially observable in a 2D view of the object.

In order to demonstrate the capabilities of the proposed method at handling textureless objects, we apply it to the use of local edge segments as observations. Practically, such features cannot be precisely and reliably observed in 2D images, e.g., due the ambiguity arising from multiple close edges, 3D geometry such as rounded edges, or depth discontinuities that change with the point of view. Such problems motivate the probabilistic approach used to represent the scene observations.

The 3D observations used to build the model are provided by an external system that performs stereopsis on a single pair of images. Such a model can thus be quickly and automatically learned, at the expense of imprecision and imperfections in the model. This again motivates the use of a probabilistic distribution of features as the object model. Other *model-based* methods proposed in the literature have used rigid learned [7,17] or preprogrammed (CAD) models [9,19], but such CAD models are, in general, not available. Our approach for object modeling is more similar to the work of Detry et al. [5], where an object is modeled as a set of parts, themselves defined as probability distribution of smaller visual features. The main contribution of this paper is the extension of those principles to the use of 2D observations.

The representations of the object model and of the scene observations that we just introduced can then be used to perform pose estimation in monocular images, using an inference mechanism. Algorithms such as belief propagation [5] and Metropolis-Hastings MCMC methods [4] were proposed in the literature to solve similar problems, and we adapt the algorithm presented in that last reference to our specific type of model and observations.

Finally, our method provides a rigorous framework for integrating evidence from multiple views, yielding increased accuracy with only a linear increase of computation time with respect to the number of views. Using several views of a scene is implicitly accomplished when using a stereo pair of images, together with a method operating on 3D observations [5]. However, our approach does not seek matches between the two images, as stereopsis does, and can thus handle arbitrarily wide baselines. Other methods for handling multiple views with a 2D method have been proposed [2,14]. In these methods however, the underlying process relies on the matching of characteristic features.

2   Object Model

Our object model is an extension of earlier work [4]. For completeness and clarity, the upcoming sections include essential background following this source.

2.1   General Form

We use a 3D model that allows us to represent a probabilistic distribution of 3D features that compose the model. These features must be characterized by a localization in the 3D space, and can further be characterized by other observable characteristics, such as an orientation or an appearance descriptor. The model of an object is built using a set

$$M = \left\{ \left(\lambda^\ell, \alpha^\ell \right) \right\}_{\ell \in [1,n]} \tag{1}$$

of features, where $\lambda^\ell \in \mathbb{R}^3$ represents the location of a feature, and $\alpha^\ell \in \mathcal{A}$ is a (possibly zero-element) vector of its other characteristics from a predefined appearance space $\mathcal{A}$. When learning an object model, the set of features M is decomposed into q distinct subsets M_i, with $i \in [1, q]$, which correspond ideally to the different parts of the object. This step allows the pose estimation algorithm presented below to give equal importance to each of the parts, therefore avoiding distinctive but small parts being overwhelmed by larger sections of the object. The procedure used to identify such parts is detailed in [4].

Our method relies on a continuous probability distribution of 3D features to represent the model. Such a distribution can be built using Kernel Density Estimation (KDE), directly using the features of M_i as supporting particles [5,18]. To each feature of M_i is assigned a kernel function, the normalized sum of which yields a probability density function $\psi_i(x)$ defined on $\mathbb{R}^3 \times \mathcal{A}$. The kernels assigned to the features of M_i will depend on the type of these features.

Reusing the distribution of 3D features of part i, ψ_i, and considering an intrinsically calibrated camera, we now define $\psi'_{i,w}$ as the 2D projection onto the image plane of that distribution set into pose w, with $w \in SE(3)$, the group of 3D poses. Such a distribution is defined on the 2D appearance space, which corresponds to $\mathbb{R}^2 \times \mathcal{B}$, where $\mathcal{B}$ is the projected equivalent of $\mathcal{A}$. For example, if $\mathcal{A}$ is the space of 3D orientations, $\mathcal{B}$ would be the space of 2D orientations observable on an image. Similarly, if $\mathcal{A}$ is a projection-independent appearance space of 3D features, $\mathcal{B}$ would be the simple appearance space of direct 2D observations of such features.

Practically, $\psi'_{i,w}$ can be obtained by setting the features of M_i into pose w, and projecting them onto the image plane (Fig. 1c). The resulting 2D features $\in \mathbb{R}^2 \times \mathcal{B}$ can, similarly to the 3D points, be used as particles to support a KDE on that space, using an equivalent projection of the kernels used in 3D.

2.2   Use of Edge Segments

This paper presents the particular application of the object model presented above to the use of local edge segments as visual features. Those features basically correspond to 3D oriented points, which are characterized, in addition to their localization in 3D, by an orientation along a line in 3D. Therefore, reusing the notations introduced above, the space $\mathcal{A}$, on which the elements α^ℓ are defined, corresponds to the half 2-sphere S_+^2, i.e. half of the space of 3D unit vectors. The kernels used to compose a 3D probability distribution ψ_i can then be decomposed into a position and an orientation part [5,18]. The first is chosen to be a Gaussian trivariate isotropic distribution, and the latter a von Mises-Fisher distribution on S_+^2. The bandwidth of the position kernel is then set to a fraction of the size of the object, whereas the bandwidth of the orientation kernel is set to a constant. The 2D equivalent of those distributions are obtained using classical projection equations. Fig. 2 depicts the correspondence between the 2D and 3D forms of a particle corresponding to an edge segment and its associated kernel.

The visual features used in our implementation are provided by the external Early Cognitive Vision (ECV) system of Krüger et al. [12,16]. This system extracts, from a given image, oriented edge features in 2D, but can also process a stereo pair of images to give 3D oriented edge features we use to build object models (Fig. 1b).

3   Scene Observations

The observations we can make of a scene are modeled as a probability distribution in a similar way to the model. The observations are given as a set

$$O = \left\{ \left(\delta^\ell, \beta^\ell \right) \right\}_{\ell \in [1,m]} \tag{2}$$

of features, where $\delta^\ell \in \mathbb{R}^2$ is the position of the feature on the image plane, and $\beta^\ell \in \mathcal{B}$ are its observable characteristics. These characteristics must obviously be a projected equivalent to those composing the object model. Here again, the features contained in O can directly be used as particles to support a continuous probability density, using KDE.

In the particular case of edge segments, the observations correspond to 2D oriented points (Fig. 1e). They are thus defined on $\mathbb{R}^2 \times \mathcal{B}$ with $\mathcal{B} = [0, \pi[$. As mentioned before, the uncertainty on the position and orientation of visual features like edge segments can arise from different sources, and no particular assumptions can thus be made on the shape of their probability distribution. The kernels used here are thus simple bivariate isotropic Gaussians for the position part, and a mixture of two antipodal von Mises distributions for the orientation part. The sum of those kernels, associated with each point of O, then yields a continuous probability density function $\phi(x)$ defined on $\mathbb{R}^2 \times [0, \pi[$ (Fig. 1f).

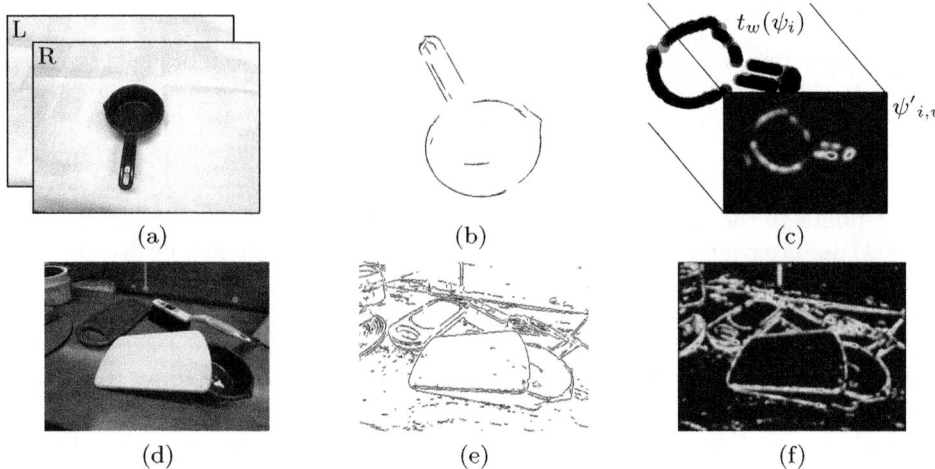

Fig. 1. Proposed method applied to edge segments (orientation of segments not represented). (a) Stereo images used to build object model; (b) 3D edge segments that compose the model; (c) probabilistic model (ψ_i) in pose w, spheres representing the position kernel (their size is set to one standard deviation), and its simulated projection in 2D ($\psi'_{i,w}$; blue and red represent resp. lowest and highest probability densities); (d) image of a scene; (e) 2D edge segments used as observations; (f) probabilistic representation of observations (ϕ).

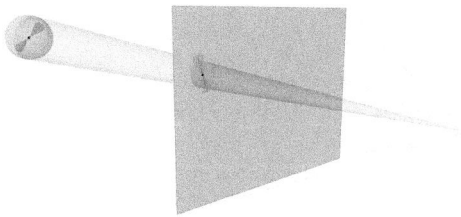

Fig. 2. Correspondence of 3D edge segment and associated kernel, with their 2D projection on image plane. Orange boundaries represent one standard deviation.

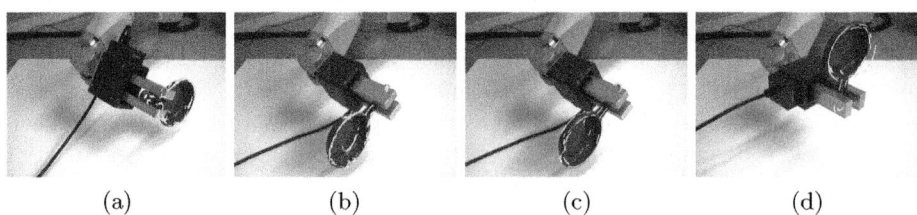

Fig. 3. Results of pose estimation; model features reprojected on input image. (a) Good result (close to ground truth); (b) good result; (c) same frame as (b) with incorrect result, orientation error of about $80°$, even though the reprojection matches observations slightly better than (b); (d) incorrect result, insufficient observations extracted from pan bottom, and orientation error of about $180°$.

4   Pose Estimation

The object and observation models presented above allow us to estimate the pose of a known object in a cluttered scene. This process relies on the idea that the 2D, projected probability distribution of the 3D model defined above can be used as a "template" over the observations, so that one can easily measure the likelihood of a given pose.

Let us consider a known object, for which we have a model composed of q parts M_i ($i \in [1, q]$), which in turn define ψ_i and $\psi'_{i,w}$. On the other hand, we have a scene, defined by a set of observations O, leading to a probabilistic representation ϕ of that scene. We model the pose of the object in the scene with a random variable $W \in SE(3)$. The distribution of object poses in the scene is then given by

$$p(w) \propto \prod_{i=1}^{q} m_i(w) , \tag{3}$$

with $m_i(w)$ being the cross-correlation of the scene observations $\phi(x)$ with the projection $\psi'_{i,w}$ of the ith part of the model transformed into pose w, that is,

$$m_i(w) = \int_{\mathbb{R}^2 \times \mathcal{B}} \psi'_{i,w}(x) \, \phi(x) \, \mathrm{d}x . \tag{4}$$

Computing the maximum-likelihood object pose $\arg\max_w p(w)$, although analytically intractable, can be approximated using Monte Carlo methods. We extend the method proposed in [4], which computes the pose via simulated annealing on a Markov chain. The chain is defined with a mixture of local- and global-proposal Metropolis Hastings transition kernels. Simulated annealing does not guarantee convergence to the global maximum of $p(w)$, and we thus run several chains in parallel, and eventually select the best estimate. In practice, a strong prior is usually available concerning the distance between the camera and the object, e.g., as information on the scale at which the object can appear in an image. The global transition kernel can benefit from this prior to favor more likely proposals, and therefore drive the inference process more quickly towards the global optimum.

As mentioned above, the proposed method naturally extends to observations from v multiple views. We define $m_{i,j}(w)$ similarly to Eq. 4 but relative to specific views j, $j = 1, \ldots, v$. Accounting for observations from all available views, Eq. 3 then becomes

$$p(w) \propto \prod_{j=1}^{v} \prod_{i=1}^{q} m_{i,j}(w) , \tag{5}$$

which is handled by the inference process similarly to the single-view case.

5   Evaluation

This sections presents the applicability of the proposed method for estimating the pose of objects on two publicly available datasets [3,10].

5.1 Experimental Setup

In this work, each model is built from one manually segmented stereo view of the object (such as Fig. 1a). The models used here are typically composed of between 1 and 4 parts, containing around 300 to 500 observations in total. Pose estimation is performed on single 1280×960 images taken with an intrinsically calibrated camera. The number of parallel inference processes (see Section 4) is set to 16. On a typical 8-core desktop computer, the pose estimation process on a single view typically takes about 20 to 30 seconds. Also, as proposed in Section 4 and detailed below, a crude estimate of the distance between the camera and the object is given as an input to the system.

The ECV observations we use (see Section 2.2) can be characterized with an appearance descriptor composed of the two colors found on the sides of the edge. This appearance information does not enter into the inference procedure. However, in the following experiments we use it to discard those scene observations whose colors do not match any of the model features. This step, although not mandatory, helps the pose estimation process to converge more quickly to the globally best result by limiting the number of local optima.

5.2 Rotating Object

We first evaluated our method on a sequence showing a plastic pan undergoing a rotation of $360°$ in the gripper of a robotic arm [10]. The ground truth motion of the object in the 36 frames of the sequence is thus known. The estimate of the distance to the object, given as input to the system, is the same for the whole sequence, and is a rough estimate of the distance between the gripper and the camera (about 700 mm). Let us note that, for some images of the sequence, this estimate is actually quite different from the exact object-camera distance, since the object is not rotating exactly around its center.

This publicly available dataset is composed of stereo images, and we used the frame corresponding to a rotation of $50°$ to learn the model, as it gives a good overall view of the object. Four types of experiments were then performed (Fig. 4). First, the pose of the object was estimated in each frame of the sequence, using one single view. One can observe that correct pose estimates can mostly be made close to the viewpoint used for learning the model (Fig. 4). A number of results have an orientation error of almost $180°$, which correspond to a special case (Fig. 3d) that can be explained by the flat and almost symmetrical object we consider. Indeed, if very few observations are extracted from the bottom of the pan, only the handle and the top rim of the object can be matched to the image. Another large number of incorrect pose estimates have orientation errors of $70–110°$; most of them correspond to ambiguities inherent to a 2D projection, as illustrated on Fig. 3b–c. Similarly, most of the translation errors occur along the camera-object axis, as an inherent limitation of 2D observations. The percentage of correct pose estimates, defined by orientation and translation errors of less than $10°$ and 30 mm resp., and evaluated over the whole sequence, is only 20%. Second, the same experiment is performed using two views. Some of the ambiguities can then be resolved, and this percentage rises to 60%. This result can be compared to the evaluation of Detry et al. [5] on a similar sequence, which achieved a score of only 40–50%. We stress that the latter method relied on 3D observations computed from stereo, whereas our method uses one or more 2D images directly, and is not limited to short-baseline stereo pairs.

Finally, we used our framework to track the pose of the object over the whole sequence, using one and two views, respectively. The pose is initialized with ground truth information for the first frame, and is then tracked from one frame to the next, using the same process as outlined in Section 4, but without the use of global proposals in the chain, and thus limiting the inference process to a local search. These experiments yield very good results (see Fig. 4), the remaining error being mostly due to the limitations of the model, learned from a single view of the object.

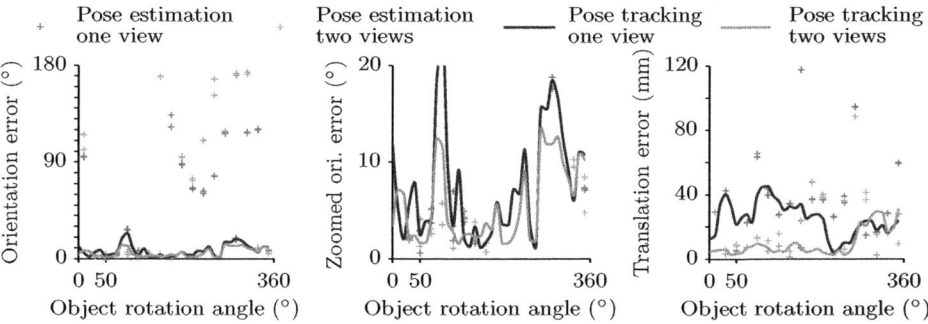

Fig. 4. Results of the "rotating object" sequence. For pose estimation, one marker represents one run of the algorithm (the same number of runs are executed for each frame). For pose tracking, the lines represent means over multiple runs.

5.3 Cluttered Scenes

We evaluated the robustness of our method to clutter and occlusions by computing the pose of various objects in several cluttered scenes [3], using a single input image. The estimate of the distance to the objects, used as input, is the same for all scenes and objects, and roughly corresponds to the distance between the camera and the table on which the objects are placed (about 370 mm). Here again, this is an only crude estimate, as the actual distance to the objects varies from 200 to 600 mm.

Several of these scenes are presented in Fig. 5, with object models superimposed in the estimated pose. Sometimes, insufficient observations are extracted from the image, and the pose cannot be recovered (e.g. second row, last image). However, the reprojection error achieved by our algorithm is clearly low in most cases; the models generally appear in close-to-correct poses. A perfect match between the reprojected model and the observations is not always possible, which is a limitation of the sparse observations and object models we use. Small differences in the reprojection on the image plane may then correspond to large errors

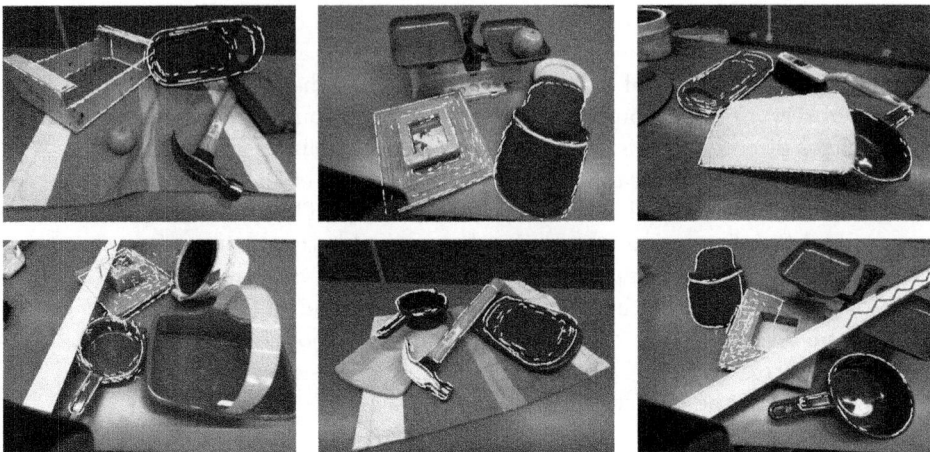

Fig. 5. Results of pose estimation (using a single view), with model features reprojected onto the input image. Most remaining errors are a limitation of the simple object models used, each learned from a single stereo pair.

in the actual 3D pose recovered. Most of these errors can be greatly reduced by using additional views of the scene, which is easily done with our method.

6   Conclusions

We presented a generic method for 3D pose estimation of objects in 2D images, using a probabilistic scheme for representing object models and observations. This allows the method to handle various types of observations, including features that cannot be matched individually; here we use local edge segments. Using these principles, we showed how to use Metropolis-Hastings MCMC to infer the maximum-likelihood pose of a known object in a novel scene, using a single 2D view of that scene. The probabilistic approach makes the pose estimation process possible without establishing explicit model-to-scene correspondences, as opposed to existing state-of-the-art methods. Together with the use of edge segments as observations, the method allows us to effectively handle non-textured objects. Further, the method extends to the use of multiple views, providing a rigorous framework for integrating evidence from multiple viewpoints of a scene, yielding increased accuracy with only a linear increase of computation time with respect to the number of views. We validated the proposed approach on two publicly-available datasets. One dataset allowed quantitative evaluation; the result of an experiment was compared to the results of an existing method, and showed an advantage in performance for our method. The pose estimation process was also evaluated with success on scenes with clutter and occlusion. Future work will extend the current implementation to the use of other visual features, thereby extending the types of objects that can be handled.

Acknowledgments. The research leading to these results has received funding from the European Community's Seventh Framework Programme FP7/2007-2013 (Specific Programme Cooperation, Theme 3, Information and Communication Technologies) under grant agreement no. 270273, Xperience. Damien Teney is supported by a research fellowship of the Belgian National Fund for Scientific Research.

References

1. Collet, A., Berenson, D., Srinivasa, S., Ferguson, D.: Object recognition and full pose registration from a single image for robotic manipulation. In: ICRA (2009)
2. Collet, A., Srinivasa, S.S.: Efficient multi-view object recognition and full pose estimation. In: ICRA, pp. 2050–2055 (2010)
3. Detry, R.: A probabilistic framework for 3D visual object representation: Experimental data (2009), http://intelsig.org/publications/Detry-2009-PAMI/
4. Detry, R., Piater, J.: Continuous surface-point distributions for 3D object pose estimation and recognition. In: Kimmel, R., Klette, R., Sugimoto, A. (eds.) ACCV 2010, Part III. LNCS, vol. 6494, pp. 572–585. Springer, Heidelberg (2011)
5. Detry, R., Pugeault, N., Piater, J.: A probabilistic framework for 3D visual object representation. IEEE Trans. PAMI 31(10), 1790–1803 (2009)
6. Ekvall, S., Hoffmann, F., Kragic, D.: Object recognition and pose estimation for robotic manipulation using color cooccurrence histograms. In: IROS (2003)
7. Gordon, I., Lowe, D.G.: What and where: 3D object recognition with accurate pose. In: Toward Category-Level Object Recognition, pp. 67–82 (2006)
8. Hsiao, E., Collet, A., Hebert, M.: Making specific features less discriminative to improve point-based 3D object recognition. In: CVPR, pp. 2653–2660 (2010)
9. Klein, G., Drummond, T.: Robust visual tracking for non-instrumented augmented reality. In: ISMAR, Tokyo, pp. 113–122 (October 2003)
10. Kraft, D., Krüger, N.: Object sequences (2009),
   http://www.mip.sdu.dk/covig/sequences.html
11. Kragic, D., Miller, A.T., Allen, P.K.: Real-time tracking meets online grasp planning. In: ICRA, pp. 2460–2465 (2001)
12. Krüger, N., Wörgötter, F.: Multi-modal primitives as functional models of hypercolumns and their use for contextual integration. In: De Gregorio, M., Di Maio, V., Frucci, M., Musio, C. (eds.) BVAI 2005. LNCS, vol. 3704, pp. 157–166. Springer, Heidelberg (2005)
13. Mittrapiyanuruk, P., DeSouza, G.N., Kak, A.C.: Calculating the 3D pose of rigid objects using active appearance models. In: ICRA, pp. 5147–5152 (2004)
14. Pless, R.: Using many cameras as one. In: CVPR (2), pp. 587–593 (2003)
15. Pope, A.R., Lowe, D.G.: Probabilistic models of appearance for 3D object recognition (2000)
16. Pugeault, N.: Early Cognitive Vision: Feedback Mechanisms for the Disambiguation of Early Visual Representation. VDM Verlag Dr. Müller (2008)
17. Rothganger, F., Lazebnik, S., Schmid, C., Ponce, J.: 3D object modeling and recognition using local affine-invariant image descriptors and multi-view spatial constraints. Int. J. Comput. Vision 66(3), 231–259 (2006)
18. Sudderth, E.B.: Graphical models for visual object recognition and tracking. Ph.D. thesis, Massachusetts Institute of Technology, Cambridge, MA, USA (2006)
19. Vacchetti, L., Lepetit, V., Fua, P.: Stable real-time 3D tracking using online and offline information. IEEE Trans. PAMI 26(10), 1385–1391 (2004)

Fusion of Audio- and Visual Cues for Real-Life Emotional Human Robot Interaction

Ahmad Rabie and Uwe Handmann

Institute of Informatics
University of Applied Sciences; HRW
Mülheim & Bottrop, Germany
{ahmad.rabie,uwe.handmann}@hs-ruhrwest.de

Abstract. Recognition of emotions from multimodal cues is of basic interest for the design of many adaptive interfaces in human-machine interaction (HMI) in general and human-robot interaction (HRI) in particular. It provides a means to incorporate non-verbal feedback in the course of interaction. Humans express their emotional and affective state rather unconsciously exploiting their different natural communication modalities such as body language, facial expression and prosodic intonation. In order to achieve applicability in realistic HRI settings, we develop person-independent affective models. In this paper, we present a study on multimodal recognition of emotions from such auditive and visual cues for interaction interfaces. We recognize six classes of basic emotions plus the neutral one of talking persons. The focus hereby lies on the simultaneous online visual and accoustic analysis of speaking faces. A probabilistic decision level fusion scheme based on Bayesian networks is applied to draw benefit of the complementary information from both – the acoustic and the visual – cues. We compare the performance of our state of the art recognition systems for separate modalities to the improved results after applying our fusion scheme on both DaFEx database and a real-life data that captured directly from robot. We furthermore discuss the results with regard to the theoretical background and future applications.

1 Introduction

Recognizing emotions is widely accepted as one relevant step towards more natural interaction in human-robot and, more general, human-machine interaction. The new scientific understanding of emotions on the one hand, and the rapid evolution of computing system skills on the other, provided inspiration to numerous researchers to build machines that will have the ability to recognize, express, model, and communicate emotions.

In order to exploit emotional cues also in technical interfaces, the recognition of dedicated emotions is in particular necessary. Indeed, humans articulate emotions using different modalities in parallel (cf. Fig. 1(a) for an example from a human-robot interaction study). On the one hand, the different modalities

R. Mester and M. Felsberg (Eds.): DAGM 2011, LNCS 6835, pp. 346–355, 2011.

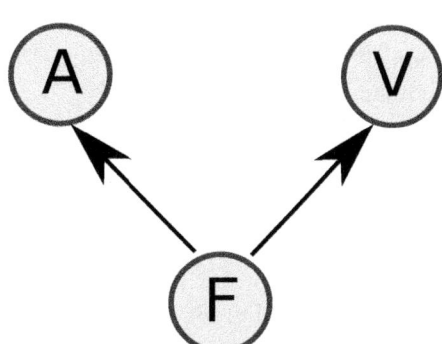

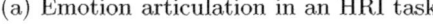

(a) Emotion articulation in an HRI task

(b) The Bayesian network structure for decision-level fusion

Fig. 1.

transport a significant amount of redundancy, allowing a more robust perception of one's emotion. On the other hand, dedicated emotions might be easier to read from one cue than another. Consequently, the recognition of emotions from multi-modal cues already has a certain tradition in research with a focus on visual and auditory cues, due to their relevance in human-human interaction. In order to apply emotion recognition in real-world interactive systems, a multimodal, online system is proposed that analyzes users' faces and voices in order to classify emotions. As we are interested in the online analysis of verbal interactions, the paper focuses on the multi-modal analysis of talking interlocutors which is different from most approaches which focus on non-talking faces.

This paper first briefly introduces the relevance and related work on multimodal recognition of emotion on natural interaction in Sec. 2. Afterwards, our systems for visual (Sec. 3.1) and acoustic (Sec.3.2) recognition are introduced. We present a comprehensive study using the DaFEx database [1] on recognizing the six basic Ekmanian emotions (anger, disgust, happiness, fear, sadness, and surprise)[2] plus a neutral class and discuss the results with regard to a fusion scheme and its accordance to theoretical models. An evaluating study of unimodal- and bimodal recogniton of five basic emotions (anger, fear, neutral, sadness, and suprise) from data captured directly from robot's camera and microphon demonstrates the ability of our bimodal system to be applied for natural, unrestricted and life-like human-robot interaction in Sec. 4.

2   Emotions in Natural Interaction

Though the study of emotion has a long tradition in psychology, approaches to the automatic recognition of emotions have emerged only in the last decade when the necessity to deal with the affective state of a user has become obvious for efficient and user-friendly human-computer interaction. For example, in tutoring systems or computer games, knowing about the user's feeling of boredom, frustration or happiness can increase learning success or fun in the game. In human-robot interaction, affective reactions of the robot, following the recognition of the user's emotional state, can make the interaction more natural and human-like.

Possible modalities to exploit for automatic recognition are language (acoustic and linguistic information), facial expressions, body gestures, bio signals (e. g. heart rate, skin conductance), or behavioral patterns (such as mouse clicks). Though one modality alone can already give information on the affective state of a user, humans always exploit all available modalities, and if an automatic systems attempts to reach human performance, the need for multi-modality is obvious. Thereby not only consent results of different modalities lead to more confident decisions, but also conflicting results can be helpful [3], e. g. to detect pretended or masked emotions, or to find out more reliable modalities for certain emotions. The most obvious modalities in human-human conversation, and also in human-robot conversation which we aim to enhance, are speech and facial expressions. Most related work has focused on the offline analysis of actors [4,5] or spontaneous emotions databases [6]. [3] present a framework for the fusion of multiple modalities for emotion recognition, however, without evaluation.

The novel aspect of our work is the using of technology that is fully capable of online recognition of emotion for natural human robot interaction. We presented an offline analysis of an actors database as previous work. With this analysis we first wanted to find a suitable fusion scheme motivated by the uni-modal results of which emotions are better recognised by which modality. This fusion scheme is then straight-forward applied in real-time scenario of human robot interaction.

3   Bi-modal Emotion Recognition

Theories of modality fusion in human perception do not agree on how information from different modalities should be integrated. For example, the Fuzzy Logical Model of Perception (FLMP) [7] states that stimuli from different modalities should be treated as independent sources of information and be combined regardless of the kind of information they contain. This view is not undisputed (i.e. [8]) and it has been argued that the FLMP does not work well when confronted with conflicting information from different modalities [9]. Perceptual results suggest that, at least for the case of emotion recognition, the modalities should be weighted according to which information that they convey best [10]: the visual modality primarily transmits valence (positive or negative value) whereas the auditory channel mainly contains information about activation.

In our work we challenge this approach by analysing the auditory and visual stimuli with respect to their general discriminative power in recognizing emotions. Note that in our work we focus on interactive scenarios and are thus targeting at systems that are able to work online. The approaches we present in this paper are, therefore, not only being tested offline on existing databases but have proven their applicability in robotic applications in real world settings [11,12]. This is in contrast to other work (e.g. [4,5]), which has focussed on offline emotion recognition only. The following three sections will provide a brief introduction on the respective unimodal analysis techniques as well on the proposed probabilistic decesion level fusion.

3.1 Visual Facial Expression Recognition

In order to recognize basic emotion visually, we take a closer look into the interlocutor's face. The basic technique applied here are Active Appearance models (AAMs) first introduced by Cootes et al [13]. The generative AAM approach uses statistical models of shape and texture to describe and synthesize face images.

An AAM, that is built from training set, can describe and generate both shape and texture using a single appearance parameter vector, which is used as feature vector for the classification. The "active" component of an AAM is a search algorithm that computes the appearance parameter vector for a yet unseen face iteratively, starting from an initial estimation of its shape. The AAM fitting algorithm is part of the integrated vision system [11] that consists of three basic components. Face pose and basic facial features (BFFs), such as nose, mouth and eyes, are recognized by the face detection module [14]. This face detetion in particular allows to apply the AAM approach in real-world enviroments as it has proven to be robust enough for face identification in human robot interaction in natural environments [15]. The coordinates representing these features are conveyed to the facial feature extraction module. Here, the BFFs are used to initialize the iterative AAM fitting algorithm. After the features are extracted the resulting parameter vector for every image frame is passed to a classifier which categorizes it in one of the six basic emotions in addition to the neutral one. Besides the feature vector, AAM fitting also returns a reconstruction error that is applied as a confidence measure to reason about the quality of the fitting and also to reject prior false positives resulting from face detection. As classifier a one-against-all Support Vector Machine is applied. The whole system is applicable in soft real-time, running at a rate of approximate (5) Hz on recent PC hardware.

3.2 Emotion Recognition from Speech

For the recognition of emotions from speech, EmoVoice, a framework that features offline analysis of available emotional speech databases, as well as online analysis of emotional speech for applications, is used [16]. The approach taken there is purely based on acoustic features, that is no word information is used. As a first step in feature extraction, a large vector of statistical features based on prosodic and acoustic properties of the speech signal was calculated for each utterance in the DaFEx database. From this large vector of over 1400 features the most relevant ones were selected by correlation-based feature subset selection [17]. This selection is necessary to increase performance as well as speed of classification. By this way, 71 features related to pitch, energy, MFCCs, to linear regression and range of the frequency spectrum of short-term signal segments, to the speech proportion and to the length of voiced and unvoiced parts in an utterance, and the number of glottal pulses remained. The full procedure of extracting features is described in [18,16]. For classification, again support vector machines were used, but with a linear kernel. The feature selection is typically done offline, but the feature extraction and classification can be done in real-time. Utterances as classification units, which are normally not available in online applications, can be replaced by an on-the-fly segmentation into parts with voice activity.

3.3   Probabilistic Decision Level Fusion

As affective states in interaction are usually conveyed on different cues at the same time, we agree with other works summarized in [19] that a fusion of visual and acoustic recognition yields significant performance gains. Hence, we followed the idea of an online integration scheme based on the prior offline analysis of recognition results on a database. In current classification fusion research, usually two types of multi-modal fusion strategies are applied, namely feature level fusion and decision level fusion. Both types combine different modalities of data to achive better recognition performance. In the former one, the feature spaces of all modalities are merged into one feature space, which is then conveyed to a single classifier. While in the latter type the classification is performed on each modality separately, then the results of each modality are fused to a final class-prediction accuracy. Due to the inherently different nature of our visual and accoustic cues, we decided for a decision-level fusion scheme. But instead of applying majority voting or other simple fusion techniques, we explicitly take the performance of each individual classifier into account and weight it according to their respective discrimination power.

   The proposed probablistic approach for this fusion are Bayesian networks with a rather simple structure depicted in Fig. 1(b). Based on the classification results of the individual visual and acoustic classifiers, we feed these into the Baysian network as *evidences* of the observable nodes (A and V, respectively). By Bayesian inference the posteriori probabilities of the unobservable affective fusion (F) node are computed and taken as final result.

   The required probability tables of the Bayesian network are obtained from a performance evaluation of the individual classifiers in an offline training phase based on ground-truth annotated databases. Therefore, confusion matrices of each classifier are turned into probability tables modeling the dependent observation probabilities of the model according to the arrows in Fig. 1(b). In the notion of Zeng *et al.* [19], our fusion scheme is referred to as model-level instead of decision-level fusion, as it takes the respective classification performance models into account.

4   Evaluation on Real-Life Data

As a previous work toward a bimodal system with online ability all systems are evaluated on the DaFEx database [1], which consists of 1008 short video clips of eight Italian actors (4 male and 4 female). Each clip comprises then deliberate presentation of one of the six Ekman's basic emotions plus the neutral one and lasts between 4 and 27 sec. The DaFEx database is divided into six blocks, in two of them namely block 3 and block 6 the actors present facial expression without speaking, in the remainder the actors speak during their emotional performance. Each actor in each of these block performs the seven emotion three times with different intensities (high, medium, and low).

The subset of DaFEx was chosen that contained only videos where the actors were speaking namely (block 1, 2, 4, and 5). Due to the small sample size, the same actors were used for training and test; but it shall be noted that both recognizers apply person independent models. However, the same leave-one-out cross-validation is used for the different modalities. Training is done on three blocks and evaluation of the performance of each uni-modals is performed on the one remaining test block. The probability tables for the Bayesian fusion model are obtained from validation of the performance on the three training blocks. The fusion performance is tested again on the test block. In cross-validation, all permutation of blocks are applied to training and test respectively.

Table 1. Recognition rates achieved by each unimodal und the bimodal for each individual emotion

	Ang	Dis	Fea	Hap	Neu	Sad	Sur	Total
Vis	94.44	73.61	58.33	80.55	79.16	72.22	62.91	**74.46**
Aco	68.05	51.38	48.61	50.00	87.49	69.44	58.33	**61.90**
Bimodal	81.94	87.50	52.78	86.11	86.11	74.99	77.77	**78.17**

Table 1 depicts the achieved significant overall improvement of the proposed fusion scheme applying our simple Bayesian networks model proposed in Sec. 3.3. The fused system has the advantage over the vision- and audio-based unimodal of about 4% and 16% points, respectively. The 2nd and the 7th columns (Dis, Sur respectively) reveal a high accuracy of the fusion model for recognizing disgust and surprise respectively in contrast to the stand alone uni-modal models, indicating that both cues obviously comprise complementary information that facilitate eased discrimination in the joint analysis. In contrast, from column (Fea) it is noticeable that both uni-modal cues comprise only redundant information so that the fusion yields no improvement with regard to discrimination ability for the recognition of fear. Overall our system achieves good results on the DaFEx database, which are comparable with those reported for human observers [1]. However, the results achieved by the bimodal system emphasize putting forward the fusion scheme of Sec. 3.3 toward efficient recognition of emotion for HRI [20].

As we are striving in this work to give the robot a bimodal emotion recognition ability that is based on analyzing facial expressions and speech information, the systems are afresh evaluated on data set with subjects in a real-life conditions. Four subjects have participated in this test (one female and three males). The whole procedure is divided into training and test phases. For one subject both phases were conducted in the same day; for two others the test was is conducted in the following day, while for the fourth subject the time interval was two days.

In the training phase the subjects are asked to display facial expressions of five emotion classes: anger, happiness, neutral, sadness, and surprise with and without speaking. The average amount of data captured from each subject for each facial expression class was 246 images. To create conditions of real-life human-robot interaction as much as possible, the subjects are allowed to move arbitrarily in front of the camera. During this phase a person-independent AAM, which is built from a subset of the DaFEx database of talking and non-talking subjects, is used to extract the emotion-related facial features. These features are then conveyed to train a person-dependent SVM.

Table 2. Confusion matrix obtained by using the facial-expression-based system in the test session of displaying emotions deliberatively; rows represent the ground truth

	Anger	Happiness	Neutral	Sadness	Surprise
Anger	**57.72**	00.60	12.19	28.54	00.95
Happiness	02.96	**67.46**	21.00	07.15	01.42
Neutral	05.21	00.00	**64.36**	30.42	00.00
Sadness	02.98	00.00	17.32	**79.18**	00.53
Surprise	05.57	00.88	31.35	10.55	**51.64**
Total	**64.07**				

In the test phase the subjects are asked to display facial expressions and utter a few sentences (in general five) expressing as much an emotions as possible [1]. The above-mentioned AAM is used to extract facial features, which are labeled with the proper emotional class by the above-trained SVM. In this session a person-independent speech-based emotion recognizer is utilized to categorize each utterance into the proper emotional class. An average of 145.25 images from each subject for each emotion are used as test data. The validation matrix for the fusion scheme of each subject was an averaged confusion matrix (CPT), which is obtained from the performance of both individual systems on the three remaining subjects.

Table 2 illustrates the result obtained by using only the facial-expression-based emotion analysis system to recognize emotions that are deliberatively displayed by the subjects. As depicted in the table, the most negative emotion − sadness − and the most positive emotion − happiness − are recognized the best. Neutral also has a relatively high recognition rate, which can serve to distinguish between emotional and non-emotional states of the interactant. The mutual confusion between sadness and neutral indicates the similarity between them when the distinguishing is based only on analyzing the associated facial expressions. The

---

[1] The sentences were emotional words free.

Table 3. Confusion matrix obtained by using the facial-expression-based system in the test session of expressing emotions via facial expressions and speech tone simultaneously; rows represent the ground truth

	Anger	Happiness	Neutral	Sadness	Surprise
Anger	**75.00**	00.00	06.25	18.75	00.00
Happiness	25.00	**43.75**	25.00	06.25	00.00
Neutral	20.00	00.00	**50.00**	30.00	00.00
Sadness	22.36	11.11	06.25	**60.28**	00.00
Surprise	16.67	00.00	12.50	22.92	**47.92**
Total	**55.39**				

fact that surprise is a transient state, difficult to hold, which changes rapidly into another one (in our test it changed generally into the neutral state), could be the reason for the relatively high confusion of surprise with neutral.

The results obtained by analyzing facial expressions during speech are illustrated in the table 3. The results present the recognition rates after applying majority voting for each utterance that doesn't include a pause longer than 200 ms. As in the evaluation with the database (offline evaluation), facial-expression-based analysis of emotion delivered lower recognition rates when the subjects were engaged in conversational sessions; 64.07% for the former and 55.39% for the latter. The higher recognition rate of anger during speech compared to anger displayed deliberatively could be because majority voting over the time of each sentence is applied in the former, while the recognition rate of the latter is computed for the entire video sequence.

Table 4. The performance of each stand-alone unimodal systems against the one of the bimodal system. All results are obtained from a test in a real-life condition.

	Anger	Happiness	Neutral	Sadness	Surprise	Total
Vis	75.00	43.75	50.00	60.28	47.92	55.39
Aco	33.04	15.42	36.25	23.06	10.42	23.63
Audio-Visual	75.00	50.00	68.75	49.03	47.92	58.14

Table 4 illustrates the results obtained from both the stand-alone and bimodal systems. The low rates delivered by the speech-based emotion analysis system - the first raw - could be because a person-independent classifier is used, which is trained on a speech-based emotion database that does not include the subjects participating in the evaluation procedure. Nevertheless, it can be seen that the whole performance of the bimodal system has an advantage over both facial-expression- and speech-information-based systems, which satisfy the goal of the fusion scheme proposed previously. However, when the performance of each channel on each emotion is considered it is notable that the recognition rate of happiness and neutral is enhanced when the bimodal system is employed, which indicates that the cues of both modalities comprise complementary information for these two emotions. In contrast, from the first and fifth rows, it is noticeable that both unimodal cues comprise only redundant information so that combining both modalities yields no improvement with regard to discrimination ability for the recognition of anger and surprise. Furthermore, the fourth column indicates that both modalities deliver conflicting information, which causes sadness to be recognized even less than the stand-alone facial-expression-based modality.

The comparison between the performance of all of the systems in the cases of offline (DaFEx database) and online (data captured in real-life conditions) evaluation shows better performance of the systems in the former case, especially of the speech-information-based system. These performance differences were greatly expected because (I) the speech-information-based system in the former was trained using data from the same subjects who had participated in the evaluation test, (II) the facial-expression-based system of the former case was trained and tested on a relatively constrained set of data (the actors displayed almost a frontal-view facial expression with constrained head movements while they were sitting in front of the camera), and (III) the degraded performance of both unimodal systems will consequentially lead to a degraded performance of the bimodal system.

5   Conclusion and Outlook

In this paper we presented our approaches on single cue analysis and multi-cue probabilistic decision-level fusion for emotion recognition. As we strive to recognize the basic emotions in real interaction, we presented a person-independent model and restricted ourselves to the challenge of talking persons in this database-based study.

The results indicate that the performance of each modality is highly varying with the respective emotion class which is in line with hypotheses of modality fusion in human perception [10,7]. Based on these results we put forward our fusion scheme where each modality is weighted according to its discriminative power for a specific emotion by applying Bayesian networks trained according to the performance of the individual classifiers. Towards our goal of real-life Human-Robot Interaction our system presents an advanced improvement not only due its reasonable accuracy in emotion recognition but also due its applicability as an online system in less constrained environments and without any further prior processing [4,6].

References

1. Battocchi, A., Pianesi, F., Goren-Bar, D.: A first evaluation study of a database of kinetic facial expressions (dafex). In: Proc. Int. Conf. Multimodal Interfaces, pp. 214–221. ACM Press, New York (2005)
2. Ekman, P., Friesen, W.: Unmasking the Face: A Guide to Recognizing Emotions from Facial Expressions. Prentice Hall, Englewood Cliffs (1975)
3. Paleari, M., Lisetti, C.L.: Toward multimodal fusion of affective cues. In: Proc. ACM Int. Workshop on Human-Centered Multimedia, pp. 99–108. ACM, New York (2006)

4. Busso, C., Deng, Z., Yildirim, S., Bulut, M., Lee, C.M., Kazemzadeh, A., Lee, S., Neumann, U., Narayanan, S.: Analysis of emotion recognition using facial expressions, speech and multimodal information. In: Proc. Int. Conf. Multimodal Interfaces (2004)
5. Caridakis, G., Malatesta, L., Kessous, L., Amir, N., Raouzaiou, A., Karpouzis, K.: Modeling naturalistic affective states via facial and vocal expressions recognition. In: Proc. Int. Conf. Multimodal Interfaces, pp. 146–154. ACM, New York (2006)
6. Zeng, Z., Hu, Y., Fu, Y., Huang, T.S., Roisman, G.I., Wen, Z.: Audio-visual emotion recognition in adult attachment interview. In: Proc. Int. Conf. on Multimodal Interfaces, pp. 139–145. ACM, New York (2006)
7. Massaro, D.W., Egan, P.B.: Perceiving affect from the voice and the face. Psychonomoic Bulletin and Review (3), 215–221
8. de Gelder, B., Vroomen, J.: Bimodal emotion perception: integration across separate modalities, cross-modal perceptula grouping or perception of multimodal events? Cognition and Emotion 14, 321–324 (2000)
9. Schwartz, J.L.: Why the FLMP should not be applied to McGurk data. or how to better compare models in the bazesian framework. In: Proc. Int. Conf. Audio-Visual Speech Processing, pp. 77–82 (2003)
10. Fagel, S.: Emotional mcgurk effect. In: Proc. Int. Conf. on Speech Prosody, Dresden, Germany (2006)
11. Rabie, A., Lang, C., Hanheide, M., Castrillon-Santana, M., Sagerer, G.: Automatic initialization for facial analysis in interactive robotics (2008)
12. Hegel, F., Spexard, T., Vogt, T., Horstmann, G., Wrede, B.: Playing a different imitation game: Interaction with an empathic android robot. In: Proc. Int. Conf. Humanoid Robots, pp. 56–61 (2006)
13. Cootes, T.F., Edwards, G.J., Taylor, C.J.: Active appearance models. PAMI 23, 681–685 (2001)
14. Castrillón, M., Déniz, O., Guerra, C., Hernández, M.: Encara2: Real-time detection of multiple faces at different resolutions in video streams. Journal of Visual Communication and Image Representation 18, 130–140 (2007)
15. Hanheide, M., Wrede, S., Lang, C., Sagerer, G.: Who am i talking with? a face memory for social robots (2008)
16. Vogt, T., André, E., Bee, N.: Emovoice — A framework for online recognition of emotions from voice. In: Proc. Workshop on Perception and Interactive Technologies for Speech-Based Systems, Irsee, Germany (2008)
17. Hall, M.A.: Correlation-based feature subset selection for machine learning. Master's thesis, University of Waikato, New Zealand (1998)
18. Vogt, T., André, E.: Comparing feature sets for acted and spontaneous speech in view of automatic emotion recognition. In: Proc. of IEEE Int. Conf. on Multimedia & Expo., Amsterdam, The Netherlands (2005)
19. Zeng, Z., Pantic, M., Roisman, G.I., Huang, T.S.: A survey of affect recognition methods: Audio, visual, and spontaneous expressions. IEEE Transaction on Pattern Analysis and Macine Intelligence 31, 39–58 (2009)
20. Rabie, A., Vogt, T., Hanheide, M., Wrede, B.: Evaluation and discussion of multimodal emotion recognition. In: ICCEE (2009)

Training of Sparsely Connected MLPs

Markus Thom[1], Roland Schweiger[1], and Günther Palm[2]

[1] Department Environment Perception (GR/PAP), Daimler AG, Ulm, Germany
[2] Institute of Neural Information Processing, University of Ulm, Germany

Abstract. Sparsely connected Multi-Layer Perceptrons (MLPs) differ
from conventional MLPs in that only a small fraction of entries in their
weight matrices are nonzero. Using sparse matrix-vector multiplication
algorithms reduces the computational complexity of classification. Training of sparsely connected MLPs is achieved in two consecutive stages. In
the first stage, initial values for the network's parameters are given by
the solution to an unsupervised matrix factorization problem, minimizing the reconstruction error. In the second stage, a modified version of
the supervised backpropagation algorithm optimizes the MLP's parameters with respect to the classification error. Experiments on the MNIST
database of handwritten digits show that the proposed approach achieves
equal classification performance compared to a densely connected MLP
while speeding-up classification by a factor of seven.

1 Introduction

Multi-Layer Perceptrons [1] have been widely employed in a vast range of classification tasks, especially for handwritten digit recognition [11]. MLP parameter
tuning is traditionally achieved using the backpropagation algorithm [18]. This
procedure has recently tied the record [3] on the MNIST database of handwritten digits [12], achieving an error of 0.35%. For this, the MLP comprised six
layers with 12 million synaptic connections. The learning set was extended by
generating artificial training examples using elastic distortions [19].

This paper focuses on posing sparseness constraints on the weight matrices
of MLPs, so that only a small fraction of entries are nonzero. Thus, sparsely
connected MLPs or briefly sparse MLPs (SMLPs) are yielded. This is motivated
in part by the fact that neurons in biological neuronal systems are not connected
to every other neuron in the network [22]. Sparse connectivity helps to reduce
both memory usage and computational complexity of the classification task.
By exploiting the structure of sparsely populated weight matrices, the principal
module of an MLP's feeding-forward mechanism can be sped up. This is especially advantageous in industrial applications, where a system may be rendered
real-time capable or where hardware cost may be reduced [15,17].

The main focus of this paper is the training of sparsely connected MLPs. The
amount of nonzero connection weights is set a-priori, and can hence be chosen
to obtain a classifier with predictable time complexity. In the first of two consecutive stages, a matrix factorization algorithm that uses sparse filter matrices for

R. Mester and M. Felsberg (Eds.): DAGM 2011, LNCS 6835, pp. 356–365, 2011.
© Springer-Verlag Berlin Heidelberg 2011

generating sparse and information-preserving representations is used to initialize the sparse MLP's parameters. In the second stage, a modified backpropagation learning algorithm finds an MLP that is optimal with respect to the classification error, simultaneously fulfilling sparseness constraints.

The remainder of this paper is organized as follows: Section 2 addresses the problem of computing sparse representations in an unsupervised manner suitable for sparse MLP initialization. In Sect. 3, an algorithm for training sparsely connected MLPs is proposed. The results of this technique applied to handwritten digits are demonstrated in Sect. 4, and compared with alternative approaches in Sect. 5. The final section contains a summary and conclusion.

2   Sparse Generative Models for SMLP Initialization

Training of sparsely connected MLPs from randomly initialized parameters is an ill-conditioned problem. Network parameter initialization constitutes the most crucial part in the whole procedure. One key idea that has recently found its way into the pattern classification community is the unsupervised pre-training of classifiers [8]. Here, the computation of sparse representations is of particular interest. Considering linear generative models, a sample $x \in \mathbb{R}^d$ is approximated by the linear combination of a matrix of bases $W \in \mathbb{R}^{d \times n}$ with a code word $h \in \mathbb{R}^n$, such that $x \approx Wh$. Traditional sparse coding [7] is achieved by requiring most entries of h to be zero. Another notion is the restriction that W be sparsely populated, which is the main focus of this section.

One of the most important mathematical models known to reproduce certain data sets using a sparse matrix of bases is Non-Negative Matrix Factorization (NMF) [14]. It aims to factorize a data matrix $X \in \mathbb{R}_{\geq 0}^{d \times M}$ of M samples with non-negative entries into the product of a matrix of bases $W \in \mathbb{R}_{\geq 0}^{d \times n}$ and a matrix of code words $H \in \mathbb{R}_{\geq 0}^{n \times M}$, both with non-negative entries. Since NMF is only allowed to make additive combinations in a linear generative model framework, sparse matrices W can be achieved [14]. However, there are data sets where NMF fails to produce sparse representations without further modifications to the algorithm itself [9].

2.1   Non-Negative Matrix Factorization with Sparseness Constraints

NMF is extended by Non-Negative Matrix Factorization with Sparseness Constraints (NMFSC) [9] so that the sparseness of the representation becomes easily controllable. In doing so, a formal sparseness measure σ based on a normalized quotient of the L^1 norm and the L^2 norm of a vector has been proposed:

$$\sigma : \mathbb{R}^d \setminus \{0\} \to [0, 1], \qquad x \mapsto \frac{\sqrt{d} - \frac{\|x\|_1}{\|x\|_2}}{\sqrt{d} - 1} . \tag{1}$$

Using σ, NMFSC must minimize the reproduction error in Frobenius norm, $E_{\mathrm{NMF}}(W, H) := \|X - WH\|_F^2$, subject to $\sigma(We_i) = \sigma_W$ and $\sigma(H^t e_i) = \sigma_H$ for all $i \in \{1, \ldots, n\}$ for constant sparseness degrees $\sigma_W, \sigma_H \in (0, 1)$. Here, e_i is the i-th canonical basis vector. σ_W controls the sparseness of the individual columns of W. σ_H controls the fraction of samples each column of W contributes to.

The biconvex objective function is minimized via alternating gradient descent on W and H, with each step followed by a sparseness-enforcing projection to meet the sparseness constraints. This sparseness-enforcing projection is computed by iterative projection on a hyperplane satisfying an L^1 norm constraint and on a hypersphere satisfying an L^2 norm constraint [9,20].

The major drawback of NMFSC is that it is only a generative architecture. However, computation of sparse code words h from arbitrary samples x is possible through a cost-intensive optimization. Unfortunately, no real-time capable algorithm to solve this code word inference problem is known.

2.2   Extension for Fast Inference of Sparse Code Words

To address this issue, an extension ensuring fast inference of sparse code words has recently been proposed [21]. There, inference is modeled as feeding forward the training samples through a one-layer perceptron, employing a non-linearity that approximates a soft-shrinkage operation. Similar to [16], the matrix of bases is used for code word inference as well.

As sparseness is enforced through NMFSC's projection operator, the non-negativity constraint is no longer needed. Hence let $X \in \mathbb{R}^{d \times M}$, $W \in \mathbb{R}^{d \times n}$ and $H \in \mathbb{R}^{n \times M}$, allowing for a more general range of applications. This enables the normalization of the training samples to zero mean and unit variance, which is advantageous in classification scenarios [13].

To extend NMFSC for fast inference, a vector of thresholds $\theta \in \mathbb{R}^n$ and a nonlinear transfer function $f : \mathbb{R}^n \to \mathbb{R}^n$ are introduced. Feed-forward code words are defined to be a one-layer perceptron's output, $x \mapsto f(W^t x + \theta)$. Here, f is chosen to be a hyperbolic tangent raised to an odd exponent greater or equal to three, that is $f : \mathbb{R} \to \mathbb{R}$, $x \mapsto (\tanh(\beta x))^q$ with $\beta > 0$ and $q \in 2\mathbb{N}_0 + 3 = \{3, 5, 7, \ldots\}$. The exponentiation has a similar effect as applying a soft-shrinkage function after a hyperbolic tangent transfer function, thus allowing for sparse inferred code words. However, this function has the advantage of being differentiable everywhere. In this paper, $\beta = 1$ and $q = 3$ were chosen. By computing the squared difference between the code word matrix and the matrix of feed-forward code words, the inference error is given by $E_{\mathrm{Inf}}(W, \theta, H) := \|H - f(W^t X + \theta \cdot J_{1 \times M})\|_F^2$. Here, $J_{1 \times M} \in \mathbb{R}^{1 \times M}$ denotes a matrix containing only ones and is employed for repeating the threshold over all M samples.

The objective function is defined to lie between reconstruction error and inference error, controlling the trade-off with a parameter $\alpha_{\mathrm{Inf}} \in [0, 1]$:

$$E(W, \theta, H) := (1 - \alpha_{\mathrm{Inf}}) \cdot E_{\mathrm{NMF}}(W, H) + \alpha_{\mathrm{Inf}} \cdot E_{\mathrm{Inf}}(W, \theta, H) \ . \tag{2}$$

Here, α_{Inf} was chosen to start from zero and reach $1/2$ asymptotically. E is minimized by alternating gradient descent. Each update of W and H is followed by sparseness-enforcing projections, ensuring that the sparseness constraints are met: $\sigma(We_i) = \sigma_W$ and $\sigma(H^t e_i) = \sigma_H$ for all $i \in \{1, \ldots, n\}$.

3   Sparsely Connected MLPs

In the preceding section, only generative models were investigated. It turns out that state-of-the-art performance in classification problems can not be achieved solely by using unsupervised learning algorithms. This is because the representations have only been optimized to retain a maximum of the information in the training samples, regardless of their class labels. However, the unsupervised algorithms provide adequate initializers for more discriminative architectures. Exploiting the emergence of sparse matrices of bases, an efficient way of training sparsely connected MLPs is proposed in this section.

3.1   Architecture

Consider an MLP with L layers, where $\mathcal{W} := (W_1, \ldots, W_L)$ and $\Theta := (\theta_1, \ldots, \theta_L)$ denote the weight matrices and the threshold vectors of the individual layers, respectively. Let $W_i \in \mathbb{R}^{d_{i-1} \times d_i}$ and $\theta_i \in \mathbb{R}^{d_i}$ for all $i \in \{1, \ldots, L\}$, where $d_0, d_1, \ldots, d_{L-1}, d_L \in \mathbb{N}$ denote the complexity of the individual layers. Given a dataset of samples and teacher signals, $\mathcal{W}$ and Θ are adjusted by minimizing the deviation between network output given the samples and the corresponding teacher signals. This deviation can be measured using the mean square error function or the cross-entropy error function [1]. In classification problems with $n > 2$ distinct classes, the teacher signals are represented using 1-of-n codes. The final layer's transfer function then is set to the softmax function [1].

In sparse MLPs, the weight matrices are enforced to meet specific sparseness constraints. Let $\sigma_{W_1}, \ldots, \sigma_{W_L} \in (0, 1)$ be sparseness degrees for every layer. The problem of training SMLPs then becomes minimizing the error function subject to $\sigma(W_i e_j) = \sigma_{W_i}$ for all $i \in \{1, \ldots, L\}$ and for all $j \in \{1, \ldots, d_i\}$. Here, σ is the sparseness measure from Sect. 2.1. In practice, posing sparseness constraints to the final layer is often not beneficial, as it constitutes the final weighting of the MLP's internal state. In the remainder of this paper, analysis is restricted to final layers without sparseness constraints. In the case of two-layer MLPs, let $\sigma_W := \sigma_{W_1}$ denote the sparseness degree of the only hidden layer.

3.2   Training Algorithm

Similar to Radial Basis Function (RBF) networks [1], a proper initialization of $\mathcal{W}$ and Θ is crucial for the success in training SMLPs. Using unsupervised pre-training, this is not limited to RBF networks [8]. By employing the learning algorithm from Sect. 2.2, layers 1 to $L-1$ are initialized in a layer-wise manner. This guarantees that the respective weight matrices are sparsely populated, and every layer is able to reproduce its individual input.

Supervised linear SVM training [6] is used to initialize the final layer. If the classification problem is not binary, each hidden unit in layer L represents one class using 1-of-n codes. Linear SVM training is then run in a one vs. all fashion, and the corresponding column of W_L and the corresponding entry of θ_L are set to contain the linear SVM's weight vector and threshold, respectively.

Supervised training of sparsely connected MLPs is achieved through sequential gradient descent, using the backpropagation algorithm [18]. With the original backpropagation algorithm, the connection matrices that were initialized to be sparsely populated lose this property during training. This indicates that sparse connection matrices do not minimize the unconstrained classification error. Minimization of the error function subject to sparseness constraints is achieved by projected gradient descent, that is the sparseness-enforcing projection from Sect. 2.1 is carried out after presentation of a few thousand samples to the network. It is important not to project too early, because then $\mathcal{W}$ will not be modified effectively during learning. By projecting too late, the changes to $\mathcal{W}$ between projections become too intense, resulting in divergence.

After training has converged, an MLP with connection matrices meeting sparseness constraints results. The connectivity rate in the weight matrices is set a-priori using sparseness degrees. The relationship between both values is non-linear, but can be calculated beforehand. Naive pruning of connections with small absolute values can increase sparseness further. The threshold for pruning has to be verified on the learning set so that the classification error is not increased.

3.3   Computational Complexity of Classification

In practice, the computational complexity of the classification routine is relevant for designing the classifier's architecture, adjusting it to specific hardware needs. Let $A \in \mathbb{R}^{d \times n}$ be a matrix and $x \in \mathbb{R}^d$ be a vector. Investigating the problem of computing the matrix-vector product $A^t x$, the kernel of this computation is a multiply-accumulate (MAC) operation, $D \leftarrow D + A(j, i) \cdot x(j)$. Here, D is a data register employed to avoid having to store the product in memory after every execution. The MAC operation is executed dn times, and $2dn$ numbers have to be fetched from memory. If A is a sparsely populated matrix with exactly k nonzero entries in each column, it can be stored as pair of a matrix $P \in \mathbb{N}_0^{k \times n}$ of positions of nonzero elements with a matrix of according values $V \in \mathbb{R}^{k \times n}$. The kernel of the sparse matrix-vector product computation then becomes the MAC operation $D \leftarrow D + V(j, i) \cdot x(P(j, i))$, and is carried out kn times. In total, $3kn$ numbers now have to be fetched from memory, also accounting for the entries of P. If $k < \frac{2}{3}d$, the sparse matrix-vector multiplication needs less read accesses than the dense counterpart does. Method effectiveness thus increases with d.

The computation of matrix-vector products is the dominating part of the overall computational complexity of MLP classification. The application of the thresholds is equivalent to initializing register D with the concrete threshold value and requires only n additional memory accesses. Transfer function evaluation can be sped up by employing a function that can be evaluated by means of algebraic operations on the argument [5]. Hence, no auxiliary data needs to be read from memory, as look-up table entries or coefficients of a Taylor expansion would be required otherwise. The final layer's transfer function can always be replaced with a linear one since the classification decision is equivalent to thresholding in binary classification problems and to finding the maximum entry in the network's output vector if more than two classes are involved.

In summary, the computational complexity of classification with MLPs depends strongly on the number of nonzero entries in the weight matrices. Sparsely connected MLPs require some overhead with respect to the read accesses, as the more complex data structure has to be stored as well. For comparison, a simple computational model that accounts for MAC operations and memory accesses is defined. Let $Z \in \mathbb{R}$ be the memory latency relative to the cost of a MAC operation. Considering a two layer $d - h - n$ MLP, the cost for classifying one sample is $(1 + 2Z) h (d + n)$ operations. A sparse MLP with a connectivity rate of $\rho \in (0, 1)$ in the first layer needs $(1 + 3Z) \rho dh + (1 + 2Z) hn$ operations. The speed-up factor $S(Z, \rho)$ is then the quotient of the two quantities and is independent of the number of hidden units h. $S(Z, \rho)$ converges decreasingly for very high memory latencies to

$$S_\infty (\rho) := \lim_{Z \to \infty} S(Z, \rho) = \lim_{Z \to \infty} \frac{\left(\frac{1}{Z} + 2\right) (d + n)}{\left(\frac{1}{Z} + 3\right) \rho d + \left(\frac{1}{Z} + 2\right) n} = \frac{2 (d + n)}{3 \rho d + 2n} . \qquad (3)$$

In this computational model, a lower bound of sparse MLP speed-up over dense MLPs is given by $S_\infty (\rho)$, which is independent of memory latencies.

4   Experiments on Handwritten Digits

The performance of sparse MLPs is evaluated on the MNIST database of handwritten digits [12]. It consists of 70 000 samples, divided into a learning set of 60 000 samples and an evaluation set of 10 000 samples. Each sample represents a digit of size 28×28 pixels and has a class label from $\{0, \ldots, 9\}$ associated with it. The samples were normalized to achieve zero mean and unit variance.

Three variants of the learning set have been employed for the experiments. The first one is the original learning set with 60 000 samples. To investigate the effect of small translations, the samples have been jittered by 1 pixel in each of 8 directions, yielding 540 000 samples. Finally, by applying additional elastic distortions [19], a learning set with 13.5 million samples was generated.

The architecture was fixed to two-layer MLPs with 1000 neurons in the hidden layer. Although employing more layers has improved classification performance [3], this paper focuses on creating classifiers with very low computational complexity. For reference, conventional densely connected MLPs have been trained on the three learning sets and tested on the 10 000 samples of the evaluation set, yielding errors of 1.9%, 0.89%, and 0.61%, respectively. Thus, similar to [2,4], adding jittered samples to the learning set significantly improves the classification error. The localization uncertainty can be explained by the original placement of the digits based on the center of mass of their pixel values [12]. This illustrates that MLPs are not able to learn invariants well, and hence rely heavily on artificial training samples added to the learning set. Adding even more samples using elastic distortions further decreases the classification error.

Two-thirds of the connections in the first layer of the MLP trained on the jittered learning set have been removed through naive pruning based on their

Table 1. Comparison of a conventional MLP with sparsely connected MLPs on the MNIST dataset. All MLPs had two layers with 1000 units in the hidden layer. Only the first connection matrix W_1 was required to be sparse, W_2 was densely populated.

Sparseness degree σ_W	none	0.75	0.80	0.85	0.90
Connectivity rate ρ in W_1 [%]	100	12.9	8.7	6.6	3.7
Number of synaptic connections	800 000	110 000	78 000	62 000	39 000
Speed-up $S_\infty\,(\rho)$ to dense MLP	1	4.9	7.1	9.1	15
Error on evaluation set [%]	0.89	0.83	0.86	0.91	0.94

absolute values. This increased the error from 0.89% to 1.2%. If only enough connections were removed so that the classification error did not increase, 55.7% of the connections still remained. Thus, only a mild speed-up factor of 1.2 could be achieved while retaining classification capabilities. If instead of naive pruning the sparseness-enforcing projection from Sect. 2.1 is used, the error increases drastically to 3.0%. This indicates that the solution found by unconstrained minimization is very distant from a minimum fulfilling sparseness constraints.

The results can be improved by training sparsely connected MLPs using the method from Sect. 3.2. As 96% of all samples possess a sparseness of less than 0.75, this value was chosen for the lower bound on the MLP sparseness. A summary of the results on the jittered learning set is given in Table 1. For $\sigma_W = 0.75$, an error of 0.83% was achieved, rendering it slightly better than the conventional MLP. Nevertheless, only 12.9% of the entries in the first connection matrix were nonzero, resulting in a lower bound to the speed-up factor of 4.9 compared to the dense MLP. For comparison, a dense MLP with a reduced number of hidden units has been trained. Though the dense MLP was adjusted for equal computational complexity as the SMLP, only an error of 1.1% could be achieved. For $\sigma_W = 0.80$, the error slightly increased, but the lower connectivity rate allowed for a speed-up of at least factor seven. The speed-ups increase more for higher sparseness degrees, while the classification capabilities degrade. However, even for very sparse connection matrices, the error remains below 1%.

Sparse MLPs for sparseness degrees 0.75, 0.80, 0.85, and 0.90 have also been trained on the learning set generated by elastic distortions, achieving significantly lower errors of 0.59%, 0.64%, 0.67%, and 0.72%, respectively. Though the SMLP with $\sigma_W = 0.75$ achieved an error statistically equal to the one of the conventional MLP, the connectivity rate in the hidden layer was 14.2%, which results in a minimum speed-up of factor 4.5.

To verify the initialization as described in Sect. 3.2, an MLP was initialized using random values and then trained on the jittered learning set with the backpropagation algorithm subject to sparseness constraints. After convergence, an error of 1.1% was achieved, which is significantly higher than the corresponding error of 0.89% using the unconstrained backpropagation algorithm. Thus, reasonable results could only be achieved using the combination of a sophisticated initialization scheme with a constrained backpropagation algorithm.

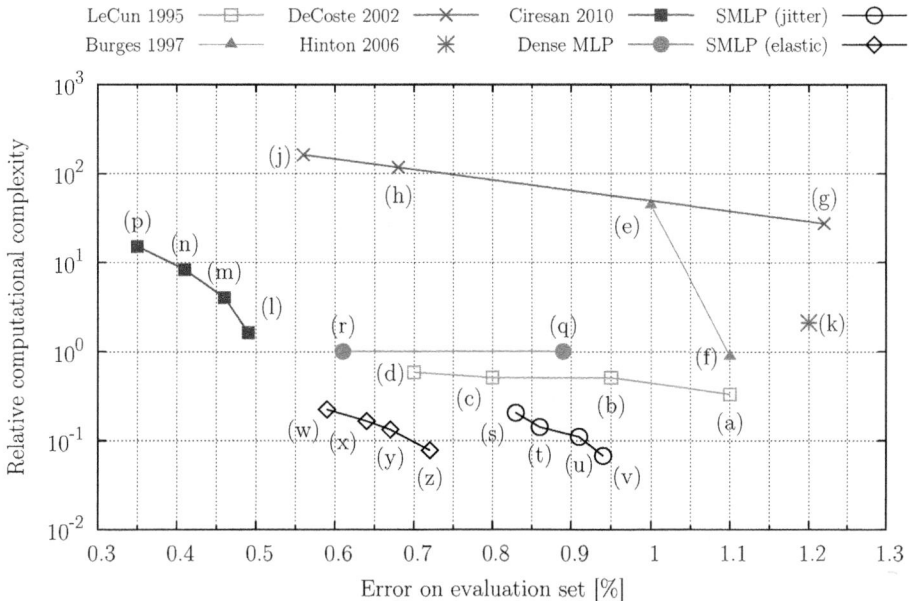

Fig. 1. Comparison of various approaches to MNIST considering classification error and computational complexity of classification. Computational complexity is given relative to the complexity of a dense two-layer MLP with 1000 hidden units. A detailed discussion is given in Sect. 5. This figure is best viewed in color.

5 Comparison with Alternative Approaches

The results described in the previous section are compared with alternative approaches from LeCun 1995 [10,11], Burges 1997 [2], DeCoste 2002 [4], Hinton 2006 [8], and Cireşan 2010 [3]. The two major points of this comparison are the error achieved on the evaluation set and the computational complexity of classification relative to a densely connected MLP with 1000 hidden units. The results of this discussion are illustrated in Fig. 1 and are referenced using signs (a)–(z). Though [19] achieved an error of 0.4% using convolutional neural networks, the computational complexity of their approach has not been published. Thus it is not included in this discussion.

A very efficient solution using a family of convolutional neural networks has been given by LeCun 1995 [10,11]: (a) LeNet-4 and (b) LeNet-5 using the original learning set, (c) LeNet-5 and (d) boosted LeNet-4 using an augmented learning set. The computational complexity has been determined based on the number of MAC operations from [11].

Burges 1997 [2] proposed a Virtual Support Vector Machine, adding samples jittered in four directions to the learning set. Their approach (e) achieves an error of 1.0%, but the computational complexity is very demanding. The computational cost can be reduced by approximating the SVM's hyperplane normal by a reduced set of vectors, resulting in a speed-up of factor 22 [2], involving a slightly larger error (f). DeCoste 2002 [4] improve on the classification error by using samples jittered in eight directions. The error improves from (g) the original learning set to (h) jittering by 1 pixel and (j) jittering by 2 pixels. Computational complexity of [2] and [4] has been determined based on the number of support vectors. The complexity in the latter case is very high, but there no reduced set approach has been applied.

Hinton 2006 [8] used a deep network of Restricted Boltzmann Machines, pre-trained using unsupervised algorithms. They (k) achieved an error of 1.2%, without having to augment the learning set using artificial training samples. Thus, their approach is completely invariant to permutations of the pixels of the input samples. Using a two-layer MLP, a significantly higher error of 1.9% was achieved using the very same learning set, see Sect. 4.

By employing very large MLPs, Cireşan 2010 [3] currently hold the record on MNIST classification. They employed elastic and affine distortions to obtain a huge learning set. MLP training was sped up by greatly exploiting parallelism on a graphics processing unit. They trained MLPs with (l) three layers, (m) four layers, (n) five layers, and (p) six layers. Unlike recent trends, they did not employ unsupervised pre-training before using the backpropagation algorithm to tune the MLP parameters.

The results obtained in this paper are quite competitive. The conventional two-layer MLP with 1000 hidden units trained on the jittered samples achieved (q) an error of 0.89%. By training on the elastically distorted samples, an error of 0.61% was achieved (r). By exploiting the sparse connection matrix of sparse MLPs, significant speed-ups can be gained while retaining similar classification performance. For the jittered learning set, SMLPs with sparseness degrees σ_W of (s) 0.75, (t) 0.80, (u) 0.85, and (v) 0.90 have been trained. On the elastic learning set, SMLPs with sparseness degrees of (w) 0.75, (x) 0.80, (y) 0.85, and (z) 0.90 have been trained, achieving significantly better classification performance but also higher computational complexity due to a higher connectivity rate.

6   Conclusions

Traditional Multi-Layer Perceptrons have been studied and applied intensely over the past decades. They have recently achieved state-of-the-art performance in handwritten digit recognition. In this paper, an algorithm for the training of sparsely connected MLPs has been proposed. In doing so, the MLP's parameters are initialized using the solution to an unsupervised matrix factorization problem. Then, the parameters are tuned to optimize classification capabilities using a projected gradient descent algorithm. A comparison with alternative approaches has shown that sparse MLPs achieve competitive classification performance, while computational complexity can be reduced using sparse matrix-vector multiplication algorithms. This enables using sparse MLPs in embedded systems, where real-time capable algorithms are mandatory, and each speed-up results in an effective reduction of hardware cost.

References

1. Bishop, C.M.: Neural Networks for Pattern Recognition. Clarendon Press, Oxford (1995)
2. Burges, C.J.C., Schölkopf, B.: Improving the Accuracy and Speed of Support Vector Machines. In: NIPS, vol. 9, pp. 375–381 (1997)
3. Cireşan, D.C., Meier, U., Gambardella, L.M., Schmidhuber, J.: Deep, Big, Simple Neural Nets for Handwritten Digit Recognition. Neural Computation 22(12), 3207–3220 (2010)
4. DeCoste, D., Schölkopf, B.: Training Invariant Support Vector Machines. Machine Learning 46, 161–190 (2002)
5. Elliott, D.: A Better Activation Function for Artificial Neural Networks. Tech. Rep. ISR TR 93-8, Institute for Systems Research, University of Maryland (1993)
6. Fan, R.E., Chang, K.W., Hsieh, C.J., Wang, X.R., Lin, C.J.: LIBLINEAR: A Library for Large Linear Classification. JMLR 9, 1871–1874 (2008)
7. Field, D.J.: What is the Goal of Sensory Coding? Neural Computation 6, 559–601 (1994)
8. Hinton, G.E., Salakhutdinov, R.R.: Reducing the Dimensionality of Data with Neural Networks. Science 313(5786), 1527–1554 (2006)
9. Hoyer, P.O.: Non-negative Matrix Factorization with Sparseness Constraints. JMLR 5, 1457–1469 (2004)
10. LeCun, Y., Jackel, L., Bottou, L., Brunot, A., Cortes, C., Denker, J., Drucker, H., Guyon, I., Müller, U., Säckinger, E., Simard, P., Vapnik, V.: Comparison Of Learning Algorithms For Handwritten Digit Recognition. In: Proceedings of ICANN, pp. 53–60 (1995)
11. LeCun, Y., Bottou, L., Bengio, Y., Haffner, P.: Gradient-Based Learning Applied to Document Recognition. Proceedings of the IEEE 86, 2278–2324 (1998)
12. LeCun, Y., Cortes, C.: The MNIST Database of Handwritten Digits, http://yann.lecun.com/exdb/mnist
13. LeCun, Y., Kanter, I., Solla, S.A.: Eigenvalues of Covariance Matrices: Application to Neural-Network Learning. Physical Review Letters 66(18), 2396–2399 (1991)
14. Lee, D.D., Seung, H.S.: Learning the parts of objects by nonnegative matrix factorization. Nature 401, 788–791 (1999)
15. Ortigosa, E.M., Cañas, A., Rodríguez, R., Díaz, J., Mota, S.: Towards an Optimal Implementation of MLP in FPGA. In: Bertels, K., Cardoso, J.M.P., Vassiliadis, S. (eds.) ARC 2006. LNCS, vol. 3985, pp. 46–51. Springer, Heidelberg (2006)
16. Ranzato, M., Boureau, Y., LeCun, Y.: Sparse Feature Learning for Deep Belief Networks. In: NIPS, vol. 20, pp. 1185–1192 (2008)
17. Rast, A.D., Welbourne, S., Jin, X., Furber, S.: Optimal Connectivity In Hardware-Targetted MLP Networks. In: Proceedings of IJCNN, pp. 2619–2626 (2009)
18. Rumelhart, D.E., Hinton, G.E., Williams, R.J.: Learning representations by back-propagating errors. Nature 323, 533–536 (1986)
19. Simard, P.Y., Steinkraus, D., Platt, J.C.: Best Practices for Convolutional Neural Networks Applied to Visual Document Analysis. In: Proceedings of ICDAR, pp. 958–962 (2003)
20. Theis, F.J., Stadlthanner, K., Tanaka, T.: First results on uniqueness of sparse non-negative matrix factorization. In: Proceedings of EUSIPCO (2005)
21. Thom, M., Schweiger, R., Palm, G.: Supervised Matrix Factorization with Sparseness Constraints and Fast Inference. In: Proceedings of IJCNN (to appear, 2011)
22. Yoshimura, Y., Dantzker, J.L.M., Callaway, E.M.: Excitatory cortical neurons form fine-scale functional networks. Nature 433(7028), 868–873 (2005)

Minimizing Calibration Time for Brain Reading

Jan Hendrik Metzen[1], Su Kyoung Kim[1,2], and Elsa Andrea Kirchner[1,2]

[1] Robotics Group, University of Bremen, Bremen, Germany
[2] Robotics Innovation Center, DFKI GmbH, Bremen, Germany

Abstract. Machine learning is increasingly used to autonomously adapt brain-machine interfaces to user-specific brain patterns. In order to minimize the preparation time of the system, it is highly desirable to reduce the length of the calibration procedure, during which training data is acquired from the user, to a minimum. One recently proposed approach is to reuse models that have been trained in historic usage sessions of the same or other users by utilizing an ensemble-based approach. In this work, we propose two extensions of this approach which are based on the idea to combine predictions made by the historic ensemble with session-specific predictions that become available once a small amount of training data has been collected. These extensions are particularly useful for *Brain Reading Interfaces* (BRIs), a specific kind of brain-machine interfaces. BRIs do not require that user feedback is given and thus, additional training data may be acquired concurrently to the usage session. Accordingly, BRIs should initially perform well when only a small amount of training data acquired in a short calibration procedure is available and allow an increased performance when more training data becomes available during the usage session. An empirical offline-study in a testbed for the use of BRIs to support robotic telemanipulation shows that the proposed extensions allow to achieve this kind of behavior.

1 Introduction

Brain Reading Interfaces (BRIs) are one particular kind of brain-machine interface (BMI) that allow to provide the machine with information about the current mental state and intent of its user such that the machine can optimize its behavior accordingly. In contrast to active Brain-Computer Interfaces (BCIs, see [3,14] for a review of works), BRIs estimate the user's mental state and intent based on passive, external observation of brain activity without requiring any active participation of the user. This observation can, e.g., be based on electroencephalography (EEG). Since no active participation of the user is required, BRIs are well-suited for scenarios like robotic telemanipulation where a sophisticated BMI is expedient but the user needs to be fully immersed in his task.

Like active BCIs, BRIs must be adapted to the current brain patterns of the user since these characteristic patterns vary between different subjects and even change over time within the same subject. This can be achieved by using machine learning (ML) techniques (see, e.g., Blankertz et al. [4] for an example in an active BCI). The common approach for using ML in BCIs is to record labeled training

R. Mester and M. Felsberg (Eds.): DAGM 2011, LNCS 6835, pp. 366–375, 2011.

data during a so-called calibration procedure that must be conducted prior to each usage session. In this calibration procedure, the user acts in a controlled and supervised scenario. The labeled data acquired is then used to adapt the ML-based BCI system to the user's current brain patterns. The drawback of this approach is that the user has to conduct this calibration procedure each time he wants to use the system. Thus, it is highly desirable to keep this calibration procedure as short as possible (or remove its necessity altogether).

Different approaches for reducing the calibration time have been proposed: Krauledat et al. [10] proposed an algorithm targeted at long-term BCI users that allows to skip the calibration procedure. This is accomplished by inferring spatial filters and classifiers that generalize well across sessions based on reusing training data from historic sessions of the same user and clustering of historic spatial filters. Fazli et al. [6] proposed a method that allows to skip the calibration procedure for both long-term and novel users. Their approach is based on an ensemble of historic spatial-filter/classifier combinations that are transferred to the current session and whose individual predictions are combined into a joint prediction by means of a gating function. Both approaches require that a large number of historic sessions be available. Further approaches for reducing calibration time are multi-task learning [2], semi-supervised learning [11], and a hybrid approach that mixes historic data with session-specific data [12].

The main contribution of this paper is to propose two extensions of the "pure" ensemble-based approach of Fazli et al. and to present an empirical comparison of these approaches in a testbed for the use of BRIs to support robotic telemanipulation. The two extensions we propose are based on the idea of combining the predictions made by the historic ensemble with session-specific predictions that become available once some amount of training data has been collected. We show that these extensions achieve good performance when only a small amount of training data is available and—in contrast to the "pure" ensemble approach— also become increasingly better for more training data. This is particularly important for BRIs, since BRIs allow to interweave the acquisition of training data with the actual usage session. Thus, the system should initially perform well based on a small amount of training data acquired in a short calibration procedure but should also be able to improve performance when increasingly more training data is gathered during the usage session. Furthermore, in contrast to related approaches like [6] and [10], the proposed extensions perform well also when only a small number of historic sessions is available. The paper is structured as follows: In Section 2, a testbed for BRIs in robotic telemanipulation is presented. Subsequently, the baseline BRI as well as different ensemble-based extensions are proposed in Section 3. In Section 4, the experimental setup and a discussion of our results are given and a conclusion is drawn in Section 5.

2   Scenario

The empirical evaluation was conducted on an EEG dataset recorded in the Labyrinth Oddball scenario (see Figure 1), a testbed for the use of BRIs in

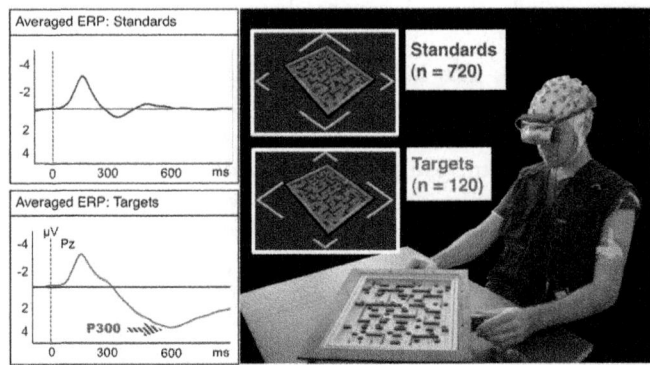

Fig. 1. Labyrinth Oddball: The subject plays a physical simulation of the BRIO® labyrinth and has to respond to rare 'target' stimuli by pressing a buzzer. Event-related potentials (ERPs) evoked by 'target' and more frequent 'standard' stimuli are depicted.

robotic telemanipulation. In this testbed, the operator has to simultaneously execute a manipulation task (playing the Labyrinth game) and to distinguish two different kinds of stimuli presented to him while playing the game. The BRI only needs to passively monitor whether the operator of the Labyrinth game correctly recognized and distinguished these stimuli. Since no user feedback is given, the testbed is well suited for evaluation of BRIs (for more details we refer to [8] and the video in [1]). The BRI's task is to discriminate between the EEG patterns evoked by recognizing so-called 'standard' and 'target' stimuli[1]. While 'standard' stimuli are frequent (720 presentations per run) but irrelevant, 'target' stimuli are rare (120 presentations per run) and require the user to press a buzzer. Such a scenario is called "oddball discrimination paradigm" and the successful recognition of the rare 'target' stimuli is known to elicit an event-related potential (ERP) called P300 [13]. In contrast to many active BCIs (e.g. [14]), the classification has to be made based on the individual instance and not on an average over several repetitions of the same condition. To avoid differences in early visual brain activity and to make sure that differences in the EEG recorded and classified after the presentation of both stimuli types are actually due to higher cognitive processing, the visual presentation (shape and color) of standard and target stimuli was kept very similar. Note that neither during the calibration procedure nor during evaluation runs feedback was given to the subject.

EEG data was acquired in 12 sessions from 6 male subjects; each subject performed 2 sessions. Sessions were recorded on different days; accordingly, the EEG cap was fitted onto the subject's head for each session anew. Each of these sessions consisted of five repetitions (called "runs") of the Labyrinth Oddball paradigm. After each of the five runs there was a short break of 10 minutes. The EEG was recorded and stored along with information about which stimulus was

---

[1] This is a kind of proxy-task for the actual task of distinguishing between recognized and missed target stimuli (see [8] for a discussion).

presented at what time and whether the buzzer was pressed afterwards. EEG was recorded continuously from 64 electrodes (extended 10–20 system with reference at electrode FCz), using an actiCap system (Brain Products GmbH, Munich, Germany). Two of the 64 channels (replacing the electrodes TP7 and TP8) were used to record electromyography signals of muscles of the lower arm and have been discarded in this study. EEG signals were amplified by two 32 channel BrainAmp DC amplifiers (Brain Products GmbH, Munich, Germany) and were sampled at 1000 Hz. The impedance was kept below 5 kΩ.

3   Methods

Baseline BRI. As a first step of the baseline BRI system used for discrimination of the 'standard' and the 'target' condition, rectangular time windows starting 0 ms and ending 1000 ms after stimulus presentation are extracted from the continuous signal recorded during the experiment. Thereupon, the extracted time windows are normalized so that the mean value of each channel becomes 0 within this window. Subsequently, the signal is low-pass filtered (cutoff frequency 12 Hz), downsampled from 1000 Hz to 25 Hz, and again low-pass filtered for a cutoff frequency of 4 Hz in order to focus on slow ERPs like the P300.

After this, the signal is spatially filtered. Spatial filtering denotes a mapping of the original n channels $x(t)$ (that directly correspond to the n electrodes) onto new pseudo-channels $\tilde{x}(t) = W^T x(t)$ that are a mixture of the signals recorded at different electrodes (see Blankertz et al. [5] for a discussion of why spatial filtering is an important step). In this work, we have generated spatial filters based on the common spatial patterns (CSP) algorithm [9]. CSP maps the data onto axes such that the variance for instances of the first class is maximized and the variance for the second class is minimized (or vice versa). With $X_i^{(c)} \in \mathbb{R}^{n \times t}$ being the i-th of the n_c examples of band-pass filtered and centered EEG segments with t samples for class c, this is achieved by a simultaneous diagonalization of the two empirical intra-class covariance matrices $\Sigma_c = n_c^{-1} \sum_{i=1}^{n_c} X_i^{(c)} (X_i^{(c)})^T$, i.e. by solving $\Sigma_1 W = \Lambda \Sigma_2 W$ where Λ is the vector of generalized eigenvalues and W is the matrix of generalized eigenvectors corresponding to the learned projections.

The values of the resulting pseudo-channels, i.e., the 26×62 samples of the 62 pseudo-channels that fall into the time window from 0 to 1000 ms, are used as features. Thereupon, each feature dimension is normalized such that its 2.5th percentile on the training data is mapped onto 0 and the 97.5th percentile is mapped onto 1. The resulting feature vectors are classified using a support vector machine (SVM) with linear kernel and complexity 0.01. Since the ratio of standard and target class instances in the dataset is highly unbalanced due to the oddball paradigm, the weight for class 'target' has been set to 2.0, while the weight of class 'standard' was set to 1.0. The feature set and all mentioned parameters have been chosen based on a preliminary investigation conducted on a hold-out dataset. The implementation of the data processing system is based on the "Modular toolkit for Data Processing" [15].

Ensemble approach. The baseline BRI outlined above adapts to the specific user by supervised training of subject- (and session)-specific spatial filters, feature normalization, and classifiers. Once trained, these three components form a subject- and session-specific classification system c_s (subsequently called a *classification flow*) that maps preprocessed time series x onto the scalar classifier prediction $c_s(x) \in \mathbb{R}$. Unfortunately, training of a classification flow requires a large training dataset that has to be recorded at the start of each session. In order to reduce the required amount of training data (possibly even to zero), Fazli et al. [6] proposed to reuse classification flows trained on N historic sessions from the same and other subjects; such a set $h = (c_{h_1}, \ldots, c_{h_N})$ of historical classification flows c_{h_i} is called an *ensemble*. An ensemble can be used to generate a vector of class predictions $h(x) = (c_{h_1}(x), \ldots, c_{h_N}(x)) \in \mathbb{R}^N$ for a given time series x.

Thereupon, a so-called *gating function* g combines the ensemble's predictions $h(x) \in \mathbb{R}^N$ into a joint prediction $g(h(x)) \in \mathbb{R}$ (in the linear case $g(x) = \sum_{i=1}^N w_i c_{h_i}(x)$). A gating function can be defined without requiring session-specific training data by, e.g., training it on historic data (compare Fazli et al. [6]) or, alternatively, without any training by predicting according to the equally-weighted mean of the ensemble's predictions ($w_i = 1/N$). Furthermore, in situations where a small amount of session-specific training data is available, it is possible to train a gating function such that higher weights w_i are assigned to historic flows c_{h_i} that have high predictive performance for the current session. We focus on the latter approach since it can be combined naturally with the proposed augmentation approaches (see below). We use an SVM with linear kernel for learning the gating function's parameters w_i since this SVM-based gating function achieved superior performance on hold-out test data of the given scenario compared to other common methods for learning gating functions. The outlined "pure" ensemble approach is depicted as the middle layer in Figure 2.

Augmentation approaches. While ensemble approaches have been successful in achieving good performance when only a limited amount (or even no) training data from the current session is available (see, e.g., [6]), it is unlikely that they can achieve competitive results when more session-specific training data becomes available since they can not exploit novel patterns or shifts present in the current session that have not been observed in any of the historic sessions. We propose to use the ensemble approach presented above not instead but in addition to the training of a session-specific flow c_s, i.e., to *augment* the session-specific flow c_s by the predictions of the ensemble h. In this approach, the available training data is used for two purposes: training of a session-specific flow c_s and training of the gating function g which determines the final classification based on the ensemble's predictions and the session-specific information. We propose and compare two alternative approaches: *Classification Augmentation* and *Feature Augmentation* (see Figure 2).

In the classification augmentation approach, the prediction of the session-specific classification flow $c_s(x)$ is treated like any of the ensemble flow's predictions $c_{h_i}(x)$: An augmented ensemble $\tilde{h} = (c_{h_1}, \ldots, c_{h_N}, c_s)$ is generated and

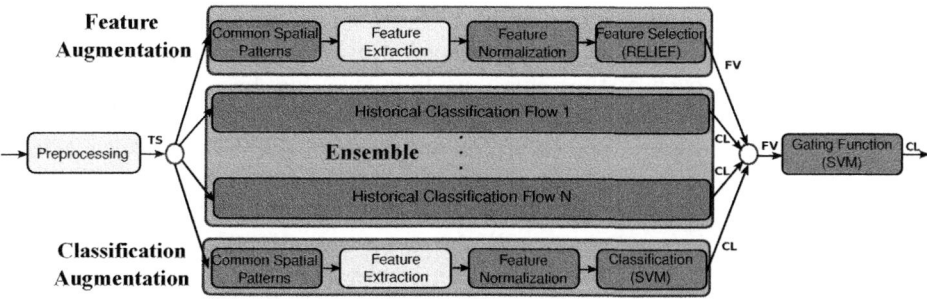

Fig. 2. Different ensemble and augmentation approaches. Feature Augmentation and Classification Augmentation are two alternative approaches for augmenting the ensemble's predictions by session-specific information. TS denotes a time-series, FV a feature vector, and CL a scalar classifier prediction.

the gating function g chooses the joint prediction $g(\tilde{h}(x))$ based on $\tilde{h}$'s output $(\tilde{h}(x) \in \mathbb{R}^{N+1})$. Both c_s and g need to be trained based on data acquired in the current session; using the same data for both tasks, however, would result in a too strong reliance of the gating function on c_s since the predictive performance of c_s would be evaluated on its own training data. Thus, the available training data needs to be split into two parts. Empirically, we have found that using $2/3$ for training of c_s and $1/3$ for training of g is a good compromise.

In contrast, in the feature augmentation approach, the session-specific information added to the ensemble's predictions is not the classifier's prediction $c_s(x)$ but the values of the n most informative features $f_1(x), \ldots, f_n(x)$, i.e., $\tilde{h}(x) = (c_{h_1}(x), \ldots, c_{h_N}(x), f_1(x), \ldots, f_n(x)) \in \mathbb{R}^{N+n}$. Thus, $\tilde{h}(x)$ consists of two very different kinds of values: classifier predictions and CSP-pseudo-channel values (the selected features). However, this does not impose a problem and has the advantage that the available training data can be used more efficiently than in classification augmentation (note that while in principle feature selection and training of the gating function should be done on disjoint training sets, we have found empirically that it is favorable to train both on the same data). The choice of n is one additional parameter of this approach. The determination of the most informative features is made using the RELIEF feature selection algorithm [7].

4   Evaluation

Experimental Setup. One historic classification flow has been trained for each historic session, resulting in 12 historic classification flows. Each of the 12 sessions has been used once as evaluation session with the remaining 11 sessions being considered accordingly as historic sessions. Two different settings have been compared: In the "LeaveOneSessionOut" setting, the classification flows belonging to all but the current evaluation session have been used in the ensemble (resulting in ensembles of $N = 11$ flows), while in the "LeaveOneSubjectOut" setting, all classification flows that have not been generated from usage sessions of the current subject are used in the ensemble (resulting in ensembles of $N = 10$ flows). For each evaluation session, the data recorded in the first run has been used as training data and each of the remaining four runs has been used once as test dataset (intra-session setup), resulting in $4 * 12 = 48$ performance samples per method. Training datasets of six different sizes $t \in \{42, 84, 168, 252, 420, 840\}$ have been randomly sampled from the 840 labeled instances of the first run, where $t = 840$ corresponds to a calibration time of approximately 16 minutes. We refer to "experimental_design.pdf" in [1] for more details.

Parameters of the SVM gating function have been selected using 5-fold internal cross-validation on the training data (complexity $C \in \{0.001, 0.01, 0.1, 1.0\}$ and target class weight $w_t \in \{1, 2, 5, 10\}$ for standard class weight 1). The parameter n of the feature-augmentation approach has been linearly increased from $n = 2$ for $t = 42$ to $n = 50$ for $t = 840$ to account for a stronger influence of the session-specific information when more training data becomes available. The scalar output of the gating function g is mapped onto the binary classes by choosing a threshold that maximizes the performance on the training data. For comparison, the results of the "zero-training" gating function that predicts according to the equally-weighted ensemble mean are given for the pure ensemble for $t = 0$. The performance of the session-specific flow c_s is given as "baseline". No value for classification augmentation is given for $t = 42$ since not enough target class training examples were available for the two-stage training procedure.

Because of the large class-skew of the classification task, standard measures such as accuracy are not well suited as performance metric. Instead, performance is measured according to the *mutual information* metric $I(T; Y) = H(T) - H(T|Y)$ with $H(T) = -\sum_{i=1}^{n} p(x_i)\log_2 p(x_i)$ being the Shannon entropy of the class label T and $H(T|Y)$ the conditional entropy of the class label T given the classifier's prediction Y. The values of the metric correspond to the bits of information about the true class label conveyed by the classifier. The main advantage of this metric is that any kind of random classifier has mutual information 0. Note that the class label's entropy (and thus $I(T; Y)$) is upper bounded by $H(T) \approx 0.533$ for the given class ratio of $6 : 1$. The optimally achieved performance (mutual information of 0.22) corresponds roughly to 94% correct classifications.

Results and Discussion. We compared the four different approaches (factor e) for different training set sizes (factor t) by repeated measures ANOVA with t and e as within-subjects factors. This statistic model was separately performed for each setting $s \in \{"LeaveOneSessionOut", "LeaveOneSubjectOut"\}$ because of the different ensemble sizes N for the two settings. Whenever the results of the two different settings were compared, the additional factor s was added to the statistic model. In order to avoid that the different values of N for the two settings affect these comparisons, one randomly selected session of another subject was removed from the "LeaveOneSessionOut" setting such that $N = 10$ in both cases. If needed, the Greenhouse-Geisser correction and—for pairwise comparisons—Bonferroni correction were applied. All tests have been performed for a significance level of $p < 0.05$ (see "statistics.pdf" in [1] for more details).

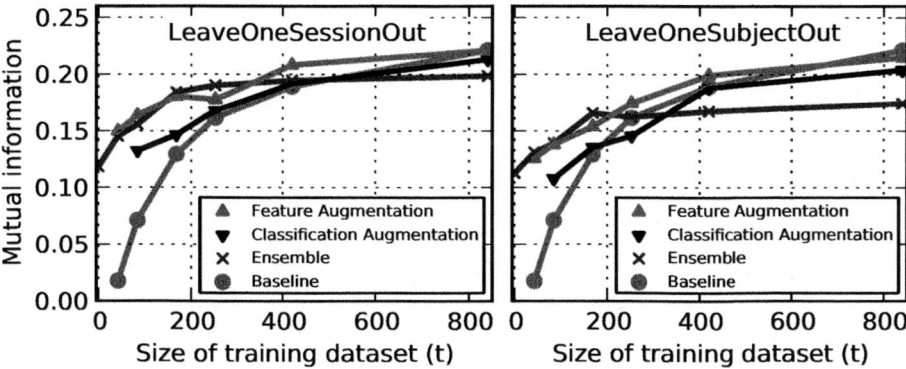

Fig. 3. Effect of training set size. Comparison of baseline, ensemble, and augmentation approaches for maximal N (LeaveOneSessionOut: $N = 11$, LeaveOneSubjectOut: $N = 10$) and for different training set sizes t.

Figure 3 summarizes the results of the study. In the "LeaveOneSessionOut" setting, the ensemble approach is significantly better than the baseline for $t \leq 252$ and worse for $t = 840$. This supports the hypothesis that historic predictors provide good performance when only a small amount of training data is available but are outperformed by session-specific predictors when larger amounts of training data have been acquired. Among the augmentation approaches, feature augmentation is clearly better with statistical significance for $t \in \{42, 84, 168, 420\}$. This may be attributed to the inefficient usage of training data in the classification augmentation approach where it is necessary to split the training data into two disjoint parts (see Section 3). Furthermore, feature augmentation can be considered to be superior to both the ensemble and the baseline approach since performance is never significantly worse than any of the two, but significantly better than the ensemble for $t \geq 420$ and better than the baseline for $t \in \{42, 84, 168, 420\}$. This indicates that feature augmentation provides an efficient way of combining historic and session-specific information by adaptively learning which source of information should be trusted more.

Results in the "LeaveOneSubjectOut" setting are qualitatively similar, with the notable difference that the ensemble's performance is significantly worse than in the "LeaveOneSessionOut" setting for all t. This shows that a historic session of the same user helps to increase the performance of the ensemble approach. As a result, in the "LeaveOneSubjectOut" setting, the ensemble is significantly better than the baseline only for $t \leq 168$ but worse for $t = 840$. Performance of the feature augmentation approach deteriorates significantly as well in the "LeaveOneSubjectOut" setting for all $t \neq 252$; however, this deterioration is less strong since the session-specific flow compensates partly for the missing historic session of the same user. Accordingly, the feature augmentation approach is still never significantly worse than the baseline but significantly better for $t \leq 168$.

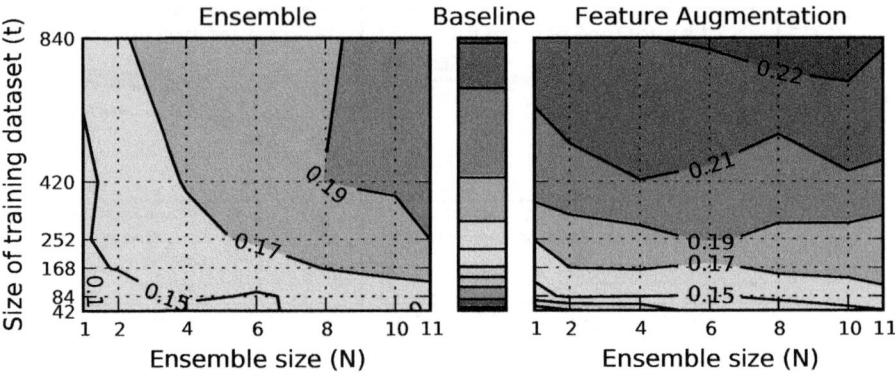

Fig. 4. Effect of the ensemble size. Mutual influence of ensemble size N and the training set size t onto performance (mutual information) in the LeaveOneSessionOut setting. For comparison, the baseline performance is shown for the same values of t.

Figure 4 shows how the size N ($N \in \{1, 2, 4, 6, 8, 10, 11\}$) of the historic ensemble and the size of the training dataset t mutually affect the performance of the pure ensemble and the feature augmentation approach (in the "LeaveOne-SessionOut" setting). These results have been separately analyzed for each setting by repeated measures ANOVA with the within-subjects factors N, t, and e. The performance of the pure ensemble approach depends strongly on the ensemble's size: Even for large t, no performance above 0.17 is achieved for $N \leq 2$ and no performance above 0.19 for $N \leq 6$. This dependence on N is even stronger in the "LeaveOneSubjectOut" setting (see "LOSubjO.pdf" in [1]). On the other hand, the feature augmentation approach depends less strongly on N, outperforming the baseline for small t significantly even when N is very small ($t < 84$ for $N = 1$; $t < 168$ for $N \in \{2, 4\}$) while never being significantly worse.

5   Conclusion

We have presented two alternative approaches for combining predictions made by an ensemble trained on historic sessions with a flow that has been trained on data acquired in the current usage session. This hybrid approach allows to achieve a better performance than the session-specific predictor when only small amounts of training data are available and a better performance than the historic ensemble when more training data becomes available. The proposed approach performs well for subjects for which historic sessions exist but also for novel subjects for which no historic sessions have been conducted. Furthermore, in contrast to related approaches like [6] and [10], the proposed method also achieves good performance when only a small number of historic sessions is available, where it still outperforms the session-specific predictor for small training datasets. Future work is to conduct online studies in which the acquisition of training data is performed concurrently to the usage session.

Acknowledgements. This work was supported through a grant of the Federal Ministry of Education and Research (BMBF, FKZ 01IW07003) and a grant of the Federal Ministry of Economics and Technology (BMWi, FKZ 50 RA 1011).

References

1. Supplementary material,
   http://www.informatik.uni-bremen.de/~jhm/dagm_sm.zip
2. Alamgir, M., Grosse-Wentrup, M., Altun, Y.: Multi-task learning for Brain-Computer Interfaces. In: Proceedings of the 13th International Conference on Artificial Intelligence and Statistics, JMLR: W&CP, vol. 9 (2010)
3. Birbaumer, N.: Breaking the silence: Brain-Computer Interfaces (BCI) for communication and motor control. Psychophysiology 43(6), 517–532 (2006)
4. Blankertz, B., Dornhege, G., Lemm, S., Krauledat, M., Curio, G., Müller, K.-R.: The Berlin Brain-Computer Interface: Machine learning based detection of user specific brain states. Journal of Universal Computer Sciene 12(6), 581–607 (2006)
5. Blankertz, B., Tomioka, R., Lemm, S., Kawanabe, M., Müller, K.R.: Optimizing spatial filters for robust EEG Single-Trial analysis. IEEE Signal Processing Magazine 25(1), 41–56 (2008)
6. Fazli, S., Popescu, F., Danóczy, M., Blankertz, B., Müller, K., Grozea, C.: Subject-independent mental state classification in single trials. Neural Networks 22(9), 1305–1312 (2009)
7. Kira, K., Rendell, L.A.: The feature selection problem: Traditional methods and a new algorithm. In: AAAI, pp. 129–134 (1992)
8. Kirchner, E.A., Wöhrle, H., Bergatt, C., Kim, S.K., Metzen, J.H., Feess, D., Kirchner, F.: Towards operator monitoring via brain reading - an EEG-based approach for space applications. In: iSAIRAS, pp. 448–455 (September 2010)
9. Koles, Z.J.: The quantitative extraction and topographic mapping of the abnormal components in the clinical EEG. Electroencephalography and Clinical Neurophysiology 79, 440–447 (1991)
10. Krauledat, M., Tangermann, M., Blankertz, B., Müller, K.: Towards zero training for Brain-Computer interfacing. PLoS ONE 3(8), e2967 (2008)
11. Li, Y., Guan, C., Li, H., Chin, Z.: A self-training semi-supervised SVM algorithm and its application in an EEG-based brain computer interface speller system. Pattern Recognition Letters 29(9), 1285–1294 (2008)
12. Lotte, F., Guan, C.: Learning from other subjects helps reducing Brain-Computer interface calibration time. In: ICASSP (2010)
13. Squires, N.K., Squires, K.C., Hillyard, S.A.: Two varieties of long-latency positive waves evoked by unpredictable auditory stimuli. Electroencephalography and Clinical Neurophysiology 38(4), 387–401 (1975)
14. Wolpaw, J.R., Birbaumer, N., McFarland, D.J., Pfurtscheller, G., Vaughan, T.M.: Brain-computer interfaces for communication and control. Clinical Neurophysiology 113(6), 767–791 (2002)
15. Zito, T., Wilbert, N., Wiskott, L., Berkes, P.: Modular toolkit for data processing (MDP): a python data processing framework. Front. Neuroinform. 2, 8 (2008)

Agnostic Domain Adaptation

Alexander Vezhnevets and Joachim M. Buhmann

ETH Zurich
8092 Zurich, Switzerland
{alexander.vezhnevets,jbuhmann}@inf.ethz.ch

Abstract. The supervised learning paradigm assumes in general that both training and test data are sampled from the same distribution. When this assumption is violated, we are in the setting of transfer learning or domain adaptation: Here, training data from a *source* domain, aim to learn a classifier which performs well on a *target* domain governed by a different distribution. We pursue an agnostic approach, assuming no information about the shift between source and target distributions but relying exclusively on unlabeled data from the target domain. Previous works [2] suggest that feature representations, which are invariant to domain change, increases generalization. Extending these ideas, we prove a generalization bound for domain adaptation that identifies the transfer mechanism: what matters is how much learnt classier itself is invariant, while feature representations may vary. Our bound is much tighter for rich hypothesis classes, which may only *contain* invariant classifier, but can not be invariant altogether. This concept is exemplified by the computer vision tasks of semantic segmentation and image categorization. Domain shift is simulated by introducing some common imaging distortions, such as gamma transform and color temperature shift. Our experiments on a public benchmark dataset confirm that using domain adapted classifier significantly improves accuracy when distribution changes are present.

1 Introduction

The fundamental assumption in supervised learning is that training and test data arise from the same distribution. However in real life applications, it is common that training examples from one *source* domain are used to build the predictor that is expected to perform a related task on a different *target* domain. This change requires domain adaptation.

The situation with domain changes and the need for domain adaptation is shared by many fields, e.g., we have to account for domain change when we train a spam filter for a new user on examples from other users. In natural language processing, this occurs in e.g., part-of-speech tagging [5], where the tagger is trained on medical texts and deployed on legal texts. In computer vision systems, classifiers are usually trained prior to deployment on data which are manually annotated by experts. This labeling process is tedious and expensive, whereas data collection is usually fast and inexpensive. For instance, collecting unlabeled

R. Mester and M. Felsberg (Eds.): DAGM 2011, LNCS 6835, pp. 376–385, 2011.

data from a video surveillance system under different settings (different camera, lighting) requires little effort, but labeling this data demands a human annotator and often even a trained domain expert. Hence, the ability to adapt to a new domain using only unlabeled data from a new target distribution is of substantial practical advantage.

To achieve good generalization in supervised learning one should keep the hypothesis class simple while minimizing the empirical risk. Intuitively, in case of domain adaptation an additional requirement should be imposed: the source and the target distributions should look the same for the good classifier. In other words, classifier should be invariant to the change of the distribution.

We consider the setting where a finite set of *labeled* training examples is available from the *source* domain, but only few *unlabeled* examples are available from the *target* domain. We proceed by first proving a bound on the *target* generalization error, which is dependant on the classifier's training error on the source distribution and its invariance to distribution changes. This bound is much tighter for rich hypothesis classes, that only *contain* invariant hypothesis, but are quite variable in general. Invariance is formulated as the inability of the classifier to discriminate between the source and the target domain. Finally, we construct an algorithm that minimizes this bound.

Along with a theoretical analysis of domain adaptation we present an experimental validation of our results. Computer vision serves as a challenging application domain for machine learning, which allows us to visually inspect our results. We experimentally show the applicability of our approach by constructing a domain adaptive version of semantic texton forest [13] (STF) for image semantic segmentation and categorization. Semantic segmentation simultaneously requires to segment and recognize objects, one of the fundamental and most challenging computer vision tasks. We study the adaptation of STF to color cast and gamma transform, which are very natural distortions in imaging. We will see that such distortions are very damaging for an STF. But with domain adaptation we are able to improve results in some cases by more than a factor of two.

The paper is organized as follows. We first shortly describe previous works. Section 3 formally defines our problem and notation. In section 4 we present our theoretical bound. In section 5 the domain adaptive random forest for semantic segmentation and categorization is discussed. Section 6 describes our experimental results followed by a conclusion.

2   Prior Work

In this paper we consider the setting of domain adaptation for an *arbitrary shift* in the data distribution and where only *unlabeled* data from the target domain is available. Much research has been done to address each constraint individually. However little has been reported when both constraints are considered. We briefly review the literature for different settings of learning under distribution shift.

Transfer learning. Transfer learning is a setting when labeled data from the target distribution is available. In [4] authors prove uniform convergence bounds for algorithms that minimize a convex combination of source and target empirical risk. A thorough experimental evaluation for this scenario (minimization of convex combination of risks) can be found in [12]. In [8] a boosting method for transfer learning is developed. [11] studies adaptation with multiple sources, where for each source domain, the distribution over the input points as well as a hypothesis with error at most ϵ are given. They prove that combinations of hypotheses weighted by the source distributions benefit from favorable theoretical guarantees.

Covariate shift. One common assumption to address the case where labels are not available is that of covariate shift. Here, only the marginal distribution $Pr[X]$ changes and the conditional remains unchanged, i.e., $Pr_{D_S}[Y|X] = Pr_{D_T}[Y|X]$. In [3] the general problem of learning under covariate shift is formulated as an integrated optimization problem and a kernel logistic regression classifier is derived for solving it. A nonparametric method which directly produces resampling weights without distribution estimation for learning under covariate shift is presented in [10]. Their method works by matching distributions between training and testing sets in feature space. Another paper [3] studies a complex problem of learning multiple tasks (multitask learning), when each task may have a covariate shift. They derive a learning procedure that produces resampling weights which match the pool of all examples to the target distribution of any given task.

Semi-supervised learning. Semi-supervised learning (SSL) [6] is another strategy to improve the classifiers accuracy by using unlabeled data. Our setting should not be confused with semi-supervised learning. As in SSL we use unlabeled data to improve our classifier. While SSL assumes data to come from the *same* distribution, our setting does not impose such an assumption. One common approach to semi-supervised learning is to treat labels of unlabeled data as additional variables which have to be optimized to maximize the possible separation margin. Such strategy could also be advocated for domain adaptation as a valid heuristic (and was used for that purpose in [1]), though it has no theoretical support. Examples of semi-supervised methods are tSVM [14] and semi-supervised random forests [7].

Domain adaptation. The setting that is closest to ours has been defined in [2]. The authors also consider the case with no assumptions about shift and they require only unlabeled data from target distribution. By studying the influence of feature representation on domain adaptation, they theoretically prove that the hypothesis space that is invariant to distribution changes improves generalization, although the problem of finding such a space is not addressed. In contrast to [2] we are interested in learning a classifier from a rich, possibly not invariant family, which generalizes well under distribution shift. We discuss this work in more details in Section 4.

3   Problem Setup

Let X be the instance set and Y be the set of labels. The joint distributions are given by $\tilde{D}_S(X \times Y)$ and $\tilde{D}_T(X \times Y)$, for the source and the target domains respectively. The corresponding marginal distributions of X are denoted by D_S

and D_T. To simplify the notation we restrict ourselves to dichotomies, i.e., to two classes. Labeled training samples are drawn from $\tilde{D}_S(X \times Y)$, but only samples of unlabeled data are gathered from D_T. Let $H \subseteq \{h : X \to Y\}$ be the hypothesis space. The probability that hypothesis h makes an error on the source domain as

$$\epsilon_S(h) = E_{(x,y)\sim\tilde{D}_S}[h(x) \neq y]. \tag{1}$$

The error on the target domain $\epsilon_T(h)$ is defined similarly. Z_h denotes the characteristic function of h,

$$Z_h = \{x \in X : h(x) = 1\}. \tag{2}$$

The symmetric set difference is abbreviated by $A \Delta B = (A \setminus B) \cup (B \setminus A)$. For example, $Pr_{D_S}[Z_h \Delta Z_{h^*}]$ is the probability that $[h \neq h^*]$ with respect to the marginal distribution of X in the source domain.

We do not make any assumptions about the nature of the domain shift. It is possible that both marginals $Pr(X)$ and conditional probabilities $Pr(X|Y)$ are changing and the resulting bound is completely agnostic.

4   Generalization Bound

Now we derive our theoretical results. Suppose there is a hypothesis in H which performs λ well on both domains:

$$\inf_{h \in H}[\epsilon_S(h) + \epsilon_T(h)] \leq \lambda. \tag{3}$$

In the work of Shai Ben-David [2], the following generalization bound was provided in a form dependant on the $\mathcal{A}$-distance between the source and the target domain:

$$\begin{aligned}\epsilon_T(h) \leq &\hat{\epsilon}_S(h) + \sqrt{\frac{4}{m}(d \log \frac{2em}{d} + \log \frac{4}{\delta})} \\ &+ \lambda + d_{\mathcal{H}}(\mathcal{D}_S, \mathcal{D}_T').\end{aligned} \tag{4}$$

In words, the $\mathcal{A}$-distance is proportional to an ability of family of predictors to distinguish between two distributions:

$$d_{\mathcal{A}}(\mathcal{D}, \mathcal{D}') = 2 \sup_{A \in \mathcal{A}} |Pr_{\mathcal{D}}[A] - Pr_{\mathcal{D}'}[A]|. \tag{5}$$

Unfortunately the question of how to find such a family of predictors was not addressed. The bound in eq. 4 states that when the features and the hypothesis family are invariant to domain shift, then we can expect to generalize well. However, the bound does not tell us how to choose the best hypothesis from the hypothesis class. Even the experimental results in [2] are not fully justified by this bound, since the feature representation was learnt *after* seeing the data. Formally, to apply this bound, all possible variants of feature representation, which could be learnt by structural correspondence learning [5], should be included into hypothesis family H, which will render the bound trivial.

We will now show a bound, which depends on the characteristics of the particular hypothesis chosen by the training algorithm, rather than on the hypothesis class that we choose from. Our bound would allow us to design an algorithm, that explicitly searches for a hypothesis that minimizes it.

We formalize *invariance* of a classifier as its inability to distinguish between the source and the target distributions:

$$\psi(h) = |Pr_{D_S}[Z_h] - Pr_{D_T}[Z_h]|. \tag{6}$$

$\psi(h)$ has a minimum at zero (high invariance), i.e., the classifier cannot distinguish between the source and the target distribution. It exhibits a maximum of one (low invariance) when the classifier can always accurately decide from which distribution a data point comes from.

Now we are ready to formulate our theorem.

Theorem 1. *Let H be a hypothesis space of VC-dimension d. Given m i.i.d. samples from $\tilde{D}_S$, $\forall h \in H$, with probability of at least $1 - \delta$,*

$$
\begin{aligned}
\epsilon_T(h) \leq &\hat{\epsilon}_S(h) + \sqrt{\frac{4}{m}\left(d\log\frac{2em}{d} + \log\frac{4}{\delta}\right)} + \lambda \\
&+ \psi(h) + \psi(h^*) + \psi(h \cdot h^*),
\end{aligned} \tag{7}
$$

where $\psi(h) = |Pr_{D_S}[Z_h] - Pr_{D_T}[Z_h]|$.

Proof. Let $h^* = \arg\min_{h \in H}(\epsilon_T(h) + \epsilon_S(h))$, and let λ_S and λ_T be the errors of h^* on the source and the target domains respectively. Note that $\lambda = \lambda_S + \lambda_T$.

To get the bound in [2] authors bounded the change, induced by the domain shift, of the difference between the best hypothesis h^* and the learnt h by the invariance of the hypothesis family to distribution shift – $\mathcal{A}$-distance. Essentially, we decompose this invariance into three parts: invariance of the learnt hypothesis, of the best hypothesis, and of their intersection. The proof is the following:

$$
\begin{aligned}
\epsilon_T(h) \leq &\lambda_T + Pr_{D_T}[Z_h \Delta Z_{h^*}] & (8) \\
= &\lambda_T + Pr_{D_S}[Z_h \Delta Z_{h^*}] - Pr_{D_S}[Z_h \Delta Z_{h^*}] + Pr_{D_T}[Z_h \Delta Z_{h^*}] & (9) \\
= &\lambda_T + Pr_{D_S}[Z_h \Delta Z_{h^*}] - Pr_{D_S}[Z_h \setminus Z_{h^*}] - Pr_{D_S}[Z_h^* \setminus Z_h] \\
&+ Pr_{D_T}[Z_h \setminus Z_{h^*}] + Pr_{D_T}[Z_h^* \setminus Z_h] & (10) \\
= &\lambda_T + Pr_{D_S}[Z_h \Delta Z_{h^*}] + Pr_{D_T}[Z_h] - Pr_{D_T}[Z_h \cap Z_{h^*}] - Pr_{D_S}[Z_h] \\
&+ Pr_{D_S}[Z_h \cap Z_{h^*}] + Pr_{D_T}[Z_{h^*}] - Pr_{D_T}[Z_h \cap Z_{h^*}] \\
&- Pr_{D_S}[Z_{h^*}] + Pr_{D_S}[Z_h \cap Z_{h^*}] & (11) \\
\leq &\lambda_T + Pr_{D_S}[Z_h \Delta Z_{h^*}] + |Pr_{D_T}[Z_h] - Pr_{D_S}[Z_h]| \\
&+ |Pr_{D_T}[Z_{h^*}] - Pr_{D_S}[Z_{h^*}]| \\
&+ 2|Pr_{D_T}[Z_h \cap Z_{h^*}] - Pr_{D_S}[Z_h \cap Z_{h^*}]| & (12) \\
= &\lambda_T + Pr_{D_S}[Z_h \Delta Z_{h^*}] + \psi(h) + \psi(h^*) + 2\psi(h \cdot h^*) & (13) \\
\leq &\underbrace{\lambda + \psi(h^*)}_{\text{constant}} + \underbrace{\epsilon_S(h) + \psi(h) + 2\psi(h \cdot h^*)}_{\text{dependant on } h}. & (14)
\end{aligned}
$$

To finish the proof one needs to apply classic Vapnik-Chervonenkis [14] theory to bound $\epsilon_s(h)$ by its empirical estimate. Using Vapnik-Chervonenkis theory again, we can bound the true ψ by its empirical estimate and an additional complexity penalty.

Observe that the bound has two parts: a constant part and the second part that is dependant on h. The constant (w.r.t. h) part is a function of the hypothesis class, which is assumed to be fixed. The part that depends on h consists of a sum of the classifier's training error $\epsilon_S(h)$ and the invariances $\psi(h)$ and $\psi(h \cdot h^*)$. The term $\psi(h)$ is the invariance of a learnt classifier, which can be controlled during training. The term $\psi(h \cdot h^*)$ measures the intersection between the learnt h and the optimal classifier h^*. It is large when the overlap between h and h^* changes a lot after the domain shift. Regretfully $\psi(h \cdot h^*)$ can neither be measured nor optimized, since we completely lack and knowledge of h^*: it pinpoints the uncertainty incurred in the absence of labeled data in the target domain. Hence in our design of the algorithm in section 5 we will only minimize the empirical estimates of $\epsilon(h)$ and $\psi(h)$.

In contrast to eq. 4 [2], we no longer rely on the invariance of the entire hypothesis class, but rather only on the specific classifier that we learn. Thus optimization of the bound can be integrated into the training process directly, as demonstrated in the following section. Our bound is also tighter for rich hypothesis classes, where invariant hypothesis is contained, but the class itself far from being invariant.

5   Algorithm

Theorem 1 provides us with an insight on how such a domain adaptive classifier could be constructed. When minimizing empirical loss on the source distribution, $\psi(h)$ should also be minimized by increasing its invariance. We implement this idea for the random forest classifier. In particular, for extremely randomized forests [9] (ERF), a predicate for splitting is selected that concurrently maximizes information gain and minimizes the empirical estimate of $\psi(h)$. Here we describe an ERF for the computer vision task of semantic segmentation – a task of simultaneous object segmentation and recognition. This ERF will also provide us with an adapted kernel for SVM based object categorization.

Semantic Texton Forest. The Semantic Texton Forest (STF) proposed in [13] is employed for semantic segmentation. Their work uses ERF for pixel-wise classification. Below we shortly describe this approach.

A decision forest is an ensemble of K decision trees. A decision tree works by recursively branching left or right down the tree according to a learnt binary split function $\phi_n(x) : X \to \{0, 1\}$ at the node n, until a leaf node l is reached. Associated with each leaf l in the tree is a learned class distribution $P(c|l)$. Classification is done by averaging over the leaf nodes $L = (l_1, ..., l_K)$ reached for all K trees:

$$P(c|L) = \frac{1}{K} \sum_{k=1}^{K} P(c|l_k). \tag{15}$$

Conceptually, a forest consists of a structure, consisting of nodes with split functions, and probability estimates in the leaf nodes. We can represent a forest as a complex function $f(g(x))$, where $g : X \to N^K$ maps the instance feature vectors to the vector of leaf indices, reached for each tree and $f : N^K \to [0,1]^C$ maps those indices to class probability estimates. Each leaf then has to store a vector $w^l = [P(y = 1|l), ..., P(y = C|l)]$.

Trees are trained independently on random subsets of the training data. Learning proceeds recursively, splitting the training data at node into left and right subsets according to a split function $\phi_n(x)$. At each split node, several candidates for $\phi_n(x)$ are generated randomly, and the one that maximizes the expected gain in information about the node categories is chosen:

$$\Delta H = -\frac{|I_l|}{|I_n|}H(I_l) - \frac{|I_r|}{|I_n|}H(I_r), \tag{16}$$

where $H(I)$ is the Shannon entropy of the classes in the set of examples I. The recursive training usually continues to a fixed maximum depth without pruning. The class distributions $P(y|l)$ are estimated empirically as a histogram of the class labels y_i of the training examples i that reached leaf l.

STF, as presented above, provides prediction on the basis of local context only. To bring a global image context into play an Image Level Priors (ILP) are used. The support vector machine (SVM) is trained to predict whether a certain object is present in the image. Output of SVM is scaled to the probability simplex and pixel level STF predictions are then multiplied by it. A kernel for the SVM is constructed by matching the amount of pixels in two given images that pass through the same nodes in the STF. We refer the reader to the original publication [13] for more details on ILP and STF training.

Domain Adaptation. To adapt a STF to a particular domain, we introduce a slight modification to the original criterion (eq 16) for choosing the best split function $\phi_n(x)$. The new criterion $\Delta \tilde{H}$ now takes shift invariance into account as desired

$$\Delta \tilde{H} = \underbrace{\Delta H^S}_{\epsilon(h)} - \alpha \underbrace{\left(\left| \frac{|I_r^T|}{|I_n^T|} - \frac{|I_r^S|}{|I_n^S|} \right| + \left| \frac{|I_l^T|}{|I_n^T|} - \frac{|I_l^S|}{|I_n^S|} \right| \right)}_{\psi(h)}, \tag{17}$$

where I_r^T and I_l^T are the data points from the target domain right and left of the split respectively. I_n^T is the total amount of the target domain data points that have been classified by a node. The same notation is used for the source data with respective superscripts $I_{(\cdot)}^S$. First term – ΔH^S stands for information gain on labeled data from source domain and optimizes an empirical estimate of $\epsilon(h)$. The second term is an empirical estimate of $\psi(h)$. This addendum deals with unlabeled data from both domains, penalizing those splits, that produce classifiers invariant, which are not invariant to the distribution shift. This modification, forces our classifier to both minimize error on the source distribution and maximize invariance of the classifier towards distribution changes. It slightly increases the training time and has no effect on the computational complexity of the final predictor. Adaptation of the image categorizer emerges in a natural way, since the adapted STF provides the (adapted) kernel for the image categorizer. The proposed approach is generic and can possibly be applied to other application fields too.

6   Experiments

We evaluate our approach on two fundamental computer vision tasks: semantic segmentation and image categorization. The benefit of using visual data for domain adaptation experiments is that we can introduce realistic distribution shifts based on common imaging distortions and visually inspect the results. For our experiments, we used the MSRC21 dataset. This dataset comprises of 591 images out of 21 object classes. The standard train/test/validation split, as in [13], contains 276/256/59 images, respectively. In order to estimate standard error deviation we used 5 random splits of the dataset into train/test/validation sets keeping the same proportions as in the standard split. We applied several common imaging distortions on the dataset to simulate distribution shift. We train our classifiers on the undistorted training images. The unlabeled set of distorted validation images is used for adaptation.

We compare our algorithm (**STF-DA**) with two baseline methods. The first baseline is a **STF** [13] trained on the undistorted training set only. We also compared our results to a semi-supervised random forest (**STF-SSL**) [7] trained on the training set and unlabeled validation set, for the following reasons. First, it can be readily integrated into the STF framework. Second, it optimizes the separation margin of the classifier over all classifier parameters and all labelings of unlabeled data, which is a valid heuristic for domain adaptation in case when no information is available on the distribution shift and labeled data for target domain are lacking. We evaluate on distorted test images. For all classifiers, we use the implementation with the parameter setting of the STF framework as provided in [13].

Image Distortions
We consider two distortions common in imaging: color temperature shift and gamma transform. Distortions are applied to test and validation set. Both distortion types change both the *marginal* and the *conditional* probabilities. Color shift affects only color features, when gamma transform inflicts a nonlinear change in all features. Moreover, the hypothesis class (random forests) are far from being invariant towards this distortions. We introduce two versions of the shift for both distortions. One is deterministic - every image is perturbed in the same way (shift parameters are constant). In the second case, for each image we randomly select a distortion parameter. In contrast to the previous works we are able to deal with this setting both in theory and in practice.

Color Temperature Shift. Color temperature is a characteristic of visible light that has important applications in lighting and photography. The color temperature of a light source is determined by comparing its chromaticity with that

Table 1. Accuracy on semantic segmentation and image categorization tasks

Distortion	Semantic Segmentation			Image Categorization		
	STF	STF-SSL	STF-DA	STF	STF-SSL	STF-DA
Temp. (det)	0.19 ± 0.02	0.20 ± 0.03	0.44 ± 0.05	0.25 ± 0.02	0.26 ± 0.02	0.48 ± 0.04
Temp. (rand)	0.37 ± 0.03	0.38 ± 0.02	0.46 ± 0.03	0.40 ± 0.02	0.40 ± 0.01	0.52 ± 0.03
Gamma (det)	0.48 ± 0.04	0.50 ± 0.03	0.52 ± 0.03	0.53 ± 0.04	0.53 ± 0.04	0.58 ± 0.02
Gamma (rand)	0.41 ± 0.03	0.42 ± 0.02	0.45 ± 0.03	0.44 ± 0.02	0.45 ± 0.03	0.49 ± 0.02

of an ideal black-body radiator. Color temperature shift is a common artifact of digital photography. The same scene shot under different lighting will have a color cast: the warm yellow-orange cast of tungsten lamps or the blue-white of florescent tubes. Most digital cameras perform white balance correction by digitally adjusting color temperature. For the deterministic case we reduced the temperature of all images by 40%. In the randomized case images have there temperature lowered by $40, 30, 20\%$ or 10% at random. Deterministic shift is very strong and renders nearly all color feature non reliable.

Gamma Transform. Due to a finite dynamic range and discretization in digital cameras, images can easily become over- or under-exposed. We mimic this effect by the gamma transform $\tilde{p}_{i,j,c} = p_{i,j,c}^{\gamma}$. In our experiments we use $\gamma = 2$ for the deterministic case. Again, we have also produced a dataset with γ being randomly chosen in the interval $[0, 4]$ to make the shift non deterministic. This shift does not change images as dramatically as color shift, but is not restricted to a certain feature subspace. One can not adapt to it by just simply discarding certain features (as it could be done in color shift case).

Results

We evaluate on semantic segmentation task measuring overall per pixel accuracy and on the task of image categorization measuring average precision (Table 1).

In all experiments, **STF-DA** outperforms both baseline algorithms. **STF-SSL** fails to bring any significant improvement over **STF**: semi-supervised learning is inappropriate to account for a distribution shift. The most significant improvements of **STF-DA** over the baselines are observed on the data with color temperature shift. Our algorithm is able to filter out unreliable color features and perform better – in the deterministic case the accuracy increases *more then twice*. Success on γ transformed data validates that our approach is applicable even when the shift affects all features and when it is not restricted to only a subset of features. The more general non deterministic shifts are also processed satisfactorily by **STF-DA**.

7   Conclusion

We have presented an analysis of domain adaptation for cases where only unlabeled examples from the target distribution are available and no assumptions are made about the shift between the target and the source distributions.

Intuitively, a good classifier should be invariant to changes in the distribution. We formalize this intuition by proving an upper bound of the generalization error of classifiers trained on the *source* domain and tested on the *target* domain. Our bound explicitly depends on classifier's invariance and its error on the source distribution. In contrast to previous work [2] that requires the whole hypothesis class to be invariant, this study demonstrates that good generalization *can* be achieved even when the hypothesis family only *contains* one invariant classifier. We experimentally confirm our findings on the challenging tasks of semantic segmentation and image categorization. We show that our adaptation algorithm significantly improves results for different imaging distortions, in some cases by more than twice.

Acknowledgements. This work has been supported by the Swiss National Science Foundation under grant #200021-117946.

References

1. Arnold, A., Nallapati, R., Cohen, W.W.: A comparative study of methods for transductive transfer learning. In: ICDM Workshop on Mining and Management of Biological Data (2007)
2. Ben-David, S., Blitzer, J., Crammer, K., Pereira, F.: Analysis of representations for domain adaptation. In: NIPS (2007)
3. Bickel, S., Brückner, M., Scheffer, T.: Discriminative learning for differing training and test distributions. In: ICML. ACM Press, New York (2007)
4. Blitzer, J., Crammer, K., Kulesza, A., Pereira, F., Wortman, J.: Learning bounds for domain adaptation. In: NIPS (2007)
5. Blitzer, J., Mcdonald, R., Pereira, F.: Domain adaptation with structural correspondence learning. In: Proceedings of the 2006 Conference on Empirical Methods in Natural Language Processing, Sydney, Australia (2006)
6. Chapelle, O., Schölkopf, B., Zien, A. (eds.): Semi-Supervised Learning. MIT Press, Cambridge (2006)
7. Leistner, C., Saffari, A., Santner, J., Bischof, H.: Semi-supervised random forests. In: ICCV (2009).
8. Dai, W., Yang, Q., Xue, G.-R., Yu, Y.: Boosting for transfer learning. In: ICML, New York, NY, USA (2007)
9. Triggs, B., Moosmann, F., Jurie, F.: Fast discriminative visual codebooks using randomized clustering forests. In: NIPS (2006)
10. Huang, J., Smola, A.J., Gretton, A., Borgwardt, K.M., Sch?olkopf, B.: Correcting sample selection bias by unlabeled data. In: NIPS (2006)
11. Mansour, Y., Mohri, M., Rostamizadeh, A.: Domain adaptation with multiple sources. In: NIPS (2009)
12. Schweikert, G., Widmer, C., Scho"lkopf, B., Ra"tsch, G.: An empirical analysis of domain adaptation algorithms for genomic sequence analysis. In: NIPS (2008)
13. Shotton, J., Johnson, M., Cipolla., R.: Semantic texton forests for image categorization and segmentation. In: Forsyth, D., Torr, P., Zisserman, A. (eds.) ECCV 2008, Part IV. LNCS, vol. 5305. Springer, Heidelberg (2008)
14. Vapnik, V.N.: Statistical Learning Theory. Wiley-Interscience, Hoboken (1998)

Will the Pedestrian Cross?
Probabilistic Path Prediction Based on Learned Motion Features

Christoph G. Keller[1], Christoph Hermes[2], and Dariu M. Gavrila[3,4]

[1] Image & Pattern Analysis Group, Univ. of Heidelberg, Germany
[2] Applied Informatics Group, Univ. of Bielefeld, Germany
[3] Environment Perception, Group Research, Daimler AG, Ulm, Germany
[4] Intelligent Systems Lab, Fac. of Science, Univ. of Amsterdam, The Netherlands

Abstract. Future vehicle systems for active pedestrian safety will not only require a high recognition performance, but also an accurate analysis of the developing traffic situation. In this paper, we present a system for pedestrian action classification (walking vs. stopping) and path prediction at short, sub-second time intervals. Apart from the use of positional cues, obtained by a pedestrian detector, we extract motion features from dense optical flow. These augmented features are used in a probabilistic trajectory matching and filtering framework.

The vehicle-based system was tested in various traffic scenes. We compare its performance to that of a state-of-the-art IMM Kalman filter (IMM-KF), and for the action classification task, to that of human observers, as well. Results show that human performance is best, followed by that of the proposed system, which outperforms the IMM-KF and the simpler system variants.

1 Introduction

Strong gains have been made over the years in improving pedestrian recognition performance. However, the initation of an emergency vehicle maneuvre requires a precise estimation of the current and future position of the pedestrian with respect to the moving vehicle. A deviation of, say, 25 cm in the estimated lateral position of the pedestrian can make all the difference between a "correct" and an "incorrect" maneuvre initiation. One major challenge is the highly dynamic behaviour of pedestrians, which can change their walking direction in an instance, or start/stop walking abruptly. As a consequence, prediction horizons for active pedestrian systems are typical short; even so, small performance improvements can produce tangible benefits. For example, accident analysis [15] shows that being able to initiate emergency braking 0.16 s (4 frames @ 25 Hz) earlier, at a Time-to-Collision of 0.66 s, reduces the chance of incurring injury requiring hopital stay from 50% to 35%, given an initial vehicle speed of 50 km/h.

The paper studies the case of a pedestrian walking towards the road curbside, and poses the question whether the pedestrian will cross or not. See Figure 1. This setting is inspired by an earlier human factors study [16], where participants were asked the same question, upon viewing similar video content. This study varied the amount of visual information provided to the participants and examined its effect on human classification performance; in the baseline case, the pedestrian was fully visible, whereas in other cases, parts of the images were masked out. Masking the complete pedestrian, and leaving only positional information (bounding box), turned out to decrease human accuracy markedly.

R. Mester and M. Felsberg (Eds.): DAGM 2011, LNCS 6835, pp. 386–395, 2011.

Fig. 1. Everyday problems vehicle drivers are faced with: Will the pedestrian cross?

Besides action classification, the aim of this paper is to accurately predict the pedestrian path. For this, an input pedestrian trajectory fragment is matched against previously stored pedestrian trajectories in a database. The retrieved trajectories in the database are used for extrapolation and path prediction. The intuition is that more complex dynamics (e.g. the process of a pedestrian stopping) are more accurately captured by such learning-based approaches than with generic modeling approaches relying on constant motion assumptions.

2   Previous Work

In this section, we focus on previous work on pedestrian motion models and path prediction. The reader is referred to [9,10] for surveys on pedestrian detection. There is furthermore a wealth of work on human activity recognition [18], including some on detecting unusual pedestrian motion patterns (e.g. [14]).

One way to perform path prediction relies on closed-form solutions for Bayesian filtering; in the Kalman Filter (KF) [3], the current state can be propagated to the future by means of the underlying linear dynamical model, without the incorporation of new measurements. The same idea can be applied to filter extensions, which involve multiple linear dynamical models, i.e. to the Interacting Multiple Model Kalman Filter (IMM-KF) [3]. An alternative approach for path prediction involves stochastic models. Possible trajectories are generated by Monte Carlo simulations, taking into account the respective dynamical models. For example [1], use Bayesian filtering by means of particle filtering and a constant motion model. [8] distinguishes lateral and longitudinal pedestrian velocity and models these independently by a random walk. In [19] pedestrian motion is modeled by means of four states of a Markov chain, corresponding to standing still, walking, jogging and running. Each state has associated probability distributions magnitude and direction of pedestrian velocity; the state changes are controlled by various transition probabilities. More recently, complex pedestrian motion models also account for group behaviour and spatial lay-out (e.g. entry/exit points) [2].

The limited amount of available training data precludes the use of modeling approaches which compute joint probability distributions over time intervals. Indeed, most pedestrian motion models consists of states that correspond to single time steps, and are first-order Markovian. This potentially limits their expressiveness and precision. In contrast [4] describe an extension of particle filtering to incrementally match trajectory models to input data. It is used for motion classification of 2D gestures and expression. A further development [17] adds an efficient tree search in the context of articulated 3D human pose recovery. In [13] this technique is applied to vehicle motion prediction, utilizing the quarternion-based rotationally invariant longest common subsequence (QRLCS) metric for trajectory matching. [5] propose a multi-level prediction model, in which the higher levels are long-term predictions based on trajectory clustering matching, whereas the low level uses an Auto-Regressive model to predict the next time step.

The main contribution of this paper is a system for pedestrian action classification (walking vs. stopping) and accurate path prediction from a moving vehicle, at short time intervals. We borrow from the efficient trajectory matching approaches of [13,17] but augment the underlying features to include motion cues. The latter is motivated by the before-mentioned study [16]. For our use in trajectory matching, however, we need to derive a low-dimensional optical flow representation. We use real video data, which results in a realistic modeling of sensor uncertainty.

3   Proposed System

An overview of the proposed system is given in Figure 2. The feature extraction step uses dense stereo [11] and dense optical flow [20] data computed over the bounding boxes returned by a pedestrian detector. Lateral and longitudinal position of the pedestrian is obtained with the center of the detector box and median disparity values inside the box, respectively. Vehicle ego motion is compensated by rotation and translation of positions to a global reference point using velocity and yaw-rate measurements from on-board sensor data. Motion features involve a low-dimensional histogram representation of optical flow. Measured pedestrian positions and motion features are subsequently used in a trajectory matching and filtering framework. From the filter state and information about the class labels of the matched trajectories, a future pedestrian position and action is derived.

Motion Features. We propose a low dimensional feature that captures flow variations on the pedestrian legs and upper body. In order to operate from a moving vehicle additional invariance to pedestrian distance and vehicle motion is important. Features are designed to allow bounding box localization errors from a pedestrian detection system. Figure 3 illustrates the feature extraction steps. Vehicle velocity and yaw-rate measurements from on-board sensor data in combination with stereo measurements are used to compute the ego-motion compensated optical flow field. Flow vectors are normalized

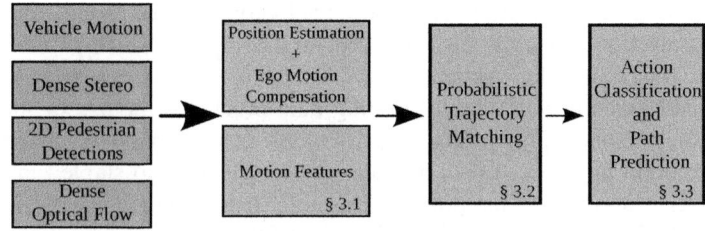

Fig. 2. Overview of the proposed system for pedestrian action classification and path prediction

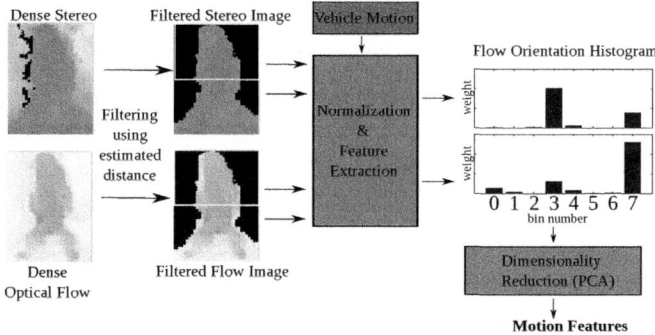

Fig. 3. Overview of the motion feature extraction procedure

with the camera cycle time and measurements from dense stereo for robustness to frame drops and invariance to different pedestrian distances to the camera. This normalized motion field is used to extract features given a bounding box detection and distance estimation z_{ped} from a pedestrian detection system. To ensure that the pedestrian is located in the box for all possible limb extensions and slight localization errors a bounding box aspect ratio of 4:3 is used. Motion vectors not belonging to the pedestrian body are suppressed by using only values at a depth similar to the estimated pedestrian distance. Remaining values in the motion field are used to compute the median object motion and extract orientation histograms. To capture motion differences between torso and legs the bounding box is split into an upper and lower sub-box. For each sub-box the median motion is removed to compensate the pedestrian ego motion. Resulting orientation vectors $v = [v_x, v_y]^T$ are assigned to bins $b \in [0, 7]$ using their 360^0 orientation $\theta = atan2(v_y, v_x)$ and bin index $b = \left\lfloor \frac{\theta}{\pi/4} \right\rfloor$. Bin contributions are weighted by their magnitude and resulting histograms are normalized with the number of contributions. A feature vector is formed by concatenating the histogram values and the median flow for the lower and upper box. Dimensionality reduction of the feature vector is archived by applying principal component analysis (PCA). The first three PCA dimensions with the largest eigenvalue are used as final histograms of orientation motion (HoM) features.

Probabilistic Trajectory Matching. A pedestrian trajectory X is represented using the ordered tuples $X = ((x_1, t_1), \dots, (x_N, t_N))$. For every timestamp t_i the state x_i consists of the lateral and longitudinal position of the pedestrian and additional features extracted from optical flow (Figure 4(a)). For motion prediction retrieval, it is possible to compare each trajectory in a motion database with an observed history using a similarity measure. With the Quaternion-based Rotationally Invariant Longest Common Subsequence (QRLCS) metric [13] the optimal translation and rotation parameters to superimpose two trajectories are derived. The distance $\text{dist}_{QRLCS}(A, B) \in [0, 1]$ between two trajectories is given by the number of possible assignments determined by an ε area around each trajectory state, normalised by the number of trajectory states. Figure 4(a) illustrates this matching process. We replaced this greedy search by a probabilistic search framework [13,17] where the search time depends on the number of sampling points.

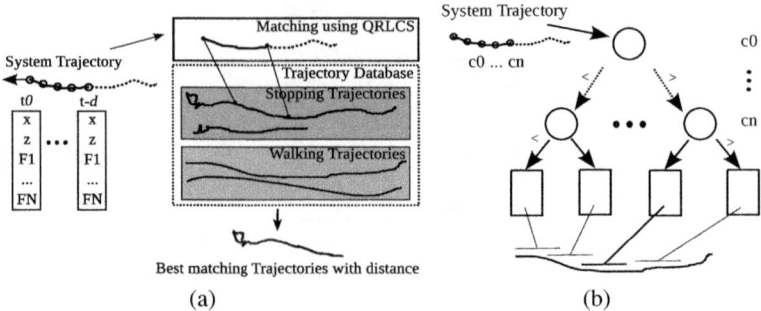

Fig. 4. a) System trajectory with history of length d containing position and feature information for every entry is matched to the training database. Resulting matching position and similarity distance to trajectories in the training database describes a possible trajectory course and class label. b) Tree representation of the trajectory training database. Leaf nodes represent trajectory snippets of fixed length. Similar trajectories are search by traversing the tree using the trajectory descriptors for every level.

Given a motion history $M_{1:t}$ up to the current time step t, the probability that a future pedestrian state ϕ_T occurs is computed by

$$p(\phi_T|M_{1:t}) = \eta\, p(M_{1:t}|\Psi_t) \int p(\Psi_t|\Psi_{t-1})\, p(\Psi_{t-1}|M_{1:t-1})\, d\Psi_{t-1} \qquad (1)$$

with a normalisation constant η and the current state Ψ_t which represents a sequence of trajectory points including position, optical flow features and its history over a temporal sliding window with a manually defined number of time steps d. $p(\phi_T|\Psi_t)$ is the probability of observing a future state ϕ_T, and is determined from the motion database. This distribution $p(\phi_T|M_{1:t})$ is represented by a set of samples or particles $\{\Psi_t^{(s)}\}_S$, which are propagated in time using a particle filter [4]. Therefore, each particle $\Psi_t^{(s)}$ represents a sub-trajectory for the current state.

A set of overlapping sub-trajectories (snippets, e.g. [12]) with fixed number of trajectory points d is created from the motion database. By piling the features for each trajectory point in a snippet into a description vector and applying the PCA method to these vectors, their principal dimensions can be ordered according to the largest eigenvalue. The resulting transformed description vector $\mathbf{v}$ is used to build a binary tree. For each level l the snippet is assigned to the left or right sub-tree depending on the sign of v_l. Figure 4(b) illustrates this search tree. Particle prediction is performed by a probabilistic search in the constructed binary tree and a lookup for the next state in the motion database. The distribution $p(M_{1:t}|\Psi_t)$ represents the likelihood that the measurement trajectory $M_{1:t}$ can be observed when the model trajectory is given. In the context of particle filters, this value corresponds to the weight of a particle and is approximated using $w^{(s)} = 1 - \text{dist}_{\text{QRCLS}}$ for each particle $\Psi_t^{(s)}$. Each particle is a representation of the assumed current pedestrian state with an assigned likelihood.

Action Classification and Path Prediction. The distribution of the predicted state $p(\Phi_t|M_{1:t})$ is approximated by means of the particle filter. An estimated state $\Phi_T^{(s)}$

Table 1. Number sequences and frames for each class with moving and non-moving ego vehicle

Sequences / *Frames*	vehicle standing	vehicle moving
ped. stopping	12 / *1526*	5 / *587*
ped. walking	9 / *1686*	4 / *750*

representing the pedestrian state in the future $T = t + \Delta T$ can be derived by look-ing ahead on the associated trajectories for the current state $\Psi_t^{(s)}$. This results in many hypotheses which are compensated using a weighted mean-shift algorithm [6] with a Gaussian kernel and weights $w^{(s)} \sim p(\Phi_T^{(s)}|M_{1:t})$.

As the final predicted state Φ_T^* the cluster center with the highest accumulated weight is selected. The trajectory database contains two classes of trajectory snippets, the class $\mathcal{C}_s$ in which the pedestrian is stopping and the class $\mathcal{C}_w$ where the pedestrian continues walking. For the predicted object state Φ_T^* derived using cluster members $L = \{\Phi_t^{(l)}\}$ and the corresponding weight $w^{(l)}$ the stopping probability can be approximated using:

$$p(\mathcal{C}_s|L) \approx \frac{\sum_{\Phi_t^{(l)} \in \mathcal{C}_s} w^{(l)}}{\sum_{\Phi_t^{(l)} \in \mathcal{C}_s} w^{(l)} + \sum_{\Phi_t^{(l)} \in \mathcal{C}_w} w^{(l)}}. \tag{2}$$

4 Experiments

Video data of two scenario types was recorded using a stereo camera (22 fps) on-board a vehicle. The first scenario features the stopping of a pedestrian at the curbstone. In the second scenario, the pedestrian crosses the street. Recorded data consisted of runs where the vehicle is stationary at a distance of 15 m to 17 m to the pedestrian and runs where the vehicle is moving at speeds of $20 - 30$ km/h. Tables 1 summarizes the recorded data with four different pedestrians.

Pedestrians were shape labeled to derive the ground-truth position in the world. The median disparity value on the pedestrian upper body and the center of gravity of the shape is used to project the 3D position. For each trajectory where the pedestrian is stopping the moment of the last placement of the foot is labeled as the stopping moment. By definition, all frames earlier to this event will have a time-to-stop value (TTS in frames) greater than zero. Frames after the stopping moment have a TTS value smaller than zero. In sequences where the pedestrian continues walking the closest point to the curbstone (with closed legs) is labeled. Analogous to the TTS definition, it is called time-to-curb value (TTC). Since the focus of the paper is not a particular pedestrian detection system, we first provide as input to the evaluated methods the ground truth 2D bounding boxes perturbed by noise. Artificially generated uniform noise is added to the height and center of the 2D bounding boxes up to 10% of the original height value.

Analyzing walking trajectories shows an average gait cycle of 10 to 14 frames for different pedestrians. A trajectory database as described in previous Section is generated in a sliding window fashion to contain sub-trajectories with a fixed length of ten frames. For test trajectories a history of 14 frames is used to capture gate cycle variations. Trajectories in which the pedestrian did not stop as well as trajectory slices with a TTS > 20 (twice the gate cycle) are member of the class $\mathcal{C}_w$. The stopping class $\mathcal{C}_s$ consists of the remaining slices.

Evaluated Models and Parameter Settings. The particle filter approximates the current probability density with $S = 400$ particles and uses a search deviation parameter of $\beta = 0.05$ for the tree search (see [13]). The mean shift position procedure operates with a kernel width value $h = 0.1$. Two feature combinations for the PF are compared: The base configuration uses the lateral and longitudinal object position (*Pos*) for the trajectory matching. The second combination uses the median horizontal object flow (*MFlowU*) in the image plane and additional motion features (*HoM*) described in previous Section. For the evaluation the training and testing data has been processed using *leave-one-out* cross validation. In order to ensure the optimal search result by the PF, the proposed system is compared against a full-search (i.e. brute force, BF) method over all training trajectories. For each trajectory slice from the training set, the BF method selects the best hypothesis based on the weight value, equal to the particle weights in the PF system.

As a second model of comparison to the proposed PF system, we use the state-of-the-art Integrated Multiple Model Kalman Filter (IMM-KF) [3]. Two process models describing pedestrian motion are used: A steady walking pace can be represented with the constant velocity (CV) model with process noise parameter q_{CV}. For non-moving pedestrians the constant position (CP) model with q_{CP} applies. For the following evaluation $q_{CV} = 0.009$ and $q_{CP} = 0.01$ has been derived from the set of training trajectories, with respect to the positions minimum mean-RMS error. Each model is provided with the same 3D position data as for the PF as a measurement input. In preliminary experiments a constant acceleration model (CA) was tested as well, but did not produce acceptable results. As mentioned in [3], this can be explained by the relatively short time span of the deceleration process, a comparatively large measurement noise and the use of the second derivative of the position data to estimate the deceleration. Measurement noise for each test trajectory is computed from the training trajectories and yields a standard deviation of $\sigma_z = 0.25$ m in longitudinal and $\sigma_x = 0.15$ m in lateral direction. The Markov matrix P describing the transition probabilities between the CV and CP model was derived from the available training data $P := [0.999, 0.001; 0.001, 0.999]$. Choosing larger values for the model transitions result in more frequent, undesired switches, especially with noisy measurements.

Pedestrian Action Classification. We first tested the ability of various systems to classify pedestrian actions, i.e. whether the pedestrian will cross or not. Figure 5 illustrates the mean performance of each system with different feature sets on stopping and walking test trajectories; depicted is the estimated probability of stopping, as a function of TTS or TTC. For the PF and BF approaches the stopping probability is approximated as described in previous Section. For the IMM-KF filter the probability of the CP model is used. To put the performance of the systems in context, we also evaluated human performance. Video data was presented to several human observers using a graphical user interfaces, where playback was automatically stopped at different TTC or TTS moments (20, 11, 8, 5, 3). For each test, the observers had to decide whether the pedestrian will stop at the curbstone or cross the street and provide a confidence using a slider ranging from 0 to 1. Sequence and playback stopping point were randomly selected before being presented, to avoid the effect of re-identification.

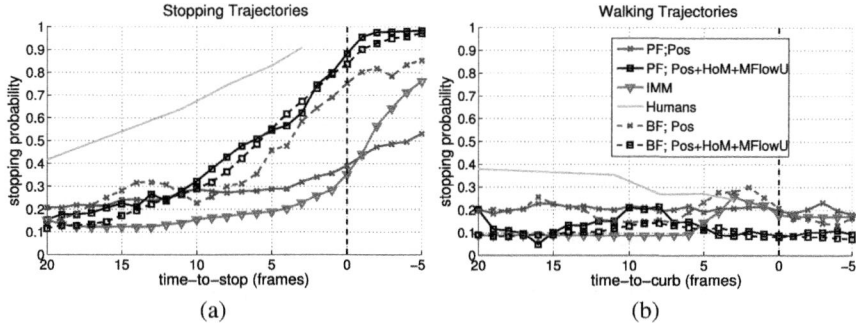

Fig. 5. Estimated probability of stopping over time for (a) stopping or (b) walking test trajectory (averaged over all respective sequences

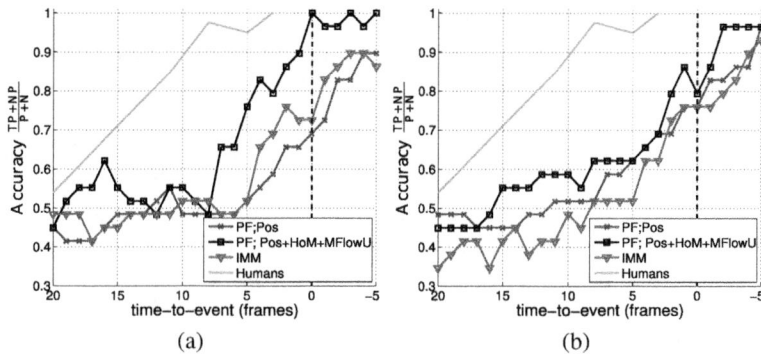

Fig. 6. Classification accuracy of the different systems over time. (a) Results for the jittered ground-truth bounding boxes. (b) Results for the bounding boxes of a HOG detector.

On trajectories where the pedestrian continues walking, all systems show a low and relatively constant stopping probability. BF and PF results for different feature combinations show a similar performance. The CV model for the IMM-KF filter remains more likely all time. On trajectories where the pedestrian is stopping, all systems initially start with a low stopping probability, since stopping is preceded by walking. But about 11 frames before the stopping event the confidence increases more markedly. Class membership of an input trajectory for each time instant is assigned by thresholding the observed stopping probability (cf. Figure 5). Based on the training set, we selected for each system a threshold that minimizes its classification error (i.e. stopping classified as walking and vice versa) over all sequences and time instants. Figure 6 illustrates the classification accuracy using these "optimal" thresholds. Human estimates of the pedestrian action class outperforms current methods. The proposed system using the feature combination Pos + HoM + MFlowU dominate the classification accuracy compared to other evaluated competetive models at all times. An accuracy of 0.8 in classifying the correct pedestrian's action is reached 570 ms and 180 ms before a possible standstill by the human and proposed system; it is only reached *after* the possible standstill with the other methods, due to sensor noise.

Table 2. Mean and standard deviation of the RMSE (in m) for *walking* and *stopping* trajectories with different systems and prediction horizons (#frames). **left:** Results using the jittered ground truth bounding boxes **right:** Results using recognitions from a pedestrian detector.

		Walking					Stopping					Walking		Stopping	
		0	3	5	11	17	0	3	5	11	17	0	17	0	17
IMM-KF	Mean	0.62	0.73	0.80	1.06	1.33	0.51	0.66	0.77	1.14	1.54	0.64	2.37	0.38	1.52
	± Std	0.51	0.57	0.61	0.73	0.87	0.48	0.57	0.65	0.93	1.23	0.69	2.52	0.28	1.26
Pos	Mean	0.32	0.42	0.48	0.70	0.89	0.25	0.35	0.43	0.63	0.86	0.28	0.68	0.25	0.83
	± Std	0.09	0.14	0.18	0.29	0.34	0.07	0.11	0.16	0.22	0.26	0.25	0.49	0.17	0.42
Pos+HoM	Mean	0.37	0.49	0.56	0.79	1.07	0.28	0.04	0.46	0.66	0.88	0.43	0.99	0.31	0.89
+MFlowU	± Std	0.17	0.21	0.25	0.31	0.39	0.11	0.18	0.22	0.31	0.43	0.45	0.79	0.20	0.61

Path Prediction Accuracy. The second set of experiments evaluates the world localization accuracy of path prediction for different prediction horizons for every time step (i.e. frame). The predicted object position for the PF is computed as described in previous Section by a look-up on the subsequent parts of the matched trajectories. Position predictions of the IMM-KF are derived by predicting the current filter state without additional measurement updates. Given a prediction time step inside the range $[20, -5]$ frames, where frame 0 denotes the manually labeled TTS/TTC moment, the predicted localization error is evaluated for different prediction horizons.

Localization error for the different prediction horizons are summarized in Table 2. As can be seen, the IMM-KF has a higher localization error for any prediction horizon than PF feature combinations. Because the IMM-KF uses the filtered velocity for path prediction, the increasing localization error can be explained by erroneous velocity estimations, without new measurements the current velocity estimates are propagated unchanged. The proposed system outperforms the IMM-KF by a factor of about 1.7 and 1.2 in stopping and walking situations, respectively, in terms of the reduction of mean RMS. The addition of motion features does not result in improved accuracy, likely because the right trajectory snippets in the database are already found with position-only features; accuracy gains can be expected by a larger training set.

Evaluation using a Real Pedestrian Detector. We also evaluated performance using the bounding boxes provided by a state-of-the-art HOG pedestrian detector [7]. Missing detections were filled in using a basic correlation tracker (one sequence had to be excluded from the evaluation because of 11 successive missing detections). For IMM-KF systems the measurements noise derived from training sequences has been adjusted to $\sigma_z = 0.48$ m and $\sigma_x = 0.37$ m. Process noise was left unchanged. We found that the position and height error of the detector boxes compared to the ground truth is normally distributed with a standard deviation of 5% of the box height but with small number of outliers with larger errors. These outliers affect both position prediction and classification performance of the IMM-KF method (cf. Figure 6(b) and Table 2). For the IMM-KF the outliers lead to frequent model switches resulting in a less accurate action class decision and velocity estimation. Classification performance of all methods decreases compared to the previous experiments. With the particle filter approach no significant change in the localization accuracy is observed compared to the results obtained previously; we attribute this to the robustness of the QRLCS metric to outliers.

5 Conclusion

We presented a system for short-term pedestrian action classification and path prediction, that makes use of learned, labeled trajectory data. On the task of classifying whether a pedestrian nearing the curb side will stop, human performance was best, followed by the proposed system, and on third spot the state-of-the-art IMM-KF and simpler system variants, without an augmented motion feature set. Regarding the path prediction accuracy, our system leads to a significant lower position error, especially for large prediction horizons. We would like to thank C. Wöhler and M. Enzweiler for helpful discussions.

References

1. Abramson, Y., Steux, B.: Hardware-friendly pedestrian detection and impact prediction. In: IEEE Intell. Veh., pp. 590–595 (2004)
2. Antonini, G., Martinez, S.V., Bierlaire, M., Thiran, J.: Behavioral priors for detection and tracking of pedestrians in video sequences. IJCV 69(2) (2006)
3. Bar-Shalom, Y., Li, X., Kirubarajan, T.: Estimation with applications to tracking and navigation. Wiley-Interscience, Hoboken (2001)
4. Black, M.J., Jepson, A.D.: A probabilistic framework for matching temporal trajectories: CONDENSATION-based recognition of gestures and expressions. In: Burkhardt, H.-J., Neumann, B. (eds.) ECCV 1998. LNCS, vol. 1406, pp. 909–924. Springer, Heidelberg (1998)
5. Chen, Z., Ngai, D., Yung, N.: Pedestrian behavior prediction based on motion patterns for vehicle-to-pedestrian collision avoidance. In: Proc. of IEEE ITSC, pp. 316–321 (2008)
6. Comaniciu, D., Meer, P.: Mean shift: A robust approach toward feature space analysis. IEEE PAMI 24(5), 603–619 (2002)
7. Dalal, N., Triggs, B.: Histograms of oriented gradients for human detection. In: Proc. CVPR, pp. 886–893 (2005)
8. De Nicolao, G., Ferrara, A., Giacomini, L.: A collision risk assessment approach as a basis for the on-board warning generation in cars. In: IEEE Intell. Veh. (2002)
9. Dollar, P., Wojek, C., Schiele, B., Perona, P.: Pedestrian detection: A benchmark. In: Proc. CVPR (2009)
10. Enzweiler, M., Gavrila, D.M.: Monocular pedestrian detection: Survey and experiments. IEEE PAMI 31, 2179–2195 (2009)
11. Hirschmüller, H.: Stereo processing by semiglobal matching and mutual information. IEEE PAMI 30(2), 328–341 (2008)
12. Howe, N., Leventon, M., Freeman, W.: Bayesian reconstruction of 3d human motion from single-camera video. In: Proc. NIPS, pp. 820–826 (2000)
13. Käfer, E., Hermes, C., Wöhler, C., Ritter, H., Kummert, F.: Recognition of situation classes at road intersections. In: Proc. ICRA, pp. 3960–3965 (2010)
14. Makris, D., Ellis, T.: Spatial and probabilistic modelling of pedestrian behaviour. In: Proc. BMVC, pp. 557–566 (2002)
15. Meinecke, M.M., et al.: Strategies in terms of vulnerable road user protection. EU Project SAVE-U, Deliverable D6 (2003), http://www.save-u.org
16. Schmidt, S., Färber, B.: Pedestrians at the kerb - recognising the action intentions of humans. Transportation Research Part F 12(4), 300–310 (2009)
17. Sidenbladh, H., Black, M.J., Sigal, L.: Implicit probabilistic models of human motion for synthesis and tracking. In: Heyden, A., Sparr, G., Nielsen, M., Johansen, P. (eds.) ECCV 2002. LNCS, vol. 2350, pp. 784–800. Springer, Heidelberg (2002)
18. Turaga, P.K., Chellappa, R., Subrahmanian, V.S., Udrea, O.: Machine recognition of human activities: A survey. CirSysVideo 18(11), 1473–1488 (2008)
19. Wakim, C., Capperon, S., Oksman, J.: A Markovian model of pedestrian behavior. In: Proc. IEEE Int. Conf. Syst., Man, Cybern., pp. 4028–4033 (2004)
20. Wedel, A., et al.: Duality tv-l1 flow with fundamental matrix prior. In: Proc. IVCNZ (2008)

Simultaneous Reconstruction and Tracking of Non-planar Templates

Sebastian Lieberknecht[1], Selim Benhimane[1], and Slobodan Ilic[2]

[1] metaio GmbH, Munich, Germany
[2] Technische Universtität München, Garching, Germany

Abstract. In this paper, we address the problem of simultaneous tracking and reconstruction of non-planar templates in real-time. Classical approaches to template tracking assume planarity and do not attempt to recover the shape of an object. Structure from motion approaches use feature points to recover camera pose and reconstruct the scene from those features, but do not produce dense 3D surface models. Finally, deformable surface tracking approaches assume a static camera and impose strong deformation priors to recover dense 3D shapes.

The proposed method simultaneously recovers the camera motion and deforms the template such that an approximation of the underlying 3D structure is recovered. Spatial smoothing is not explicitly imposed, thus templates of smooth and non-smooth objects can be equally handled. The problem is formalized as an energy minimization based on image intensity differences. Quantitative and qualitative evaluation on both real and synthetic data is presented, we compare the proposed approach to related methods and demonstrate that the recovered camera pose is close to the ground truth even in presence of strong blur and low texture.

1 Introduction

Template tracking is one of the fundamental problems in computer vision and a multitude of impressive techniques have been proposed in the literature [12,1,4,9]. They mainly concentrate on planar templates and estimate camera motion by energy minimization. The applications of template tracking are wide and include, but are not limited to, vision-based control, human-computer interfaces, augmented reality, robotics, surveillance, medical imaging and visual reconstruction. In many applications, the planarity assumption is good enough, but in general that is not the case. For that reason Silveira and Malis [17] and Bartoli and Zisserman [2] considered computing 2D warpings of the reference templates while tracking them. The real depth and camera motion are then obtained by decomposing the estimated warpings.

Motivated by the fact that the world is not planar and driven by the emerging needs of simultaneous recovery of the structures and motion of the camera, we address the problem of simultaneous tracking and reconstruction of a non-planar template in real time. The model of the template is represented as a triangular mesh. We start with a planar shape and simultaneously recover camera motion

R. Mester and M. Felsberg (Eds.): DAGM 2011, LNCS 6835, pp. 396–405, 2011.

and deform the shape such that the underlying 3D structure is approximately recovered. As we use all pixels of the template, the object does not necessarily have to be well textured and contain many feature points. This is different from classical Structure from Motion (SfM) and Simultaneous Localization and Mapping (SLAM) techniques that primarily rely on sparse feature points, such as e.g. Klein and Murray's PTAM [10] of which Newcombe and Davidson [13] use the camera poses and sparse feature map to create a dense reconstruction. They perform very well, but depend on the amount of the observed features and tend to be sensitive to the amount of blur.

Unlike methods which rely on prior deformation models [16,15] and assume fixed camera position, we solve for camera motion and do not impose any constraints on the model deformation, therefore we can equally reconstruct and track templates that are smooth or have creases. However, since the problem is ill-posed, we have made certain assumptions: we use templates of a predefined size, assume that in its initial/reference position the entire template is visible and is not self-occluded, and finally we restrict mesh vertices to only move along the camera rays, thus having one degree of freedom per vertex.

We evaluated the performance of our method on both synthetic and real video sequences. Further, we performed quantitative analysis and compared the method to ground truth measurements and to standard planar template tracking methods and PTAM. Our experiments indicate that, even with the approximate shape we recover, the tracking precision increased and turned out to be much more stable than tracking of planar templates and deals better with blur and low-textured surfaces than PTAM.

In the remainder of the paper, we first discuss related works, then describe our method in detail, finally present experimental results and conclude.

2   Related Work

Template tracking has always been assuming the planarity of the object of interest to be tracked. Since Lucas-Kanade [12], the real-time constraint was enforced and in recent works [1,3] it became standard. Improvements in convergence speed and robustness in the calibrated camera setting were especially achieved by the method of Benhimane and Malis [4]. For those reasons, we in part relied on their method.

Other researchers [14,7,17] also proposed to find deformations of an object in a sequence of acquired images. These methods generally consist of estimation of the parameters of the warping function that registers the reference image, in which the object is mainly planar, to the input image where the object is deformed. Pilet et al. [14] and Gay-Bellile et al. [7] relied on feature points. While the former can deal with a huge amount of outliers, the latter is relatively sensitive to them. Datta et al. [5] use affine warps and integrated the idea of articulated points as hard constraints into the minimization, i.e. they force patches to move according to their connectivity. Hilsmann et al. [8] re-texture the surface of a deforming object realistically by estimating both the changes in geometry and photometry, they also explicitly model external occlusions to further improve the quality of the augmentation. Silveira and Malis [17] use 2D warps and present a generic framework for template tracking which can undergo deformations. In all of these cases, the warping is done in image space and therefore does not provide a 3D shape, but instead 2D warpings of the images as in deformable registration. To recover the 3D shape, the recovered 2D warpings are decomposed into a rigid motion and according depths.

On a separate track, deformable surface tracking from monocular videos has been developed. Because of the inherent ambiguity, deformation models have been introduced to constrain deformations of particular objects like *e.g.* paper and clothes [16,15,19]. These approaches generally output the 3D surface meshes. However, they do not provide the relative camera/object motion in the image sequence, require heavily textured objects and generally do not work in real-time.

Simultaneous recovery of the camera motion and the 3D shape is also related to SfM [18] and SLAM [6] techniques. Both techniques strictly rely on image features and incremental reconstruction of an observed scene, while neither of them operates on the dense pixel level. The system proposed by Newcombe and Davidson [13] indeed produces a dense reconstruction using a movable camera; it relies on PTAM [10] to precisely recover the motion of the camera, they also use its sparse feature map to initialize a dense optical flow method [20].

Most of the previously mentioned methods are using feature points and/or define constraints on the possible model deformations. Relying on features usually implies that the observed object has to be well textured. Instead of using a set of extracted feature points in the image, we use all available pixels of the template which in turn enables tracking of low textured templates. We simultaneously recover the camera motion and the approximate shape of the non-planar template. Our method exhibits fast convergence, is robust under blur, works in real-time and recovers quite precise camera pose given the on-line reconstruction of the approximate template's shape.

3   Method

The task of the algorithm is to estimate updates of the mesh M and the camera pose $\mathbf{T}$ given a novel image $\mathcal{I}$ of the object and relying of estimates on mesh and pose, denoted as $\widehat{M}$ and $\widehat{\mathbf{T}}$ obtained in the previous frame. We assume that, ignoring occlusion and drastic lighting changes, the reference image $\mathcal{I}^*$ can be constructed from $\mathcal{I}$ by back-warping each face f given the true pose and the recovered mesh. Given that we only know their approximations $\widehat{\mathbf{T}}$ and $\widehat{M}$, we produce an estimated image $\widehat{\mathcal{I}}^*$ by applying a homography $\mathbf{G}$ to each face of the mesh. This is illustrated in Figure 1(a). As the mesh is defined piece-wise planar, warping a single face f is conducted by the homography:

$$\mathbf{G}(\mathbf{T}, \mathbf{n}_f^*) = \mathbf{K}(\mathbf{R} + \mathbf{t}\mathbf{n}_f^{*\top})\mathbf{K}^{-1}\mathbf{G}_f. \tag{1}$$

Here, $\mathbf{K}$ denotes the known 3×3 camera intrinsics, $\mathbf{n}_f^* \in \mathbb{R}^3$ is the normal of face f scaled by the inverse of the distance d_f^* of the face to the camera center $\mathbf{c}^*$

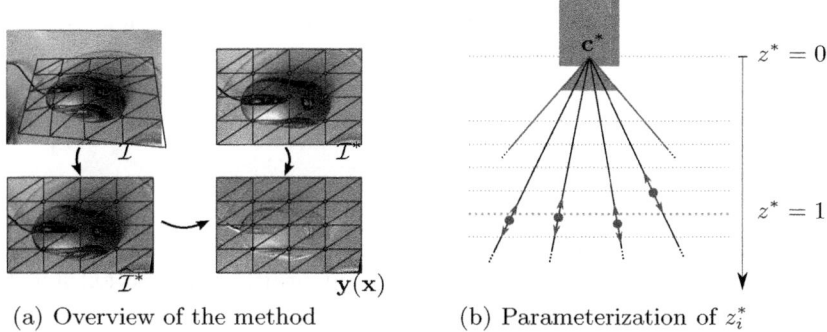

(a) Overview of the method   (b) Parameterization of z_i^*

Fig. 1. (a) The mesh is overlaid onto the object, with highlighted movable vertices. Out of the camera image $\mathcal{I}$ the estimate of the reference image $\widehat{\mathcal{I}}^*$ is unwarped. The error $\mathbf{y}(\mathbf{x}) = \widehat{\mathcal{I}}^* - \mathcal{I}^*$ is subject to iterative minimization. (b) The vertices of the mesh are free to move along their respective projection ray, *i.e.* (u_i^*, v_i^*) are fixed but z_i^* may change.

in the reference frame; the camera pose $\mathbf{T}$ is decomposed to get $\mathbf{R} \in \mathbb{SO}(3)$ and $\mathbf{t} \in \mathbb{R}^3$. Finally, the homography $\mathbf{G}_f$ is used to apply a 2D translation of the face to its specified position within $\mathcal{I}^*$. We assume that the updates $\mathbf{T}(\mathbf{x}), \mathbf{n}_f^*(\mathbf{x})$ of the estimates $\widehat{\mathbf{T}}, \widehat{\mathbf{n}}_f^*$ are reasonably small. They are parameterized in terms of the camera pose and the mesh deformation $\mathbf{x} = (\omega_x, \omega_y, \omega_z, \nu_x, \nu_y, \nu_z, \psi_1, \psi_2, \ldots, \psi_n)$ where the first six parameters represent the update of the pose $\widehat{\mathbf{T}}$ of the camera, represented by the Lie algebra of $\mathbb{SE}(3)$. The remainder of $\mathbf{x}$ represents the update of the inverse depths $\psi_i = 1/z_i^*$ of the movable vertices.

Deformations of the mesh M^* are modeled by moving vertices along their respective rays emanating from the camera center $\mathbf{c}^*$ in the reference view, see Figure 1(b). Every vertex $\mathbf{v}_i^*$ is defined via its 2D coordinates $\mathbf{v}_i^* = (u_i^*, v_i^*, 1)^\top$ in $\mathcal{I}^*$ and its depth z_i^* w.r.t. the camera center $\mathbf{c}^*$. The normal $\mathbf{n}_f^*$ of a face f is computed from its vertices $\{\mathbf{v}_i^*, \mathbf{v}_j^*, \mathbf{v}_k^*\}$ and inverse depths:

$$\mathbf{n}_f^*(\mathbf{x}) = \frac{\mathbf{n}^*}{d^*} = \mathbf{K}^\top \left[\mathbf{v}_i^* \, \mathbf{v}_j^* \, \mathbf{v}_k^*\right]^{-\top} \left[\psi_i \, \psi_j \, \psi_k\right]^\top . \tag{2}$$

This formula was developed by combining the inverted pinhole projection $\mathbf{a} = (x, y, z)^\top = z\mathbf{K}^{-1}(u, v, 1)^\top$ with the plane equation $\mathbf{n}^\top \mathbf{a} = d$. Note that this parameterization of $\mathbf{n}_f^*(\mathbf{x})$ is linear w.r.t. the inverse of the depths.

For the sake of simplicity, we consider only a single face consisting of m pixels and define the $m \times 1$ error vector $\mathbf{y}(\mathbf{x})$ as concatenation of the error measures

$$y_i(\mathbf{x}) = \widehat{\mathcal{I}}^* - \mathcal{I}^* = \mathcal{I}(\mathbf{q}_i) - \mathcal{I}^*(\mathbf{p}_i^*) \tag{3}$$

$$= \mathcal{I}\left(\mathbf{d}\left(\mathbf{G}\left(\widehat{\mathbf{T}}\mathbf{T}(\mathbf{x}), \mathbf{n}_f^*(\widehat{\mathbf{x}} + \mathbf{x})\right)\mathbf{p}_i^*\right)\right) - \mathcal{I}^*(\mathbf{p}_i^*) \tag{4}$$

where $\mathbf{q}_i$ are pixel coordinates in the input image obtained by back-warping to the reference image and $\mathbf{d}((u, v, w)^\top) = (u/w, v/w, 1)^\top$ represent normalized homogeneous coordinates. The current estimates of the depths is stored in $\widehat{\mathbf{x}}$, thus the update $\mathbf{n}_f^*(\widehat{\mathbf{x}} + \mathbf{x})$ used in Equation (4) is equivalent to the update $\frac{1}{\widehat{z}^*} \leftarrow \frac{1}{\widehat{z}^*} + \psi$. To increase numerical stability, we add a regularization term to the cost function via a function $\mathbf{r}(\mathbf{x}) : \mathbb{R}^{6+n} \to \mathbb{R}^{6+n}$ for n movable vertices in the mesh, discussed in section 3.1. The cost function can be written as

$$\phi(\mathbf{x}) = \frac{1}{2} \left(||\mathbf{y}(\mathbf{x})||^2 + \lambda \, ||\mathbf{r}(\mathbf{x})||^2 \right) \tag{5}$$

where the scalar λ is used to balance the squared norms of $\mathbf{y}(\mathbf{x})$ and $\mathbf{r}(\mathbf{x})$. The update $\mathbf{x}$ is computed by linearizing the quadratic cost function and therefore solving the linear system

$$\left(\mathbf{J}_\mathbf{y}^\top \mathbf{J}_\mathbf{y} + \lambda \mathbf{J}_\mathbf{r}^\top \mathbf{J}_\mathbf{r} \right) \mathbf{x} = - \left(\mathbf{J}_\mathbf{y}^\top \mathbf{y}(0) + \lambda \mathbf{J}_\mathbf{r}^\top \mathbf{r}(0) \right) \tag{6}$$

where $\mathbf{J}_\mathbf{y}$ and $\mathbf{J}_\mathbf{r}$ are Jacobians of the data and the regularization terms. This system is solved iteratively for $\mathbf{x}$ using $e.g.$ its pseudo-inverse or Cholesky decomposition. The Jacobian $\mathbf{J}_\mathbf{y}$ can be written as the product $\mathbf{J}_\mathbf{y} = \mathbf{J}_{\widehat{\mathcal{I}}^*} \mathbf{J}_\mathbf{d} \mathbf{J}_\mathbf{G}$ where $\mathbf{J}_{\widehat{\mathcal{I}}^*}$ is the gradient of the estimated reference image, $\mathbf{J}_\mathbf{d}$ and $\mathbf{J}_\mathbf{G}$ are the Jacobians of the projection and the homography. In the spirit of [4], this first order linearization can be approximated to second order as $\mathbf{J}_\mathbf{y} = \frac{1}{2} \left(\mathbf{J}_{\widehat{\mathcal{I}}^*} + \mathbf{J}_{\mathcal{I}^*} \right) \mathbf{J}_\mathbf{d} \mathbf{J}_\mathbf{G}$ by including the gradient of the reference image $\mathbf{J}_{\mathcal{I}^*}$. As shown in the evaluation, this in general increases the convergence frequency of the Gauss-Newton optimization with low additional costs. The convergence area is increased by employing multiple levels of an image pyramid.

3.1   Regularization

In case the camera is close to the reference camera, the matrix $\mathbf{J}_\mathbf{y}^\top \mathbf{J}_\mathbf{y}$ becomes increasingly ill-conditioned, $i.e.$ tiny changes in $\mathbf{y}(0)$ may provoke huge changes in $\mathbf{x}$. This is because the projection rays of the current camera are approximately aligned with those of the reference camera (depicted in Figure 1(b)). In this degenerate configuration, arbitrary movements of the vertices, respectively their inverse depth ψ_i, result in almost identical unwarped reference images $\widehat{\mathcal{I}}^*$.

However, this configuration can be easily mitigated by adding a regularization term to the cost function that restrains the vertices in that case. We define $\mathbf{r}(\mathbf{x})$ as $\mathbf{r}(\mathbf{x}) = (\mathbf{0}_{1 \times 6}, r_1(\mathbf{x}), r_2(\mathbf{x}), \dots, r_n(\mathbf{x}))^\top$ which currently only operates on the n movable vertices. We compute $\forall i \in 1, 2, \dots, n$:

$$r_i(\mathbf{x}) = \left(1 + \lambda_s e^{-\lambda_r ||\widehat{\mathbf{t}}||^2} \right) \left(\frac{1}{\widehat{\psi}_i + \psi_i} - \mu_i \right). \tag{7}$$

The first part of the regularization term is a weighting factor that penalizes the degenerate configuration just discussed. The scalars λ_s and λ_r determine the scale and range of the penalty concerning the baseline, empirically $\lambda_s = \lambda_r = 10$ gave good results. The second part of Equation (7) is responsible for damping the deformations and moving them towards their most likely true value. It penalizes changes of the depths with respect to a reference depth μ_i of the vertex.

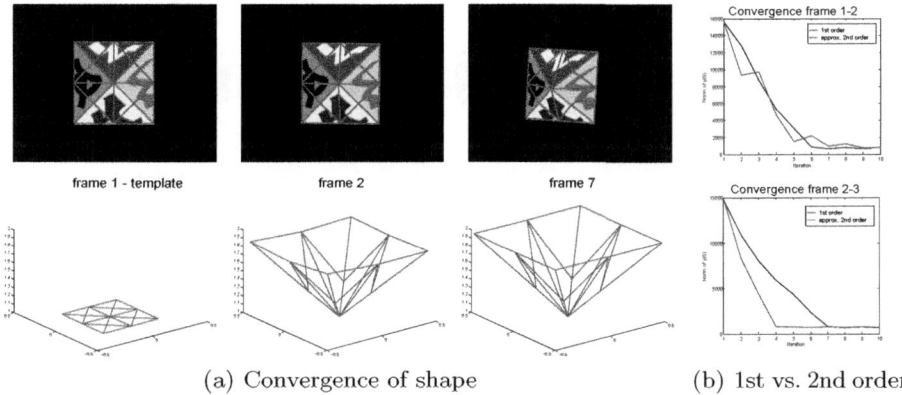

(a) Convergence of shape   (b) 1st vs. 2nd order

Fig. 2. Evaluation on synthetic data. (a) Sequence of synthetic pyramid, 16 faces and 12 moving vertices were used. Note that the shape quickly converges towards true shape from the template image (frame 1) to frame 2. (b) The proposed second order approximation of $\mathbf{J_y}$ converges 2-4 iterations earlier in case of slight deformations.

A naïve way of determining μ_i may consist in computing it as running average, *e.g.* updated after every image as $\mu_i \leftarrow 0.9\,\mu_i + 0.1/\widehat{\psi}_i$. This method is simple yet effective in case of a continuously moving camera. However, when the camera becomes stationary, μ_i will converge towards the value optimal for only this local configuration and information from distant successful registrations will be lost over time.

An improved version of determining μ_i tries to preserve previous knowledge about the camera motion. For this, we spatially sample height estimates of the proposed method on a hemisphere around each vertex using the geometry of the camera ray of the vertex in $\mathcal{I}^*$ and the current camera ray in $\mathcal{I}$. The samples are weighted using the angle between the rays, small angles are down-weighted as they represent (near-) aligned camera rays and thus lead to the degenerate configuration just discussed. Further we include into the weight the normalized cross-correlation of the adjacent faces of the vertex in both $\mathcal{I}^*$ and $\widehat{\mathcal{I}}^*$ to mitigate the influence of severely incorrect estimations of the camera pose or vertex heights. Typically, the value of μ_i changes rapidly in the beginning as the shape transforms from the initial estimate towards a more likely shape, but after that becomes relatively stable given sufficient camera movements.

4   Evaluation

The proposed method was quantitatively evaluated both on synthetic and real video sequences for which ground truth of the camera pose was available; in case of the synthetic sequence also the estimate of the shape was evaluated. Further, we evaluated the method qualitatively on smooth objects and on objects with creases, using a moving camera. Equally we tested our method on a smoothly deforming object with a fixed camera. Comparison against PTAM [10] was conducted in presence of several levels of blur. Videos of the evaluations can be found in the supplementary material.

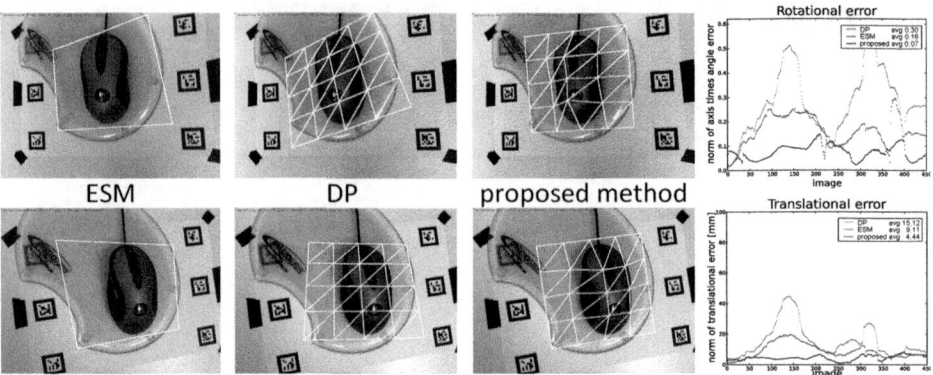

Fig. 3. Evaluation on real data. Comparison of ESM [3], DP [4] and proposed method. Poses were compared to ground truth from a mechanical measurement device.

4.1   Quantitative Evaluation

Synthetic sequence. A synthetic pyramid was created first seen from the top, then moving towards the lower left corner of the image while rotating. We used a mesh of 16 faces and 13 vertices from which only the central vertex was fixed. No regularization was employed as neither noise nor degenerate configurations are present and only a maximum of five iterations per frame on pyramid level 0, *i.e.* on the original resolution, were allowed. The method shows low errors in both pose and shape of the object. The synthetic evaluation is illustrated in Figure 2 and in the supplementary material. When comparing the first order linearization of $\mathbf{J_y}$ with the presented approximated second order linearization, we observed that they have similar convergence rate when there is strong motion in the depths like in frames 1-2 in Figure 2(b) . However, when the estimation of the structure is changing just slightly like in frames 2-3 shown on the bottom in Figure 2(b), 2 to 4 iterations may be saved and our results match those of Benhimane and Malis [4] in terms of convergence.

Real sequence. To perform a quantitative evaluation with real camera images, we have created a sequence using a real camera mounted on a mechanical measurement device that provided a ground truth pose of the camera computed similarly to Lieberknecht *et al.* [11]. We made a sequence for tracking low textured target, a computer mouse on a mouse pad. Similar to the synthetic sequence, this sequence starts with an almost fronto-planar view such that we can create a reasonable reference image from it by rectifying the first image given the ground truth pose. The sequence was used to evaluate our method, ESM [3] and the calibrated multi-planar tracking method [4] referred to as DP. The algorithms were given identical parameters, *i.e.* 2 pyramid levels and 5 iterations per level. Poses were computed from the 2D–3D correspondences of the corners of the templates. As can be seen in Figure 3, our method outperforms planar methods in terms of accuracy on the pose of the camera. Furthermore, we evaluated the robustness of the proposed method with respect to blur introduced by consecutively

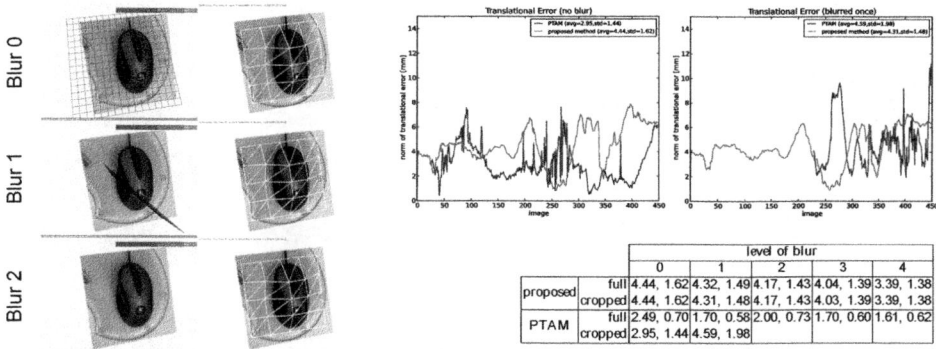

Fig. 4. Quantitative evaluation against blur. A (5×5) mean filter was applied consecutively 0–4 times to evaluate the robustness of the method to blur. *Left:* Frame of the blurred image sequences given to PTAM (left) and proposed method (right). In case of PTAM the plane indicates the ground plane PTAM fits to available features after initialization. In our case we show the deformed 3D mesh model. *Right:* Error in translation for cropped images and blur levels 0 and 1, below a table displaying the mean error and standard deviation of the methods.

applying a (5×5) mean filter. This kind of blur can be found in real data when the object is out-of-focus given a fixed-focus camera. We observed that the accuracy of the method did increase slightly as the blur increased. The same sequences were given to PTAM. As poses of PTAM are defined in an rather arbitrary coordinate system, we aligned them by minimizing the sum-of-squared distance to the ground truth, solving for a 6-DOF transformation and 1-DOF scale. In order to make fair comparisons, we focused only on the area belonging to the object and cut the markers out. To avoid synthetic stable features, like those on the edges of the cut, we slightly randomized the borders of the mask. PTAM could not successfully initialize starting from the second level of blur, as depicted in Figure 4, since there were very few features on the lowest image pyramid level to be tracked. However the accuracy of PTAM is superior when using the full image as shown in Figure 4. The proposed method is giving the same results both for full and cropped image.

4.2 Qualitative Evaluation

To analyze how the method works in case of a smooth object and in case of object with creases, we evaluated it by tracking a cup and a truncated pyramid. The method was able to track both objects well and approximated the shapes reasonably. As noted in [5], best results are obtained when the structure of the mesh is able to express the structure of the underlying object. Furthermore, we evaluated the robustness of the method when tracking deformed objects. Although this violates the rigidity assumption, the method copes well with slight deformations as shown in Figure 5. In the cup sequence, after estimating the shape we manually disabled the estimation of the depths and used the method only for tracking the pose. We show that the pose is well estimated even under severe occlusion of up to 50% of the mesh. On a 2.5 GHz dual core notebook, the speed is typically 10–30 ms

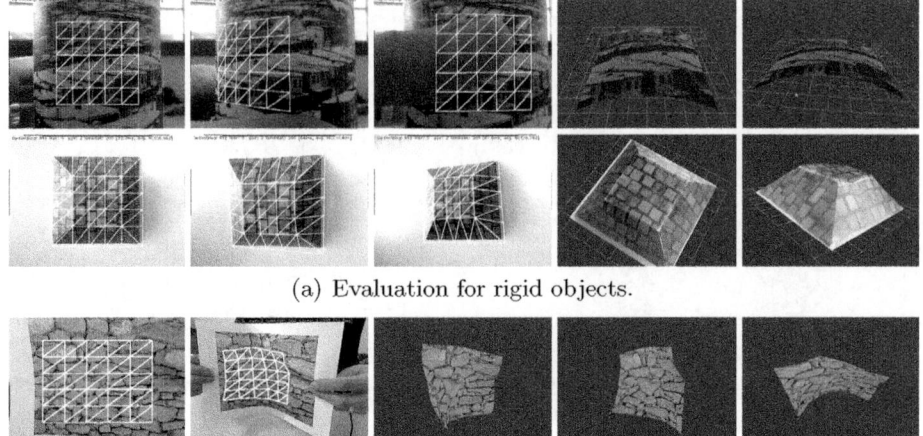

(a) Evaluation for rigid objects.

(b) Evaluation for a deforming object.

Fig. 5. Qualitative evaluation of recovered shapes. The first frame of the sequence (shown left-most) is used as template. (a) Shape recovery of the rigid objects from moving camera where also the camera motion is estimated. (b) Recovering shape of the deforming object where the camera is not moving. Although the method was not designed for such situations, we still managed to apply it to recover moderate object deformations.

per frame when estimating the camera pose and around 40–60 ms when additionally estimating the deformations. The timings were obtained using pyramid levels 3 and 2, at most 5 iterations per level and a mesh of approximately 200×200 pixels on level 0. Most of the time is spent in the direct computation of $\mathbf{J_y^\top J_y}$.

4.3   Discussion and Future Work

During the evaluation, we observed that the main source of error originated from fast translational camera motion as this violates our assumption of small motion considerably. However, we believe that this could be mitigated by using active search, *e.g.* by employing a motion model. To further increase robustness, we plan to investigate in a regularization term that penalizes deformation caused by errors in camera tracking. In addition, we plan to add the possibility of dynamically extending the deformed template as camera moves around.

5   Conclusion

We presented a real-time method for simultaneous tracking and reconstruction of non-planar templates. While we remove the planarity constraint inherent to classical template tracking, we still benefit from all available pixels of the template when building our objective function. We do not impose any constraints on the model deformation, therefore we can equally reconstruct and track templates that are smooth or have creases. The tracking precision of our method is very good compared to the ground truth. This proves that even with only an approximate shape of the template recovered on-line, the tracking is more stable compared to planar template tracking methods. Furthermore, and in contrast to SfM and SLAM methods, the proposed algorithm still works well for low textured objects and in presence of strong blur.

References

1. Baker, S., Matthews, I.: Lucas-kanade 20 years on: A unifying framework. IJCV 56(3), 221–255 (2004)
2. Bartoli, A., Zisserman, A.: Direct estimation of non-rigid registrations. In: BMVC (2004)
3. Benhimane, S., Malis, E.: Homography-based 2d visual tracking and servoing. Special Joint Issue IJCV/IJRR on Robot and Vision. Published in The International Journal of Robotics Research 26(7), 661–676 (2007)
4. Benhimane, S., Malis, E.: Integration of euclidean constraints in template based visual tracking of piecewise-planar scenes. In: IROS (2006)
5. Datta, A., Sheikh, Y., Kanade, T.: Linear motion estimation for systems of articulated planes. In: CVPR (2008)
6. Davison, A.J., Reid, I.D., Molton, N.D., Stasse, O.: MonoSLAM: Real-time single camera SLAM. PAMI 26(6), 1052–1067 (2007)
7. Gay-Bellile, V., Bartoli, A., Sayd, P.: Direct estimation of non-rigid registrations with image-based self-occlusion reasoning. PAMI 32, 87–104 (2009)
8. Hilsmann, A., Schneider, D.C., Eisert, P.: Realistic cloth augmentation in single view under occlusion. Computers & Graphics (2010)
9. Jurie, F., Dhome, M.: Hyperplane approximation for template matching. PAMI 24, 996–1000 (2002)
10. Klein, G., Murray, D.: Parallel tracking and mapping for small AR workspaces. In: ISMAR (2007)
11. Lieberknecht, S., Benhimane, S., Meier, P., Navab, N.: A dataset and evaluation methodology for template-based tracking algorithms. In: ISMAR (2009)
12. Lucas, B., Kanade, T.: An Iterative Image Registration Technique with an Application to Stereo Vision. In: IJCAI (1981)
13. Newcombe, R., Davison, A.: Live dense reconstruction with a single moving camera. In: CVPR (2010)
14. Pilet, J., Lepetit, V., Fua, P.: Fast non-rigid surface detection, registration and realistic augmentation. IJCV 76(2), 109–112 (2008)
15. Salzmann, M., Fua, P.: Reconstructing sharply folding surfaces: A convex formulation. In: CVPR (2009)
16. Salzmann, M., Urtasun, R., Fua, P.: Local deformation models for monocular 3d shape recovery. In: CVPR (2008)
17. Silveira, G., Malis, E.: Unified direct visual tracking of rigid and deformable surfaces under generic illumination changes in grayscale and color images. IJCV 89(1), 84–105 (2010)
18. Triggs, B., Mclauchlan, P.F., Hartley, R.I., Fitzgibbon, A.W.: Bundle adjustment – a modern synthesis. In: Proceedings of the International Workshop on Vision Algorithms: Theory and Practice (2000)
19. Varol, A., Salzmann, M., Tola, E., Fua, P.: Template-free monocular reconstruction of deformable surfaces. In: ICCV (2009)
20. Wedel, A., Pock, T., Zach, C., Bischof, H., Cremers, D.: An Improved Algorithm for TV-L1 Optical Flow. In: Cremers, D., Rosenhahn, B., Yuille, A.L., Schmidt, F.R. (eds.) Statistical and Geometrical Approaches to Visual Motion Analysis. LNCS, vol. 5604, pp. 23–45. Springer, Heidelberg (2009)

Multi-target Tracking in Crowded Scenes

Jie Yu[1], Dirk Farin[1], and Bernt Schiele[2]

[1] Corporate Research Advance Engineering Multimedia
Robert Bosch GmbH, Germany
[2] MPI Informatics, Saabrucken, Germany

Abstract. In this paper, we propose a two-phase tracking algorithm for multi-target tracking in crowded scenes. The first phase extracts an over-complete set of tracklets as potential fragments of true object tracks by considering the local temporal context of dense detection-scores. The second phase employs a Bayesian formulation to find the most probable set of tracks in a range of frames. A major difference to previous algorithms is that tracklet confidences are not directly used during track generation in the second phase. This decreases the influence of those effects, which are difficult to model during detection (e.g. occlusions, bad illumination), in the track generation. Instead, the algorithm starts with a detection-confidence model derived from a trained detector. Then, tracking-by-detection (TBD) is applied on the confidence volume over several frames to generate tracklets which are considered as enhanced detections. As our experiments show, detection performance of the tracklet detections significantly outperforms the raw detections. The second phase of the algorithm employs a new multi-frame Bayesian formulation that estimates the number of tracks as well as their location with an MCMC process. Experimental results indicate that our approach outperforms the state-of-the-art in crowded scenes.

1 Introduction

Tracking is a key issue in various video-based applications, such as surveillance, video retrieval systems, robotics, etc. However, multi-target tracking, especially in crowded scenes, is still one of the most challenging problems, due to difficulties such as occlusions, association complexity and measurement noise.

In recent years, much progress in object detection has been made and many detector-based tracking approaches e.g. [1,10,18] have been proposed. In contrast to background-model based approaches, detector-based tracking is robust against changing backgrounds and moving cameras. It can also be used in crowded scenes, where learning and updating the background model are often impractical.

However, object-model learning is also challenging. For some object classes with large appearance variations, e.g. people, detectors can not distinguish objects from the background reliably, e.g. due to clutter and partial occlusions. Such uncertainties cause erroneous detections when using a single-frame object detector only. Whilst temporal context can improve detections, the sparse and discrete nature of single-frame detectors (that use e.g. a non-maximum suppression to

R. Mester and M. Felsberg (Eds.): DAGM 2011, LNCS 6835, pp. 406–415, 2011.

sparsify detections) are unsuitable for this purpose, as too much information is discarded. In contrast, their dense and continuous raw detection-scores are more suitable for modeling the temporal context. In our work, we propose an efficient way to explore the spatial-temporal volume of dense detection-scores and extract tracklets from this volume. With an inhomogeneous Poisson process [8], we describe the tracklets as multi-frame observations without confidences originated from the corresponding tracks. Thus, based on the density of tracklets, the number of targets as well as their states can be estimated in a multi-frame tracking framework.

This paper presents three main contributions. Firstly, an efficient method to explore the spatial-temporal context of targets based on the continuous detection-scores is introduced in Section 3.1, Secondly, a new tracking framework based on multi-frame observations is proposed. In this framework, we use the density of tracklets rather than their detection-confidences as measurements for multi-frame tracking, to avoid the problem of instable detection-confidences due to occlusions and cluttered background. Finally, the experiments (Section 4) show a significant improvement of detection performance by employing tracklet detections. Our tracking algorithm outperforms the state-of-the-art method in crowded scenes.

2   Related Work

Significant progress in object detection recently has motivated research interest in detector-based tracking. Some approaches resolve the tracking problem by associating tracklets, i.e. short measurement sequences, using a global matching algorithm, e.g. [1,10]. These approaches are globally optimal in the sense of maximum-a-posteriori (MAP) probability. But they are often unsuitable for time-critical online applications. Moreover, detection-scores below the threshold-value are discarded, which could have been helpful information for linking tracklets. Wu and Nevatia [18] process online-tracking by associating detection responses of multiple confidence levels, which are generated by varying the thresholds. This algorithm is actually a compromise between efficiency (hard decision) and completeness (continuous scores).

Other algorithms make use of the intermediate output of detectors for tracking directly on the dense detection-score volume (TBD). In this case, detection decision, e.g. from thresholding, is delayed and tracking is performed on the raw measurements. It was first proposed for tracking weakly detected objects in radar applications where the SNR is low [15]. Recently, TBD has also been used for detector-based tracking. One category is online-boosting based tracking, e.g. [2]. They employ supervised or semi-supervised learning methods to distinguish the specific object from the background. However, drifting as a result from self-enforced wrong updates remains an issue. Another category is based on detectors trained offline [5], [14], [6]. In the work of Breitenstein et al. [5], they integrate the continuous detection-scores in a particle-filter framework. However, to avoid the exponential growth in the number of particles needed to represent the joint state space, they use independent particle sets for each target, which may

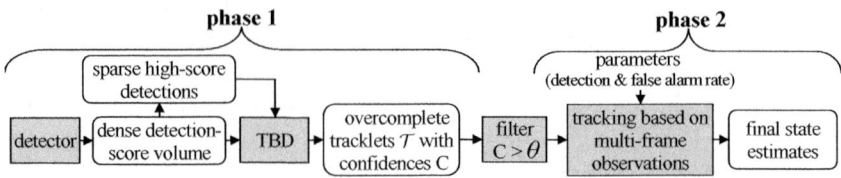

Fig. 1. The pipeline of our tracking system. TBD stands for tracking-by-detection.

have problems with interacting objects and occlusions. [14] generates a global spatial-temporal volume by combining detection-scores with ground-plane and background information. In this confidence volume, they apply a particle-filter to find the trajectories. Due to the lack of individual information in detection responses, such an optimization on responses over a long time is not robust against frequent interactions or occlusions between targets.

Building on the idea of tracklets, e.g. used in [1], we explore the local spatial-temporal volume of dense detection-scores in the form of tracklets, which are shown to improve detection significantly. As long tracks are not considered, it is more robust against occlusions. Based on the density of these tracklets, instead of the instable detection-confidences, a multi-frame tracking framework is proposed to estimate the target states.

3   Multi-target Tracking Based on Dense Detection-Scores

Fig. 1 depicts our tracking framework which consists of two phases. First, over-complete tracklets are extracted by exploiting the local spatial-temporal context of detection-scores. Then, based on the density distribution of tracklets, we propose a Bayesian framework to estimate the target states jointly.

3.1   Generation of Tracklets

In many of the previous detector-based approaches, the high-score detections are used as input for tracking. However, these detections are sparse and unreliable in situations such as occlusions or complex backgrounds. For example, the detection-score often decreases when the object is partially occluded and thus discarded by thresholding. But in the temporal context, these responses are important cues for detecting the object completely and accurately over frames. On the other hand, some stochastically generated false alarms, which usually have high detection-scores for only one or two frames, can also be characterized by their large changes of the detection-scores over a short duration. In these situations, a frame-based threshold discards too much useful information. Thus, instead of using single-frame detections, tracklets $\mathcal{T}$ are extracted from the response volume as observations for tracking, where each tracklet $T \in \mathcal{T}$ is a sequence of target states $\{x_k, x_{k+1}, \cdots, x_{k+l-1}\}$ with a fixed length l.

We apply the detector on the input images $\mathcal{I} = \{\mathbf{I}_1, \mathbf{I}_2, \cdots, \mathbf{I}_k\}$ and obtain the detection responses $\mathcal{F} = \{\mathbf{F}_1, \mathbf{F}_2, \cdots, \mathbf{F}_k\}$, where $\mathbf{F}_t$ are the responses at frame

t. Ideally, tracklets $\mathcal{T}$ could be determined from the response volume $\mathcal{F}$ jointly. However, such a global optimization on $P(\mathcal{F}, \mathcal{T})$ is computationally expensive, especially when the number of targets is high. As a compromise, we determine an overcomplete set of tracklets, where each tracklet $T \in \mathcal{T}$ is found separately in a local response volume. Intuitively, such local volumes should be chosen around high-score detections. More specifically, for each high-score detection d at frame t, a temporal window $[t, t + l - 1]$ and a spatial neighborhood, depending on the assumed maximal velocity of a target (see (3)) and the size of the temporal window, are specified. In this spatial-temporal volume, we define the observation of a state x as a small spatial neighborhood around x at each frame s, denoted as $\mathbf{F}_{s|x}$. Let $\mathcal{F}_{t,d}$ be the set of the frame observations $\mathbf{F}_{s|x}$ in the local spatial-temporal volume, a tracklet is determined by maximizing the joint probability:

$$T^* = \arg \max_T P(\mathcal{F}_{t,d}, T) \, . \tag{1}$$

Using a hidden Markov model of first order, i.e. assuming state x_s is only dependent of the previous state x_{s-1}, the joint probability can be reformed as

$$P(\mathcal{F}_{t,d}, T) = P(\mathcal{F}_{t,d}|T)P(T) = \underbrace{\prod_{s=t}^{t+l-1} P(\mathbf{F}_{s|x}|x_s)}_{observation} \underbrace{\prod_{s=t+1}^{t+l-1} P(x_s|x_{s-1})}_{transition\ prob.} \underbrace{P(x_t)}_{init.\ prob.} \, .$$
$$\tag{2}$$

Initial probability models the a-priori state distribution of objects. The scene knowledge can be modeled in this distribution. Without explicit information, we set $P(x_t)$ as a uniform distribution.

Transition probability is modeled by a gating function, which assumes a maximum velocity δ of targets:

$$P(x_s|x_{s-1}) = \begin{cases} 1/c & \text{if } x_s \in \Delta(\delta, x_{s-1}) \, , \\ 0 & \text{otherwise,} \end{cases} \tag{3}$$

where $\Delta(\delta, x_{s-1})$ is a spatial neighborhood of x_{s-1} defined by δ and $c = |\Delta(\delta, x_{s-1})|$ is the normalization factor.

Observation Model is approximated by the maximal response f_r from $\mathbf{F}_{s|x}$ and $P(f_r|x_s)$ can be learned by fitting the responses on a validation dataset.

Thus, optimal tracklets initialized by the high-score detections can be determined by using the Viterbi Algorithm. In this way, weak detections between high-score detections can be recovered and only a relatively low joint probability $P(\mathcal{F}_{t,d}, T)$ is assigned to 'isolated' false alarms. By setting a threshold θ on $P(\mathcal{F}_{t,d}, T)$, such false positive detections can be eliminated. As the optimization in a local volume is sensitive to initializations (starting frames and positions), overcomplete tracklets are generated, i.e. initialized from all high-score detections. In this way, our approach is robust against missing or inaccurate detections (see Fig. 3). Besides, dense tracklets would be generated in volumes with "continuous" high scores. Hence, the density of tracklets provides an alternative to detection-confidences as measures for the state-estimation.

3.2   Multi-target Tracking from Tracklets

The tracklets generated as described previously are an overcomplete set of track fragments. The remaining problem considered in this section is to estimate the number of targets and their tracks based on the observations of overlapping tracklets. To this end, we propose an approach similar to multiple hypothesis tracking (MHT) [7,4], which is a multi-target tracking with deferred decision. In our tracking model, tracklets T are considered as multi-frame observations and an inhomogeneous Poisson model [8] is used to describe the generation process of the set of tracklets from the tracks to be estimated. The main difference to conventional data-association based methods like JPDA [13,11] is that no explicit association has to be made. In this model, the density of tracklets, instead of their detection-confidences, are used as measurements, because of the discrete nature of the Poisson process. Besides, detection-confidences are instable due to e.g. occlusions, clutters, or bad illumination.

The advantage of multi-frame observations is that they provide clues for not only positions of targets at each frame, but also their temporal developments. Because tracklets are overlapping, it is easier to identify related tracklets than in the case of single-frame detections. Thus, the number of hypotheses that must be considered is reduced. This leads to a lower computational complexity.

Problem formulation: The multi-target state is $\mathcal{X}_t = \{X_t^1, \cdots, X_t^n\}$, where n is number of targets up to frame t and each track X_t^i is a sequence of target states. The observations are the tracklets $\mathcal{T}_t = \{T_t^1, \cdots, T_t^m\}$ from Section 3.1. The standard Bayesian formulation is applied to update the belief about the multi-target state:

$$P(\mathcal{X}_t|\mathcal{T}_t) \propto P(\mathcal{T}_t|\mathcal{X}_t)P(\mathcal{X}_t) \, . \tag{4}$$

In the following, the observation model and the prior model are detailed. For notational simplicity we omit the time index t.

Observation model: The inhomogeneous Poisson point process is used to model the likelihood function [8]. It assumes that the received observations $\mathcal{T}$ are generated by (conditionally independent) superposition of observations from $n + 1$ sources, of which n are the targets $\mathcal{X}$ and the extra one is for the background clutter. Compared to the conventional likelihood model, complexity is significantly reduced as no explicit association between targets and observations is made and multiple observations originating from a target are allowed. Both the number of the observations and their spatial distribution are considered in this model. The joint likelihood of m observations $\mathcal{T} = \{T^1, \cdots, T^m\}$ for multi-target $\mathcal{X} = (X^1, X^2, \cdots, X^n)$ are [8]:

$$P(\mathcal{T}|\mathcal{X}) = \frac{e^{-\mu}}{m!} \prod_{j=1}^{m} \lambda(T^j|\mathcal{X}) = \frac{e^{-\mu}}{m!} \prod_{j=1}^{m} \sum_{i=0}^{n} \lambda_i(T^j|X^i) \, , \tag{5}$$

where $\mu = \sum_{i=0}^{n} \mu_i$ is the number of expected observations in the image area A, μ_i is the expected observations from target X^i, and $\lambda_i(p|X^i)$ describes the spatial density of observations in A with $\mu_i = \int_A \lambda_i(p|X)dp$. λ_0 models the observations from clutter. We assume λ_0 uniformly distributed in A, i.e. $\lambda_0(p|X^0) = \rho$. This model was originally defined for single-frame observations. It can be easily extended for multi-frame observations:

$$P(\mathcal{T}|\mathcal{X}) = \underbrace{\frac{e^{-M}}{(m \cdot l)!}}_{\text{expected \#observations}} \underbrace{\prod_{j=1}^{m} \left(\rho^l + \sum_{i=1}^{n} \Lambda_i(T^j|X^i) \right)}_{\text{observation spatial density}}, \qquad (6)$$

where l is the length of tracklets and $M = \sum_i M_i$ is the expected number of observations originating from targets $\{X^i\}_{i=1\cdots n}$. Let $A_{i,j}$ be the intersection frames of X^i and T^j. The multi-frame observation spatial density $\Lambda_i(T^j|X^i)$ is

$$\Lambda_i(T^j|X^i) = \rho^{l-|A_{i,j}|} \prod_{s \in A_{i,j}} M_i g(z_s|x_s), \qquad (7)$$

where $g(z_s|x_s)$ assumes a Gaussian distribution of observations z_s around the corresponding target x_s at each frame s. Substituting (7) into (6), we have

$$P(\mathcal{T}|\mathcal{X}) = c_1 e^{-M} \prod_{j=1}^{m} \left(1 + \sum_{i=1}^{n} \prod_{s \in A_{i,j}} c_2 g(z_s|x_s) \right), \qquad (8)$$

where c_1 is a constant independent of the tracks $\mathcal{X}$ and $c_2 = \frac{\mu_i}{\rho}$ models the signal-to-noise-ratio. In the implementation, the expected number of observations for each target is determined by $M_i = |X^i| \cdot l \cdot P_d$, where P_d is the detection rate.

However, for two very close targets, i.e. not only at one frame but several frames in our case, there is a problem of merged observations (see Fig. 2(a)). This leads to an ambiguity in the state estimation regarding the number of targets and the distribution for each target. In Fig. 2(b), two tracks and several tracklets (multi-frame observations) are visualized. The spatial intensities of tracklets $\sum_i \Lambda_i$ is indicated by the line width. While the overlap with a track increases the spatial intensity (e.g. T^1 and T^2, either a spatial deviation (T^3) or a temporal inconsistency (T^4) reduces the spatial intensity. It shows that tracklets provide strong clues in spatial as well as in temporal dimension for state estimation.

Prior probability: By assuming an independent and constant-velocity motion of targets, we penalize sudden changes in velocity:

$$P(\mathcal{X}) = \prod_{X \in \mathcal{X}} P(X) = \prod_{X \in \mathcal{X}} P(\|X''\|_\infty), \qquad (9)$$

where X'' the second-order motion-vector , i.e. accelerations at each frame, and $\| \bullet \|_\infty$ is the maximum norm. A Gaussian function $G(0, \sigma_m)$ is used to model the prior probability $P(\|X''\|_\infty)$. The parameter σ_m is learned from some training sequences. Accelerations are normalized according to the target size, so that they are invariant to the 3D projection. Intuitively, $\|X''\|_\infty$ increases as tracks get longer. Therefore, different σ_m are learned for different track lengths.

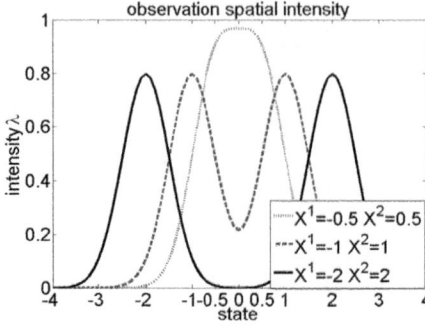
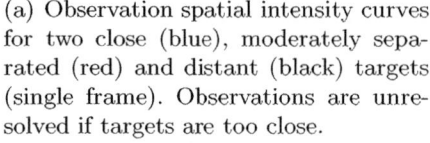
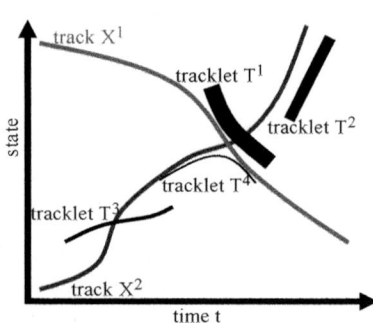

(a) Observation spatial intensity curves for two close (blue), moderately separated (red) and distant (black) targets (single frame). Observations are unresolved if targets are too close.

(b) Examples of tracks and tracklets. The spatial and temporal consistency of tracklets to tracks is important for the observation spatial intensities $\sum_i \Lambda_i$ (visualized by the line width of tracklets).

Fig. 2. Examples of observation spatial intensity for (a) single- and (b) multi-frame observations. We assume a Gaussian distribution of observations around the corresponding target.

State estimation: After specifying observation likelihood (8) and prior probability (9), multi-target states $\mathcal{X}$ can be estimated by maximizing the posterior distribution in (4). Let O be all frame-states of tracklet $\mathcal{T}$. A possible solution of $\mathcal{X}$ is a set of tracks $\{X^1, \cdots, X^n\}$, where each track X^i consists of a sequence of states from O and n is an unknown variable. Additionally, a maximum velocity of any target is assumed to reduce the solution space. For the reason of efficiency, the Markov chain Monte Carlo (MCMC) approach is employed to sample instead of enumerating all possible solutions. Similar to the multi-scan MCMCDA algorithm in [11], a variation of transition types are defined to initialize, terminate, split, merge, extend, reduce and switch tracks by sampling with the MCMC algorithm. As multi-frame observations are used, the convergence rate is fast. For example, about 2000 iterations are sufficient to track more than 20 targets in our experiments. Furthermore, a temporal window $[t - L + 1, \cdots, t]$ of size L can be set, so that only the last L frames are revisited for the estimation.

4   Experiments

In this work, a cascade Adaboost classifier [17] trained on head-and-shoulder-patches is used, as the head-and-shoulder part of most people is visible in crowded scenes. For the evaluation, we use video sequences of crowded scenes from PETS2007 [16], MCTTR [9] and PETS2009 [12].

Detection Performance: First, we want to show the improvement of detection performance by using the proposed tracklets (the first phase of our algorithm, Section 3.1). In this experiment, we vary the length of tracklets. To compare

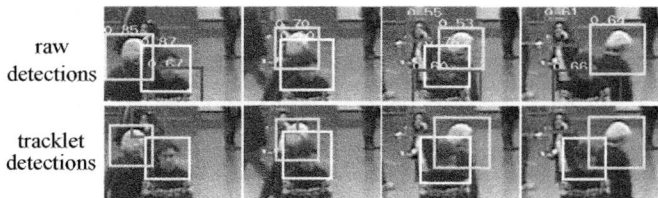

raw detections

tracklet detections

Fig. 3. Raw detections (first row) vs. tracklet detections (second row). The detection-scores of the objects (numbers above bounding boxes) are not stable, which leads to missing detections. These missing detections are recovered by our tracklet approach. Furthermore, false alarms are also reduced.

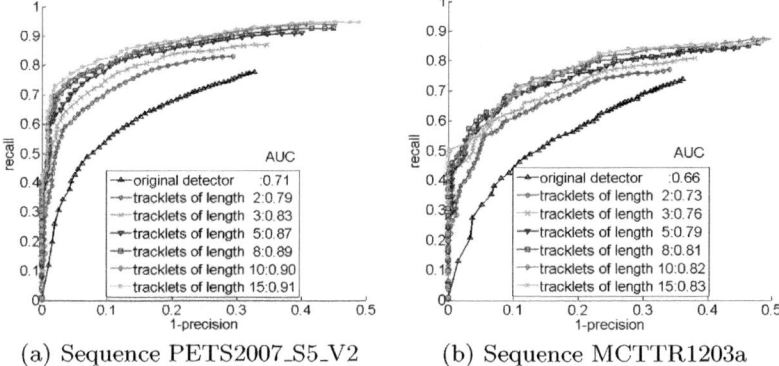

(a) Sequence PETS2007_S5_V2   (b) Sequence MCTTR1203a

Fig. 4. Comparison of detection-performance of tracklets and the original detector (black lines). Tracklets achieve much better results than the original detector. The improvement increases with the length of tracklets.

with the original detector, precision-recall curves are computed by adjusting the threshold value for the joint probability $P(\mathcal{F}_{t,d}, T)$. In Fig. 4, recall rates are significantly improved by tracklets which exploit the temporal context of strong detections. Further, many false positives of the original detector, even with high detection-scores (left-side of the curve), are eliminated. It proves the effectiveness of tracklets by removing the sporadic false alarms with high detection-scores. The performance increases also with the length of tracklets. However, the improvements saturate at length 10.

Tracking Performance: The proposed tracking algorithm is based on tracklets detections. Fig. 5 shows some tracking results from our complete two-phase approach proposed in Section 3. By modeling false alarms explicitly in the likelihood model and introducing the motion model, our approach is robust against some outliers in the generated tracklets (Fig 5(a)). However, some false alarms still remain (Fig. 5(c)). Most of them do not change appearance much over time, hence relatively constant detection-responses are obtained. In this situation, the proposed approach can not distinguish them from the correct target, as the detector is the only source of information for tracking. Combination of different detectors could probably alleviate this problem.

(a)   (b)   (c)

Fig. 5. (a) Tracking output (yellow lines) from tracklets (red lines). The track estimates are robust against the outliers in tracklets. (b) Tracking output (yellow lines) are compared to the ground truth (blue lines). Targets far from the camera (too small) are not tracked well. (c) Examples of false alarms by tracking. Most of them have relatively constant detection-responses, i.e. with stable appearance over time.

Table 1. Quantitative evaluation. Compared to the results in [6] on PETS2009, our algorithm has much better precision (MOTP) and similar accuracy (MOTA).

Seq.	HD RailwA	HD RailwB	PETS2007 S5-V2	MCTTR 1203a	PETS2009 S2-L2	PETS2009 S2-L3
MOTP	83.8%	82.7%	81%	78.8%	79.1% (51.3% [6])	80.1% (52.1% [6])
MOTA	83.9%	72.4%	72.6%	60.7%	55.1% (50.0% [6])	61.0% (67.5% [6])

The CLEAR MOP metrics [3] are used to evaluate the tracking performance quantitatively. The precision score MOTP (intersection over union of bounding boxes) and the accuracy score MOTA (composed of false negative rate, false positive rate and number of ID switches) are computed. The results are shown in Table 1. We also compare our method with the results reported in [6] for PETS2009. Our algorithm achieves a much higher precision score (MOTP). It benefits from our head-shoulder model (suffering less occlusion problems in such crowded scenes) and the exploitation of the dense spatial-temporal volume. The accuracy (MOTA) of our algorithm is similar to that of [6]. Our tracking system is implemented in C++. The runtime depends on the number of targets and tracklets. For the sequence MCTTR1203a with about 20 targets, the processing time of tracking is about 0.8 second/frame. Further optimization is possible.

Summary: The proposed tracklet approach improves the detection performance significantly. Based on that, our algorithm provides robust tracking in challenging crowded sequences and outperforms a state-of-the-art method.

5   Conclusions

In this paper, we propose a novel tracking framework based on the dense output of the detector. From local spatial-temporal volumes of dense detection-scores, tracklets are extracted to improve the detection performance. Instead of using detection-confidences directly, which are usually instable due to occlusion and clutter, overcomplete tracklets are generated and their density is considered as measurements for tracking. By modeling the tracklets and their density with an inhomogeneous Poisson process, target states are estimated efficiently in a Bayesian tracking framework. Compared to the state-of-the-art method, our algorithm achieves better tracking results in crowded scenes.

References

1. Andriluka, M., Roth, S., Schiele, B.: People-tracking-by-detection and people-detection-by-tracking. In: Proc. CVPR (2008)
2. Avidan, S.: Ensemble tracking. In: Proc. CVPR (2005)
3. Bernardin, K., Stiefelhagen, R.: Evaluating multiple object tracking performance: the clear mot metrics. Journal Image Video Process 2008, 1–10 (2008)
4. Blackman, S.: Multiple hypothesis tracking for multiple target tracking. IEEE Trans. on Aerospace and Electronic Systems 19(1), 5–18 (2004)
5. Breitenstein, M., Reichlin, F., Leibe, B., Koller-Meier, E., Van Gool, L.: Robust tracking-by-detection using a detector confidence particle filter. In: ICCV (2009)
6. Breitenstein, M. D., Reichlin, F., Leibe, B., Koller-Meier, E., Van Gool, L.: Online multi-person tracking-by-detection from a single, uncalibrated camera. IEEE Trans. on Pattern Analysis and Machine Intelligence PP(99), 1 (2010)
7. Cox, I.J.: A review of statistical data association techniques for motion correspondence. International Journal of Computer Vision 10(1), 53–66 (1993)
8. Gilholm, K., Godsill, S., Maskell, S., Salmond, D.: Poisson models for extended target and group tracking. In: Proc. SPIE (2005)
9. Home Office: Multiple camera tracking scenario data, http://www.homeoffice.gov.uk/science-research/hosdb/
10. Huang, C., Wu, B., Nevatia, R.: Robust object tracking by hierarchical association of detection responses. In: Forsyth, D., Torr, P., Zisserman, A. (eds.) ECCV 2008, Part II. LNCS, vol. 5303, pp. 788–801. Springer, Heidelberg (2008)
11. Oh, S., Russell, S., Sastry, S.: Markov chain monte carlo data association for multi-target tracking. IEEE Trans. on Automatic Control 54(3), 481–497 (2009)
12. PETS workshop: PETS (2009), http://www.cvg.rdg.ac.uk/PETS2009/
13. Roecker, J.: A class of near optimal jpda algorithms. IEEE Trans. Aerospace and Electronic Systems 30, 504–510 (1994)
14. Stalder, S., Grabner, H., Van Gool, L.: Cascaded confidence filtering for improved tracking-by-detection. In: Daniilidis, K., Maragos, P., Paragios, N. (eds.) ECCV 2010. LNCS, vol. 6311, pp. 369–382. Springer, Heidelberg (2010)
15. Tonissen, S., Evans, R.: Peformance of dynamic programming techniques for track-before-detect. IEEE Trans. on Aerospace and Electronic Systems 32(4), 1440–1451 (1996)
16. UK EPSRC REASON Project: PETS (2007), http://pets2007.net/
17. Viola, P., Jones, M.: Robust real-time object detection. International Journal of Computer Vision 57(2), 137–154 (2002)
18. Wu, B., Nevatia, R.: Detection and tracking of multiple, partially occluded humans by bayesian combination of edgelet based part detectors. International Journal of Computer Vision 75(2), 247–266 (2007)

Efficient and Robust Shape Matching for Model Based Human Motion Capture

Gerard Pons-Moll, Laura Leal-Taixé, Tri Truong, and Bodo Rosenhahn

Leibniz University, Hannover, Germany

Abstract. In this paper we present a robust and efficient shape matching approach for Marker-less Motion Capture. Extracted features such as contour, gradient orientations and the turning function of the shape are embedded in a 1-D string. We formulate shape matching as a Linear Assignment Problem and propose to use Dynamic Time Warping on the string representation of shapes to discard unlikely correspondences and thereby to reduce ambiguities and spurious local minima. Furthermore, the proposed cost matrix pruning results in robustness to scaling, rotation and topological changes and allows to greatly reduce the computational cost. We show that our approach can track fast human motions where standard articulated Iterative Closest Point algorithms fail.

1 Introduction

Markerless motion capture is an active field of research [2, 3, 9, 10, 23]. The high dimensionality of the state space and the inherent depth ambiguities make estimating 3D motion from 2D images a difficult and interesting problem. The integration of priors learned from training data is now a very popular approach to mantain robustness in difficult conditions [13, 19–22, 26]. Although human pose estimation benefits from learned priors, many applications require a general solution without imposing strong assumptions on the dynamics of the activity to be captured. The majority of algorithms are generative and model based, in which a surface mesh of the subject is matched with 2D image observations. Generative approaches aim at modelling the likelihood with a cost function that measures how well the model explains the image observations. Local optimization (LO) methods estimate the pose by iteratively linearizing the cost function to find a descent direction. Here, recovery from false local minima is a major issue. To overcome such limitations particle based global optimization algorithms have been proposed [9, 10]. However, this last group of approaches, while robust, are computationally very expensive and do not provide a smooth and temporaly consistent motion like local approaches. It has been reported that (LO) can easily get trapped in local minima during fast motions. One reason for that is that correspondences between model and image observations are typicaly obtained with variations of the well known *Iterative Closest Point* (ICP) algorithm [4, 7, 8, 19, 25]. We argue that this practice has led LO algorithms to the inferior performance for capturing highly dynamic activities. In fact, provided with the correct correspondences, LO converges to the correct solution in almost all the cases, even for large displacements.

In this paper, we show how the performance of standard LO is greatly improved by employing a robust and efficient model image association algorithm based on bipartite

R. Mester and M. Felsberg (Eds.): DAGM 2011, LNCS 6835, pp. 416–425, 2011.

graph matching. In order to increase the robustness and decrease the computational cost of the matching problem, extracted shape features such as the turning function of contours and gradients are used to reduce the space of possible associations. By representing the contours as strings, upper and lower bounds for the matches are found using the Longest Common Subsequence (LCS) algorithm. This enables robust tracking even for highly dynamic activities as we will show in the experiments.

2   Related Work

Shape matching is a rich sub-field of computer vision research in itself (see for example [5, 27]). ICP is one of the most popular algorithms for finding correspondences, mainly due to its simplicity. Nonetheless, ICP gets trapped in local minima for sequences with fast motions due to the fact that only the localy closest points are considered. Richer shape descriptors such as Shape Context [15, 29] or Chamfer distance [9] reduce ambiguities in the matching costs. The advantage of Shape Context as used in [15, 29] is that it uses a global optimization algorithm, namely the Hungarian matching algorithm, which provides a globally optimal assignment. This property is particularly useful for fast motions, but unfortunatelly global matching is computationaly very expensive. Contour-based matching exploits the order of the points to improve data association [1]. As presented in [6, 14], shape contours can be expressed as strings, and therefore, the shape matching problem can be solved using string matching methods, which are fast and can be efficiently implemented using dynamic programming. In the context of human pose estimation, sophisticated shape descriptors and matching algorithms have been used in discriminative approaches where the goal is to learn direct mappings from shape or image features to the pose space [2, 3, 11, 15, 21].

However, few works (*e.g.* [24, 29]) have focused on integrating robust shape matching constrains in a generative model based pose estimation algorithm. The main reason is the high complexity of optimal assignment algorithms. As we will show in this work, rich shape descriptors can be used not only to resolve ambiguities in the matching process but also to reduce the computational complexity. This enables us to use a global shape matching method to feed a model based tracker with robust correspondences. Hence, the resulting tracker has the desirable properties of global optimization algorithms such as recovery from tracking failures with reasonable computational complexity.

3   Tracking System

We model human motion by a skeletal kinematic chain containing $N = 22$ joints that are connected by rigid bones. The global position and orientation of the kinematic chain are parameterized by a twist $\xi_0 \in \mathbb{R}^6$ [16]. Together with the joint angles $\Theta := (\theta_1 \ldots \theta_N)$, the configuration of the kinematic chain is fully defined by a $D = 6 + N$-dimensional vector of pose parameters $X = (\xi_0, \Theta)$. We assume here for simplicity that all joints are modelled by concatenating 1 *DoF* revolute joints, for a description of the parameterization using free axes of rotation to model *ball joints* we refer the reader to [18]. Let $\mathcal{J}_i \subseteq \{1, \ldots, n\}$ be the ordered set of parent joint indices of the i-th bone. The absolute rigid motion $\mathbf{G}_i^{TB}$ of the bone is given by concatenating the global transformation matrix $\mathbf{G}_0 = \exp(\hat{\xi}_0)$ and the relative rigid motions matrices $\mathbf{G}_i$ along the chain by

$$\mathbf{G}_i^{TB} = \mathbf{G}_0 \prod_{j \in \mathcal{J}_i} \mathbf{G}_i = \mathbf{G}_0 \prod_{j \in \mathcal{J}_i} \exp(\theta_j \hat{\xi}_j). \tag{1}$$

where $\exp(\theta_j \hat{\xi}_j)$ is the exponential map of the j-th joint and ξ_j is the constant twist of the j-th joint in the chain. A surface mesh of the actor is attached to the kinematic chain by assigning every vertex of the mesh to one of the bones. Let $\bar{\mathbf{p}}$ be the homogeneous coordinate of a mesh vertex $\mathbf{p}$ in the zero pose associated to the i-th bone. For a given pose X, the vertex in a rest position $\bar{\mathbf{p}}$ is transformed using $\bar{\mathbf{p}}(X) = \mathbf{G}_i^{TB}\bar{\mathbf{p}}$.

In order to find correspondences between model points and image features we project the mesh points belonging to the occluding contour $\mathbf{p}_i \in \mathcal{O}$ obtaining a set of 2D projections $\hat{\mathbf{r}}_i \in \mathcal{M}$. Then we match the model projections $\hat{\mathbf{r}}_i \in \mathcal{M}$ to the image contour points $\mathbf{r}_j \in \mathcal{I}$ using the algorithm explained in Sect. 4. Given a set of 2D-2D correspondences we minimize the sum of squared distances between the 3D counter part of the model projections $\mathbf{p}_i$ and the projection rays L_i casted by the 2D image contour points $\mathbf{r}_i$. Let $L_i = (\mathbf{n}_i, \mathbf{m}_i)$ be the Plücker coordinates of the line corresponding to the image point $\mathbf{r}_i$. Then, the cost function for N correspondences can be written as

$$e(\mathbf{X}_t) = \sum_i^N \|\mathbf{e}_i(\mathbf{X}_t)\|^2 = \sum_i^N \|\mathbf{p}_i(\mathbf{X}_t) \times \mathbf{n}_i - \mathbf{m}_i\|^2 \tag{2}$$

where the scalar $e(\mathbf{X}_t) \in \mathbb{R}$ is the total error and $\mathbf{e}_i(\mathbf{X}_t) \in \mathbb{R}^3$ is the individual error associated with the i-th correspondence. To minimize Eq. (2) we use the Levendberg Marquadt algorithm. Let $\mathbf{e} = (\mathbf{e}_1, \ldots \mathbf{e}_N) \in \mathbb{R}^{3N}$ dennote the vector valued error function containing the individual correspondence errors. Then at each iteration the descent step ΔX is found as

$$\Delta X = -(\mathbf{J}^T \mathbf{J} + \mu \mathbf{I})^{-1} \mathbf{J}^T \mathbf{e} \tag{3}$$

where $\mathbf{J} \in \mathbb{R}^{3N \times D}$ is the analytical Jacobian matrix of the vector valued error function w.r.t the pose parameters $\mathbf{J} = \frac{\Delta \mathbf{e}}{\Delta \mathbf{X}}$ and μ is the adaptive damping parameter of the Levendberg Marquadt (LM) algorithm. As with any local method LM can get trapped in local minima. Fortunately, provided with the correct correspondences and adequate adaptive damping parameter μ it converges to the correct solution even for fast motions as we will show in the experiments.

4   Motion Capture with String Matching

To minimize Eq. (2), we must find correspondences between the set of projected mesh points $\hat{\mathbf{r}}_i \in \mathcal{M}$ and the set of contour points $\mathbf{r}_i \in \mathcal{I}$ of the image. We formulate the shape matching as a Linear Assignment Problem and propose to use Dynamic Time Warping on the string representation of the contours to discard semantically dissimilar matchings, thereby greately reducing computational time and increasing robustness to scaling, rotation, holes and topological changes.

4.1 Linear Assignment Problem

Let us define a weighted bipartite graph $G = (V, E)$, where its vertexes (or nodes) are partitioned into two distinct sets: the projected points of the occluding contour of the mesh $\mathcal{M}$ and the contour image points $\mathcal{I}$. All the edges $(i, j) \in E$ of the graph connect a vertex from one of the vertexes sets to the other ($E \subseteq \mathcal{M} \times \mathcal{I}$). Each edge (i, j) has a weight or cost $C(i, j)$, computed using the Euclidean distance. The shape matching problem is then reduced to finding the maximum weighted bipartite matching, which can be formulated as a Linear Assignment Problem (LAP) by defining a set of flags $x_{i,j}$, which take the value 1 when nodes i and j are matched, and 0 otherwise. In this setting, the LAP is formulated as the minimization of the objective function:

$$\min \sum_{i,j} C(i,j)x_{i,j} \quad \text{subject to:} \quad \sum_i x_{i,j} = 1 \text{ for } i \in \mathcal{M} \quad \sum_j x_{i,j} = 1 \text{ for } j \in \mathcal{I}.$$

The algorithms used to solve the LAP can be classified into three categories, depending if they are based on: *maximum flow*, e.g. Hungarian algorithm; *Linear Programming*, e.g. Simplex algorithm; and the methods based on *shortest paths*, like the LAPJV presented by Jonker and Volgenant [12]. In this paper, we use the LAPJV algorithm since its notably faster than the commonly used Hungarian algorithm. Next, we present how we use DTW on 1D shape representations to prune the graph.

4.2 String Representation of Shapes

To map a contour $\mathcal{A}$ onto a 1D string we first parametrize it by the arclength s. Thereby, a contour $\mathcal{A}$ is represented by a set of n ordered points along the curve $\mathcal{A}(s) = (x(s), y(s))$, $s \in \{1 \ldots n\}$ forming a polygon. As a 1D descriptor, we use the cumulative angle function, or turning function $\Theta_{\mathcal{A}}(s)$ of a polygon that measures the angle between the counterclockwise tangent and the x-axis as a function of the arclength s. To leverage the influence of noise and the number sampled points in the contour, we compute the turning function as the cumulative angle differences between robust contour gradients $\nabla I(s)$. Hence, the 1D string representation of the contour is:

$$\Theta_{\mathcal{A}}(n) = \sum_{s=0}^{n} \arccos \left(\frac{\nabla I(s) \cdot \nabla I(s+1)}{\|\nabla I(s)\| \cdot \|\nabla I(s+1)\|} \right) \left(\hat{\mathbf{z}} \cdot \frac{\nabla I(s) \times \nabla I(s+1)}{\|\nabla I(s)\| \cdot \|\nabla I(s+1)\|} \right),$$

where the gradient $\nabla I(s) = \nabla I(x(s), y(s))$ is computed at $x(s), y(s)$ on the silhouette image using Gaussian derivative filters. This results in a more robust and smoother version of the turning function. The second term, where $\hat{\mathbf{z}} = [\,0\,0\,1\,]^T$ is the unit vector in the z direction, simply keeps track of the turning direction taking the value +1 for right hand turns and -1 for left hand turns. Note that this representation is already translation invariant. Now, matching two contours $\mathcal{M}$ and $\mathcal{I}$ simplifies to a comparison between the corresponding strings which have in general different lengths $\Theta_{\mathcal{M}}(s)$, with $s \in \{1, 2 \ldots n\}$, $\Theta_{\mathcal{I}}(t)$ with $t \in \{1, 2 \ldots m\}$. To obtain a scale invariant solution we use the Dynamic Time Warping (DTW) which finds the optimal alignment between strings allowing non-linear deformations along the arclength dimension s as we will explain in Sect. 4.3. This further allows us to be robust to topology changes such as

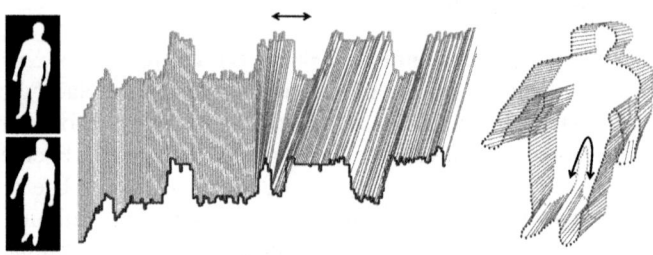

Fig. 1. Matching the turning function with the Longest Common Subsequence (LCS). The LCS allows the string to be compressed and stretched, which allows us to correctly match silhouettes with holes or disappering contours (like the contour between the legs marked with a black arrow).

self occlusions that often occur during tracking. To bring both strings into a common starting salient point, we find the region in both shapes with highest consequent similarity. The problem, which is known as Longest Common Consecutive Substring (LCCS) match, consists in finding the longest strings which are substrings of both $\Theta_{\mathcal{M}}(s)$ and $\Theta_{\mathcal{I}}(s)$ and can be efficiently solved using Dynamic Programming. The substring found is used to bring both sequences to a common starting point. As a result, the turning function is more robust against rotations (see Fig. 2(a)).

4.3   The Wagner-Fischer Algorithm

The most common problem we face when matching human silhouettes are topology changes such as disappearing contours, as shown in an example in Fig. 1. In the first frame, the legs are separated enough so that they can be distinguished in the silhouette. In the next frame though, the legs are too close to each other, and the contour that separates them suddenly dissapears. Intuitively, this means that one contour needs to be warped in a non-linear fashion to match another contour. Dynamic Time Warping (DTW) is a well-known technique to find an optimal alignment between two given sequences, allowing the sequences to be stretched or compressed in order to be better matched. When the sequences consist of discrete symbols, i.e., strings, the objective is to find the Longest Common Subsequence (LCS). The LCS algorithm used in this paper was proposed by R. Wagner and M. Fisher [28], and is based on the *edit distance*, also called the *Levenshtein distance*. Let $A = A_1, A_2 \ldots A_m$ and $B = B_1, B_2 \ldots B_n$ be two strings. The *Levenshtein distance* between A and B, $D(A, B)$ is computed in $O(m, n)$ time in a dynamic programming fashion:

$$D(i,j) = \begin{cases} D(i-1,j-1), & \text{if } A_i = B_j \\ \min \begin{cases} D(i-1,j-1)+1, \\ D(i,j-1)+1, \\ D(i-1,j)+1, \end{cases} & \text{if } A_i \neq B_j \end{cases}$$

where $i = 1 \ldots m$ and $j = 1 \ldots n$. Once we have the edit distance matrix $D(A, B)$, a recursive function is used to find the assignments. Note that the assignments are not

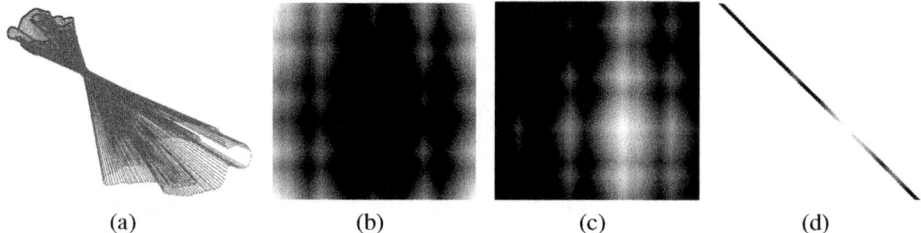

(a)   (b)   (c)   (d)

Fig. 2. (a) Matching of two rotated and scaled shapes with the proposed method. (b) Original distance matrix. (c) Distance matrix after LCCS. (d) Final distance matrix, only the values inside the LCS boundaries are computed; as we can see, most of the edges (in white) are erased, efficiently reducing the computational time and increasing the matching accuracy of the algorithm.

necessarily unique and they depend on the order how we run the LCS algorithm. Therefore, we run the LCS twice, once in each direction, and consider these assignments to be the upper and lower bound of the set of possible assignments. By erasing the elements of the cost matrix $C(i, j)$ in Eq. (4) which are outside these bounds, we reduce most of the edges, (Fig. 2(d)), therefore reducing computational time (see Section 5.1).

5   Experiments

In this section we evaluate our proposed algorithm by comparing it to a standard articulated ICP. For validation, we use the publicly available database (MPI08) [17], which contains a wide variety of human motions ranging from simple ones such as walking to really challenging ones such as lying down, throwing and non-scripted freestyle motions. The database is recorded in an indoor setup with 8 calibrated cameras. It consists of 4 subjects performing 14 different motion patterns. In total, more than 10 minutes of video footage are used for our validation study. Unless otherwise specified, we used 7 cameras for tracking and *left out* one frontal camera for validation. The overlap measure between the validation camera and the mesh silhouette projection is used as error metric. For a sequence of T frames the error measure is computed as

$$e = \frac{1}{T} \sum_{f=0}^{T} \left(1 - \frac{\mathcal{I}_{val}^{f} \cap \mathcal{I}_{templ}^{f}}{\mathcal{I}_{val}^{f} \cup \mathcal{I}_{templ}^{f}} \right) \qquad (4)$$

where $\mathcal{I}_{val}^{f}$ and $\mathcal{I}_{templ}^{f}$ are the silhouette image of the validation camera, and the rendered model silhouette at frame f respectively.

5.1   Computational Time

We compare the computation time for solving the LAP using different 4 different methods, i.e. (1) Hungarian on the distance matrix, (2) Hungarian on the pruned cost matrix obtained with the method explained in Section 4, (3) LAPJV on the distance matrix

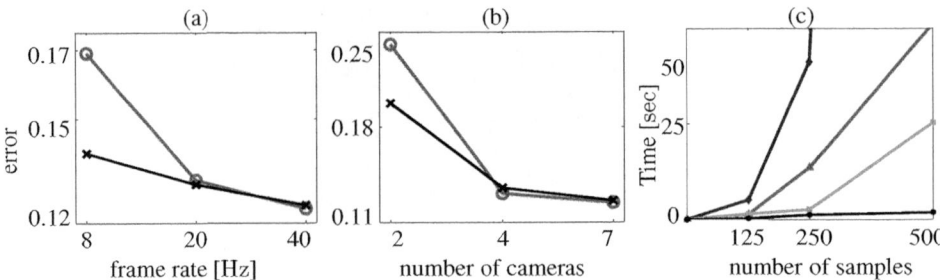

Fig. 3. (a) mean error vs frame rate of a walking sequence: ICP (red •) vs. proposed (black •) , (b) mean error vs the number of cameras: ICP (red •) vs. proposed (black •), (c) comparison of computation time for the methods: Hungarian (blue •) , Hungarian+SM (red •), LAPJV (green •) and proposed (black •)

and (4) our proposed method (LAPJV + pruned cost matrix). In Fig. 3(c) the computational time for matching is shown as a function of the number of sampled points in the contour. Our approach scales much better with the number of sampled points than the other 3 methods thanks to the graph pruning. In addition, the processing time per frame is comparable to that of a simple articulated ICP even though we use global matching.

5.2   ICP vs. Proposed Method

To test the robustness of the proposed approach to fast motions we tracked one of the walking sequences of the database with reduced frame rates. In Fig. 3 **(a)** we show the mean error as a function of the frame rate for the ICP and the proposed method. The proposed method outperforms ICP for low frame rates as ICP easily gets trapped in local minima during matching. Similar results are obtained when the number of cameras are reduced, see Fig. 3(b). In Fig. 5 the tracking error of ICP vs. our proposed method is

Fig. 4. Freestyle sequence: Top row (ICP) and bottom row (proposed)

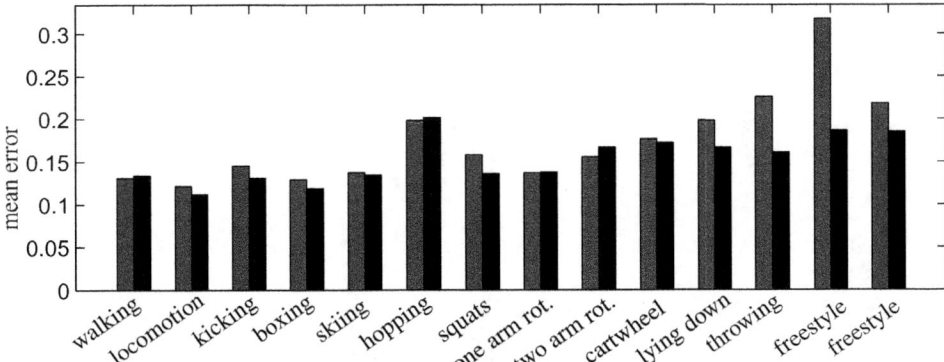

Fig. 5. Mean error for the sequences in the MPI08 database for methods (ICP) in red ● and (proposed) in black ●. Each of the 14 motion patterns was performed by 4 different subjects.

Fig. 6. Freestyle sequence for (ICP) top row and bottom row (proposed). The segmented image is shown with the reconstructed skeleton overlaid.

shown for all the 54 sequences present in MPI08 database. For every motion pattern we show the mean error of the 4 sequences corresponding to each actor. Our method performs better in almost all the sequences. A small improvement is achieved for simple motion patterns such as walking or locomotion because there ICP already performs very well. However, for complex motions such as throwing, lying down and freestyle we obtain much more accurate results. Several qualitative results showing the original segmented image with the reconstructed poses of ICP and the proposed method can be seen in Figs. 4 and 6. Finally, we show the reconstructions obtained our proposed method together with the mesh overlaid on the original images in Fig. 7.

Fig. 7. Tracking results of a cartwheel sequence with our proposed method: top row original image with the model overlaid in yellow and bottom row the reconstructed pose. Even when the segmentation is not correct (see the arm missing in the last image), the pose is correctly recovered.

6   Conclusions

We have presented a robust shape matching approach based on strings for Markerless Motion Capture. Under a generative pose estimation algorithm, we define a Linear Assignment Problem to find correspondences between model projections and image features. Shape features such as contour and the turning function are used to represent the shapes as 1-D strings. Dynamic Time Warping is then used on the shape strings in order to find upper and lower bounds for the correct matches. The proposed cost matrix pruning effectively lowers the computational complexity and removes most of the non-optimalities typical of local data association algorithms. Quantitative and qualitative experiments show that our method outperforms the commonly used Iterative Closest Point (ICP) for sequences with fast motions. We also show that the proposed method allows tracking at a lowered frame rate, since it is more robust to scale and rotation and is able to deal with topological changes. In future work we will explore the use of string matching algorithms for consistent identification and localization of body parts.

References

1. Adamek, T., O'Connor, N.: Efficient contour-based shape representation and matching, pp. 138–143. MIR (2003)
2. Agarwal, A., Triggs, B.: Recovering 3D human pose from monocular images. TPAMI 28(1), 44–58 (2006)
3. Bo, L., Sminchisescu, C.: Twin gaussian processes for structured prediction. International Journal of Computer Vision (2010)
4. Bregler, C., Malik, J., Pullen, K.: Twist based acquisition and tracking of animal and human kinematics. IJCV 56(3), 179–194 (2004)

5. Bronstein, A., Bronstein, M., Bronstein, M., Kimmel, R.: Numerical geometry of non-rigid shapes. Springer-Verlag New York Inc., Secaucus (2008)
6. Bunke, H., Buhler, U.: Applications of approximate string matching to 2D shape recognition. Pattern Recognition 26(12), 1797–1812 (1993)
7. Corazza, S., Mündermann, L., Gambaretto, E., Ferrigno, G., Andriacchi, T.: Markerless motion capture through visual hull, articulated icp and subject specific model generation. IJCV 87(1), 156–169 (2010)
8. Demirdjian, D.: Combining geometric-and view-based approaches for articulated pose estimation, pp. 183–194 (2004)
9. Deutscher, J., Reid, I.: Articulated body motion capture by stochastic search. IJCV 61(2), 185–205 (2005)
10. Gall, J., Rosenhahn, B., Brox, T., Seidel, H.P.: Optimization and filtering for human motion capture. IJCV 87, 75–92 (2010)
11. Hofmann, M., Gavrila, D.: Multi-view 3d human pose estimation combining single-frame recovery, temporal integration and model adaptation. In: CVPR, pp. 2214–2221 (2009)
12. Jonker, R., Volgenant, A.: A shortest augmenting path algorithm for dense and sparse linear assignment problems. Computing 38(4), 325–340 (1987)
13. Lee, C., Elgammal, A.: Coupled visual and kinematic manifold models for tracking. IJCV (2010)
14. Marzal, A., Palazón, V.: Dynamic time warping of cyclic strings for shape matching. In: ICAPR, pp. 644–652 (2005)
15. Mori, G., Malik, J.: Recovering 3d human body configurations using shape contexts. TPAMI, 1052–1062 (2006)
16. Murray, R., Li, Z., Sastry, S.: A Mathematical Introduction to Robotic Manipulation. CRC Press, Baton Rouge (1994)
17. Pons-Moll, G., Baak, A., Helten, T., Müller, M., Seidel, H.P., Rosenhahn, B.: Multisensor-fusion for 3D full-body human motion capture. In: CVPR, pp. 663–670 (2010)
18. Pons-Moll, G., Rosenhahn, B.: Ball joints for marker-less human motion capture. In: WACV, pp. 1–8 (2009)
19. Rosenhahn, B., Brox, T.: Scaled motion dynamics for markerless motion capture. In: CVPR (2007)
20. Salzmann, M., Urtasun, R.: Combining discriminative and generative methods for 3d deformable surface and articulated pose reconstruction. In: CVPR (June 2010)
21. Shakhnarovich, G., Viola, P., Darrell, T.: Fast pose estimation with parameter-sensitive hashing. In: ICCV, pp. 750–757 (2003)
22. Sidenbladh, H., Black, M., Fleet, D.: Stochastic tracking of 3D human figures using 2D image motion. In: Vernon, D. (ed.) ECCV 2000. LNCS, vol. 1843, pp. 702–718. Springer, Heidelberg (2000)
23. Sigal, L., Balan, L., Black, M.: Combined discriminative and generative articulated pose and non-rigid shape estimation. In: NIPS, pp. 1337–1344 (2008)
24. Sminchisescu, C.: Consistency and coupling in human model likelihoods. In: FG (2002)
25. Sminchisescu, C., Triggs, B.: Covariance scaled sampling for monocular 3D body tracking. In: CVPR, vol. 1 (2001)
26. Urtasun, R., Fleet, D.J., Fua, P.: 3D people tracking with gaussian process dynamical models. In: CVPR, vol. 1, pp. 238–245 (2006)
27. Veltkamp, R., Hagedoorn, M.: State of the art in shape matching. Principles of visual information retrieval 87 (2001)
28. Wagner, R.A., Fischer, M.J.: The String-to-String Correction Problem. J. ACM 21(1), 168–173 (1974)
29. Zhao, X., Liu, Y.: Generative estimation of 3D human pose using shape contexts matching. In: Yagi, Y., Kang, S.B., Kweon, I.S., Zha, H. (eds.) ACCV 2007, Part I. LNCS, vol. 4843, pp. 419–429. Springer, Heidelberg (2007)

Image Comparison on the Base of a Combinatorial Matching Algorithm

Benjamin Drayer

Department of Computer Science, University of Freiburg

Abstract. In this paper we compare images based on the constellation of their interest points. The fundamental technique for this comparison is our matching algorithm, that is capable to model miss- and multi-matches, while enforcing one-to-one matches. We associate an energy function for the possible matchings. In order to find the matching with the lowest energy, we reformulate this energy function as Markov Random Field and determine the matching with the lowest energy by an efficient minimization strategy. In the experiments, we compare our algorithm against the normalized cross correlation and a naive forth-and-back best neighbor match algorithm.[1]

1   Introduction

The comparison of complex structures plays an important role in biological and medical research. In many cases the problem of how similar two structures are is posed on a scale where we have one to one correspondences such as eye to eye, leg to leg or mouth to mouth. A good strategy is to first perform a registration (e.g. an elastic registration such as [2]) and then measure the similarity of the pixel intensities e.g. with differences or with the normalized cross correlation (NCC). Difficulties arise, when there are no one-to-one correspondences guaranteed as shown in Figure 1.

| | | |
| (a) | (b) | (c) |

Fig. 1. While (a) and (b) match better according to the shape of the leaves, (a) and (c) are considered more similar regarding the number and arrangement of leaves. In this paper we define a matching based similarity measure that allows to consider both criteria.

---

[1] Recommended for submission to YRF2011 by Junior-Prof. Dr. Olaf Ronneberger.

R. Mester and M. Felsberg (Eds.): DAGM 2011, LNCS 6835, pp. 426–431, 2011.

Obviously every intensity based similarity measure fails, when one leaf corresponds to no or several leaves. This problem also arises in microscope imaging, where we can register and compare different recordings on a rough scale to a certain degree. But when we go in detail, in our case the cell level, the slight differences between the same organs in different individuals become noticeable. One cell may correspond to no cell, to one cell or to many cells and vice versa.

To solve this problem, we apply a similarity measure based on correspondences between interest points of the images. Our main contribution is the matching algorithm that establishes these correspondences. An intuitive way for such a matching is a forth- and back-matching of the best neighbors. The disadvantage of this naive method is, that it cannot favor the one-to-one correspondences. As a result, we get un-proportional many multi-matches and the structure of the image is lost. Whereas our matching algorithm, matches not one key point to its closest neighbor, but it matches a local arrangement so that the one-to-one correspondences are favored and local constellations are properly taken into account.

2   Interest Points and Features

In our application, the substructures that we want to match are roundish. We detect them with a Laplacian of Gaussian as done in [4]. The Laplacian of Gaussian gets a high response not only on round structures but also on elongated structures such as edges and ridges. As in [4], [1], we remove the unstable key points caused by elongated structures and we reject the interest points in the background with an Otsu thresholding.

Considering 2D images, we describe the interest points with local, normalized color histograms. When we deal with 3D images, we compute rotation invariant features based on the spherical harmonics [3], where the spherical harmonics are computed on multiple spheres at different scales in order to better describe the volume around the interest point.

3   Matching Algorithm

With each matching f, we associate an energy in such a way that the one-to-one correspondences are favored. Minimizing the energy function in a brute force manner is too expensive and since the energy function is non-convex, a gradient descent is not an option. Therefore we reformulate the energy as a markov random field and use a combinatorial approach.

For the matching, we consider the sets $\mathcal{A}$ and $\mathcal{B}$, each containing vectors with geometrical and appearance information of the respective interest points. With $d(\mathbf{a}, \mathbf{b})$ we denote the distance between the interest points in the feature space, where $\mathbf{a} \in \mathcal{A}$ and $\mathbf{b} \in \mathcal{B}$. The distance is the l_2-norm, normalized by the average distance of the best neighbor (in $\mathcal{A}$) of each interest point in $\mathcal{A}$.

With f we denote the matching relation from $\mathcal{A}$ to $\mathcal{B}$. Equivalently, we can write that as

$$f : \mathcal{A} \to \mathcal{P}(\mathcal{B}), \tag{1}$$

where $\mathcal{P}$ denotes the power set.

In order to judge the quality of a certain matching, we compute an energy function $E : f \to \mathbb{R}_+$. This energy function consist of the cost for the matchings from $\mathcal{A}$ to $\mathcal{B}$ and the costs for the not matched points in $\mathcal{B}$. With $E_f(\mathbf{a})$ we denote the cost that is contributed by $\mathbf{a}$ under the mapping f:

$$E_f(\mathbf{a}) = \begin{cases} p_\emptyset & f(\mathbf{a}) = \emptyset & \text{(miss match)} \\ d(\mathbf{a}, \mathbf{b}) & f(\mathbf{a}) = \{\mathbf{b}\} & \text{(single match)} \\ p_m + \sum_{\mathbf{b}_i \in f(\mathbf{a})} d(\mathbf{a}, \mathbf{b}_i) & |f(\mathbf{a})| > 1 & \text{(multi match)} \end{cases} \tag{2}$$

where $p_\emptyset$ and p_m are constants that penalize miss- and multi-matches. In our experiments, we choose the average of the distance for $p_\emptyset$ and $p_m = 10$.

So far this energy favors a one-way best neighbor match. We introduce another energy term for the not matched elements from $\mathcal{B}$. This term $E_f(\mathbf{b})$ forces the one-to-one correspondences and therefore it also preserves the local structure. Let $\mathbf{a}_1$ and $\mathbf{a}_2$ be the two closest elements to $\mathbf{b}$. Then we define a miss-match penalty function:

$$p(\mathbf{b}) = \min(\lambda d(\mathbf{a}_1 - \mathbf{b}) + (1 - \lambda) d(\mathbf{a}_2 - \mathbf{b}), \ p_\emptyset), \tag{3}$$

with $\lambda \in [0, 1]$. For our experiments, we choose $\lambda = 0.5$.

For the assignment of the miss-match cost, we need information of the inverse matching relation. The inverse matching relation f_{inv} of $\mathbf{b}$ is:

$$f_{\text{inv}}(\mathbf{b}) = \{\mathbf{a} \in \mathcal{A} | \mathbf{b} \in f(\mathbf{a})\}. \tag{4}$$

The energy term $E_f(\mathbf{b})$ becomes:

$$E(\mathbf{b}) = \begin{cases} p(\mathbf{b}) & f_{\text{inv}}(\mathbf{b}) = \emptyset \\ 0 & else \end{cases}. \tag{5}$$

Altogether the energy function of mapping f is:

$$E(f) = \sum_{\mathbf{a} \in \mathcal{A}} E_f(\mathbf{a}) + \sum_{\mathbf{b} \in \mathcal{B}} E_f(\mathbf{b}). \tag{6}$$

3.1   Reformulation as Markov Random Field

The brute force solution for this problem is too expensive (exponential runtime), even if we restrict the amount of mappings in such a way that an $\mathbf{a}$ can only be mapped to an arbitrary subset of its k closest $\mathbf{b}$ Therefore, we reformulate the problem as a Markov Random Field of the form:

$$E = \sum_{\mathbf{a} \in \mathcal{V}} V_{\mathbf{a}}(l_{\mathbf{a}}) + \sum_{(\mathbf{a}_i, \mathbf{a}_j) \in \mathcal{E}} V_{\mathbf{a}_i \mathbf{a}_j}(l_{\mathbf{a}_i} l_{\mathbf{a}_j}) \tag{7}$$

and can apply sophisticated algorithms such as the *max-sum* solver [5] to minimize the energy in a reasonable time.

The set of nodes $\mathcal{V}$ is $\mathcal{A}$. The set of labels for each $\mathbf{a}$ are the 2^k possible subsets of its k closest $\mathbf{b}$. In our implementation, we choose $k = 5$. The set of edges $\mathcal{E}$

consists of pairs of nodes $(\mathbf{a}_1, \mathbf{a}_2)$ that have at least one common $\mathbf{b}$ in their sets of k closest $\mathbf{b}$, otherwise they don't form an edge.

The unary potential becomes:

$$V_{\mathbf{a}}(l_{\mathbf{a}}) = \begin{cases} p_\emptyset & l_{\mathbf{a}} = \emptyset \quad \text{(miss match)} \\ 0 & |l_{\mathbf{a}}| = 1 \quad \text{(single match)} \\ p_m & |l_{\mathbf{a}}| > 1 \quad \text{(multi match)} \end{cases} \quad (8)$$

The pairwise potential becomes:

$$V_{\mathbf{a}_i, \mathbf{a}_j}(l_{\mathbf{a}_i}, l_{\mathbf{a}_j}) = \sum_{\mathbf{b} \in \{f(\mathbf{a}_i) \cap f(\mathbf{a}_j)\}} \frac{E_{\mathbf{a}_i, \mathbf{a}_j, \mathbf{b}}(l_{\mathbf{a}_i}, l_{\mathbf{a}_j})}{\binom{|f_{\text{inv}}(\mathbf{b})|}{2}}, \quad (9)$$

where

$$E_{\mathbf{a}_i, \mathbf{a}_j, \mathbf{b}}(l_{\mathbf{a}_i}, l_{\mathbf{a}_j}) = \begin{cases} p(\mathbf{b}) & \mathbf{b} \notin l_{\mathbf{a}_i} \wedge \mathbf{b} \notin l_{\mathbf{a}_j} \quad \text{(miss match)} \\ d(\mathbf{a}_i, \mathbf{b}) & \mathbf{b} \in l_{\mathbf{a}_i} \wedge \mathbf{b} \notin l_{\mathbf{a}_j} \quad \text{(single match)} \\ d(\mathbf{a}_j, \mathbf{b}) & \mathbf{b} \notin l_{\mathbf{a}_i} \wedge \mathbf{b} \in l_{\mathbf{a}_j} \quad \text{(single match)} \\ d(\mathbf{a}_i, \mathbf{b}) + d(\mathbf{a}_j, \mathbf{b}) & \mathbf{b} \in l_{\mathbf{a}_i} \wedge \mathbf{b} \in l_{\mathbf{a}_j} \quad \text{(multi match)} \end{cases} \quad (10)$$

We normalize by $\binom{|f_{\text{inv}}(\mathbf{b})|}{2}$, since this is the number of pairs $(\mathbf{a}_1, \mathbf{a}_2)$ that have $\mathbf{b}$ in common.

4 Experiments

We show the performance of our algorithm with two experiments. First, we compute correspondences for different constellations of fruits and second, we apply the matching algorithm on microscopic data of the zebra fish embryo. The correspondences are the base for the similarity measure, where only one-to-one correspondences are taken into account (multi-matches inconsistencies are reduced to their best edge). The similarity measure is:

$$s(\mathcal{A}, \mathcal{B}) = \frac{2}{|\mathcal{A}| + |\mathcal{B}|} \sum_{(\mathbf{a}, \mathbf{b}) \in \mathcal{S}} \frac{1}{1 + d(\mathbf{a}, \mathbf{b})}, \quad (11)$$

where $\mathcal{S}$ denotes the set of one-to-one correspondences.

In Figure 2 we compare our algorithm against the NCC. In the first row of this Figure, we try to match a mixture of apples and kiwis, where the position and the amount of the objects vary. In the second row, we almost keep the position of the fruits, do not vary the amount, but we change the kiwis to apples and vice versa. For the NCC, the case in the second row is more similar, whereas with our matching algorithm we correctly determine that the images in the first row are more similar.

The second part of this experiment (Figure 3) shows the superiority of our multi-matching algorithm over the best neighbor match. By comparing the two

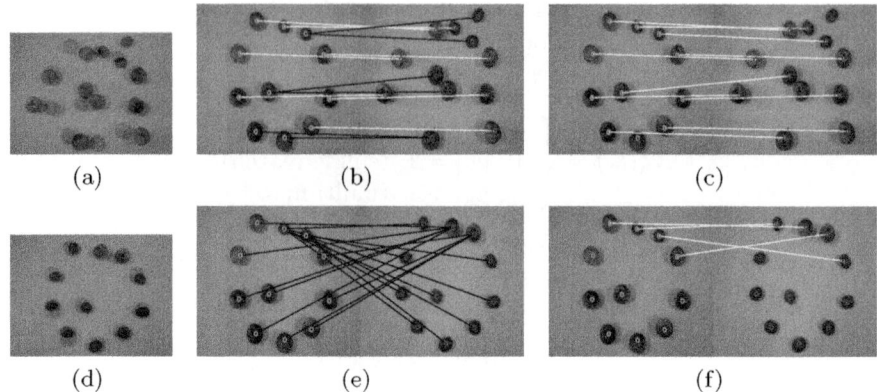

Fig. 2. (a) overlay of the images, similarity=0.2969 (NCC) (b) all edges of multi-match. (c) confident edges of multi-match, similarity=0.836 (d) overlay of the images, similarity=0.7401 (NCC) (e) all edges of multi-match. (f) confident edges of multi-match, similarity=0.331.

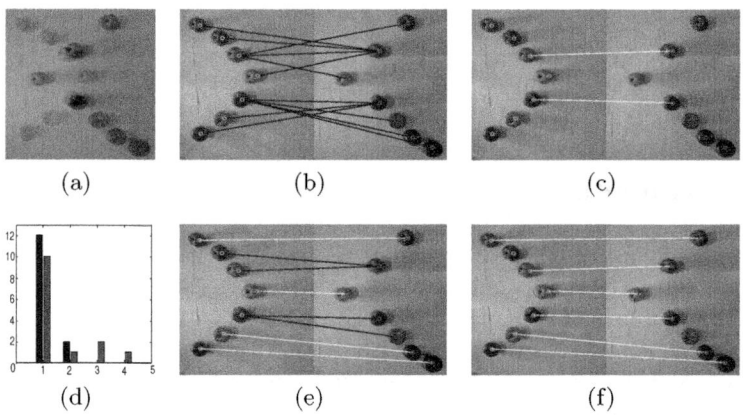

Fig. 3. (a) overlay of the images. (b) all edges of best match. (c) confident edges of best match, similarity=0.412. (d) distribution of matches for the best match (red) and multi-match (blue) algorithm. (e) all edges of multi-match. (f) confident edges of multi-match, similarity=0.748. The blue edges indicate multiple correspondences, the yellow edges indicate one-to-one correspondences.

sets of apples, arranged as bows we see advantageous effects of matching a local neighborhood, especially the preserving of the local structure. The histogram of the matches in Figure 3(d) shows the strong favoritism of the one-to-one correspondences of our approach.

In Figure 4, we show the performance of our matching algorithm on microscopic recordings of the zebra fish embryo. The recordings are taken on the cell level and a dataset measures $800 \times 500 \times 500$ voxel. Based on our matching

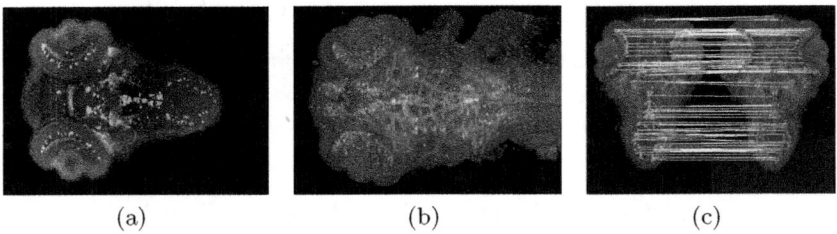

(a)   (b)   (c)

Fig. 4. (a) cells (red) and gene expression (green), (b) maximum intensity projections of the gene expression (c) matching of the same gene expression (of different individuals), green and red circles are the found interest points, yellow lines indicate the correspondences. Due to better visibility this is a maximum intensity projection in z-direction from 220 to 250 μm.

algorithm, we can correctly classify a large database of gene expressions, but as this is a part of a joint unpublished project, only one example can be shown here.

5 Conclusion

In this paper we presented a matching algorithm for a correspondence based similarity measure. We showed the advantages of our comparison method over the normalized cross correlation and the best neighbor match algorithm. Furthermore, we got promising results when we applied the algorithm on microscopic recordings of the zebra fish.

References

1. Allaire, S., Kim, J.J., Breen, S.L., Jaffray, D.A., Pekar, V.: Full orientation invariance and improved feature selectivity of 3D SIFT with application to medical image analysis. In: Computer Vision and Pattern Recognition Workshops (January 2008)
2. Glocker, B., Komodakis, N., Tziritas, G., Navab, N., Paragios, N.: Dense image registration through mrfs and efficient linear programming. Medical Image Analysis 12(6), 731–741 (2008)
3. Kazhdan, M., Funkhouser, T., Rusinkiewicz, S.: Rotation invariant spherical harmonic representation of 3d shape descriptors. In: Proceedings of the 2003 Eurographics/ACM SIGGRAPH Symposium on Geometry Processing, SGP 2003, pp. 156–164. Eurographics Association, Aire-la-Ville (2003)
4. Lowe, D.G.: Distinctive image features from scale-invariant keypoints. Int. J. Comput. Vision 60(2), 91–110 (2004)
5. Werner, T.: A linear programming approach to max-sum problem: A review. IEEE Trans. Pattern Anal. Mach. Intell. 29, 1165–1179 (2007)

Large Displacement Optical Flow for Volumetric Image Sequences[*]

Benjamin Ummenhofer

Department of Computer Science, University of Freiburg

Abstract. In this paper we present a variational optical flow algorithm for volumetric image sequences (3D + time). The algorithm uses descriptor correspondences that allow us to capture large motions. Further we describe a symmetry constraint that considers the forward and the backward flow of an image sequence to improve the accuracy of the flow field.

We have tested our algorithm on real and synthetic data. Our experiments include a quantitative evaluation that show the impact of the algorithm's components. We compare a single core implementation to two parallel implementations, one on a multi-core CPU and one on the GPU.

1 Introduction

For the analysis of biological or medical volumetric data sets, the motion or growth of objects is of great interest. We propose the use of the three-dimensional optical flow field to analyze the motion of such processes. In contrast to conventional volumetric tracking methods, we do not need to segment the tracked objects, which is of great advantage when dealing with objects at the resolution limit of the microscope. The flow field provides dense motion information for every voxel.

An optical flow method for the analysis of biological data should fulfill three requirements. First, the method should be able to capture large displacements because the time resolution of microscopes is limited and fewer exposures prevent the samples from damage. Second, the method should be accurate, so that objects can be tracked over many time steps. Third, the method should be fast. Short runtimes in the area of the frame rate of the microscope allow to use the results to automatically manipulate objects during an experiment.

Our algorithm can capture large displacements by integrating descriptor matching into a variational framework as presented by Brox et al. [3]. We have adapted their *Large Displacement Optical Flow* to volumetric datasets by using a three-dimensional extension of the *Histogram of Oriented Gradients* by Dalal and Triggs [4]. Similar 2D + time HOG descriptors have been used in the context of action recognition by Kläser et al. [6].

---

[*] Recommended for submission to YRF2011 by Prof. Dr. Thomas Brox.

R. Mester and M. Felsberg (Eds.): DAGM 2011, LNCS 6835, pp. 432–437, 2011.
© Springer-Verlag Berlin Heidelberg 2011

We have also integrated the *Symmetrical Optical Flow* proposed by Alvarez et al. [1]. Similar to them, we add an energy term that considers the symmetry between the forward and the backward optical flow. The consideration of the symmetry improves the accuracy of the optical flow field.

To achieve fast runtimes we have implemented our algorithm on parallel hardware such as shared memory computers and graphics processing units (GPU).

2 Variational Model

Like Horn and Schunck [5], we describe the problem of computing the optical flow as an energy minimization problem. Let $I_1(\mathbf{x})$ and $I_2(\mathbf{x})$ be the functions of the first and the second image of an image sequence with $\mathbf{x} = (x, y, z)^T$. The optical flow from the first to the second image (the forward flow) is denoted as $\mathbf{w}_1 = (u_1, v_1, w_1)^T$, where u_1, v_1, w_1 are functions of a position $\mathbf{x}$. The energy functional for the forward flow reads

$$E_1(\mathbf{w}_1) = E_{\text{grey}}(\mathbf{w}_1) + E_{\text{grad}}(\mathbf{w}_1) + E_{\text{smooth}}(\mathbf{w}_1) + E_{\text{match}}(\mathbf{w}_1) + E_{\text{symm}}(\mathbf{w}_1). \tag{1}$$

The distinct energy terms are

$$E_{\text{grey}}(\mathbf{w}_1) = \int_\Omega \Psi\left(|I_2(\mathbf{x} + \mathbf{w}_1) - I_1(\mathbf{x})|^2\right) d\mathbf{x} \tag{2}$$

$$E_{\text{grad}}(\mathbf{w}_1) = \gamma \int_\Omega \Psi\left(|\nabla I_2(\mathbf{x} + \mathbf{w}_1) - \nabla I_1(\mathbf{x})|^2\right) d\mathbf{x} \tag{3}$$

$$E_{\text{smooth}}(\mathbf{w}_1) = \alpha \int_\Omega \Psi\left(|\nabla u_1(\mathbf{x})|^2 + |\nabla v_1(\mathbf{x})|^2 + |\nabla w_1(\mathbf{x})|^2\right) d\mathbf{x} \tag{4}$$

$$E_{\text{match}}(\mathbf{w}_1) = \beta \int_\Omega \delta(\mathbf{x})\rho(\mathbf{x})\Psi\left(|\mathbf{w}_1(\mathbf{x}) - \mathbf{w}_D(\mathbf{x})|^2\right) d\mathbf{x} \tag{5}$$

$$E_{\text{symm}}(\mathbf{w}_1) = \zeta \int_\Omega \Psi\left(|\mathbf{w}_1(\mathbf{x}) + \mathbf{w}_2(\mathbf{x} + \mathbf{w}_1(\mathbf{x}))|^2\right) d\mathbf{x}\,, \tag{6}$$

with the robust penalizer $\Psi(s^2) = \sqrt{s^2 + \epsilon^2}$ and the constant $\epsilon = 0.001$. The descriptor flow $\mathbf{w}_D$ in E_{match} is computed from descriptor correspondences. As we do not compute descriptor correspondences for every voxel, we define that δ is 1 where we have a descriptor correspondence and 0 elsewhere. The function ρ defines a weight for each descriptor correspondence and is explained later. The backward flow is denoted as $\mathbf{w}_2$. All energy terms are weighted relative to the grey value constancy constraint E_{grey} with the factors α, β, γ and ζ.

The minimization of the above energy functional is done similarly to [2], [3]. The functional (1) is minimized in two nested fixed point iterations. The outer fixed point iterations are in the flow $\mathbf{w}_1$ and are combined with a coarse-to-fine strategy. The inner fixed point iterations compute an increment $d\mathbf{w}_1$ and resolve remaining nonlinearities in the equations caused by the Ψ functions.

In the following we describe the computation of the descriptor correspondences and the integration of the symmetrical optical flow into the minimization scheme.

2.1   Descriptor Matching

The idea of the descriptor matching is to integrate a flow $\mathbf{w}_D$ computed from descriptor correspondences between the first and the second image into the variational approach. This is done by the energy term E_{match}. The term drives the optical flow field towards a solution that contains the large displacements.

The flow $\mathbf{w}_D$ is computed on a sparse grid. For each of the grid points we compute a HOG descriptor in I_1 and find the best matching descriptor in the second image I_2. An example is given in Fig. 1, where the feature vector $\mathbf{f}_1$ of the descriptor is matched to the descriptor with feature vector $\mathbf{f}_2$.

To reduce the number of wrong correspondences we apply a consistency check by reverse matching. The best reverse match $\mathbf{f}_1'$ must be within a threshold radius R, otherwise the descriptor correspondence is rejected. A resonable choice for the radius R is the spacing of the grid points.

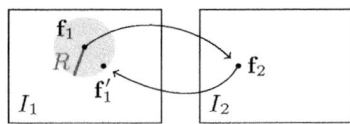

Fig. 1. The descriptor with feature vector $\mathbf{f}_1$ is matched to $\mathbf{f}_2$. The descriptor correspondence $(\mathbf{f}_1, \mathbf{f}_2)$ is rejected if the distance between the reverse match $\mathbf{f}_1'$ and $\mathbf{f}_1$ is greater than R.

Correspondences that pass the test are weighted with the function

$$\rho = \frac{d_2 - d_1}{d_2} \cdot \left(1 - \frac{r}{R}\right) , \qquad (7)$$

where r is the distance between $\mathbf{f}_1$ and $\mathbf{f}_1'$. The d_1, d_2 are the SSD dissimilarity measurements between the best and the second best match (e.g. $d_1 = |\mathbf{f}_1 - \mathbf{f}_2|^2$).

2.2   Symmetrical Optical Flow

The idea of the symmetrical optical flow is that the flow vectors of the forward and backward flow at corresponding points are inverse to each other. This leads to the constraint $\mathbf{w}_1(\mathbf{x}) = -\mathbf{w}_2(\mathbf{x} + \mathbf{w}_1(\mathbf{x}))$ found in the energy term E_{symm}.

The full energy functional of the symmetrical optical flow is

$$E(\mathbf{w}_1, \mathbf{w}_2) = E_1(\mathbf{w}_1) + E_2(\mathbf{w}_2) , \qquad (8)$$

where E_2 is similarly defined as E_1 in Eq. (1). Note that we have chosen that E_1 is not a function of $\mathbf{w}_2$ and E_2 is not a function of $\mathbf{w}_1$. This allows us to alternately compute the forward and the backward flow.

Both flows are estimated once for each level of the coarse-to-fine strategy. On the coarsest level we initialize both flows using the non-symmetrical energy functional that is Eq. (1) without the symmetry term E_{symm}.

3   Results

We have tested our algorithm on synthetic and real data sets. Fig. 2 shows two of the data sets. To prove the abilities of our algorithm we have tested the effects of the symmetrical optical flow and the descriptor matching on both data sets.

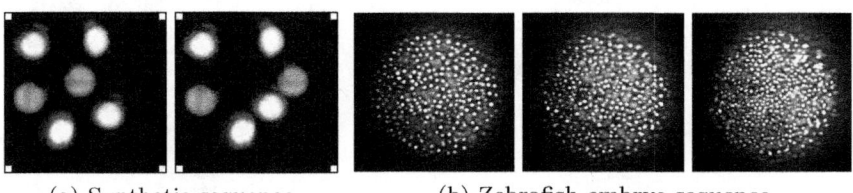

(a) Synthetic sequence   (b) Zebrafish embryo sequence

Fig. 2. Datasets: (a) The synthetic image sequece shows 6 objects in motion. One of the objects is displaced more than its diameter between frames. (b) Zebrafish embryo image sequence recorded with a confocal microscope.

3.1   Synthetic Image Sequence

Table 1 shows the results compared to the ground truth of the synthetic data set. The errors are only computed at the objects in the scene, as the background has no information and its motion is undefined. The results show that the error is

Table 1. Results on the synthetic image sequence with different features activated. Parameters are $\gamma = 3$, $\alpha = 20$, $\beta = 100$, $\zeta = 5$.

	Without E_{match},E_{symm}	Without E_{match}	Without E_{symm}	All features
Angular error	36.44°	35.27°	15.07°	12.30°

dominated by the object with the large displacement. Activating the descriptor matching allows to capture the large displacement and significantly reduces the error. The symmetrical optical flow improves the accuracy but cannot cope with the large displacement.

3.2   Zebrafish Embryo Sequence

To test the performance on this sequence, we compute trajectories from the optical flow field and compare them with the true trajectories of the objects.

Fig. 3 shows the trajectory computed for a fast moving nucleus without (a) and with (b) the symmetry energy term. The computed trajectories are very accurate and allow to track the objects over many time steps. The trajectory shown in Fig. 3(b) is more accurate and diverges after 48 time steps, while the trajectory computed from the flow without the symmetry term diverges after 32 time steps from the actual object trajectory.

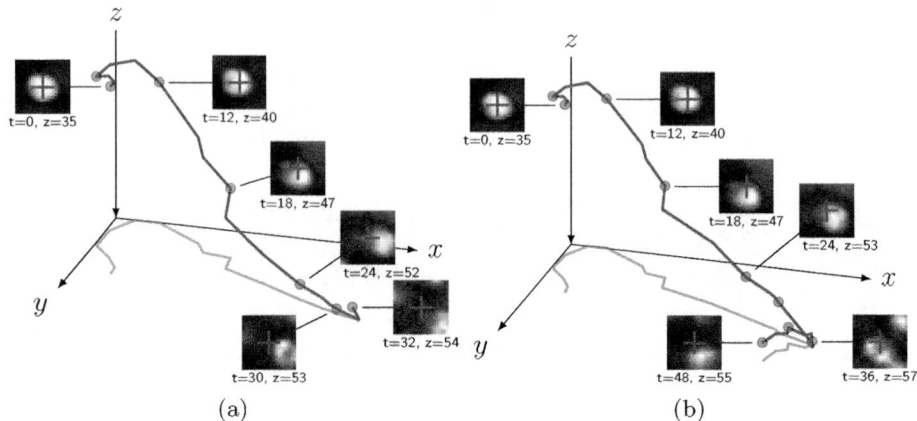

(a)   (b)

Fig. 3. Trajectory of a nucleus computed from the optical flow without (a) and with (b) the symmetry energy term E_{symm}. The length of the trajectory in image (a) is 69μm over 32 time steps. The length of the trajectory in image (b) is 90μm over 48 time steps.

Some of the displacements in the data set can only be captured with descriptor matching. Fig. 4(a,b) shows a nuclei that moves about the size of its diameter. Without the descriptor matching the resulting optical flow field shown in Fig. 4(c) tries to shrink the object (because it is gone). With the descriptor matching enabled, the object motion is correctly described by the flow field shown in Fig. 4(d). The image also shows some distortions that can be explained with false descriptor matches.

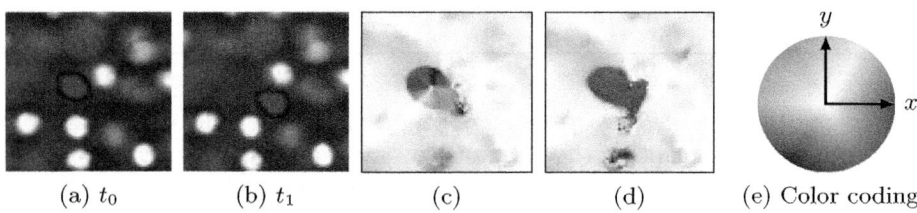

(a) t_0 (b) t_1 (c)   (d)   (e) Color coding

Fig. 4. (a) and (b) show a nucleus (highlighted red) that moves about the size of its diameter between time steps. The images (c) and (d) show the x and y components of the optical flow field computed without (c) and with (d) descriptor matching. The color coding for the optical flows is depicted in image (e).

3.3 Runtime

Table 2 shows a runtime comparison for the CPU and the GPU version of our implementation. The tests were run on a computer with an Intel Xeon 6 cores CPU at 3.33GHz. For the GPU version we used an Nvidia GTX 460 and an Nvidia Quadro 6000.

Table 2. Runtimes for the zebrafish sequence with a resolution of $205 \times 205 \times 41$

	Xeon 1 thread	Xeon 6 threads	Quadro 6000	GTX 460
Runtime in seconds	806.724	267.429	121.489	155.710

The GPU version is quite close to the capture speed of the microscope which is 60 seconds. There is still room for optimization of the GPU code, which will allow to use our method in real time applications with respect to the capture interval of microscopes. For instance, we plan to adapt our generic CG solver to the specific structure of our system matrix.

Acknowledgments. We want to thank Sungmin Song and Wolfgang Driever from the *Wolfgang Driever Lab, Biology I* at the University of Freiburg for providing the data sets used in this work.

References

1. Alvarez, L., Deriche, R., Papadopoulo, T., Sánchez, J.: Symmetrical Dense Optical Flow Estimation with Occlusions Detection. International Journal of Computer Vision 75(3), 371–385 (2007)
2. Brox, T., Bruhn, A., Papenberg, N., Weickert, J.: High accuracy optical flow estimation based on a theory for warping. In: Pajdla, T., Matas, J. (eds.) ECCV 2004. LNCS, vol. 3024, pp. 25–36. Springer, Heidelberg (2004)
3. Brox, T., Malik, J.: Large displacement optical flow: descriptor matching in variational motion estimation. IEEE Transactions on Pattern Analysis and Machine Intelligence 33(3), 500–513 (2011)
4. Dalal, N., Triggs, B.: Histograms of Oriented Gradients for Human Detection. In: IEEE Computer Society Conference on Computer Vision and Pattern Recognition, vol. 1, pp. 886–893 (2005)
5. Horn, B., Schunck, B.: Determining optical flow. Artificial Intelligence 17(1-3), 185–203 (1981)
6. Kläser, A., Marszałek, M., Schmid, C.: A Spatio-Temporal descriptor based on 3D gradients. In: British Machine Vision Conference (September 2008)

Visual Motion Capturing for Kinematic Model Estimation of a Humanoid Robot[*]

Andre Gaschler

Technische Universität München, Germany
gaschler@cs.tum.edu

Abstract. Controlling a tendon-driven robot like the humanoid Ecce is a difficult task, even more so when its kinematics and its pose are not known precisely. In this paper, we present a visual motion capture system to allow both real-time measurements of robot joint angles and model estimation of its kinematics.

Unlike other humanoid robots, Ecce (see Fig. 1A) is completely molded by hand and its joints are not equipped with angle sensors. This anthropomimetic robot design [5] demands for both (i) real-time measurement of joint angles and (ii) model estimation of its kinematics. The underlying principle of this work is that all kinematic model parameters can be derived from visual motion data. Joint angle data finally lay the foundation for physics-based simulation and control of this novel musculoskeletal robot.

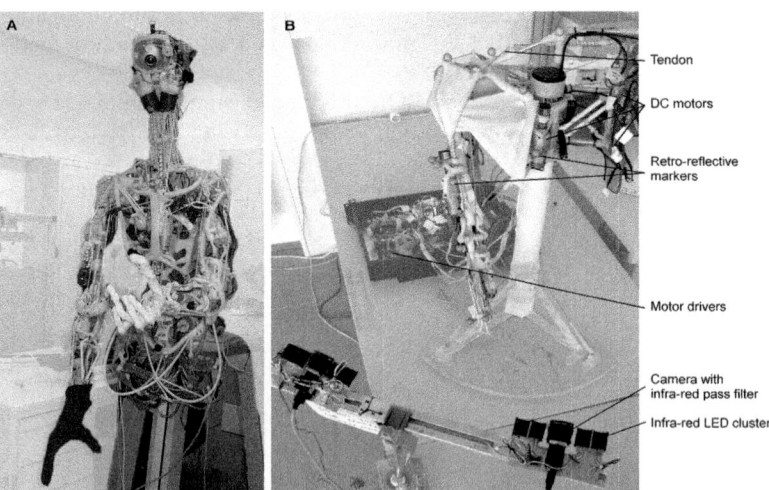

Fig. 1. A: Musculoskeletal humanoid robot Ecce **B:** Shoulder test rig with visual motion capture system, both robots developed within the Eccerobot project [6]

---

[*] Recommended for submission to YRF2011 by supervisor Alois Knoll.

R. Mester and M. Felsberg (Eds.): DAGM 2011, LNCS 6835, pp. 438–443, 2011.

1   Introduction

As for almost all robot control tasks, modeling the kinematic structure and obtaining real-time joint angle data is of crucial importance. Controlling the muscle-based humanoid robot ECCE (Fig. 1A) is still an unresolved problem, but without knowledge of its precise kinematics, only few control approaches can be used at all [1]. However, the novel muscle-based humanoid ECCE is completely molded by hand in a rapid-prototyping process, its skeleton is hand-crafted using the thermoplastic polymorph [6] and its artificial muscles are made of tendon-driven actuators. Therefore, we first need to estimate its kinematic parameters in order to allow approaches to robot simulation and control.

Beyond the need for precise kinematic parameters, real-time measurement of joint angles is also of crucial importance for robot controller design. However, the robot is equipped with ball-and-socket joints, in which direct angle sensors can hardly be incorporated. Creating a three-dimensional angle sensor for a spherical joint is a challenging task: For another tendon-driven robot Kotaro, Urata et al. developed a custom-made sphere joint angle sensor using a micro camera and image processing of markers in the joint socket [11].

Our requirements are slightly different, as we need a means for joint angle measurement that is inexpensive, commercially available and very precise, but not necessarily internal. We therefore decided to use external motion sensing, which can be dedicatedly installed and calibrated at all three robots of the ECCEROBOT project. For that, we first tested a Polhemus Liberty^{TM} magnetic motion capture system. However, the magnetic sensors showed a jitter of up to 5 mm and 3 degrees during motor operation, rendering the magnetic tracking approach impractical for our setup. After further review of motion capture systems, we decided on a *visual stereoscopic solution with passive retro-reflective marker balls and infra-red illumination*, similar to [7]. This solution is available from commodity hardware, cost-effective and allows us to arrange the markers over the full length of the robot's limbs, effectively increasing the precision of orientation and joint angles in comparison to systems with fixed marker sizes. In the following, the setup of our motion capture system is briefly described.

2   Visual Motion Capture System

The overall setup of our motion capture system is shown in Fig. 1B. Each robot limb is equipped with 4 to 6 marker spheres with retro-reflective coating. A stereo camera setup of two PointGrey Flea 2 cameras with 6 mm Pentax optics and a baseline of 477 mm is installed roughly 1 m from the robot. Each camera is enclosed by four $\lambda = 880$ nm LED clusters and equipped with $\lambda_{thresh} = 750$ nm infra-red pass filters.

Marker thresholding, connected component search and 2D coordinate extraction are efficiently implemented at sub-pixel accuracy similar to the standard methods [7]. After that, the 3D coordinates of the marker balls are obtained by optimal 3D triangulation. All these image processing steps are described at length in [4].

2.1 Efficient Rigid Body Detection

Once the 3D marker positions are available, the combined matching and orientation problem of the known rigid marker targets needs to be solved in order to recover the poses of the robot's limbs. Mathematically, the rigid body detection is the problem of aligning a selection Π_M of m from k known marker points M with a selection Π_P of m from n measured points P under a rigid transformation RT. Π_M and Π_P are binary matrices that select and permute 3D points of M and P, respectively. Our rigid body detection step finds a compromise between the number of matching points m and the residual geometric error of the alignment:

$$\underset{\Pi_M, \Pi_P, RT}{\arg\min} \ \|\Pi_P P - RT \ \Pi_M M\|_2 \ \frac{1.5^{k-m}}{m} \quad \text{s.t.} \ \ m \geq 3 \qquad (1)$$

Here, the constant 1.5 is a design parameter to penalize low numbers of matching points. Even though this problem is similar to the largest clique search and can be theoretically infeasible for even small numbers of points, we can dramatically shrink the search space by applying an upper threshold t that rejects all matchings over a certain geometric distance, in our case $t = 5$ mm. As an initial step, a priority queue of 2-matchings is built, which can be ordered by geometric distance in $O(n^2)$ [7]. From that, we select only a certain quantile, in our case the best 50 matchings—note that this is the only heuristic we apply in our algorithm. On this set, the actual search is conducted in a RANSAC-like fashion [2], recursively adding candidate points. In every recursive step, the residual geometric distance is checked against the threshold t, leaving very few evaluations for real-world problems [4]. For $m \geq 3$, transformations RT are recovered by Umeyama's method [10]. Finally, the poses RT of the limbs of the robot are output.

We believe that our approach is particularly efficient thanks to the heavily pruned search tree, compared to the extensive search in [8] or a maximum-clique search [7]. Furthermore, it is able to handle very low numbers of inliers in contrast to rigid point set registration approaches based on interative closest point [9] or eigenstructure decomposition [12].

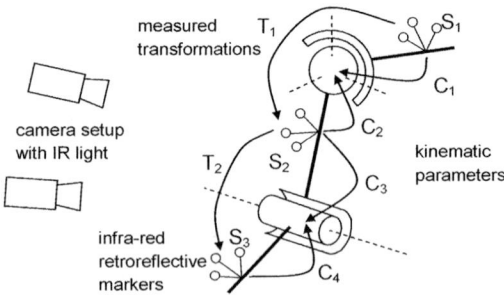

Fig. 2. Kinematic parameter estimation using visual motion capturing

3   Kinematic Model Estimation and Joint Angle Calculation

Now that the pose of the robot is available from the motion capture system, we are to calibrate its kinematic model and then calculate the joint angles.

3.1   Ball Joint Model Estimation

First, we consider the calibration of ball-and-socket joints based on the method described in [3]. As shown in Fig. 2, a ball joint can be parameterized by the position of the center of rotation with respect to the two frames of reference given by the attached marker targets. Let c_1 and c_2 be the rotational center in the reference frames S_1 and S_2, respectively. Measuring several joint poses T_i, we can assume $c_1 \approx T_i c_2$ for all i. Separating the rotational and translational parts of T_i such that $T_i = [R_i \; t_i]$, we obtain a linear least squares problem:

$$\underset{c_1,c_2}{\arg\min} \; \underbrace{\begin{bmatrix} I & -R_1 \\ I & -R_2 \\ & \vdots \end{bmatrix}}_{M} \begin{bmatrix} c_1 \\ c_2 \end{bmatrix} - \begin{bmatrix} t_1 \\ t_2 \\ \vdots \end{bmatrix} \tag{2}$$

This problem is easily solved by standard numerical libraries and we obtain the kinematic parameters c_1 and c_2.

3.2   Hinge Joint Model Estimation

As hinge joints are essentially a special case of ball-and-socket joints, we can again apply Eq. 2. However, the minimization then yields a random point on the rotational axis of the hinge joint, possibly far away from the physical setup. Gamage et al. [3] resolve the rotational axis ambiguity by replacing the measurement matrix M by its closest rank-5 approximation M_5, which leads to a well-defined position for the center of rotation c. The null space of M_5 yields the axis of rotation c_z in both reference frames, which we define as the z-axis of the rigid transformations to the axis coordinate frames. With the further choice $c_y = c \times c_z$ and $c_x = c_z \times c_y$ and normalization to unit vectors, we finally obtain a *unique parameterization of the hinge joint* coordinate frame $C = [c_x \; c_y \; c_z \; c]$, for C_3 and C_4, respectively. As described in [4], we further perform a non-linear minimization on our kinematic model in order to minimize the actual marker ball residual errors.

Finally, we have obtained a unique parameterization for both ball joints and hinge joints. This allows us to model the kinematics of the robot ECCE. For the shoulder test rig in Fig. 1B, we measured 22 distinct joint poses from several viewpoints and could calibrate the robot kinematics up to a residual error of 1.29 mm for the position of the center of rotation and 0.83 mm for the axis of rotation. Note that this error is far better than in earlier manual measurements, when we could estimate the robot's kinematics at an error of $\approx$10 mm.

Table 1. Error Evaluation Results

A. Accuracy of 3D position		**B.** Precision of joint angles			
Marker Target Position [mm]			Translation	Rotation	Joint angle
		Transformation [mm]		[degrees]	[degrees]
S_1 Torso	0.8082	T_1 Shoulder	0.4833	0.2382	0.2060
S_2 Upper Arm	0.8214	T_2 Elbow	0.5638	0.2304	0.0546
S_3 Lower Arm	1.2083				

3.3   Joint Angle Calculation

With the kinematic parameters at hand, we finally calculate joint angles given the transformations T from Section 2. For ball joints, the rotation can be recovered from the measured pose T by solving the orthogonal Procrustes problem as described in [10]. For hinge joints, the angle calculation reduces to a 2-dimensional problem in the plane perpendicular to the rotational axis. The rotation angle α can be obtained by employing the two-valued arctangent function, details are given in [4]. Our final motion capture system delivers real-time joint angle data at a 20–30 ms delay on a dual core 2.4 GHz system.

3.4   Error Evaluation

In order to verify the accuracy of our motion capture system, we evaluated both the accuracy of 3D positions compared to known motions over a fixed distance, as well as the precision of all data while the changing camera angle.

First, the robot setup was moved over a known distance of 400 mm, while the joint angles were unchanged. This measurement was repeated several times and under several angles, the root mean square error of measured distances compared to the known distance is shown in Table 1A.

Second, we measured the precision of motion capture (see Table 1B) data while moving the camera to widely different angles over a sequence of 2000 frames. It is our strong belief that most sources of errors—except overall scaling—will show up when changing the viewpoint. From these results, we draw the conclusion that our system delivers joint angles at an error well below 1 degree.

4   Conclusion

In this work, we have developed a versatile motion capture system that serves two purposes: First, we can estimate the kinematic model of the musculoskeletal humanoid ECCE. Second, we can deliver real-time data of its pose and its joint angles, which opens up several areas of application. Both static and dynamic data may be captured and put to use for our future work in robot simulation and control.

4.1   Future Work

One of the central objectives of the ECCEROBOT project is to employ physics-based robot simulation both off-line for controller development as well as on-line as an internal model for robot control [6,5]. Our motion capture system is therefore of great use for simulation parameter estimation and creation of a simulation model. Evolution strategies are currently applied in order to optimize the physics-based simulation model based on our joint angle measurements [13].

Acknowledgments. The author would like to thank Konstantinos Dalamagkidis and Alois Knoll (Robotics and Embedded Systems, Technische Universität München) for their valuable advice, as well as Steffen Wittmeier for his help with the robot platform.

References

1. Cheah, C., Liu, C., Slotine, J.: Adaptive tracking control for robots with unknown kinematic and dynamic properties. Intl. J. of Robotics Research 25(3), 283 (2006)
2. Fischler, M., Bolles, R.: Random sample consensus: A paradigm for model fitting with applications to image analysis and automated cartography. Communications of the ACM 24(6), 381–395 (1981)
3. Gamage, S., Lasenby, J.: New least squares solutions for estimating the average centre of rotation and the axis of rotation. J. of Biomechanics 35(1), 87 (2002)
4. Gaschler, A.: Real-Time Marker-Based Motion Tracking: Application to Kinematic Model Estimation of a Humanoid Robot. Master's thesis, Technische Universität München, Germany (2011)
5. Jäntsch, M., Wittmeier, S., Knoll, A.: Distributed Control for an Anthropomimetic Robot. In: Intl. Conf. on Intelligent Robots and Systems, pp. 5466–5471 (2010)
6. Marques, H., Jäntsch, M., Wittmeier, S., Holland, O., Alessandro, C., Diamond, A., Lungarella, M., Knight, R.: Ecce1: The first of a series of anthropomimetic musculoskeletal upper torsos. In: Humanoid Robots, pp. 391–396 (2010)
7. Pintaric, T., Kaufmann, H.: Affordable infrared-optical pose-tracking for virtual and augmented reality. In: Proc of Trends and Issues in Tracking for Virtual Environments Workshop, pp. 44–51 (2007)
8. Steinicke, F., Jansen, C., Hinrichs, K., Vahrenhold, J., Schwald, B.: Generating Optimized Marker-based Rigid Bodies for Optical Tracking Systems. In: Intl. Conf. on Computer Vision Theory and Applications (2007)
9. Trucco, E., Fusiello, A., Roberto, V.: Robust motion and correspondence of noisy 3-D point sets with missing data. Pattern recognition letters 20(9), 889–898 (1999)
10. Umeyama, S.: Least-squares estimation of transformation parameters between two point patterns. Pattern Analysis and Machine Intelligence, 376–380 (1991)
11. Urata, J., Nakanishi, Y., Miyadera, A., Mizuuchi, I., Yoshikai, T., Inaba, M.: A three-dimensional angle sensor for a spherical joint using a micro camera. In: Proc. Intl. Conf. on Robotics and Automation, pp. 4428–4430 (2006)
12. Wang, X., Cheng, Y.Q., Collins, R.T., Hanson, A.R.: Determining correspondences and rigid motion of 3-d point sets with missing data. In: Computer Vision and Pattern Recognition, pp. 252–257 (1996)
13. Wittmeier, S., Gaschler, A., Jäntsch, M., Dalamagkidis, K., Knoll, A.: Calibration of a physics-based model of an anthropomimetic robot using evolution strategies. In: Intl. Conf. on Intelligent Robots and Systems (submitted, 2011)

Object Recognition System Guided by Gaze of the User with a Wearable Eye Tracker

Takumi Toyama*

German Research Center for Artificial Intelligence (DFKI) GmbH, Germany

Abstract. Existing approaches for object recognition typically rely on images captured on an ordinary digital camera and therefore the recognition task sometimes becomes difficult when the image contains other objects (cluttered) and the object of interest is not clearly indicated. In this work, we integrate a wearable eye tracker into the object recognition system in order to recognize which object the user is paying attention to in the scene camera. To demonstrate the usability of such a *gaze*[1] *based object recognition* interface, we developed a prototypical application named Museum Guide 2.0 which can be used in a museum as a mechanical guide for visitors.

1 Introduction

A significant advance of object recognition technologies has been seen in recent years and it provides us with great opportunities to design practical applications for object recognition such as Google Goggles[2], kooaba[3] or ViPR[4]. Thus, nowadays people can easily access information about objects simply by taking a picture of them with these applications. In these applications, an ordinary digital camera which captures a fixed-shaped (usually square) image of the scene is typically used. However, in the image taken by such a camera, the object of interest may not be captured perfectly (occlusion) or other objects may also be captured (clutter) and therefore the task of object recognition becomes difficult. A drawback of an ordinary camera-based object recognition method is that the user's interests or attentions do not explicitly appear within the image and thus it is not easy to estimate where they exist in the image taken.

To estimate where the user's interest exists in a certain environment, an eye tracker is a suitable device because eye movements are immediately connected to human intuition. Recent studies on eye movements revealed how human eye movements are controlled and showed that the eyes fixate on a scene to acquire enough information for understanding the scene [1]. A number of developers

---

* Recommended for submission to YRF2011 by Prof. Andreas Dengel.
[1] Gaze is referred to as a long steady look at an object which is composed from several fixations in this work.
[2] http://www.google.com/mobile/goggles/
[3] http://www.kooaba.com/
[4] http://www.evolution.com/core/ViPR/

R. Mester and M. Felsberg (Eds.): DAGM 2011, LNCS 6835, pp. 444–449, 2011.

in the area of human-machine interaction (HCI) have been inspired by these studies and have proposed a lot of applications taking advantage of eye tracking information [3,4].

In this work, we investigate how object recognition can be guided by eye tracking information to recognize the object the user is interested in and how such a framework can be used in a human-machine interactive interface. We developed a prototypical application named *Museum Guide 2.0* to demonstrate the usability of such a *gaze-based interface* for object recognition. Museum Guide 2.0 acts as an unintrusive personal guide for a visitor in a museum. When it detects that the user is looking at a specific art object, it will provide audio information on that specific object via headphones.

2   Proposed Application

Figures 1 and 2 show an abstracted image of the Museum Guide 2.0 scenario and a brief workflow model of the system, respectively. The system works as follows: A head-mounted eye tracker observes the visitor's eye movements and synchronizes detected eye fixations with the captured real world images. The built-in object recognition subsystem recognizes which of the objects in the database is currently being fixated by the user. As soon as gaze on a specific object is detected, the application provides audio information on that specific object.

We have several challenges in this scenario. First, how to use fixation information to guide object recognition. Second, in order to apply any kind of benchmarking to the system output, we need to define so-called ground truth based on our context. What is required for the system in the Museum Guide 2.0 scenario is to detect the user's gaze on a specific object which can be observed as a time interval rather than a frame in a video stream. Therefore, we need to transform observed eye movements over several frames in a video stream into gaze on specific objects and thereby we define our criteria for benchmarking. Third, we need to judge whether the recognized object for each frame is being gazed at by the user or not.

3   Real-Time Gaze Based Object Recognition

We propose *real-time gaze based object recognition* that overcomes the challenges stated above.

3.1   Eye Tracking Method

We use the SMI iViewX^{TM} HED [5] as a head-mounted eye tracker. In this system, the user's eye is illuminated by infra red light. The eye camera of this eye tracker captures images of the illuminated eye and the image analysis software in the

---

[5] http://www.smivision.com/en/gaze-and-eye-tracking-systems/products/
iview-x-hed.html

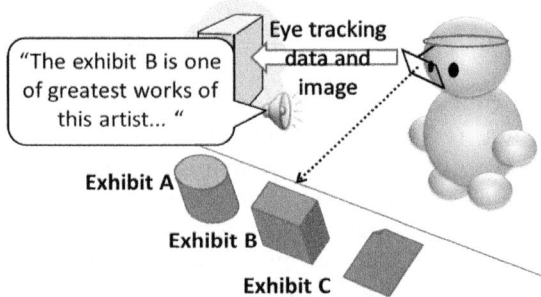

Fig. 1. Museum Guide 2.0. The system detects the gaze of the user on particular objects and instantly provides information regarding the respective object.

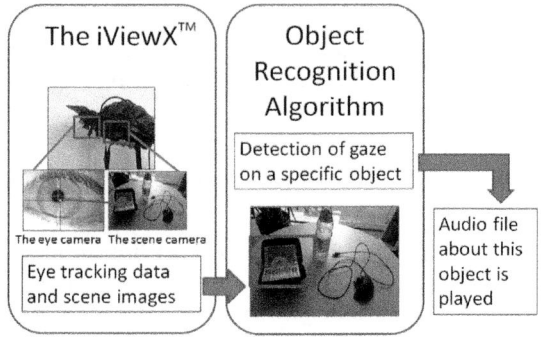

Fig. 2. A brief workflow model of Museum Guide 2.0

system maps the center of the pupil in the image into the scene camera. When it detects a fixation, the mapped point is sent to the object recognition framework as the user's fixation point.

3.2 Basic Object Recognition Method

We adopt a SIFT based object recognition method [2] as the base of our object recognition framework. To prepare the database for object recognition, SIFT features are extracted from images of each object (an exhibit in the museum). Each query image is recognized as a specific object by matching SIFT features between the query and the database.

3.3 Fixation Guided Object Recognition

Since we can obtain the fixation point for each frame which can be considered as the interest point of the user, object recognition system can be guided in order to recognize the object being watched by the user. Thus, instead of extracting SIFT features from the entire image of the frame, we limit the region for feature extraction to a local area whose center position is the fixation point.

3.4   Gaze-Based Ground Truth Processing

For benchmarking the system, we need to obtain ground truth from video stream data. Manual labeling for each frame is the most primitive way to obtain ground truth of video stream data. However, for the sake of the gaze-based interface, we would prefer to define a sequence of frames whose fixations are on one specific object as gaze based ground truth which corresponds to a time interval in which the user likes to get information from the museum guide. In this work, manually labeled video data is processed to obtain gaze based ground truth that is composed from the gaze on each object.

3.5   Gaze Detection Based on Recognition Results

In order to match processed ground truth, the system needs to judge whether the user is gazing at the object or not from object recognition results. We propose three different methods to detect the user's gaze from object recognition results.

Non-weighting plain method directly outputs an object recognition result for each frame. *Accumulation of n frames method* accumulates histograms obtained from object recognition processes. Each value in the histogram corresponds to the frequency of matched SIFT features for each object. If the highest value in the histogram exceeds the threshold value, it is recognized as gaze on the object. *Pseudo ground truth generative method* counts the number of frames that have the same object recognition label X. When the number of such frames reaches T_{dur} value, the system recognizes the user is gazing at object X. Simultaneously, if the consecutive T_{noise} frames are not recognized as object X, the count is set to 0.

When the gaze on a specific object is detected by the system, it triggers the event for providing information about the object.

4   Experiments and Results

For benchmarking the system, we recorded 10 test video files where the users were strolling in our museum wearing the SMI iViewX^{TM} HED eye tracker. We used 12 objects and placed them on a table in our museum. All frames of the video files were labeled manually as the name of the object being fixated by the user.

First, to evaluate the benefit obtained by using fixation positions in object recognition, we compare the fixation guided object recognition method with two conventional methods that work on the camera image without considering the eye position (baseline methods). As shown in Figure 3, "Entire image" uses the entire image of a frame for recognition (extracting SIFT features from the entire area) and "Center area" limits the region for recognition to the center area of the image regardless of eye position (but the size of the region is the same as the fixation guided method). In this experiment, the result is evaluated frame by frame without considering *gaze-based ground truth* stated in the previous

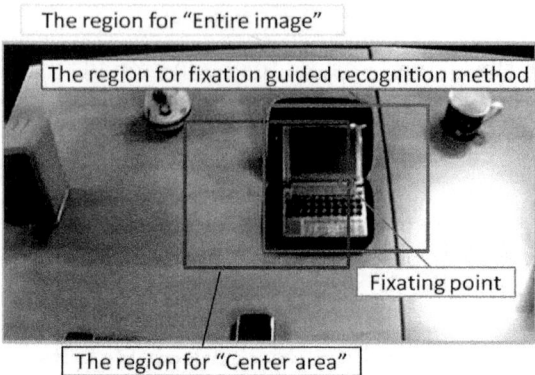

Fig. 3. Example of regions for each recognition method. *Entire image* uses the whole image, *Center area* crops the region from the center of the image and *fixation guided recognition method* crops the region according to the fixating point.

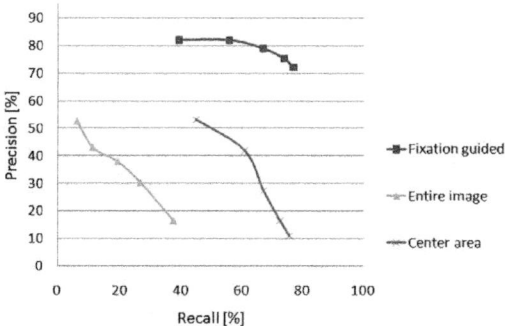

Fig. 4. Results of fixation guided object recognition, showing that methods using fixation information clearly outperformed simple object recognition methods (Entire image, Center area) that did not use any eye tracking information

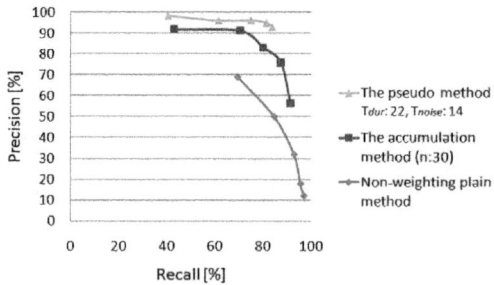

Fig. 5. The results of gaze based object recognition. The pseudo method outperformed other two methods.

section. Figure 4 shows the results obtained by changing output thresholds from 0.5 to 0.9 for the highest value in the histograms computed by object recognition processes. The fixation guided object recognition method completely outperformed the two baseline methods indicating that eye position indeed helps in improving the object recognition system.

Next, we evaluated the gaze detection methods on recogniton results. By processing the manually labeled data, we obtain sequences of frames that the users were gazing at the objects (long time intervals of gaze on particular objects). Here, we compared three methods (a pseudo ground truth generative method, an accumulation of n frames method and a plain method). Figure 5 shows the result of each gaze detection method. As shown in this figure, the pseudo method (pseudo ground truth generative method) outperformed the other methods. By using this method, the system could detect the users' gaze with more than 90% of precision and 80% of recall.

5 Conclusion

We have proposed an object recognition system that makes use of eye tracking information to detect the user's gaze on a particular object. The experimental results showed the fixation guided recognition method could recognize the object that the user was looking at and the advantage of using eye information by comparing it with two baseline methods. Furthermore, they also showed the proposed gaze detection method could reasonably detect the user's gaze on objects.

Regarding future work, we would like to expand the database to adapt the application not only to the museum scenario but also to other scenarios and compare the recognition method with other recognition methods which use the segmentation approach or a saliency map to estimate the user's attention.

References

1. Henderson, J.M.: Human gaze control during real-world scene perception. Trends in Cognitive Sciences 7(11), 498–504 (2003)
2. Lowe, D.G.: Distinctive image features from scale-invariant keypoints. International Journal of Computer Vision 60(2), 91–110 (2004)
3. Majaranta, P., Ahola, U.K., Špakov, O.: Fast gaze typing with an adjustable dwell time. In: Proceedings of the 27th International Conference on Human Factors in Computing Systems, CHI 2009, pp. 357–360. ACM, Boston (2009)
4. Nacke, L., Stellmach, S., Sasse, D., Lindley, C.A.: Gameplay experience in a gaze interaction game. In: Proceedings of the 5th Conference on Communication by Gaze Interaction COGAIN 2009: Gaze Interaction For Those Who Want It Most, Lyngby, Denmark, pp. 49–54 (2009)

Spectral Clustering of ROIs for Object Discovery*

Paul Bodesheim

Chair for Computer Vision
Friedrich Schiller University of Jena
Paul.Bodesheim@uni-jena.de
http://www.inf-cv.uni-jena.de

Abstract. Object discovery is one of the most important applications of unsupervised learning. This paper addresses several spectral clustering techniques to attain a categorization of objects in images without additional information such as class labels or scene descriptions. Due to the fact that background textures bias the performance of image categorization methods, a generic object detector based on some general requirements on objects is applied. The object detector provides rectangular regions of interest (ROIs) as object hypotheses independent of the underlying object class. Feature extraction is simply constrained to these bounding boxes to decrease the influence of background clutter. Another aspect of this work is the utilization of a Gaussian mixture model (GMM) instead of k-means as usually used after feature transformation in spectral clustering. Several experiments have been done and the combination of spectral clustering techniques with the object detector is compared to the standard approach of computing features of the whole image.

1   Introduction and Related Work

Unsupervised image categorization for object discovery is a challenging task in computer vision. Algorithms try to group images according to categories of the pictured objects only using the visual content. This can be done by utilizing similarities between representations of images assuming that images containing objects of the same class provide similar feature vectors. A clustering of all vectors then implies a clustering of the corresponding images.

Commonly used approaches for object discovery include spectral clustering techniques, which are characterized later in this paper. A main part of those methods rely on graph partitioning based on optimizing the *Normalized Cut* [11]. Closely related to *Normalized Cuts Spectral Clustering* is a dimensionality reduction technique called *Laplacian Eigenmaps* [2], where at last, the same eigenvalue problem of the graph Laplacian as for the Normalized Cut optimization needs to be solved. A good overview of spectral clustering and graph Laplacians is provided by von Luxburg [5].

---

* Recommended for submission to YRF2011 by Prof. Dr.-Ing. Joachim Denzler.

R. Mester and M. Felsberg (Eds.): DAGM 2011, LNCS 6835, pp. 450–455, 2011.
© Springer-Verlag Berlin Heidelberg 2011

Another alternative to discover objects in images is the usage of *Topic models* [12,13]. Object categories are determined by estimating the parameters of a statistical model, which involves hidden (latent) topic variables [12]. Both approaches for object discovery, spectral clustering and topic modeling, are compared by Tuytelaars et al. [14]. In the present paper, we focus on spectral clustering techniques and present their combination with a general object detector.

2   Spectral Clustering Techniques

Spectral clustering techniques are methods that rely on the eigen-decomposition of a modified similarity matrix containing pairwise similarities of feature vectors [14]. Using the eigenvectors and eigenvalues of such matrices, feature vectors can be transformed by projections into a low-dimensional feature space prior to clustering.

In this section, four selected methods, which meet that definition of spectral clustering, are described briefly. They have in common that each of them uses pairwise similarities of feature vectors $x^{(1)}, \ldots, x^{(M)} \in \mathbb{R}^N$ calculated by a kernel function κ and collected in a kernel matrix K with $K_{ij} = \kappa\left(x^{(i)}, x^{(j)}\right)$.

Each method realizes a specific feature transformation and the transformed data points are always clustered using standard techniques. While k-means is usually applied, we use a GMM, which generalizes k-means by estimating arbitrary covariance matrices.

2.1   Nonlinear Component Analysis

Kernel methods treat the kernel matrix K as a matrix containing inner products of the feature vectors in a higher-dimensional space $\mathbb{F}$, which mostly depends on the input space in a nonlinear way. The following two approaches of nonlinear component analysis both project the data points on principal axes in $\mathbb{F}$ without computing vectors in this space, but they differ in the selection of the axes.

Kernel Principal Component Analysis (Kernel-PCA). For *Kernel-PCA*, those principal axes are chosen, which offer largest variance of data points in $\mathbb{F}$. Thus, Kernel-PCA is equal to standard PCA in this higher-dimensional space. As in standard PCA, a centering step is necessary to ensure centered data points in $\mathbb{F}$ [10]. The largest eigenvalues and corresponding eigenvectors of the centered kernel matrix $\bar{K}$ solving $\bar{K}v = \lambda v$ are required to compute transformed feature vectors $\tilde{x}^{(1)}, \ldots, \tilde{x}^{(M)}$ [10].

Kernel Entropy Component Analysis (Kernel-ECA). Using *Kernel-ECA* for feature transformation also results in computing projections of data points on principal axes. Different to Kernel-PCA, the eigenvectors are not chosen according to the largest eigenvalues of the centered kernel matrix, but with respect to their contribution to an approximation of the quadratic Renyi entropy [8] $H(p) = -\log \int p^2(x)\, dx$. As stated by Jenssen [4], the aim is to select principal axes with highest contributions to this entropy. The contribution of the

m-th principal axis to an approximation of this entropy is $c_m = \left(\sqrt{\lambda_m}\mathbf{1}^\mathsf{T}\boldsymbol{v}^{(m)}\right)^2$ with eigenvalue λ_m and the corresponding eigenvector $\boldsymbol{v}^{(m)}$ of $\boldsymbol{K}$. Compared to Kernel-PCA, there is no centering step of the kernel matrix involved [4].

2.2   Normalized Cuts Spectral Clustering

For Normalized Cuts Spectral Clustering, a weighted and undirected graph is constructed treating feature vectors as vertices and pairwise similarities as edge weights. Thus, it is possible to use the kernel matrix $\boldsymbol{K}$ to represent a full graph. The two methods of this section optimize the Normalized Cut [11] of the graph determined by $\boldsymbol{K}$. In general, the optimization can be done by minimizing the Rayleigh quotient $\frac{\boldsymbol{y}^\mathsf{T}(\boldsymbol{D}-\boldsymbol{K})\boldsymbol{y}}{\boldsymbol{y}^\mathsf{T}\boldsymbol{D}\boldsymbol{y}}$, which ends in computing eigenvectors according to the smallest eigenvalues of the generalized eigenproblem $(\boldsymbol{D}-\boldsymbol{K})\,\boldsymbol{y} = \lambda\boldsymbol{D}\boldsymbol{y}$, where $\boldsymbol{D}$ is a diagonal matrix containing row sums of $\boldsymbol{K}$ [11]. The eigenvalue λ is equal to the Normalized Cut with respect to $\boldsymbol{y}$, which in theory is a binary vector describing the corresponding bipartition of the graph.

Random Walks Laplacian Eigenmaps (Random Walks LEM). The work of Meila and Shi [6] gives an interpretation of spectral partitioning with random walks using the stochastic matrix $\boldsymbol{P} = \boldsymbol{D}^{-1}\boldsymbol{K}$. Instead of the generalized eigenproblem, they solve $\left(\boldsymbol{I} - \boldsymbol{D}^{-1}\boldsymbol{K}\right)\boldsymbol{y} = \lambda\boldsymbol{y}$, with $\boldsymbol{I}$ the identity matrix, by computing eigenvectors of $\boldsymbol{P}$ according to the largest eigenvalues. Since eigenvectors of $\boldsymbol{P}$ are also solutions for the generalized eigenproblem [5], these eigenvectors minimize the Normalized Cut as well. Forming a matrix $\tilde{\boldsymbol{X}}$ containing the eigenvectors of $\boldsymbol{P}$ in its columns, the rows of $\tilde{\boldsymbol{X}}$ represent the transformed feature vectors $\tilde{\boldsymbol{x}}^{(1)}, \ldots, \tilde{\boldsymbol{x}}^{(M)}$. Because of the strong connection between Normalized Cuts Spectral Clustering and Laplacian Eigenmaps (cf. Sect. 1) as well as the random walks point of view [6], this method is termed *Random Walks Laplacian Eigenmaps (Random Walks LEM)* throughout this paper.

NJW-Algorithm. The *NJW-Algorithm* [7] uses eigenvectors of the normalized Laplacian matrix $\boldsymbol{L} = \boldsymbol{D}^{-\frac{1}{2}}\left(\boldsymbol{D} - \boldsymbol{K}\right)\boldsymbol{D}^{-\frac{1}{2}}$ by computing eigenvectors according to the largest eigenvalues of $\tilde{\boldsymbol{L}} = \boldsymbol{I} - \boldsymbol{L}$. Compared to Random Walks LEM, this leads to scaled eigenvectors $\boldsymbol{z} = \boldsymbol{D}^{\frac{1}{2}}\boldsymbol{y}$ [11]. Transformed feature vectors are computed as done in the algorithm called Random Walks LEM, but with an additional normalization of the rows of $\tilde{\boldsymbol{X}}$ having unit length [7].

3   Object Detection and Categorization of ROIs

As in [14], feature extraction is often performed on the whole image. To avoid clusterings based on background textures, it is desirable to compute features only at regions, which are covered by an object. The key idea of this paper is to integrate a general object detector into an unsupervised learning framework for object discovery. For this purpose, the general object detector of Alexe et al. [1] is applied to generate bounding boxes as object hypotheses independent of the object's class and feature extraction can be limited to these rectangular areas. Using this detector, we get an arbitrary number of bounding boxes, each of them having a score between 0 and 1 measuring how likely the rectangle contains an object of any class. The scoring and thus the detector works generic across categories using some object cues such as closed contour and color contrast [1].

At first glance, applying this detector is not possible in an unsupervised framework, because the detector needs to be trained with images and ground-truth-information about ROIs. But if the training images are completely independent of the clustered images, there is no information utilized about the latter. So, when we use the detector with the default parameter setting, which comes with the software of Alexe et al. [1] and whose values are obtained using images containing objects of classes different to those that should be discovered, it can be seen as an unsupervised scenario as well.

First Approach: One ROI per Image. In a first approach, we sample a fixed number of ROIs for every image, but using only the ROI of each image with the highest score given by the detector. Feature extraction, transformation and clustering is simply done for those ROIs and the category label of one ROI directly specifies the label of a single image.

Second Approach: Multiple ROIs per Image. The second approach employs the idea of Russell et al. [9] for object discovery, where multiple segmentations of each image are used with the assumption that at least one segment covers one single object in a sufficient way. In the case of ROIs, assuming that at least one ROI is a good bounding box for an object in the image, multiple ROIs per image are sampled at the beginning, e.g. b ROIs with highest score. Subsequent, feature extraction is performed on all ROIs as well as feature transformation and clustering. In the end, there are b labels for each image, one per ROI. To avoid images with multiple labels and to compare the results with the first approach, it is necessary to have one label for each image. Using a GMM for clustering, one can determine a single ROI per image, which has the highest probability for being a member of the specific category and the image is assigned to the label of this ROI.

4   Experimental Results

In experiments, all images of 20 object categories of the *Caltech-256* dataset selected by Tuytelaars et al. [14] are grouped. *PHOG* features [3] as well as the χ^2-kernel [14] are applied, and also a kernel particular for *PHOG* similarity [3], which we term PHOG-kernel. As proposed by Tuytelaars et al. [14], the conditional entropy is measured to evaluate a clustering. A low conditional entropy corresponds to a high quality of the clustering.

In Fig. 1, the conditional entropy of achieved clusterings is displayed depending on the dimension of the transformed feature vectors, where ⟨*IMAGE*⟩ stands for feature calculation on the whole image, ⟨*1 ROI*⟩ for applying the first approach proposed in Sect. 3 and ⟨*1 of 10 ROIs*⟩ for the usage of ten ROIs per image selecting the best one as described in the second approach. It can be seen clearly that only using one ROI per image leads to poor clusterings according

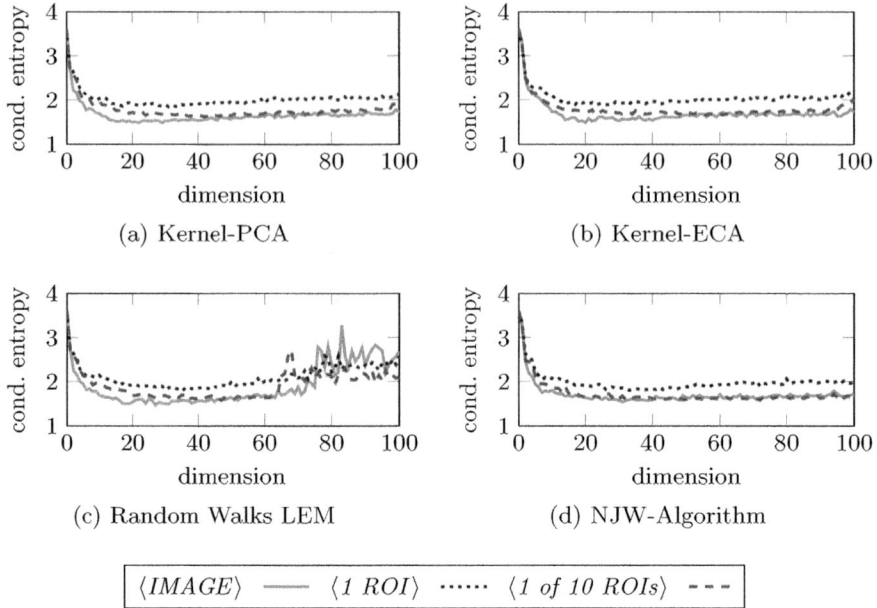

Fig. 1. Conditional entropy of the clusterings depending on the dimension of the transformed feature vectors (number of eigenvectors used for transformation), obtained by four spectral clustering techniques (a)–(d) and three mentioned approaches using PHOG-kernel [3] and a GMM (best viewed in color)

Table 1. Conditional entropy of the clusterings with χ^2-kernel compared to results of [14], where different features are evaluated (that's why there are intervals denoted)

SPECTRAL CLUSTERING TECHNIQUE	$\langle IMAGE \rangle$ (20 EIGENVECTORS)	$\langle 1 \ of \ 10 \ ROIs \rangle$ (40 EIGENVECTORS)
Kernel-PCA & GMM	1.55	1.61
Kernel-ECA & GMM	1.60	1.62
Random Walks LEM & GMM	1.56	1.67
NJW-Algorithm & GMM	1.61	1.66
Kernel-PCA & k-means [14]	$1.64 - 2.35$	–
NJW-Algorithm & k-means [14]	$1.58 - 2.54$	–

to the conditional entropy, whereas multiple ROIs show better performance. As stated before, we also calculated features on the whole image. Indeed this leads to the best results, but especially the NJW-Algorithm produces nearly equal outputs comparing $\langle IMAGE \rangle$ and $\langle 1 \ of \ 10 \ ROIs \rangle$. For clarity and due to the lack of space, Fig. 1 only shows the results obtained by the GMM since in further experiments, clusterings using k-means achieve a higher conditional entropy.

In comparison to the results of Tuytelaars et al. [14] using 20 eigenvectors for feature transformation, the clusterings are better for $\langle IMAGE \rangle$, notably obtained by Kernel-PCA with a conditional entropy of 1.55 (cf. Table 1). Also

⟨*1 of 10 ROIs*⟩, using twice the number of eigenvectors, because there is an additional performance gain for a dimension higher than 20, achieves good results near the lower bound given by the intervals of Tuytelaars et al. [14].

5   Conclusions

The presented results show the ability of applying a general object detector in an unsupervised object discovery framework, where the usage of multiple ROIs per image leads to better performance. Although the proposed method of spectral clustering of ROIs does not provide a clear quantitative performance benefit, our approach of first detecting an object in general and subsequent discovering the category is promising and improvements should be aspired in further work.

In our studies, it turned out that a GMM for grouping transformed feature vectors, compared to commonly used k-means, boosts the quality of categorizations obtained by spectral techniques.

Acknowledgements. I want to thank Erik Rodner, advisor of my diploma thesis, for his great support and Michael Kemmler for helpful suggestions.

References

1. Alexe, B., Deselaers, T., Ferrari, V.: What is an object? In: CVPR, pp. 73–80 (2010)
2. Belkin, M., Niyogi, P.: Laplacian eigenmaps for dimensionality reduction and data representation. Neural Computation 15(6), 1373–1396 (2003)
3. Bosch, A., Zisserman, A., Munoz, X.: Representing shape with a spatial pyramid kernel. In: CIVR, pp. 401–408 (2007)
4. Jenssen, R.: Kernel entropy component analysis. TPAMI 32(5), 847–860 (2010)
5. von Luxburg, U.: A tutorial on spectral clustering. Statistics and Computing 17(4), 395–416 (2007)
6. Meila, M., Shi, J.: Learning segmentation by random walks. In: NIPS, pp. 873–879 (2000)
7. Ng, A.Y., Jordan, M.I., Weiss, Y.: On spectral clustering: Analysis and an algorithm. In: NIPS, pp. 849–856 (2001)
8. Renyi, A.: On measures of entropy and information. In: Proceedings of the Berkeley Symposium on Mathematics, Statistics and Probability, vol. 1, pp. 547–561 (1960)
9. Russell, B.C., Freeman, W.T., Efros, A.A., Sivic, J., Zisserman, A.: Using multiple segmentations to discover objects and their extent in image collections. In: CVPR, pp. 1605–1614 (2006)
10. Schölkopf, B., Smola, A., Müller, K.R.: Nonlinear component analysis as a kernel eigenvalue problem. Neural Computation 10(5), 1299–1319 (1998)
11. Shi, J., Malik, J.: Normalized cuts and image segmentation. TPAMI 22(8), 888–905 (2000)
12. Sivic, J., Russell, B.C., Efros, A.A., Zisserman, A., Freeman, W.T.: Discovering objects and their location in images. In: ICCV, pp. 370–377 (2005)
13. Sivic, J., Russell, B.C., Zisserman, A., Freeman, W.T., Efros, A.A.: Unsupervised discovery of visual object class hierarchies. In: CVPR, pp. 1–8 (2008)
14. Tuytelaars, T., Lampert, C.H., Blaschko, M.B., Buntine, W.: Unsupervised object discovery: A comparison. IJCV 88(2), 284–302 (2010)

Robust Classification and Semi-supervised Object Localization with Gaussian Processes*

Alexander Lütz

Chair for Computer Vision
Friedrich Schiller University of Jena
Alexander.Luetz@uni-jena.de
http://www.inf-cv.uni-jena.de

Abstract. Traditionally, object recognition systems are trained with images that may contain a large amount of background clutter. One way to train the classifier more robustly is to limit training images to their object regions. For this purpose we present a semi-supervised approach that determines object regions in a completely automatic manner and only requires global labels of training images. We formulate the problem as a kernel hyperparameter optimization task and utilize the Gaussian process framework. To perform the computations efficiently we present techniques reducing the necessary time effort from cubically to quadratically for essential parts of the computations. The presented approach is evaluated and compared on two well-known and publicly available datasets showing the benefit of our approach.

1 Introduction and Related Work

Image categorization became a well studied problem in the area of image understanding during the last years. Traditionally, one represents already labeled training images by certain features and trains a classifier based on features and labels. In a second step labels of unknown images can be estimated by evaluating the response of the classifier for each image. The main assumption is the presence of only one single dominant object per training image with only few clutter and occlusion. Otherwise, the extracted features would not be representative for the category given by the image label. Going one step further, researchers attempted to overcome this limitation by using more complex classifiers [11] or by extracting a large set of features [12,3]. Nevertheless, this leads to higher computation times as well as higher memory demand in many cases. For this reason, we introduce a new method to determine object regions in training images only given the category label. Therefore, we interpret the object region in an image as a kernel function hyperparameter and optimize the model likelihood with respect to these hyperparameters. This allows obtaining convenient training images for a robust training of a classification system. To reduce the computational effort we apply two lemmata that allow computing inverse and determinant of a matrix in quadratically time in contrast to cubically effort with standard approaches.

---

* Recommended for submission to YRF2011 by Prof. Dr.-Ing. Joachim Denzler.

R. Mester and M. Felsberg (Eds.): DAGM 2011, LNCS 6835, pp. 456–461, 2011.
© Springer-Verlag Berlin Heidelberg 2011

Many publications directly deal with the detection or localization of objects in images [5,8]. Many of these approaches use sliding window techniques to collect hundreds of possible object regions, classify each region and return the one classified with lowest uncertainty or best score. Obviously, this is not possible, if the classifier was trained on images rather than on regions. An alternative are generic object detectors, as proposed by Alexe et al. [1]. They perform detection of arbitrary objects by defining object cues for the presence of an object — like strong color contrast or high edge density.

To our knowledge, just a few publications directly address the determination of object regions in training images by using class labels only. Chum et al. [4] select the region in an image which achieves the highest similarity score to all other images of its class, measured by similarities of visual words and edge densities. Bosch et al. [2] present a method similar to [4] that also obtains object regions in images by maximizing a similarity score, but evaluates the similarity function only on a subset of the training images, instead of considering every training example. In contrast to these approaches, we select the image region, which gives highest probability to explain the class labels by considering only the part of the image covered by the region.

The remainder of the paper is organized as follows. In Sect. 2 we will briefly review classification with Gaussian processes, present our approach for object localization with hyperparameter optimization and show techniques for efficient computations. Experimental results are given in Sect. 3 that show the benefit of our approach. A summary of our findings and a discussion of future research directions conclude the paper.

2 Object Localization with Hyperparameter Optimization in a Gaussian Processes Framework

Brief review of Gaussian Process Classification. Assume a given set of training images $(\mathcal{I}_1, \ldots, \mathcal{I}_n)$ represented by certain features $X = (x_1, \ldots, x_n)$ and a vector $t_L \in \{-1, 1\}^n$ containing the labels of the images. Then we are interested in estimating the general relationship between unseen examples $x_* \in \mathcal{X}$ and their class labels t^*. If we use a kernel function $\kappa : \mathcal{X} \times \mathcal{X} \to \mathbb{R}$ that maps each pair of features to a similarity score we can model the relation in a probabilistic way using Gaussian processes (GP) [11]. The main assumption is that every label t_i is created by a continous latent variable y_i. Then every two labels y_i, y_j are expected to be jointly Gaussian and their covariance is specified by applying the kernel function $\kappa(x_i, x_j)$ to their inputs. As in [11] we assume the y_i to have a zero mean, which leads to $P(y|X) \sim \mathcal{N}(0, K)$ with $K_{i,j} = \kappa(x_i, x_j)$. The choise of κ is crucial for the performance of the classification system, because it defines how strong the estimated label differs given a change in the feature vector. Therefore, to adjust the chosen kernel function to the training data one possibility is to use a parameterized kernel function and to optimize its hyperparameters with respect to the training data. In the Gaussian process framework, optimization can be done by maximizing the model likelihood $P(t_L|X,\beta)$, which states how well the class labels can be explained given the training data under the chosen model.

Object localization with hyperparameter optimization. If the object region in an image is interpreted as a hyperparameter of the kernel function, object localization becomes equivalent to optimization of hyperparameters. Let $\beta = (\beta_1,\ldots,\beta_n)$ be the vector of hyperparameters with β_i as a representation of the object region for the ith image, such as upper left and lower right corner of a rectangle. Then the determination of the object regions can be done by

$$\beta^* = \operatorname*{argmax}_{\beta} P(t_L \mid X,\beta). \qquad (1)$$

If we expect only additional Gaussian noise in the labels, the logarithmic likelihood in the GP regression framework can be written in closed form [14]

$$\log P(t_L \mid X,\beta) = -\frac{1}{2}\log\det(K_\beta+\sigma^2 I) - \frac{1}{2}t_L^T(K_\beta+\sigma^2 I)^{-1}t_L + \text{const}. \quad (2)$$

In (2), K_β denotes the GP covariance matrix computed with the parameterized kernel function, which in our case is equal to restricting the training images to the regions specified by β.

If we have a multi-class classification task that is $t_L \in \{1,\ldots,m\}^n$, m one-vs-all-classifiers can be used. Assuming independent outputs of the m classifiers, we can again compute the joint likelihood [11]

$$\log P(t_L \mid X,\beta) = \sum_{j=1}^{m}\log P(t_L^{(j)} \mid X,\beta), \qquad (3)$$

with binary label vectors $t_L^{(j)}$ whose entries are equal to one if the corresponding entry of t_L is j and -1 otherwise.

To perform the optimization of (2) and (3) one typically uses non-linear optimization techniques like gradient descent. Caused by the descrete parameter space this is not possible in our case. Therefore and due to the combinatorial complexity, we use a greedy strategy as an approximation. In detail, we fix every dimension of β except one and perform likelihood optimization according to this dimension. This is done for every dimension and repeated for several times, which is known as cyclic coordinate search [13]. In practice this corresponds to fixing every image region except for one and choosing the region for this specific image that maximizes the likelihood with respect to the already computed regions of all other images.

Methods for efficient computations. To reduce the computational effort we draw advantage of our greedy approximation scheme. While performing the optimization of one single dimension, the resulting kernel matrix changes only in one row and one column. This is equal to a rank-2-update of K. Therefore we can apply Woodbury's formula [9] to compute the inverse of the slightly changed covariance matrix K' by utilizing the already computed inverse of K.

Table 1. Recognition rates averaged over all categories of Caltech-101. Entry x/y denotes restricting training images to x and test images to y.

# training examples per category	global / global	ROI est. / GT ROI	GT ROI / GT ROI
5	39.12	40.63	49.11
10	44.89	45.55	55.17
15	48.76	49.42	58.59

This results in a computational effort from only $\mathcal{O}(n^2)$ compared to $\mathcal{O}(n^3)$ with standard approaches like Cholesky decomposition. With our implementation, this leads to a time effort of just 0.04 s for inverting a 2000×2000-Matrix on a standard PC in contrast to 12.04 s with a complete Cholesky decomposition. Apart from that, we also benefit from using the determinant lemma (see chapter 18 of [10]). With the Schur-Complement of K on hand — which we already needed for the efficient determination of the inverse — we are able to compute the determinant in constant time for rank-2-modifications of K.

3   Experimental Results

To demonstrate the benefit of our approach, we performed experiments on Caltech-101 [7] and Pascal VOC 2008 [6]. We extracted PHOG-features [2] and BoF-features (identical setup as presented in [15]) for every image to use both structure and color information. The results were combined with uniform weights. As supposed in [11] we also tested weight optimization but this decreased the results slightly. We want to point out that we did not focus on choosing the most promising features or optimize their extraction. To generate region hypotheses for the greedy optimization scheme we performed a sliding window approach. Therefore, we scaled the initial image region by a factor ranging from 1.0 to 0.6 with step size of 0.1. To perform the optimization of (2) or (3) in Sect. 2, we initialized the bounding boxes with the whole image regions and repeated the iterations over all training images for 10 times. For the multi-class classification task we measured recognition rates averaged over all classes whereas we chose the average precision measure for the binary case.

Evaluation. Although Caltech-101 is not the most convenient dataset for evaluating the performance of an object localization system, it is one of the standard datasets for classification tasks. Therefore, we present the results achieved with our approach on this dataset.

As we can see in Table 1, our approach improves the quality of the training step slightly, although there is still some space left for improvement compared to the results based on ground truth regions for training. This is due to the fact, that many images of Caltech-101 show only one dominant object. Nevertheless, the automatically determined object regions are visually meaningful as shown in Fig. 1.

Classifying images from Pascal VOC 2008 is a more challenging task. On this difficult dataset our method showed superior performance compared to the

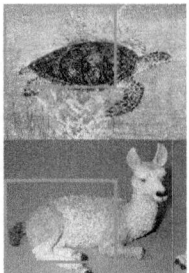

Fig. 1. Good (left) and bad (right) results achieved with our approach on Caltech-101 with 15 training images per category (best viewed in color)

Table 2. Average precision rates achieved on Pascal VOC 2008 bicycle

# training examples per category	global / global	ROI est. / GT ROI	GT ROI / GT ROI
15	6.13	11.63	56.67
30	8.46	35.74	55.03
50	7.48	42.84	57.28

Fig. 2. Good (left) and bad (right) results achieved with our approach on Pascal VOC 2008 bicycles with 50 training images per category (best viewed in color)

standard approach, which can clearly be seen in Table 2. Although the results obtained with our approach are a little lower than the ground truth results, the improvement is up to a factor of six for our simple feature set. This clearly points out the advantages of our approach for a robust training especially in difficult classification tasks. The results confirm the fact that images restricted to their object regions give an essential benefit for building classifiers more robustly. Fig. 2 shows some exemplary results on Pascal VOC 2008 bicycle achieved by our approach. Note that the bad examples are cases where the bicycle regions are too small compared to the minimum scaling factor or are not highly representative for the bicycle category.

4   Conclusion and Future Work

We have shown that reducing images to their object regions allows building classifiers more robustly. Our approach showed superior performance by improving classification results up to a factor of six for challenging tasks compared to classification based on whole images. To overcome computational limitations we proposed techniques for efficient computations. As future work we plan to replace the sliding window approach with a generic object detector to reduce both computation time and probability of choosing non-meaningful image regions. It could also be interesting to evaluate the utility of our approach in an active learning setup. Apart from this, we want to use our approach to localize multiple objects per image in the test step.

Acknowledgements. I am grateful for the support of my advisor Erik Rodner.

References

1. Alexe, B., Deselaers, T., Ferrari, V.: What is an object? In: Proceedings of the CVPR, pp. 73–80 (2010)
2. Bosch, A., Zisserman, A., Munoz, X.: Image classification using random forests and ferns. In: Proceedings of the ICCV, pp. 1–8 (2007)
3. Bosch, A., Zisserman, A., Munoz, X.: Representing shape with a spatial pyramid kernel. In: Proceedings of the CIVR, pp. 401–408 (2007)
4. Chum, O., Zisserman, A.: An exemplar model for learning object classes. In: Proceedings of the CVPR (2007)
5. Dalal, N., Triggs, B.: Histogram of oriented gradients for human detection. In: Proceedings of the CVPR, pp. 886–893 (2005)
6. Everingham, M., Van Gool, L., Williams, C.K.I., Winn, J., Zisserman, A.: The PASCAL Visual Object Classes (VOC) challenge. IJCV 88, 303–338 (2010)
7. Fei-Fei, L., Fergus, R., Perona, P.: Learning generative visual models from few training examples: An incremental bayesian approach tested on 101 object categories. In: Workshop on Generative-Model Based Vision (2005)
8. Felzenszwalb, P.F., Girshick, R.B., McAllester, D., Ramanan, D.: Object detection with discriminatively trained part based models. PAMI 32 (2010)
9. Hager, W.W.: Updating the inverse of a matrix. Society for Industrial and Applied Mathematics (SIAM) Review 31(2), 221–239 (1989)
10. Harville, D.A.: Matrix Algebra From a Statistician's Perspective. Springer, Heidelberg (2007)
11. Kapoor, A., Grauman, K., Urtasun, R., Darrell, T.: Gaussian processes for object categorization. IJCV 88, 169–188 (2010)
12. Lazebnik, S., Schmid, C., Ponce, J.: Beyond bags of features: Spatial pyramid matching for recognizing natural scene categories. In: Proceedings of the CVPR, pp. 2169–2178 (2006)
13. Nocedal, J., Wright, S.J.: Numerical Optimization. Springer, Heidelberg (1999)
14. Rasmussen, C.E., Williams, C.K.I.: Gaussian Processes for Machine Learning. In: Adaptive Computation and Machine Learning. The MIT Press, Cambridge (2006)
15. Rodner, E., Denzler, J.: One-shot learning of object categories using dependent gaussian processes. In: Proceedings of the DAGM, pp. 232–241. Springer, Heidelberg (2010)

Color Image Segmentation
Based on an Iterative Graph Cut Algorithm
Using Time-of-Flight Cameras*

Markus Franke

Multimedia Information Processing Group
Department of Computer Science
Christian Albrechts University of Kiel, Germany

Abstract. This work describes an approach to color image segmentation by supporting an iterative graph cut segmentation algorithm with depth data collected by time-of-flight (TOF) cameras. The graph cut algorithm uses an energy minimization approach to segment an image, taking account of both color and contrast information. The foreground and background color distributions of the images subject to segmentation are represented by Gaussian mixture models, which are optimized iteratively by parameter learning. These models are initialized by a preliminary segmentation created from depth data, automating the model initialization step, which otherwise relies on user input.

1 Introduction

The extraction of relevant visual information from images through segmentation is one of the most important steps in image processing and is used in many applications, like medical imaging, driver assistance systems, and 3DTV content creation. While for many segmentation approaches user input is mandatory, the use of TOF cameras for segmentation purposes is another promising method. These cameras measure per-pixel depth data through correlation of emitted and reflected infrared light. Although technical progress has been made in the development of TOF cameras, their limited resolution and dependency on reflectance properties often require post-processing of the captured data.

In this work, depth data aquired from a camera setup containing TOF cameras is used to support an interactive segmentation algorithm [9], taking advantage of its optimization capabilites to compensate for the unreliability of the depth data at the border region of foreground and background.

The remainder of this paper is structured as follows: After an investigation of related work in Section 2, the segmentation procedure is described in Section 3. Section 4 presents experimental results, while conclusions are drawn in Section 5.

---

* Recommended for submission to YRF2011 by Prof. Dr.-Ing. Reinhard Koch.

R. Mester and M. Felsberg (Eds.): DAGM 2011, LNCS 6835, pp. 462–467, 2011.
© Springer-Verlag Berlin Heidelberg 2011

2   Related Work

Available image segmentation techniques can generally be classified into two categories: Interactive approaches incorporate user input to narrow down the number of feasible segmentations, while automatic approaches do not rely on user input.

A common approach to automatic segmentation is the integration of previous knowledge about the scene, e.g. removing a known, uniform background to extract the foreground [10]. However, this method is obviously not applicable to the segmentation of natural images, as it requires a special capturing environment. Interactive segmentation approaches e.g. require the user to indicate definite foreground or background regions [3,9]. While generally high quality results are produced, processing a large number of images is time-consuming. Utilizing depth data captured by TOF cameras for segmentation purposes is also subject of current research [1,11,4]. The authors in [11,4] automatically create a trimap from depth data and subsequently perform matting in an uncertainty region around the foreground. Our work combines automatic trimap generation with iterative segmentation as described in the following section.

3   Color Image Segmentation

Our segmentation technique expands the interactive segmentation algorithm from [9] by incorporating depth data into the creation of a preliminary segmentation, which relies on user interaction otherwise. This also limits the segmentation to an uncertainty region around foreground objects.

3.1   Data Acquisition

Figure 1 shows a picture of the camera setup, with the central color camera C and the two used TOF cameras $T1$, $T2$. The color camera is a Sony X300 (1920×1080 px), the TOF cameras are PMD CamCube 3.0 cameras (200×200 px). Due to their limited resolution, two of them are combined to obtain a depth image of the same view as the color camera. The TOF cameras are rotated slightly in order to cover the full viewing area of the central camera. In an attempt to minimize the amount of disocclusions, the depth images from cameras $T1$ and $T2$ are then simultaneously warped into the central view using a triangle mesh warping technique [1]. Note that from the camera setup shown in Figure 1 only the three cameras mentioned above are used.

The resulting warped depth image (see Figure 1) features black pixel areas for which no depth data is available, representing occluded regions not seen by any of the TOF cameras. The image is also not free from artifacts, especially at the border region of foreground and background, resulting from the large resolution difference between the color image and both original depth images, and also from general depth measurement errors. In order to disregard these artifacts when generating a preliminary segmentation from the depth image, a trimap is created as described in the following paragraph.

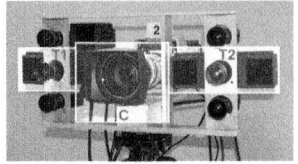  

Fig. 1. From left to right: Camera setup, color image from central camera C, warped depth image from cameras $T1$, $T2$

3.2 Trimap Generation

In a first step, the warped depth image is tresholded to create a binary image B with foreground and background pixel regions. The respective threshold can be selected by user input or can also be aquired automatically [8,5]. In order to incorporate the uncertainty of the foreground border region, a trimap is generated from the binary image B through morphological operations. Let B_e be the result of performing erosion on image B and let B_d be the result after dilation of B. Then the definite foreground region of the trimap is given by $T_{fg} := B_e$ and the uncertainty region around forground objects is given by $T_{un} := B_d - B_e$. Another dilation of the dilated binary image B_d creates the image B_{dd}. Then the background region of the trimap is given by $T_{bg} := B_{dd} - B_d$. This limits the background region to a narrow strip around the uncertainty region. Thus, the black pixels of the trimap are disregarded during segmentation and are also not considered for the creation of the background Gaussian mixture model during clustering. This not only increases performance, but also prevents interference of the color models by spatially distant background regions. Hence, the foreground, uncertainty, and background regions form the trimap $T := T_{fg} \cup T_{un} \cup T_{bg}$, as displayed in Figure 2(b).

3.3 Color Clustering

Based on the definite foreground and background pixel regions (T_{fg}, T_{bg}), two Gaussian mixture models GM_{fg} and GM_{bg} are created by clustering the corresponding color image pixels. We use a hierarchical clustering approach based on color quantization [2]. Here each Gaussian mixture model starts with all pixels in a single cluster C_1. This cluster is then split in two by means of principal component analysis, by first calculating the covariance matrix of C_1 and then finding its largest eigenvector e using singular value decomposition. Due to the involved diagonalization of the covariance matrix, the variance of the now uncorrelated color data points is greatest along the direction of e. Cluster C_1 is then split into clusters C_1', C_2 by a plane perpendicular to e and passing through the mean value of C_1.

This process is continued iteratively by repeatedly splitting the cluster with the largest variance, until the desired cluster limit has been reached. Instead of setting this limit to a fixed number as proposed in [9], we compare all within-cluster variances to the total variance among all clusters to abort the splitting process automatically. The calculated foreground and background pixel clusters are then used to initialize the individual components of the respective Gaussian mixture model.

3.4   Segmentation by Energy Minimization

After the Gaussian mixture models are initialized, the segmentation is performed based on the iterated graph cut approach described in [9]. We abort the iterative energy minimization when the fraction of pixels changing classification is below 0.01% of total image pixels.

The minimization of the energy functional employs the maximum flow algorithm described in [7]. As each of the nonterminal graph vertices v has a connection to both the source s and the sink t, all paths of the form (s, v, t) are augmented before execution of the maximum flow algorithm to increase performance. Additionally, after each iteration of the segmentation algorithm, the flow on the image graph is reused from the previous iteration [3]. This significantly improves performance of all iterations but the first, as only those edges subject to a positive capacity change can form new augmenting paths. Likewise, as the maximum flow algorithm starts its search for augmenting paths from a set of active vertices, this set is consequently limited to those vertices connected to updated edges. Also, the most recent search tree after termination of the maximum flow algorithm is reused for the following execution [6], preventing the time-consuming rebuilding of the search trees at execution start.

4   Experimental Results

The segmentation algorithm was evaluated on frames of three video sequences captured by the camera setup explained in Section 3.1. Figure 2 shows the influence of the initial clustering on the segmentation results by comparing the used clustering algorithm to a conventional k-means approach. Also note that the segmentation results varied using k-means due to its randomly chosen starting cluster centers, whereas the results using the hierarchical clustering remained invariant due to its deterministic nature.

4.1   Segmentation Performance

The run-times given in this section were obtained on a PC with a 3.16 GHz Intel Core 2 Duo CPU and 7.8 GB of RAM. Table 1 shows performance results for the maximum flow calculation only, Table 2 displays total segmentation times. Note that the pixels marked black in the trimap are not used to build the image graphs. The lower resolution images were obtained by downsampling the color images using a mean-shift filter, scaling down erosion and dilation parameters for the trimap generation accordingly. Experiments show that reducing the resolution to 960×540 pixels has almost no impact on segmentation quality but significantly reduces computation time.

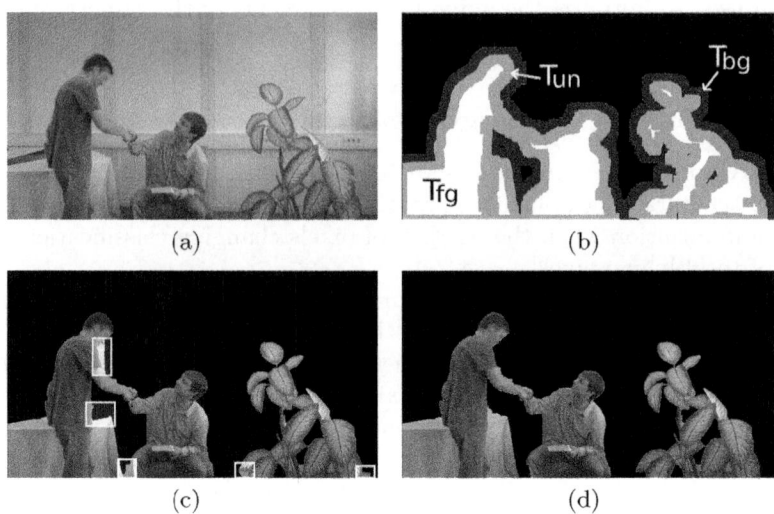

Fig. 2. (a) Input image; (b) trimap generated from depth image; (c) segmentation result using k-means (10 iterations); (d) segmentation result using our approach. Differences in the results are highlighted by white rectangles

Table 1. Performance of the maximum flow algorithm averaged over 9 test images. Note that the last row only shows the average run-time excluding first iterations, as those are not affected by reusing the flow and the search trees.

	resolution			
	240 × 135 px	480 × 270 px	960 × 540 px	1920 × 1080 px
standard Kolmogorov [7]	0.05s	0.10s	0.42s	1.88s
+ augm. terminal paths	0.02s	0.06s	0.22s	1.03s
+ reusing flow and trees	0.01s	0.02s	0.06s	0.24s

Table 2. Performance of the segmentation algorithm averaged over 9 test images, reusing the graph, flow, and search trees after the first iteration. The last row shows total segmentation time, with an estimated average of 9 iterations until convergence.

	resolution			
	240 × 135 px	480 × 270 px	960 × 540 px	1920 × 1080 px
first iteration	0.13s	0.37s	1.24s	5.12s
subsequent iterations	0.04s	0.12s	0.30s	1.06s
total time	0.45s	1.33s	3.64s	13.60s

5   Summary and Conclusion

We presented an approach to automatic color image segmentation. By using depth data captured by TOF cameras, we managed to automate the initialization procedure of the probabilistic color models. We also automatically determined an optimal number of clusters for the hierarchical color clustering by evaluating the within-cluster variances. By reusing the flow and the search trees used during maximum flow calculation throughout the iterative segmentation, we arrived at a performance suitable for the segmentation of image sequences. Future work includes efforts to achieve temporal stability when segmenting video sequences of images by introducing temporal edges, linking consecutive video frames together. This way the amount of flickering caused by temporal artifacts can be reduced by incorporating knowledge about previous segmentation results [8,5]. Also part of our investigation is the automatic removal of the background in interior scenes, which is done by estimating multiple depth tresholding planes through clustering of surface normals [5].

References

1. Bartczak, B., Schiller, I., Beder, C., Koch, R.: Integration of a time-of-flight camera into a mixed reality system for handling dynamic scenes, moving viewpoints and occlusions in real-time. In: Proceedings of the 3DPVT Workshop, Atlanta, GA, USA (2008)
2. Bouman, C., Orchard, M.: Color quantization of images. IEEE Transactions on Signal Processing 39(12), 2677–2690 (1991)
3. Boykov, Y.Y., Jolly, M.P.: Interactive graph cuts for optimal boundary and region segmentation of objects in N-D images. In: ICCV, pp. I:105–112 (2001)
4. Crabb, R., Tracey, C., Puranik, A., Davis, J.: Real-time foreground segmentation via range and color imaging. Computer Vision and Pattern Recognition Workshop 0, 1–5 (2008)
5. Frick, A., Franke, M., Koch, R.: Time-consistent foreground segmentation of dynamic content from color and depth video. In: Mester, R., Felsberg, M. (eds.) DAGM 2011. LNCS, vol. 6835, pp. 462–467. Springer, Heidelberg (2011)
6. Kohli, P., Torr, P.H.S.: Dynamic graph cuts for efficient inference in markov random fields. IEEE Trans. Pattern Analysis and Machine Intelligence 29(12), 2079–2088 (2007)
7. Kolmogorov, V., Boykov, Y.Y.: An experimental comparison of min-cut/max-flow algorithms for energy minimization in vision. In: Figueiredo, M., Zerubia, J., Jain, A.K. (eds.) EMMCVPR 2001. LNCS, vol. 2134, pp. 359–374. Springer, Heidelberg (2001)
8. Paris, S., Durand, F.: A topological approach to hierarchical segmentation using mean shift. In: CVPR, pp. 1–8 (2007)
9. Rother, C., Kolmogorov, V., Blake, A.: "Grabcut": interactive foreground extraction using iterated graph cuts. ACM Trans. Graph 23(3), 309–314 (2004)
10. Smith, A.R., Blinn, J.F.: Blue screen matting. In: Proceedings of the 23rd Annual Conference on Computer Graphics and Interactive Techniques, pp. 259–268 (1996)
11. Wang, O., Finger, J., Yang, Q., Davis, J., Yang, R.: Automatic natural video matting with depth. In: Proceedings of the 15th Pacific Conference on Computer Graphics and Applications, pp. 469–472 (2007)

Application of Multi-modal Features for Terrain Classification on a Mobile System

Marc Arends

Active Vision Group, University Koblenz-Landau, 56070 Koblenz
marends@uni-koblenz.de

Abstract. This paper[1] presents an approach of an extended terrain classification procedure for an autonomous mobile robot with multimodal features. Terrain classification is an important task in the field of outdoor robotics as it is essential for negotiability analysis and path planning. In this paper I present a novel approach of combining multi modal features and a Markov random field to solve the terrain classification problem. The presented model uses features extracted from 3D laser range measurements and images and is adapted from a Markov random field used for image segmentation. Three different labels can be assigned to the terrain describing the classes *road*, for easy to pass flat ground, *rough* for hard to pass ground like grass or a field and *obstacle* for terrain which needs to be avoided. Experiments showed that the algorithm is fast enough for real time applications and that the classes *road* and *street* are detected with a rate of about 90% in rural environments.

1 Introduction

The problem of planning an optimal path through an unknown outdoor environment is a fundamental task in the field of mobile robotics. A save path can only be found if the mobile system knows which terrain is negotiable and which is not. Robots fulfilling this task can be used to automatize work in agriculture, transportation or even for reconnaissance in hazardous territories. The field of applications is enormous, therefore there is a lot of research in this field.

Different types of sensors are used to collect data about the robots surroundings. The representation of the terrain is a discretized 2D grid consisting of cells of equal size, each representing a piece of environment. The acquisition of this structure is introduced by Neuhaus et al. [7] and is the foundation of the classification process presented in this paper. The goal of this work is to classify each cell, allowing a prediction, which cell is difficult or easy to pass by using laser and image data to gain information about the structure and the appearance of the terrain. The features work as input of a Markov random field that allows the modeling of the assumption that terrain cells of the same class tend to appear in groups in the environment.

In this paper the hardware setup is presented in sec. 2. The related work is described afterwards in sec. 3. In sec. 4 I discuss the combination of used

---

[1] Recommended for submission to YRF2011 by Prof. Dr.-Ing Dietrich Paulus.

R. Mester and M. Felsberg (Eds.): DAGM 2011, LNCS 6835, pp. 468–473, 2011.

features and sec. 5 describes the application of the Markov random field. The results of the performed experiments are presented in sec. 6 and sec. 7 contains my conclusion.

2   Hardware Setup

The algorithm described in this paper is designed to be used for a combination of 3D-laser scans and camera images, mounted on a mobile robot. The sensors used for the task are a 3D laser range finder (LRF), a *Logitech HD Pro Webcam C910* which is attached to the front and two *Philips SPC1300NC* cameras pointed to each side. The LRF is a *Velodyne HDL-64E S2* which provides about 1.8 million range measurements per second using 64 lasers rotating 360 degrees around its own vertical axis. As it is not always possible to use a robot, the sensors can be attached on a car to record sensor data. The recorded data can be replayed in the used software framework in the same chronological order and speed it was recorded. This allows its usage for developing and evaluating algorithms without actually employing a robot.

3   Related Work

As mentioned before there has been a lot of research in the field of terrain classification. The approach I present in this paper is an extension to the algorithm described by Neuhaus et al. [7] which is already implemented in the used robotics framework. It provides the partitioning of the terrain into a cell based 2D grid map and the computation of laser based terrain features.

Approaches using LRFs to acquire information about the geometry of an environment are widely spread. A method to gain information about the geometry of terrain to predict the negotiability is described by Wolf et al. [10], where a concatenation of 2D laser scans is used to create 3D data. Another approach introduced by Vandapel et al. [8] is based on the arrangement of single 3D laser points in a point cloud. They defined a descriptor which can be used for the segmentation of a 3D scan into different geometric regions.

Besides the acquisition of the terrain geometry there exist methods which use the remission values of a laser scan to distinguish between vegetation and non-vegetation e.g. by Wurm et al. [11] or by Wellington et al. [9]. These approaches allow the detection of obstacles like bushes or high grass.

The combination of image and laser features is not new to terrain classification either. Wellington et al. [9] combine the color of the terrain with laser features to improve the detection rate.

The application of Markov random fields for segmentation tasks is a common technique in the field of image processing. However these random fields can also be used for classification and segmentation work in terrain classification, if a discretized 2D terrain representation is used (see [9,10]).

4 Multi-modal Features

Features are essential for negotiability analyses. I want to distinguish between three different terrain classes. These are *road, rough* and *obstacle*. The class *road* describes surfaces, which are basically flat without rough elements like small stones, grass or small plants which can be passed by the robot and are part of cells of the class *rough*. High vegetation, walls and everything which is not negotiable by the system is classified as *obstacle*.

The geometric characteristics of a terrain cell can be applied with a laser range finder. I utilize a roughness feature f_r (see [7]), which is calculated with the help of the *local distance disturbance* and provides a good quantization of how rough the surface of a cell is. The local distance disturbance describes the difference of a laser measurement that hits a small bump and one that would not have hit the same bump. Applying this information, a roughness value can be calculated as follows.

$$f_r = \frac{\sigma^2}{d_{Cell}^2} \tag{1}$$

where σ^2 describes the distance variance of a laser scan and d_{Cell} the distance of the cell hit by the corresponding scan. A detailed description of the calculation of this features is described by Neuhaus et al. [7]. Distinguishing between *rough* and *obstacle* cells is not always possible with this feature because these two cells often have an equal rough surface. As an obstacle is defined as something which is too steep for a robot to pass, I apply the difference of the highest and lowest laser measurement within a cell as a feature f_h (see [3]). These two laser features are adequate to describe the detected classes and combining them should lead to a successful differentiation between them.

However it is not always possible to provide enough laser scans within a cell to calculate these features correctly. This is the reason why I decided to use image features in addition. I make the assumption that the texture of a terrain cell allows a prediction about its geometry. This is based on the difference in appearance of e.g. the texture of a rough cell containing grass in comparison to the texture of a road cell containing an asphalted surface. To examine the texture of an image Haralick et al. [4] proposed a number of calculations to acquire texture features. These features are computed on co-occurrence matrices displaying how often a pixel value is inside the neighborhood of another value. These matrices need to be computed for every cell, which needs to be analyzed. For this, the color images need to be converted to gray level images, because the possible number of different color values is to large for fast computations. However, calculating the matrices and all the features for all cells is still expensive in terms of runtime. Therefore I chose to use only 3 features which can be calculated by iterating over a co-occurrence matrix once, namely the *second angular moment* f_{sam}, *variance* f_v and the *inverse difference moment* f_{idm}. The detailed description of these calculation is described by Haralick et al. [4]. An alternative texture calculation is the computation of a homogeneity feature f_{fh} described by Knauer et al. [5]. Making the assumption that a rough terrain cell has an inhomogeneous texture makes this reasonable. This can be calculated fast by using a summed area table of difference images, which only needs to be calculated for a whole image in contrast to the co-occurrence matrices. The homogeneity of an subimage spanned by two points is calculated as follows

$$f_{FH} = \frac{Sat(x_{lr}+1, y_{lr}+1) + Sat(x_{ul}, y_{ul}) - Sat(x_{ul}, y_{lr}) - Sat(x_{lr}, y_{ul})}{(x_{lr} - x_{ul}) \cdot (y_{lr} - y_{ul})} \quad (2)$$

where $Sat(x, y)$ represents an entry in the summed area table at position (x, y), x_{ul}, y_{ul} stand for the x- respectively the y-coordinate of the upper left point and x_{lr}, y_{lr} for the x- respectively the y-coordinate of the lower right point. The last feature included is the averaged color f_c of each cell, having the belief that roads, rough terrain and obstacles like trees or bushes are different in their color.

The introduced features allow different combinations of feature vectors, containing laser and image data. Therefore I can use features of different modalities for a classification task. A probabilistic model is acquired to respect the different kinds of features in one computation to classify the terrain.

5   Terrain Classification with a Markov Random Field

A label describing a class has to be assigned to each cell according to its calculated features. For this task a Markov random field is applied allowing the consideration of features and the classes of neighboring cells to find a terrain classification. An introduction and a more detailed description of Markov random fields in the field of classification can be found in several books (i.e. [6]). I use a Markov random field model presented for image segmentation tasks by Deng et al. [1], which assumes features to be Gaussian distributed and uses parameters to weight their impact against neighbor classes for the calculation. For a classification result ω with regards to the observed feature vectors f, this model allows to compute the a posteriori probability $P(\omega|f)$. The maximization of the probability can be achieved by applying a Gibbs sampler described by Geman and Geman [2]. This sampler works with a so called Gibbs random field. According to the *Hammersley-Clifford theorem* a Markov random field is a Gibbs random field, which leads to the following equation

$$P(\omega|f) = \frac{1}{Z} \exp\left(-\frac{1}{T}(E_n + \alpha E_f)\right) \quad (3)$$

where Z is a normalizing constant, T the temperature parameter, E_n the energy form of the probability for the labeling according to the neighborhood relationships and E_f the energy form of the distribution of the calculated features with a weighting factor α. The calculation of the energies is described by Deng et al. [1] and can also be applied to this context. The acquired image and laser data and a corresponding classification result can be seen in fig. 1.

(a)   (b)

Fig. 1. Acquired laser and image data (a) and corresponding classification result with red obstacles, brown rough terrain and gray road (b)

6   Experiments

To evaluate the algorithm with different feature combinations, classifications of single terrain scenes are compared to a ground truth of the same scene, which was acquired by a human annotator. Table 1 shows the results for the true positive ratio (TPR) and false positive ratio (FPR) for each class in a field scenario. The columns represent the used features: laser based (L), Haralick features (H), the homogeneity feature (FH) and the color information (C).

Table 1. Results of the classification algorithm

Class/value	L	L + H	L + FH	L + C
Road/TPR	91.049 %	91.914 %	90.432 %	91.049 %
Road/FPR	1.523 %	1.146 %	1.158 %	1.372 %
Rough/TPR	74.618 %	73.828 %	75.158 %	75.293 %
Rough/FPR	1.190 %	1.103 %	1.306 %	1.422 %
Obstacle/TPR	92.826 %	91.785 %	92.881 %	92.552 %
Obstacle/FPR	3.565 %	4.426 %	3.221 %	3.118 %

7   Conclusion

The results of the experiments show that the developed algorithm works well in a field environment. However the application of image features in addition to the laser features do not result in a significant change of the detection rate. A reason for this are high standard deviation values for the image features, which are needed in the Markov random field. The variety of textures for the different classes is much higher as predicted, therefore these values do not have enough weight in comparison to the laser features.

In future work other image features should be examined if they provide better possibilities for classifying terrain. I propose to fuse the image and laser data after classifying a whole image and not only parts of it, as it is possible that information is lost due to high distances.

References

1. Deng, H., Clausi, D.A.: Unsupervised image segmentation using a simple mrf model with a new implementation scheme. Pattern Recogn. (2004)
2. Geman, S., Geman, D.: Stochastic relaxation, gibbs distribution, and bayesian restoration of images. In: IEEE Transactions on Pattern Analysis and Machine Intelligence (1984)
3. Happold, M., Ollis, M., Johnson, N.: Enhancing supervised terrain classification with predictive unsupervised learning. In: Proceedings of Robotics: Science and Systems (2006)
4. Haralick, R.M., Dinstein, I., Shanmugam, K.: Textural features for image classification. In: Proceedings of IEEE Transactions on Systems, Man, and Cybernetics, pp. 610–621 (1973)
5. Knauer, U., Meffert, B.: Fast computation of region homogeneity with application in a surveillance task. In: Proceedings of ISPRS Commission V Mid-Term Symposium Close Range Image Measurement Techniques (2010)
6. Li, S.Z.: Markov Random Field Modeling in Computer Vision. Springer, Heidelberg (2009)
7. Neuhaus, F., Dillenberger, D., Pellenz, J., Paulus, D.: Terrain drivability analysis in 3d laser range data for autonomous robot navigation in unstructured environments. In: Proceedings of the IEEE International Conference on Emerging Technologies and Factory Automation, pp. 1686–1689 (2009)
8. Vandapel, N., Huber, D., Kapuria, A., Hebert, M.: Natural terrain classification using 3-d ladar data. In: Proceedings of the IEEE International Conference on Robotics and Automation, pp. 5117–5122 (2004)
9. Wellington, C., Courville, A., Stentz, A.: Interacting markov random fields for simultaneous terrain modeling and obstacle detection. In: Proceedings of Robotics Science and Systems (2005)
10. Wolf, D.F., Sukhatme, G., Fox, D., Burgard, W.: Autonomous terrain mapping and classification using hidden markov models. In: Proceedings of the IEEE International Conference on Robotics and Automation, pp. 2026–2031 (2005)
11. Wurm, K.M., Kümmerle, R., Stachniss, C., Burgard, W.: Improving robot navigation in structured outdoor environments by identifying vegetation from laser data. In: Proceedings of the IEEE/RSJ International Conference on Intelligent Robots and Systems, pp. 1217–1222 (2009)

Author Index